THE BLACK CUILLIN

FOR MY PARENTS

THE BLACK CUILLIN

THE STORY OF SKYE'S MOUNTAINS

Calum Smith

First published 2020
by Rymour Books
with Hog's Back Press
45 Needless Road
Perth
PH2 0LE

© Calum Smith 2020

ISBN 978-0-9540704-3-4

Cover design by Ian Spring
Typeset in Garamond
Printed and bound by
Imprint Digital
Seychelles Farm
Upton Pyne
Exeter

All rights reserved. No part of this publication may be reproduced, stored in a retrieval system, or transmitted, in any form or by any means, electronic, mechanical, photocopying, recording or otherwise, without the prior permission of the publishers.

The paper used in this book is approved by the Forest Stewardship Council

CONTENTS

Contents	5
Acknowledgments	6
Illustrations	7
Introduction	9
1: The Lake of Terror (1745-1864)	15
2: The Dearest of Islands (1865-1887)	43
3: Norman Collie and John Mackenzie	69
4: The Rocky Mountains of Skye (1888-1894)	93
5: Joyous Days upon the Mountainside (1895-1905)	121
6: The Book of Abraham	147
7: The British Alps (1906-1918)	169
8: Goodbye to all That (the Twenties)	195
9: Always a Little Further (the Thirties)	219
10: The Magic of Skye (1946-59)	245
11: The Sixties and Seventies	271
12: The Competitive Edge	295
Postscript	321
References	323
Sources	331
Index	339

ACKNOWLEDGEMENTS

I would especially like to thank my brother, Donald, for introducing me to the hills, and for his help with the publication of this book. Also, Ian Spring for his enthusiasm for this project, and his support and advice throughout the process.

Many, many people have selflessly helped with the preparation of this book, whether providing information or reading over and commenting on part, or all, of the manuscript. In the later category I would like to acknowledge the help given by the late Donald Bennett, and the late Peter Hodgkiss. I would also like to select John Harwood for particular thanks for his evocative reminiscences of the Cuillin in the 1960s and 1970s. I am most grateful to Fred Schley for permission to use his wonderful painting for the cover design.

My heartfelt thanks also go to the following for their contributions to the book: Dave Alcock, Rab Anderson, Chris Bonington, Richard Brooke, Bill Brooker, Sinclair Bruce, Robin Campbell, Fiona Campbell of the Sligachan Hotel, Ginger Cain, Karen Caldwell (University of St Andrews), Mike Dent, Mike Dixon, Mick Fowler, Blair Fyffe, Willie Gallacher, Davie Gardner, Phil Gribbon, Murray Hamilton, P Hatfield (Eton College archivist), Con Higgins, Kev Howett, Mike Lates, Gary Latter, Cameron Lees, John Llewellyn (Rucksack Club archivist), Cyril Loftus, Hamish MacInnes, Donald MacKenzie, Ian MacNaught-Davis, Ruby McCann, Rennie McOwan, Christine Mill, Rob Milne, Colin Moody, Martin Moran, Grahame Nicoll, Andy Nisbet, Geoff Pigott, Tom Prentice, Jim Renny, Dave Ritchie, George R Russell, Vic Saunders, Hazel Scott, Chris Simkins, Jim Simpson, David Stone, Greg Strange, Bob Toogood, Reinier Vellekoup (SYHA), Patsy Walsh, Ian Whitney (FRCC archivist), Chris Wilson.

During my research the following people and organisations were especially helpful: The staff of Mitchell Library, Glasgow; University of Glasgow Library and Special Collections; University of Strathclyde Library and Special Collections; St Andrews University Library and Special Collections; University of Dundee Archive Service, Portree Library, Dualchas (Portree), Alpine Club Library, National Library of Scotland, National Museums of Scotland Research Library, University of North Wales (Bangor) Archives; Gurkha Museum, Winchester; University Hall, St Andrews.

A big thank you to the following for great memories of climbing on gabbro: George Corbett, Sam Galbraith, Richard Gatehouse, Fraser Gray, Si Newton, Gordon Pryde, Sandy Reid, Doug Rennie, Ian Spring, Jim Tannahill.

Dennis Gray and Jim Perrin are legends in the world of climbing and climbing literature and I cannot thank them enough for reading my work and for their enthusiastic testimonials.

Above all, I would like to thank my parents for their love and support. This book is dedicated to them.

ILLUSTRATIONS

Between page 92 and page 93

The Cuillin from near Elgol
An engraving of J M W Turner's *Coriskin* (1831)
The summit of Sgurr nan Gillean
John MacCulloch's 1816 geological map of Skye
John MacCulloch
James David Forbes
Reverend William Knight
The stone shoot by which Alexander Nicolson ascended Sgurr Alasdair
The Sligachan Inn in the 1850s
Alexander Nicolson
The Bad Step on Loch Scavaig
Collie's Ledge on Sgurr Mhic Choinnich
Henry Chichester Hart
A diagram made by E W Steeple for the 1923 SMC guidebook
The East Ridge of Inaccessible Pinnacle
Charles Pilkington, Eustace Hulton and Lawrence Pilkington
Abseiling the West Ridge of the Pinnacle
The shadow that brought the Cioch to Collie's attention
John Mackenzie with pony
Norman Collie in 1886, aged 27, the year he first visited Skye
John Mackenzie and client on the West Ridge of Sgurr nan Gillean
Advert for the Sligachan Hotel
John Mackenzie and Norman Collie in later life
Pinnacle Ridge on Sgurr nan Gillean
The Sligachan Inn during the 1890s
A page from the Sligachan Climbers' Book, dated 11 September 1894

Between page 244 and page 245

The north face of Am Basteir and the Bhasteir Tooth
The first pitch of Naismith's Route (Severe) on the Bhasteir Tooth
A diagram of Naismith's Route from the first SMC guide to Skye (1907)
An article by George Abraham in *The Sphere* (1908)
The diagonal line of Cioch Direct
Approaching the Parallel Cracks pitch on Cioch Direct
George Abraham
E W Steeple and A H Doughty relaxing at Mary Campbell's cottage
Direct Route (Severe) on Sron na Ciche's Eastern Buttress
E W Steeple and party on the Bealach a'Mhaim in September 1910

William Wallwork
Wallwork's Route (Very Difficult) on the Cioch Upper Buttress
Ben Humble and Bill Murray with a group of admirers at Loch Coruisk
The common room at Glenbrittle Hostel around 1970
Bastinado (E1) on Cioch Buttress,
Trophy Crack (E1) on Cioch Upper Buttress
An SYHA guide to Skye from the 1960s
Vulcan Wall (HVS) on Sron na Ciche's Eastern Buttress
The view north from Bruach na Frithe
Tom Patey on a winter traverse attempt in 1962
Phill Townsend on an early ascent of King Cobra (E1)

INTRODUCTION

The Black Cuillin is the main mountain range of Skye, described as 'black' to distinguish it from the 'Red' Cuillin, named for the reddish tinge of the granite as opposed to the darker gabbro.

However, when I first encountered it – as a student looking through the window of Glen Brittle youth hostel one sunny evening, it was a golden hue! This aspect is also noted by the poet, Alexander Smith in the early nineteenth century: 'If you think these poems exaggerated go out at Sligachan and see [the mountains] all golden and on fire with the rising sun!'[1]

From that moment, the Cuillin has been fixed in my mind through that vivid memory and has remained a fascination. At the time it seemed too high, too rugged, too far away to be climbed. But in due course I did, and those days were some of the happiest of my life.

This book is the story of those mountains and of those who climbed them. Although, in order for them to be climbed, they first had to be 'discovered'. In 1587, Johann Müller described mountains as the 'theatre of the Lord, displaying monuments of past ages, such as precipices, rocks, peaks, chasms and never-melting glaciers'.[2] This view, however, was an exception. For many centuries mountains were regarded as an accident, an aberration – interfering with the proper practice of agriculture, commerce and trade. Such was the view, largely, of Johnson and Boswell – when they conducted their tour of Scotland in 1773 – and of Captain Burt, an eighteenth-century military surveyor, who imagined an Englishman, blindfolded and released in Glen Nevis, dying of fright! However, Smith outlines a process taking place through the late eighteenth and early nineteenth century that was to change this: 'In the space of a few decades after the 1745 Jacobite rebellion, a process began that would transform the popular view of the Highlands from that of a treacherous and bellicose backwater, awash with barbarism and misrule, to one of the most fashionable tourist destinations in Europe'.

It is considered that the Romantic period 'discovered' the mountains as objects of interest, with the Romantic poets – notably Gray, Coleridge, Byron and, especially, Wordsworth – among the first to venture to, and write about, the mountains.[3] The writer and climber David Craig notes: '…we may say that the possibility of loving mountains dawned in the 1780s',[4] This belief is contingent on the 'discovery' of the Scottish mountains as an object of interest to the artist and the 'invention' of a new form of 'perspective', the picturesque, a term coined by William Gilpin,[5] and epitomised in John Ruskin's 'Of Mountain Beauty' in *Modern Painters*: 'We have found that where at first all seemed disturbed and accidental, the most tender laws were appointed to produce forms of perpetual beauty…'[6]

Early visitors to the Scottish mountains, enthralled by Scott's *Lady of the Lake* and lured by Thomas Cook's tours, largely populated the Trossachs and more southern areas. Skye was of a different vintage and Scott, indeed, noted (of the Cuillin) in his notes to *The Lord of the Isles*: 'It is as exquisite a savage scene as Loch Katrine is a scene of Romantic beauty.'[7] The 'savage scene' is perhaps epitomised in this verse from *The Lord of the Isles*:

… seems that primeval earthquake's sway,
Hath rent a strange and shatter'd way,
Through the rude bosom of the hill,
And that each naked precipice,
Sable ravine, and dark abyss,
Tells of the outrage still.

What enabled this new appreciation of mountain scenery was Edmund Burke's concept of the sublime; 'the oxymoron of agreeable horror', as Simon Schama has it. From the eighteenth century, artists had begun to depict mountains. William Daniell pictured the Cuillin from Loch Coruisk as jagged peaks but accompanied by people and boats as signs of civilisation.[8] The Romantic transformation saw the mountain landscape portrayed for its own sake. The most extraordinary depiction of the Cuillin is J M W Turner's *Coriskin*, in which the Cuillin ridge is depicted, apparently, from above! In order to achieve this, Turner himself undertook some climbing as Smith records: 'Turner eventually favoured an elevated viewpoint, high on Sgurr na Stri, where he includes two figures in the foreground. In a letter to Cadell he related how he slipped on the rocky ascent and only saved himself by grabbing handfuls of turf'.[9]

By the nineteenth century, Skye, and the Cuillin, had been well mapped by, among others, Timothy Pont, Aaron Arrowsmith, John MacCulloch and John Thomson (who, in 1832, had produced the first reliable chart of the comparative height of the Scottish mountains). However, the island was still comparatively inaccessible. Due to the popularity of the Grand Tour in the early nineteenth century, central Europe was familiar to gentleman travellers. In 1865, the news surfaced of Edward Whymper's ascent of the Matterhorn. An ascent made only the more sensational due to the fact that four of his companions were lost in the ascent – of the fourth, Lord Douglas, nothing was found other than a shoe, gloves and a coat sleeve![10] This predated the more serious ascents in Skye. However, around the turn of the century, many members of the Alpine Club ventured to Skye and it became known as 'Britain's Alps'. During the Great War, with the Alps out of bounds, some climbers came to the Cuillin. Their activities were, of course, grossly outweighed by the loss of young life during the conflict. After 1918, it was some time before life returned to anything like normality on an island devastated by the War.

I have dwelt at some length on the early years of the discovery of the Skye mountains which are dealt with and contextualised in full in this book. However, writ large upon this account of the early years of mountaineering in Skye are the exploits of certain individuals. Norman Collie and John Mackenzie were quite different, the former a university research chemist, the latter a crofter's son from Sconser, who became the best known of Skye mountain guides, although the climber Ashley Abraham noted of him: 'He is more a companion than a guide. When in his company one feels that his predominating qualities are his love for the mountains, his genial and kindly nature, his unremitting care, and a fine sturdy independence of spirit; the mere accident that Providence has not seen fit to endow him with worldly riches does not detract from these'. Ashley Abraham himself, along with his brother George, were originally Lake District climbers who came to Skye and published the first, influential guide to the hills, *Rock Climbing in Skye*. All of these pioneers frequented the Sligachan Inn – although only 'gentlemen' were allowed in the smoking lounge. Today they are equally commemorated in a small museum within the modern hotel.

The second half of this book deals with many of the individual climbs and climbers from the twentieth into the twenty-first century. It is far from just a factual account, however, being populated by a whole range of fascinating characters who frequented the Cuillin: the writers Lytton Strachey, and John Buchan, the notorious Algernon Charles Swinburne, the even more notorious occultist sometimes known as 'the wickedest man in the world', Aleister Crowley, Sandy Mackendrick, who directed *Whisky Galore*, and Maynard Miller, one of the first scientists to identify global climate change in the 1950s..

Then there are J B Meldrum, who lived to 107 and was made an honorary member of the Alpine Club at the age of 100. The Alpinist Dorothy Pilley who, 'had several first ascents to her credit including the North Ridge of the Dent Blanche in 1928, and the Victoria Memorial on Armistice Day 'with the help of a soldier and a sailor'. A journalist with political aspirations who became a noted authority on Chinese culture, religion and art, she preferred to be called plain 'Pilley', as was the current post-suffragist fashion. Adventurous to the last 'she spent her final New Year at the Glen Brittle Hut, aged 92, drinking gin till the early hours.'

Smith enlivens his account of these climbing characters with accounts of their travels, their careers, the equipment they used and their habits, down to the details, for example, of what they drank: the local tipple, Talisker, but also Mummery's Blood, a gruesome mixture of Bovril and navy rum.

More recently, noted climbers in the Cuillin have included the ubiquitous Chris Bonington and the irrepressible Tom Patey, climber, general practitioner and accordion player, noted for several climbing-related songs. Along with Hamish MacInnes, David Crabb and Brian Robertson, Patey made the first winter traverse of the Cuillin Ridge in 1965.

INTRODUCTION

When I was a climber it would generally take two days to traverse the entire ridge, even in the summer. Today the record for the journey is under three hours in summer and under five hours in winter – the former achieved by the runner and mountaineer Finlay Wild and the latter by Uisdean Hawthorn, who knocked more than an hour off the previous best in 2018.

This is a useful reminder that times have changed. When I climbed, in the seventies and eighties, I was acutely aware of the history and traditions of the hills I climbed. For a significant portion of climbers today, that no longer pertains. Indeed, since the advent of indoor walls, many younger climbers may have never been to a mountain, let alone the Cuillin. I still believe, however, that the athletic pleasure of indoor climbing hardly compares to the adventurous exploits of our time, when even the best guidebooks could be extremely misleading. There are also still many climbers of the current generation who embrace the challenge of the mountains. Dave MacLeod, Scotland's finest climber and undoubtedly the best all-round climber in the world, excels at all the disciplines of climbing. Inspired by the spectacular sword fight filmed on the top of the Cioch for the movie *Highlander*, he set up the hardest rock climb in the Black Cuillin directly up the frontal arête of the Cioch – The Gathering (E8). One of his recent videos, about the joys of creating new routes, is titled *The Unknown*: ' ...the unknown is an essential part of the adventure'. Recently, Natalie Berry, editor of UKclimbing.com and one of Scotland's best competition climbers (on artificial walls) has joined him on his videos and taken up traditional rock climbing and winter climbing.

It has also to be said that this book, unlike many early accounts of mountaineering, is not just an account of wealthy gentlemen and their leisure activities. The people of Skye, who maintained the land, facilitated transport and accommodation and acted as guides, whilst maintaining their own, often meagre living, feature too. The privations of the Clearances are considered: 'People were moved off any good arable or grazing land which was then incorporated into the farms. Eight townships near Elgol, 400 people, were cleared to create two sheep farms, Camasunary and Kirkibost. In the Glen Brittle area there were originally four townships around Loch Brittle, four more villages on Loch Eynort and three on Loch Harport. By 1830 Kenneth McCaskill merged all of these into a single sheep farm. In what was known locally as the 'Reign of Terror', many families were cleared'. Much of this culminated in the famous 'Battle of the Braes' in April 1882, but poverty persisted. In 1924 the Scottish Mountaineering Club set up a 'Skye Relief Fund' to aid the crofters whose crops had failed in a year of wet weather.

The lives of the Skye folk were marked by their mountain environment.[11] And it is an environment that still has to be maintained. In 2000, I was reading a magazine in my doctor's surgery when I came across an advertisement offering the Black Cuillin for sale by the Clan MacLeod – putatively the owners.

Thankfully, it was not sold, although it still belongs to the MacLeods. There have been massive changes that impinge upon the wilderness areas of Skye, as noted by Smith in his postscript. Notably the recent burgeoning popularity of Skye as a tourist destination which has resulted, apparently, in signs posted in the summer on the mainland side of the Skye Bridge to the effect that the island is 'full'.

Personally, many of the accounts of first ascents in this book are of great interest, as they will be to many climbers who have had the pleasure of repeating these routes since their inception. My own experience of climbing in Skye includes many days camping outside the Sligachan Hotel when the ubiquitous Skye 'horizontal rain' allowed no more than a quick dash to the bar and back whilst ruefully watching the burn encroach upon your tent, but also one glorious summer on the ridge – circumnavigating the Thearlaich-Dubh gap and the Inaccessible Pinnacle – and climbing some of the classic routes detailing in this volume: Cioch West, Cioch Grooves, Integrity, Crack of Double Doom, The Snake, White Slab Direct, Grand Diedre, Con's Cleft and others.

Recently I watched the amazing *Free Solo,* a documentary movie about climbing at the most extreme. It reminded me of my own free soloing exploits: many moons ago, about 10pm in Coire Lagan after a full day's climbing.

CALUM: Let's finish off with Cioch Direct.

IAN: Don't be daft. It'll be dark by the time we get the ropes out.

CALUM: Let's not bother with the ropes.

It was graded severe, but I didn't fancy the chimney crux, so I climbed it on the right wall, a grade harder. And the sun was setting as we walloped down the stone shoot to the tent!

Today our climbing experiences are of the less strenuous variety, but we still go to the hills to walk and to watch, and the mountains of Skye, described so well by Robin Smith as 'a wedding of thrusting rock and sucking sea', still exercise their fierce fascination.

ON FRITHARD HILL[12]

A flock of whitecap waves,
The dizzying swoop of a
Herring gull.

Then there is nothing else but you:
The brooding bard,
The Black Cuillin.

For on Frithard Hill I stand,
Holding between thumb and forefinger
The gravid gabbro of eternity.

Ian Spring, 2020

INTRODUCTION

Notes:

1. Alexander Smith, *A Summer in Skye* (Hawick: Byways Books, 1983).
2. See Simon Schama, *Landscape and Memory* (London: Harper Collins, 1995).
3. See Simon Bainbridge, *Mountaineering and British Romanticism* (Oxford: OUP, 2020).
4. David Craig, *Native Stones: a book about climbing* (London: Martin Seeker & Warburg, 1987). See also Ian Mitchell, *Scotland's Mountains before the Mountaineers* (Edinburgh: Luath Press, 1998). (The published edition is wrongly dated 1988) and James L Caw, *Scottish Painting 1620-1908* (Edinburgh: Black, 1908). He notes: 'The change in attitude [to the mountains] which coincides with Scott's reign was not less than a revolution'.
5. William Gilpin, *Observations relative chiefly to Picturesque Beauty, made in the year 1776, on several parts of Britain: particularly the High-lands of Scotland* (London, 1803)
6. John Ruskin, *Modern Painters* (London: Smith, Elder & Co, 1843-1860).
7. Walter Scott, *The Lord of the Isles* (Edinburgh: Archibald Constable & Co, 1815).
8. See Lindsay Errington, *The Discovery of Scotland*: the appreciation of Scottish scenery through two centuries of painting (Edinburgh: National Galleries of Scotland, 1978).
9. The mountains were not only depicted by visual artists but also lauded in poetry and song. The first true songs and poems by active Scottish mountaineers come from the period of early exploration of Skye and are mostly recounted in B H Humble, *Songs of Skye* (Stirling: Eneas Mackay, 1934). See Ian Spring, 'Scottish Mountaineering Songs', in *Hamish Henderson and Scottish Folk Song* (Hog's Back Press: Edinburgh, 2015), pp 29-57.
10. See Fergus Fleming, *Killing Dragons: the conquest of the Alps* (London: Granta, 2000).
11. 'This romantic Scotland could not have existed without its mountains… mountain folk and mountain rocks could symbolise the spirit of a people… ' Donald Horne, *The Great Museum: the re-presentation of history* (Pluto Press: London, 1984), p. 169.
12. Frithard Hill is a viewpoint in Plockton, Wester Ross, looking across to Skye.

Chapter One

The Lake of Terror

The Black Cuillin, the most rugged mountain range in the United Kingdom, is located on the Isle of Skye off Scotland's west coast. It forms a continuous chain of narrow ridges, jagged gabbro pinnacles and wild, ice-scoured corries around the basin of Loch Coruisk. The traverse of the Main Ridge, eight miles and 10,000ft of ascent, is the finest mountaineering expedition in the British Isles in summer, while in winter it provides an equally superb but more serious challenge.

One of the earliest references to the Cuillin mountains of Skye is by Donald Monro, 'High Dean of the Isles', who in 1549 embarked on a tour to many of the Hebridean islands. Regarding Skye, he wrote that there are 'many grate hills, principally Cuilluelum [Cuillin] and Glannock [Glamaig]'. Monro also mentions that Sligachan is a good place for salmon.

Timothy Pont was the son of a Reformation minister who spent the last two decades of the sixteenth century surveying Scotland on foot. His cartography (with any gaps filled in by others) was published in Joan Blacu's *Atlas* (1654) making Scotland one of the best mapped countries in the world at the time. On the map 'The Yle of Skie' the Cuillin are marked as 'Culluelun or Gulluin Hils' but located to the north of Sligachan. In Glenbrittle there are settlements either side of the river: 'Kilmolruy' on the west side, and 'Glenbretil' on the east. It is to areas such as the Cuillin that Pont is referring to when he makes an ominous cartographic note, 'Extreme Wilderness; Many Woolfs in this country; and black flies… seen souking men's blood.'

In the 1690s, Martin Martin, scion of a farming family from the north of Skye, made a series of voyages at the behest of Sir Robert Sibbald to gather information on the Hebrides and their inhabitants. He published his findings in 1703 as *Description of the Western Isles of Scotland*, a commentary that revealed his local knowledge, 'The Quillin, which exceed any of these Hills in height, is said to be the cause of much Rain, by breaking the clouds that hover about it, which quickly after pour down in Rain upon the quarter on which the wind then blows.' As early as 1700 significant themes are starting to emerge: 'grate hills', midges, rain.

One celebrity visitor to the island was Prince Charles Edward Stuart who, following defeat at Culloden, arrived clandestinely in Skye after hiding out in the Outer Hebrides. At Portree, Flora MacDonald handed her charge over to

Malcolm MacLeod as the Prince's disguise changed from the cross-dressing Betty Burke, Flora's Irish maid, to Lewie Caw, MacLeod's manservant. Travelling south they evaded government troops stationed at Sligachan by taking to the hills, before meeting a boat at Elgol to take the Prince to Mallaig and eventually France.

Local tradition has them passing at night down Glen Sligachan then through Mam a' Phobuill between Marsco and Beinn Dearg Mheadhonach (known locally as Mam a' Phrionnsa, the Prince's Pass). The Prince previously planned for just such an eventuality by walking long distances barefoot. Nothing, however, prepared him for the morasses of Glen Sligachan where he initiated a tradition of floundering in its bogs that would be upheld by generations of tourists, walkers and climbers. In the *Lyon in Mourning*, a contemporary account of the Prince's movements, we hear how he 'happened to fall into a bogue almost to the top of his thighs, and MacLeod behoved to pull him out by the armpits and thereby was bogued himself'. The Glen Sligachan path, cursed by many early visitors and described in contemporary guide-books as 'the worst mountain path in Scotland', was substantially improved in the 1990s.

In the space of a few decades after the 1745 Jacobite rebellion, a process began that would transform the popular view of the Highlands from that of a treacherous and bellicose backwater, awash with barbarism and misrule, to one of the most fashionable tourist destinations in Europe. The Disarming Act of 1746 signalled the start of an assault on traditional Highland society and culture; it removed the judicial authority of clan chiefs and banned Highland dress, bagpipes and the owning of weapons. Coupled with the post-Culloden atrocities it emasculated any threat from marauding clans that might be perceived by those in England and Lowland Scotland. Paving the way for the first tourists were adventurous travellers, keen to explore and record the natural history and antiquities; government-sponsored surveys assessing what resources of value existed and, in tandem, men of science eager to scour this previously unavailable scientific hunting ground.

In 1764 the Reverend John Walker, 'the mad minister of Moffat' and later professor of natural history at Edinburgh University, was appointed by Lord Kames to make a survey of the Highlands (due to its belligerent reputation little was actually known about the region): 'The Quillen Mountains, which are amongst the highest in the British Isles, are situated upon the West Coast, about the middle of the Island. The Mountains or rather skeletons of Mountains appear at a distance like a huge Congeries of Buildings and Spires in Ruins; and on approaching their Summits, all is sharp, ragged and naked, without either Earth or Herbage.'[1] This is the earliest mention of walking on the Cuillin mountains and enticingly suggestive of the first recorded ascent of a Main Ridge peak.

After the death of John Walker in 1803, Leith-born Robert Jameson took over as professor of natural history at Edinburgh University. Jameson was a key figure in the development of geology and natural history. Early nineteenth century Edinburgh was a hotbed of geological debate between the followers of James Hutton (Plutonists) and Abraham Werner (Neptunists) regarding the origin of rocks and whether the predominant agent was volcanic activity or water. Jameson, a devout Wernerian, reputedly hid from students and potential rivals any geological specimens that might contradict his own Neptunist views. His visit to Skye was part of an expedition to collect information for his 1800 publication, *Mineralogy of the Scottish Isles,* and, like his predecessor John Walker, Jameson was keen to explore the higher peaks: 'Rue-dunan, where we landed after Canna, is situated at the bottom of the Cuillin mountains, and at the head of Loch Brittle. The mountains rise here with the utmost grandeur; but the continual covering of clouds, prevented me from investigating them with so much accuracy as I wished.'[2] Jameson also ascended Glamaig and Beinn na Caillaich.

Between the surveys of John Walker and Robert Jameson, the Cuillin were also documented by Thomas Pennant, a Welsh naturalist and travel writer bent on recording the landscape, natural history and antiquities of the West Highlands. He was also a compassionate chronicler of the grinding poverty that prevailed prior to the kelp boom at the end of the eighteenth century. In 1772, Pennant's party made their second visit to Scotland, a land he famously described as 'little known to its Southern Brethren as Kamschatka'. In Skye they ascended to the large cairn on Beinn na Caillich in the Red Cuillin. Pennant's ecstatic description of the summit view has become a favourite for Skye anthologies: 'The prospect to the west was of desolation itself; a savage series of rude mountains, discoloured, black and red, as if by the rage of fire… The serrated tops of Blaven affect with astonishment: and beyond them, the clustered height of Quillin, or the mountain of Cuchullin, like its hero, stood like a hill that catches the clouds of heaven.'[3]

Samuel Johnson and James Boswell were inspired by Pennant's writing to tour the Hebrides. The writer, lexicographer and Tourette's sufferer was 64 years old when he arrived on Skye in September 1773. Many commentators express disappointment at Johnson's failure to describe the lofty peaks of Skye, but to Johnson mountains were just something that got in the way of the view. Boswell, on the other hand, does mention them, 'the Cuillin, a prodigious range of mountains, capped with rocky pinnacles in a strange variety of shapes', accurately comparing them to the mountains of Corsica.

In the Highlands, at this time, travellers often made a will before embarking on a long journey. Pennant, Boswell and Johnson proved it was now possible for the soft southern traveller to set a tentative foot north of the Highland Line without being dirked or robbed. The accounts of these early visitors drew attention away from the more exotic destinations of the Grand Tour to curiosities nearer home, a trend the Napoleonic Wars encouraged. But it was the Romantic movement's special relationship with wild places that accelerated the change in attitude. The Romantics hoped to counter the domination and destruction of nature, characterised by the Industrial Revolution, with an attitude of reverence and respect. Samuel Johnson describes Glen Sheil thus, 'An eye accustomed to flowery pastures and waving harvests is astonished and repelled by this wide extent of hopeless sterility.' From being areas to be feared and avoided, full of dark superstition, the advent of Romanticism made rugged Highland scenery extremely popular, with the Cuillin high on the not-to-be-missed list.

In London, James Boswell befriended James Macpherson, a schoolmaster from near Kingussie in Inverness-shire, 'a large, handsome man with thick legs; morose, sceptical, licentious and unamiable'.[4] It was this unlikely figure who was a catalyst in forging the rise of the Romantic movement. After touring Skye and neighbouring islands to collect Gaelic oral material, Macpherson published a series of epic poems between 1759 and 1763, purporting to be a translation of the third-century bard, Ossian's tales of the legendary hero Fingal. These chimed with the contemporary Caledonian mood, providing traumatised, post-Culloden Scotland with a politically undemanding ancestry it could be proud of. Ossian became a symbol of traditional values and stability at a time of great cultural and social upheaval.

Ossian inspired Scotland's first wave of literary tourism. In the forty years following Macpherson's publications, there was a burgeoning demand for a personal encounter with the Ossianic essence: the gloomy mists, raging torrents, tempestuous seas and mountain storms. The Cuillin became a major focal point in this upsurge of interest. The poet Robert Buchanan referred to the mountains as the 'Temple of Ossian' with their two 'entrance porches', Scavaig and Sligachan. The name was even 'Ossianised' to Cuchullin after a character in the poems based on the Irish hero Cuchulain who was Lord of Skye, or the 'Isle of Mist' as it was known. It was a literary connection early tourist guidebooks milked: 'Even the gloomy mountains of Cuchullin that rise in majestic splendour in its neighbourhood, are objects not unworthy of attention, as well from their altitude as from the mighty hero of the Celtic bard, whose name they bear, and who here often pursued the stag, and upon their cloudy summits held their aerial feast of shells.'[5]

Ossian became a publishing sensation; taking Europe by storm. The huge acclaim soon turned to controversy as its authenticity was questioned. The forgery claims were confined to England where they were not unrelated to the anti-Scottish sentiment prevalent at the time. (In London James Boswell continuously felt the need to apologise for being Scottish.) The poems suggested that the despised Highlands, and by association all of Scotland, had a literary heritage older and superior to its southern neighbour. Indeed, one of Samuel Johnson's prime motives for his trip north was to prove the poems fraudulent; he regarded Macpherson as a charlatan as he could not conceive a 'primitive' country like Scotland producing any work of literary merit. The writer Alexander Smith had no such doubts: 'If you think these poems exaggerated go out at

Sligachan and see what wild work the pencil of moonlight makes on a mass of shifting vapour. Does that seem nature or a madman's dream? Look at the billowing clouds rolling off the brow of Blaavin, all golden and on fire with the rising sun! Wordsworth's verse does not more completely mirror the Lake Country than do the poems of Ossian the terrible scenery of the Isles.[6] By 1805 Macpherson's books were outselling everything save the Bible and Shakespeare, with Napoleon carrying a copy on his campaigns.

The Napoleonic wars produced an unprecedented demand for gunpowder, so much so that the millstones used in its manufacture were wearing out. Britain needed to be hastily surveyed for a source of suitable rock, free of grains of quartz which could trigger explosions. The man given the task was John MacCulloch, a full-time chemist at the Board of Ordnance, who in 1811 was sent to Scotland for the millstone survey. Two years later he concluded that the limestone of Skye, found between Broadford and Torrin, was best suited for the purpose. Before plans for quarrying were implemented, Napoleon's defeat at Waterloo meant the crisis was over.

MacCulloch was then redeployed as a geologist with the Trigonometrical Survey, the forerunner of the Ordnance Survey. This was largely run by Thomas Colby who led an early attempt to climb Sgurr nan Gillean in July 1819. Colby's Royal Engineers established triangulation stations in Scotland that laid down the foundation for today's maps. Their survey was a tale of almost superhuman effort and endurance. In 1819 Colby drove the Sappers to cover 1,100 miles (1,770km) of remote Highland terrain in just 45 days. As well as constantly having to survey the rough, mountainous country, they also had to transport carts loaded with their heavy instruments, clothing and camping equipment. However, the Cuillin knocked some of the wind out of their sails when they were forced to turn back near the top of one of the peaks. It is often dangerous to speculate on such locations, but a description by R K Dawson, one of Colby's lieutenants, strongly suggests the west ridge of Sgurr nan Gillean:

> Not being provided with ladders or ropes the perpendicular rock at the summit effectually baffled our efforts for several hours to find a crevice by which to ascend it. We gained, however, a ridge which reaches out from the perpendicular cliff with a superb column at the end of it, and so narrow is this ridge that we were obliged to sit astride upon it, in which position little more than the strength of an infant was required to hurl a stone to the bottom of the corrie in the south side without impinging upon the face of the cliff, a depth of about 2,000 feet.[7]

Between 1815 and 1819 MacCulloch spent much time on Skye conducting geological surveys. His references to the Cuillin are largely limited to Bla Bhein and the Red Cuillin, considering the latter 'tamely rounded and disagreeably distinct'. MacCulloch was first to use the name 'Red Cuillin' due to the number of the hills that had *dearg* (Gaelic for red) in their title. On ascending Beinn na Caillich he is, like Pennant before him, greatly affected by the view of the Black Cuillin, 'The upper peaks are mere rocks and with acclivities so steep and so smooth, as to render all access impossible.'[8]

MacCulloch claimed to have made seven attempts to scale the Black Cuillin but he provides few details save pointing out that the most promising direction to climb them is from Loch Brittle or the head of Loch Sligachan. The Cuillin pioneer J D Forbes remarked: 'Such a want of success appears incredible.' MacCulloch's defence is characteristically vague, at least where the high tops are concerned: 'I formerly represented the cliffs which impede the examination of the Cuchullin hills. Since that period I have obtained access to a larger portion of them, but still there is much unseen, probably inaccessible to human footsteps.'[9]

MacCulloch claimed to have 'discovered' the principal rock of the Black Cuillin, which he named hypersthene after the Greek for immense strength, a term that remained in vogue until 1871 when it was renamed gabbro (after a town in Tuscany): 'I have chosen the term hypersthene rock to designate this new and important member of the trap family, since it is explicit and introduces no confusion into the existing nomenclature.' He published the results of his geological work in *A Description of the Western Islands of Scotland* (1819). The book included a geological map of Skye, the last of three versions he made. The first of these (1816) was based on the cartography of William Faden and Murdoch Mackenzie. MacCulloch later criticised their inaccuracy and, with some justification, lamented the difficulty of plotting his hard-won observations on an inaccurate base map. For his later versions (1817/1819) he turned to Arrowsmith's more reliable 1807 map.

The redoubtable Aaron Arrowsmith was the first to map Scotland with any degree of accuracy. He represents the Cuillin as a row of three mountains at the head of Loch Brittle, 'The Culinn Hills'. He also names some of the more accessible peaks such as: 'Glamaig', 'Benna Dearg', 'Marscow', 'Belveg' (Belig) and 'Garrabine' (Garbh-bheinn). Glenbrittle village is called 'Coilnamine', still unconnected by road to the rest of Skye. Glen Sligachan is marked as 'Strath na Creach' but there is still no sign of Loch Coruisk.

Most early maps of Skye were either for military and naval use, or estate rentals. Cartography was a crucial tool in the subjugation process that followed the Jacobite rebellions. There was little reason to accurately survey non-strategic and unproductive land like the high Cuillin, so maps tend to allude to them rather than show actual relief. Examples of this cartography include Matthew Stobie's maps of the MacDonald estate (1766) and Murdoch Mackenzie's nautical chart (1776). The latter only highlights significant landmarks visible from the sea with the 'Culen Hills' represented as a prominently shaded wedge.

One of the main estate surveys was by John Blackadder who was commissioned to map the MacDonald lands (c1811). At this particular juncture Highland cartographers held many people's future in their hands as the information they recorded could decide who was cleared off the land, who emigrated and who stayed; sometimes who lived and who died. Blackadder considered the runrig system as inefficient and his maps were used as a tool to amalgamate the best arable land into large scale sheep farms, clearing people to smallholdings on the coast where they might have some income as long as the kelp industry remained viable. Much of the lower land around the Black and Red Cuillin was subject to this process.

John MacCulloch was the first map-maker to show the Cuillin as a defined crescent-shaped ridge. In one of his papers to the Geological Society (1815) he explains that 'the lofty and formidable group of the Cuchullin hills are either nameless, or only recorded in the traditional geography of the shepherds'. The only summit MacCulloch names on the Main Ridge is Gars-bheinn ('Garsven'), which he regards as one of the highest peaks. He reckons the height of the Cuillin as around 3,000ft, with Bla Bheinn higher still. He was the first to show Loch Coruisk and Loch na Creitheach as well as adding several mountain names such as 'Blaven' and 'Scuir na Streigh' (Sgurr na Stri, the Hill of Strife). This last name originates from a long-running boundary dispute between the MacLeods of Dunvegan and the MacDonalds. The latter claimed that the march ran up the middle of Loch Coruisk whereas the MacLeods regarded the border as the glens running between Camasunary and Sligachan. The argument increased in significance in the twenty-first century when John MacLeod, Chief of Clan MacLeod, attempted to sell the Cuillin to pay for repairs to Dunvegan Castle. This opened a can of worms as his ownership of the mountains came into question. However the longstanding debate established, though the exact boundary was still uncertain, that his land adjoined the MacDonald estate.

After the maps of Arrowsmith and MacCulloch, the next major cartographic development was John Thomson's *Atlas of Scotland* (1832). On his map of Skye Thomson used several names for the Cuillin mountains and corries not previously documented. Many of these appear to be spelt phonetically, perhaps giving more clues to their original derivation: 'Sgurdubhnahua' (Sgurr na h-Uamha), 'Bruchnafrea', 'Scurvadie', 'Sgurnanack' (Sgumain/Alasdair), 'Scurdubhniedaewin' (Sgurr Dubh an Da Bheinn), 'Tarinelar' (Sgurr a' Ghreadaidh?), 'Coirecass' (Coire Riabhach on Sgurr nan Gillean), 'Coirachgorme' (Coire a' Ghreadaidh), 'Coirebanochir' (Coire na Banachdich), 'Coirelaen' (Coire Lagan). The settlement in Glenbrittle is named 'Leasoll'.

Almost every writer used a different spelling for the Cuillin, Walter Scott hedging his bets with four different variations: Quillen, Cuillin, Coolin, and Cuillen. Cartographers preferred Culin, Culen or Cullen. William Daniell informs us that of all the variations for Coruisk such as Coruisg, Coriskin, and Coruisq, Mackinnon of Corrie considered the last to be correct (despite Gaelic having no 'q'). However it is Cuchullin and Coruisk, the versions favoured by the influential MacCulloch, that are most often adopted.

MacCulloch's official work was curtailed in 1820 due to financial cuts. When he discussed his concerns with Thomas Colby, MacCulloch was 'not very coherent and talked of hanging and shooting himself'. The surveys had taken its toll on his health and he now concentrated on teaching and writing. In 1824 MacCulloch published his most controversial work, the four-volume *The Highlands and Western Isles of Scotland*. In this prolix, occasionally engrossing, topographical work MacCulloch relates how he made several attempts to reach Loch Coruisk. He exaggerates the remoteness of the setting as 'only known to the Shepherds of Strathaird' and claims it is inaccessible by land except at one point, the pass over Druim Hain from Glen Sligachan. The first time he tried to walk to the loch he was forced to turn back at the Bad Step, a rocky slab that had to be negotiated on the path along Loch Scavaig: 'I made the attempt, not being inexperienced in such adventures; but soon finding myself on the bare face of a smooth rock, far elevated above the deep sea that was rolling below, with nothing but rocks around and overhead, suspended like Mahomet's tomb, between heaven and earth, I became glad to retreat.'[10] He eventually hired a boat and crew to bypass the obstacle. In the contemporary herring boom Loch Scavaig was often bustling with life, yet MacCulloch perpetuates the romantic myth of the 'lost world of Coruisk':

> When suddenly, on turning the angle of a high rock, a valley burst on my view, which, in a moment, obliterated Loch Scavig, together with all the records of all the valleys that had ever left their traces on the table of my brain. The name of this extraordinary place is Coruisk… I felt as if transported by some magician into the enchanted wilds of an Arabian tale, carried to the inhabitants of Genii among the mysterious recesses of the Caucasus.[11]

MacCulloch's account of the trip caused a furore, especially his portrayal of local people as indolent and incompetent. A whole book, James Browne's vituperative *Critical Examination* (1825), was written in response. In it Charles MacDonald of Gillian stated, 'I affirm that the whole of his account of the sail to Scavaig is a tissue of lies.' MacCulloch was a complex character, described by Alexander Smith as 'caustic, censorious and epigrammatic'. The geologist Charles Lyell was more compassionate, attributing his faults to 'ill-health feeding on a sensitive nature'.

MacCulloch's *The Highlands and Western Isles of Scotland* was dedicated, in a brazen marketing ploy, to his friend Sir Walter Scott who would excel even Ossian as a publicist for the Cuillin. Scott encouraged the tourist by inhabiting the wild Highland landscapes of his poems and novels with wholesome heroic figures far removed from the reality of an impoverished and destitute people after the post-Napoleonic collapse of the kelp and cattle markets. With many associated bestsellers, Scott was lionised by the public as a major celebrity, rivalled only by Shakespeare as a literary icon. In 1814 he was invited by the engineer Robert Stevenson, the novelist's grandfather, on the Lighthouse Commissioners' annual tour of inspection of Scottish lighthouses in their cutter, the *Pharos*. He took this opportunity to visit Skye and research locations for one of his last long narrative-poems, *The Lord of the Isles*. On 25 August they landed at Camasunary where Scott's party was guided by a farm boy, John Cameron, to the outlet of the River Scavaig:

> Advancing up this huddling and riotous brook, we found ourselves in a most extraordinary scene; we were surrounded by hills of the boldest and most precipitous character, and on the margin of a lake which seemed to have sustained the constant ravages of torrents from these rude neighbours… I never saw a spot on which there was less appearance of vegetation of any kind: the eye rested on nothing but brown and naked crags, and the rocks on which we walked by the side of the loch were as bare as the pavements of Cheapside.[12]

In his notes to *The Lord of the Isles,* Scott wrote, 'It is as exquisite a savage scene as Loch Katrine is a scene of Romantic beauty.'[13] Despite Scott's often rhetorical description, he does provide some factual information, noting the perched boulders and observing some were of a different origin than the exposed rock. He also isolates individual peaks, 'on the left-hand side, which we traversed, rose a higher and equally inaccessible mountain, the top of which seemed to contain the crater of a exhausted volcano'. Scott's party walked to the head of Loch Coruisk where, in *The Lord of the Isles,* he set the meeting of the fugitive Robert the Bruce with Cormac Doil.

On his return home Scott wrote to the Chief of Clan MacLeod at Dunvegan asking for an introduction at the castle for William Daniell, a landscape artist and aquatint engraver who proposed travelling clockwise around Britain illustrating prominent coastal features including Dunvegan and 'the lake of terror which lies at the foot of the Coolin'. Daniell started at Land's End in 1813, finishing at the same point ten years later after a total of six trips carried out during the more amenable summer months. The west coast of Skye was largely accessed by sea, the east coast by land. At points of interest he made detailed pencil sketches annotated with details of colours and textures.

The results were published in *A Voyage Round Great Britain,* one of the towering topographical works of the early nineteenth century, containing over

300 aquatint plates engraved by Daniell from his own drawings. Four of these, completed in the summer of 1815, feature the Cuillin. One shows a large rowing boat surrounded by steep mountains. This is not Loch Scavaig as one first presumes, but Coruisk, for the boats have been manhandled from the salt water to the fresh.

Prior to the eighteenth century landscape paintings were rarely created for their own sake as they were regarded as an inferior class of picture. There followed a transition from composite or imaginary landscapes to paintings of precise, identifiable locations. Crucial to this, in the late eighteenth century, was William Gilpin who travelled through Britain cataloguing views and formulating simple rules for the composition of attractive rural scenes. He recommended that artists judiciously recompose the scene according to his rather arbitrary 'picturesque' principles. The Romantics, meanwhile, were advocating a sense of union with the natural world. All this conspired to make landscape painting the height of fashion as a series of stock viewpoints and vistas evolved. And where the artist went the tourist was sure to follow, hot in pursuit of the perfect picturesque prospect.

The story of the Cuillin is inextricably bound up with the development of the tourist industry, which in the Highlands had its foundation in the period between 1790 and 1810. By the 1790s picturesque taste and the Ossian cult were vindicating the Scots after the pejorative comments made by the likes of Samuel Johnson. Early visitors to Scotland initially confined themselves to a round of historical and picturesque sights in the more accessible Lowlands and Southern Highlands, like the Falls of Clyde, Loch Lomond, Rosslyn Chapel, and the Hermitage (Ossian's Hall) at Dunkeld. With the publication of Scott's *Lady of the Lake* in 1810, visitors thronged to the new tourist honeypot of the Trossachs. With *The Lord of the Isles* in 1815 attention shifted north to Loch Coruisk and the Cuillin, with tourist guidebooks promoting these as requisite highlights of the Ossianic circuit.

If the picturesque was about aesthetics, the sublime (often spelt with a capital) was about emotional reaction. Dublin-born Edmund Burke, one of the most influential of the Romantic thinkers, summed up the sublime as 'a state of mind awakened by the great and energetic aspects of nature'. He suggested that pleasure and pain were represented by the concepts of beauty and sublimity; beauty was associated with regularity and inspires love, whereas the more rugged sublimity causes strong feelings of fear and awe that in turn arouse instincts of self-preservation. It was the most powerful response nature could inspire. In Scotland, the Cuillin, and especially Loch Coruisk, were regarded by many as the apotheosis of sublimity, the Romantic ideal of a landscape where the elemental forces of nature were still in control, impervious to technological advance and uncontaminated by social or industrial change.

When William Daniell's party visited Loch Coruisk, despite fine, settled weather and an 'ample supply of cold meats with wine and other good cheer', Daniell felt compelled to toe the Burke line: 'The frowning grandeur of the savage and sterile scene spread a gloom over our spirits which, for a time, were indescribably oppressive… The contemplation of such a wilderness, even under the mild aspect of a summer's day is sufficiently appalling, but what must be its horrors in the agitation of a midnight tempest.'[14] He goes on to recount a tourist visiting Coruisk who 'was seized with an access of melancholy which deprived him of all energy. He could imagine no parallel to this feeling, but the rapid precipitation from sadness to despair which is the usual precursor of suicide.'[15] Into the 1860s tourist guidebooks continued to describe Loch Coruisk with the likes of 'beauty reposing in the lap of terror'.

The Romantic artists championed a move away from topographical accuracy towards using ever-changing weather and light to fuel an emotive response to nature. J M W Turner was regarded as the apogee of the Romantic style and was commissioned by Walter Scott's publisher, Robert Cadell, to illustrate a later edition of *The Lord of the Isles,* as he reckoned someone of Turner's prestige would double sales. Scott, heavily in debt, set great store on this, but fretted whether the artist would manage to visit Coruisk due to its remoteness and the lateness of the season.

When Turner eventually arrived in Skye, in September 1831, he made a series of drawings of the Cuillin from various viewpoints including Ord, Torrin and Elgol. He considered Loch Coruisk 'one of the wildest of Nature's landscapes', making sketches around the loch as well as from the west side of Loch Scavaig below Gars-bheinn. Turner eventually favoured an elevated viewpoint, high on Sgurr na Stri, where he includes two figures in the foreground. In a letter to Cadell he related how he slipped on the rocky ascent and only saved himself by grabbing handfuls of turf.

Turner visited Cadell on his return to Edinburgh, news the publisher passed on to Scott: 'He is great in his praise of Coriskin and wanted to know if you prefer any one point more than another.' The resulting watercolour, *Loch Coriskin*, was also engraved as the frontispiece of the first volume of Scott's *Poetical Works*. In *Modern Painters* the critic John Ruskin described it as 'the perfect expression of the inferior mountains'. Many weren't so sure and voiced their doubts about the accuracy of Turner's portrayal. The painting makes much more topographical sense as a mirror image which may be linked to the use of a Claude glass, a darkened lens used to aid composition and reduce contrast. The watercolour can be viewed every January in the National Gallery of Scotland in Edinburgh.

Many other artists came to capture the sterile grandeur and grisly proclivities of the Cuillin. George Fennell Robson was born in Durham, one of 26 children. He often used Scott's writing to help select the most commercial subjects for his painting. Robson regularly stayed with the farmer at Camasunary, when he produced several watercolours of Loch Coruisk. In one, probably inspired by Scott's *The Lord of the Isles*, he inserted three kilted Highlanders at the loch side;

another version has a bird of prey on a rock in the foreground, a third a herd of goats. The version with the Highlanders, displayed in London's Victoria and Albert Museum, was reviewed in the *London Literary Gazette* (1826), 'A scene of more sublime desolation could hardly have been given to the eye, or more happily executed by the hand of the artist, than that which is here depicted for the contemplation of the admirers of Nature in her awful grandeur.' The Cuillin pioneer Alexander Nicolson picked out John MacWhirter's *Loch Coruisk* for particular praise, but felt the view of the Cuillin from the sea was even finer. Artists who used this viewpoint included Sam Bough, Sir Thomas Dick Lauder and Reverend John Thomson of Duddingston. The latter's work, from a sketching trip in 1836, was also engraved for a later edition of Scott's *The Lord of the Isles*.

From the sublime to the ridiculous. In 1822 Walter Scott stage-managed the visit of George IV to Edinburgh, the first to Scotland by a reigning monarch since 1650, when the king appeared wearing a bright red mini-kilt with pink pantaloons to hide his varicose veins. However the royal pageant succeeded in changing attitudes regarding the clans, as did the prestige gained by Highland regiments in the Napoleonic wars. Symbolically it was the start of post-Culloden reconciliation, a process, it could be argued, that continues today. It was also the beginning of a re-branding exercise that gave the Highlands a glamorous new image. The Cuillin and Coruisk became an integral part of a Highland Grand Tour that incorporated picturesque attractions like Iona, Staffa and Ben Nevis, as well as the parallel and unparalleled sublimity of Glen Roy and Glen Coe respectively. Writers like Walter Scott imbued these landscapes with myth and legend whose authenticity the Victorians loved to debate. Steamers heading north were packed with tourists eager to render their own views and interpretations. *The Scottish Tourist Companion* (1823) endorsed their choice of destination: 'Scotland presents to the inquisitive traveller a scene more interesting than perhaps any other spot of equal extent on the globe.'

From the 1820s steamers were available from Glasgow to Oban. After the opening of the Caledonian Canal in 1822 there was a connecting service between Oban and Inverness. From the canal the independent traveller bound for Skye now had a choice of two new Parliamentary roads, part of a government road building programme between 1803 and 1825. From Fort William they could take the 'Road to the Isles', with its strong Jacobite connections, to the Treigh ferry, near the Arisaig Inn, for Ardvasar. From Arisaig you could also hire a boat to take you directly to Loch Slapin and the Spar Cave, 'the principal object of curiosity in the island of Skye'.

After the abandonment of the Bernera Barracks near Glenelg in the 1790s the military road there, from Fort Augustus via Glen Moriston, fell into neglect. In 1812 a new road, from Invergarry to the Skye ferry at Kyle Rhea, was constructed by Thomas Telford, a shorter route by way of Loch Loyne that was designed to open up the area and help boost the economy. There were inns every ten miles or so: Tomdoun, Cluanie (originally called Reabuie), Sheil, Kylerhea. In remote areas early inns were more akin to emergency shelters geared to the needs of cattle rather than the requirements of the genteel traveller, which explains the constant drone of complaint from southern visitors, mostly concerning bedding and cuisine.

It is to the same centuries-old droving route that the Sligachan Inn, the well-known Cuillin watering hole, owes its existence. The Inn had a strategic location on the main route taking cattle from the Western Isles through Skye to the Michaelmas trysts (markets) at Crieff and Falkirk. After 1800 over 7,000 black cattle were annually driven south from the island, and Sligachan was the gathering point where herds from the Outer Isles joined those from Portree and the north of Skye.

The original Sligachan Inn was situated at Kinloch near the head of Loch Sligachan where there was a ford. Its remains can be seen by following a path along the river from the present campsite. The location was significant as a shelter for drovers and travellers who might have to wait days for the water to subside when the bridgeless River Sligachan was in spate. Mrs Sarah Murray is one of few visitors to have left a description of the original hostelry, 'a hut of an inn, too bad to sleep at, but there may be had, as I was told, tolerably good eating and drinking'.

Sligachan was the location of an important cattle market. The *Clarion of Skye* (October 1953) recalls the first market in October 1794 when 4,000 people attended, and 1,400 black cattle and 200 horses and ponies were sold. By the mid-nineteenth century there were three cattle markets a year at Sligachan. With the gradual decline in droving this was consolidated into one large annual market on the third Friday in September. Tourists often had to be turned away as the inn was full of tipsy drovers. The wall around today's campsite demarcates the original cattle stance. (Droving on Skye continued well into the 1950s).

In 1805 Lord Stanhope reported there were still no proper roads on the island. Through the next decade their construction was stimulated by Telford's new road to Kyle Rhea as well as the development of new fishing ports like Stein in the north-west of the island. In 1815 the road from Sligachan to Portree was completed. John Macpherson, the Chamberlain of Skye, wrote: 'The opening of the road from Bridge of Sligachan to Portree conduces to the comfort of the public as it prevents the necessity of ferrying at Sconser which is difficult in winter, particularly with swimming horses.' Three years later Macpherson described 'the desperate circumstances' of Mackenzie, the innkeeper at Sconser, as the new road with its Telford bridge over the River Sligachan now enabled travellers to reach Broadford from Portree in one day.

Joseph Mitchell was the engineer responsible for inspecting the new stretch of road connecting Sligachan to Broadford, completed in 1825. Visiting the

Sligachan Inn he stumbled across an uncannily modern scene: 'The tents, if they could be called such, were temporary, formed of blankets and were miserable. The whole aspect of the place, a bare and barren mountainside, was wild and savage. It had been raining all night and as most of the people had been either up drinking or sleeping on the ground during the night, they had a dirty and dishevelled appearance.'[16]

Two visitors who would have fitted seamlessly into this scene were the geologists Adam Sedgwick and Roderick Murchison, who arrived on Skye in 1827. During their earlier visits to Arran, Staffa and Mull they had gradually gone native; on one occasion they 'slept at a whiskey-shop, and breakfasted in the same room with the pigs'. Personal hygiene was becoming a problem as Professor Sedgwick, who had taken to wearing a plaid and was often mistaken for a drover, commented, 'the two shirts I had with me would have fetched a good price from a tallow-chandler'. He was eventually reunited with his luggage, including some much-needed soap. In Skye the weather was wild: 'Our attempt to cross the Cuchullins almost ended fatally. Lord MacDonald's forester was our guide; but in a dreadful storm of wind and rain, accompanied with the usual mists, he lost his way. After wandering many hours in a state of great misery we at length escaped from a labyrinth of precipices by the help of my needle, and found our way to a farm-house.'[17]

One of the first tourists to record a visit to the new Sligachan Inn was the Reverend Charles Lesingham Smith in 1835. He had just completed a five-year stint as a mathematics lecturer at Christ's College, Cambridge. Lesingham Smith was delighted to find a recent building, 'a perfect palace', infinitely superior to the old inn. On 5th September, after a hearty breakfast of mutton chops and eggs, he hired a local gamekeeper, Duncan MacInyre, to guide him over Druim Hain to Coruisk: 'All is bare and gloomy, and one cannot contemplate without an appalling thrill such a desolation of sterility.' As they then made very good time to the head of the loch his guide suggested they take a more direct way back, zigzagging up the rocky slopes to the ridge and then down into Harta Corrie. Smith was initially cautious about the shortcut, but decided to consider the proposition over lunch when he enjoyed some more mutton, biscuits and 'made a considerable vacuum in my whisky flask':

> Well we began to ascend, and at first succeeded admirably; though the labour was indeed tremendous, 'I am sure we shall do well' said I, 'Best not be too sure Sir, one step may send us all the way back.' We now came to a steeper part, where we were obliged to crawl upon our hands and knees, and I found my umbrella a sad nuisance; but the Forester's two dogs were much worse,

for they were constantly in my way. Sometimes we climbed up a cleft, in the bare rock just like a chimney; and sometimes the one was obliged to push the other up; and he in return, pulled up the first. A single false step would have hurled us to destruction, and there was moreover very great danger that the first man would loosen some stone that might sweep down the hindmost. I once sent down a tremendous rock, the percussion of which against the crag below, sent up a strong smell of sulphur; fortunately for the Forester he was above me. In the midst of all these difficulties we arrived at a spot where the crag rose up so smoothly and perpendicularly that it was vain to attempt ascending it; we were obliged therefore to turn back a little, and angle around as he called it. But in the end we surmounted every obstacle and stepped forth proudly and joyously upon the topmost crag! And what a scene of unparalleled sublimity and grandeur was spread around us![18]

Although Lesingham Smith's route has traditionally been regarded as the first scramble to be recorded in the Cuillin, it was in fact a long-established link for shepherds and others between Sligachan and the top of Loch Coruisk. However this was, as his guide verified, the first ascent by a gentleman. Smith is the first writer to mention 'Harticory' and 'Lotecory'. The route used was marked on some maps as 'Hartie Corrie Pass'. The Reverend Smith came to a sad end in 1878, certified insane after he was convinced he was being poisoned by his nephew.

The year after Smith's adventure, in 1836, another visitor is credited with the start of mountaineering proper, not just in Skye but Scotland as a whole. His name was James David Forbes and his ascents of Sgurr nan Gillean in 1836 and 1845 are often regarded as the formal birth of Scottish mountaineering. After studying law he turned to science where he achieved an international reputation as a geologist and one of the foremost British experts on glaciology. In 1833 Forbes, a determined careerist, won a bitterly-fought contest to become professor of natural philosophy at Edinburgh, aged 24, a position he held until his health broke down in 1859.

Forbes's first three visits to Skye, between 1836 and 1845, cover a tumultuous period in the island's history: two devastating potato famines and the cataclysmic effects of the Great Disruption of 1843 when one-third of congregations left the established church to form the Free Church of Scotland. His initial visit, in July 1836, was part of a walking tour of the Highlands when he made a list of useful Gaelic words and phrases in his notebook: 'which is the way?', 'give me a drink', a reflection of how little English was spoken in some areas. On arrival at Broadford he wrote his sister Jane: 'I confess I have not yet got reconciled to be continually wet and to sit wet as the denizens of this happy country are, but I am gradually being initiated into the mysteries of being soaked five times a day.'[19]

He first explored Spar Cave and then the north of the island, before walking through Glen Sligachan to Camasunary where he met Duncan MacIntyre and hired him as a guide (the fee of ten shillings is carefully logged in his notebook). He took Forbes towards Loch Coruisk where they climbed up to a viewpoint 'to the east of Coruisk', presumably Sgurr na Stri. From here Forbes would have been drawn to Sgurr nan Gillean with its remarkable outline of Pinnacle Ridge. Sgurr nan Gillean was reputed to be the highest of the Cuillin, but was widely regarded as unclimbable and its name, 'peak of the young men', was said to originate from the untimely fate of those who attempted it. The dramatic shapes of the Cuillin were obvious challenges to the young men of Skye, and if any succeeded in scaling them there are reasons why details have not survived. They would have formed part of a Gaelic oral tradition not easily accessible to outsiders. It was also in the early mountaineers' interest to suppress any local climbing tradition that diminished the status of their own ascents.

By this time MacIntyre had made several attempts on Sgurr nan Gillean either by himself or with various clients who had engaged him. These were all from the Coire a' Bhasteir side, but he now thought a possible route might be found round on its southern flanks. He still felt the summit itself would be unattainable. In this he was proved wrong for, on 7th July 1836, the pair reached the top in two-and-a-half hours 'with little difficulty and no risk'. They had traversed around the foot of Pinnacle Ridge and easily gained the ridge between Sgurr Beag and Sgurr nan Gillean. Although now known as the Tourist Route, the final 200ft (60m) involves some scrambling as Forbes discovered: 'The extreme roughness of the rocks (all hypersthene) rendered the ascent safe, where with any other formation it might have been considerably perilous. Indeed, I have never seen a rock so adapted for clambering. At that time I erected a cairn and temporary flag, which stood, I was informed, for a whole year.'[20]

In May 1843 Forbes was back in the Cuillin when he made more geological notes before returning to Edinburgh for his marriage to Alicia Wauchope, daughter of a Leith wine merchant. After recovering from a serious illness, he travelled to Skye with Mrs Forbes in May 1845, 'digesting the severities of science amidst the beauties of nature'. That summer he also visited an old friend in Portree, Louis Albert Necker de Saussure, whom he first met in Edinburgh in 1831. Necker had first visited Skye in September 1807, part of an ambitious geological field trip he documented in *A Voyage to the Hebrides* (1822). (As was common at the time, this book may have been an unauthorised translation.)

But why was a member of an illustrious Swiss family, a professor of mineralogy and geology in Geneva, living for over twenty years in a remote Highland village? In the 1830s, 'distressed and disgusted by home politics', and suffering increasingly from depression, he became restless and travelled extensively, including a series of lengthy trips back to Scotland. He spent the winter of 1839-40 in Portree. Letters to his mother relate how the landscape of Skye evoked in him the spirit of Ossian. Necker eventually resolved to settle permanently on what he calls 'Ile des Brouillards', a decision influenced by a family fall out, as well as unstipulated romantic complications. He arrived in Portree in April 1841 (to the news of his mother's death) and took up lodgings with John Cameron, tenant of the Portree inn, at the family home, 10 Bosville Terrace, now part of the Bosville Hotel, where he was able to look out on 'Les Cullen' from his room.

During the summer of 1845 Forbes started to explore the Cuillin with Necker, taking scientific notes and observations: 'The Cuchullin ridge constitutes a more connected chain of craggy peaks whose fantastic outlines, in certain positions, may vie with any in the world.' They walked completely around the range as well as crossing some of the easier passes. Necker also assisted Forbes with the analysis of geological specimens found on the Cuillin. Forbes made his second ascent of Sgurr nan Gillean with Duncan MacIntyre when they ascended Fionn Choire to the summit of Bruach na Frithe and then, from Bealach nan Lice, traversed under the south face of Am Basteir. The Bhasteir Tooth reminded him of one of the peaks of the Dauphiné, 'a gigantic nutcracker, menacing heaven with its open jaws'. They proceeded to climb Sgurr nan Gillean by a long-forgotten route from Lota Corrie, probably a line of weakness on the left side of Sgurr nan Gillean's south face. Using a barometer, Forbes was attempting to calculate the height difference between Sgurr nan Gillean and Bruach na Frithe. His results were inconclusive due to a fall in pressure, but by careful interpolation of this change at Sligachan, as well as correlating his observations with those made by Necker at Portree, he estimated the height of Sgurr nan Gillean between 3,200ft and 3,220ft, with Bruach na Frithe 40ft lower (Sgurr nan Gillean is 3,162ft/964m, Bruach na Frithe 3,143ft/958m).

Until Louis Agassiz's travels in Scotland in 1840 and the announcement of his fieldwork in *The Scotsman* in October of that year, 'Discovery of Former Existence of Glaciers in Scotland,' it was largely unrecognised that the Scottish Highlands had been subject to glaciation. On his explorations in the Cuillin Forbes observed further evidence that supported Agassiz. At the entrance to Coir' a' Mhadaidh, as well as in the lower reaches of Coir' a' Ghrunnda, he noted semicircular ridges of boulders very similar to the terminal moraine a glacier would leave. Around Loch Coruisk he itemised a number of features that were indicators of the former action of ice: the perched blocks, roches moutonnées, striations and grooves parallel to the valley trend, and smooth surfaces at variance with the roughness of gabbro. Roches moutonnées were named by Necker's grandfather, the mountain scientist Horace de Saussure, not after sheep as thought by many geography teachers, but because he considered they resembled the curls of wigs, called moutonnées due to the mutton fat used to hold them in place.

Forbes's fieldwork of May 1845 was published a year later as 'Notes on the Topography and Geology of the Cuchullin Hills in Skye and on the Traces of Ancient Glaciers which they Present'. In summary, Forbes's main arguments against the traditional geomorphological theories were twofold. The hypersthene (gabbro) was extremely hard, resistant to erosion and would require a very powerful agent working over a long time to produce the existing forms; secondly, the radial pattern could only have been produced by local glaciers, not sea ice. Yet, when he writes to William Whewell on 8th January 1846 he still feels uncertain about his evidence: 'I have lately written a paper on the geology of the Cuchullin Hills in Skye, in which I think I have all but demonstrated the existence of ancient glaciers there, having been myself convinced most entirely against my will.'[21] Later the same year he wrote Necker, to whom he had sent a draft of his article: 'I assure you, that I have the greatest reluctance in the world to introduce such cold neighbours for you as glaciers in the Cuillin Hills.' Archibald Geikie, Director of the Scottish branch of the Geological Survey, had no such doubts and described Forbes's paper as 'the most detailed and satisfactory account which has yet been given of the proofs that the Highlands of Britain once nourished groups of glaciers'.[22]

Forbes went on to create the first map solely of the Cuillin, part of his 1846 article, which he called *Eye Sketch for a Map of the Cuchullin Hills in Skye*. He used a scale of about a half-inch to the mile. On it, Forbes names eight of the Cuillin corries, admitting to forgetting Coir' a' Ghrunnda which he calls 'Bottomless Corry'. Along with its predecessors, Forbes's map demonstrated the amount of variation that existed with regard to Cuillin place names: Druim nan Ramh is called 'Drumnanrahue' by Thomson, 'Strona Stree' by Forbes and is marked as 'Sgor na Ramh' on A & C Black's 1862 map. The same cartographers call Sgurr na Stri: 'Scuir na Streigh', 'Trodhu' and 'Sgor na Stri' respectively. This impressive peaklet near the entrance to Loch Coruisk was often referred to as 'Trodhu' by Victorian tourists, and this name was even resurrected for use on the 1912 Bartholomew half-inch map. Most of the Cuillin mountain names were standardised with the publication of the first Ordnance Survey (OS) maps to cover the mountains in 1885.

Forbes's map was a highly credible effort considering it was produced from sketches in the field without the help of proper surveying equipment. The extent of his explorations can be inferred from the map; those areas surveyed on foot are presumably given most detail: Coruisk, Coir' a' Ghrunnda, Coire Lagan, Coire Riabhach. If Forbes scaled further peaks (he intended climbing Bla Bheinn but was prevented by an accident) one of the most likely contenders is Gars-bheinn; he makes several references to the geology of this mountain and provides details of the steep descent down the ridge to Loch Scavaig.

Forbes's cartography of the Cuillin and understanding of their origin contributed considerably to making the mountains less objects of apprehension, and more of a desirable destination for the new breed of intrepid mountain tourist. He is remembered by the Aiguille Forbes and its classic Forbes Arete in the Mont Blanc Massif. Professor Necker maintained a reclusive, nocturnal lifestyle until his death in 1861. He is buried in the old Portree Churchyard, but his name lives on in an optical illusion he devised, the Necker Cube, now used as a test of perception.

By the mid-nineteenth century Queen Victoria began to visit Balmoral and this royal endorsement, combined with the first cross-border rail routes in the 1840s, ensured parts of the Highlands were thronged with visitors. The Cuillin area, through association with Walter Scott, Ossian, Bonnie Prince Charlie and J M W Turner, proved irresistible to the tourist. Bradshaw's railway guides were consulted, portmanteaus packed with angling equipment and sketching materials; pencils sharpened to journalise the horrid gloom, abysmal precipices, unfathomed lakes and dense vapours. Newspapers and magazines also boosted Skye's reputation as a fashionable holiday destination:

> 'In respect of wild solitude', said the editor of the *Inverness Courier*, 'Coruisk is probably the most extraordinary spot in all Scotland. The Harz Mountains and the Brocken, of which so much has been said by German poets, and which have been made a seat of wildness and superstitious horror in Europe by Goethe's famous *Walpurgis Nacht*, are very tame beside any of the wilder parts of the Highlands of Scotland, and can bear no comparison with the Cuchillins and Coruisk.'[23]

Throughout the Highlands there was a tradition that well-connected travellers used a letter of introduction to secure accommodation at a manse or the home of a local dignitary. In the 1840s there were at least ten inns on Skye, but to allow gentry to sleep in a potentially flea-ridden bed was anathema to genteel Highland custom. Around the Cuillin the most prominent sources of hospitality were Mackinnon at Corriechatachan (Corry) outside Broadford, where Boswell got tipsy, the Reverend Mackinnon at Kilbride, and Macalister at Kirkibost. The Macalisters owned Strathaird estate, the triangle formed by Elgol, Loch Coruisk, and Bla Bheinn, from 1786 until 1884. Strathaird House was built in 1826 where the family were very hospitable to guests, though not so charitable to their tenantry—500 were evicted in 1852.

Three years earlier, in Inverness, the judge Lord Henry Cockburn jailed several men from North Uist for resisting forced emigration. Cockburn, a prominent Whig politician honoured with a street name in Edinburgh, stayed with Mackinnon at Corry in 1841 when he was keen to view the Cuillin with a fresh, objective eye after the hyperbole of Scott and MacCulloch. The boats used for Loch Scavaig generally held four oarsmen and up to six passengers plus their guide. The lengthy approach from Torrin, four hours there, four hours back, allowed Cockburn time to admire the surrounding mountains:

> Black, steep, hard, and splintered, they seemed to stand amphitheatrically, and rising from the very level of the sea, their irony and shiny tops, stream up to the height, MacCulloch says of 3000 feet (but I suspect that this is too much) and are fixed in every variety of peak and precipice, and ridge, and pillar, made more curiously picturesque by forms so fantastic, that were it not for their position and their obvious hardness, it might be supposed that they were artificial… Yet, hard though they be, I thought I saw places where even I could have found my way out: and Mackinnon assures me that the shepherds find their way in by the hills, whenever it is necessary.[24]

Many visitors to the Cuillin continued to be either sponsored by the government, like John MacCulloch, or were well-heeled artists and writers with access to their own transport, invariably by sea. With the expansion of the steamer services the options for travel were extended to a greater demographic. There were as yet few piers, and passengers often had to disembark in small boats or, at low tide, clamber ashore over seaweed and slippery rocks. Portree harbour, designed by Thomas Telford, was completed in 1820.

Initially most steamers in the West Highlands and islands were run by G & J Burns. By 1840 there was a weekly Glasgow to Skye steamer, as yet only in the summer months, making it possible to reach the island direct from the Clyde in two days, rather than nearer two weeks by sail. After the business was sold to David Hutcheson & Company, the steamer network continued to expand through the twin demands of the tourist eagerly heading north to see the enchanted world of Ossian, and ships going south carrying economic migrants tearfully bound for Australia or Canada. The geologist Archibald Geikie, a frequent visitor to Skye, was an eye-witness to the notorious evictions from Suisnish and Boreraig in 1852. Some of the villagers were transported towards a new life in Australia aboard the *Hercules*: 'The Cuillin mountains were in sight for several hours of our passage: but when we rounded Ardnamurchan Point, the emigrants saw the sun for the last time glitter upon their splintered peaks, and one prolonged and dismal wail rose from all parts of the vessel; the fathers and mothers held up their infant children to take a last view of the mountains of their Fatherland which in a few minutes faded from their view forever.'

Geikie also pointed out that the first concern of the early steamers was to supply the islanders' needs, often making long detours to pick up sheep or cattle. Consequently tourists were a low priority and had to share the decks with 'odoriferous barrels of herring'. Once on Skye visitors found that the island was promoting its very own Grand Tour: Spar Cave (named after the minerals that lined its walls), the Cuillin and Loch Coruisk, as well as Glen Sligachan which now, despite the bogs, had scenic prestige second only to Glen Coe. One tourist described this itinery: 'Experience enables the writer to assure travellers that this route can present nature, from the depths of a remarkable cavern to the lonely crests of mountains, together with every variety of cool moisture, from a scotch mist on the Corrie to a rather deeper ford, or the deeper depths of the mosses in Sligachan.'

Spar Cave, whose interior Walter Scott likened to a mermaid's bath, was located near Strathaird Point about two miles east of Elgol, about halfway on the sea route from Torrin to Loch Coruisk. The cave was first explored by Mrs Gilliespie of Kilmarie in 1808 and its popularity was cemented when, three years later, a whole book was written about it by K Macleay from Oban. However its reputation, as once a showcase of the Celtic world, was now in decline as one visitor confirmed, 'Steam-boats come here, and vomit forth their gaping multitudes.' There was a flourishing souvenir trade in broken-off stalactites; the walls were blackened by tar torches with some parties even burning tar barrels for a better view. Eventually a locked door was built to prevent further vandalism from 'Cockney tourists'. Lord Cockburn said of it, 'At present the only reward for going in consists in the pleasure of getting out.' Its place was taken by other attractions in the north of the island: the Storr and the Quiraing where enterprising Napoleonic war veterans had set themselves up as guides.

A basic infrastructure started to develop to meet the new demand for sight-seeing, increasingly focused on the Sligachan Inn, 'the real headquarters of the tourist in Skye despite the pitiless rains'. Tourist guidebooks recommended an itinerary where visitors could tick off Coruisk, the Cuillin and Glen Sligachan in a single day. After a night at Mr MacKenzie's inn at Broadford, you forwarded luggage to Sligachan with a note to secure accommodation there. You then made your way to Torrin to hire a boat for Loch Scavaig, visit Loch Coruisk and then continue on foot over Druim Hain to Glen Sligachan, and eventually the inn. Nowadays the village of Torrin provides an attractive foreground for pictures of Bla Bheinn. It was not always so photogenic. When a Mr Fixby visited in 1854, he concluded that the likes of David Livingstone were travelling to the wrong places:

> Ladies and gentlemen who flutter their cambric at Exeter Hall, who weep for the darkness of Heathendom, and send Bibles, and blankets, and converted Israelites to the uttermost parts of the earth, should bethink themselves of a mission to Torrin… a genuine exhibition of human wretchedness and degradation, that the wilds of America, or the lagoons of Africa could scarcely surpass.'[25]

Nor were the inhabitants well regarded. The boatmen of Torrin were demonised, the shame of Skye's nascent tourist industry; duplicitous rapscallions warned about in tourist guidebooks and denounced in the national press. At the 'huts and hovels' of Torrin there was a scene reminiscent of any tourist hotspot worldwide, a ragtag band aggressively touting for your business. If boats were hired there were frequent accounts of disputes, with tourists sometimes jettisoned miles from their destination. Parties were often rowed to the anticlimactic Spar Cave, 'a mountain sewer' according to another disappointed visitor, but no further: 'The Torrin boatmen are as truthless and as lawless as a pack of pirates.'[26]

The innkeepers at Broadford tried their best, vouching for reliable crews, but the disagreements continued. The boatmen maintained that 'old Mr Mackinnon' had formulated a contract where the fare from Torrin to Loch Scavaig was fixed at one pound plus a bottle of whisky, a dram every two hours being the set ration. It was assumed that food too would be provided by the tourists as part of the deal: oatcakes, cheese, cold mutton. But several guidebooks warned against indulging the crews, especially with whisky. The confusion was exacerbated by language difficulties, and the morale-boosting contractual riders were often lost in translation. If no lunch appeared by Spar Cave all would not be plain sailing. A disgruntled visitor, far from home, abandoned in the rain miles from food or shelter, outrageously swindled by impertinent oafs with barely a word of English— what is one to do? Of course—a letter to *The Times*:

> Sir, At Torrin we hired a boat with four boatmen to row us as far as Loch Scavaig, they agreeing to stop where we chose and guide us on our way, at the usual charge and allowance of whisky. About halfway to our destination we were dreadfully annoyed to find that the four boatmen would not proceed further, and they became most insolent… My object in troubling you with this letter is to draw the attention of the authorities in the island to making some regulations for the conduct of these men, who are a disgrace to the civilisation of our country. (*The Times*, 22nd October 1864).

Black's Tourist Guide to Scotland, first issued in 1839, was an extremely popular and influential publication, promoting the Cuillin as 'a scene of grandeur and of desolation altogether unequalled in any other part of the British Isles'. The guidebook became many early visitors' Bible with most tourists faithfully following its advice. A goal of many at Coruisk was to stand on the very spot where Walter Scott placed Robert the Bruce in the *Lord of the Isles*. After seeing the sights and perhaps walking around the loch, travellers without a guide were recommended to return by boat to Camasunary and then take the rough but safe path to Sligachan. The guidebook advised 3 to 4 hours for this eight-mile walk, warning walkers to carry sufficient provisions including a whisky flask, 'the later to be reserved for use where it will be most required, in passing through Glen Sligachan'. If you had a guide, or one of the boatmen was 'qualified to act in that capacity', it was deemed safe to tackle one of the short cuts to Sligachan such as Druim Hain or that used by Lesingham Smith over the ridge to Harta Corrie.

One of Black's rivals was Anderson's *Guide to the Highlands and Western Islands of Scotland*. This was one of the first publications to warn of the hazards that could be met off the beaten track: 'A solemn silence generally prevails, but is often and suddenly interrupted by the strife of the elements. The streams become quickly swollen, rendering the progress of the wayfaring stranger not a little hazardous, while fierce and fitful gusts issue from the bosom of the Cuchullins.'[27]

More adventurous visitors were keen to climb a Cuillin peak. Sgurr nan Gillean and Bla Bheinn were the best known, and the two peaks for which guides could be obtained. Bla Bheinn came more to the fore through the creative work of two friends, both with Skye connections. Alexander Smith, a short, delicate man with a pronounced squint in his right eye, was a Kilmarnock-born poet and novelist. Smith accompanied the Glasgow artist Horatio McCulloch on a painting trip to Skye where he met Flora MacDonald, a cousin of the artist's wife, whom he later married. It was from near the MacDonald home that McCulloch painted *The Cuillins from Ord*. He continued to paint Coruisk and the Cuillin throughout the 1850s, with Cuillin pioneer Alexander Nicolson ranking his view of Glen Sligachan as 'among the chief works that have ever been produced in illustration of High Scenery'.

Since 1854 Alexander Smith was secretary and registrar at the University of Edinburgh where he was falling prey to the stresses of Victorian academia. Every August he returned to Skye with his family, an eagerly awaited escape from the noise and grime of the capital, 'In Skye I am free of the century.' As well as the poem 'Blaavin', the visits inspired his lyrical classic, *A Summer in Skye*, much of it written in a shoreline bothy on Loch Eishort. The dramatic view over to Bla Bheinn and the Cuillin permeates every page, 'the outline wild, splintered, jagged, as if drawn by a hand shaken by terror or frenzy'; 'sleek as satin, rose a range of hills, clear against the morning, jagged and notched like an old sword-blade':

> In the morning they wear a great caftan of mist; but that lifts away before noon and they stand with all their scars and passionate torrent-lines bare to the blue heavens, with perhaps a solitary shoulder for a moment gleaming wet to the sunlight. After a while a vapour begins to steam up from the abysses, gathering itself into strange shapes, knotting and twisting itself like smoke; while above, the terrible crests are now lost, now revealed, in a stream of flying rack.[28]

One of Smith's earlier works *Life Drama* (1853) was very well received with its author proclaimed the 'Scottish Shelley'. Hoping to capitalise on his new fame Smith headed south with his friend John Nichol, later professor of English at Glasgow University. In England their paths soon parted although they remained close friends until Smith's untimely death from typhoid, aged 38.

At Balliol College, Oxford, Nichol befriended the diminutive Algernon Charles Swinburne, of whom Queen Victoria commented: 'I have heard it said that Swinburne is the finest poet in my dominion.' She was presumably unaware of his staple literary themes: sadomasochism, lesbian passion and anti-Christian sentiment. Swinburne also had a reputation as a notorious drunkard and an enthusiastic patron of the Circus Road flagellation brothels. With John Nichol he made the first recorded ascent of Bla Bheinn.

In 1857, the summer of Alexander Smith's wedding at Ord in Sleat, Swinburne joined Nichol and the Reverend Henry Crosskey, a 'most ardent student of glacial geology', for a trip to Skye. In a letter to his brother-in-law, William Jack, professor of mathematics at Glasgow University and one of the original members of the Scottish Mountaineering Club (SMC), Nichol gave an account of their adventures:

> In Skye itself certainly the most wonderful spectacles are the bay of Scavaig, and the head of Coruisk. Imagine a deeper Glen Sannox, hemmed in by more tremendous crags, yet black and lowering, with a bluish-grey lake like Acheron beneath them, with the floating mists like dread phantoms of evil spirits around it, and you have a faint idea of Coruisk. The splintered shafts of the Coolin hills seem to rise right from the entrance of the bay. It is best seen as we saw it from a boat lying a little way from the landing, but at every turn there is some new sublimity. We climbed Blaven, the highest peak, with no great danger.[29]

Although Swinburne and Nichol's ascent of Bla Bheinn (presumably accompanied by Crosskey) is the earliest recorded, the mountain's location and comparative lack of difficulty make it highly unlikely that it had not been climbed before. Indeed, the popular *Black's Tourist Guide,* published before Swinburne and Nichol's visit, gives the impression that ascents were relatively commonplace, albeit with a guide: 'The ascent of Blaven may be made from Broadford or Sligachan; but in neither case should it be attempted without a guide; for not only is it beset with dangerous crags and precipices, but it is peculiarly liable to be suddenly enveloped in the mists which ascend from the low ground and from the sea.'[30] *Nelson's Hand-book to Scotland* (1860) provided further information on the mountain:

> It forms a steep, sharp, fantastic pinnacled ridge, alike rude and grand, about 3,000 feet high, and commands a glorious view. Its skirts on Loch Slapin terminate in cliffs, torn with fissures and riddled with caves; its sides and shoulders exhibit a profusion of crags and clefts; and a pass in one of the lines of ascending it consists for about six feet, of a summit-edge of rock

scarcely more than a foot broad. No stranger should dream of climbing the mountain without a guide.

As well as tourist guidebooks, information on the Cuillin could be culled from contemporary travel writers. One such was Walter Cooper Dendy, a London psychiatrist who studied medicine along with the poet John Keats, and who coined the term psychotherapy. A keen botanist, he was one of the first to document Cuillin flora. He was also one of the first to mention 'Sgurr nan Eig' and translates Bla Bheinn as 'mountain of the blast'. The latter was often spelt phonetically as 'Blaven', and sometimes referred to as 'Ben Blaven'.

Dendy records a crossing of the Bad Step which he calls the 'Slippery Step'. This short section of scrambling on the Loch Scavaig approach to Coruisk was still proving an obstacle to inexperienced walkers. One guidebook said this about it: 'Many travellers have given themselves the fatigue and trouble of reaching this singular crossing, and upon seeing it have turned back in despair, vowing they would rather go a hundred miles about than venture to walk across.' Another visitor, James Leitch, elaborated on the difficulties involved: 'Below the line which the tourist must traverse there is a great stretch of sloping rock, down which, if his footing failed, he would be hurled into the growling sea, and from its greedy jaws there could be no salvation.'[31] Descriptions like this gave the Bad Step a daunting reputation out of all proportion to the actual difficulties.

The prevalence of visitors from down south was resulting in the adoption of the occasional English place-name. The Bad Step was previously referred to as the Leac (a rocky slab) while Spar Cave was known to locals as Slochd Altrumain, 'Cave of the Nursling'. The Bloody Stone, a large boulder in Harta Corrie, was marked on some early maps as Clacha Ghirue, and called by some Clach na Ghiorrach. At Loch Scavaig there was the Mad Stream, named after its appearance in spate and first mentioned by John Wilson in 1841.

The Sligachan Inn was run from around 1849 until 1856 by John MacLennan from Ross-shire who had previously been proprietor of the Glensheil inn. Sligachan continued to attract large numbers of visitors as communications improved. There were two steamers a day to Portree which was connected to the inn by mail-gig. The inn now comprised: 'Two public rooms, two parlours, six bedrooms and other apartments with two stables and coach-houses, etc. Includes several acres of arable land, walled enclosure and some adjoining hill pasture.'[32] The stables and coach-houses were in an L-shaped building on the site of the present bar. However in the winter of 1856-57 there was a fire which destroyed much of the interior of the inn. After repairs were completed Simon MacKenzie ran the hotel for ten years until May 1867.

Initially MacLennan received good reviews, one visitor commenting in 1854, 'One of the most comfortable road-side inns I have ever had the good luck to put up at, and quite equalling the best of the hotels of a similar class in Westmoreland'. However towards the end of MacLennan's tenure standards started to slip; there were many complaints that it was overpriced with few comforts and slovenly service. One disgruntled guest was Charles Inglis who visited with his brothers in September 1856 when they accomplished an early guideless ascent of Sgurr nan Gillean: 'We arrived late at night amidst scenes of great confusion. Fancy an inn with a great number of hungry travellers calling, blaming, stamping and bell-ringing, and no-one attending to them, or apparently likely to attend to their wants for some time to come.'[33] When C R (Charles) Weld visited a few years later he offered a Swinburnian explanation: 'when you hear that his wife was not allowed access to the liquor closet, you will understand that she was not fit for the office of landlady.'[34]

Weld was a brother-in-law of Lord Tennyson, a shrewd lawyer who was also secretary of the Royal Society. But not shrewd enough—he was sacked in 1861 'for introducing a lady into his rooms during his wife's absence'. Weld set off down Glen Sligachan with a guide and pony to climb the fine viewpoint of Sgurr na Stri. Here he set out this challenge: 'Now, turning to the north, and sweeping the horizon from east to west, what do we see? Peaks, and pinnacles, jagged crests and fantastic outlines; a wilderness of weird shapes, dark, solemn, and awful. Giant Sgor-na-Gillian is there, the monarch of the Cuchullins; and hear it, brother members of the Alpine Club, another peak a little to the south, laid down by enterprising Captain Wood on the Admiralty chart as being 3,212 feet high and *inaccessible*.'[35] *Anderson's Guide* (1863) also suggests there are unclimbed peaks awaiting the mountaineer. Referring to local shepherds, it states, 'to them the steepest hills in the neighbourhood are accessible, but they declared some of the pinnacles to be so needle-pointed that a man could hardly venture to stand on top of one of them'.

Captain Henry Charles Otter was in overall charge of the Admiralty survey of the west coast of Scotland which started in Skye around 1852, using wooden paddle steamers like HMS *Porcupine* and HMS *Avon*. (After the Royal Navy assisted with the birth, a native of St Kilda was christened Mary Jemima Otter Porcupine Gillies). The survey of most of the coast of Skye was undertaken by Commander James Wood with the assistance of Messrs Jeffrey and Taylor. Although their priority was coastal navigation they were under instruction to also survey the adjacent three miles inland. This was a slow process as the Ordnance Survey had not yet reached the West Highlands and islands, and so no suitable base map existed. Because of this anomaly, the early Admiralty surveyors and the later Ordnance Surveyors are often confused. The Cuillin section of the Admiralty chart, surveyed around 1857, was the first to map the mountains with any degree of accuracy, albeit only the western peaks nearer the sea.

As mentioned by Charles Weld, one of few Cuillins to be named on the chart was 'Inaccessible Peak'. Wood's survey team were some of the first to record a visit to Gars-bheinn (height given as 2,902ft): 'The summit of Gars-bheinn is like a knife-edge and so narrow as scarcely to leave room for the erection of a cairn.' Spot heights on their map suggest they traversed the Main Ridge north to Sgurr nan Eag (height given as 3,006ft). There is a strong possibility that their 'Inaccessible Peak' was actually Sgurr Alasdair and not what is now called the Inaccessible Pinnacle. The position of 'Inaccessible Peak' on the Admiralty chart fits Sgurr Alasdair better than Sgurr Dearg, and if Wood's team approached the former from the south, as the spot heights suggest, the Thearlaich-Dubh Gap and/or its South-West Ridge, would certainly have created an impression of inaccessibility to non-mountaineers. This argument is supported by Alexander Nicolson, the first ascentionist of Sgurr Alasdair in 1873, who states the peak 'had foiled the Ordnance men' (presumably the Admiralty surveyors as the Ordnance Survey did not start in this area until 1875). It would not be the last cartographic confusion in the Cuillin.

Chapter Two
The Dearest of Islands

Alexander Nicolson was a pivotal link between the preliminary explorations of the early scientists and the more intense scrutiny of the later mountaineers. He was born in September 1827, the son of Malcolm Nicolson, a tacksman to MacLeod of Dunvegan. To Alexander Nicolson there was nothing gloomy or threatening about the Cuillin; they were home ground, a familiar sight from his childhood days at Husabost on Loch Dunvegan (he was known on Skye as 'Alick Husabost'), 'The sight and feeling of these Skye hills filled his heart with an expanding joy in which his whole soul was absorbed, everything else sunk and forgotten.'[1] In 1845 Nicolson left Skye for Edinburgh University where he began a close friendship with John Veitch from Peeblesshire who would later succeed Professor George Ramsay as second president of the Scottish Mountaineering Club. Veitch later recounted his first meeting with Nicolson after a university exam: 'A tall, slim, fair lad he was dressed in a long brown greatcoat; something in the look of the grey blue eyes, and the gentle, but somewhat languid expression of the face attracted me.'[2]

After studying classics and philosophy, Nicolson began theology classes at the New College in Edinburgh, recently established for students of the Free Church of Scotland. There followed a critical period in his life when he began to have doubts about the doctrines of the Free Church, 'The officer's uniform in that excellent body is painfully tight.' By 1851, Nicolson realised he could not adhere to the Westminster Confession of Faith and writes to John Veitch: 'I can never be a minister of the Free Church; and all but equally certain, of none other. Such is the lamentable conclusion. The future is as blank and doubtful as can be.'[3]

Nicolson now tried his hand at a variety of careers including journalism with which he also became increasingly disillusioned. Although often berated for his lack of ambition this was, however, an industrious period when he juggled several different jobs at the one time. These included working as a sub-editor on the *Encyclopædia Britannica,* doing cataloguing in the Advocates' Library, as well as lecturing and tutoring in the evenings. One of his students was another lover of the Cuillin, the geologist Archibald Geikie, who remembered him as 'a big-boned Celt with a look of strength and kindliness in his large and strongly-marked features'.

After working for the publishers Chambers, Nicolson became an Inspector of Parish Registrars for the Lothian area from 1855 until 1857. In 1860 he embarked on a career in law, supplementing his meagre advocate's income with some law reporting for the *Scottish Jurist*. In Parliament Hall, where cases were discussed, little business came his way. The reason for this is unclear (and somewhat mysterious) as he certainly had no shortage of influential friends in the city—his funeral was attended by a 'who's who' of Edinburgh society. It was an embittering experience which he expressed in a song, 'Sam Hall, a New Version': 'I've paced for many a year / That big hall / I've paced for many a year / With a smile to hide the tear / For the agents won't come near / Hang them all!'

In 1865 Nicolson was appointed assistant commissioner by the Scottish Education Committee who required a Gaelic speaker to compile a report on the state of the schools in the Western Isles, groundwork for the Education Act of 1872 which ironically had calamitous long-term consequences for Nicolson's native tongue. The post gave him the opportunity to return to Skye, his 'dearest of islands', where he could also spend some time in the Cuillin. One fine June day in 1865 he engaged Duncan MacIntyre, son of Forbes's guide, to accompany him on the established route up Sgurr nan Gillean: 'The crest is very narrow, broken, and rocky, interrupted every now and then by a gash, or a mass of rock, over which you must get as carefully as you can, for on each side there is a steep descent into considerable depths. In two or three places you must use hands and feet vigorously, and if you have not a head to feel a sense of glory in looking into space beneath you, you won't enjoy it.'[4]

On the summit they found a comfortable couch of moss and lichen, a common feature before erosion by countless boots (the pinnacle on Druim nan Ramh is one of few summits still in this condition). Nicolson was now curious to find out what lay along the west ridge towards Am Basteir. They left the summit plinth by squeezing through the Window, for a while known as 'Alasdair's Hole', before scrambling down to where a small pinnacle, called the Gendarme, blocked the ridge. They avoided this by descending a chimney on the right, described by Nicolson as a 'horrid cleft'.

Throughout his life Nicolson composed songs which he sang to amuse dinner audiences at the many clubs and societies he was a member of. On his return to Edinburgh, in 1865, he wrote his best known composition, 'The Island of Skye, an Edinburgh Summer Song', in which he mentions the Cuillin: 'The Matterhorn's good for a fall / If climbing you have no skill in / But a place as good to make raven's food / You can find upon Scoor-nan-Gillean.'

In August 1879 Nicolson returned to Sgurr nan Gillean to tackle the west ridge in an upwards direction. At Sligachan he was delighted to discover that their original route was now being referred to as Nicolson's Chimney (Difficult). It was regarded by some as an easier descent than the ordinary route. On this occasion he 'found the rockwork a good deal abraded and softened since 1865'. In the party was David Hepburn, a London-based dental surgeon and early SMC member who was a regular visitor to the Cuillin in the 1890s. Hepburn provided further details of what he claimed was the first time the west ridge had been ascended:

> The party consisted of Angus MacPherson (guide), Mr Nicolson, the Reverend Mr Black and myself. We had with us a strong staff about six feet long and a long highland plaid. The chimney at first gave way to a long consultation but eventually we decided to attack it. By means of the crook the plaid was hitched over an overhanging point and after considerable difficulty Angus MacPherson succeeded in drawing himself up and reported that an advance was feasible. By means of the plaid firmly gripped by Angus the remaining three scaled the chimney one by one and without much further trouble reached the summit.[5]

In 1872, Nicolson accepted the office of sheriff-substitute in Kirkcudbrightshire, a move he bitterly regretted. He felt he had been cold-shouldered by the Edinburgh legal establishment and rusticated to a judicial backwater. After the conviviality of Edinburgh, Galloway seemed a dull and unstimulating environment where his song writing becomes tinged with bitterness over his new circumstances, as in 'A Lay of Kirkcubree': 'If a man's chief end were vegetation/ no better place is in creation.' From around this time there is a sense of despondency surrounding the genial Skyeman.

The year after his move south, in August 1873, one of Nicolson's friends, Professor (Reverend) William Angus Knight, also made a first ascent in the Cuillin. Knight was a former student of James David Forbes at Edinburgh University: 'As a lecturer he was dignified, but very cold; the academic counterpart of the Mer de Glace at Chamonix.' Knight was also friendly with John Veitch, as well as John Nichol for whom he was both biographer and senior literary executor. He was minister at St Enoch's Free Church in Dundee until 1876 when he became a candidate for the post of professor of moral philosophy at St Andrews University. Both Nicholson and Nichol provided him with testimonials, the latter commenting, 'few are so free and so far from the rivalry which is the bane of literary life'. Knight's application was successful and at St Andrews he consolidated his position as an authority on the Lake poets.

The Reverend Knight arrived at Sligachan fighting fit after an alpine season of fourteen peaks including the Matterhorn. Along with an unnamed companion he was keen to repeat Forbes' route on Sgurr nan Gillean. They engaged Angus MacPherson who was the 'principal guide' at the time. When they eventually attained the summit Knight noticed that the shapely fourth top of Pinnacle Ridge, then known as Needle Rock, presented an unclimbed challenge. But MacPherson was not keen on this journey into the unknown. In Britain ropes were not yet used as safety aids. MacPherson eventually capitulated to Knight's financial bribe, an offer which had to be doubled at the col. From here on he was cajoled to the twin summit where first ascent rituals included the building of a cairn and the singing of a Gaelic song. Flushed with success Knight proposed that his guide accompany him on a 'three days' expedition, ascending each peak of the Coolin in succession and sleeping out amongst them'. This is the first reference to the possibility of a Main Ridge Traverse in one continuous expedition. MacPherson politely declined.

Safely back at Sligachan they were delighted to pick out their cairn through a telescope. They had completed what Clark and Pyatt, in their authoritative history *Mountaineering in Britain*, regarded as the first genuine rock climb on Skye. Knight mentioned the climb to Alexander Nicolson who repeated it with Alexander Gibson, and changed the name to 'Little Horn'. This did not catch on and the format of Knight's Peak slowly gained acceptance. In the 1997 edition of *Munro's Tables* Knight's Peak was promoted to a Top despite protests that it lacked the necessary stature, providing the list with a bête almost as noire as the Inaccessible Pinnacle. In September 2013, to a sigh of relief from acrophobic Top baggers, surveyors used state of the art GPS mapping tools to calculate that it was actually six inches short of the critical 3,000ft.

Alexander Nicolson and John Veitch returned to Skye in 1873 to find a much-changed island; it was bustling with visitors due to the recent improvements in transport. The Hutcheson brothers introduced passenger-only 'swift steamers', the nautical equivalent of the express train, which revolutionised travel in the West Highlands. For Skye you boarded the *Iona* on Glasgow's Broomielaw at 7am, reaching Ardrishaig on Loch Fyne around noon where you transferred to a smaller track boat to negotiate the Crinan Canal; you then took the *Mountaineer* for the bustling port of Oban. After a sprint down the gangway to secure the limited accommodation in town, you continued the next morning to Broadford or Portree, a long summer's day sail of 12 to 14 hours. The 'swift steamers' did not run during the winter when the only alternative was the 'all-the-way' vessels like the *Clansman* and *Clydesdale* which took the long route from Glasgow to Portree, and beyond, around the often stormy Mull of Kintyre. When the Hutcheson brothers retired in 1879 another partner, the iconic David MacBrayne, carried on in his own name.

In 1870 the Dingwall and Skye Railway was completed as far as Strome Ferry. The company ran out of money and the planned extension to Kyle was not finished until 1897. In the interim steamers like the *Oscar* and *Ferret* provided a daily ferry connection between Strome Ferry and Portree, now only 15 hours from London. Touring Skye was the height of fashion. Thomas Carlyle paid a visit as did Prince Arthur, Queen Victoria's favourite, who signed the Visitors' Book at Sligachan. In 1880 William Gladstone also stayed at the inn and visited Loch Coruisk as he cruised the Western Isles on the *Grand Tully*, part of a voyage around Britain as he recovered from health problems. When the vessel was at anchor in Loch Scavaig several of the Torrin boatmen rowed alongside and insisted on seeing what the prime minister looked like. Curiosity satisfied, they continued on their way. Thirty of the official party then went ashore in two boats, with Gladstone leading sea shanties as he returned to the vessel to work on his despatch boxes. Two years later these would contain papers relating to events nearby.

Alexander Nicolson went on to write articles in *The Scotsman* promoting Skye as a tourist destination, advising travellers to experience the best of both worlds by approaching on the steamer from Oban and leaving by the new Strome Ferry to Inverness railway. Most tourists still chose to approach Sligachan from the south, using the recommended itinerary by way of Torrin, Loch Scavaig and Druim Hain or, alternatively, through the glens from Camasunary. Nicolson informed his readers that Mr Ross's inn (later the Broadford Hotel) had an improved arrangement with the Torrin boatmen. In 1871 there was an added attraction when a 60-foot sperm whale was washed up near the head of Loch Scavaig. In the prevailing hot weather the throng of inquisitive visitors soon thinned out.

The fact that no tourists died in their quest to see Loch Coruisk is remarkable. They were venturing into a potentially dangerous and remote area with little idea of the potential hazards. The tourist guidebooks available were not always accurate: there was not necessarily a boat at Camasunary with which to avoid the Bad Step, nor were the likes of milk and scones readily available there. Some had the nous to equip themselves appropriately with waterproof capes, merino shirts and suitably stout footwear, and to hire a guide or arrange for ponies to meet them in Glen Sligachan. Many parties blundered on without guide or guidebook, adequate clothing or any inkling as to the potential ferocity of Skye weather. They often carried no food or drink with them, expecting to find sustenance at a cottage or inn along the way.

Many tourists had already done the Storr and the Quiraing, and assumed the Coruisk day would be a similarly straightforward undertaking. Underestimating the distance and the difficulties, they frequently got lost in the mist, soaked and benighted; often prey to hunger, exhaustion and exposure. The staff at Sligachan were left to pick up the pieces: there were search and rescue parties with hurricane lamps at all hours and in all weathers, reviving and caring for casualties on their arrival. The Skye weather put great strain on the drying facilities of isolated inns like Sligachan which eventually had a store of spare clothes for guests drenched on the hills, or who had fallen victim to the peaty pitfalls of the Coruisk path. Many of these 'cast-offs' were of surprisingly good quality and some visitors came home in much smarter attire than when they left.

When Veitch and Nicolson arrived on Skye in August 1873 they headed straight for Sligachan where they were lucky to obtain two of only twelve beds available. They reckoned the inn could easily fill a hundred during the peak season of August and September. Many visitors to Sligachan, however, only made a hurried day trip away from the promenading pzazz of Portree, as Nicolson pointed out, 'With at least three streets, limited possibilities for the display of costume are clear points of superiority over the desolate though glorious solitude of Sligachan.'

Under the MacDonald family, who were innkeepers from 1868, the Sligachan Inn's reputation continued to flourish. The poet Robert Buchanan, who was inspired by the Cuillin scenery to write his *Coruisken Sonnets,* described the inn as 'the cleanest, snuggest, cheapest little place of the sort in all the Highlands'. In 1873 John Alexander Butters took over from the MacDonalds. That March Butters married Sarah, niece of Mrs Campbell of the Portree Hotel. The Butters soon set about enlarging the premises with some major alterations. In 1879 they created seven new bedrooms, a new bar, wine and beer cellars, drying room and, most significantly for mountaineers, the addition of a smoking-room which would become the clubbable focus for Skye's inchoate climbing scene. Later, a substantial extension to the inn was constructed to the north, near the stables, at right angles to the original building, and for a time the main entrance was located there. Butters also developed the hotel's gardens.

Once settled in, Nicolson and Veitch explored Coir' a' Mhadaidh, climbing Sgurr Thuilm where they found the summit marked with a wooden cross, possibly left by James Wood's Admiralty survey around 1857. In this age of rapid change Nicolson, who had recently holidayed in Switzerland, was relieved to find there were no funicular railways to the Cuillin summits. The two friends then visited Camasunary, a favourite oasis of most visitors. He concedes if there has to be a Swiss-style hotel in the Highlands, then this was the spot for the 'Grand Hotel du Blaveinn'. On the subject of tourist development he presciently warned of the implications of a bridge to Skye: 'I hope, however, that it will not be attempted in this generation as the next thing would probably be the continuation of the railway through Glen Sligachan, which I am sentimental enough to prefer being without.'[6] (In February 1896 the Inverness-shire MP, James Baillie, proposed a light railway from Kyleakin to Portree, and from Sligachan to Dunvegan.)

In Nicolson's lifetime the landscape of his native Skye changed dramatically. As sheep superseded black cattle, farms were enlarged and consolidated into bigger units so rents could be maximised. People were moved off any good arable or grazing land which was then incorporated into the farms. Eight townships near Elgol, 400 people, were cleared to create two sheep farms, Camasunary and Kirkibost. In the Glen Brittle area there were originally four townships around Loch Brittle, four more villages on Loch Eynort and three on Loch Harport. By 1830 Kenneth McCaskill merged all of these into a single sheep farm. In what was known locally as the 'Reign of Terror', many families were cleared: some to the nearest shore, some to the then uninhabited island of Soay, some to the villages along Loch Harport and further afield. The destitute condition of these landless cotters was made life-threatening by the potato famines of the 1840s, fostering mass emigration to Canada and Australia. (One native of Glen

Brittle cleared at this time was Angus McMillan who, in 1838, left for Australia where he became a well-known pioneering farmer. As is sadly too often the case, the oppressed became the oppressor with McMillan responsible for several massacres of the indigenous population.)

Two small settlements managed to survive the upheaval: Bualintur on the west side of the River Brittle, and Culnamean on the east (sometimes spelt Colinamine). The Skye folklorist Frances Tolmie reckoned that the former was named after a pre-Christian burial ground. (Blaeu's atlas of 1654 shows a church there.)

After Veitch's departure Nicolson walked from Sligachan over Bealach a' Mhaim to Glen Brittle where he visited Donald Cameron, the tenant farmer. The farm was originally known as Rhundunan (not to be confused with the old McCaskill home out at the point of Rubha an Dunain), but when Cameron took over in 1863 it was renamed Glenbrittle farm. In conversation with Nicolson, Cameron informed him that one of the adjacent peaks had never been climbed and had even foiled the Admiralty surveyors.

Nicolson walked up into Coire Lagan where, despite it being a wet and windy day, he caught a brief glimpse of an attractive symmetrical peak, 'one of the wildest objects I ever saw'. The next day with A MacRae, a shepherd and experienced hillman, he climbed Sgurr na Banachdich and continued along the ridge to Sgurr Dearg. He didn't attempt the summit rock tower, now known as the Inaccessible Pinnacle: 'That pillar, as seen from a distance, has a very peculiar and puzzling appearance; from some points it looks like a chimney can, from others like a 'wild beast's horn'.'

The unattainable pinnacle was clearly higher than Sgurr Dearg, but to Nicolson this was of no great consequence. He wrote: 'It might be possible with ropes and grappling irons, to overcome it; but the achievement seems hardly worth the trouble.' Steep rocky outcrops like the Innaccessible Pinnacle (often referred to as the 'In Pin') were often pragmatically regarded as features which extended *from the summit* with the highest easily accessible point considered 'the top'. For example even the Pilkington brothers, who did the first ascent of the pinnacle in 1880, describe it as 'that curious slab of rock which leans so weirdly over the summit of Sgurr Dearg'. When Scottish mountains over 3,000ft were compiled by Hugh Munro in 1891 Sgurr Dearg, though listed as 3,234ft to the pinnacle's 3,250ft, was still regarded as the mountain's top, the Munro summit. All this supports the argument that the 'Inaccessible Peak' marked on the admiralty chart was Sgurr Alasdair and not Sgurr Dearg.

Nicolson and MacRae then skirted below the unnamed peak at the head of the corrie (Sgurr Mhic Choinnich) until it was possible to enter a large gully curving upwards towards their objective, the unclimbed peak. The loose stone shoot led laboriously, but without incident, to the summit where they celebrated with the construction of a cairn, a dram and no doubt a Gaelic song. The new peak needed a name but this was not as simple as it seemed. Nicolson thought Sgurr Sgumain (a stack, like a haystack) was appropriate, but MacRae assured him this already referred to the western peak, as used today. Nicolson later proposed the name 'Scur-a-Laghain' after the corrie, but this did not catch on. Coire Lagan was translated by the Ordnance Survey as 'the muddy corrie', and spelt 'Coire Labain' on the first OS map in 1882. Eventually the peak took on the name Sgurr Alasdair (Gaelic for Alexander).

The Ordnance Survey used a series of Name Books to record place names. The information documented in these books included the name, 'as written on the plan', variations to its spelling with the source used for this, and a general description of the location. Some of these sources ('authorities') used by the OS in the Cuillin area included Mr Nicolson, the teacher at Carbost, Neil McKenzie at Sligachan, Mr McKinnon, the shepherd at Glen Drynoch, and Mr McIntyre, teacher at Sconser.

The handwritten logbooks were often annotated in officious red ink, for example, 'adopted by order'. In 1877, four years after Sgurr Alasdair's first ascent, the OS recorded the mountain in their Name Book as Sgurr Sgumain: 'The name is applied to one of the most prominent peaks in the Coolin Hills. It is very rocky and difficult to ascend.' (Sgumain is one of the more straightforward of the Cuillin.) The source given was Alexander MacRae, the shepherd at Glen Brittle House. Paradoxically, this could well have been Nicolson's companion on the first ascent of Alasdair (and if not, would be a relative or neighbour imbued with the same cultural tradition).

There is little comment regarding the mountain's new name until the 1920s when the naturalist Seton Gordon states that the Cuillin guide John Mackenzie had mentioned to him that the original name of Sgurr Alasdair was Sgurr Biorach (the pointed peak). This was confirmed later by Skye poet Sorley MacLean who said he had been told the same thing by Mackenzie: that the mountain was traditionally known as Sgurr Biorach by local people. In his poetry, including his epic 'An Cuilithionn' (The Cuillin), MacLean continues to use this name.

Once Alexander Nicolson returned from Glen Brittle to Sligachan he set off with a companion down Glen Sligachan to tackle the unclimbed Sgurr Dubh Mor from Coruisk. It was not the challenge of unclimbed peaks that motivated him but a poet's desire for the aesthetic experience. Where many found Coruisk intimidating, even during the day, Nicolson sought out the adventure of a new peak with an unknown descent by moonlight. On the way he visited two artist friends, some of the first to construct small huts as a summer base near Loch Coruisk. Aware it was a full moon Nicolson and his companion were in no hurry, not setting off up An Garbh-choire until 4pm. Just before sunset they reached the summit of Sgurr Dubh Mor, 'a very narrow rocky ridge with a thick bed of green, spongy moss'.

In the dimming light they descended the seldom visited Coir' an Lochain, a complex route even in good visibility, first down a field of huge boulders to the lochan where there are more gigantic blocks of gabbro. From here several short impasses were negotiated with Nicolson again improvising his plaid as a rope (he also claimed to use it as a cushion, carpet, bed-clothes, rucksack, curtain, awning and sail). He was lowered down the obstacle by his younger companion who then stepped down onto his shoulders. This process was repeated several times until, fingers skinned by the rough rock, they eventually reached the level ground at the head of Loch Coruisk, arriving back at Sligachan at 3am after what Nicolson described as 'the hardest adventure I have had among these hills'.

Nicolson's explorations of the Cuillin with John Veitch, David Hepburn and other friends helped dispel the aura of inaccessibility. He presented wild landscapes like Coruisk and Lota Corrie as no longer places to be feared but spots to be savoured for their atmosphere of peace and serenity. Although Nicolson made no more first ascents in the Cuillin he continued to record his experiences with articles in the likes of *The Scotsman* and *Good Words*. He provided sound and still apposite advice for dealing with the island's frequent bad weather: be patient and you will get your reward for, as he reminds us: 'If they are in a hurry, Skye and its clouds are in none, and the Cuillin will unveil their majestic heads, in due time and no sooner. To see them do so is worth a week of waiting.'[7] In 1883 Nicolson returned to Skye on more sombre business as the villages around the Cuillin found themselves on the front pages of Fleet Street.

Throughout 1882 over 130 years of clearance, poverty, overcrowding and famine came to a head, aggravated by a poor summer and winter storms which decimated much of the potato and hay crops, the fishing, and the peats. Historical archives in the Highlands are clogged with censorious correspondence between landowners, factors and agents discussing unpaid rents, grazing disputes and the setting of all manner of petty impositions. Any improvements to a croft resulted in a rent increase; the aspirations of ordinary people were stifled as much of the land was exclusively devoted to sheep and deer. Any sign of dissent could be met with the threat of eviction. But now, through the likes of the Highland Land League, the crofting community began to organise, instilling a newfound mood of defiance throughout the Hebrides.

Alexander Nicolson's father had sold the estate of Husabost to Dr Nicol Martin, a cousin of the sheriff. Here there were now twenty summonses of eviction against tenants who were also subject (unlawfully) to provide ten days unpaid labour to the proprietor. Land disputes like this led to civil disorder, culminating in the 'Battle of the Braes' in April 1882 when fifty constables were dispatched from Glasgow to quell the trouble (events covered in the Runrig song 'Recovery'). Alexander Nicolson was shocked by the outbreak of lawlessness and wrote pamphlets and newspaper letters entreating the crofters not to break the law. Many took exception to his views.

Sconser, three miles east of Sligachan, was the home of the well-known Cuillin guide John Mackenzie and his family. Knowing there were journalists in Portree covering the disturbances in the Braes, the people of Sconser sent a representative to entreat the press to visit their homes and hear their story. To John Mackenzie and his fellow villagers the simmering resentment was about land, land that fifty years ago was common grazing, available to all, but which was taken over for the sole use of the landowner's deer or tacksmens' sheep. Crofters around the Cuillin had to look on as the new sheep farms of Glenbrittle, Glen Drynoch and Camasunary were allowed to keep flocks on what they regarded as their birthright. Glamaig was now the 'Forbidden Mountain', as much a bone of contention as Ben Lee, on the opposite side of Loch Sligachan, was to the people of the Braes. In short, there was a general policy that the traditional common grazing of the crofters was taken from them by the landlord, with no commensurate reduction in rent, and given to sheep farmers or let to shooting tenants.

The growing population of Sconser (over forty families, 250 people in 1882) was swollen by people cleared from neighbouring townships like Tormichaig and Moll in the 1850s when Lord MacDonald enlarged the deer forest. Sconser was described by one visitor, in February 1883, as 'a wretched little hamlet'. Some of the villagers were forced to huddle on land near the shore, not allowed to keep sheep as they might spread disease to the farmer's more valuable breeds, or dogs which might harass the deer. To add insult to injury the deer ate their hard-won potatoes and corn as, before wire fencing, stone walls were no match for hungry deer. Much of the Red Cuillin was now referred to as Lord MacDonald's deer forest and even well-to-do visitors were not exempt from being denied access. In August 1882 someone wrote the following entry in the Sligachan Visitors' Book (the page was later ripped out):

> We the undersigned visitors at the Sligachan Hotel, in thanking Lord MacDonald and his agent for their courteous and hospitable notice affixed to this hotel, prohibiting all persons from walking on the adjacent hills, beg to congratulate his Lordship and agent on the picturesque beauty of the happy homes of the peasantry on the MacDonald estate. In other parts of the Empire the stern requirements of Christianity and the Sanitary Inspector have deprived even the pigsty of the attractions presented by these inhabitants. It is refreshing to find a spot where the simplicity of cottages and architecture is not yet marred by the meretricious adjuncts of roofs, doors, windows, chimneys. Long may Lord MacDonald continue the beneficent Chieftain of a happy and subservient, though probably rheumatic, tenantry.

When Gladstone's government set up a Royal Commission under Lord Napier, Alexander Nicolson was one of six commissioners appointed to investigate the causes of the widespread agitation. It was no coincidence that the very first meeting of the commission was at the Braes, on 8th May 1883. The first to give evidence was Angus Stewart, great grand-uncle of Sorley MacLean. In broken English he made two requests: to be examined in Gaelic and immunity from eviction for what he had to say. The Glasgow magazine *Quiz* depicted Nicolson's more formal side at the Royal Commission hearings: 'Sheriff Nicolson has rather a solemn face and his closely-shaven cheeks give him an almost theatrical appearance. His accent is decidedly nasal and the eyeglass pressure on the nose exaggerates this characteristic.'[8] By 18th May the Commission reached Bracadale, the nearest meeting for those living under the main mass of the Cuillin. John McCaskill, a shoemaker and cottar, was asked if he had any statement to make on behalf of the people of Fernilea (north of Carbost) whom he represented. His reply was recorded in the Napier Commission Minutes of Evidence:

> I can speak concerning the commencement of the clearances. I have learnt from older people than myself that they commenced seventy years ago at first and then by Dr McLean, as a former delegate said, from the Talisker side. McCaskill had only Rhu Dunan in his possession at that time. Glenbrittle was occupied by crofters in comfortable circumstances and it is likely he [McCaskill] asked for Glenbrittle; but, at all events, he got it, and cleared it, and made a sheep run of it. We don't know how many families there were, but at that time there was a church in Glenbrittle, and there is nobody there now to use it. The church is now in ruins and the manse is converted into a shepherd's house. McCaskill was clearing on the Glenbrittle side, and the doctor [McLean] was clearing on the Talisker side.

The commission ended its Skye leg at Portree where one witness was Alexander MacDonald, Lord MacDonald's current factor in charge of the parts of Skye where the disputes originated. MacDonald was a very influential figure. Like many individuals in the Highlands at this time, he had a monopoly on powerful posts, many of which were normally incompatible. He was the factor of several estates, a land owner in his own right, Skye's only lawyer, a bank agent, sheriff officer and the prime collector of rates and taxes. Alexander Nicoldon, however, had a personal point to make to him:

> *Sheriff Nicolson*: But are the public generally prohibited from wandering over the hills and the deer forest?
> *Alexander MacDonald*: There is no occasion to prohibit them. They are allowed on the Macleod estate to go to Coruisk.
> *Sheriff Nicolson*: But on the other side?

Alexander MacDonald: There is nothing to be seen.

Sheriff Nicolson: There are some fine hills. Is there not a threatening notice in the hotel at Sligachan to the effect that trespassers will be prosecuted with the utmost rigour of the law?

Alexander MacDonald: It's very probable, and that notice may be very necessary; but I do not believe it is intended to be carried out in its full sense. I am sure that, if you choose to go up on the hill, we will not object to it.

Sheriff Nicolson: I beg your pardon. I and two friends were subjected to the indignity of being assailed by a gillie on these hills.

Alexander MacDonald: I am sorry to hear it.

Sheriff Nicolson: And what is worse, we were called 'Glasgow tailors' in a letter addressed to Mr Butters the landlord, complaining of the intolerable trespass upon our hills.

Alexander MacDonald: But he was a Sassenach and did not know better.

Over the next few years the land struggle continued but the government appeared to stall regarding the implementation of the Commission's recommendations. Throughout the 1880s financial speculation over Scottish estates escalated as sheep-farming became less profitable due to cheaper wool from the Antipodes, and English sporting estates more expensive and difficult to manage. The Strathaird estate was sold in 1884 by the Macalisters to a Mr Bower who leased Camasunary farm to Walter Laidlaw. Four years later Strathaird was bought by Sir William MacKinnon, the shipping magnate. The new owner set about making a series of improvements: the construction of the lodge at Camasunary, a large house at Kilmarie, the last three miles of road to Elgol, and estate cottages, now the offices of the John Muir Trust.

On many estates there was wholesale conversion to deer forests, with deer so numerous watchmen had to be employed in villages like Sconser and Luib to protect crops. The MacDonald deer forest, with Sconser Lodge and adjacent shootings and fishing, was regularly advertised for let in *The Times*. In the *Highland Sportsman* the newly stocked 'Cuchullin' deer forest was marketed along with the lodge at Drynoch, containing 'dining-room, drawing-room, four bedrooms, dressing-room, five servants' rooms, kitchen, butler's pantry, wine and beer cellars'.

The social unrest continued, hastening an Act of Parliament, the *Crofters' Holdings (Scotland) Act, 1886*. This landmark legislation offered security of tenure and fair rents but failed to address the problem of lost land or landless cottars. Even into the new century the MacDonald estate continued to take legal action against the Sconser crofters for grazing sheep on the hills.

In 1885 Alexander Nicolson moved from Galloway to a similar position in Greenock. It was an unhappy transition as he found it hard to cope with the commercial pressures of the 'sugar capital' after sleepy Kirkcudbright. He seemed happiest on visits to his favourite hotel at Sligachan which he regarded as not only the best in Skye but in all the Western Isles. In 1885 Mr and Mrs Butters left for the Sutherland Arms in Lairg, to be replaced by the Sharps who upheld the high standards of their predecessors. The Visitors' Book is full of Nicolson's purrs of contentment: 'Here a day is worth two in most places.' He only records one negative theme, the boggy path up Glen Sligachan: 'If there is any worse path in the world, it is unknown to me.'

During his time at Greenock, Nicolson's health began to fail with fainting fits and periodic bouts of depression. He retired on grounds of ill-health in November 1889 and returned to Edinburgh to live with his sister and nieces. His professional underachievement is often commented on. *The Scotsman* stated: 'He had the warmest of warm hearts, but the greatest dislike of settled industry.' His lecturer at New College, the Reverend A C Fraser, concurred, 'a Celtic genius of easy disposition and desultory habits'. Yet Sheriff Nicolson was a resounding success with other people, 'perhaps the most popular man in Edinburgh'. One of his friends there reminisced:

> No one was more welcome at the dinner table, or when he chanced to drop in of an evening. Yet the old fire no longer burned in him as of old. Doubtless Edinburgh held a good many ghosts for him. His old friend, Alexander Smith, was no longer there to rhapsodise with him about Blaven and Scoor na Gillian, and recall pleasant days in the little Inn at Sligachan.[9]

When, late in life, Nicolson joined the Scottish Mountaineering Club, William Naismith sang his praises in a letter to William Douglas, comparing him to the geologist Archibald Geikie (whom Nicolson, in one of his songs, rhymes with Auld Reekie): 'He is a great acquisition to the club and I hope we shall have a lot more from his pen, for besides his pleasant style he seems a real mountaineer and a right good Scot, just such another as old Geikie.'[10]

The last memory of many climbing friends was at the SMC Dinner in December 1892 when he sang his favourite song, 'The Island of Skye, an Edinburgh Summer Song'. One month later, aged 66, he suffered a fatal heart attack. Sheriff Nicolson wrote his own epitaph: 'I would rather be remembered as the composer of one good song, than as the writer of many respectable and superfluous books.' His old friend John Veitch added: 'He was one of the most lovable men I have known, simple, guileless, unworldly and in all things true, with a humour peculiarly his own, and a feeling for poetry, especially Gaelic song, evidently born with him and due to his Celtic and Scandinavian heredity.'[11]

William Naismith was part of a new generation of young thrusters, climbing rocks for interest and difficulty rather than purely to attain the summit. His first visit to Skye was at Easter 1880 when he was aged 24, nine years before he became one of the founding fathers of the Scottish Mountaineering Club. Prior to this trip Naismith's only recorded experience is of relatively easy hills and low-level walks, often starting out from his home near Hamilton.

At Sligachan he and his companions set off for Sgurr nan Gillean through the unfrequented An Glas-choire in misty conditions. There was still no semblance of a path and to navigate the way back Naismith placed stones on prominent rocks whose location he carefully numbered and entered in a notebook. He confirmed that the gabbro was 'grand holding for hobnail'. They then set off for Camasunary where they spent the night. The following day they traversed Bla Bheinn before the inevitable dark trudge back to Sligachan through the interminable bogs and burns of Glen Sligachan.

The next day, 26th April, they visited Coire na Creiche. Through a gap in the mist Naismith spotted a fine pointed peak which they duly climbed by an obvious couloir. Finding no evidence of any previous visit, they built a small cairn. It was a few years until Naismith was able to confirm, on the Ordnance Survey map, what peak it was.

The OS surveyed the Cuillin between 1875 and 1877. They were led by Captain Macpherson who based himself at the Sligachan Inn which he described as 'a large two storey house having first class accommodation for man and beast'. The OS six-inch map was published in 1882. The one-inch map was reduced from this and went on sale three years later; it had contour lines at 100ft intervals up to 1,000ft and 250ft above (the six-inch map had none). However the early OS maps were hard to obtain; they were not readily available in shops but had to be ordered specially. When Naismith finally obtained a copy of the map, he found his peak marked 'Sgurr a' Mhadaidh' which he translates as 'Dog Peak'. In fact it wasn't; he had actually made the first ascent of Bidein Druim nan Ramh's North Top.

There was much cartographic confusion over this part of the Main Ridge. Both the one-inch and six-inch map mark Bidein as near to the actual location of An Caisteal, while Sgurr a' Mhadaidh's whereabouts on the map approximates to that of Bidein, especially so on the one-inch version. The Ordnance Survey rectified their mistake on the second edition of the one-inch map, published in 1896. However, the eastern branch of Coire na Creiche remained Coir' a' Mhadaidh, and the western branch Tairneilear, until the mid-1960s. The geologist Alfred Harker reckoned that Coir' a' Mhadaidh covered not just the smaller corrie but what is referred to as Coire na Creiche, 'a name of suspiciously new appearance'.

Colonel T Pilkington White, one of the engineers in charge of the Ordnance Survey team mapping the Cuillin, later explained how handicapped his men were as they had little knowledge of mountaineering. Yet, despite their inexperience, they managed ascents of Sgurr nan Gillean, Bruach na Frithe, Sgurr na

Banachdich, Sgurr Dearg, Sgurr Sgumain, Garsbheinn, Bla Bheinn and Garbhbheinn. The Original Series OS maps were not extensively updated and revised until the publication of the Popular Edition in the late 1920s.

Some of the name derivations recorded by the Ordnance Survey in the 1870s differ from those in popular use today: Sgurr a' Mhadaidh was 'hill of the wild beast', Sgurr a' Ghreadaidh was 'the burning peak'. On Sheriff Nicolson's advice the OS used the anglicised Harta Corrie while the adjacent 'Lobht a' Choire' was spelt Lota Corrie on the map (they translated this as 'floor of the corrie', though more accurately it is like a storey in a building). Curiously, these two features are the only ones in the Cuillin spelt with the anglicised 'corrie'. Regarding Harta Corrie the OS conceded that 'the meaning of the name is obscure'. In an 1866 article James Leitch made the credible suggestion that it might be derived from 'gleann ard o'choire', the glen of the high corrie.[12]

Charles Pilkington became so frustrated with the limitations of the Ordnance Surveys's cartography that he eventually created and marketed his own map of the Cuillin. Charles and his brother Lawrence were born in St Helens, Lancashire, in 1850 and 1855 respectively. Although members of the famous Pilkington glass-making family, no positions in the company were available so the brothers went to work for an uncle who owned coalmines at Clifton, outside Manchester. By 1888 they were both directors of Clifton and Kearsley Collieries. Their first climb together was Pillar Rock in 1869. In Skye they are best known for their first ascent of the Inaccessible Pinnacle in 1880. Despite the brothers undoubted ability, and regular visits to venues like the Lake District, their only British first ascents are in the Cuillin.

The recording of the Pilkingtons' early Cuillin exploration is somewhat vague and to interpret events it is useful to examine at what standard they are climbing elsewhere. Their level of fitness was self-evident: in 1883 they managed to cover about 60 miles (95km) and 13,800ft (4,200m) in the Lake District within 24 hours. Their alpine record is also impressive. From 1872 to 1883, if not in Scotland, they were in the Alps either with Eustace Hulton or their cousin Fred Gardiner. To the consternation of the Alpine Club old guard they began to dispense with guides, making some impressive first ascents like the Jungfrau directly up the Guggi Glacier in 1881 and the Disgrazia by the north face the following year. Lawrence later confirmed that Charles was usually the leader of the party: 'He was always even-tempered and resourceful.'

When the Pilkington brothers first visited Skye in 1879 they only crossed 'a humble pass or so', as mountaineering was secondary to their prime interests of shooting and fishing, sports all the rage due to the prevailing Balmoralmania. Due to poor shooting in 1880 they relocated to Sligachan where they made a precocious but unsuccessful attempt on the north-west face of Sgurr nan Gillean. Perhaps as guideless pioneers of La Meije the summer before, they were overconfident on British 'hills'. They did observe though, that the mountain's west ridge might provide an interesting route of ascent, one they duly completed the next day. On their map, most likely that in *Black's Guide to Scotland*, they also noticed an unclimbed summit named 'Inaccessible Peak' (3,212ft). The brothers interpreted this as the summit pinnacle of Sgurr Dearg, what is now known as the Inaccessible Pinnacle, and resolved to try and be the first to climb it.

As the morning of 18th August was misty the brothers thought it advisable to hire an unnamed guide from the Sligachan Hotel to help them locate this feature in the poor visibility. This is often assumed to be John Mackenzie, but Angus MacPherson was also actively guiding from the inn until around 1886. Nowadays just about everyone reaches the Inaccessible Pinnacle from the Glen Brittle side, but in the nineteenth century almost all approaches began at Sligachan and one of the standard routes to the southern peaks started through Harta Corrie. The Pilkingtons and their guide went this way: over Druim nan Ramh to the head of Loch Coruisk and then up Coireachan Ruadha to Sgurr Dearg. Here the Pilkingtons chose to attempt the longer but less steep east ridge, leaving their guide at the base of the pinnacle. The quantity of loose rock they encountered confirmed the popular opinion that any previous attempts had been unsuccessful. Both brothers have left accounts of their first ascent of the pinnacle's East Ridge (Moderate), now one of the most popular rock climbs in Britain:

> Charles: 'As the mountain on which it stands also shoots away on either side, the eye seems to plunge immediately to the bottom of Glen Coruisk, 2,500 feet below, giving an additional feeling of insecurity to anyone who, clinging to the narrow east edge (on which he may be seated astride) feels the whole slab vibrate with the blow of a falling rock that he has levered out from the crest above, as actually happened on the first ascent.'[13]

> Lawrence: 'I shall always remember that as the noisiest climb I ever had. There was a foot or more of loose rock which had been shattered by the lightning and frost of ages. This formed the edge of the pinnacle and had to be thrown down as we climbed up. The noise was appalling: the very rock of the pinnacle itself seemed to vibrate with indignation at our rude onslaught.'[14]

Charles Pilkington mentions that the second ascent of the Inaccessible Pinnacle was made by an unnamed local shepherd in 1881 who climbed it in bare feet. Again this has generally been assumed to be John Mackenzie, but if so one would expect Pilkington to credit him by name—he does so later in the same article in the *Alpine Journal*, 'The Black Coolins', with regard to Mackenzie's ascent of the pinnacle's shorter side, the West Ridge. When Norman Collie repeated the pinnacle in 1887 he lists the previous ascents but makes no mention of this particular 'second ascent' despite having access to local information through his close association with John Mackenzie.

In the autumn of 1883 Lawrence Pilkington returned to Skye without Charles but with two Alpine Club friends, Eustace Hulton and Horace Walker. Walker, a Liverpool lead merchant, was one of the leading lights during the golden age of the Alps where he had a pedigree stretching over fifty years from 1854 to 1905. In 1865 he was a member of the party that made the first ascent of the Brenva Ridge on Mont Blanc, the same day as the Matterhorn disaster. His name lives on in Pointe Walker, the true summit of the Grand Jorasses with its much sought-after Alpine classic, the Walker Spur.

The Pilkington brothers had contrasting luck with the Skye weather. Charles was the lucky one. In the Badminton Library volume, *Mountaineering,* Charles gave some unorthodox advice on how to locate Scotland's best mountains: get hold of a meteorological map and head for the areas where rainfall was over 80 inches per annum. Few visitors to Skye manage to avoid talk of the weather. In 1860 George Symons published his first annual volume of *British Rainfall*, the start of his quest to scientifically measure this popular topic of conversation. From 1871 until 1884 there was a rain gauge at Sligachan when the innkeepers, first Angus MacDonald then John Butters, took on the role of volunteer observers. During this period the highest annual total was 151 inches in 1884, the lowest 55 inches in 1879.

For protection from the frequent downpours early visitors to Skye had the choice of an oiled-silk cloak or faithful umbrella. By the time of the Pilkingtons' visits the 'deluge-proof' mackintosh raincoat was available, but was not popular on the hills as the rubber coating trapped a pungent build-up of condensation. Not that Charles Pilkington would have needed a waterproof: 'My personal experience of Skye weather is that it is the driest place in the British Isles, for I have been there three times, spending at least ten days on each occasion, and have only had four hours rain in the three visits.'[15] However, the autumn of 1883 epitomised Lawrence's contrasting fortune:

> For three weeks it rained more or less every day: when the barometer fell it rained cats and dogs; when the barometer rose a sea mist crept up the hills in the morning, and turning into a persistent rain that did not clear off until the evening. Indeed it was only by getting up determinedly at 5am whenever the glass showed signs of rising and walking sometimes eight or nine miles to the foot of our peak and then waiting hours for a break in the weather, that we were able to make any ascents at all.[16]

Nor did this level of dedication guarantee any success. Lawrence was keen to introduce his friends to the Inaccessible Pinnacle but after walking all the way from Sligachan to Sgurr Dearg, this time via Bealach a' Mhaim and Glen Brittle, they were unable to even find the summit stack in the mist. When they eventually did climb it the contrast with the first ascent was pronounced, 'Not a single loose rock on the ridge… No sound.' Considering the poor weather and that most approaches were on foot from Sligachan, the achievements of Lawrence Pilkington's party in 1883 were impressive. These included the first ascent of Bidein's Central Peak, the third ascent of the Inaccessible Pinnacle and both Sgurr Alasdair and Sgurr Dubh by new routes. Eustace Hulton, a Manchester businessman in the cotton trade, described the day on Bidein via the classic Druim nan Ramh ridge:

> Ascending from Harta Corrie we gained the ridge between it and Loch Coruisk, which from this point seemed to lead straight to the summit; but we soon found the direct ascent cut off by a series of dykes, and were forced to work along below the crest to our right until we gained the foot of the mass of rock forming the peak itself. Here we regained the crest and traversed a ledge on the Coruisk side of the mountain until it lost itself on the face of the cliff. A long reach and a lift from below enabled us to gain the next point, whence a series of narrow ledges and long lifts, first above Glen Coruisk and then above Harta Corrie brought us to the top of our mountain, a fine moss-covered summit, with no stone-man [cairn] to mark a former ascent. We meant to have descended by the North Ridge, but the rocks looked so smooth that we did not attempt it.[17]

Details of their new climbs on Sgurr Alasdair and Sgurr Dubh Mor are sketchy. There was no formal recording mechanism for new routes prior to the start of the *Scottish Mountaineering Club Journal* in 1890. The *Alpine Journal* was happy to publish details of the first ascent of peaks in Great Britain, like the Inaccessible Pinnacle, but British rock climbs were regarded as too trivial for inclusion. Lawrence Pilkington, Eustace Hulton and Horace Walker made the second recorded visit to Sgurr Dubh Mor 'by a fine rough scramble from Corrie Lachain, one of the upper hollows of Glen Coruisk'. This complex and unfrequented face is another whose early history is poorly documented. It would be a hundred years before another route was recorded here, Paddy and Mick's Route (Moderate).

Their other new route on the Coire Lagan face of Sgurr Alasdair is presumably that described by Charles Pilkington in his article 'Sgurr Alasdair' (*SMC Journal*, 1891) where they headed up the screes towards Bealach Sgumain before striking out left onto the rocks between Collie's Climb and the South-West Ridge. Horace Walker, in his application to join the Scottish Mountaineering Club, also mentions an ascent of Sgurr a' Mhadaidh in 1883 which would make it the first recorded ascent of the mountain, but this claim is clouded by the continued confusion between this peak and Bidein Druim nan Ramh.

The next year, at the age of 29, Lawrence's climbing days were all but over. In Piers Ghyll, a gully above Wasdale in the Lake District, his thigh was crushed by falling rocks and he was carried off the hill on a farm gate. He never fully recovered and was increasingly drawn to business and his other passions, music and poetry. He published two novels and five volumes of poetry which include verses celebrating the Cuillin.

After Walker and Hulton's visit with Lawrence Pilkington in 1883, there was little new activity on Skye until the Reverend A H Stocker and A G Parker's ascent of the short side of the Inaccessible Pinnacle, the harder West Ridge (Severe), on 19 August 1886. Stocker was a pioneer of some of the first climbs in Snowdonia: routes on Lliwedd with T W Wall in 1883, and Parker the following year. These were some of the earliest records in Britain of large cliffs being climbed for their own sake. In 1888 Stocker also made the first ascents of some peaks in the Drakensberg in South Africa.

Stocker recorded their new climb on the Inaccessible Pinnacle in the *Alpine Journal,* comments which again reflect the skill and competence of these early rock climbers: 'The north face of the west edge is broken by three ledges, the highest of which slopes unpleasantly outwards. It is but a step from the first ledge to the second, from which the highest is easily reached. The only difficulty, hardly worthy of the name, consists in crossing the sloping ledge and working on to the west edge of the Pinnacle. The whole climb is about seventy feet, and takes less than five minutes.'[18] The West Ridge was traditionally graded Difficult until the 2011 SMC guide when it skipped a grade to Severe. (In his 1908 book, *Rock-Climbing in Skye*, Ashley Abraham gave the same grade, Difficult, to both East and West Ridges.)

Stocker and Parker also descended the original route, the East Ridge, completing the first traverse of the pinnacle. Abseiling was then unknown and routes were climbed down in much the same way as ascended, the leader going last and protecting himself by passing the rope over rock projections known as hitches. Cragsmen were adept and well-practiced in down climbing when they assisted each other with their shoulders and arms. Occasionally, on very steep sections, the rope was draped over a hitch and descended hand over hand, a method known as the double rope technique. Ostensibly this meant the rope was descended 'sailor fashion' with the feet being used as a brake. A second ascent of the West Ridge was recorded by Reginald Broomfield from Oxford two weeks later:

> On 4 September John Mackenzie and I left Sligachan at 11am and reached farmhouse 1.30. Commenced ascent of Sgurr Dearg at 1.45 and reached foot of the so-called Inaccessible Peak at 4.05. The ascent and descent occupied fifty minutes and proved fairly difficult. We used a rope both in ascending and descending though I think this precaution hardly necessary.[19]

Also in Skye that September (1886) was Walter Haskett Smith who, three months earlier, made the first ascent of Napes Needle in the Lake District, a solo climb that is regarded as an iconic event in the birth of British rock climbing. He didn't hang about when he repeated the Inaccessible Pinnacle's East Ridge, 'a fine piece of rock requiring care rather than skill (ascent four minutes, two minutes on top, descent six minutes)'.[20] The genial Haskett Smith is also author of the world's first rock climbing guide, *Climbing in the British Isles*.

With all these ascents in 1886 the Inaccessible Pinnacle was not living up to its name and the phallically correct 'Old Man of Skye' comes increasingly into vogue. In fact with most of the loose rock on the original route despatched to the screes, the word was now out that the climb comprised a series of dangle-holds, the Victorian term for what we now call jug-handles. Charles Pilkington would later sum up the changes:

> The Inaccessible Pinnacle of Sgurr Dearg is the Matterhorn of the district, and the east ridge is now safe enough for a man with a steady head, but is very narrow with a sheer drop on one side; great care should be taken in the descent, one man only moving at a time, and let the last man be steady and keep the rope tight. The western ascent, not nearly so fine, is very short, and has, moreover, one difficult and dangerous step, where no help can be given to the leader, and where, if he fell, he could not be held by the rope; once up, however, he can, if required, give very effective aid to those below.[21]

In late May 1887 Charles Pilkington and Horace Walker returned to the Cuillin for a week's mountaineering with James Heelis, a Manchester solicitor. They managed to tick off most of the peaks accessible from Sligachan before turning their attention to the small matter of the unclimbed Clach Glas. After approaching the mountain down Glen Sligachan, they completed the first ascent by what is now known as Pilkington's Gully, a line on the west face that leads to the summit ridge: 'Gaining the upper part of the ridge, to the right or south side of the actual summit, we found a knife-edge of tremendous steepness coming down towards us. We put on the rope and nerved ourselves for the attack; we just had a look around the edge first, and seeing a piece of slanting rock, we crossed it, and pulling ourselves out of the neck of a little gully, walked up the imposter in a few minutes.'[22] This photogenic rock feature is now referred to as 'the Imposter'.

In 1884 Glenbrittle farm was taken over by MacLeod of Dunvegan who installed Henry Laidlaw from Rosshire as farm manager. In 1887 Glen Brittle House was unlet and Pilkington's party managed to negotiate accommodation there, engaging John Mackenzie as porter to transport their baggage from Sligachan by pony and cart. This was the first record of climbers using the shooting lodge which later became a popular mountaineering base. On their way to Glen Brittle they took in Bidein's North Peak where they were bemused to find the cairn left by William Naismith seven years earlier. His ascent was not common knowledge until his article in the 1890 *SMC Journal* (and even this had a very limited circulation). From the summit of the North Peak Horace Walker recognised the Central Peak as the one he had climbed with Lawrence Pilkington and Eustace Hulton four years earlier, after their ascent of the Druim nan Ramh ridge. However, none of them fancied the look of the next section, the direct route from the gap up to the Central Peak. They opted to descend the gully between the North and Central Peaks and then skirt round to the top of the Central Peak by way of the West Peak.

Like Alexander Nicolson, Pilkington's party found that a feature of many of the tops was a comfy carpet of moss that encouraged an even longer stop to savour the view and rest the muscles. Bidein's highest top was no exception and here Charles Pilkington noticed that the needle on his prismatic compass was behaving oddly—the rocks were magnetic, rendering the bearings useless. The geologist John MacCulloch was one of the first to point this out yet, despite further warnings by Pilkington, Naismith and others, this information did not seem to permeate beyond a close-knit few. Until the end of the century repeated 'discoveries' of the rocks' magnetism are recorded in the Sligachan Climbers' Book.

Charles Pilkington's party spent the next two days exploring Coire Lagan. While John Mackenzie and Heelis, the party's photographer, remained in the corrie, Pilkington and Walker tackled the unclimbed East Peak of Alasdair. A later description suggests Gully E as their route of ascent: 'A capital scramble can be made on it, by leaving the Stone Shoot when halfway up and taking to the rocks to the left: you must climb where you can, aiming a little to the north of the summit.'[23] For the new peak Pilkington proposed the name 'Sgurr Labain' after the corrie it overlooked, but as with Nicolson's similar suggestion for Alasdair this did not gain general acceptance. In Norman Collie's list of Cuillin heights, published in 1893, it remains 'Sgurr Alasdair, East Peak'. However by 1896 it is established as Sgurr Thearlaich (Charles's Peak).

The next day Pilkington, Walker and Heelis felt honour-bound to repeat Stocker and Parker's West Ridge on the Inaccessible Pinnacle along with John Mackenzie. From the summit the party of four descended the original route and continued under An Stac to the distinctive unclimbed peak at the head of Coire Lagan, 'a fine easy climb with precipitous rocks on either side of the ridge'. After building a cairn they considered the pleasant task of nomenclature, jokingly referring to it as 'Pic Mackenzie'. This name was actually used for several years until the publication of Pilkington's map in 1890 when the Gaelic version there, Sgurr Mhic Choinnich (Mackenzie's Peak), became the accepted format.

As the fine weather continued, Charles Pilkington's party took the coastal route from Glen Brittle round to Coruisk where they called in at the cabin of Alfred Williams, a Salisbury artist and Alpine Club member who relished living in wild and remote places. Near the outlet to Loch Coruisk he had constructed a rough hut as a base from which to paint his 'Coruisks'. In the afternoon they set off to attempt the Dubh Ridge but were beaten back 'by a trap dyke high up on the north ridge'. Pilkington blamed the superb view down Loch Scavaig for their dilatory start and sluggish progress, but later, in a letter to William Douglas, William Brown let the cat out of the bag, 'too much of William's Bass [beer]'. After a night at Glen Brittle, Pilkington's party returned to Sligachan by way of an unrecorded route on the west face of Sgurr a' Ghreadaidh. They continued along the crest of the ridge to make the first ascertained visit to Sgurr a' Mhadaidh's main top before then completing the first recorded passage of the Thuilm Ridge, the shattered west ridge descending towards Sgurr Thuilm.

On their last day they took up a suggestion of Alfred Williams's to try the unclimbed Sgurr na h-Uamha. This peak has a confused history. In 1871 four army officers claimed the ascent of 'the sharp peak opposite Sgurr na Stri. Rather difficult in places and no traces of previous ascent, built a cairn on top'. B H Humble thought this vague description referred to Sgurr Dubh Beag, others thought Sgurr na h-Uamha, but it could be applied to almost any mountain in the range.

John Mackenzie had made two unsuccessful attempts on Sgurr na h-Uamha, one from Harta Corrie and the other by the north ridge which connected the peak to Sgurr nan Gillean. Charles Pilkington's party opted for the latter route which they approached by Glen Sligachan and then up through An Glas-choire. From the corrie they were attracted by a slanting gully, 'a capital scramble', now known as North-East Face (Grade 3), which led to easier rocks and the summit. They considered this the first ascent, something they would not have done had they come across the cairn built by the army officers. This brought to a conclusion one of the most productive weeks of mountain exploration ever seen in the British Isles which included the first recorded ascents of no less than four peaks: Clach Glas, Sgurr Thearlaich, Sgurr a' Mhadaidh and Sgurr na h-Uamha.

After the ascent of Sgurr Thearlaich in early June 1887, the last major unclimbed summit on the Main Ridge, the emphasis shifted towards completing the links between the peaks. Norman Collie is particularly associated with this but he was pre-empted by a polemical Irishman, H C (Henry Chichester) Hart. Born in Dublin of a prominent Donegal family, Hart was one of the first Irish mountaineers, as well as an exhaustive explorer of Ireland in a quest to find rare flowering plants. At six-foot-one he was a noted athlete at Trinity College, Dublin, where he studied science, though later in life turned to Elizabethan literature. The Irish writer Standish O'Grady described Hart as 'the handsomest, noblest looking, most superbly formed Irishmen of modern times'. For a wager

THE BLACK CUILLIN

Hart completed a 75-mile (121km) return walk from Dublin to Lugnaquilla, highest point of the Wicklow Hills, within 24 hours. This is now commemorated in the Hart Walk, a popular challenge for endurance walkers and runners, which takes place every August Bank Holiday.

Although renowned for his fitness and stamina, Hart could be hard to get on with. A fellow botanist, Robert Lloyd Praeger, described him as 'dictatorial, impatient, difficult to handle'. Later in life he became 'a confirmed drunkard'; his wife divorced him on grounds of cruelty and adultery in 1897 when he was living in a Brighton hotel with a married woman. Hart compiled the Irish section of Haskett Smith's seminal *Climbing in the British Isles,* where the author also portrays him as something of a slippery customer: 'After months of mysterious silence he would glide into sight, great with solid mountaineering matter, gleaming with pearls of botany, and gems of geologic lore; but alas! In another moment he would glide away into unknown depths where the harpoon of the penny post was harmless and telegrams tickled him in vain.'[24]

In July 1887, accompanied by John Mackenzie, H C Hart made at least two traverses of considerable chunks of the Main Ridge. On 1st July, after starting at Sgurr nan Gillean, he and his guide continued along the ridge to make the first recorded traverse of all the tops of Bidein and Sgurr a' Mhadaidh, 'over some very bad places'. At Sgurr a' Ghreadaidh they were forced off the ridge as the weather closed in, descending to Glen Brittle to start the long slog back to Sligachan. Three days later they returned to the ridge near where they left off. They then continued along the crest, including a traverse of the Inaccessible Pinnacle and all the peaks of Alasdair, to descend to Glen Brittle House for some welcome tea, and a pony and trap home. Hart was particularly impressed by the performance of his companion: 'Mackenzie is a first-rate climber; I gave him a "leg up" on the pinnacle and he didn't do the "tooth" on Sgurr nan Gillean, but in every other place he followed my lead without a mistake. I would advise him however to fix up his own shoes at heel and toe which once gave him a fall.'[25] Whether Mackenzie was so impressed with Hart is not recorded. Chances are this was the type of client he dreaded, one who tore along the ridge at breakneck speed over unclimbed pinnacles, with no stop for a breather or dram unless some rare flower was spotted.

Mackenzie and Hart were the first to traverse Sgurr Mhic Choinnich, in July 1887, but exactly what route did they take? And if they used Collie's Ledge, why was this named after the well-known Cuillin pioneer Norman Collie, Mackenzie's close friend, and not Hart? These are interesting questions and deserve some detailed analysis. (It should be noted that eponymous place names do not necessarily relate to first ascents; they can also refer to the discovery or first mention of a feature, or to some noteworthy occurrence.)

In the Sligachan Hotel Visitors' Book, Hart recorded how they negotiated this section of the ridge as 'climbed [Inaccessible] pinnacle up one side down the other and then crest with slight descent for a drop'. The term 'drop' is often used by Victorian climbers for a very steep section which was normally roped down, whereas 'descents' were down-climbed. But Hart also states, 'used no ropes at any time'. We also know Hart was particularly assiduous about sticking to the crest as closely as possible.

In 1890 Charles Pilkington wrote: 'Mr Hart climbed along the ridge from Sgurr Mhic Choinnich to this peak [Sgurr Alasdair], and, I believe, found the drop from Mhic Choinnich rather difficult; it certainly looks very steep'.[26] This statement, and Hart's own account, suggest that he and Mackenzie followed the crest of Sgurr Mhic Choinnich to its end where they attempted to descend the steep rocks to the bealach. Although going down the top part of Sgurr Mhic Choinnich's West Buttress to Collie's Ledge was an easier option, this does not fit with the above descriptions, and would also invite mention of the discovery of the distinctive, pavement-like ledge.

One's initial reaction to all this is that a direct descent to the bealach was too challenging for unroped climbers at this time, even with combined tactics which were an integral part of down-climbing. However nothing should be dismissed with regard to these early pioneers who have the capacity to constantly surprise with their technical ability, fitness, and assured movement in exposed positions with little or no protection. It was also contemporary protocol that desperate epics were recorded in a matter-of-fact manner or, preferably, not at all.

After reading the notes left by Hart in the Sligachan Visitors Book, W E Corlett decided to investigate the area for himself, on 3rd August 1889, but found things problematical even with the help of a rope: 'Followed South Ridge until Pic Mackenzie was reached and after a deal of trouble by using the rope liberally managed to descend the drop on far side of it.'

When Collie and Mackenzie reached Sgurr Mhic Choinnich the guide would naturally have first tried the route he knew, the one he had done with Hart the year before. With Collie still a relatively inexperienced rock climber they appear to have thought better of this and to have eventually retraced their steps to find and explore part of the traverse line that became known as Collie's Ledge. In an article in the *Alpine Journal* (1918) Collie made the following comment: 'This cost us about two hours, trying first to get down directly to the dip below, and next trying to find a traverse across the west face.'

Whatever the exact line of Hart and Collie's routes, over the following years the top section of Sgurr Mhic Choinnich's West Buttress, a Difficult chimney of excellent rock, became the established link between the mountain's summit and Bealach Mhic Choinnich. Ashley Abraham's book *Rock-Climbing in Skye* has a diagram showing two other lines to the left of this chimney which he labels 'Easy Routes from the col to Sgurr Mhic Choinnich.' Although none of these options appear to tally with Pilkington's description of Hart's drop as 'very steep', they do fit the account Collie gives in 1893: 'Directly beyond the peak of Sgurr Mhic

Choinnich on the south side there is a very precipitous drop. This can be turned by descending on the Corrie Labain side just before reaching the summit of Sgurr Mhic Choinnich and then keeping to the left till the bealach is reached.'[27] Abraham describes a similar route but attributes it to Hart and Mackenzie. To complicate matters even more there was another ledge system parallel to but below Collie's Ledge which was a recommended option for several years. It is marked on diagrams (Figs 12 and 13) in the 1923 SMC guide.

When the writer John Buchan, a keen climber, discussed the possibility of traversing the Main Ridge from north to south in a single day, he mentioned having to tackle 'the awkward direct descent of Sgurr Mhic Choinnich'. For several decades Hart and Mackenzie's route was kept in mind as an option but rarely actually taken. The route gradually became neglected, then forgotten, due doubtless to the easier alternatives nearby. By the 1923 SMC guide there is no mention at all of Hart's explorations, but we do get the first reference to 'Collie's Ledge': 'Professor Collie *in 1890* [author's italics] made a way up to the left of King's Chimney by following an obvious ledge which slants up to the left from about 20 feet above the col… Collie's Ledge leads without difficulty round on to the Coire Lagan side.'

The topographical configuration of Sgurr Mhic Choinnich, and the fact that the northern start of the ledge is not obvious and can be easily missed, suggests that the traverse of the full length of the ledge would most likely be first done by a party travelling in a south to north direction. Among all the conjecture it seems fairly safe to conclude that Collie was first to traverse the bulk of the ledge round on the Coire Lagan face, first in descent in 1888, and then more fully in the opposite direction two years later. Whatever the order of events, this generation of British mountaineers were sticklers for accuracy as well as unerringly honest in their exploratory claims. In short, the name Collie's Ledge would not have been adopted without good cause and would not have gained general acceptance if credit was due elsewhere.

Whatever route Hart and Mackenzie took traversing Sgurr Mhic Choinnich, they would have been, like many mountaineering historians, glad to leave the complexities of the mountain behind them. They then ascended Sgurr Thearlaich, the first to climb it directly from Bealach Mhic Choinnich. It was the last link in the connection of all the peaks around Coire Lagan, a round that is one of the classic outings in the Cuillin.

Due to the lack of detailed information and the distance of many peaks from Sligachan, a typical day in the Cuillin was often limited to either one or two peaks or the round of a corrie. The length of Hart's trips are highly impressive considering the unfamiliar ground and the quantity of loose rock; the lack of paths, nail marks or polished rock later taken for granted as navigational aids, and also the fact that he tried to keep to the crest of the ridge. Hart was a noted botanist and on his frenetic expeditions in Skye he managed to find time to record *Cerastium alpinum* (Sgurr na Banachdich), *Azalea procumbens* (Sgurr nan Gillean) and even located a botanical rarity, the Alpine Rock-Cress (*Arabis alpina*), found only in a few Cuillin corries and nowhere else in Britain.

Hart's Cuillin exploits are even more remarkable in that, like William Knight, he did not use a rope, writing: 'Of roped climbed the author has no experience outside the Alps.' The low status accruing to British mountains at this period (and the general ignorance of ranges like the Cuillin) resulted in the use of the rope in Britain being seen as unnecessary and therefore unsporting. This was the first instance of Britain adopting its own distinctive code of ethics. Reports of climbs were often appended with 'climbing fairly done' or 'no ropes or other illegitimate means'. Today ropes are such an integral part of climbing it is hard to think of them not being an essential piece of kit. However in Skye, prior to the Pilkingtons, this was indeed the case. Alpenstocks, shoulders, plaids and wooden staffs were all acceptable means of upward assistance, but not a rope.

The Pilkingtons introduced the use of the rope to Skye, probably in 1880 on their first ascent of the Inaccessible Pinnacle. In a letter to W A B Coolidge, Charles Pilkington alludes to the use of a rope on this climb when he offers his guide, 'to take him up and let him down'. The brothers do not specifically mention its use until Charles's 1887 visit when he commented that 'forty to fifty feet is generally enough'. Around 1885 the rope began to be used in the Lake District and by 1889, save for one or two die-hards, its use in the Cuillin was no longer regarded as ethically unsound. In the Sligachan Visitors' Book, Hart appended Charles Pilkington's entry with 'Ropes all the time' but got his comeuppance when his own account was annotated: 'A rope with a noose at the end and a long drop would have suited this idiot.' Haskett Smith was more sympathetic when he summed Hart up as 'essentially a scholar and man of science, complicated by being an athlete and an Irishman'.

The Pilkington brothers were instrumental in raising John Mackenzie's climbing standard by helping him to improve his technique and teaching him basic rope management. This enabled Mackenzie, still without proper climbing boots, to follow Henry Hart on their unroped traverse of the Inaccessible Pinnacle and the following year lead an inexperienced Norman Collie up its tricky West Ridge.

Hart returned to Skye in 1890 when a fellow guest at the Sligachan Inn was Alexander Nicolson. The evening that Nicolson was packing for his return to Edinburgh, Norman Collie arrived for a short stay. It has not been recorded whether the two men met but symbolically two distinct eras in the Cuillins' history rubbed shoulders. Collie, a London-based research chemist, spearheaded a process of more systematic exploration, laying the ground for the new sport of rock climbing.

Chapter Three
Norman Collie and John Mackenzie

Of all the names associated with the Cuillin, those of Norman Collie and his climbing partner and guide, John Mackenzie, most readily come to mind. Both men have Cuillin peaks named after them: Sgurr Thormaid (Norman's Peak) and Sgurr Mhic Choinnich (Mackenzie's Peak). Collie was born on 10th September 1859 at Alderley Edge in Cheshire, the second of five children, but much of his childhood was spent in Scotland: a few months at Bridge of Allan and then five years at Glassel on Deeside. At the latter he discovered his love of wild places, climbed his first hills and saw his first mountain, Lochnagar. Throughout his life Collie maintained he felt Scottish and in later years renewed his acquaintance with north-east Scotland through contact with the Cairngorm Club.

His mother, Selina Winkworth, disliked Scotland and when Norman was eleven the family moved to Clifton in Bristol. After undistinguished performances at Charterhouse and latterly as a day boy at Clifton College, he studied chemistry at University College, Bristol. Here, under E A Letts, he found his professional vocation as a research chemist. He then studied for his doctorate at Würzburg University in Germany (in Britain to become a chemist you took a form of apprenticeship). A letter home in December 1882 reveals how little student life has changed: 'I am still worse or I never should have asked you for money. I have got nothing at all and Richardson has only eight shillings and I owe him some money. So in four days we shall starve.'

His uncle, Stephen Winkworth, a Bolton cotton spinner, helped him out financially. A member of the Alpine Club, he would also have a seminal influence on Collie's development as a mountaineer, both as role model and means of introduction to the likes of A F (Fred) Mummery and Geoffrey Hastings with whom Collie later formed a strong team climbing new routes in the Alps. Norman's family life was a stimulating environment, especially among his aunts: Catherine was a well-known translator of German hymns – as a quick browse through any church hymnbook will reveal; Susanna was a German scholar and Emily a suffragette. All the sisters were friendly with Charlotte Brontë, Mrs Gaskell and the soprano Jenny Lind.

After Collie gained his PhD in 1884 he taught at Cheltenham Ladies' College, 'the girls' Eton', a disheartening time for him that was alleviated by summer fishing holidays in north-west Scotland. It was on the last of these trips, in 1886, that Collie found himself precipitated into a lifelong love affair with the Cuillin, taking his first steps to becoming one of the finest all-round mountaineers of his generation. The next year, aged 28, he became assistant to Professor William Ramsay at University College London, a post he held until 1896. This period covered his major Cuillin and Alpine exploration before his pioneering instincts demanded more avant-garde destinations. Ramsay was uncle of G C Ramsay, professor of humanity at Glasgow University and first president of the Scottish Mountaineering Club. He quickly took to his new colleague, 'Collie is a delightful fellow with a genius for research' and invited him to spend the Christmas of 1887 with his own family: 'My beloved friend and demonstrator, Dr Collie, whom to know is to esteem, took the part of Father Christmas, having assumed a cotton wool moustache and beard.'

The University College lab was a dusty jumble of chemical jars and complex apparatus; there was even an Egyptian mummy lying discarded in the cellar below (the building now houses the Slade School of Fine Art). Mountaineering would have been a popular topic of conversation in the lab as Collie's colleagues included A M (Alexander) Kellas, whom George Mallory took such a shine to on the first Everest expedition in 1921; and Morris Travers, Ramsay's right-hand man, who was a member of the party, along with Collie, that made the first ascent of Castle Ridge on Ben Nevis in 1895. One of Collie's students E C C (Cyril) Baly, who has an eponymous climb in Coire Lagan, described him as 'a born teacher gifted with a salutary sarcasm'. Although Ramsay regarded Collie as 'a very clever experimentalist and a most enthusiastic researcher', he grumbled that the moment the term ended Collie headed for the hills.

Collie initially lived in a suite of rooms at 16 Campden Grove, Kensington, until a move was made to 20 Gower Street round the corner from University College. At home he surrounded himself with objets d'art: Indian embroideries, ivories, bronzes, fine bindings and especially Chinese porcelain on which he was an acknowledged expert. There are two contrasting vignettes of Collie in London: the solitary, gaunt Sherlockian figure in Jaeger dressing gown with malt whisky and after-dinner pipe, wreathed in tobacco fug by a blazing fire; and the gregarious and devoted host, organiser of celebrated dinner parties, witty raconteur who far from a recluse delighted in conviviality and good company. It was especially among his mountaineering friends that this affable side blossomed. Frequent visitors to the cluttered Gower Street flat included Hugh Stutfield, W P Ker, the painter Colin Phillip, Charles Bruce, W C (Cecil) Slingsby and Francis Younghusband. Collie would greet them at the door beside the imposing sculpture of a Mayan God he used as an umbrella stand. Younghusband was particularly interesting company: an imperialist adventurer, spy, and mystic who advocated free love and believed there was a 'world leader' living on planet Altair.

Collie was a deeply enigmatic character. Although generally well respected, his reserve was often construed as arrogance and he was consequently disliked by some. However when he found the company stimulating his engaging side inevitably broke through. His alpine articles reflect a droll sense of humour lacking in his later, more wistful pieces. On naming the Dent du Requin he suggests Aiguille Noire, 'so that it might not be confused with Mt Blanc'. On summit celebrations: 'Sometimes the varied emotions are allowed a safety valve in shouting or trying to distinguish all the other mountains in the Alps. We, however, kept our feelings sternly suppressed by means of corned beef.'[1] On Mummery's leadership: 'This was questioned by the more cautious members of the party, who were not so accustomed as he to thousands of feet of granite set at a terribly steep angle.'[2] Like many academically gifted people Collie often preferred his own thoughts to fawning small talk, presenting an air of haughtiness as a carapace against mediocrity. Geoffrey Winthrop Young agreed:

> His benign look could turn to one of rallying amusement or to a meditative and pipe-puffing remoteness, or if he saw or heard something offending his sense of decency out came the pipe, the mouth compressed and there was a moment's fixed and scowled glare followed by a stony aloofness, again it would change to courteous interest or to a vivacity of pleasure and quick utterance at something really new or striking.[3]

The pipe was his trademark, hanging over the lower lip, giving him his characteristically sardonic, hangdog expression. Collie was an accomplished glass-blower, an indispensable skill for a chemist to make his own apparatus which he invariably did with lit pipe in mouth. His students ribbed him that he only smoked cigarettes when filling his pipe. Indeed, his only near accident in the mountains was in the Rockies when a slip dislodged his pipe and he risked life and limb to catch it.

In the early 1880s Collie had his first glimpse of the distinctive serrated skyline of the Cuillin from Wester Ross. Learning there was good fishing there, he crossed to Skye in the summer of 1886 but, like the Pilkingtons before him, found the rivers too low. Taking to sea-bathing, a jellyfish sting resolved him to stick to pastimes on dry land. In the Sligachan Hotel Visitors' Book the entry for 14 August 1886 includes Norman Collie, Cheltenham; Arthur Leslie Collie, Kensington, London (a younger brother) and A W Collie, Oxford (another brother, Alexander). After walking to view Coruisk the three brothers began to explore the mountains, visiting Coire a' Bhasteir where they spotted two climbers high above them on Sgurr nan Gillean, as Norman Collie recalled: 'Hundreds of feet above me, on what appeared to me to be rocks as steep as the walls of a house, they moved slowly backwards and forwards, but always getting higher, till they finally reached the summit.'[4]

They eventually discovered that the climbers were A H Stocker and A G Parker who were in the process of creating a new climb on the Fourth Pinnacle, the same week they had made the first ascent of the Inaccessible Pinnacle's West

Ridge. Collie felt compelled to copy their example, and used the inn's telegraph office to contact Buckinghams, the London rope manufacturer, to send one of their manila alpine ropes with its distinctive red thread. When this arrived the Collie brothers spent the next two days attempting Sgurr nan Gillean unsuccessfully by three different routes. Initially they were rebuffed by the Gendarme on the West Ridge, then by Pinnacle Ridge, and finally by a direct attempt on the main peak from Coire a' Bhasteir. To unlock the key to Sgurr nan Gillean they decided to seek advice from the local expert, the guide John Mackenzie, and a few days later engaged him for an ascent of Am Basteir. Having first climbed Sgurr nan Gillean as a 10-year-old, Mackenzie already had twenty years' experience of the Cuillin when he first met Collie. It was the start of a very special friendship that lasted until Mackenzie's death in 1933, an extraordinary relationship that bridged the social and cultural gulf between the two men.

Although Collie and Mackenzie are often thought of together, our view of their relative contribution is skewed towards Collie as we are more familiar with his mountaineering exploits through his books and articles. He has also been the subject of two biographies: W C Taylor's *The Snows of Yesteryear*, and *Norman Collie, A Life in Two Worlds* by Christine Mill, as well as an extensive Royal Society obituary by E C C Baly. Mackenzie's life, views and opinions formed part of an oral tradition that is now mostly lost. But we shouldn't underestimate his influence. Collie had a few weeks break in Skye while Mackenzie was a permanent fixture at Sligachan, well respected, and cognizant of all that was going on in the hills and at the inn.

John Mackenzie was born on 20th April 1857, the third of a family of eight, at the family croft in the village of Sconser. His father, Archie, died when he was 15, his mother in 1899. Mackenzie was born at a time of near famine and would live through several similar episodes. During the 1850s there was a series of crop failures in many parts of Skye and at times people were surviving on meal distributed to the needy, which was mixed with shellfish and edible seaweed to make it last. One journalist described the villagers of Sconser in 1851 as 'in a state of extreme destitution': 'In one hut here we found a family, consisting of the parents and seven children, without any food save a few herrings… The children, both in Sconser and the Braes were almost in a state of nakedness and the men and women were in the most part clothed in rags.'[5] C R Weld visited Sconser in 1859 when John Mackenzie would have been two years old:

> Our road lay along the slopes of the hills dipping into Loch Sligachan. Near the entrance of the loch are some score of dwellings which, until I saw human beings emerging from them, I did not imagine for a moment were built to shelter humanity. The walls, constructed of uncemented stones, were scarcely six feet high, and they were unprovided with windows or chimneys. The roofs consisted of rough thatch, which, when saturated with soot, is

THE BLACK CUILLIN

removed, and serves as manure. Little patches of blighted oats and potatoes surround the huts, but so unpropitious is the climate, that these crops rarely arrive at maturity. Indeed, it would be difficult to conceive a harder struggle with nature than these poor people have to submit to for bare existence.[6]

In 1873, when Mackenzie was 16, the Parish Sanitory Inspector wrote of improved housing and good potato crops, but the age-old custom of sharing accommodation with cattle persisted. This was a major contributory factor for his visit to the village, six cases of typhoid. However, the booming late-Victorian tourist industry helped to provide much needed income in the summer months. The young Mackenzie was initially employed as a pony-boy escorting tourists down Glen Sligachan to view Loch Coruisk. As he gained experience he progressed from ghillie to porter to mountain guiding.

Mackenzie is recorded as accompanying Wilberforce Newton (Will) Tribe, a Bristol share broker and brother-in-law of the Hopkinson brothers, on the first ascent of Sgurr a' Ghreadaidh in 1870. However the date seems suspect as Mackenzie would have been 14 years old, Tribe 15. The mountain was definitely ascended in 1871 by Matthew Forster Heddle from Hoy in the Orkneys. Like the geologist John MacCulloch, Heddle graduated in medicine before gravitating toward the earth sciences, becoming in 1862 professor of chemistry at St Andrews University where James David Forbes was now principal. Forbes gave Heddle a testimonial for his new post, but later fell out with him due to what he described as his 'strange and perverse conduct'.

Over the next 25 summers, Heddle, who had ten children, chose to spend much of his time exploring the northern highlands and islands for mineral localities. He discovered at least 17 species new to Scotland and has Mattheddleite named in his honour. No less an authority than Hugh Munro said of him: 'There can be little doubt that Professor Heddle had climbed far more Scottish mountains than any man who has yet lived.'[7] Between 1881 and 1891 he often accompanied the naturalist John A Harvie-Brown on his Hebridean yacht trips which included several visits to the Cuillin. In Talisker Bay there is a sea-stack named after Heddle which now sports a couple of rock climbs.

During the late 1880s John Mackenzie took over from Angus MacPherson as chief guide at Sligachan Inn. Mackenzie's career lasted over fifty years in which he made over 1,000 ascents of Sgurr nan Gillean alone. He claimed to have had only one accident, in a gully on Sgurr a' Bhasteir in 1902 when he slipped due to a missing boot-nail. He maintained he turned back only once, when a wildcat with kittens blocked his path and refused to give way. Mackenzie wrote little of his experiences, but in a newspaper interview he talked of a benightment on one of the remoter peaks when his party, soaked to the skin, was forced to sit out a wild September night till first light at 6am.

John Mackenzie has often been regarded as the first British mountain guide.

Over on Deeside the advent of the Royal Family at Balmoral led to a demand for guides to lead mountain walks, but unlike Mackenzie they did not develop into rock climbers. In fact his main rivals to the title are his predecessors at Sligachan: Angus MacPherson and before that, Lessingham Smith and J D Forbes's guide, Duncan MacIntyre (and his son who guided Alexander Nicolson in 1865). John Mackenzie was in demand not just for his unrivalled knowledge of the Cuillin and its flora and fauna, but also for the confidence and reassurance that he transmitted to more nervous clients. Ashley Abraham wrote of him:

> He is more a companion than a guide. When in his company one feels that his predominating qualities are his love for the mountains, his genial and kindly nature, his unremitting care, and a fine sturdy independence of spirit; the mere accident that Providence has not seen fit to endow him with worldly riches does not detract from these. The Coolin are to him an open book, every page of which he knows by heart. Their history is at his fingertips; it is a great delight to sit with him on the top of some grim tower and question him on the topography of the surrounding peaks.[8]

Through his close relation with many climbers, especially Norman Collie, Mackenzie is often regarded as a one-man corporation of guides working in isolation on Skye. In reality he was the leading light in a largely family concern that included his brothers Murdo (eight years younger) and Donald (seven years older) as well as nephews Archie and Rory. This was just as well since the better known John was often fully booked with regular clients like Norman Collie. Murdo regularly helped out in busy periods, with one client, H Sinclair Brooke, giving him a glowing endorsement in the Sligachan Climbers' Book: 'I gladly recommend Murdoch Mackenzie as a guide. He did excellently in the bad weather in which the above climbs were carried out and he is getting to value and use to good advantage, the rope.'[9] Murdo's preference, however, was to take clients fishing; he was also kept busy looking after the family croft where he bred West Highland terriers. Archie made his debut in 1901 when he assisted William and Jane Inglis Clark on Sgurr na h-Uamha: 'A porter, a young lad Archie Mackenzie, nephew of John, proved very satisfactory and evidenced a desire for serious rock climbing with a view to becoming a guide.' Rory was to the fore for a few years from 1908 onwards.

The Cuillin had Collie's undivided attention from 1886 until 1891, a formative period that shaped the rest of his life. He had stumbled onto a wild paradise, discovered his forte as a mountaineer and in John Mackenzie found the perfect partner. By the end of 1887 Mackenzie was Scotland's most experienced rock climber with at least three ascents of the country's hardest technical rock climb, the West Ridge of the Inaccessible Pinnacle. (This route is now graded Severe and described in the 2011 SMC guide as, 'Quite a hard classic climb lacking in protection and positive holds.') In these early days Collie was in a curiously isolated position: part of the London establishment, yet learning to climb in a remote and relatively unexplored range outside the normal sphere of influence of the Alpine Club. With few mountaineering role models he was initially attracted by the more familiar scientific challenge of surveying and establishing the heights of the Cuillin:

> Although there are no new peaks to conquer the Ordnance maps still remain; and should any one seek for information whilst actually on the hills from, let us say, the one-inch map, problems more difficult to solve than the ascents of many of the dark weather-worn pinnacles of rock are often found, and one must certainly possess that faith which is said to be able to move mountains, before a proper understanding of this map can be obtained which harmonises with the environment.[10]

Discovering that only seven of the peaks and none of the passes had been measured by the Ordnance Survey, he began his own systematic examination to check existing heights and establish new ones. Assuming that all Ordnance Survey heights were accurate, he then moved rapidly to an unsurveyed point where he measured the height by aneroid, a barometer operated by a spring rather than using mercury, that functioned as a crude altimeter. Collie constructed a portable version with flexible stem that fitted inside a tobacco tin. Over several observations, which he finally checked using a clinometer, his system appeared to give reasonable results. His completed list included the heights of all the prominent peaks and passes in the Cuillin including Caisteal a' Garbh-choire, the first record of an ascent of this distinctive rock tower.

Collie's list was used by Hugh Munro for the Skye section of his Tables published in 1891. It also confirmed Sgurr Alasdair as the highest of the Cuillin, much to the delight of Sheriff Nicolson: 'I am sorry that since this was written Sgurr nan Gillean has been discrowned. I was still more sorry that the highest place was assigned by the Ordnance Survey to Sgurr Dearg which I never loved. But since then I have been pleased to know that so good an authority as Dr Collie has assigned the highest place to Sgurr Alasdair, confirming the aneroid calculation I made in 1874.'[11]

Nicolson also went on to assert that the correct spelling was 'The Coolin', or in Gaelic 'A' Chuilionn', and mentioned that the currently popular spelling 'Cuchullin' was 'a name due, so far as I know, only to the makers of guidebooks, who thought it grander than the other, and all the better for being more difficult to pronounce'. It should be noted though that back in 1877 the Ordnance Survey used 'Cuillin Hills' after being assured by Nicolson that this was the correct spelling. For many years there was, not surprisingly, a lot of confusion as to how to correctly spell the mountains. The SMC and other mountaineers initially chose to adopt the anglicised 'Coolin' which remained in popular use until the First World War.

When it came to documenting his explorations in the Cuillin, Collie developed a reputation for being parsimonious with detail in both his writing and conversation. This was neither due to selfishness nor his well-documented eccentricity, but a sincere and far-sighted attempt to protect his favourite range from the commercial developments he had seen in the Alps. Nor is John Mackenzie a reliable help in unravelling the confusion over some of their explorations. Mackenzie had sound reasons for occasionally wearing a blank expression and keeping details in-house. Loyalty to Collie, his close friend and main client, meant discretion had to be used if discussing routes or areas Collie had an interest in developing.

Consequently, there is only a superficial record of Collie and Mackenzie's explorations. Their climbing partnership spanned at least thirty years during which Mackenzie was also privy to the plans and schemes of many other leading mountaineers. Geoffrey Winthrop Young, who described Collie's climbing style as 'a tense supple uprightness', also wrote this about him: 'Much of his early wandering went unrecorded; and in later life he might now and again chuckle grimly over accounts of new climbs on Scottish cliffs, and remark with the familiar saturnine sidelift of his lips, 'They'll find a little cairn there, when they get up!'[12]

Collie's reticence to record information mellowed in later years with an article in the *Alpine Journal* of 1918 entitled 'The Island of Skye'. It is, however, tantalisingly vague at times, referring as it sometimes does to events thirty years before. From his first visit to Sligachan in 1886, until his first Alpine season in 1892, Collie regularly had a two-week break at the inn, usually in late August/ early September. In the article he compresses the exploration of these energetic summers into a few succinct lines: 'It was in 1888 that I first made my way along the whole ridge and climbed all the peaks of the Coolin. The first ascent of the Bhasteir Tooth was made, and in 1889, with W W (William Wickham) King, the first traverse of the Alasdair Dubh Gap from the south was accomplished.'[13]

To see through the mist surrounding Collie's early climbs on Skye it is necessary to seek assistance from his climbing partners. W W King has left accounts of his climbs with Collie, but these are unsurprisingly inaccurate as he was about 90 years old when he wrote them; he refers to Collie's brother as 'John'.

For Norman Collie one day always stood out, 23rd August 1887. He and Mackenzie spent eighteen hours traversing the Main Ridge from Sgurr a' Mhadaidh to the Thearlaich-Dubh Gap, 'one of the hardest days I ever had in the mountains'. After an alpine start from Sligachan they joined the ridge at Bealach

THE BLACK CUILLIN

na Glaic Moire before following the crest over the four tops of Mhadaidh. From here on Collie was on new ground: over the sharp ridges of Ghreadaidh and Banachdich to the foot of the Inaccessible's West Ridge. At this time Collie was still a relatively inexperienced rock climber and, by his own admission, had to be pulled up the crux moves by Mackenzie, the fourth ascent of the route.

After continuing over Sgurr Mhic Chionnich and Sgurr Alasdair the pair dropped into Coir' a' Ghrunnda before tackling the awkward descent of Coir' an Lochain to the Coruisk River. A final steep pull over Druim nan Ramh led to Harta Corrie and the path for Sligachan: 'Everything was wrapt in gloom, and only the sound of the streams could be heard faintly up at the head of the corrie. One seemed cut off entirely from the outside world, and the lonely grandeur of the place; the stillness of the night was a thing I have never forgotten.'[14]

On this 1887 trip to Skye, Collie was again accompanied by his brothers Arthur and Alexander but they are not mentioned in Collie's accounts; to the Victorians personalities were a poor second to topographical detail. There was also a protocol that personal details were either not mentioned or censored.

The next year (1888) Collie chose September for his third visit to Sligachan, this time with only one brother, Arthur. It was on this trip Collie first met W W King, a solicitor from the West Midlands. Both of them agree that the Bhasteir Tooth was first climbed that summer. A E (Ernest) Maylard confirmed that this was accomplished by way of the Lota Corrie Route: 'Collie, with the guide, John Mackenzie, had spent about five hours one afternoon seeking some accessible route to this hitherto unconquered pinnacle. He at last accomplished it by making a considerable descent into Lota Corrie, and then ascending a steep gully on the south-east side.'[15] In July 1887 H C Hart mentions going 'over the spike of Bhasteir' with John Mackenzie, and may well have beaten Collie to it. However, in October 1889 when Richard Ball and Mackenzie traversed from Sgurr nan Gillean to the Bhasteir Tooth, and then descended Lota Corrie Route, Mackenzie claimed that this was the second ascent of the Bhasteir Tooth.

That summer of 1889 Collie was again joined on Skye by W W King who brought along a friend from his hometown of Stourbridge outside Birmingham, F P Evers, a coroner who lived to be 110. Evers was the nephew of Colonel T Pilkington White, one of the Royal Engineers who had taken part in the Ordnance Survey mapping of the Cuillin. Collie led them up Pinnacle Ridge and then down the West Ridge to the Gendarme or Tooth, a small but exposed pinnacle described in the 1923 SMC guidebook: 'This is a fearsome-looking place, narrow and shattered, with a great boulder planted on the ridge and blocking the way.'

To pass the pinnacle you had to embrace it boldly with both arms, swing a leg across an exposed drop and try to locate a hidden foothold on the far side. The Gendarme created a two-pipe teething problem until it lost its balance in the icy winter of 1987. Or was it pushed? David Shotton of the University of Nottingham Explorers Club related in the *Angry Corrie* (No. 71) how his party came across a severely decayed tooth at Easter 1987. Frost-shattered to half its original size the unstable remnants of the Gendarme needed little encouragement to join the screes of Lota Corrie.

Collie and King also climbed the Inaccessible Pinnacle's North-West Corner (Difficult) the 'pretty little chimney' first noticed by A H Stocker in 1886. This was sometimes referred to as Collie's Variation though Collie himself characteristically denied his was the first ascent. (The climb was affected by rock-fall during the 2006-7 winter.) Collie and King also traversed Clach Glas and Bla Bheinn along with Mackenzie. The Skyeman was still using ordinary shepherds' boots which lacked the specialised edge nails of the mountaineering variety. On the final slabs of Clach Glas disaster was not far away when Mackenzie had a rare slip. It was a close shave but the bottle of Talisker remained intact. Collie was taking no second chances and at the first opportunity obtained proper climbing boots for his friend.

When they returned to the Sligachan Inn they bumped into Ernest Maylard, secretary of the newly formed Scottish Mountaineering Club. The tall, bearded Maylard was pictured by A E Robertson as 'quiet and somewhat reserved in manner, not particularly genial to those he did not know well'.[16] For over thirty years he was a consultant surgeon at Glasgow's Victoria Infirmary where he developed a new technique, the Maylard Incision. It is him we have to thank for the idea of the CIC Hut on Ben Nevis. Regarding Skye, Maylard related how Collie guided himself and King over the length of the ridge from Sgurr a' Mhadaidh to Sgurr nan Gillean in a time of 10 hours 45 minutes, inn to inn, when they only required the use of the rope on one occasion: 'I regret to say that not one of us left the Cuchullins without irreparable damage to our knickerbockers.' On the journey home Maylard invited Collie and King to stay at his home in Blythswood Square in Glasgow which he shared with wife Jane and four servants. He also introduced them to other SMC members and arranged their successful applications for SMC membership in 1891.

For many years there was a great deal of confusion surrounding the Thearlaich-Dubh Gap, the dramatic gash that cuts off the Alasdair group from the peaks to the south. The gap was for a time regarded as inescapable. Even in the 1920s the SMC guidebook was giving ominous advice: 'It is recommended that a party of tourists should not all descend into the gap at one time, in case they might have to remain there permanently.' It developed something of a reputation after thwarting Collie and Mackenzie in 1887, and even more so when it defeated Clinton Dent's highly experienced Alpine Club party three years later when they concluded that the obstacle was 'impracticable'.

As mentioned above, Collie claimed that in 1889, with W W King, 'the first traverse of the Alasdair-Dubh Gap from the south was accomplished'. (But what exactly is Collie saying here? Does he mean they were the first to cross the gap, or just the first to traverse it south to north?) W W King gives 1891 for the 'ascent of both sides of the Thearlaich-Dubh Gap with Collie and Mackenzie', but this time the gap was not traversed in the conventional sense. After ascending the Thearlaich-Dubh Gap Gully from Coir a' Ghrunnda, Collie led the first recorded ascent of the short side (Very Difficult), then, after descending back into the cleft, King led the opposite wall (Severe).

In his 1893 article in the *SMC Journal,* 'On the Height of Some of the Black Cuchullins in Skye,' Collie describes the crossing, this time from north to south: 'If the ridge from the east peak of Sgurr Alasdair be followed in a southern direction a difficult piece of climbing will be met with, where it is necessary to descend into a narrow cleft in the ridge: this is probably not possible without a rope. After descending into the cleft the opposite perpendicular side has to be climbed, and the hand and footholds will be found somewhat scanty.'

So out of the way and undocumented was this part of the southern Cuillin that when the Reverend E H Kempson and E Kempson crossed the gap in April 1895 they recorded it in the Sligachan Climbers' Book as a possible new route: 'The ascent of the North East Peak from the col on the Main Ridge between Sgurr Dubh and Sgurr Alasdair affords a very interesting climb which I have not seen mentioned before.' The Reverend Kempson, currently a master at Harrow and later Bishop of Warrington, was father of Edwin, the 1930s Everest climber.

The next year (June 1896) John Mackenzie and Sydney Williams repeated the crossing from the south. Williams helped dispel some of the mystery surrounding the *mauvais pas* by publishing a detailed description with annotated diagram in the *SMC Journal*. He explained that there were few holds at the start of the long, north side and that he and Mackenzie only succeeded by throwing the rope into a crack about 20ft above the start.

Six weeks after this, the SMC team of John Bell, William Brown and the Napier brothers negotiated the gap in the opposite direction (north to south) when they found the ascent of the short side particularly difficult. Bell had recently been in conversation with John Mackenzie when the TD Gap was one of the topics under discussion. Mackenzie enigmatically insisted that it had never been climbed. William Brown passed on this bombshell in a letter to William Douglas: 'Mackenzie has never done this. He told Bell so three days before we crossed it. Furthermore he says he was not aware that it had ever been done.' This, despite Mackenzie and William's crossing of the gap being witnessed by Lamont, Rennie and Douglas from the Dubh Ridge. Cross-examined about the contradiction Mackenzie continued to deny point blank that he had ever done the traverse of the Thearlaich-Dubh Gap.

Many other first ascent claims of Collie's are also shrouded in pipe smoke. In his 1893 article Collie claims that all the gullies on the Coire a' Bastier side of Pinnacle Ridge, with the exception of Third-Fourth, were climbed prior to 1890. The name Doctor's Gully hints at his involvement. He alludes to climbs on the faces of the five pinnacles, possibly doing a new route with King on the Second Pinnacle in 1889. In his book *Himalayan Wanderer,* Charles Bruce mentions his visit to Skye with Collie in 1899: 'We had had a very hard day at Glen Brittle in which we accomplished what Collie says was a new route up Sgurr Alasdair.' William Douglas, who was attempting to compile a guide to Cuillin climbs (first published in September 1907 *SMC Journal*), was understandably exasperated by all this vagueness, 'In the absence of more definite information, we must credit those who first record their ascent as being the first to make it'.[17]

By 1891 we hear that, 'the comfortable little Inn at Sligachan, with its genial and hospitable host, is rapidly becoming a favourite resort for all lovers of rock-climbing.'[18] Lota Corrie Route (Moderate) and the Thearlaich-Dubh Gap (Severe) opened the Cuillin to the growing fad for 'ridge-wandering'. Hill-goers were more confident about tackling longer segments of the Main Ridge as there was now more information available such as Charles Pilkington's article, 'The Black Coolins' in the *Alpine Journal* (1888), as well as the publication of Pilkington's map (1890).

The formation of the SMC in 1889 finally gave mountaineering in Scotland the fillip it required. Norman Collie was one of those who played a pivotal role in transforming the SMC from a hillwalking club to a mountaineering club. When Collie joined the SMC in 1891 there were no Scottish rock climbs of any consequence outside of Skye. One SMC member, Thomas Fraser Campbell, went on to say: 'The alleged necessity of ropes and axes to make the ascents of Scottish mountains was looked upon as rather childish, while those who made winter ascents were apt to be classed as mere freaks.'[19]

Collie started to visit Wasdale Head, the main centre for rock climbing in the Lake District, where he made first ascents of classics like Moss Ghyll (Severe) on Scafell as well as, on the same mountain, the first winter ascent of Steep Ghyll (V), quite possibly the hardest climb in the world at the time. These visits brought him into contact with Alpine Club members like Geoffrey Hastings and Joe Collier. These connections led to his Alpine Club membership in 1893. In turn he encouraged English-based Alpine Club members like Collier and G. A. (Godfrey) Solly to attend SMC meets, telling them they would meet 'a number of fellows who were going to the hills but not doing much climbing'. They would introduce up-to-date climbing techniques to the Scots. The *SMC Journal* reflected this transition with a move away from topographical articles towards the more technical aspects of the sport.

The new editor of the *SMC Journal*, William Douglas, was forever badgering members for contributions, and was particularly keen to tap Collie's knowledge of Skye. He initially got little co-operation as Collie curtly responded that he did not see the point in route descriptions as they were like 'a railway timetable'. However, Collie would finally acquiesce to the persuasive Douglas. In 1893 the

SMC Journal published his article on surveying the Cuillin heights which, since their publication in *Munro's Tables* two years earlier, had been further revised and refined. The article was appended by a mini-guide to sections of the Main Ridge which gave advice on descents, ropes, water, etc. Although brief this was significant as the first attempt to formally record and bring together Cuillin route descriptions. It was another four years till Collie wrote a further article on Skye: 'A'Chuilionn' was a lyrical panegyric which, despite few specific climbing references, was incorporated into the first SMC guide, The Island of *Skye,* in 1907.

From 1892 until 1895 Collie was seduced by the Alps which included the first ascent of the Dent du Requin in 1893 and the first guideless ascent of the Old Brenva Route the following season. He was also part of an audaciously naive attempt on Nanga Parbat in the Himalaya on which Mummery tragically died. Collie was back in Skye for the bumper summer of 1896 which saw a move away from the familiar ridges to tackle the large but relatively untouched faces of the Cuillin peaks.

Collie arrived on the island that September with a friend, E B Howell, to join William Naismith, J A (James) Parker and William Garden. The name E B Howell is not found in any mountaineering records save Skye that summer. He may have been Evelyn Berkeley Howell, later a political agent with the Indian Civil Service. Good details survive of Collie's activities in 1896 due to notes kept by Naismith, 'the historian of the party'. In a letter to William Douglas he summed up that memorable season: 'Collie and I did practically everything we had in view. I never felt in better form. We skipped along the Pinnacles in the most callous way unroped. Collie says he never had so much rock climbing anywhere at the same time.'

The first day of the month saw Collie lead Howell up the South-East Ridge of Sgurr a' Ghreadaidh (Difficult) described in the *SMC Journal* as 'the finest climb on the mountain and the best bit of mountaineering in Skye'. On the final ridge Collie and Howell avoided any difficulties on the left. At a time when all distances were relative to Sligachan this climb, when approached through Harta Corrie and over the shoulder of Druim nan Ramh, was regarded as fairly accessible. This, Collie's enthusiastic description, plus its label of 'longest climb on Skye' at over 2,000ft (610m), ensured it became a popular classic. However it is really two distinct routes separated by a short walk. As the first section is open to much variation it was a tricky option in mist and was the scene of several benightments.

Two days later Collie and Howell were joined by Naismith for what became known as Collie's Climb (Difficult) on Sgurr Alasdair where a final shattered arete led to a sudden finish on the summit. Although now considered a rather loose classic (H M Kelly later used 'dangerous'), Collie summarised his route as a delightful climb, very steep but with excellent holds. The previous summer (July 1895) Norman Heathcote and his sister Evelyn climbed in the same area when they commented: 'The face of Alasdair is practicable in several ways but it is very steep and unless you choose a good route, you will meet with difficulties.' The Heathcote siblings also made the first recorded ascent of The Spur, in August 1895, a fine scramble to the left of Waterpipe Gully.

James Parker then joined Naismith for a route on the excellent rock of Sgurr na h-Uamha's south ridge which they described as 'probably new'. Their doubts stemmed from reading in the Sligachan Visitors' Book that William E Corlett had already climbed this mountain direct from Harta Corrie on two separate occasions, firstly on a very wet day in July 1890 and again the next year with regular partner E Kidson. Yet Parker and Naismith found no evidence of nail marks and reckoned that the other routes were further to the right. After traversing Sgurr na h-Uamha the SMC pair descended into Lota Corrie to create an undisputed new line (Route One, Difficult) on Sgurr a' Fionn Choire, a peaklet then known as Biod a' Fionn Choire.

The next day Naismith and Parker joined Collie for the North-West Buttress of Sgurr a' Mhadaidh (Very Difficult), another climb that gained initial popularity. It provided 1,200ft (370m) of rock climbing up four tiers of rock. The third tier had an overhanging section which was avoided by a detour to the right, then regaining the original line by a 'stomach traverse' above the overhangs: 'A traverse back to the middle line of the buttress was accomplished by Dr Collie, who wormed himself along a very narrow and sensational groove, sixty feet long, across the face of an AP cliff, and invited the rest to follow him.'[20] AP (Absolutely Perpendicular) was part of a rudimentary grading system that also included OH (Overhanging), DS (Difficult Slopes) and ES (Easy Slopes).

After a rest day on Sunday, Naismith led a new start to Sgurr nan Gillean's Pinnacle Ridge which featured a fine chimney on the First Pinnacle (Naismith's Route, Difficult). The second Naismith's Route in three days was then created on Clach Glas's west face where rough slabs led to the crux, a steep corner. Now graded Difficult, this climb became a popular start to the Clach Glas-Bla Bheinn traverse when the most frequented approach was down Glen Sligachan from the inn. The nimble-footed Naismith was a serial pinnacle-bagger and the same day provided him with six, including a repeat ascent of the Half-Crown Pinnacle to check if the coin he left on top in 1893 had been claimed (now twelve and a half pence, but well worth risking your neck for in the 1890s).

On 11th September Collie, Howell, Naismith and John Mackenzie made an early repeat of the Dubh Ridge on Sgurr Dubh Mor. They followed this with an overnight camp at Loch Coruisk to ensure an early start on the unclimbed Sgurr Coir' an Lochain. After two and a half hours of climbing over wet and slippery rocks on the north face, they eventually arrived at the compact, shapely summit: 'Though no part was especially difficult, nearly every step required care, and good anchorages were few and far between.' (Original Route, Difficult.) Finding no sign of previous visitors to the summit, Collie's party built a small cairn which remains intact today completing the lost world atmosphere of this magnificent viewpoint, William Naismith's all-time favourite. It was two days after Collie's thirty-seventh birthday, 12th September 1896, when this, the last virgin peak in the British Isles, was climbed. Original Route has had few repeats, with modern guidebooks adding little to the pioneers' brief description.

It should be borne in mind that, unless on the rare occasion lodgings could be arranged at Glen Brittle, forays into the southern Cuillin inevitably involved long energy-sapping tramps back to the inn. Sligachan was eventually reached either by descending to Coruisk and then continuing over Druim Hain into Glen Sligachan or, as the above party did, take the Main Ridge to Sgurr a' Mhadaidh and then descend the Thuilm Ridge to gain the Bealach a' Mhaim path.

In Collie's accounts of his trips abroad he waxes lyrical about the pleasure and contentment derived from nights spent out in the mountains. In the Cuillin camping was possible if the heavy equipment was transported by pony but the ascent of Sgurr Coir' an Lochain is the only record of Collie doing this. Throughout the early exploration of the Cuillin there are few references to bivouacking, even in fine settled weather, possibly because great store was placed on the etiquette of returning to the inn in time for dinner.

Although modestly graded, much of the 1896 exploration was on big faces with complex route-finding problems. The traditional progression from enclosed chimneys and gullies to ridges, and finally exposed faces, was less well defined in the Cuillin than elsewhere in Britain. In Skye the psychological barrier had already been challenged on routes like the Inaccessible Pinnacle and Sgurr nan Gillean's Pinnacle Ridge, and conversely many of the gullies did not succumb till much later. One such 'last great problem', Second-Third Gully on Sgurr nan Gillean, only fell with the arrival of extrovert Manchester surgeon Joe Collier, at the time one of Britain's top rock climbers.

Collier led Naismith, Parker and Walter Reid up the crux of Second-Third Gully (Difficult) just before the start of a dramatic thunderstorm that heralded an end to the long spell of fine weather which had made possible such an unprecedented frenzy of exploration. In a letter to Douglas, Naismith kept him up to date with events: 'This is the last gully to fall. The difficulty consisted of a huge cave with overhanging roof which had to be passed by liberal back and knee work up to jammed stones from which we climbed to a second set of jammed stones and then was easy.'

Back at Sligachan, as the rain pelted against the windows, everyone was glad of the opportunity to relax, lounge about and cool sunburnt faces; leisurely light pipes and embroider their recent exploits on Herculean walls, OH chockstones, and Sisyphean stone shoots. In his letter Naismith continued: 'This was without exception the most awful day of rain I ever saw… it came down in solid blocks and the river was tremendous in spate. Nobody ventured beyond the door but we passed a jolly day in the smoking room on all sorts of competitions between

England and Scotland who were nearly equally divided, and finally we all left next morning.'[21]

Professionally, 1896 was a busy year for Collie when he was elected a Fellow of the Royal Society and left University College to take up a new appointment as professor of chemistry at the Pharmaceutical College in Bloomsbury Square. He continued to take an interest in the inert gases, jointly publishing with Ramsay several papers on helium and argon. Professor Ramsay celebrated Collie's new appointment with the composition of a song which he sang at the Lab Dinner:

> When first I came to London town as Williamson's successor
> And donned his figurative gown as chemical Professor,
> With Plimpton who, with Rideal too, I felt uncommon Jolly,
> And in my mind I had in view our friend J. Norman Collie,
>
> In Cheltenham his mission lay to train the girls in science,
> And demonstrate to them each day some chemical appliance.
> But weariness on him depressed, and deepest melancholy,
> Right glad he was to come to us, our friend J Norman Collie.
>
> And now the Pharmaceutical has made him his professor,
> He's found a chair and settled there, its undisturbed possessor.
> And now he's only got to wed some Sally, Jane or Polly.
> Come fill a bumper, drink a health: our friend J Norman Collie.

Although Collie took his professional life very seriously he felt a great need to escape the rectitude and propriety of Victorian Britain. 'The lazy, delightful, disreputable' camp life in the mountains had always satisfied this but now the Alps seemed played out, the Himalayan experience soured by Mummery's death; the boorishness of the cities had even reached the Cuillin as he cynically pointed out: 'Now the climbers "run" over the Pinnacle Ridge and no doubt the next generation will take their maternal grandmothers up the inaccessible summit of Sgurr Dearg. One by one the recollections of all our most cherished climbs will be punctured flat and unprofitable as a collapsed bicycle tyre—the new nickel-plated, pneumatic-cushioned, electrically-driven modern mountaineer, on his fascinating career.'[22]

For seven of the eight summers from 1897 till 1904 Collie eschewed the established mountaineering venues to seek new experiences and stimulating company in remote, unexplored regions. He visited the Canadian Rockies six times, occasionally burying unopened bottles of whisky at the end of each trip, to be dug up on the next. His regular guide Fred Stephens became John Mackenzie's occidental alter ego, a life-long friendship with a regular exchange of letters over the next 25 years. Collie also made three visits to the 'Cuillin of the North', the Lofoten Islands in Norway, which he ranked second only to Skye in terms of climbing pleasure. His last trip to the Rockies was in 1911 with Arnold Mumm, a wealthy London publisher, when it took them seven days to travel 25 miles through burnt and fallen timber. Collie's article in the *Alpine Journal* expresses a palpable sense of bereavement in leaving for the last time this remote wilderness with its stirring adventures and boisterous characters:

> No longer would we sit over the campfires in our tent and listen to the stories of Fred Stephens about bear hunts, prospectors, hunters and the endless other subjects that are of interest to the dwellers of the wilds. No longer should we laugh over the small jokes and the happenings that go to make up life in camp. We were soon to be engulfed by the great whirlpool of everyday life where the dollar counts for more than the man, and where the chains of custom bind one to the conventional life of civilised society. Those who have never tasted the freedom of camp life amongst the great mountains can hardly understand the immense peacefulness that it all means.[23]

In 1899 Collie came to Skye as part of a large group that included legendary bon viveur Charlie Bruce who helped out on the Nanga Parbat expedition in 1895. Bruce is one of few people to have been awarded an Olympic medal for mountaineering. He had tremendous rapport with the Gurkhas he commanded, returning in his old age to visit them in the sergeants' mess, 'singing songs and telling dirty stories in the Nepali language'. It is hard to imagine a more contrasting character to Norman Collie than this raconteur of barrack-room humour, yet the two men got on exceptionally well. Bruce had brought with him one of his most tried and tested men, Harkabir Thapa from the village of Malbanse in eastern Nepal, south of Everest.

Harkabir was awarded the Indian Order of Merit, the nearest equivalent to the VC that soldiers of the British Indian Army could receive. In 1892 he was a member of Martin Conway's Karakorum survey when he reached the summit of Pioneer Peak. Conway regarded him as his right-hand man: 'He was remarkably intelligent; he taught himself by mere observation, how to set up, level and orient the table, and the tricks of the various cameras. He was an admirable companion, and we soon became the best and most inseparable friends. I can find no words too high to express my appreciation of him.'[24]

Although not a name readily associated with British mountaineering, Harkabir Thapa was present when the Cioch was first 'discovered' and was also responsible for inspiring one of Scotland's premier hill races. After some time in the Alps Bruce's party arrived on Skye in September 1899, much to his delight, 'Unbeatable wildness and savagery!' While ascending Sgurr Alasdair they were delayed by the rescue of a cragfast sheep but their late descent serendipitously brought to their attention the evening shadow of the Cioch cast on the neighbouring slab. Collie photographed it, but it would be another seven years before he was able to investigate the phenomenon more closely.

At the Sligachan Inn another guest in residence was medical student A F R 'Sandy' Wollaston who was selected for the first Everest expedition in 1921 where he became friendly with George Mallory. In Skye Wollaston delighted in the ridge traverses, bathing in the corrie lochans, and recording the wild-life. He did several climbs including the central chimney of Nead na h-Iolaire, then known then as 'Ladies' Chimney', while Norman Collie taught him the rudiments of mapping. Wollaston went on to recall how Harkabir carried a huge rucksack barefoot over the rough ground of the Cuillin, and after dinner entertained the guests by doing contortions and chopping pennies in half with his kukri.

The origins of the annual Glamaig Hill Race go back to this 1899 visit, commemorated with a large Nepali inscription in the Sligachan Visitors' Book. The Gurkha hill-running tradition started in 1890 when, in protest against the Indian Army's attitude that Gurkhas could not compete physically with Punjabis or Sikhs, Bruce inaugurated the annual Khud Race, 'unsurpassed as a spectacle among athletic contests'. At Sligachan, in bare feet and wearing only shorts, Harkabir ran the four-and-a-half miles and 2,400ft (730m) up Glamaig and back in one and a quarter hours. MacLeod of Dunvegan refused to believe the time and a rerun had to be organised to assuage clan scepticism and uphold Gurkha regimental pride. Harkabir was roused from a well-deserved nap, but Bruce found him 'perfectly game'. Watched by cheering crowds, many following his progress through telescopes, he arrived back in 55 minutes (37 up, 18 down). Percy Caldecott, who had timed the run, later recalled the feat in a letter:

> To this day I can see in my mind the spray thrown up by Herkia [sic] as he ran along, regardless of pools or any other obstruction. The speed with which he climbed Glamaig was incredible, more like a spider than anything else. On reaching the top he waved his arms to us, and then immediately started the descent, which he made at the run. He came down this in what one might call a series of jumps, and each time his foot landed, he slid for some distance as the scree moved with him. The most wonderful thing about it was that he arrived at the bridge barely out of breath.[25]

The story of Harkabir's run led to the inauguration in 1988 of the annual Glamaig Hill Race, held every July. It has one of the toughest descents of any Scottish hill race where the key is to stay on scree for as long as possible. In 1995 the race was won by a member of the Gurkha Regiment, Dilli Rai, while in the centennial event in 1999 a team of four Gurkhas took part. Both male and female records date from 2018 when Finlay Wild of Lochaber Athletic Club beat his own record by five seconds with a time of 44 minutes 22 seconds, and Jill Stephen beat Trish Calder's 28-year-old record by one second with a time of 56 minutes 09 seconds. Both wore footwear.

In 1902 Collie returned to his old haunts at University College as first professor of organic chemistry. Two years later Professor Ramsay was awarded the Nobel Prize for his work on the noble gases. History credits Ramsay and Morris Travers for the isolation of krypton, neon and xenon. Although there is little evidence to support it, Collie insisted on his place in these important achievements: 'If anyone ever happens to write an obituary of me, I want two things said: I first discovered neon and I took the first X-ray photograph [for medical purposes].'[26] At one point Collie was in possession of almost the world's entire supply of neon, which could easily have fitted inside a test tube.

However Collie *was* the first to construct a neon lamp, as E C C Baly confirms, 'There is no doubt that Collie was in fact responsible for the development of the illuminated neon signs which were a familiar sight before the outbreak of war.' Had Collie exploited his idea he would now be celebrated as the man who lit up Las Vegas. Sadly, the Cioch will never be illuminated in his honour as it was left to a Frenchman, Georges Claude, to construct the first commercial neon tube sign.

For Collie, 1906 saw the beginning of a renewed interest in the Cuillin. With his close friend, the artist Colin Phillip, he spent his summers at the remote Glen Brittle House, cocooned from the hurly-burly of the Skye tourist circuit. Although Phillip spent much of his life in London and Devon he returned regularly to the Highlands where he indulged his passion for collecting mountain place-names from local people. Gilbert Thomson of the SMC wrote: 'It is doubtful if any man ever possessed such an extensive knowledge of the Scottish mountains.'[27]

Collie was now 47 years old. Though climbing the Cuillin was still high on the agenda, other interests gradually took precedence. His first two summers at Glen Brittle House were particularly active in terms of climbing but there are few records after this time. The publication of the 1907 SMC guide *The Island of Skye* and Abraham's *Rock-Climbing in Skye,* in quick succession, resulted in an upsurge of interest in the range which undoubtedly jaundiced Collie to any further publicity. In 1906, however, there was unfinished business with the Cioch after their shadowy introduction seven years earlier. Collie's curiosity could contain itself no longer and he set out alone to investigate:

> I soon saw that the rock was a very real and interesting tower quite removed from the great rock face, standing out in a most imposing way over the corrie

below. From the top of the precipice to the bottom is at least 1000 feet, perpendicular in many places, and a narrow knife-edge of rock, about 100 feet long, runs out from it rather less than half-way down. At the end of this knife-edge is placed the tower that casts its shadow across the great slab. I do not know of any great mass of rock like it in Great Britain. It is not part of the rock face, but stands away from it, and its face has a sheer drop of about 500 feet into the corrie below.[28]

The next day he returned with John Mackenzie and a rope:

As it turned out, the climb was full of excitement, for one never knew what was round the next corner. We traversed slabs, we worked up cracks, and went right away from the Cioch into the gully on the east side of it, losing sight of it altogether. Then we fortunately found a queer traverse unlike any traverse I have ever seen, that led out of the gully across the perpendicular face of the cliff, and back in the direction of the Cioch. But the Cioch itself we could not see until having got round several corners suddenly it came into view and we found ourselves on the end of the knife-edge. We sat down on that knife-edge, and slowly made our way to the great rock tower at its end up which we climbed, and John and I were mightily pleased with our climb. After that everyone in Glen Brittle had to climb it and I believe that during that July and August John and I made the first ten ascents of the Cioch.[29]

The next June (1907) the Rucksack Club party of Steeple, Woodhead and Bowron repeated the Cioch climb armed with a rough route description they had gleaned from Charles Pilkington, Collie's close friend. He revealed that Collie had originally attempted to gain the neck by way of Cioch Gully, but beaten by the final steep flake had followed the terrace round under the nose to gain the cracks in the left side of the main slab. When Buckle and Barlow repeated the climb in August 1906, a month after the first ascent, they also started up Cioch Gully. The initial popularity of this approach may explain the three or four routes recorded on the west side of the Cioch itself. Abraham, in his influential book *Rock-Climbing in Skye,* described in detail the route now popularly used to the Cioch, which begins by traversing ledges from the Sgumain Stone Shoot, and this soon superseded the original approach.

Later on Collie worked out a more direct descent from the top of the Cioch, another example of his skill in route-finding. From the Cioch neck he roped down the top pitch of Cioch Gully, the one he failed to ascend on the Cioch's first ascent, and then traversed along the terrace to below the Cioch Nose where a slab gave access to a hidden chimney, down which it was possible to reach the easy lower section of Cioch Gully. This is now a scramble known as Cioch Gully and South-West Chimney (Grade 3).

Although John Mackenzie was the first to step on top of the Cioch, which he also named, the climb is known as Collie's Route. Contemporary etiquette required that guides were rarely credited, their reward being their fee. When, or if, their partnership ceased to be a financial arrangement is not documented but in the likes of the Sligachan Inn, despite being great friends, Mackenzie could not be accepted as a social equal; he was denied access to the smoking-room and had to dine in the ghillies' quarters. This may explain the location of Collie's chair in the hotel porch, neutral territory where he and Mackenzie could socialise, jaw about the day and plan for the morrow. In the fishing records Mackenzie was entered as Mr Morton to hide the fact he was local. 'Morton' was soon adopted as his nickname by locals and family alike, while younger brother Murdo became 'Myles'. In the Hebrides nicknames are semi-official and can last for generations. Even today John Mackenzie's family recall him as 'Morton'.

In these later years Collie hints at a wealth of exploration in the Cuillin, but after the discovery of the Cioch he only ever recorded five routes: 'During 1906 and the years that followed there were few parts of the Western Coolin that John and I did not wander over. On Sron na Ciche alone we found enough new climbing to last for a long time; also the faces of rock in all the other corries besides Coire Lagan had to be investigated.'[30] In 1906 Collie and Mackenzie recorded the classic Window Buttress (Very Difficult) on Sgurr Dearg. This has an initially steep section up to the eponymous Window which gives access to easier ground and eventually the final steep tower. Within two years the climb had spawned at least two variation starts.

The last climbs Collie and Mackenzie recorded were two 1907 routes, Zigzag Route (Moderate) and Amphitheatre Arete (Moderate). However it was by no means the end of their pioneering as Geoffrey Winthrop Young pointed out: 'It will never be known just how much Collie and Mackenzie did in the Coolin. They explored every corner, but left no records. I believe his reticence nearly broke the hearts of the compilers of the Skye Guide.'[31]

Collie and Colin Phillip leased Glen Brittle House between 1906 and 1909, and 1912 to 1915 when they virtually kept open house. By 1909 Phillip is giving this as his permanent address to the Fell and Rock Climbing Club who in turn nicknamed him 'Coolin Phillip'. Also often in residence were Phillip's wife and nieces, the Prothero sisters, who are commemorated in Ladies' Pinnacle in the Sgumain Stone Shoot, and can be seen in some of Collie's photographs, notably contemplating the crux on the Inaccessible Pinnacle's West Ridge in ankle length skirts.

Over the summer there was a constant stream of friends and acquaintances taking tea in the drawing-room or garden after a day on the hills. Some stayed for longer periods when they joined the obligatory tour of the newly discovered Cioch. Winthrop Young visited and was in a party that made a direct variation to Collie's Route that cut out the detour into Eastern Gully. In *Mountains with a Difference* Young provides a description of his host: 'Collie was lean, almost cadaverous, with deep-grooved ivory features, lank greying hair, and long amber eyes like a sheepdog's, with a sardonic sideways gleam through his gravity.'

E C C Baly, now assistant to Collie at University College, used his visit in 1909 to put up two new climbs: his eponymous route on Sgurr Dearg's South Buttress and the Upper Rake (Grade 1) on Sgurr a' Mhadaidh, an alternative to the adjacent Foxes' Rake. Another visitor to Glen Brittle House was Hugh Munro who, through the compilation of his Tables, entered the dictionary as the name for Scottish mountains over 3,000ft (915m). His obituary in the *SMC Journal* describes him as, 'a strange mixture of courtesy and pugnacity'. Surprisingly, the number of Munros and Tops is not constant but fluctuates over the years due to surveying inaccuracies, isostatic rebound, and the need to keep Munro-baggers on their toes. In Skye there are currently eleven Munros and, after Knight's Peak's demotion in 2013, eight Tops on the Main Ridge, plus Bla Bheinn (one Munro and one Top).

Although Munro, he was not Sir Hugh until 1913, was more a hillwalker than a rock climber, he was a gutsy individual whose adventurous life was punctuated by acts of real courage. Under constant threat from the twin scourges of socialism and rheumatism, he served as a cavalryman in the Basuto War, stood as a Conservative in proletarian Kirkcaldy, and pioneered extreme glissading – done wearing a kilt. Unable to obtain the services of John Mackenzie who was currently engaged by A E Robertson at Sligachan, Munro was chaperoned around the trickier sections of the ridge by Colin Phillip's nieces, the Prothero sisters. One day was so hot that Munro was forced to climb Sgurr nan Eag during the cool of the night when he was rewarded with a temperature inversion at dawn.

Hugh Munro and Colin Phillip were etymological sparring partners, liking nothing more at Glen Brittle House than argue the night away, over a Talisker or two, about the derivation of Cuillin place names. Was there a genuine connection between the Irish hero Cuchulain and the name Cuillin? Or were they named after the Gaelic *cailin* (maidens), *cuileanan* (pups) or *coal lainn* (slender spears). Did An Stac refer to the Inaccessible Pinnacle itself? Was the western branch of Coire na Creiche called Tairneilear or Mhadaidh?

In 1928 Collie retired as the head of the chemistry department at University College. He continued as Emeritus Professor doing some scientific work for another five years. His later life was one of seeming contentment characterised by professional recognition and an active mountaineering committee life. He held the prestigious presidency of the Alpine Club from 1920 until 1922 when Dorothy Pilley recalled him at Alpine Club tea parties: 'His appearance was very distinguished; spare, rugged and hawk-like, reminding one of the Sherlock Holmes drawings in the *Strand Magazine*.'[32] With Glen Brittle House no longer available after the war Collie and Mackenzie continued to have a regular two-week break in the glen, now basing themselves at Mrs Chisholm's cottage. During the rest of the season Mackenzie was still guiding on a regular basis when one regular client, possibly secret admirer, was the Yorkshire poet Dorothy Una Ratcliffe:

> To see Loch Coruisk properly you should choose a day of sun and cloud, and take John Mackenzie as your companion. He has spent a lifetime exploring the Coolins; he knows each peak better than many fathers know their children, he appreciates their beauty as a man appreciates the beauty of his sweetheart, and to one of them he has given his name, Sgurr Mhic Coinnich. He is an old man now, but you might sail the four seas for many a moon before finding as strong, as active or as handsome a man as John Mackenzie, with his distance-seeking eyes, his long, straight nose, his beard, white as the Coolins' snows.[33]

After retiring from University College in 1928, Collie's summer break on Skye became longer though it was increasingly devoted to fishing and painting. David Robertson, who married George Mallory's daughter Berry, met Collie in 1933: 'I remember him at his table in the inn at Sligachan, on the Isle of Skye: long face with strong features, and habitual aloofness relieved now and again by a quiet smile.'[34] That same year came the cruellest blow, John Mackenzie's death aged 77. Collie's eulogy for his friend is heart-felt:

> As a companion on a long summer day he was perfect. Always cheerful, keenly alive to everything: the wild birds, the fish in the rivers, the deer on the hillside, and all natural things. There is no one who can take his place. Those who knew him will remember him as a perfect gentleman, one who never offended either by word or deed. He has left a gap that cannot be filled. There was only one John, simple-minded, most lovable, and without guile.[35]

Mackenzie's death deeply effected Collie and he became increasingly reclusive and intolerant of strangers. His isolation was aggravated by increasing deafness. Hamish Corrie was another who recalled his presence at Sligachan: 'A most striking figure and a remarkable personality; sardonic and dry as dust in manner, he did not suffer fools gladly. The gaunt and ravaged face, austere and withdrawn, below the battered deerstalker which he always wore.'[36]

Collie renewed his contact with north-east Scotland through the Honorary Presidency of the Cairngorm Club in 1922, travelling north at the age of 78 to attend their Jubilee Dinner in November 1938. He became friendly with one of the younger members of the Cairngorm Club, Hugh Welsh, who went on to provide an intimate picture of Collie living out his last years at Sligachan:

> Shy and reserved with strangers and difficult of approach, Dr Collie on closer acquaintance became one of the most interesting and affable of men. There were few subjects on which he could not talk easily and with great knowledge

and authority, but perhaps climbing in his beloved hills was his favourite subject. He had a photographic memory and could describe in minute detail every hand and foothold of climbs done years before. He did not talk freely until he came to know and like you; then his conversation was intimate and full of delight. From the time of my first contact with him in 1934 at Sligachan, it was my good fortune to be regarded as one of his friends, and I shall always have exceedingly pleasant recollections of my association with him.

My first impression was that of a solitary, unfriendly man living in a world of memories. But by degrees he unbent and I was admitted to the small circle of close friends who came to Sligachan… His favourite chair in the outer vestibule was known as 'Collie's Corner' and woe betide anyone who presumed to occupy it! From there he could look out upon Glamaig and the Red Hills and down Loch Sligachan to Raasay and envelop himself in a cloud of tobacco smoke and memories.

I often wondered what he thought about as he gazed out with far-regarding listening eyes. Sometimes when spoken to he seemed to return from a great distance, as if he had been living over again some of his early exploits. He was intolerant of strangers, and as a result was thought rude and unfriendly… but he was at his best after dinner with his audience of a select few, for then his conversation was sparkling and memorable no matter what was the subject. But whenever strangers appeared he drew into himself and retired either to his own room or Mr Campbell's, where we later on joined him to continue our enjoyment.[37]

Collie was on Skye in 1939 when war was declared. He was considering moving permanently to the island as he was concerned about the bombing in London, but the decision was now made for him. At Sligachan he became increasingly isolated as Skye was now designated a restricted zone where travel was carefully vetted. On one of his regular fishing trips to the Storr Lochs Collie got wet through. The resultant chill developed into serious illness and severe pain. He died on 1st November 1942, aged 83, to be buried alongside John Mackenzie in the secluded churchyard at Struan, nestling into the moors they both loved so passionately.

An engraving of JMW Turner's *Loch Coriskin* (1831)

The Cuillin from near Elgol

The summit of Sgurr nan Gillean

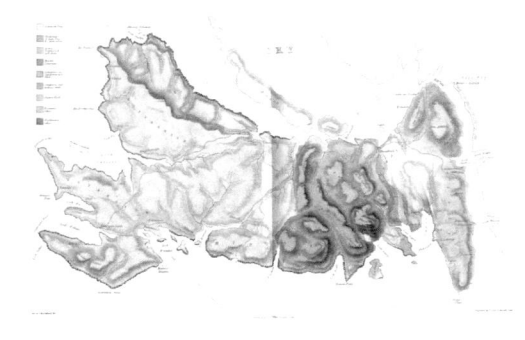

Left: John MacCulloch's 1816 geological map of Skye, the first of three versions he made

John MacCulloch  James David Forbes  Reverend William Knight

The stone shoot by which Alexander Nicolson made the first ascent of Sgurr Alasdair, the sharp peak on the right, in 1873

The Sligachan Inn in the 1850s

Alexander Nicolson

The Bad Step on Loch Scavaig

Collie's Ledge on Sgurr Mhic Choinnich

Right: Henry Chichester Hart who, with John Mackenzie, completed the first traverse of Sgurr Mhic Choinnich, in July 1887

Below: A diagram made by E W Steeple for the 1923 SMC guidebook

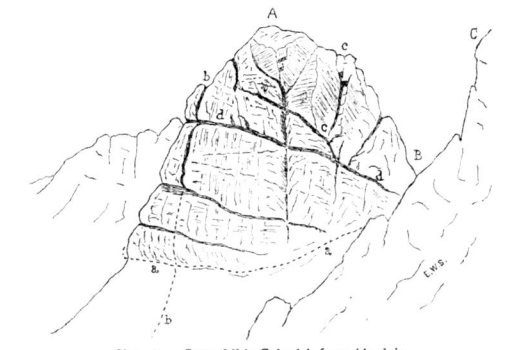

FIG. 12.—Sgurr Mhic Coinnich from Alasdair.

A. Sgurr Mhic Coinnich. B. Bealach Mhic Coinnich. C. Sgurr Thearlaich. *a*. Traverse from below col. *b*. West Buttress Route. *c*. King's Chimney. *d*. Collie's Ledge (for continuation of which see fig. 13).

The East Ridge of Inaccessible Pinnacle

L to R: Charles Pilkington, Eustace Hulton and Lawrence Pilkington

Abseiling the West Ridge of the Pinnacle

The shadow that brought the Cioch to Collie's attention. His original route followed the bottom left of the slab into the gully on the left, then returned right by a diagonal fault to the pinnacle neck

John Mackenzie with pony

Norman Collie in 1886, aged 27, the year he first visited Skye

John Mackenzie and client on the West Ridge of Sgurr nan Gillean near the summit. Taken in July1893 when Mackenzie was 36 years old (© SMC)

Advert for the Sligachan Hotel

John Mackenzie and Norman Collie in later life

Pinnacle Ridge on Sgurr nan Gillean

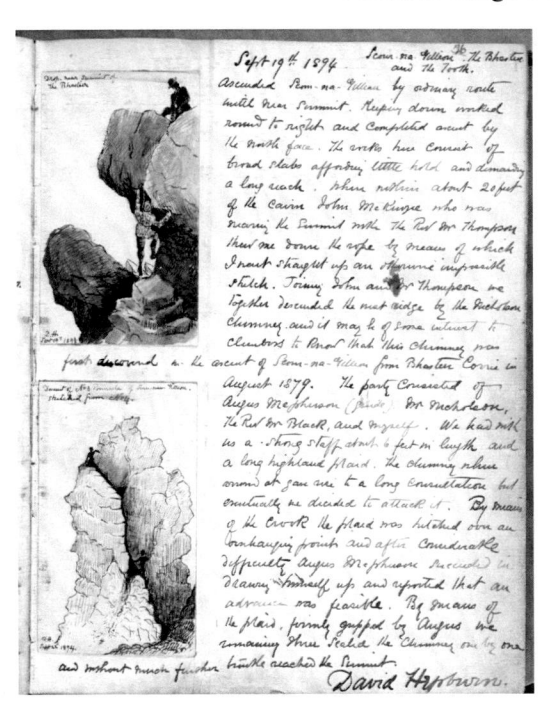

The Sligachan Inn during the 1890s when it was run by the Sharp family

A page from the Sligachan Climbers' Book, dated 11 September 1894, in which David Hepburn recalls the first ascent of Nicolson's Chimney. The drawings depict two routes in the Cuillin, now superceded by easier alternatives: the steep crack climbed to gain the summit of Am Basteir, and the original descent of the Third Pinnacle on Sgurr nan Gillean

Chapter Four

The Rocky Mountains of Skye

By the 1890s travelling to Skye was a more congenial experience than previously with a greater choice of increasingly comfortable options. The road over the Mam Ratagan to Glenelg was improved, and by 1897 the railway finally reached Kyle of Lochalsh. Portree harbour was now the hub of an extensive network of steamer services. Many of the vessels sported the distinctive MacBrayne livery of black hulls and scarlet funnels topped by a band of black, matching the puffy clouds of coal smoke. Many steamers were now passenger-only, and increasingly luxurious. Well-travelled tourists often found them superior to the famous Rhine riverboats. Hotels, however, were generally very expensive, prone to all manner of extra charges, giving the Scottish Highlands a reputation as one of Europe's more costly holiday destinations.

The Glasgow to Stornoway mail-steamer, crack vessels like the *Clansman* and *Claymore,* called at Armadale, Broadford, Loch Sligachan and Portree. There was also the *Gael* on her popular excursion trip from Oban to Gairloch. Every Tuesday from mid-June to mid-September, weather permitting, the *Gael* made a diversion to Loch Scavaig. The MacBrayne excursion guide, *Summer Tours in Scotland,* was not alone when it fell into lyrical rhapsody:

> As we approach Loch Scavaig, the Cuchullin hills attract our attention. To the left may be seen the little isle of Soay, the lonely home of a few fishermen. We steam in near the head of the loch and, after anchoring, are rowed ashore in large and comfortable boats. A few minutes' walk brings us with beating hearts in full view of Loch Coruisk – the solitude only intensified by the plaintive sough of the wind and the ceaseless gargle of the mountain torrent.

These trips were inaugurated by Messrs Hutcheson & Co. on 30th August 1855 when the very first paddler left Oban for Loch Scavaig, allowing tourists to view the Holy of Holies without the long trek from Sligachan or row from Torrin. The *Inverness Advertiser* (28th August 1855) announced: 'For one day, however, a visit to the savage Coolins is to be made a matter of ease and luxury.' It was not till the 1870s that the excursions became a regular part of the schedule with five trips per summer. The roll of honour for the Loch Scavaig outing includes a select list of Highland steamers: *Gael, Mountaineer, Fusilier, Glencoe,* and *Dunara Castle.*

Tourist services on the island were also improving with a fairly sophisticated network of integrated public transport (coach, boat and pony) to help visitors see 'the most fantastic skyline in the country'. The route of routes remained Broadford to Sligachan by way of Loch Scavaig, Coruisk and Glen Sligachan. There was now also the option of a day trip from Portree: steamer to Broadford then carriage to Torrin where a new steam-launch departed at noon for the head of Loch Scavaig, returning at 4pm. During the summer season the Coruisk area was thronged with those intrigued by the guidebook hyperbole: 'An awful silence reigns in this Avernus of the North, where all is hard, dark, and motionless.'

There was an alternative route to Coruisk for those who preferred more exercise. A ferry from Torrin across Loch Slapin could be used to avoid the three mile detour around the head of the loch. The next section was on foot to Camasunary where guides often carried clients across the river to keep their feet dry, a simple courtesy rarely extended by today's professionals. Mention of the nearby Bad Step still spread dread through the minds of nervous pedestrians, though occasionally a boat could be hired at Camasunary to avoid the obstacle. The Sligachan Inn produced a booklet which warned that the Bad Step 'will be found somewhat trying and sensational to those not accustomed to climbing'.

There seemed to be little consensus over what the Bad Step actually involved, and the more dramatic the description the more it deterred people from attempting it. Many tourists consequently decided to take the easier option and view the Cuillin from the more accessible Sligachan side. They often made Portree their base, using carriages to get a closer view of the mountains. From the Royal Hotel there was a public coach service every morning for Sligachan where ponies could be hired to join the daily equestrian procession, many wearing the latest hats and tartan fashions, to see the 'black tarn of Coruisk'. Near the top of Glen Sligachan the path divides, the right fork heading uphill towards the cairn on the skyline and its much-anticipated view of the loch. However some tourists without a guide missed the junction and kept straight on. They then mistook Loch an Athain for Coruisk, and arrived back at the inn wondering what all the fuss was about.

Ponies were also used for the approaches to Bla Bheinn and Bruach na Frithe; they helped to keep the feet dry though in heavy rain it was sometimes preferable to walk. The demand for ponies reached its peak in the 1890s when the stables at Sligachan had to be considerably enlarged to cater for the increased number of animals. This peaked at fifteen though the number dwindled to just a couple by the 1920s. The writer Malcolm Ferguson described the ride up the Glen Sligachan 'path':

> By far and the roughest and wildest bridle path I have ever seen. I was quite amazed to see our sure-footed pony scrambling his way along, in some places over bare rock, but with a peculiar rough surface, resembling a steel rasp or

as if studded with small tacks, and not at all slippery, otherwise neither man nor horse could ascend by the regular path. Indeed, one could hardly slide on it. In other places the little pony was wading to its belly in bogs and stagnant dibs of water, from end to end the pathway is thickly covered with rough stones of all sorts and sizes.[1]

By the foot of Druim Hain the ponies were in need of rest and there was a halt for grazing: pasture for ponies, picnic hamper for tourists. Although the ponies were capable of taking you up Druim Hain many elected to do this last steep section on foot. After sweating their way to the top some complained the view was a swiz as you could only see a small corner of the fabled loch. Most concurred that the serrated skyline of the Cuillin was very fine indeed, but this was not what they had come to see. The keenest and fittest traversed towards Sgurr na Stri for a more expansive view but most resolved that next time they would approach by sea to have a better look at what guidebooks referred to as the 'hidden pearl of the Cuillin'. Baddeley's tourist guide (1892) agreed. It recommended a circular excursion as an altogether finer experience: continue down Glen Sligachan to Camasunary, hire a boat for Coruisk to avoid the Bad Step, and return to Sligachan over Druim Hain:

Portree to Sligachan (coach), 10 miles.
Camasunary (pony), 18 miles.
Loch Scavaig (boat), 21 miles.
Loch Coruisk (foot), 22 miles.
Foot of Druim Hain (Glen Sligachan), 25 miles.
Sligachan (pony), 30 miles.
Portree, 40 miles.

Baddeley also warned readers that the Sligachan Inn could appear deceptively near from the top of Druim Hain, and not to be tempted to linger longer than advisable to watch the sunset. The Glen Sligachan footpath was in reality a series of quagmires tenuously linked by sections of solid path, but in mist or fading daylight walkers were often led into a bog with little chance of finding the connecting track on the other side. After hours of stumbling through the darkened mire many arrived at the inn resembling creatures from the primordial swamp, traumatising any young children not yet in bed.

Another, more ambitious, circular route was talked of highly as it took you into the heart of the Cuillin: down Glen Sligachan to Camasunary, across the Bad Step to Loch Coruisk and then return to the inn by way of the Bealach Glac Mhor, a pass on the Main Ridge between Bidein and Mhadaidh. A guide was recommended and the route should certainly not be tackled alone or in misty or doubtful weather.

One visitor who ignored this advice was W W (Walter) Greg, a leading Shakespearean scholar of the twentieth century. In *Who's Who* his recreations are listed as 'minding his own business'. In September 1893 there proved little chance of this, as Greg dominated the national newspaper headlines after being missing from Sligachan for three days. When he had not returned by 8pm on the initial day two experienced guides set out with lanterns and spent the night looking for him but found no trace. The next day a large party composed of guides, ghillies and visitors, searched the hills, again with no success.

There was concern Greg may have had an accident on the Bad Step. The height of the ledge above the sea was often given as too high, leading some unwary walkers into difficulties. A contemporary account in *The Telegraph* about the missing Greg made great play of the perils of the place: 'At the Bad Step the rocks fall so abruptly into the sea that you can only pass along a sharp ridge, where you must go sideways with the feet against the edge and the back leaning against the cliffs. The sea foams and thunders upon a bed of black crags sixty or seventy feet beneath, and one slip of the foot means that you will plunge from this world into the next.'

Greg had, however, taken the circular route but fallen while descending Coire na Creiche, sustaining some nasty cuts and injuring his thigh. With heavy rain setting in, Greg was obliged to spend the night where he fell. The next day he continued slowly down and was eventually found, exhausted, in Glen Brittle on his third day out, 'to the immense relief of his widowed mother, who was accompanying her son on his Highland trip'.

At Sligachan, during spells of fine weather, favoured visitors were taken aside and the pinnacles of Sgurr nan Gillean pointed out: 'These, it is authoritatively reckoned, contain more real rock climbing than the ascent of the Matterhorn.' Ropes and nailed boots began to clog the hotel's hallway; alpenstocks and knapsacks competed with fishing baskets and rods for space in the porch, while the smell of wet tweed and dubbin permeated past the trophies of stuffed and mounted salmon through to the ladies' room and the coffee house. Chambermaids were up till all hours darning socks and patching gabbro-worn knees and trouser seats. Anxious owners often inserted notes inside their climbing boots: 'Please do not dry near a fire or attempt to clean with black boot polish.' One visitor described the bustling atmosphere of the inn at the height of the season:

> There were about thirty persons dining as we passed their room window towards the porch. Stepping as we did from the midst of the storm and half-darkness, we must have moved their pity. The hotel was full. We spent the night in the smoke-rooms, on camp beds hard enough to have satisfied a Spartan general. Our atmosphere was a foul compound of stale tobacco, peat reek and half-dried coats, waistcoats and trousers, several suits of which hung about the fireplace. Outside, the night was wild. The wind bellowed without

pause, and the rain volleyed against the panes as if it would surely smash them…The alpine ropes in the vestibule tell the same tale. So do the cut and scarred hands and attenuated breeches of the men who, over Talisker, in the smoke-room, narrate their exploits among the pinnacles and edges.[2]

In May 1890 many of those recounting adventures in the smoking-room were members of the Alpine Club, one of the last formal club visits to Skye. Charles Pilkington brought together some of the mountaineering elite of the day, though it could be argued many were past their prime. Lawrence Pilkington was still convalescing from his injuries but was well enough to conduct the colliery choir, compose poetry (some in praise of the Cuillin) and write novels of northern mining towns. Characteristically the Skye weather would be excellent. Charles Pilkington stimulated interest in the mountains with an 1888 article 'The Black Coolins' in the *Alpine Journal* where he set out what you needed to know:

Go early in the year, at the end of May or beginning of June when the days are long. Take a rope and one of Silver's gourds, for water is hard to get on the rocks and you are often rock-climbing for hours at a stretch. Sligachan Hotel is most comfortable and only twenty-four hours from London via Euston or King's Cross, Inverness, Strome Ferry and Portree. Mr Sharp, the landlord, is very obliging and knows how to carry out any arrangements you may wish to make. Mackenzie is a pleasant, willing companion and a good rock-climber. He quickly learnt the use of a rope amongst loose rocks and recognised its value. He likes climbing for its own sake and enters thoroughly into it.[3]

Charles Pilkington used the Ordnance Survey six-inch map (1882) and the one-inch map (1885) to produce his own version *The Cuchullin Hills*, 'The upper ridges are corrected, and the positions of peaks defined.' Using a scale of two inches to the mile he helped those navigating the peaks by emphasising the orientation of the Main Ridge and giving more definition to the location of the main summits. Sgurr a' Mhadaidh was clarified as having four tops, Bidein Druim nan Ramh as having three; the Alasdair group was sub-divided into Sgurr Alasdair, Sgurr Sgumain and North-East Peak (Sgurr Thearlaich). Only two paths were marked: from the Sligachan Inn over Bealach a' Mhaim to Glen Brittle and from Sligachan to Loch Coruisk.

Pilkington's map first went on sale in 1890 and despite mixed reviews proved popular: 'It gives a good idea of the ground and has been pronounced by competent authorities to be more correct than the Survey sheets.' But Ernest Maylard disagreed: 'To look at Charles Pilkington's admirable map, one might just conclude that such a walk was of easy accomplishment, for there is little upon it to indicate the real roughness of the road. The six-inch Ordnance Survey, however, gives a much more vivid picture of the difficulties to be met with, and shows at a glance that this ridge is beset with innumerable obstacles in the shape of broken pinnacles and deep clefts.'[4]

Pilkington's 1890 Skye party included the current, Clinton Dent, and three future presidents of the Alpine Club: Pilkington himself, Horace Walker and Hermann Woolley. They were joined by Eustace Hulton, W C (Cecil) Slingsby, Geoffrey Hastings and Edward Hopkinson. Cecil Slingsby was a Yorkshire Dalesman from Carleton-in-Craven near Skipton, often remembered as the 'Father of Norwegian Mountaineering'. Slingsby was a well-liked and gregarious individual, one of Norman Collie's closest friends. Collie's only recorded fall was on a Christmas visit to Slingsby's when, returning to the dining room from the hall, he opened the wrong door and tumbled into the cellar.

As an enthusiastic member of practically every climbing club in Britain, Slingsby provided an important focus for many of these disparate groupings: the Alpine Club (formed 1857), Scottish Mountaineering Club (1889), Climbers' Club (1898), Yorkshire Ramblers (1899), Wayfarers' Club (1906), Fell and Rock (1907) and the Rucksack Club (1902). Some of these networks were more than mountaineering friendships. Slingsby had close ties with the Snowdonia climbing community through his daughter Eleanor's marriage to Geoffrey Winthrop Young and he was also a cousin of the five mountaineering Hopkinson brothers and developed close ties with the Pilkingtons after they assisted with Lawrence's rescue in Wasdale. Edward Hopkinson and Lawrence Pilkington became near neighbours at Alderley Edge outside Manchester, while Charles Pilkington and Horace Walker also lived close to each other.

One of Slingsby's early partners in the Lake District was fellow mill-owner Geoffrey Hastings. He was a member of the ill-fated expedition to Nanga Parbat in 1895 where he mysteriously failed to adhere to Indian Government regulations and ultimately had to resign from the Alpine Club. Hermann Woolley, a pharmacist, did not seriously take up mountaineering until he was over forty years of age and is most associated with the Caucasus where he made several first ascents during the 1880s and 1890s including Pik Woolley. Also in the Skye party was Clinton Dent, 'a noted conversationalist and connoisseur of old plate, furniture etc'. He was the first person in print to seriously propose a full-scale attempt on Everest, in 1892. Collie named Mount Dent in the Rockies in his honour.

Skye was an attractive destination for the 1890 Alpine Club 'expedition' as it was an almost unexplored range with a few unclimbed summits. The locals spoke English (or so they thought!) and were willing to act as porters or guides. Waiting to welcome them to Skye, at the foot of the steamer's gangplank, was John Mackenzie sporting the new climbing boots he had recently received from Collie. They were soon ensconced at the Sligachan Inn where the bustling atmosphere of the time was evoked by author and traveller C F Gordon Cumming: 'The Inn, though small, is comfortable enough and affords shelter to a wondrously varied multitude of tourists and travellers, members of the Alpine Club, distinguished artists, statesmen, ecclesiastics, botanists, geologists, yachting parties, pleasure-seekers of all sorts, drovers, excisemen, down to that class of tourist who "does" Skye as a sort of unpleasant duty.'[5]

From the Sligachan Inn, Pilkington introduced his friends to Pinnacle Ridge (Difficult), or Pinnacle Route as it was then called, helping establish the time-honoured tradition as route of choice for the preliminary day. Some confusion surrounds the first ascent details for this climb, one of the most popular in the range. In *Rock-Climbing in Skye,* Ashley Abraham writes that the Pilkington brothers climbed this classic ridge, finding no traces of a previous ascent until Professor Knight and Angus MacPherson's cairn on the Fourth Pinnacle. When researching his book on Skye, Abraham was in contact with Charles Pilkington, yet for the ascent of Pinnacle Ridge gives 1880, a year in which Lawrence Pilkington stated that their only Cuillin expedition was the Inaccessible Pinnacle. However, Lawrence's accounts can appear slightly inaccurate as he wrote them over fifty years after the event. In his 1888 article in the *Alpine Journal,* 'The Black Coolins', Charles Pilkington alludes to an ascent of Pinnacle Ridge at Whitsun 1887 but gives few details; they 'spent the rest of the day amongst the pinnacles', but he does not state specifically whether they completed the whole climb. During the 1890 ascent he makes it clear that he *has* done the route before, leaving 1887 as firm favourite for the year of first ascent.

From the Sligachan area Pinnacle Ridge appears as four distinct peaks but when actually climbing the route the first two are not apparent as separate peaks, a long-running source of confusion. The third peak contains the crux descent, now usually abseiled. It should be remembered that this now common technique was unknown in Britain until after the First World War. Until then every effort was made to down-climb, before the rope was draped over a hitch and descended by hand. Leaving the summit of the Third Pinnacle the original route went down on the right, overlooking Coire a' Bhasteir, where an awkward and exposed move tended to throw the climber off balance. At Whitsun 1890 the Alpine Club party discovered an easier variation on the left which soon became the preferred route. William Naismith described these two options in the 1892 *SMC Journal*:

> The descent of this Pinnacle is by way of a shallow gully on the Bhasteir side of the ridge, and the drop into the gully is a little trying. The usual way follows the crest of the ridge for forty feet beyond the cairn, and then, turning to the right, goes down ten feet of perpendicular rock. The holds though good are far apart, and if the last man has not a long reach, he had better pass the middle of a sixty-foot rope round a convenient block above, and hold both ends as he descends. It is not a place to go down with a run, because the rocks below slope steeply and end in a precipice. Mr Charles Pilkington discovered an alternative method of reaching the gully in question without a

rope, namely by its left side, at a point some thirty feet nearer the top. Once you get into it, the gully is simple enough.[6]

Back at the Inn, Pilkington directed four of his friends down Glen Sligachan to the north face of Bla Bheinn where he had spotted potential for pioneering three years earlier. About halfway up the climb the party divided into two: Slingsby and Hastings, Woolley with Dent, to create two parallel routes near the other, less well-known, Pinnacle Ridge (Moderate). The next day all of the Alpine Club party initiated what became a favourite excursion linking Sligachan with Glen Brittle. They crossed Bealach a' Mhaim into Coire na Creiche and then climbed Sgurr a' Mhadaidh's Thuilm Ridge to the summit. From here they negotiated the ups and downs of the Main Ridge to the Inaccessible Pinnacle which Dent likened to 'a tooth-comb stuck in the middle of a hair brush for the convenience of packing'.

The youngest of the party at thirty, Geoffrey Hastings was nominated to lead the short side of the pinnacle. On their arrival at Glen Brittle House the party split, with Slingsby and the veteran Walker returning to Sligachan to reassure the ladies of their safety. Later in the week Charles Pilkington's wife, Mabel, repeated the Inaccessible Pinnacle to become the first female to visit the Bolster Stone, 'all previous attempts being by members of the sterner sex'. After a lightning strike this distinctive boulder now forms the actual summit.

On their way back to Sligachan the main party of Pilkington, Hastings, Dent and Woolley walked up to Coire Lagan and took in Sgumain's West Buttress Route (Grade3/Difficult). Although this route was subsequently described in guidebooks as starting in the lower corrie, Pilkington's party began near the lochan, presumably taking the broken rocks on the left of the steep buttress to reach the crest by way of a prominent rake where routes like Sunset Slab now end. The lower part of the climb was added later and marked on a diagram in the Sligachan Climbers' Book (22 July 1896). Charles Pilkington left a description of the upper part of the route which finishes on the terrace below the upper tier:

> On reaching the top of the buttress, you are surprised to find that it stands well away from the mountain, to which it is joined by a narrow and rotten ridge; following this, you will find yourself immediately under the steep upper rocks of Sgumain. A narrow ledge on the face to the right will take you out of all difficulties, but by turning up over some steep rocks when half-way along the ledge, the top of Sgumain can be gained by struggling up an awkward and conspicuous crack.[7]

From the summit of Sgumain they continued to Alasdair by the first recorded ascent of its South-West Ridge, though this may well have been descended by previous parties. From the summit of Sgurr Alasdair they planned to continue to Sgurr Dubh but were categorically stymied by the impasse of the Thearlaich-Dubh Gap, then known as the Alasdair-Dubh Gap. That a president of the Alpine Club was defeated on British soil was the source of much *schadenfreude* to Scottish mountaineers for years to come. They were forced to skirt the obstacle by retracing their steps down to Bealach Sgumain and then traversing under Alasdair's south face to Sgurr Dubh na Da Bheinn. Here the party separated: Pilkington and Hastings climbed Sgurr Dubh Mor before joining Dent and Woolley in An Garbh-choire. In his book *Mountaineering,* Dent recalled the descent of this rocky corrie, 'as exasperating as any to be found in any part of the world'.

Back at Sligachan, Slingsby was joined by Hastings and Edward Hopkinson for his eponymous route on Sgurr nan Gillean's Third Pinnacle. Hopkinson was a Cambridge mathematician who was a leading exponent in the burgeoning world of electrical engineering. He was one of five high-achieving brothers, sons of a wealthy mill owner, who upset the fledgling Scottish climbing scene with their anti-guidebook ethos, especially their unpublicised exploration of Ben Nevis in 1892. Slingsby's party approached Sgurr nan Gillean by their well-known aquatic ascent of the Bhasteir Gorge: 'A bold attempt by Hastings to find a way by a little ledge, while still observing the ordinary proprieties in the matter of costume proved fruitless.' Harold Raeburn turned the waterfall pitch on the right wall some years later. Once established on the Third Pinnacle they were beaten by the chimney now taken by Luscher's No. 1. They then traversed left to tackle the crucial slab pitch which was the key to Slingsby's Route (Severe), a climb Ashley Abraham reckoned was even more sensational than Eagle's Nest Ridge Direct on Great Gable. Slingsby later revealed the technical jiggery-pokery required for the final crux cave:

> Hopkinson went up into the cavern and held tight the rope while Hastings and I built up an insecure footstool of stones about eighteen inches high. On this Hastings stood, held by Hopkinson with the rope. I climbed on Hastings's knee, then his shoulder, and tried for handholds; but all in vain. I was then shoved up a bit farther, and got my right elbow in a little corner which sufficed to give me the necessary leverage. Hastings steadied me with his axe. This enabled me to surmount a really bad place, above which I soon reached good ground and the others followed.[8]

Clinton Dent went on to summarise the exploration and multifarious adventures of the large party in a witty article in the *Alpine Journal,* 'The Rocky Mountains of Skye', which for many years served as an interim guide to the mountains. Dent also mentioned a new route on Bidein Druim nan Ramh, but did not provide any details. However Slingsby later confirmed that during this trip he was a member of a party that traversed from the North to the Central

Peaks finding no scratch marks on the rocks. This proved to be the first recorded ascent of the North Ridge of the Central Peak which, though relatively short, has an authentic alpine ambience. Normally abseiled in the rush to complete a Main Ridge Traverse, it has often been neglected as a rock climb in its own right, with an accurate description or grade hard to come by.

Clinton Dent concluded his account of their Skye trip with a warning that not all the rock is sound and that care was required, particularly on new routes. He recommended employing John Mackenzie, especially in misty weather: 'He is a capital climber and takes great interest in all the modern refinements of new routes and variations, and is an excellent companion.'[9] Dent also offered his opinion on the best method for getting to grips with the remoter southern peaks: 'A party of three or four provided with an alpine tent pitched say, on the north shore of Loch Coruisk or in the corrie running up from the loch, would find ample occupation for three or four days in climbing the peaks around. There is a good place for camping on the neck of land on the west side between Loch Coruisk and Loch Scavaig.'[10] It would not be long till this suggestion was taken up.

The first record of camping in the Cuillin is by William Daniell's party in 1819 which included clan chiefs and other local grandees. They spent two days exploring Loch Coruisk and its islands, staying overnight in a tent pitched near the mouth of the River Scavaig, which can be seen in one of Daniell's prints. In Britain camping and climbing were first combined in the Lake District in 1885. Four years later T Pilkington White pitched a small marquee and bell tent at Camasunary from where he made an early ascent of the Druim nan Ramh ridge, as well as an attempt on the unclimbed Clach Glas where he was defeated by an 'apparently impassable rock turret'.

The first record of camping in Glen Brittle is in 1890 when a party employed John Mackenzie as their camp attendant to cook dinner, tend the fire and collect their mail from Sligachan. Howard Priestman and brothers Walter and Harrison Barrow camped in the glen two years later when they enjoyed ten days of magnificent weather. In 1899, a Climbers' Club party had more typical weather at the head of Loch Coruisk when they had to abandon their tents due to torrential rain. When they retrieved them they were three times their original weight. The first generation of specialised mountaineering equipment was designed with the Alps in mind and it was not until the outdoor boom of the interwar period that protection from Skye-like rain entered the equation.

At Easter 1892, another Alpine Club party put into practice Dent's suggestion of camping overnight at Coruisk. Their ambitious plan was to climb initially from Sligachan, spend a couple of nights at Glen Brittle and then cross to

Coruisk where their camping equipment was to be delivered by pony from the inn. The team of four included some of the leading lights in the second wave of guideless climbing in the Alps that began around 1890. J H (Herbert) Wicks was a wealthy merchant specialising in trade with Brazil. Up to the First World War he was involved in over 200 alpine climbs including the first guideless ascent of the Charmoz where he is commemorated in the name of a pinnacle, Baton Wicks. G H (George Henry) Morse was manager of the family brewing firm in Norwich, and like Hugh Munro, T K Rose, W W Greg and Edward Hopkinson was yet another Cuillin regular to be knighted (as opposed to the commoner benighted). Ellis Carr was a member of the Carlisle biscuit family, sometime flute player with the *Wandering Minstrels,* and illustrator of Haskett Smith's climbing guides. Together, Wicks, Morse and Carr did the first ascent of the Pic Sans Nom in the Mont Blanc Massif in 1890.

The quartet was made up by J H (John Henry) Gibson, a Writer to the Signet (senior solicitor) from Edinburgh who had recently moved to England. A few months earlier, in January 1892, on the A' Chir Ridge in Arran, he made history as the first person to place a piton in British rock. At the time this was not an issue as climbing in Britain was as yet too young a sport to have developed its own distinct ethics. Of the early Scottish-based SMC members, Gibson probably had the greatest experience with five alpine seasons which included guideless ascents of the Aiguille de Talèfre and the Grépon. Naismith and others considered Gibson the best rock climber in Scotland and, when Gibson married and moved south, hoped he might reek revenge on the Sassenachs for the ignominy of Tower Ridge's first ascent. Ellis Carr was regarded by many as the finest amateur mountaineer of his day, particularly talented on ice, while Morse was another exceptionally good rock climber. It was just as well this was a group of seasoned alpinists as a less capable team could easily have got into difficulties in the prevailing conditions: 'The snow lay in large masses, and a wind, generally north-easterly and always cold, numbed the fingers, and made any halting when out of the sun the reverse of agreeable.'[11]

Carr, Gibson, Morse and Wicks climbed from Sligachan for a week, visiting most of the main peaks north of Sgurr Alasdair. Although many of their impressive achievements might now be classed as first winter or semi-winter ascents, no differentiation was made at the time; snow and ice in Britain were regarded as only factors that made rock climbing more awkward. With most serious climbers of the day spending their summers in the Alps, first ascents in Britain were often made at the only other holiday times, the harsher conditions of Christmas or Easter. The 1890s saw a series of long severe winters when Loch Lomond was frequently frozen over. On Skye at Easter 1892 there was often fresh snow on the ground in the morning; it frequently snowed during the day and descents were often glissades on solid névé. North and east-facing parts of the Cuillin appeared to be in winter condition; those with western or southern aspects, exposed to any sun, had more of an alpine feel. Their ascent of

Pinnacle Ridge was probably in the former category and if so a sound claimant for the first winter ascent. Gibson's understated writing style makes it difficult to interpret the technical difficulties experienced, but in the background fresh snow, ice-bound rocks and biting winds are rarely far away.

The day after Pinnacle Ridge they abandoned any thought of climbing in Coire na Creiche as it was snowing so heavily, and went directly to Glen Brittle to be welcomed by Henry Laidlaw, the estate manager. The next day they made a ground-breaking, semi-winter ascent of the Inaccessible Pinnacle's East Ridge after failing on the shorter side: 'The western edge of the pinnacle is, for one or two steps, quite difficult enough to make it imperative to discard one's gloves, and the bitter north-east wind and snow on the rocks rendered it impossible to climb without them.'[12] After this impressive achievement they continued to the summit of Sgurr Mhic Choinnich. They were unable to work out the direct descent to the col, so retraced their steps to Bealach Coire Lagain from where they made quick progress to the warmth of Glenbrittle farm.

The next day they reached Bealach Mhic Choinnich by way of the tops of Sgumain, Alasdair and Thearlaich. Despite deteriorating conditions they stoically decided to try and force a route from the col up to the summit of Sgurr Mhic Choinnich, 'in order to retrieve our reputation'. Although there are easier options further left round Collie's Ledge, Gibson's description appears to fit the stepped buttress to the right of King's Chimney, quite possibly the same route that Hart and Mackenzie descended in July 1887. The configuration of this area is not obvious from below but would have been apparent on their descent of Sgurr Thearlaich. Gibson elaborates:

> It is I fear almost impossible to give any description of the way up this face of Sgurr Mhic Coinnich that could be recognised by any one wishing to take the ascent [the King's Chimney and West Buttress options are easily described]. Still, any climber standing on our col could hardly fail to notice a broad ledge running round on to the Corrie Labain side of the mountain. The ledge must be followed for 15 or 20 yards until the foot of a sheer wall some 12 feet high is reached. Up that wall he has got to climb, and that done, an easy ridge leads him to the top.[13]

William Naismith also describes this area in notes he made for an updated version of the 1907 SMC guide which finally appeared in 1923: 'On the face opposite Thearlaich there are three chimneys, all of which have been climbed.' (Only King's Chimney made it to the new guide.) Having gained the summit, and with reputation intact, Gibson's party descended to Loch Coruisk to rendezvous with their camping equipment:

> Mr Sharp of Sligachan Hotel was found to be a man of his word. Tent,

wraps, provisions, were discovered reposing on the large boulder that forms such a conspicuous object in the foreground of the well-known photograph of the loch. As the Whymper Tent only held three comfortably, Carr had a little Mummery Tent, the poles of which are inverted ice axes, brought round with the rest of our baggage from Sligachan for his special accommodation and this being rigged up alongside the larger erection was at once nicknamed the 'dependence'. Spare clothes, a warm fire, and a varied meal of Irish stew, cooked in a Silvers' self-cooking soup tin, coffee, cold beef, tinned peaches, and whisky, made us feel more at peace with ourselves and the world at large.[14]

The Silvers' mentioned were S W Silver & Co., one of the main Victorian retailers of outdoor equipment (others included Jaeger, Benjamin Edgington, and Hill & Sons). Silver's self-cooking apparatuses were ordinary tins of soup, etc. which had a container attached filled with cotton wick steeped in spirits. To heat up, you simply stripped off the seal and set it alight. The Whymper tent, developed in the 1860s by Edward Whymper, was an A-framed version that was the prototype for most mountaineering tents for the next hundred years; made of Willesden canvas it could be set up by two people in three minutes. (Whymper, if he hadn't climbed the Matterhorn, would be remembered as an innovative equipment designer.) The smaller but lighter Mummery was draughtier and much less comfortable. (That same year, 1892, saw Edgingtons' produced a silk version of the Mummery that fitted in a pocket, as well as the invention of the Primus stove in Sweden.)

For Carr, Gibson, and Wicks one frosty night camping at Coruisk was more than enough as the limitations of their ground insulation began to make itself felt. The tent was flooded with light when the moon rose and any further sleep was halted by a curious sheep 'unused to campers'. Keen to return to a warm bed at Sligachan, they cut and kicked steps in the snow to the Main Ridge then traversed the tops of Banachdich, Ghreadaidh and Mhadaidh. It is a real testament to the skill and fitness of these Victorian mountaineers that challenging sections of the Cuillin Ridge were despatched under wintry conditions in a matter-of-fact manner with few technicalities deemed worthy of detailed comment. On their last day they ascended the Druim nan Ramh ridge to finish with a traverse of Bidein in fresh snow.

The topographical layout of this keystone section of the Main Ridge was causing a lot of head scratching. The Ordnance Survey placed Bidein's three tops in a straight line when in reality they formed a triangle. J H Gibson attempted to clarify the cartographic confusion with a sketch map in the *SMC Journal* where he used the analogy of a toasting fork: Druim nan Ramh as the handle and the two western corries (Mhadaidh and Tairneilear) between the forks.

Prior to the 1890s most winter excursions on the Cuillin were confined to isolated ascents of the peaks near Sligachan. For example, Alexander Nicolson climbed the ordinary route on Sgurr nan Gillean in February 1872, an opportunistic ascent while visiting Skye in a professional capacity to investigate contraventions of the Vaccination Act (see comments on typhoid in Sconser in Chapter 3). An unnamed climber, writing in *Temple Bar* magazine, ascended Bruach na Frithe by its North-West Ridge in January 1883 when he was accompanied by a spaniel from the inn. But the most regular out of season visitors were a party of masters from Eton College who were active in the Cuillin for five Easters between 1890 and 1894.

The most frequent Eton visitors to Skye included classics master H F W (Herbert) Tatham, A C (Arthur) Benson and T C (Thomas) Porter. The latter has half a scientific concept named after him, the Ferry-Porter Law which relates to the psychophysics of vision. Benson came from a far from conventional family. His father was the bipolar Archbishop of Canterbury, his brother Hugh was a Catholic priest, his mother a lesbian, sister Margaret an Egyptologist; another brother, E F Benson, was the camp author of the *Mapp and Lucia* novels. Arthur Benson himself is best remembered as writer of the lyrics of 'Land of Hope and Glory' and, in climbing circles, as tutor and suitor of George Mallory at Magdalene College in Cambridge.

After Herbert Tatham was killed on a walking holiday in the Alps in 1909, Benson described him as a 'big, bluff and burly creature'. In consistently icy conditions the Eton masters made successful ascents of all the central Cuillin peaks between Bidein and Sgurr Dearg as well as the first recorded winter ascent of Sgurr Alasdair at Easter 1891. They vie with J H Gibson's party for further first winter ascent claims. All this winter exploration of the Cuillin during the early 1890s predates the famous SMC Easter Meets at Fort William and should also be regarded as seminal events in the birth of Scottish winter climbing.

Almost without exception those climbing on the Cuillin in the late Victorian period were well-heeled professionals kitted out in the best of gear then available. In the mid-nineteenth century clothing for the Scottish mountains was little different from that worn by ordinary Skye folk: heavy tweeds and hobnailed boots or brogues. By the 1890s outdoor wear for the hills was more specialised, strongly influenced by flourishing pastimes like deer stalking, fishing and cycling. The embodiment of the Victorian outdoor lifestyle was the Norfolk jacket. This favourite garment buttoned from the throat to the thighs with the sewn-in belt giving further leeway for adjustment. Later sophistications included silk or flannel linings and a choice of elasticated or buttoned cuffs.

Flannel or coarse woollen waistcoats comprised the next layer. Plus-fours (four-inch fold below the knees) were fine for hill-walking but the voluminous knee obscured footholds when rock climbing. For this knickerbockers (knee breeches, sometimes called plus-twos) were ideal, often with double thickness at seat and knees. Next to the skin silk underwear spelt a thankful end to chafing from clammy cotton combinations. For warmth on winter expeditions in the Cuillin, as outlined above, climbers used wool, especially for the extremities. The best quality came from Jaeger & Co: Shetland pullovers, mufflers, balaclava helmets and close-knitted mittens. One piece of military kit that was particularly useful in the Cuillin were puttees, long narrow pieces of cloth wrapped around the lower leg which stopped small stones and snow permeating down boots and socks. In cold conditions these 'horse bandages' could be improvised as a scarf or head-wrap. There are also records of them being used, in conjunction with an ice axe, to splint broken legs.

Early photographs of mountaineers on the Cuillin rarely show anyone carrying a rucksack. John Mackenzie was an exception, presumably due to the onerous responsibility shouldered for the safety of the Talisker bottle, a whisky described by Alexander Nicolson as 'one of the most esteemed and potent products of the barley bree'. A large dram of 'Carbost' was standard issue for taking the sting out of a chill north-easterly, or for direct aid on a particularly exposed section of ridge. Rucksacks were generally Willesden canvas laced at the mouth with no flap at top, but they did not become a regular piece of kit until after the First World War (when they were spelt without the Hun umlaut). When rock climbing, rucksacks would often be regarded as a hindrance due to the amount of back and foot work involved in Cuillin chimneys and gullies. However the main reason for their absence was the prevalence of pockets: the Norfolk jacket had as many as twelve pockets as well as a large game version extending around the skirt. Waistcoats and knickerbockers doubled this number. Apart from the rope, which was carried over the shoulder, pockets could hold everything required for the exigencies of a day out on the Cuillin: tobacco tin or snuffbox, pipe, fusees, sandwiches, map, watch, silk muffler, Buckingham's twine, oil of citronella, cold cream, safety pins.

Around this time the Cuillin began to be featured in the illustrated magazines that the Victorians devoured. The authorship of one piece in *The Graphic* was the source of much speculation among smoking-room regulars. 'It might be Collie,' thought Naismith, 'but I hardly think so.'[15] No longer were holidaymakers on Skye content to gawp at the Cuillin from Sligachan or take the excursion to see Loch Coruisk. The line between tourist and mountaineer was becoming increasingly hazy. Now reaching the summits, especially Sgurr nan Gillean, was a requisite trophy of the popular tourist itinerary. Alexander Nicolson gave his wry take on this, 'The employment of a guide slightly diminishes the glory, but it certainly saves time, and it may possibly save the traveller's neck, if that be of any consequence.'[16]

The *Cornhill Magazine* urged guests at Sligachan to take on the nearby challenges: 'Scour na Gillean, the master peak, is less than three miles from your wash-hand basin.' Murray's guidebook provided advice on how this could be achieved: 'It may be reached with a guide in three hours from the Inn, not less. It is somewhat difficult and requires a steady head. There is no beaten path. It is not suited for ladies: and when mists arise, is dangerous for strangers to the mountain. The Pinnacle Route along the peaks should only be attempted by members of the Alpine Club, to whom it offers attractions in the way of rock work unsurpassed in Great Britain.'[17]

Through the 1890s, information on how to tackle the renowned Sgurr nan Gillean turns up in many diverse, and often unexpected, sources. Baddeley's guidebook describes the final section of the Tourist Route as 'a cyclopean causeway, unrelieved by flower or verdure'. One writer in the *Manchester City News* (23rd September 1893) did their best to put you off:

> Only in one direction may the novice gain the crest, and even then not without a little test of nerves and endurance. People often scramble to the final ridge and shirk the cone. They can be excused for this measure of funk. The final climb is an unmitigated clamber of rocks which are complemented in being termed a staircase. If you can imagine a staircase set at an angle of seventy to seventy-five degrees, and composed of enormous granite blocks, the whole representing an unbalustraded corridor but a few feet wide, and with alarming precipices on either side, you will have some idea of Scour-na-Gillian's crest.

Gilbert Thomson recorded his ascent of Sgurr nan Gillean in *The Essayist*, magazine of the Pollokshields Free Church Literary Institute. A sanitary engineer and later one of the stalwarts of the Scottish Mountaineering Club, Thomson visited Sligachan with a friend on a touring holiday when he was advised to hire a guide: 'Each was provided with a stout stick, a field glass and a pocketful of sandwiches and it would be difficult to say which of these was the more important.' Their ascent was successful and, as was the custom, they left their names in a bottle hidden in the cairn. Their guide 'a sturdy Highlander' related how it was common for ladies to be carried across the last narrow and exposed section. Some parties refused to cross this final obstacle but sent their guide over to fetch the bottle, put in their names and sent it back.

In the country gentleman's magazine, *The Field*, sandwiched between the greyhound results and the racing tipsters, we find one visitor engaging a guide for an ascent of Pinnacle Ridge, 'the ample satchel of John Mackenzie well stocked with a good lunch and a supply of Talisker': 'Mackenzie anchors himself round a corner paying out the rope, and I am sent on to get down as best I can amid cheery shouts of direction and encouragement from the hidden guide. I scramble down as far as possible, then leave go with the hands and drop, landing as high as possible up the gully floor as I can. 'Good I'm down. Carry on, Mackenzie,' I call. His red face beams round the rocks and, the rope being hitched over a little projecting knob, he comes carefully over and drops alongside me.'[18] John Mackenzie's fame was spreading far and wide. In the Austrian magazine *Sport im Bild* (1896) continental admirers could catch up with his exploits on the 'Jungenmänner-Spitze', 'Nicholson's Kamin' and the 'Bhasteir Schlucht'.

Another tourist to stay at Sligachan was Mrs Edward Crowley with her precocious 17-year-old son Alick. At the inn the young Crowley struck up a friendship with the surgeon Joseph Lister, pioneer of antiseptic surgery, who introduced him to some climbers, possibly Lake District regulars R E and J P Gibson who were also resident at the time. They agreed to take him up Pinnacle Ridge the next day – he was hooked. He later traversed Sgurr a' Ghreadaidh and Sgurr a' Mhadaidh on his own to bring his tally of the newly-listed Munros to twelve.

Crowley also made an early ascent, possibly the second, of Lota Corrie Route although it had often been descended. Continuing to Am Basteir he was unable without assistance to negotiate the steep wall where a shoulder was normally required: 'Very wet and misty. The peak of Bhasteir could not be quite gained without extreme risk, a gap some thirty feet from the top barring progress.'[19] The Cuillin made an enormous impact on Alick Crowley, starting a passion for mountaineering that continued throughout his life. His home in Streatham was soon renamed *Coire-na-Creiche* and he called a climb on Beachy Head, Cuillin Crack. When he changed his name from Alexander to Aleister, part of a Celtic persona he adopted, it is not inconceivable that he was influenced by a similar, though correctly spelt, name change in the Cuillin.

Crowley spent the summer of 1894 in the Alps with Ernest Maylard who, the same year, supported his application for membership of the Scottish Mountaineering Club. In a letter to a fellow SMC member Maylard commented: 'It would be a real kindness to the fellow if he could somehow or other get quietly taken down.' On his regular visits to Wasdale Head, Crowley befriended Norman Collie who proposed him (unsuccessfully) for the Alpine Club. Had Crowley not missed the 1895 SMC Easter Meet due to illness, he would doubtless have accompanied his friends Collie and Travers on the first ascent of Castle Ridge on Ben Nevis. Aleister Crowley became one of the pioneers of high altitude mountaineering. He also developed a reputation as one of the world's most notorious occultists, the self-styled 'Great Beast 666', vilified in the tabloid press as 'the wickedest man in the world'. He was the only SMC member selected for the cover of the Beatles' *Sgt. Pepper's Lonely Hearts Club* album.

In the Cuillin, through the 1890s, the activities of the Alpine Club were gradually superseded by the emergent Scottish Mountaineering Club which formally came into existence in March 1889. The objects of the new club, whose 94 original members included eleven professors, eight knights or baronets, and two members of parliament, were: 'To encourage mountaineering in Scotland in winter as well as summer; to serve as a bond of union amongst all lovers of mountain climbing.' Charles Pilkington was one of seventeen Alpine Club members who joined, helping ease the birth pangs of the new club. However, it would be a while before pioneering on the Scottish mainland by native climbers reached the quality and quantity of rock climbing now available on Skye.

Despite the advances in winter climbing on Skye during the first half of the 1890s, the concurring summer seasons proved uneventful. With Collie absent in the Alps or Himalaya, the period from 1892 until 1895 was one of consolidation as members of the SMC found their feet before eventually making a big impact during the bumper summer of 1896. Although the first official SMC Skye Meet was not until 1903 there was a large informal presence on the island throughout the 1890s. This included many of the club's rising stars: William Naismith, William Tough (pronounced Tooch), William Brown, the Napier brothers and marine engineer J H (John) Bell, not to be confused with the later Dr J H B Bell.

With no guidebook available and demand for John Mackenzie oversubscribed, the start of the *SMC Journal* in 1890 helped fill the information gaps. Early articles by the likes of Tough, Naismith and F W (Fred) Jackson were invaluable in enabling those not of an exploratory nature to repeat routes safely. Sheriff Nicolson persuaded Walter Brunskill to provide details of the Inaccessible Pinnacle, still a largely unknown quantity. Tough also published articles in the newly established *Cairngorm Club Journal,* (a rivalry not welcomed by the SMC) where he summarised the accumulated wisdom: June was the best month for a visit, the compass was unreliable and the use of a rope, preferably 60ft (18m), was recommended, as was the wearing of gloves.

Tough recorded an ascent of the Inaccessible Pinnacle with John Mackenzie when he felt he had cracked the access problem to Glen Brittle by hiring a pony and trap from Sligachan. After climbing the pinnacle's long side in a howling gale, Tough's hands were so numb he was unable to lower his partner down the short side. They were forced to down-climb the East Ridge where, to compound matters, Tough lost a favourite pipe. The journey home was not a pleasant one: 'Wet, cold, pipeless, the alternate driving and walking over these wretched 15 miles was a miserable experience.'

Under the hospitable management of the Sharp family, from 1885 until 1902, the Sligachan Inn began to establish its mountaineering character, a focus of thirst-quenching anticipation where climbers could regale tourists, anglers and bona fide topers with tales of derring-do on boilerplate slabs and cyclopean walls. The Sharps, as with their successors, had to learn to cater for the errant schedules of their mountaineering clientele. Many returned from the hill well after midnight to find a meal still waiting, as the boundaries between dinner and breakfast became increasingly blurred.

THE BLACK CUILLIN

William Sharp provided a Climbers' Book to supply information for those new to the Cuillin. There was initially little enthusiasm to make entries and he had to rely on the dependable Naismith and Douglas: 'Mr Sharp has asked us to give some notes of two climbs of 13-14 July [1893] which may perhaps be of use to future parties who are not familiar with the Coolin.' With Pinnacle Ridge they clarified that the pinnacles were numbered going upwards, a source of some previous confusion, and on the West Ridge proposed 'gendarme' in favour of 'tooth'. Mrs Sharp continued to run the Inn after the sudden death of her husband in 1895, described in the press as 'gunshot wound to the head'.

The day after their climb of Pinnacle Ridge, Naismith and Douglas were joined by John Mackenzie for an anti-clockwise round of Coire Lagan. They started with an ascent of Sgurr Sgumain from the lochan when they followed ribs to the right of the North-West Ramp to join Pilkington's West Buttress Route at the loose arete below the terrace. Back at the inn they recorded their day in the Sligachan Climbers' Book: 'Weather magnificent, used rope as rock not of rough gabbro but of slabby, splintery rock, the ledges dipping the wrong way.' At the Inaccessible Pinnacle they recommended that you down-climbed the short side to just above the crux where the rope could be draped over a good hitch to descend the steep lower section. Naismith, Douglas and Mackenzie ended their day with one of the great rewards of climbing on Skye, a fiery sunset over the Western Isles.

Fred Jackson, a Manchester Quaker, also shared his knowledge of the Cuillin with notes and sketches in the *SMC Journal*. Jackson was especially enamoured by Clach Glas and Bla Bheinn, the traverse of which (Difficult) forms one of the finest scrambles in the British Isles. In the early days the mountains were approached through the glens from Sligachan. Nowadays the usual start is from near Loch Slapin, a route that became more accessible with the construction of the road to Elgol in the early 1890s and the completion of the railway to Kyle of Lochalsh in 1897.

The first record of a complete traverse was in July 1887 by William and Percy Marshall from Birmingham and London respectively. Accompanied by John Mackenzie they walked down Glen Sligachan before ascendeding the west face of Bla Bheinn near Willink's Gully, and then continuing to Clach Glas, 'The ridge is rough and has some awkward places.' For several years this was the format favoured by the Sligachan guides.

In July 1893 Fred Jackson repeated the Marshalls' traverse as member of a party that included William Naismith and his sister, as well as a pair from Oxford University, Patrick Duncan and W M Geldart. On the steep descent of Bla Bheinn they used a rope to negotiate the 'stiff chimney'. Near its foot Naismith and Murdo Mackenzie made the first ascent of Half-Crown Pinnacle (Difficult).

Nowadays the most popular direction for doing the ridge is north to south, starting with Clach Glas. This was first accomplished by W E Corlett and E R

Kidson in 1890. Fred Jackson also became an enthusiast for tackling the traverse in this direction, advocating an alternative approach from Sligachan, an intricate route that used deer tracks through the Red Cuillin. He recommended leaving the Glen Sligachan path about two miles from the inn before following the stream to the col between Marsco and Beinn Dearg; rough paths were then followed to gain the bealach between Ruadh Stac and Garbh-bheinn. In July 1895 Jackson followed this route along with T K (Thomas) Rose and guide Donald Mackenzie (who often feature in Jackson's sketches). An original member of the Climbers' Club, Rose was an assayer with the Royal Mint, ideal credentials for becoming the club's first treasurer.

Rose's party were soon tackling the dramatic rock tower of Clach Glas, 'A glance downwards revealed a prospect of immediate dissolution and eternity'. From the summit they descended past Pilkington's 'Imposter' to the col below Bla Bheinn. Jackson outlined the next part of the route in the *SMC Journal*: 'The north end of Blaven is a perfect maze of shattered pinnacles. We therefore proceed over open, grassy ground to where two stone shoots are distinctly seen a little way ahead. The second of these is the better and shorter one to take; both lead into the enclosed place, Naismith's Half-Crown Pinnacle forming the eastern side. Facing south we next climbed a pretty sixty-foot chimney leading to the final walk to the top of Blaven.'[20]

At the Scottish Mountaineering Club AGM, in December 1894, a motion was passed to start publishing climbers' guides to Scotland (initially only one volume was envisaged). They did not want a Sassenach like Haskett Smith beating them to it, and in this they were successful for his planned third volume to cover north of the border failed to materialise. (Ellis Carr spent a long holiday in the Highlands in 1895 drawing illustrations for the ill-fated Scottish guidebook.) The first SMC guide to the Cuillin, *The Island of Skye,* did not appear until 1907, but in the interim accurate topographical information was urgently needed. Revised editions of both the one-inch and six-inch maps were issued in 1895-96 but these only corrected the most obvious errors. A new, more accurate survey was required, but the Ordnance Survey had neither the technology nor the mountaineering expertise to deal with such a complex and difficult area.

Nor had they the linguistic skills. Gaelic place names can be something of a minefield due to the often convoluted manner of their cartographic adoption. In the Hebrides the OS received assistance from the Highland folklorist Alexander Carmichael who was excise officer at Carbost in the 1860s. (The writer Neil Gunn held the same post in the 1920s.) Carmichael, a long-standing friend of Sheriff Nicolson, corrected and revised thousands of Gaelic place names for the Ordnance Survey's officer Captain Macpherson (with no pay and little thanks) often visiting the location and correcting the name from 'the living voice on the spot'. After learning the OS had decided to use some phonetic spelling, Carmichael expressed his frustration in a letter to their headquarters in Southampton: 'The system pursued by the Ordnance Survey in regard to taking up place names is altogether erroneous. Non-Gaelic speaking men go about among non-English speaking people to take down Norse-Gaelic names with their English meanings!'[21]

Carmichael had hit the nail on the head, putting his finger on a fundamental problem that often forced the OS to hedge their bets. In Skye they chose the Gaelic 'Coir-uisg' to name the corrie, while the anglicised version, 'Coruisk', was used for the loch. Similarly the Gaelic 'Camas Fhionnairidh' was adopted for the bay, and 'Camasunary' for the nearby farm. They also had doubts over Loch Scavaig: should they use the Gaelic 'Loch Sgath Bheag' (as on the Admiralty chart), or the eventually winner, the Norse 'Scavaig'?

The hills on the east side of Loch Coruisk was another area where differing claims for nomenclature had to be resolved. For Sgurr Hain the Ordnance Survey rejected both Sgurr na Nighinn (peak of the girl) and Sgurr na Aighin in favour of Sgurr an Eidhne (peak of ivy). Similarly Druim Hain was named Druim an Eidhne until the 1929 Popular Edition. The name Druim Hain was interpreted as 'Druim an Eoin' (the birds' ridge). To avoid any confusion between An Ruadh-stac, on the eastern flank of Druim Hain, and Ruadh Stac, across the glen in the Red Cuillin, the OS simply changed the former name to Meall Dearg.

Appearing in print can give a contentious place name undue authority over an under-examined local tradition. The names adopted by mapmakers are often just one clue in a bigger puzzle. But it was exceedingly expensive to alter any errors on the copper plates used to produce the maps. This did not stop William Douglas of the SMC also pointing out the Ordnance Survey's limitations:

> There are still a number of unnamed peaks in the Coolin range, such as the peak between Gars-bheinn and Sgurr Eag, the west peak of Sgurr Dubh, the peak to the south of Sgurr Dearg; Banachdich and Mhadaidh might be split up and the various tops named, the peak of Bidein Druim nan Ramh (if it is a peak of Bidein) that lies west of the Bealach na Glaic Moire, the peak that lies between Bruach na Frithe and Bhasteir on the main ridge, all these and others ought to be named, and thus simplify future description . But who is to do this?[22]

Douglas himself made an attempt by collating information he gleaned from the likes of Norman Collie, Colin Phillip, and William Naismith. These three made up an informal committee to try and sort out the topographical muddle and produce the required names, generally linking them to some salient feature. Colin Phillip suggested Sgurr an Fheadain, from a whistle or chanter, a name commonly applied to clefts in hills, in this case Waterpipe Gully. Naismith advised that a draft of Douglas's list of peaks and passes should be submitted to Phillip who has 'the most extraordinary knowledge' of the mountains. Throughout his time in the Highlands, Colin Phillip regularly collected oral evidence of place-names from local people.

One Bla Bheinn shepherd referred to Clach Glas as An Stac while the peak below the Inaccessible Pinnacle, marked by the Ordnance Survey as An Stac, was known to locals as Stac nan Eun. John Mackenzie, however, claimed he christened the latter peak Sgurr na Caileag (Gaelic for girl) after a female client, and maintained that An Stac referred to the Pinnacle itself, which makes philological sense. Clach Glas, incidentally, has never been named on a one-inch or 1:50,000 OS map. Colin Phillip also noted that the local name for Bruach na Frithe's north-west ridge was Sron an Tobar, named after the spring at its foot, Tobar nan Uaislean, 'the well of the gentlemen' (the early climbers).

William Douglas compiled a detailed list of the heights of the peaks and cols of the Cuillin with additional information on the easy passes. This format, appended to many climbing guides, was not superseded for almost a hundred years. With few of the conventional aids for navigation, like compasses or OS maps, providing effective help in the Cuillin, having the heights of bealachs was a real boon in 'thick weather'. Used in conjunction with an aneroid barometer, a rudimentary altimeter, Douglas's list provided one of few practical aids for navigating the Main Ridge in misty conditions.

Douglas started work on his 'Names, Heights and Positions of the Coolin Peaks' in 1892 but it was not published until the 1897 *SMC Journal* where it demonstrated some of the changes in nomenclature. The Inaccessible Peak became Pinnacle, the North-East Peak became Sgurr Thearlaich (spelt Tearlach initially) though the Alasdair-Dubh Gap only gradually changed to Thearlaich-Dubh. Sgurr a' Fionn Choire, An Caisteal, Caisteal a' Garbh-choire and Sgurr a' Choire Bhig were listed for the first time; Sgurr Dubh was sub-divided into Sgurr Dubh Mhor, Sgurr Dubh Beag and Sgurr Dubh na Da Bheinn. In 1898 Douglas had a composite map produced at a scale of about three inches to the mile, based on the OS First Edition six-inch map: 'The Names and Heights not in the Survey Map have been added to this map in block letters.' The map also included five soundings in Loch Coruisk made in September 1886.

Douglas also clarified names in the Bhasteir area where Collie had used 'Basteir Tooth' for the whole mountain. There was further confusion with the use by some of 'Basteir Rock'. Colin Phillip felt that 'Am' should be placed in front of Bhasteir, a convention that was not adopted until some years later. The revised edition of *Munro's Tables* stated that Am Bhasteir was also known as Sgurr Dubh a' Bhasteir. (It also mentions that Banachdich was sometimes spelt Banachaig.) Early interpretations of Basteir include 'the deadly place' and 'the place where deer are often shot'. With the arrival of the early mountaineers it was popularly translated as 'the executioner' due to the Tooth's resemblance to an axe. However, in the 1920s, Ronald Burn argued effectively that Basteir derives from a word for cleft.

The bealach below the Tooth, marked on the First Edition (1885) one-inch OS map as Bealach a' Leitir was changed to Bealach nan Lice on the Second Edition (1896). Sgurr Coir' an Lochain was named by Collie and Phillip despite suggestions that it was known by shepherds as Sgurr Dubh Coire Lochain. In much the same way as the Inaccessible Pinnacle is often called the 'In Pin', the Edwardians created their own pet names for the mountains: 'Gerty', 'Charlie', 'Sandy', and 'Mick'. As late as 1991 new peaks were still being discovered! Robin Campbell's eagle eye spotted the unnamed Cuillinette extending south from Sgurr nan Gillean's west ridge for which he proposed the name Sgurr Coire an Lobhta.

Geologists on Skye got off to a bad start. To the untutored local eye the Victorian proponents of this heretical new science appeared to be southern eccentrics aimlessly breaking up rocks with large hammers, for all the world like studious convicts. Other tools of the trade included sledgehammers, blasting powder and dynamite. They soon became objects of scorn and ridicule. A young Charles Darwin got the ball rolling with Robert Jameson, one of the first geologists to visit the Cuillin: 'During my second year in Edinburgh I attended Jameson's lectures in geology and zoology, but they were incredibly dull. The sole effect they produced on me was the determination never as long as I lived to read a book on geology or in any way to study the science.'[23] One tale doing the rounds featured at some time almost every geologist to visit Skye, including Roderick Murchison, Adam Sedgwick and Archibald Geikie. The geologist entrusts a local lad to carry a heavy bag of specimens back to his lodgings. The enterprising youth, once out of eyeshot, dumps the contents of the bag to later refill it with other stones near his destination.

John MacCulloch was derided by fellow geologists and Skye folk alike. Mackinnon of Strath encapsulated their opinions by ordering chamber pots with MacCulloch's portrait decorating the bottom. J D Forbes used a withering put-down, 'His favourite method of studying geology was from a boat.' The poet Robert Buchanan regarded geologists as 'frequently duller company than the Free Church minister or the dominie'.[28] After this damning comparison some ground was regained with the much-respected Archibald Geikie who was appointed to the Geological Survey in 1855 as a mapping assistant. He first visited Skye as a student, staying at Kilbride in Strath with the Reverend John Mackinnon, the first of a dynasty of ministers that served the area for over a hundred years. The quarries advocated by MacCulloch had eventually started operations and Geikie observed that some of what were referred to as the 'hovels of the peasants' were actually constructed from marble, albeit blackened from years of peat smoke. Transporting a fresh batch of rock samples, Geikie was constantly quizzed by locals as to how much money he would get for the stones. He became known in Strath as *Geikie na Clachan,* but rival geologist J W (John) Judd would call him something much stronger.

Climbers' controversies, like the pick versus spike, ice axe debate that raged through the 1890s, were small beer compared to the acrimonious scientific feuds of the day. Most walkers ascending the Druim Hain path from Glen Sligachan were oblivious that the hillside to their right was the focal point of a vitriolic geological dispute that eventually focused on whether the Black or Red Cuillin were older; in other words did the gabbro or granite (granophyre) come first? Judd insisted the Red Cuillin were the more ancient. The accepted premise was the jaggier the outline the younger the mountains, for example Rockies – young, Appalachians – old; the geological principle being that younger rocks intruded into older rocks. The spat between Judd and Geikie hinged on a critical area of Druim Hain, above Glen Sligachan, where there was a distinct junction between the gabbro and the granite.

Geikie photographed his evidence in the gullies there, demonstrating that the granite did indeed intrude into the gabbro, and proving that the Red Cuillin *were* younger despite appearing more weathered. This vindication was a major intellectual coup for Geikie, bringing to an end one of the most heated controversies of 19th-century British geology. This particular war of words was part of an ongoing rivalry between members of the Geological Survey and the 'amateur' university geologists, primarily over their respective methods: Geikie's work relied on field observations while Judd's evidence was derived from laboratory work based on the examination of thin sections.

In 1881 Geikie was promoted to director-general of the British Geological Survey and later honoured with a rock named after him, Geikielite. In 1893 he became an honorary member of the SMC. Two years later Geikie appointed the 'master petrologist', 46-year-old Alfred Harker from Hull, to a part-time position with special responsibility for surveying and mapping the Cuillin. Initially using Sligachan as his base, Harker carried this out in the summer from 1895 until 1900, returning to Cambridge for the winter to study the material gathered in the field.

The fleet-footed Harker befriended many of the members of the SMC he came across in Skye, becoming a member himself in 1900. A E Robertson recalled him: 'I first met him at Sligachan in July 1898. Coming down to breakfast one morning I saw at a table by himself a tall, thin, dark, shy-looking man rapidly eating an enormous breakfast. Thereafter he strapped on sundry satchels and map cases and I watched him disappear up Glen Sligachan at an incredible pace.'[24]

For his 1899 season Harker moved his base to Glen Brittle, building a cabin (the remains still exist) supplemented by tents, inside the gorge of the Allt Coire na Banachdich near the foot of the Eas Mor waterfall above Glen Brittle House. He stayed there with his assistant, usually John Mackenzie's nephew Archie, taking Sunday off to visit Carbost or Sligachan. He sent Geikie regular progress reports, mostly positive save for a criticism of the coloured index the Geological Survey had chosen for their maps, which he thought was 'not well adapted to the rather special requirements of the district'. In August 1899 Harker reported: 'The work has been very interesting, though of course rough with a great deal of climbing and not much "area" to show for it. The prolonged fair weather throughout the past month has been very trying owing to the absence of wind. The thermometer has reached 75 degrees and I find that almost intolerable in the moist climate in a dead calm with the air full of midges.'

In 1907, Harker was presented with the Geological Survey's Murchison Medal: 'His brilliant mapping of the Cuillin hills of Skye, completed in 1901, was a tribute not only to his skill as a field geologist and petrographer but also to his prowess as a mountaineer and brought to a close the historic controversies of Geikie and Judd on the igneous history of the island.' Another colleague praised the thoroughness of his hammer work, 'No stone was left unturned.'[25] Harker's map was published in 1904, the same year as his classic geological memoir, *The Tertiary and Igneous Rocks of Skye*, which served as a model for all subsequent survey work on the island. G M (Malcolm) Brown, a leading post-war Cuillin geologist, wrote of Harker's 'seemingly superhuman achievement'.

Harker also published a paper on the glaciation of the Cuillin, 'Ice-Erosion in the Cuillin Hills, Skye.' He thought the Cuillin an excellent choice for this type of study as, at the period of maximum glaciation, the mountains were covered by a localised ice cap around which the main Scottish ice sheet flowed. Evidence, therefore, was not complicated by being over-ridden by larger ice sheets; there was also little glacial drift and the rock was generally uniform, ie, gabbro.

Alfred Harker certainly left his mark on the world – and beyond. The mineral Harkerite, first found on Skye, is named in his honour, as are Mount Harker in Antarctica, Harker Glacier (South Georgia), Harker's Gully on Marsco, and Dorsa Harker, a feature on the Moon. If, as seems inevitable, Munro-bagging develops into a world-wide phenomenon, Mount Harker, at 2,999ft, will provide fuel for controversy.

William Douglas, at the conclusion of his 'Names, Heights, and Positions of the Coolin Peaks', admitted that there were bound to be inaccuracies, and welcomed any corrections or further information. Alfred Harker responded with an article in the 1900 *SMC Journal*, 'Notes on the Cuillin Hills'. He provided new heights and topographical detail which built on Douglas's framework. What Harker especially improved was the description of the difficulties involved descending from the passes on the Main Ridge, which had previously been a bit vague. His name soon became synonymous with an easy pass. In poor visibility few parties headed down from the tops through the 'clammy vapours' without a tentative: 'Hope it's a Harker.'

Harker also suggested new names such as Sgurr na Bhairnich (the Limpet) and Sron Bhuidhe on Sgurr na Banachdich. A E Maylard was the first to point out that Sgurr na Bhairnich lacked a name and the eventual choice of nomenclature probably reflects his description of the peak as having 'an unstable mass of rock on top'. Sron Bhuidhe (the yellow shoulder) was so-called after a band of orange-yellow rock, conspicuous when viewed from the east. Colin Phillip suggested Sgurr a' Leighiche (the Doctor's Peak) for the unnamed peak between Banachdich and Ghreadaidh, in honour of his friend Collie. Alfred Harker altered this to Thormaid (Norman), following the tradition of Gaelic first names like Alasdair (Alexander) and Thearlaich (Charles). Many years earlier John Mackenzie gave the name Sgurr Beag to Phillip for the small peak on the ridge south of Sgurr nan Gillean. This was mistakenly passed on to Douglas as Sgurr a' Beoch, an error rectified by Harker. This peak had in the past also been known as Sgurr an Fithich (peak of the ravens).

William Douglas considered the southern termination of the Cuillin backbone to be Sgurr Dubh Beag on the Dubh Ridge, while the continuation to Gars-bheinn was for long regarded as a sub-branch of the Main Ridge. Both Harker and Hugh Munro disagreed, and it was duly modified on Harker's list. This anomaly goes some way to explaining the apparent lack of interest in the peaks south of Sgurr Dubh an Da Bheinn prior to this. From the early surveyors until 1896 there is only one record of a visit: W E Corlett and E R Kidson who traversed from Sgurr Dubh to Gars-bheinn in 1891. Corlett and Kidson are a little known team who carried out some significant explorations in the Cuillin during the early 1890s. Kidson was from Nottingham, while Corlett was a wealthy solicitor from Liverpool. Described by Geoffrey Winthrop Young as 'dark and restless', William Corlett was a founder member of the Climbers' Club, as well as chairman of Higson's Brewery, familiar to many Merseyside climbers for their pint of 'Higgies'.

In 1907 Douglas, with the help of Collie, Naismith and Harker, collated most of the available information on the Cuillin to fill the whole September issue of the *SMC Journal* as the first SMC Skye guide. Illustrated with many fine photographs by A E Robertson it was a tremendous success and almost immediately sold out. For the grading of rock climbs the guide used the categories originated by O G Jones, but referred to them numerically, ie, 1, 2, 3, 4 (a 3A was added later) equating to Easy, Moderate, Difficult, Exceptionally Severe. This esoteric numerical system was used in Skye on the grounds that the unique properties of gabbro made comparisons with other areas misleading. It persisted until 1948. There were originally only two Cuillin climbs in the hardest category (4): Third-Fourth Gully on Sgurr nan Gillean and Waterpipe Gully Direct. The influence of the SMC guide was overshadowed the following year (1908) by the publication of Ashley Abraham's more glamorous *Rock-Climbing in Skye* with its dramatic action shots and inclusion of recent favourites like Window Buttress.

The 1907 SMC guide was complemented by a map of the Cuillin reduced from the OS Second Edition of 1903. The scale was similar to Douglas's 1898 version but the area covered greater as it included the Red Cuillin and the Bla Bheinn range which the earlier map omitted. The spelling of the title differed too: 'The Coolins Skye', as advocated by Alexander Nicolson, on the 1898 map; 'The Cuillin Hills Skye' for the 1907 map. The latter map was printed in black with red lines added by Harker to indicate the safest ways across the range: 'The routes marked in red on this map are no evidence of a right-of-way, or even of a track or path. Users of this map are requested to respect proprietary and sporting rights.' Broken lines were used to indicate sections where scrambling would be encountered. Harker even used arrows to show preferable routes of ascent and descent, for example recommending the right side (looking up) of the Sgumain Stone Shoot for ascending, the opposite side going down; descend Lota Corrie on left (scree), ascend on other side (rock).

The mountaineers of the 1890s removed the last vestiges of mystery from the Cuillin. The knowledge they accumulated was disseminated throughout the small, close-knit climbing community. It enabled Skye to experience a golden age around the turn of the century when the mountains almost rivalled the Alps as a destination for a mountain holiday by British climbers.

Chapter Five

Joyous Days Upon the Mountainside

Climbers loafing around the smoking-room in September 1895 were flabbergasted to read a recent entry in the Sligachan Climbers' Book. 'Constant, interesting and sometimes difficult climbing,' it read, referring to Skye's last great problem, the Waterpipe Gully of Sgurr an Fheadain. This prominent cleft had a formidable reputation, compounded when it defeated Norman Collie and W W King in 1891. The modest note was signed by J Kelsall from Bradford and Arthur W Hallitt, a consultant chemist from Halifax, names unfamiliar to the smoking-room cognoscenti. So awesome was the reputation of the gully that a successful ascent by two unknowns was considered poppycock; many scoffed at the claim thinking it a ruse or prank. Leading cynics included T A Falcon and E Gray who, the next May, tried unsuccessfully to complete the climb.

Falcon, who was from Devon, was a regular at Sligachan through the 1890s. He made himself unpopular through, amongst other things, his criticism of Donald Mackenzie, John's brother, in the Sligachan Climbers' Book (a serious breach of etiquette), where he recommended Donald as 'guide to any climber who prefers a degree of uncertainty in his day's undertaking'. Falcon was also a vehement critic of climbing style, especially what he considered the overuse of the rope. When Falcon and Gray attempted Waterpipe Gully they found few nail marks in the gully but several on the adjoining ridge. This added fuel to Falcon's doubts regarding the first ascent which he was quick to express in the Climbers' Book with some fashionably restrained invective. But the two Yorkshiremen had indeed climbed the gully. Their attention was first drawn to it by Walter Greg who, two years earlier, found unwanted fame in the national press after his accident in Coire na Creiche.

Accompanied by Greg, Kelsall and Hallitt had a cursory examination of the lower gully before returning on their own, on 9th September, for a more serious attempt. They soloed the initial section, avoiding some harder pitches on the right, to where a 'stack of rock' divided the gully into two branches. Here, about halfway up, 30-year-old Arthur Hallitt slipped and cut his hands. They put on the rope for the remainder of the climb which Kelsall led to the top.

Kelsall and Hallitt's departure from the climbing world was as sudden and mysterious as their arrival. It is not unusual for talented climbers to suddenly burst onto the scene, and later consolidate their reputation, but to pioneer by far the hardest climb in Skye, indeed at the time one of the most challenging in

Britain, now graded Very Severe, and then vanish from all climbing records is truly extraordinary. For many years the gully was considered to have no equal in the British Isles: over 1,300ft (400m) with 25 pitches, 'some of them monsters'.

The next year (1896) the strong Scottish Mountaineering Club team of John Bell, William Brown and the two Napier brothers arrived on Skye. As well as exploring the south of the range they were keen to repeat Waterpipe Gully and put the rumours to the test. John Napier was a paper-maker in Denny near Stirling while his brother Robert worked as a chartered accountant in Glasgow. The previous month Brown, a lawyer, teamed up with William Tough for the first ascent of the Tough-Brown Traverse, Lochnagar's first rock climb. Poignantly Brown had only five years to live, dying of a 'wasting disease' aged 33.

Their first attempt on Waterpipe Gully was made on 21st July on their way from Sligachan to Glen Brittle House. That morning found them tentatively staring up into the depths of the chasm and tossing a coin for the lead. (This practice was condemned by many as it could result in a weaker member of the party taking on most of the responsibility – it was one of the main causes of the 1903 Scafell tragedy). Brown won the toss but after five-and-a-half hours climbing was forced to concede defeat at the 'stack of rock'. Here he chose the wrong option of the tempting-looking branch on the left and eventually they were forced to escape by the gully wall. Brown later wrote to William Douglas in Edinburgh: 'We tried *the* gully. It is a whopper. The fun begins at once. My hands are so badly cut I can scarcely write.'

Had the SMC party carried a first aid kit Brown would have led them to the top with ease. One contemporary version called the 'Mountaineers' Pocket Case', endorsed by the Alpine Club, contained opium, quinine, laudanum (opium dissolved in alcohol), chalk and opium powders, and cocaine solution.

It was a sober-minded foursome who ruefully headed down to Glen Brittle House. This was an ideal base to tackle the southern Cuillin but was only available under special circumstances or if you had the right connections. So rarely was this favour granted that the SMC party even discussed whether they should mention it to anyone. The next day Brown rested the injuries to his hands while Bell and the Napier brothers ascended Sgurr Sgumain by a line below its steep north face, the North-West Ramp (Grade 3).

The following day Brown felt well enough to accompany the others up the Alasdair Stone Shoot and then across the Thearlaich-Dubh Gap to Sgurr Dubh: 'This is by far the finest ridge wander in the Coolins.' On Sgurr Dubh the party split with John Napier and William Brown the first of many to consider, wrongly, that the return to Glen Brittle by way of Coruisk and then around the coast was little more than a pleasant diversion. They did not arrive back until 11.15pm. Despite torrential rain, John Napier and John Bell resolved to have one last stab at Waterpipe Gully. At Brown's highpoint they used a shallow chimney in the 'stack of rock' to finally gain the right branch of the gully. Above, a series of short chockstone problems led to the last main pitch where they were forced to ascend the watercourse directly. After this final soaking they were able to categorically confirm that Kelsall and Hallitt's description was 'accurate in every particular'.

Safely back at Sligachan Inn, Bell wasted no time in writing the news of their success to William Brown who had earlier left for home: 'Dear Brown, We have done the Gully. Yesterday was vile so did nothing. Today nearly as bad but at 10.45 John Napier and I started out. We reached the place where we stuck in two hours from Sligachan… We might just as well gone for a swim.' T A Falcon stubbornly continued to impugn the validity of the first ascent. The screes only began to settle after the respected team of Norman Collie, William Naismith and William Garden repeated the climb in 1896, corroborating the accuracy of the original description: 'The climb is an interesting and not especially difficult one to everyone accustomed to gullies.' After a fractious froth of discord it was back to understated business as usual.

However the first major pitch of Waterpipe Gully, 'the 80-foot Pitch', had been avoided on the first ascent by a detour on the right. In June 1899, this and all other pitches were taken directly by a Climbers' Club team led by Roger Thompson. Due to the length of the climb and large size of party they were absent from Sligachan for over 18 hours, 12 of which were spent in the confines of the gully (from 1pm to 1am). They eventually arrived back at 4.45am 'to a most luxurious supper'.

The summer of 1896 would be a vintage season 'when a large muster of the mountaineering clan filled Sligachan from June to September'. It was no coincidence that Norman Collie, now Professor Collie, was back on the island taking stock after the trauma of Nanga Parbat the previous year. The peaks near to Sligachan were now thoroughly investigated, but the dilemma of how best to access the more inaccessible southern end of the range remained. William Tough's hiring of a pony and trap from Sligachan to Glen Brittle helped little and he admitted later he would have been quicker on foot: 'Walk! That is walk openly and avowedly, and make no pretence of hiring a conveyance.'

It was artists rather than mountaineers who came up with the best solution to this problem. The roster of artists who painted Loch Coruisk is a long one: John William Inchbold (1855) a protégé of John Ruskin, George Barnard (1859), art teacher at Rugby School, Richard Ansell (1860), J C Hook (1881). Alfred William Hunt was a disciple of Turner as well as a champion of the then almost unknown Robson. Hunt's 'lost masterpiece' of Loch Coruisk, painted in 1869, turned up on the BBC's *Antique Road Show*.

As the fame of Loch Coruisk created a steady demand for paintings of this subject, artists started to construct temporary huts at the loch as a summer base for their creative endeavours. In the 1870s, David Murray from Glasgow and L A MacDonald, a Skyeman, stayed at Coruisk for two months 'in what was little more than a tin box', exhibiting and selling their paintings in Edinburgh the following winter. Alexander Nicolson visited them prior to his ascent of Sgurr Dubh Mor. In 1895 John MacNiven, a Glasgow artist known for his paintings of the River Clyde, spent the summer at Loch Coruisk with a companion. Tragically MacNiven collapsed and died near the loch and his friend had to wait several days until the evacuation of the body could be organised.

The next year the Salisbury artist Alfred Williams built himself a hut near Loch Scavaig. After retiring from the malting company he helped establish, Williams spent much of his time painting in the wilds. In 1896, aged 64, he stayed at his Coruisk cabin from mid-April until the end of June when visitors included the Abraham brothers, well-known photographers from Keswick, on their first trip to Skye. That May Alfred Williams was joined by his son Sidney when they took advantage of some fine settled weather to engage John Mackenzie for the first recorded ascents of the north-east ridges of both Gars-bheinn (Grade 1) and Sgurr a' Choire Bhig (Difficult). Their major achievement, however, was the first ascent of Sgurr Dubh's east ridge, now better known as the Dubh Ridge (Moderate), though they avoided the steep drop off Sgurr Dubh Beag by ledges on its south flank.

This popular classic, over 3,000ft (915m), is the longest rock climb in Britain if started near Loch Coruisk. For many years the route's lower slabs were avoided by a higher start in An Garbh-choire as advocated by Ashley Abraham in his book *Rock-Climbing in Skye*. The next month (June 1896) the SMC team of John Rennie, William Douglas and William Lamont arrived by sea at the foot of the Cuillin. They had spent a week sailing from the Clyde aboard Rennie's yacht, *Ronaval*, before dropping anchor in Loch Scavaig, 'one of the most sublime spots in all bonnie Scotland'. For those under sail Loch Scavaig was a favourite anchorage in settled weather. It was also the golden age of the steam yacht when vessels made pleasure trips with picnics ashore. However fierce squalls could come out of nowhere and many craft were reluctant to linger. Mooring rings were eventually bolted onto the rocky islets by the Northern Yacht Club.

Rennie was a wealthy bachelor from Helensburgh who had a private income through family coalmines near Kilsyth. On 9th June Lamont and Rennie climbed the south-east ridge of Gars-bheinn, and then continued past the top of the Chasm to provide the first details of this southernmost section of the range: 'The ridge was followed from Gars-bheinn, past top unnamed on Pilkington's map, to Sgurr nan Eag, thence to lump at bealach between Coir a' Ghrunnda and the Garbh-corrie [Caisteal a' Garbh-choire]. The ridge is much broken and gashed in places. There is a deep rent to east of Sgurr nan Eag, bridged by jammed boulders at top.'[1]

William Douglas missed out on this trip due to ill health, probably an asthma attack. Two days later he was well enough to join Rennie and Lamont for a repeat of the Dubh Ridge. A blazing hot day, they scrambled up the warm boiler-plate slabs to the summit of Sgurr Dubh Beag and, after a leisurely lunch in the warm sun, tackled the tricky descent avoided by Williams and Mackenzie, now usually abseiled:

> The connecting ridge was seen some eighty feet below, but nothing of the intervening space. The rope was unwound and a man sent down to explore. He soon returned with the joyful intelligence that it would 'go' all right, for the *mauvais pas* resolved itself into a pitch of about fifteen to twenty feet of vertical rock with a break in it about half way down. The first man was soon lowered, the second man followed, and the last, finding an excellent hitch for the rope, came down sailor fashion with his back to the wall.[2]

Rennie, Lamont and Douglas's nautical approach to Coruisk was regarded as an innovative alternative to the lengthy approach walks. It was copied by a large SMC party the next Easter weekend when they proposed to use the SS *Erne* as a floating hotel. On 16th April 1897, this well-appointed steam yacht entered Loch Scavaig with a cargo of 29 climbers picked up in Oban the previous evening. South-westerly gales, however, meant any boats launched for the shore would find it difficult to return, so they reluctantly opted for the more sheltered waters of Knoydart. On dry land Norman Collie, Geoffrey Hastings and Walter Haskett Smith had hoped to rendezvous with them at Loch Scavaig. Collie later wrote William Douglas: 'We were all afraid you were going to be drowned.' A hundred years later, in May 1997, the SMC commemorated the occasion with a Centennial Yacht Meet when classic craft, including the 1898 steam yacht *Carola*, rafted together for two days in Loch Scavaig, this time in perfect weather.

John Rennie was impressed by Alfred Williams and other artists who 'are in the habit of living in portable wooden homes'. After seeing Williams' prototype on his visit to Coruisk, Rennie decided to design his own version. The 'Rennie Hut' was a triangular structure made of wooden sections covered with roofing felt. The plan was to assemble three prefabricated huts, two bedrooms and one kitchen, at Loch Coruisk, and use them as a climbing base for five weeks during the summer of 1897. As well as Rennie, the party included William Douglas, William Brown and Harrison Barrow, grandson of John Cadbury, founder of the chocolate company.

After disembarking from the MacBrayne steamer, the *Gael*, they hired a Soay fisherman, John MacRae, to help ferry provisions to the far end of Loch Coruisk well away from inquisitive tourists. Five years earlier MacRae gave evidence to the Napier Commission when he described the harshness of his island life: 'I have been through England, Scotland, Ireland and France, and I have not seen such an awful place for people to be living in as Soay.' Through correspondence with Rennie, MacRae agreed to look after the timber delivered, and advised them to take fishing rods for the plentiful trout in the loch. It took three days and seven trips to ferry all the equipment, including the timber and nails, four iron camp beds, a coke stove and four bags of coke, to the site chosen for the huts. They were not totally isolated as fresh food was delivered by the steamer every Tuesday; mail could be collected by the long hike over to Sligachan and there were also visits from SMC friends, for example Harold Raeburn.

Initially the weather alternated between storms and calmer, more sultry spells. In the former they slept fitfully with their clothes on and boots within easy reach, but in the drier breaks some climbing was possible. In one of the mountaineering highlights William Brown led the party up an unclimbed buttress on Sgurr a' Mhadaidh. Now known as Brown's Climb (Difficult) this provided 'a capital climb up continuously steep rocks without having to pass any exceedingly difficult pitches'. The second part of their stay displayed all the capricious vicissitudes of Skye in August. According to his brother Walter, Harrison Barrow returned home to Birmingham with a severe case of rheumatism. Douglas's diary says it all:

> 13 August. Rain! Rain! Rain! Real Skye rain and no mistake, and all the waterworks of the Coolins were going high pressure. It continued like this all day… On our return to camp we found the loch had raised its level by nearly three feet.
> 14 August. The storm still continues
> 15 August. Raining still
> 16 August. A tremendous gale last night
> 17 August. If the gale of the 16th was bad
> 18 August. The mist came down
> 19 August. The mist again baffled our efforts.
> 20 August. Rain all day!
> 21 August. The beginning of the end.
> 22 August. The weather has gone against us.
> 23 August. A most glorious day, which had unfortunately to be spent in packing.[3]

With the completion of the railways from Strome Ferry to Kyle of Lochalsh in 1897, and Fort William to Mallaig in 1901, the dynamic of travel on Skye shifted dramatically. The new Kyle line spelt an end to the steamer from Strome Ferry to Portree. The Portree mail-boat now waited at Mallaig for the arrival of the Fort William train and, instead of reaching the Cuillin from Portree, many tourists and mountaineers now chose to disembark at Broadford. The changes encouraged a flurry of activity on the newly accessible eastern faces of Clach Glas and Bla Bheinn. In June 1900 Sidney Williams teamed up with Duncan Grant, a Broadford shepherd, to explore and name the principal gullies there. The pair spent three days working out a route up the spur that falls to the east of Bla Bheinn's summit, East Ridge (Moderate), and on Clach Glas they also discovered an easy ramp across the east face, now known as Sid's Rake.

If Charles Pilkington was blessed with fine weather on his Skye trips, William Inglis Clark invariably attracted the storm clouds, especially on Clach Glas and within lightning strike of the Bhasteir Tooth. In July 1895, with his cousin J Gall Inglis, Clark was chased off Clach Glas by a storm, an incident that resulted in dinner at Sligachan near midnight. Enthused by Sydney William's explorations, Clark returned to Skye in 1901 with his wife Jane. After the scenic train journey to Mallaig and an idyllic sail on the steamer, they were not long disembarked at Broadford when they noticed the wind was getting up. Undeterred, they set off for Clach Glas where they considered an attempt on B Gully. Due to the amount of water in the gully they decided instead to tackle the rocks on the right. These led to below the pinnacles climbed by Naismith and Parker in September 1896, from where they headed directly for the top, a scramble now known as the Ramp Route (Moderate). On the summit they were exposed to the full blast of the wind which was so fierce they were unable to take their planned descent by way of Bealach Clach Glas. An epic retreat ensued back down the east face. True to form, Clark's storm clouds remained with him for the next ten days, relenting with a glorious day for the journey home.

The Clark family were influential figures in the growing Scottish climbing community: son Charles was a promising climber who reached the summit of the Matterhorn when he was fourteen, while sister Mabel and mother Jane were founder members of the Ladies' Scottish Climbing Club. William Inglis Clark achieved due immortality with the name of a draughty rock peak in the Dolomites, Punta Clark.

Clark had the same bad luck with weather on the Bhasteir Tooth as he had on Clach Glas. In June 1896 he and two friends descended Lota Corrie Route to a point near the screes when a ferocious hailstorm and heavy rain forced them to re-ascend towards the summit of Am Basteir. Here combined tactics were usually required for the final rocks, but Clark fortuitously discovered an alternative route round to the right that has since become the *voie normale*. Two years later Clark and his wife were forced to abandon an attempt to reach the Bhasteir Tooth from Am Basteir due to atrocious weather. On the same holiday the Reverend A E Robertson and Clark ascended Lota Corrie route, only to be caught by 'a perfect hurricane of wind and rain' that left them spread-eagled on the summit slabs. They had no choice but to again turn and descend, an epic Robertson recorded in his diary:

Places where we had come up with ease had to be taken with the utmost care coming down. A slip would have been fatal. Only one man moved at a time, rope carefully hitched. Steady was the word. 'Keep your hair on and don't get excited!' We got off the rocks in due time, but oh how cold I was! I don't think I was ever so cold in my life. Soaked to the skin. Part of the way down was a gully which by this time was a torrent. At one place I had to lie with the water flowing over me, while I played out the rope to Clark. When clear of the rocks we took to our heels and ran. Ran! We ran for miles, ending by coming up to the Inn at the double.[4]

This soaking, an event that led to an unfortunate overdose of medicinal whisky, was in June 1898 when William and Jane Inglis Clark were some of the season's first arrivals at Sligachan. It would be a momentous year when the final jigsaw pieces of the Main Ridge were slotted in place. The Clarks were accompanied by James Parker, a civil engineer in the railway industry who became a stalwart of the Cairngorm Club as well as the first secular Munroist. That summer, Parker and the Clarks supported A E Robertson with ascending the tricky Skye peaks, the crux of his quest to beat Hugh Munro in climbing all the Scottish three-thousanders. The Victorians were natural history buffs who accumulated displays of exotic ferns, birds' eggs, butterflies, fossils and minerals, etc. Now the mountains themselves were becoming part of the 'collecting' tradition, an interest that shows little sign of abating.

Robertson was the son of a Victorian merchant from Helensburgh, and was presently minister at Braes of Rannoch. The Cuillin were the climax of a bicycle-propelled, two-month Munro-bagging trip, culminating in Sgurr na Banachdich on 2nd July, the last of a total bag of 74. The Reverend Robertson finally succeeded in becoming the first person to ascend all the Munros in 1901. Or did he? Certainly not, claim conspiracy theorists after spotting discrepancies in Robertson's 'compleation' (there is some doubt to whether he climbed Ben Wyvis).

The fortnight in Skye included some of Robertson's most memorable mountain days: Pinnacle Ridge where he took the lead for a direct variation on the final rocks, and an early ascent of the 'picturesque and sensational' An Stac Buttress below the Inaccessible Pinnacle. Robertson, Parker and Inglis Clark were put up for three nights by Henry Laidlaw, the farmer at Glen Brittle, a handy base for bagging the southern Munros (Sgurr Mhic Choinnich and the Inaccessible Pinnacle were not yet classified as such).

The high season of 1898 saw the cream of the SMC check in to Sligachan in dribs and drabs throughout August. First to arrive were G P (George Percival) Baker, Godfrey Solly and James Maclay. Baker was a 42-year-old from Kent, engaged in the oriental carpet business, who had spent the previous summer in the Rockies with Collie. He amassed one of the finest textile archives in the world, and with his brother started a fabric company which now has a Royal Warrant supplying Britain's royal palaces. Solly was a solicitor and one-time Mayor of Birkenhead. In 1892 he led a party, including Baker, on the first ascent of Eagle's Nest Ridge Direct (Mild Very Severe) on Great Gable, a route so ahead of its time they discussed the advisability of recording it. This was a current safety issue. It was felt information on severe climbs should be kept amongst a select, competent few, and that word of mouth was the best vehicle for doing this.

Maclay, Solly's brother-in-law, was a strict teetotaller but his brother, concerned about unforeseen emergencies, insisted he carried a full hip flask at all times. A heady blend of brandy and chartreuse, this was referred to by wags as 'the temperance drink', the source of much ribbing as well as feigned ailments such as cramp, giddiness and circulatory problems. Maclay, Solly and Baker joined forces for the first ascent of Maclay's Gully (Very Difficult) on Sgurr nan Gillean's First Pinnacle, one of the nearest climbs to the Inn.

The temperance contingent at the Inn was further strengthened by chartered accountant William Naismith, a church elder who as a matter of principle never climbed on a Sunday. One SMC colleague, A M (Sandy) Mackay, recalled their days on the hills: 'I never remember him growling at a bad sky, or discouraged by a bad bit. Out he went, on he went, gaily always, and the condition just yielded to optimism. He never had a boast – hence some of his best efforts, like the Tooth itself, passed at first as if ordinary affairs.'[5] Naismith's natural conservativeness and modesty prevented him from entertaining any attempts to ordain him as SMC president. However, it did not stop him trying his hand at a remarkably varied range of sports: boxing, in which he sparred with Gilbert Thomson, horse-riding, ice-skating, canoeing, and even ballooning over Glasgow. The only flaw in Naismith's moral integrity appeared to be a streak of chauvinism when beaten to first ascents by what he termed 'glaikit Englishers'.

Naismith was accompanied in Skye by W W King and William Douglas. As well as partnering Collie in the Cuillin, King accompanied Naismith on several alpine trips. A Midlands-based solicitor, he is inexorably linked to the chimneys of the Cuillin where he is commemorated in two contrasting climbs: King's Chimney on Sgurr Mhic Coinnich and King's Cave Chimney on Am Basteir.

The 'modest but indispensable' William Douglas was a publisher with the Douglas & Foulis Company in Edinburgh. His father, David Douglas, was a friend of Alexander Nicolson. A genial man, he was nevertheless renowned, as *SMC Journal* editor, for hectoring more slovenly members to reach for the quill. His forthcoming marriage, with its attendant responsibilities, was almost treated like a bereavement by his club-mates: 'Now he cultivates climbing roses and Alpine plants in his garden.' Despite the threat of domesticity Douglas remained very much a pivotal mainstay of the SMC, a focal point for more active members who made a point of keeping him in touch with their adventures on the hills, and tittle-tattle from the meets. His name lives on in the Douglas-Gibson Gully on Lochnagar (along with aforementioned J H Gibson), and his eponymous, hypertrophied boulder on Ben Nevis.

On 8th August 1898, the all-William team of Douglas, King and Naismith drove by pony and trap to Glen Brittle from where they made their way up Sgurr Sgumain by 'a gully from the lochan'. Precise details of their climb have not survived but one option is a repeat of Heathcote's Gully (Moderate). An artist and early writer on St Kilda and its rock climbing tradition, J Norman Heathcote was a first cousin of Dame Flora MacLeod of Dunvegan. He also lived in a castle, Conington near Peterborough. His companion for the Sgurr Sgumain climb was the Reverend George Broke, Rector of Holme, a neighbouring parish in Cambridgeshire where he instigated the idea of a floating church, the Fenland Ark, to serve inaccessible parts of the area.

After their climb on Sgurr Sgumain, Douglas, King and Naismith ascended the Thearlaich-Dubh Gap Gully (Grade 2) to Sgurr Thearlaich. They then continued to Mhic Choinnich where, after first attempting a line to the left, they made the first ascent of King's Chimney (Very Difficult). They returned to Sligachan over Druim nan Ramh and then down through Harta Corrie. King says surprisingly little about King's Chimney, now an integral part of the Main Ridge Traverse. Although an accurate diagram was drawn in the Sligachan's Climbers' Book, many subsequent parties either failed to correctly identify the climb or were put off by its appearance. As today's climbers assess a route from below by the prevalence of cracks for placing modern protection, those of the 1890s were looking for hitches: spikes and bollards behind which they could pass the rope to safeguard each other. Despite the name, King's Chimney was in reality an open corner. Features like this were not popular at the time, presumably because they generally provided fewer hitches than the more broken chimneys, gullies or ridges.

Harold Raeburn was keen to repeat King's Chimney, and four weeks later set out with John Mackenzie on foot from Sligachan. This was a day that once again demonstrated the fitness of these pioneering climbers. The weather was exceedingly hot but, after cooling off in Loch Coire Lagan, Raeburn succeeded in completing the second ascent of the route: 'This is a fine climb which looks hopeless from below but is, if a hitch is made round one of the jammed blocks in the chimney, quite safe and owing to the splendid holds, not difficult.' They continued along the ridge to the Inaccessible Pinnacle where Raeburn added a direct start to its North-West Corner. They then followed the Main Ridge to An Dorus where they set off for the Inn by way of Bealach a' Mhaim. Raeburn, as ever watching the clock, recorded the day's times: left Sligachan 8.08am, back 7.16pm.

In August 1889 the ubiquitous W E Corlett and E Kidson were some of the first to seriously examine the climbing potential of the Bhasteir Tooth, but concluded that a direct ascent was impossible. Several years later William Douglas took a breather below this dramatic prow of rock. Munching a jam sandwich, he managed to mentally link the cracks and ledges on the south face into something of a possibility. Naismith expressed great interest in Douglas's discovery but was concerned about the exposed, tenuous-looking final moves. It wouldn't be long till he was having a closer look.

A week after the first ascent of King's Chimney, Naismith teamed up with J F Dobson and A M Mackay for the first ascent of Forked Chimney by the left branch (Very Difficult) on Sgurr nan Gillean. Mackay, currently a 23-year-old student at Cambridge, was later Lord Advocate, the chief law-officer for Scotland. At Cambridge Mackay became a regular climbing partner of Geoffrey Winthrop Young who described him as 'in his day one of the best mountain climbers in Scotland'. Mackay excelled at many other sports: he captained Aberdeen University Cricket Club, played rugby for London Scottish, represented Scotland at tennis, and was also a fine golfer, curler and billiards player. Mackay was still smarting from two months earlier, when he was knocked out of the Wimbledon Men's Singles at the first round, in straight sets.

After Forked Chimney, Naismith and Mackay set off to the Bhasteir Tooth to examine the final section of the proposed route using a rope from above. Mackay takes up the story of Naismith's Route (Severe):

> Looking from above over the edge, it did really seem to me undercut. But I roped him, and then I lay, squatting far back, and let him down gingerly over the sharp edge. Slowly Naismith used the rock handrail which goes sloping down in a westerly direction for about twenty-five feet to the first rest. And I do not know if any feat of nerve needs more stiffening than to be the first to dangle on a hand traverse. Back he came and reported all was well so far, but had grave doubts of the approaches below. Down the long leg to the Lota Corrie we went and up to the col, and quite soon we were far out on an almost level stretch. One thing which photographs rather fail to make clear is the alarming rate at which the scree drops away there, so that when you have gone out what looks like only thirty yards, you already have a direct fall of apparently 200 feet or more to hard-looking gabbro boulders.
>
> From that point Naismith became more doubtful, the middle pitch looks so very steep. On he went, and this portion proved to have good holds, although monstrous steep. All at once, it seemed, he was at the hand traverse, and tackled it forthwith, and I admired his little toes scraping, and no more, on the rough incline. But now he was triumphant. It could go.[6]

Naismith himself described the route as 'delightfully sensational, but easy, and saves the long descent into Lota Corrie'. The day after this spectacular face climb, Naismith teamed up with G B (George Bennett) Gibbs, a bank clerk just arrived from his native Sunderland. They made an abortive attempt on Sgurr a' Mhadaidh's Deep Gash Gully, then known as the Tairneilear Chasm, spending three hours trying to overcome the formidable second pitch. Naismith also made two attempts on the Bhasteir Nick Gully, the dank labyrinthine slit between Am Basteir and the Tooth, now better known as King's Cave Chimney (Very Difficult). At its top William Inglis Clark had previously investigated small holes breathing draughts of cold air. From below there was a sight to gladden the heart of any Victorian climber: a wet, greasy gully disappearing up into a dank and dingy cave. Although John Bell and John Napier had had a cursory examination from below two years earlier, in July 1896, no one had yet succeeded in penetrating the narrow tunnels and Stygian recesses that linked these features.

Naismith descended his Tooth climb two days after the first ascent and was now keen to climb up the enclosed chimney and complete the circumvention of the whole pinnacle. He opened the campaign with King and Gibbs on 17 August but they were forced to retreat and return the next day with some vital equipment, the string and spare bootlaces that the convoluted rope manoeuvres required. They were again unsuccessful on what was sadly Naismith's last day. (He eventually did the climb on a subsequent visit in 1912.) King, who was sidelined from the Tooth climb due to a strained thumb, announced, with the addition of a geological hammer to his equipment rack, that the days of the subtle approach were over.

With John Mackenzie added to the party the critical breakthrough came on 25th August. It was a windier day than usual and King noticed a draught of fresh air coming down from the back of the cave, a slot leading up to daylight. As this looked extremely narrow they decided to forego lunch. King was eventually able, in true pot-holing style, to follow the cold draught to its source: 'We heard a joyful yodel high up in the free air.' Gibb's account in the *SMC Journal*, 'The Bhasteir Nick Gully, or Twelve Hours in a Cave,' is typical of the best of its time, illustrated with attractive full-page diagrams.

Between Naismith's departure and the eventual ascent of King's Cave Chimney, Gibbs and King also spent a couple of days exploring the Glen Brittle corries. Along with Dobson they climbed the pinnacled ridge that divided Coire a' Ghreadaidh into two, the North-West Ridge (Moderate) which leads over the summit of Sgurr Eadar da Choire to the Main Ridge. Later the same day they re-ascended to the summit by way of a chimney, possibly what is now known as Hamish's Chimney (Difficult). Two days later Gibbs and King teamed up with John Mackenzie for the first ascent of Banachdich Gully (Very Difficult) the prominent, square-cut and often wet cleft that splits the slabs of Coire Banachdich.

After a night in Glen Brittle, Gibbs and Mackenzie climbed the Inaccessible Pinnacle where they tied two 60ft (18m) ropes together and lowered them to King who was keen to examine the pinnacle's prominent South Crack (Very Difficult) on a top-rope: 'The initial part is the most difficult and a slip here would be most serious. It was not found necessary to come upon the rope but its

THE BLACK CUILLIN

moral support was very great.'

The late arrivals of the 1898 season included Harold Raeburn, William Garden, A W (Arthur) Russell and Alec Fraser, an Edinburgh insurance clerk. The 33-year-old Raeburn was especially keen to make up for lost time. With G B Gibbs he completed the first 'traverse' of the Bhasteir Tooth: up Naismith's Route and down King's Cave Chimney. Arthur Russell, a law student when he joined the SMC in 1896 (he remained a member until 1967), was a keen cyclist who regularly used a combination of bike and train to approach the hills. Russell recorded the latter part of the 1898 season in his diary, which included details of the first ascent of Foxes' Rake (Moderate), a classic scramble on Sgurr a' Mhadaidh (see 31 August below):

28 August. After breakfast Garden and I went up with Raeburn and Gibbs to Bhasteir Corrie, heavy hail showers and mist prevented any good photos of Sgurr nan Gillean. Luncheon in the Bhasteir Cave, passing the spot where Foster's friend had hurt himself a few days previous. Then round to the other side of the Bhasteir, where Garden and I watched the others do the Traverse climb, a very good thing, some 150 feet. Then back to the Cave to await their descent by the Cave route and home by Fionn Choire, climbing a boulder on the way and seeing two deer.

29 August. Raeburn and Gibbs off to Blaven and Clach Glas. Garden and I with John Mackenzie made for Sgurr nan Gillean by Pinnacle Route. It turned out a real Skye day, very wet and strong gale so that on the top we could not do the ridge to the Bhasteir. The descent of the central pinnacle was made by the right-hand route into the gully. The descent from the summit by the ordinary Tourist Route in thick mist and rain. Fast home over the moor; five hours out.

31 August. Alec Fraser had arrived last night so Raeburn, he and I started out for Sgurr a' Mhadaidh, Garden taking an off-day, passing Bealach a' Mhaim and over Coire na Creiche and into Coir' a' Tairneilear. No mention of right-hand buttress so we attacked it and found an easy ledge running up its face which brought us out on the Thuilm Ridge near the 2990 top. Quitting the ridge we climbed up by a small cave chimney and passed along to the right-hand peak 3020 and then back over the various other peaks to the Bealach na Glaic Moire. Over the various peaks of Bidein and on to the Castles, descending straight to the col and up over Bruach na Frithe and down by Fionn Choire.[7]

In 1903, Mrs Sharp left the Sligachan Inn for the Golf Hotel in Montrose, looking forward to a conventional routine where dinner was served in the evening and breakfast in the morning. She presented the SMC with the Sligachan Climbers' Book. The club lodged the original book, covering the period 1893 to 1903, in their library but made a typewritten copy with additional route descriptions, photographs, articles and a map. This was compiled and bound by William Douglas to create a 'handsome volume' that from the spring of 1905 was a vital source of information at the Inn. Blank pages were left for future routes and comments. Douglas also included a draft of his own guide to the Cuillin, welcoming additions and corrections in the interim until its publication in the 1907 *SMC Journal.*

Although intended for the use of all climbers the volume remained the property of the SMC to whom it was returned every November for indexing. On page one, Inglis Clark laid down the law: 'Climbers are requested to assist loyally in preserving the book from defacement or destruction: to this end it must be returned to the Manager of the Hotel after use and must not be allowed to lie about on tables or the like.' The Climbers' Book, an invaluable record of climbing in the Cuillin going back to 1893, went missing in the early 1990s. The original in Edinburgh had been updated with some typewritten notes ending around 1920, but only the Sligachan version covered the period after this. When an article was written mentioning its disappearance, someone somewhere had a pang of conscience. In the porch of the Sligachan Hotel, near Norman Collie's old chair, a polythene bag was discreetly left with the missing book inside.

After Mrs Sharp's departure in 1903 the hotel was run by a consortium, the Sligachan Inn Company. John Campbell, who trained at the prestigious St Enoch Station Hotel in Glasgow, was appointed manager. The son of Samuel Campbell, proprietor of the Broadford Stores, contemporary accounts are generous in their praise of his Skye courtesy and hospitality:

Ashley Abraham: 'Its manager, Mr Campbell, has an excellent knowledge of the requirements of climbers and spares no pains to make them comfortable. I remember with feelings of gratitude sundry dinners eaten long after midnight, when my party returned wet and tired, expecting little more than the roughest and scantiest meal.'[8]

G D Valentine: 'Small, quiet and unobtrusive, he never raised his voice, and his face was seldom seen, but his influence was felt at every turn, and made all wheels run smoothly.'[9]

Soon after John Campbell started as manager there was another extension to the building to cope with increased demand. By 1905 there were eleven single and seventeen double bedrooms. Leslie Shadbolt recalled how bachelors were housed in a corrugated-iron annexe on the site of which was built, in 1930, the imposing south wing of the hotel. Evenings at the Inn were spent relaxing in the smoking-room, planning climbs and tracing prospective routes on the six-inch OS map and photographs that lined the walls, while the main window framed the real thing. Anything too ambitious could be soberly reassessed over a pipe on the Telford bridge. The parapets here were used as a training venue, or to demonstrate, along with instructive commentary, the day's most memorable moves. Climbing inns like Sligachan proved a safety valve from the stifling conventions of the Victorian home. The Sligachan smoking-room provided scope for the exuberant capers and gymnastic competitions that climbers revelled in. A favourite routine involved feats of strength on a rope slung from the roof beams. Another popular pastime was singing, raising the afore-mentioned rafters with rousing choruses like the SMC club song:

Oh, my big hobnailers! Oh, my big hobnailers!
How they speak of mountain peak,
And lengthy stride o'er moorland wide!
Oh, my big hobnailers! Oh, my big hobnailers!
Memories raise of joyous days
Upon the mountain side!

Among regular visitors there was a fair share of musical talent: Hugh Munro was a flautist, Sandy Mackay a keen fiddler; Alastair McLaren and William Garden were talented pipers. The latter was inspired by the Cuillin to compose a slow air entitled *Coire na Creiche*. While Garden was resident at the Inn, guests enjoying a nap were rudely awoken as he piped patriotically between the hotel door and the bridge. It was not uncommon for the Inn to stage impromptu dances when mountaineer, angler and tourist joined forces for a Highland Reel or lively quadrille.

One visitor who almost certainly would not have joined in was Lytton Strachey, eminent biographer and one of the subjects of the 1995 movie *Carrington*. He chose Sligachan as a restorative mountain resort to expurgate the ill-effects of an unrequited infatuation with Rupert Brooke (he was also smitten with George Mallory). When asked what he thought about the dark peaks of the Cuillin, the foppish Strachey pronounced them, in his shrill falsetto, 'simply absurd'. But he was not the only literary celebrity to visit.

The writer John Buchan set a short story, *The Knees of the Gods*, at Sligachan Inn; a dystopian mountaineering world where whisky and tobacco are banned, where the Main Ridge is only a challenge at night in winter, and Waterpipe Gully after a week's rain: 'The ancient barn-like shape had been changed. The well-worn sofa had gone; gone, too, the moth-eaten deer's horn above the fireplace, the rickety writing-tables, the few well-thumbed books. The place was furnished like a sitting-room at the Ritz, but it was none the less the smoking-room of the Sligachan Inn.'[10]

Buchan was introduced to climbing by Stair 'Sandy' Gillon, a student friend at Oxford who, in October 1904, proposed him for membership of the SMC. Buchan wrote in his autobiography, *Memory Hold the Door*: 'But my favourite ground was our Scottish hills, especially Skye and the Coolins. In them it was still possible to make first ascents, and I came to know every crack and cranny from Gars-bheinn to Sgurr nan Gillean. It was my ambition to be the first to traverse the whole range in a summer's day, but I put off the enterprise too long and others got in before me.'[11]

John Buchan was more expansive in a speech he made in Glasgow in 1907: 'There is a small band of climbers, of which I am a humble member, who go every year to Skye, and we are not prepared to put our beloved Coolins second to anything. Several of us have climbed in many lands and at least one is a famous pioneer in the Himalayas, so our opinion is not based on ignorance. I am not going to talk much about Skye, because when I begin it is impossible to stop me.'

In his writing Buchan frequently drew on his knowledge of the range to create composite landscapes for his rollicking spy adventures like *The Three Hostages* and *Mr Standfast*. In the former he uses Cuillin place-names: 'Sgurr Dearg', 'Mad Burn', and 'Pinnacle Ridge'. In the latter, as a backdrop for stalking German spies, he introduced elements of Window Buttress and the Cioch:

> The sun was westering, and its light fell upon the rock-wall above the place where I had abandoned my search for the spoor. As I gazed at it idly I saw a curious thing. It seemed to be split in two and a shaft of sunlight came through between. There could be no doubt about it. I saw the end of the shaft on the moor beneath, while all the rest lay in shadow. I rubbed my eyes, and got out my glasses. Then I guessed the explanation. There was a rock tower close against the face of the main precipice, and indistinguishable from it to any one looking direct at the face. Only when the sun fell on it obliquely could it be discovered.[12]

Buchan made several autumn visits to the Cuillin between his return from South Africa, restless and unsettled in 1903, and his marriage in 1907. In 1905, Buchan and his brother Walter had a climbing holiday on Skye when they engaged John Mackenzie. In a letter to Sandy Gillon, John Buchan wrote: 'John says we are the fastest people on the hills he has ever seen except the Gurkhas whom Major Bruce brought up here some years ago.' The energetic Buchan ticked off many of the classic climbs but his only new route was a variation on Sgurr nan Gillean in October 1905, 'The most sensational piece of cliff climbing I have ever done.' John Mackenzie was keen to name the climb 'Buchan's Chimney' but it is now known as the Right Branch of Forked Chimney. Buchan elaborated on the climb in an article in *Blackwood's Magazine*:

> The hardest ascent I ever made in Skye was the highest pinnacle of Sgurr nan Gillean by one of the chimneys from the Bhasteir Corrie. I am still in doubt about that chimney. It may have been what was called in the Sligachan Inn Book, the Forked Chimney, but if so we lost the road, for after the first pitch it bore no resemblance to the official description. As we made the ascent, the first hundred feet lay up an easy chimney, whose only fault was that it was too narrow for foot and back and too wide for knee and shoulder. The whole climb was barely four hundred feet, but it took five hours, and the writer will think twice before repeating it.[13]

The exhilaration of this new climb stayed with Buchan for a long time and he used the experience in his 1924 novel *The Three Hostages*. (Incidentally, the location and some of the plot of *The Thirty-Nine Steps* were possibly inspired by events that occurred in March 1915, the time Buchan was working on the novel, when an SMC party led by John Rennie was recruited to hunt for German spies reputedly hiding out in the Galloway hills.) Several years after his adventures in *The Thirty-Nine Steps* Richard Hannay returned to take on a gang of criminals led by Dominick Medina in *The Three Hostages*. In the novel's dramatic climax, Hannay is pursued up Sgurr nan Gillean's Bhasteir face by his sinister adversary:

> I came to a fork. The branch on the left looked hopeless, while that on the right seemed to offer some chances. But I stopped to consider, for I remembered something. I remembered that this was the chimney which I had prospected three weeks before when I climbed the Pinnacle Ridge. I had prospected it from above, and had come to the conclusion that, while the left fork might be climbed, the right was impossible or nearly so, for, modestly as it began, it ran out into a fearsome crack on the face of the cliff, and did not become a chimney again till after a hundred feet of unclimbable rotten granite. So I tried the left fork, which looked horribly unpromising. The first trouble was a chockstone, which I managed to climb round, and then the confounded thing widened and became perpendicular. I remembered that I had believed that a way could be found by taking the right-hand face, and in the excitement of the climb I forgot all the precautions. It simply did not occur to me that this face route might bring me in sight of eyes which at all costs I must avoid.[14]

Medina eventually falls to his death. Buchan's location for his demise is no coincidence as in reality this area was a notorious black spot for accidents. Although George Abraham wrote in 1910 that there had, as yet, been no accidents to roped parties climbing in the Cuillin, there had been at least four fatalities involving unroped parties. (In 1905 there were nearly 200 deaths in the Alps.) Coincidentally, all four accidents occurred on Sgurr nan Gillean. In September 1870 there was another 'melancholy incident' when John Thom from Liverpool was killed descending the mountain after becoming benighted.

In 1891 there was a fatality in the Nicolson's Chimney area due to giddiness, the same ploy John Buchan uses to despatch Medina in *The Three Hostages*. In 1901, Aberdonian lawyer Alexander Whincup was fatally injured after falling near the Doctor's Gullies. Two years later Malcolm Allen from London died from a fractured skull sustained in a fall. His body was discovered at the foot of the First Pinnacle after search parties led by John Mackenzie, and including Dr J Ellis Milne of Aberdeen, had been out for two days and a night. One explanation for some of these incidents may lie in the confusion over the location of the climbs there. Deep Chimney was originally known as Jammed Block Chimney, and in the 1907 SMC guide Nicolson's Chimney was mistaken for Doctor's Gully.

The start of John Campbell's tenure at Sligachan coincided with a resurgence of SMC activity on Skye, following a quiet spell resting their laurels after the vintage summer seasons of 1896 and 1898. Two short but very significant events stand out: the 1903 and 1905 Easter Meets at the Inn. At the helm was William Inglis Clark, the SMC secretary from 1901 until 1913 who effectively fulfilled the role of club fixer, for example negotiating reduced rates for members at the Sligachan Inn. His diplomatic skills were increasingly required at a time when disturbance of the stalking was leading to greater restrictions on the hills. Keepers were occasionally positioned to prevent access to Harta Corrie and some farmhouses, like Camasunary, were forbidden to take in visitors unless by prior arrangement.

These changes were soon apparent to Claude and Guy Barton, leading Lake District activists. After camping without permission at Coruisk in July 1903, the brothers received a belligerent four-page letter from the proprietor: 'Camping in Strathaird has never been allowed without permission, first asked and obtained. Where odd camps have been found belonging to people like yourselves, camping under a misapprehension, the campers have been promptly removed.' Three years later, the Gimson brothers and J S Sloane, who were inspired to emulate the 1897 SMC camp at Loch Coruisk, but under canvas, did ask for permission to camp for a fortnight and were 'most hospitably entertained' by the proprietor R L (Lawrence) Thomson, at Camasunary on their way home.

The SMC had two official meets each year, at New Year and at Easter. The Reverend A E Robertson gave a flavour of what they entailed:

> At these times a hotel is fixed on or near some good climbing ground. There a goodly gathering assembles for three or four days, perhaps twenty to thirty members turning up at New Year, thirty to forty at Easter. It is a merry party, and good humour and fellowship prevail. Dividing themselves up into small parties of three or four, they tackle the various climbs according to the individual experience of the party, the more experienced doing the more difficult climbs. In this way men of kindred interests are brought together,

friendships are formed, and the sport advanced.[15]

For the Easter Meets of 1903 and 1905 Inglis Clark was at the height of his organisational powers, negotiating with R L Thomson for accommodation at Camasunary where, between the lodge and the farm, there were sufficient beds for six (the farm is now a roofless building near the lodge). Thomson bought Strathaird in 1897 (he also owned the island of Eigg where he kept his coffin under the bed) and since 1902 leased the sporting and fishing rights in the Coruisk basin from Norman McLeod of Dunvegan. Originally known as MacEwen, Thomson had made his money as an arms dealer supplying weapons for revolutions in Chile, Peru and Afghanistan, as well as being an agent for Jardine Mathieson.

At Glen Brittle, Clark also arranged with Mr E Palmer Morewood for the use of Glen Brittle House where two bedrooms and the attic could accommodate five, 'Though not luxurious, members will be sufficiently comfortable.' The limited beds at these strategic locations were allocated by ballot. With provisions delivered by pony from Sligachan, the triangular arrangement made possible longer and more ambitious expeditions. In an SMC circular Clark proposed an itinerary for attendees, based on that used by the Abraham brothers in 1896:

First Day: Ascent of Sgurr nan Gillean by Pinnacle Route, returning to Sligachan (a) Sgurr na h-Uamha and Bloody Stone; (b) by the Gendarme to the Bhasteir Tooth with descent either to Lota or Bhasteir Corrie.
Second Day: Traverse of Clach Glas and Blaven, sleeping at Camasunary.
Third Day: Over Sgurr na Stri, or by Bad Step to Loch Coruisk, and thence by Sgurr Dubh Mor to the 'Gap' and Sgurr Alasdair, sleeping at Glen Brittle.
Fourth Day: Direct to the Inaccessible, thence along main ridge to Fionn Choire and Sligachan.

For the excursion to Skye at Easter 1903 Clark had reserved a heated through-carriage from Edinburgh to Mallaig for connection with the Portree steamer. In the *SMC Journal*, W C Smith praised 'Clarkie' for the party's comfortable journey: 'The transit from Edinburgh to Portree was accomplished in the smoothest possible manner in about twelve hours, and at a phenomenally low cost. All difficulties disappeared before the organising genius of the Secretary. A saloon carriage served as sleeping, smoke, and map room until Crianlarich, when it began to be used for the purposes of a Highland breakfast, a somewhat lengthy operation.' He even arranged with Mr Macbrayne for 12 members to be disembarked by small boat at Sconser.

The Easters of 1903 and 1905 were both at the end of prolonged, snowy winters. Photographs taken on the Meets vouch for the quantity of snow and ice present. These two winters saw the conclusion of the initial exploration of the Cuillin under snow, when most of the main peaks including the Bla Bheinn-Clach Glas traverse had now been done in winter or alpine condition. Accounts of 1903, when 'we had snow down to sea-level every night till the last day of the Meet', are peppered with the mention of iced rocks and stinging hail. Two years later conditions were almost as severe though the lower and south-facing rocks tended to be clear of snow.

As with the Alpine Club party and the Eton masters during the Easters of the early 1890s, many of the achievements of these SMC meets were not given due credit as first winter ascents. At the turn of the century, outside of gullies, there was still no clear distinction between winter and summer climbing; iced or snowed-up ascents were regarded as rock climbs done under challenging conditions. This resulted in many routes being recorded as summer excursions although first climbed under severe winter conditions, a confusion that has obfuscated some outstanding achievements by late nineteenth/early twentieth century mountaineers who have not received the credit due to them, none more so than Harold Raeburn. From North Trident Buttress (III) on Ben Nevis in 1904, until Observatory Ridge (IV) in 1920, Raeburn was involved in every major first winter ascent in Scotland.

Raeburn, who was from an Edinburgh brewing family, dedicated his 1920 book *Mountaineering Art* to close friend W N (William) Ling. They partnered each other from the Dolomites, through the Alps and Norway, to the Caucasus. Ling, a Carlisle grain merchant, helped Raeburn forge strong links with the Lake District and its Fell and Rock Climbing Club. Ling described his friend as: 'Gifted by nature with a marvellous sense of balance, a wiry frame, and an extraordinary suppleness of limb, he added to these a cool judgement, entire fearlessness, and an indomitable will which refused to be beaten.'[16] Accounts of the 1903 Skye Easter Meet certainly back this last statement up, when Raeburn frequently led his party up intimidating ground in ferocious conditions.

On the Friday of the 1903 Meet, Raeburn and Ling left Sligachan for the Dubh Ridge in the company of two cousins, Charles and Harry Walker, commemorated in their 1904 ascent of Cousin's Buttress (Very Difficult) on Ben Nevis. The Walkers were managers in the family business, the Caldrum Works in Dundee, one of the largest jute mills in Britain. It would be a day of bitterly cold winds when it was sometimes difficult to keep your balance. The four breakfasted at the Inn for 6am and were off down Glen Sigachan in fine weather just over an hour later. They crossed Druim Hain to Loch Coruisk where there were now stepping stones to help cross the river. They then started up the slabs of the ridge, down-climbing the drop from Sgurr Dubh Beag to reach the summit of Sgurr Dubh just after 2pm. They continued, in increasingly wintry conditions, to the Thearlaich-Dubh Gap. When ascending the long side it was standard practice for the leader to throw the rope up over a projection or 'hitch' to protect themselves, but Raeburn was unable to do this: 'It was very cold here, and the snow was being blown through the gap, plastering the rocks and obscuring the holds.'[17] He virtually soloed the climb, a phenomenal feat in the prevailing circumstances. Crossing the Gap from one side to the other took the party of three exactly one hour in exacting conditions (compare and contrast with contemporary times).

From the top of the gap Raeburn's party continued over Alasdair and Sgumain into Coire Lagan and, eventually, the comfort and warmth of Glen Brittle House where they were greeted by Mr Morewood, 'glass in hand', and his 'stately Norwegian maid named Ingred'. What the SMC party were not aware of was that their host was on the run from the law for a notorious crime. Several years earlier Palmer-Morewood and his four brothers gathered for Christmas at the family home, Alfreton Hall in Derbyshire. The four younger brothers confronted and brutally attacked the eldest, Charles, reputedly holding a revolver to his head, to try and force him to sign a document to their financial advantage. He resisted but was beaten unconscious and left naked in a pool of blood. The brothers were arrested but only charged with assault. Released on bail they absconded to, as rumour had it, Spain or America. But Ernest Augustus Palmer-Morewood had eventually made his way north to a remote Highland glen. The *New York Times* reported the case as indicative of the moral decline of the British upper classes. Oblivious to the scandal, Willie Ling dealt with more pressing matters, the day's times:

Leave Sligachan, 7.10.
Druim Hain col, 9.25.
Loch Coruisk, 9.40.
Second breakfast, top of Mad Burn, 10.20 (20 minutes).
Sgurr Dubh Beag, 1.10.
Sgurr Dubh Mor, 2.10.
Sgurr Dubh an Da Bhein, 2.40.
Thearlaich-Dubh Gap, top south side, 2.50.
Thearlaich-Dubh Gap, top north side, 3.50.
Sgurr Thearlaich, 4.05.
Sgurr Alasdair, 4.20.
Sgurr Sgumain, 5.05.
Glen Brittle House (Mr
 and music),
 7.20 (despite getting lost in mist).
Total: 12 hours 10 minutes.

At the other end of the range conditions were no less challenging for the Sligachan contingent. Frank Goggs, Euan Robertson and Charles Nettleton, a man famous for giving Aleister Crowley a black eye, were forced to abandon their attempt on Pinnacle Ridge at Knight's Peak. Although the next day, Saturday, brought yet more hail squalls, Raeburn, Ling and the Walkers returned up through Coire Lagan to the col between Sgurr Thearlaich and Sgurr Mhic Choinnich. After roping up, they descended the icy gully on the Coruisk side till they were able to reach the day's objective, a climb on Sgurr Mhic Chionnich starting from the East Face Rake. Raeburn led them 'with much dash and skill' up snow covered slabs until overhanging rock forced them right to easier ground, a climb now known as Raeburn's Route (III). Ling reckoned their new route 'would probably not go in summer when the rocks were bare'.

Despite jets of hail stinging their eyes they continued from the summit of Sgurr Mhic Choinnich to the foot of the Inaccessible Pinnacle. The wild conditions did not deter them from roping up to attempt the pinnacle, but halfway up the climb the cold and hail was so intense they gave up, a phrase rarely used with regard to these early pioneers. They now opted to descend Coire na Banachdich where the waterfalls were being blown aloft by the wind. On reaching the road the group split up; Ling and the Walkers had the short straw, heading into the wind for the long walk over to Sligachan, while Raeburn had a short stroll to Glen Brittle House where he met up with Hugh Munro and D S Campbell. Six years earlier, on the abortive SMC Yacht Meet to Loch Scavaig, Raeburn made a promise to Munro to lead him up the Inaccessible Pinnacle, the one tick in his Tables causing him sleepless nights. The next day (Sunday), Raeburn and Munro, who claimed to have travelled 800 miles to attend the meet, were at the foot of the climb but as it was yet again plated in ice, they did not even contemplate an attempt.

The previous evening Raeburn had warned the new arrivals at Glen Brittle House, James Parker, A E Robertson and Inglis Clark, that conditions on the tops were too severe for rock climbing. So on Sunday morning the trio plumped for the 'easiest' option to reach the next night's accommodation at Camasunary: up Coire Lagan to Bealach Coire Lagain and then descend to Coruisk by way of Coireachean Ruadha. Crossing the bealach involved them in over two hours of step-cutting. Further delays caused by the cameras of Clark and Robertson were beginning to frustrate Parker who had to be back at work in London early Tuesday morning. Once they reached Loch Coruisk, Parker struck off for Sligachan on his own over Druim Hain. With the weather now deteriorating he had to battle down the glen in the dark through snowstorms, bogs and snowdrifts. Parker's consolation, which he only learnt later, was that Clark and Robertson had great difficulty crossing a snowy Bad Step in the twilight and, despite managing to stay dry all day, got soaked wading the river at Camusunary.

In winter Harold Raeburn was constantly experimenting with footwear. He tried different patterns of nails, concluding that clinker-nailed boots with some Swiss-made tricounis at the instep were best for all-round work in Scotland. In Britain crampons, originally called climbing irons or claws, were rarely used.

These climbing aids are of great antiquity going back to Roman times. They were even used by whalers to keep their balance when butchering carcasses. The modern mountaineering design stems from Oscar Eckenstein (1908/12) whose double-hinged version had ten points (there were no front points till the Grivel version in 1929). Almost all mountaineers in Britain still favoured step-cutting with Raeburn arguing that it was more effective for stopping a fall as well as facilitating retreat. George Abraham regarded crampons as prone to mechanical failure and blamed them for disasters to parties in the Alps. In winter a combination of nailed boots and good step-cutting technique proved so effective that crampons didn't cut the ice with British climbers until Vibram-soled boots replaced nails from the 1950s onwards.

Raeburn was also an innovator regarding rock climbing, one of the first to advocate outcrop training. The scabrous gabbro attacked the hands producing a tumescent condition known as 'strawberry fingers' for which he recommended golfing mitts. For the feet he was one of the first in Scotland to try felt-soled scarpetti (kletterschuhe) as used in the Dolomites. Although he reckoned they would not last long 'on the razor-edged crystalline rocks of the Coolin', he decided to test them out on the 1905 SMC Easter Meet to Sligachan.

Raeburn was accompanied on the meet by a Swedish friend, Erik Ullen, a professor at Uppsala University. On the first day the pair teamed up with Godfrey Solly and Cecil Slingsby for a climb on An Caisteal's Harta face. The venue was chosen to obtain shelter from the fierce north-westerly blizzard that blew all day. Raeburn changed to scarpetti for the dry lower slabs of the central buttress, reaching the summit in four hours. This ascent, now known as Raeburn's Route (Difficult), has traditionally been regarded as a summer rock climb but the final tier of cliffs were under winter condition as Raeburn related: 'The chimney was steep and held a good deal of ice, snow, and water.' From the summit of An Caisteal Raeburn and Ullen descended into Lota Corrie before heading for their night's accommodation at Camasunary.

Although the Easter of 1905 was nearly two weeks later than the 1903 meet, the following morning gave rise to a familiar feel: bitter squalls of hail alternating with sunny spells. Raeburn wanted to take advantage of their base to explore the very south of the range, the section of the ridge from Gars-bheinn to Sgurr nan Eag. After climbing Gars-bheinn by its North-East Ridge they set off into the wind along the Main Ridge. By Sgurr Dubh an Da Bheinn they were in the mist. It speaks volumes for Harold Raeburn that he was still game to once again tackle the Thearlaich-Dubh Gap in exacting circumstances:

> It did not look an inviting spot in the present conditions. It was now snowing very heavily, soft, sticky, large flakes that drove levelly through the cleft and quickly plastered even vertical rocks with white. It stuck also on our faces, filled up our eyes and ears, and drifted into our mouths whenever we ventured

to open them…The short descent on the Dubh side was easily done with the aid of a hitched rope, and we dropped on to the sharp snow arete of the col … The best way to climb it, the only possible way under such conditions as we had, is to take to a narrow chimney or crack slightly overhanging the gulf on the Coruisk side. This goes better without a sack. Good holds are to be found near the top of this, and one hand can be used to clear the ice and snow off the little projecting nose at the top of the vertical portion.[18]

At the end of the difficulties they untied the rope but it soon had to be put back on for the descent of Alasdair's South-West Ridge where fresh snow lay over patches of ice. A reflection of Raeburn's competitiveness, and the era's, is demonstrated in how contemporary articles are punctuated with timings that reflect the frenetic pace kept up on the hills. Raeburn's party descended the Sgumain Stone Shoot and 'thirty-six minutes (6.14-6.50pm) after leaving the chaotic boulders of our couloir', reached Glen Brittle where they were greeted at the door by Charlie Inglis Clark and an anxious-looking Hugh Munro. Munro was increasingly desperate to have another go at ticking off the Inaccessible Pinnacle but, due to the prevailing conditions, it was again agreed that any attempt on the pinnacle should be postponed until the weather mellowed.

Munro had a torrid time getting assistance to tackle his nemesis. John Mackenzie was often either fully booked at Sligachan, or engaged for the whole season by Norman Collie at Glen Brittle. Munro never did manage the pinnacle and at his death was just two short of all the peaks on his eponymous list. The next day (Sunday), after an unsuccessful attempt on an icy Banachdich Gully, Raeburn, Ullen, Munro and Clark had the compensation of traversing the Banachdich-Ghreadaidh ridge where they found a lot more ice than they had come across on the southern peaks the day before. Raeburn described the route as 'sensational and decidedly more difficult than the East Ridge of the Weisshorn'.

Those staying at Camasunary also had their share of excitement. On the same day that Raeburn and Ullen were traversing the Thearlaich-Dubh Gap, Harry Walker, William Inglis Clark and T E (Thomas) Goodeve, a railway engineer in Crewe, tackled a winter ascent of Bla Bheinn's Pinnacle Ridge: 'The mountain was heavily coated with snow which however had disappeared from the rocks, leaving them frostbound.'[19] Clark was leading one section when he realised that directly above him was an unstable mass of large blocks. He found himself unable to move up or down as his body was holding the stones in place and the slightest touch would destabilise them. Clark ordered the others to untie from the rope and get rapidly out of the line of fire as he would soon have to move, release the rocks, and hope for the best. Walker courageously stayed put to belay Clark, suffering severe bruising from the rock-fall.

The next morning, despite their close shave, they were all up for 5.30am and away for 7am. They ascended Coire Dubh to the foot of the west face of

Clach Glas where they made the first winter ascent of Pilkington's Gully, the way the mountain was first ascended. After climbing the first two pitches they moved right onto the buttress which proved challenging due to the amount of fresh snow that covered the smooth slabs. They eventually reached Sligachan at 7.15pm.

Harold Raeburn was regarded by Godfrey Solly as 'a character in no way given to self-advertisement'. This contributed to his winter ascents of Green Gully (IV) on Ben Nevis (1906) and Crowberry Gully (III/IV) in Glen Coe (1909) not being recognised until the 1970s. As mentioned above, his winter ascents in Skye were also technically advanced and certainly deserve more recognition. He was described by one contemporary as 'physically and mentally hard as nails'. This determination and drive may well have contributed to his early death. In 1920 he visited Kangchenjunga and also explored the approach to Everest. The next year, aged 56, he was appointed climbing leader of the 1921 Everest Reconnaissance Expedition which included George Mallory. (Ling was offered a place but declined.) Accounts of Raeburn describe him as increasingly cantankerous. In expedition photographs George Mallory comes across as the joker in the pack. In one of the 1921 group portraits Mallory stands behind the seated Raeburn and appears to be pretending to urinate on him. On the approach to Everest Raeburn caught dysentery and was carried, accompanied by the expedition doctor Sandy Wollaston, to a mission in Sikkim to recover. After an absence of three months Raeburn, almost unbelievably, rejoined the expedition and pushed his weakened body to over 22,000ft (6,700m).

The Everest experience, whether emotionally or physically, was one from which he never recovered. In February 1922, not long after his return to Britain, he tried to commit suicide by throwing himself in front of a taxi-cab. He was taken to a nursing home but during the night tried to smash his skull with a poker. Raeburn was then admitted to Craig House, an Edinburgh psychiatric hospital where he spent his last four years until his death in 1926. At one stage he was labouring under the delusion that he had murdered another member of the Everest expedition, Alexander Kellas, Norman Collie's laboratory colleague who probably died from the same dose of dysentery. Raeburn's death certificate read, 'Exhaustion from melancholia.'

Chapter Six

The Book of Abraham

In 1908, the publication of Ashley Abraham's classic book, *Rock-Climbing in Skye*, with its effusive description and stunning photographs of this dramatic new sport, brought the Cuillin to a wider audience. Abraham's joie de vivre shines through every page as the mountains of Skye even rival his local fells: 'The Coolin were the first mountains I saw, outside the English Lakeland, and after my first visit, in spite of a not unnatural jealousy for the honour of my own district, they took the first place in my esteem.'[1]

Although he had two other brothers, Sydney and John, Ashley Abraham is primarily associated with his older brother, George. Born in 1872 George was the slimmer of the two; quiet and unassuming, a neat and cautious climber of the new 'balance school'. Ashley, four years younger, was the more ebullient and extrovert, a natural enthusiast. After Ashley's marriage to Lucy Kennedy, the two brothers lived next door to each other in a semi-detached house on Chestnut Hill, the steep road leading out of Keswick towards Thirlmere: George at *Idwal* (he first met his wife, Winifred Davies, at Lake Idwal in Snowdonia) and Ashley at *The Screes*.

Together the brothers pioneered classic climbs like New West Climb (Very Difficult) on Pillar, the Keswick Brothers' Climb (Very Difficult) on Scafell and Crowberry Ridge Direct (Severe) in Glen Coe where the iconic Abraham's Ledge is named after them. Geoffrey Winthrop Young wrote: 'We never thought of the brothers apart. They complemented each other perfectly: George the more often leading, graceful, supple and balanced; Ashley, a moving column of strength and aggressive energy in support.'[2]

The family photography business in Keswick, G P Abraham Ltd, was founded by their father, George Perry Ashley Abraham, in 1866. Their dramatic mountain photography, displayed at their Lake Road premises (later George Fisher's mountaineering shop), grabbed the attention of many visitors. At Easter 1896, these included a London science teacher who had met Ashley the previous Christmas at Wasdale Head. O G (Owen Glynne) Jones was a man on a mission. He arrived at the shop intent on recruiting the brothers' photographic skills for a book he was writing about Lake District rock climbs. After only a few hours the three new friends were heading into the fells, the start of a brief but highly fruitful collaboration. Although regarded by George Abraham as the finest climber he had ever seen, Jones developed a reputation as a brash and reckless exhibitionist. Norman Collie, who on one occasion rescued Jones from the top of Napes Needle, had little time for him. William Naismith confirmed this in a letter to William Douglas in 1896: 'Collie by the way cannot abide Jones.'

In a mutually beneficial arrangement, Jones found professional photographers with mountaineering experience to illustrate his book, while the brothers obtained a powerful leading climber capable of posing in precarious positions for the long exposures required. With Jones's tutelage and leadership the brothers' climbing ability developed dramatically, enabling them to pioneer an exciting new form of mountain photography that first bore fruit with the classic *Rock-Climbing in the English Lake District*, published in 1897. The book was a bold and innovative production compared to Haskett Smith's 'little red books' and also introduced the earliest version of the existing British grading system, devised by Jones. Although some grudging praise was offered by the climbing establishment, the Abraham brothers continued to be tainted through their association with Jones's dare-devilry, as well as their promotion of potentially dangerous rock climbs, a thorny ethical issue of the day. George was over eighty before he was elected a member of the Alpine Club.

After Jones's death in a fall on the Dent Blanche in 1899, the brothers started work on a book detailing Snowdonia rock climbs, *Rock-Climbing in North Wales*, published by their father in 1906. The Welsh book was a less happy experience as the Pen-y-Pass climbing set was a more close-knit, exclusive community compared to Wasdale Head. Many of them regarded the Abrahams' book as a vulgar intrusion into the spiritual sanctity of *their* mountains, out of true with the prevailing ethos of understatement and high-minded reticence. The prickly Oscar Eckenstein became apoplectic over an innocent comment in the text regarding him. As well as their overtly commercial approach, the brothers were also criticised for the hints of retouching and tilting in their photographs. It was their last credited collaboration before Ashley completed the trilogy with a solo project featuring Skye.

The effect of the Abrahams' books on the mountaineering world cannot be over-emphasised. This was ground-breaking stuff. Although photography was hardly new it was only recently that printing technology had advanced to the extent that their photographs could be reproduced in books and articles with the quality they deserved. Prior to the 1880s there was no way of reproducing photographs directly onto a page; they were either rendered as engravings, just like sketches, or printed separately and glued in. In *Rock-Climbing in Skye* the thirty illustrations are printed using the collotype process, the first method invented for reproducing photographs, and the only way to produce continuous tone prints without using a screen. The method was slow and expensive but produced high quality results.

The Abraham brothers first heard about the mountains of Skye when they met Norman Collie at Wasdale Head. On their first visit to the island, in 1896,

THE BLACK CUILLIN

they based themselves at the Sligachan Inn from 30th April until 14th May. It took them three days to reach Portree from Keswick. After travelling by steamer from Oban to Portree, patience exhausted by frequent stops to load and unload goods and cattle, they eventually arrived at the Inn for some welcome food: 'Whether this was supper or breakfast no one knew or cared.' On this, their first time in the Cuillin, their prime motivation was photography rather than mountain exploration; they were content to climb and record classic routes like the Inaccessible Pinnacle, Pinnacle Ridge and the Druim nan Ramh ridge.

Despite their late arrival at Sligachan they were up early, keen to tackle the famous Pinnacle Ridge. Here Ashley Abraham was instrumental in popularising the leftward descent from the Third Pinnacle as an easier alternative to the original, more awkward route on the right overlooking Coire a' Bhasteir. They were at the summit cairn four hours after leaving the Inn despite some snow and ice which required step-cutting. Descending Sgurr nan Gillean's west ridge they noticed how unstable parts were, with the whole Gendarme area seeming to vibrate in the wind. Ashley's description of the distinctive pinnacle brings this much-missed feature back to life: 'The climber hugs him as closely as though he were a human being and the climber a vagrant after a club dinner.' Ashley predicted that the Gendarme would eventually fall off – which it did in 1987.

Druim nan Ramh (Moderate) gave them another classic day, a panoramic viewpoint with Coruisk to one side and Lota Corrie on the other. After negotiating the initial small gap they continued over the Druim Pinnacle until below the spectacular final tower. They then traversed ledges on the Coruisk side until near Bealach Glaic Mhor, from where they scrambled up the West Peak and then down to the Bridge Stone, a large jammed boulder at the gap below the highest point. At the summit of the Central Peak, despite the late hour, they lingered to enjoy the gloaming before starting the tricky descent to the North-Central gap. Abraham is one of the first to provide a detailed description of this complex section of the ridge, now often abseiled:

> Running due north was a veritable knife-edge of rock; along this we scrambled, with our fingers in Corrie Mhadaidh and the rest of us in Harta Corrie. The ridge ceased at a steep drop of about fifteen feet. Slightly on the Harta Corrie side was a narrow ledge, down which we climbed to the bottom of the steep part. Thence easy going along the skyline brought us to a cairn of three stones, beyond which the rocks were perpendicular. Again a traverse had to be made to the right, and then the route was straight downward, over two huge rock-steps, to the col between the Central and North Peaks.[3]

The Abraham brothers were later invited to stay with Alfred Williams at his huts near Coruisk, an opportunity that made possible a three-day expedition combining some of the classic routes. It was a heavily laden party that started off on the trudge down Glen Sligachan. As it was a Sunday they were unable to hire a pony to help with the transport of their equipment. After leaving their loads at the foot of Druim Hain they set off for Clach Glas, 'one of the shapeliest peaks in Great Britain' according to George. He also referred to it as 'the Matterhorn of Skye', an epithet many other writers adopted.

It is often difficult to interpret the correct sequence of the Abrahams' explorations in the Cuillin as the main source, *Rock-Climbing in Skye*, details routes in geographical, not chronological, order. In his book Ashley describes their Clach Glas-Bla Bheinn traverse as starting with an ascent of Arch Gully (Moderate): 'This is not difficult, but a big chock-stone pitch about halfway up lends distinction to the scramble.' This account, however, may be from a later occasion or a composite of more than one visit as he goes on to relate how they returned to the Inn in the evening by the 'ankle-twisting abomination' of the Glen Sligachan path.

On their trip in May 1896, they were eager to reach William's base at Coruisk by nightfall which left little time for exploration; areas of potential, like Clach Glas's West Face, were noted but left for another day. Similarly they had to avoid the temptation to attempt any of Bla Bheinn's pinnacles and restrict themselves to the normal route by the short wall and 60-foot (18m) chimney. It was then a speedy descent back to their baggage and a beautiful evening walk over Druim Hain to Coruisk. Although Williams' hospitality was up to his usual high standard they had a poor night's sleep: 'The heather mattress with which he provided us was all that could be desired, but unfortunately some rats gnawed at the underside of the flooring boards for the greater part of the night. The rest of the time they spent clambering up one side of our hut and glissading down the other'.[4]

It didn't stop them getting up and away very early to savour the sunrise at the head of Loch Coruisk. From here they ascended into Coireachan Ruadha and climbed slabs to the summit of Sgurr Thearlaich (a Grade 3 scramble known as North-East Rib). After continuing to Sgurr Alasdair they descended to Glen Brittle, the first trees they had seen for weeks, and 'a goodly store of luxuries' sent over from Sligachan. The next day they returned to the Inn by way of the Inaccessible Pinnacle and then the ridge to Sgurr a' Mhadaidh where they dropped into Coire na Creiche to pick up the path over the Bealach a' Mhaim. The Abraham brothers' combination of routes provided a three-day itinerary that in years to come many parties tried to emulate.

The two weeks in Skye produced about fifty images which were marketed as *Skye: A Series of Mountain Photographs*. One Scottish Mountaineering Club reviewer thought some rather theatrical in that they had been 'too manifestly posed'. Nevertheless they were purchased for the club library, a mouth-watering preview for those planning trips to the island.

During the Edwardian era a craze for collecting picture postcards developed. Some of the early Skye photographs were reproduced as postcards, a lucrative trade at the time, and were also widely used to illustrate journal and magazine articles. George was especially active in the latter, between 1904 and 1913, writing pun-packed prose for magazines like *Pall Mall, Cassell's, Wide World* and *The Sphere*, many of which featured the Cuillin. They even had an article in *National Geographic* after its foreign editor visited their Keswick shop in 1935. The avuncular Ashley preferred the limelight, literally, of the lecture circuit where he regularly showed lantern slides to appreciative audiences. The shop at Lake Road, built in 1887, incorporated a lecture theatre, the 250-seat Victoria Hall. The brothers were astute business operators. Although prolific authors, few articles appeared in mountaineering journals which offered no fee. Even potential first ascents had to wait until the main business of photography was completed.

The Abrahams used an Underwood field camera made from heavy mahogany with brass fittings. Focusing was achieved by winding a leather bellows back and forwards until the image appeared sharp on a ground glass plate. This could only be seen in the dark under a focusing cloth which also kept out light when an unexposed plate was inserted. The large size of plate ensured fine definition after being printed and enlarged. There was no choice of shutter speed as on modern cameras; the emulsion on the plates needed lengthy exposures for which the lens cap was removed for the required time, making a tripod essential. With the advent of pre-packaged, dry glass plates you no longer had to be near a darkroom to quickly process the light-sensitive emulsion.

But the Abraham brothers were not the first to photograph the Cuillin. The earliest recorded mountaineering photos were by James Heelis, one of Charles Pilkington's 1887 party, when he employed John MacKenzie to help carry the cumbersome camera equipment. Unfortunately none of his photographs appear to have survived. The earliest existing prints are by Herman Woolley, part of the 1890 Alpine Club group. The next year William Norrie of Fraserburgh, who was photographer for the naturalist John A Harvie-Brown on his Hebridean trips, took a series of pictures around Coruisk and in Coire Lagain.

Photography at this time was restricted to professional photographers like the Abraham brothers or serious amateurs like Howard Priestman, William Douglas or Walter Brunswick. In 1888 George Eastman patented and marketed his 'Kodak' camera, preloaded with celluloid film. You sent the whole camera away to have the film developed and printed: 'You take the pictures we do the rest' was the famous slogan. Now almost everyone could start taking their own snaps of the hills.

Although photographers admired the convenience of these new 'detective' cameras many still wanted the quality and control offered by the older plate cameras. To satisfy this niche, manufacturers produced a range of small quarter-plate cameras, ideal for mountain photography. Watson's, a major British camera supplier, had a branch in Edinburgh where SMC photographers had a choice of the Alpha (quarter and half-plate), The Fram (preloaded with film), the Van Neck (could take either a magazine for 12 glass plates or the Eastman roll-film holder) or the Watson's Dainty, a small quarter-plate camera that fitted in a pocket and was designed with outdoor enthusiasts in mind.

These developments ensured that photographing mountains like the Cuillin was now a more practicable pastime when compared to the weight of equipment carried by the Abraham brothers. In 1892 Howard Priestman did a lot of photography while camping with the Barrow brothers in Glen Brittle. The following year William Douglas recorded his expeditions on camera, some of which were used to illustrate the new Sligachan Climbers' Book. The *SMC Journal* and the 1923 SMC Skye guidebook provided other outlets for the club's photographic talent which included A E Robertson, William Inglis Clark, J R Young, Harry MacRobert and James Parker. Robertson was particularly influenced by the Abrahams' photographs and often tried to replicate their compositions.

In the two years prior to the publication of *Rock-Climbing in Skye* in 1908, Ashley Abraham made four more trips to the island for further research and photography. The first of these was at Easter 1906 when the opening of the West Highland Line to Mallaig and connecting steamer to Portree made for a quicker and more comfortable journey north. However the continuation of late winters meant things weren't so straightforward on the hills. Even reaching the summits proved problematical. With the snow level at 2,000ft (610m) Abraham's party were defeated twice by icy conditions on Sgurr nan Gillean: first on the verglassed rocks below the Gendarme, and three days later on Pinnacle Ridge when they were forced to retreat from the top of the Third Pinnacle. They eventually succeeded in reaching the summit by the Tourist Route in alpine conditions.

An attempt on Raeburn's Route on An Caisteal had to be abandoned due to ice coating the lower slabs. Disillusioned by these setbacks they tried to find a climb free from snow and ice, reckoning that the south ridge of Sgurr na h-Uamha might fit the bill, 'And not a vestige of ice or snow was to be seen.' On the summit they had magnificent views of the Main Ridge and the snow-capped mainland peaks including Ben Nevis. However in no time they were engulfed by a heavy snow shower that soon grew into a full-scale blizzard. Their descent by the North Ridge, possibly a first in winter conditions, developed into a near epic: 'Below it the rocks were glazed with ice, upon which rested about a foot of snow. This had to be cleared away and the rock beneath exposed before progress could be made.'[5]

Ashley returned to Skye two months later, in June, when warmer weather had cleared the mountains of snow. For this major climbing and photographic trip he recruited two friends, Henry Harland from Hull and Alfred Binns from

Sunderland. Harland was a director of the family printing and numerical ticketing firm. A staunch Methodist he was happy to produce any ticket imaginable save those used for greyhound racing. One of Harland's first climbs was an audacious solo ascent of Kern Knotts Crack (VS) on Great Gable, at a time when it was seldom even attempted roped.

After O G Jones's tragic demise in the Alps, Harland became the Abrahams' new supermodel, often kitted out in a white jersey to highlight his position at the crux of the climb. Binns was a Lake District regular, a life-long friend of the Keswick brothers, whose key role in the team was that of rear man with the unenviable task of transporting and safe-guarding the heavy camera equipment that included fragile glass plates and lenses, up constricted Cuillin chimneys and gullies. This cumbersome yet delicate load was often too large to pass behind the chockstones that characterised many climbs, and Binns was forced to untie, rethread the rope, and surmount the outside of the obstacle.

Harland was the eldest of the team at 36, while Binns was 35 and Ashley Abraham 30. These boon companions were summed up by William Naismith as 'a cheery party who worked well together and backed up one another loyally'. Binns and Harland feature in many of the well-known Abraham photographs including that of Naismith's Route on the Bhasteir Tooth. It was common for the brothers to mask out some of the background with tape or paint to allow the main subject to stand out. Evidence of this retouching can be seen in the version that appears in George's *British Mountain Climbs* where a great chasm dramatises the Tooth. The route itself they found 'sensational, even speaking from the Coolin standard in such matters; and fairly long stretches are to be passed before good resting places are available'.[6] That June the trio spent much of their three-week stay repeating the established routes within reach of their base at Sligachan. This included Waterpipe Gully where Harland led the party up the climb in torrential conditions in seven-and-a-half hours, 'A heavy rush of water announced the fact that he was out of its channel and safely at the top of the pitch.' When water levels subsided they returned to the gully 'to dispose themselves in artistic attitudes'. The resulting photographs were yet more hard-won images to be reproduced in various books and articles.

Descending Coire a' Bhasteir late one fine evening Ashley's attention was caught by the low sun highlighting the rocks on the face of the Third Pinnacle. He sat down, lit his pipe and ruminated over the possibilities of creating a new route to the top of the buttress. The initial rocks looked straightforward as far as a prominent ledge where a steep slab led up to below a black-looking cave. The next day Ashley was back at the crag along with Harland and Binns, purposely building a cairn at the foot of the rocks. (Unknown to them the route had already been climbed by Slingsby, Hastings and Edward Hopkinson in 1890.) At the foot of the steep slab they decided that they needed to examine the difficulties from above. After traversing left they ascended Second-Third Gully until they had a good view of the hard section where a crack appeared to split the upper slab with what appeared to be a good anchor at the top. However the day would once again reveal the Abrahams' priorities: they were professional photographers completing a mountaineering assignment, not climbers taking photographs.

As the light had improved they decided to temporarily abandon the climb and return to the Bhasteir Tooth where they had cached their camera equipment until conditions were right for some shots of this spectacular feature. It was after 6pm before the photography was completed and they were able to return to the Third Pinnacle. Harland then led the exposed slab to the black cave. As was usually the case, the exit from the cave proved to be the crux: Harland used Abraham's shoulders, Abraham used Binn's and the latter resorted to the rope and anything else he could get his hands on.

The Abrahams have been credited with introducing combined tactics, where you stand on a companion's shoulders to reach better holds, to British rock climbing. They perfected the technique on their climbs with O G Jones in Wales, when Ashley's 15 stone (95kg) were used as a solid launching pad with George acting as a sort of flying buttress to his brother. George often pointed out a scar on his nose where Jones had perched to gain a few more inches. Ashley Abraham's shoulders feature a great deal in *Rock-Climbing in Skye*. A popular pastime, when foul weather kept climbers indoors at Glen Brittle or Sligachan, was to count how many instances of them being used you could find in the book.

In the early days of rock climbing it was common to resort to the use of shoulders. As climbs got harder more specialised variations of this were contrived to help gain extra height, for example outstretched arms, alpenstocks jammed into cracks or rucksacks on the head. Ashley often protected his cranium with a large handkerchief tucked under his hat. In the context of the time these techniques were not just a crude method of cheating, as often viewed nowadays. Used systematically, combined tactics could prove an effective and fairly sophisticated method for overcoming even sustained difficulties, with sometimes two people climbing together as a unit (see Slanting Gully later in this chapter). To many, combined tactics were the default resort when things looked tricky ahead. This should be borne in mind when comparing and contrasting climbing grades and standards between different eras (including a banked-up Second Step on Everest in 1924?).

These tactics were only slowly seen as unsporting with the Edwardians eventually trying to eliminate them like aid points. Harold Raeburn was a leading critic: 'In some accounts of British climbs which have been published, this method seems to have been rather freely resorted to.'[7] Ashley Abraham disagreed, arguing that the shoulder was a legitimate means to conserve the leader's strength for the upper part of an unprotected pitch. One of his Wasdale Head friends, Lehmann Oppenheimer, felt that it added to the sense of communal effort: 'The climb is done by the party rather than by the individual members of it.'

THE BLACK CUILLIN

The Abraham brothers' photographs document the evolution of climbing techniques from the naive beginnings of British rock climbing through to the adoption of some rudimentary belaying practice. Well into the new century many inappropriate methods prevailed in Britain which had evolved for use in alpine conditions. Safety on glaciers required a party of four or at least three, a convention that was unquestioningly transferred to British rock. Alpenstocks continued to be carried, partially from alpine habit, but also to aid the removal of loose stones or to fend off falling rocks. A version more suited to British hills, Hillman's spiked stick, was in use up to the First World War when it proved particularly useful in Skye for testing the depth of peat bogs or for vaulting swollen burns.

By the end of the nineteenth century rock climbers in Britain stopped moving together, at least on harder sections, but still stayed as close as possible, proceeding in a series of short steps and using every available stance to minimise the length of potential falls. The second protected the leader by passing the rope around a spike or block of rock so that, in the event of a fall, the weight theoretically came on this and not the hands. These were often called a belay pin which, as George Abraham pointed out, could vary in size from 'an eggcup to a country church spire'. They should not be confused with the modern use of the term belay which implies anchoring oneself to the rock. This was rarely done, perhaps copying the alpine need for speed, or possibly because the brevity of most pitches was felt to negate its use.

Within the context of the time this lack of anchoring had some advantages such as flexibility in escaping rock-fall, a much commoner hazard in those pioneering days. The Abrahams did occasionally tie themselves to the rock when taking photographs, for example in Waterpipe Gully, to protect themselves from the dizzying effect of the focusing cloth. Seconds were prepared to stand in cramped and precarious positions if it meant being able to safeguard the leader with a good hitch. For example the long side of the TD Gap was often climbed in three pitches to make use of all the hitches available.

It is remarkable how few accidents or injuries occurred considering the looseness of the terrain and the nature of most early routes: chimneys or gullies which were natural channels for falling rocks. Loose rock was so prevalent that climbers developed specific techniques to deal with the problem: in confined spaces a party climbed in close order while open slabs were ascended in a series of zigzags. An unwritten rule was that there should be no more than one party on the same route. On the ascent of Waterpipe Gully by Ashley Abraham's party, one climber descended back down on a tight rope to dislodge loose material and make the way safer for subsequent climbers. These public-spirited antics also gave legitimacy to the early pioneers' delight in boulder trundling.

Great emphasis was placed on the leader not climbing up what he couldn't climb down, a mantra repeated in instructional books into the 1970s. The SMC's

General Guide-Book (1933) emphasised safety over style: 'Where necessary use your knees, teeth or eyebrows to secure yourself. There are no meticulous rules of deportment in rock climbing.' The same guide advised beginners: 'If you do not lead, trust to your leader and to your own powers before trusting to the rope. In fact, do not trust the rope.' Safety was seen as not falling. The rope was perceived as more of a convention than a safeguard, its main function often wryly regarded as a preventative to losing each other in the mist. The Alpine Club tested climbing ropes at a laboratory but Harold Raeburn remained unimpressed – reckoning that a 12-stone (76kg) man falling 10ft (3m) would break the best climbing rope available.

Up until the 1920s there was only one choice of rope, the same manila hemp that Norman Collie telegraphed John Buckingham's for on his first visit to Sligachan. This company was taken over by Arthur Beale (not to be confused with the French company Beal) who in 1918 brought out an improved rope marked with three red worsted threads, one in the centre of each strand, to distinguish it from others on the market: 'Beware of fraudulent imitations.' The latter included Frederick & Co. of Leeds who sold two versions of alpine rope: green strand for better quality, red for cheaper, and the Edinburgh Roperie and Sailcloth Company whose ropes had a blue strand. For durability hemp ropes were often soaked in pine tar. You generally tied on with a bowline though there was a special knot for those in the middle, the 'running knot to hold', also known as the middleman noose. When climbing the knot was often slid to the side or round the back to keep the rope 'out of the way'. There were three main diameters or 'weights': full (11mm), three-quarters (10mm) and line (8mm).

George Abraham recommended 60ft (15m) for two climbers, 80ft (24m) for three and 100ft (30m) for a party of four (20ft of rope weighed 1lb). He felt that 120ft (36m) was advisable for some of the harder Skye climbs like Slanting Gully and the South Crack of the Inaccessible Pinnacle. However most climbers considered anything over 100ft (30m) a sensationally long run-out. Into the 1920s a 40ft (12m) rope was regarded as perfectly adequate for climbing in the Cuillin, and was even used on some first ascents. When it got wet, hemp became very stiff and awkward to use. In exceptionally cold conditions it was often impossible to untie frozen knots and some parties arrived back at their accommodation still roped together, with seating for dinner having to be hastily rearranged.

Towards the end of their stay in June 1906 the weather turned more settled, so Ashley Abraham, Harland and Binns hired transport to Glen Brittle and a porter to help carry food and bedding up into Coire Lagan. From this new base they first tackled the cliffs of Sgurr Alasdair to the left of Collie's Route, a line with some fine situations. They found the rock to be primarily basalt with only small outcrops of the rougher, more accommodating gabbro, and it provided so few belays that Ashley recommended seconds 'should possess no nerves and little imagination'. Now known as Abraham's Climb (Difficult) it was repeated a few years later by a party led by Francis Greig. On the section overlooking the Stone Shoot the rocks start to steepen as Greig related:

> The holds here are very small, and the leader, as he cautiously works his way straight up, has always in his mind the uncomfortable thought that the second man is resting in a bad position where there is absolutely no hitch to be got for the rope. Above and to the left of this difficult pitch a welcome little saddle of rock projects from the face of the cliff. The leader sits astride this tiny rock rib, which just holds three men, and gives splendid anchorage for those coming up the stiff pitch below.[8]

From the summit of Sgurr Alasdair, Abraham's party continued down to the Thearlaich-Dubh Gap to capture more illustrations for the book, before returning to their bivouac in Coire Lagan. If conditions were right Ashley Abraham was a real enthusiast for sleeping out or camping in the corries and his lively descriptions inspired many others to copy his example:

> Pipe after pipe was enjoyed in huge content, while the night came stealing over the face of the water, and the moon peeped round the shoulder of Sgurr Sgumain, illuminating the peaks above us with a weird, uncertain light. It has been my good fortune to lie on the summit of the Matterhorn and look away across the sea of peaks to Mont Blanc, sixty miles distant; to sit at the old gîte on the Weisshorn, and see the night chase the evening mists up the sides of the Dom and Täschhorn, and to watch the sun rise and flush red over the grand dome of Mont Blanc; but I can recall none of these things, beautiful and memorable as they were, so vividly to mind as that perfect night up in lonely Corrie Lagan.[9]

The next day was their last one in the Cuillin, and Harland and Binns were eager for something meaty to round off their stay. Abraham had an idea. He remembered W W King's top-roped ascent of the Inaccessible Pinnacle's South Crack eight years earlier (a line King spotted on one of the Abrahams' early photos). After a brief inspection of the final moves on a rope from above, they descended to start the climb. South Crack (Hard Very Difficult) is deeper and more defined than appears from below. At times Abraham could only guess at Harland's progress by the occasional puff of tobacco smoke. The hardest part was about 30ft (9m) up where the climber is forced to make a short detour onto the left wall: 'A small foothold on the right wall is the key to the situation and, after testing this well and determining as far as possible the necessary distribution of the balance a foot or two higher, Harland moved slowly upward and soon gained the wider part of the crack where he again disappeared from my sight.'[10] South Crack provides a fine alternative to queuing for the popular East Ridge on this iconic Munro. When it was Abraham's turn to climb he found much to recommend his readers: 'This long stretch of crack reaches a degree of excellence which approximates very nearly to the superlative.'

The Cuillin screes have long had a reputation for destroying boots. In 1835 Charles Lesingham Smith's footwear survived the Alps but not the Cuillin. Similarly James David Forbes' boots fell to bits in Skye and he had to have replacements made by a local cobbler, a transaction that led to a long and contentious correspondence. The Abraham brothers saw boots for the hills change from the ubiquitous hobnailed variety in general use by all and sundry, and very familiar to crofters like John Mackenzie and his neighbours in Sconser, to a more specialised climbing boot. The traditional tackets at the edges were replaced by V-shaped nails called clinkers, while in the centre of the sole, hobs often gave way to star-shaped muggers. However all this nailing conducted cold to the feet which was combated with cork insoles.

George Abraham advocated lighter boots with less nailing but even these required a very controlled, deliberate style of climbing with the leader balancing one clinker on the crux holds for as long as was required. In 1912 traditional nails had competition from the new hard steel tricounis designed by Swiss jeweller Felix Genecand. The interwar period was awash with debate over what type and pattern of nails were best. The lighter, soft steel clinker, despite a need for larger welts and a tendency to fall out more easily, was seen as better for rock climbing in Scotland, while the tricounis' forte was snow and ice where the clinker was best avoided. There were seven different types of tricouni, the most iconic being the two-piece No.6 which fastened to the edge of the boot.

But what type of nail pattern was best? The tricouni manufacturers suggested twenty nails for each boot: six in the heel, eleven around the edges and three in the middle. Instructional books of the period are full of diagrams suggesting various permutations. Robert Lawrie, the paragon of bespoke boot-making, and first choice for early Everest expeditions, narrowed the options down to six distinct patterns: tricounis around the sole, clinkers round heel and muggers in the centre of the soles. However, a consensus was never reached and individual preferences continued to dominate until nails were superseded by Vibrams in the 1950s (these rubber soles mimicked the pattern of nailed boots: clinkers round the edges, muggers in the centre). No longer were you able to tell what parties had a head start on you up the Coire Lagan path where nailed boots left their own unique imprint in the peaty mire. (This footpath and some others were vastly improved in the mid-1990s.)

Many climbers rejected cumbersome nailed boots for harder climbs and adopted light, tight-fitting plimsolls, 'the cheaper the better' as the soles were thinner. This footwear was usually referred to as 'rubbers' but had different regional names: 'pumps' in Manchester, 'sannies' in Glasgow, 'dappers' in Wales, 'gutties' in Northern Ireland. Many regarded the new footwear as 'bad form' and the debate over their use continued for decades. Rubbers were best for face climbs in dry conditions while nails remained the first choice for cracks, chimneys and especially wet rock. Plimsolls could be carried in a pocket for use at the crux; for damp sections socks were often worn over them. When Francis Greig led Abraham's Route on Sgurr Alasdair he wore rubbers but was caught in a downpour at the crux. With his hobnailers back in the last man's rucksack he was forced to climb using his knees for almost twenty minutes.

In June 1907, Ashley Abraham, Binns and Harland returned to Skye with Dr and Mrs A J Wallace in the latter's Sunbeam motorcar. They were also accompanied by Geoffrey Bartrum, a regular at Winthrop Young's Pen-y-Pass parties. The plan was to use this newly popular method of transport to climb from Glen Brittle on good days yet still enjoy the comfort of Sligachan if the weather was inclement, which it was during their first week. The incessant rain provided opportunities to peruse the Climbers' Book and finalise plans. When the weather finally cleared they hired a pony and ghillie to establish a base, Harland's home-made tent, in Coire na Creiche: 'We had exchanged the comforts of Sligachan and its palatial accommodation for the discomfort of one small room eight feet by six, which as far as we knew, might at any moment become deluged with water. And yet, in spite of this, and incredible as it may sound, we were absurdly happy.'[11]

They had intended to camp in the corrie for a week but after just one night the inevitable flooding meant it was back to Sligachan to sit out three more days of stormy weather. But their first day back made up for it. Their aim was to climb Collie's North-West Buttress on Sgurr a' Mhadaidh. However a shout from Binns, who had wandered off to the right, resulted in a change of plan: 'Directly above them was a beautiful narrow chimney, surmounted at the top by a small chock-stone. Above it, receding one beyond the other as far we could see, were chimneys, chock-stones, pitch after pitch, and the clean-cut walls of a gully of most alluring appearance. A great black cave, high up, completed a picture that was calculated to gladden the sight of any rock-climber worthy the name.'[12]

This would become Slanting Gully (Severe) a route that cuts through the height of the cliffs of Sgurr a' Mhadaidh, divided into two sections by Foxes' Rake. A series of interesting pitches on good rock led towards the prominent slanting rake. Harland initially took the lead with Abraham and Bartrum coming next for physical and moral assistance in the shape of shoulders and shouts of encouragement. Bringing up the rear, as usual, was Binns with the plate camera. They knew Foxes' Rake was near the halfway point and were keen to see what lay above. What eventually materialised took them all aback: 'And not without cause, for two thin vertical cracks, each about 40 feet high, and both overhanging at the bottom, were what we saw. These converged at their upper extremities into a small cave, which also overhung. Above this rose the narrow continuation of the gully, which dwindled again higher up to an overhanging crack, which scarcely needed a second glance before being pronounced unclimbable.'[13]

Although it was already 7pm they were prepared to risk a night out if it meant completing the route. Abraham wanted to photograph the first section, the Cracks Pitch, so Bartrum took over as the leader's mobile footholds. Harland led off up the left-hand crack and stopped when he needed assistance. Bartrum then climbed up to him and offered his shoulder. These tactics were repeated until Harland was able to use crude jamming techniques to reach the cave and a good anchorage. The rope was then thrown down, first to Abraham who now had the heavy camera rucksack, and then Binns. A series of jammed boulders led to the overhanging crack: 'This looked just about as impossible as a crack can look.' Harland, game as ever, made a last futile effort but his arms had had enough. In the dimming twilight they decided to traverse ledges to the right where an arete of fine gabbro led to easier ground, and for Ashley Abraham that magical feeling of inner contentment which comes with the end of a grand day's climbing on the Cuillin. In the darkness they descended to the Thuilm Ridge and then into Coire a' Ghreadaidh and their little white tent.

Slanting Gully had stretched the party to their limit but had also demonstrated their professional commitment in cramped and precarious positions by producing a fine photograph of the Cracks Pitch, one of many used to illustrate *Rock-Climbing in Skye*. Repeat ascents were made by Francis Greig's party in June 1908 when they avoided the Cracks Pitch by slabs on the right, and E W Steeple's party a year later (in two hours). They appeared to confirm Abraham's opinion that it was the finest gully in Skye. For a few years Slanting Gully was one of the most sought-after challenges on the island until some high-profile names, most notably J M Archer Thomson, considered it overrated. Rock-falls contributed to a further decline in popularity. However, by 2011 Slanting Gully was back in favour with a three-star rating in the SMC guide.

Thomson, one of the leading rock climbers of the day, spent a wet week on Skye in September 1911. He was a prominent member of the Pen-y-Pass group that met regularly in Snowdonia, some of whom had fallen out with the Abraham brothers over their commercial approach to the mountains. Thomson haughtily viewed the Abrahams' books as a form of vulgar entertainment, and was determined to bring the acclaimed brothers' down a peg or two, and belittle their achievements by climbing Slanting Gully in better style: straightening it out and extending it to its true finish on the summit ridge.

Thomson's party consisted of two ropes of two: himself and a Welsh friend H O Jones on one, Leslie Shadbolt and Alastair McLaren, a team well-known for their first traverse of the Main Ridge, on the other. They all enjoyed the high profile Cracks Pitch. Thomson then made a direct ascent of the Overhanging Crack which the Abrahams had avoided on the right. He cattily commented: 'The authors of *Rock Climbing in Skye* whose interesting account of their attack has been pointed out to me would seem to have judged somewhat harshly of the amenities of the place.'[14] Thomson's party also added a further 250ft (75m) continuation above the Upper Rake, where the original climb finished, to the summit ridge.

Also in Skye at this time were H E L (Harold) Porter and N C (Nigel) Madan, currently a student at Oxford. Porter, from Birkenhead, was a regular climbing partner of George Mallory in North Wales and the Alps. In the 1920s, Porter went on a climbing trip to New Zealand where he popularised the use of crampons (playing his own small part in the story of Everest). Porter's Col between Mount Cook's Low and Middle Peaks is named in his honour. In the Cuillin, Porter and Madan put up yet another possible finish to Slanting Gully, Two Pitch Gully (Very Difficult) to the right of Thomson's route, a better climb than the bland name suggests. Porter described the top pitch as 'sensational and equal to anything in Slanting Gully'. The accounts of Two Pitch Gully and Slanting Gully were the first in Skye to use the technical terms 'bridging' and 'jamming'. In 1923 George Abraham described the latter technique, often regarded as a product of the 1950s: 'A capital upward pull may be got by thrusting the hand as high as possible into the crack and then doubling the clenched fingers.'

When Abraham's party eventually returned to the Sligachan Inn after their ascent of Slanting Gully they were presented with a note left for them by E W Steeple, on his way to catch the steamer at Portree, outlining his explorations with a Rucksack Club party at the Glen Brittle end of the range. This included a new route on the Cioch, the classic Cioch Nose (Very Difficult), described in the 2011 SMC guidebook as 'a superb little climb'. Steeple's party had also managed the first ascent of Sron na Ciche's Central Gully (Very Difficult) where they were forced to avoid a steep chimney in the upper section due to a 'copious waterfall'.

Buoyed by this news, Abraham's party used the Wallaces' car to reach Glen Brittle and see for themselves the much talked about Cioch. The brothers were friendly with Colin Phillip as they were all early members of the Fell and Rock Climbing Club, of which Ashley was also president in this its inaugural year. Phillip would contribute translations and pronunciations of Cuillin place names for the Skye book. Norman Collie also helped with some information, but doubtless regarded Abraham's project as anathema, unnecessary and unwarranted Baedekerism.

Ashley Abraham was guided up Collie's Route to the Cioch by one of Colin Phillip's nieces, Miss Prothero, who had been part of the first female ascent. From the Sgumain Stone Shoot they crossed Eastern Buttress by a traverse line which took them into Eastern Gully. By now this approach to the Cioch had superseded the original route by way of Cioch Gully. Abraham was impressed both by the alpine scale of the cliffs and the subtle ingenuity of Collie's year-old route: 'A delightful route puzzle, the solution of which acquaints one with most of the things that gladden the heart of a climber: gullies, slabs, knife-edges, pitches, aretes, even a cave to go through, all are in evidence on the easy way up the Cioch.'[15]

The party descended from the pinnacle down Slab Corner (Difficult) the first mention of this conspicuous feature (James Thomson recorded an ascent in 1911). Once back down on the Cioch Terrace most of the party set off to explore the extensive Cioch Slab, making several traverse lines at different heights while Ashley photographed. Several years later George Abraham also climbed Collie's Route (Moderate) but was less enthusiastic than his brother, thinking time would settle its reputation as a fairly average outing. Ashley's party also repeated Central Gully, above and to the right of the Cioch, where he was impressed by the atmospheric scenery of the Amphitheatre.

Ensconced back at Sligachan, Harland and Abraham decided to have another attempt at Black Chimney (Severe) on Sgurr nan Gillean's First Pinnacle, a route they had failed on previously. They eventually succeeded by using combined tactics and a technique that George Abraham claimed to have devised: threading the rope behind a chockstone to protect the leader. This entailed untying the rope, passing it behind a jammed rock and then retying. (Slings were not used until after the First World War when they were initially referred to as 'rope-rings'.) This procedure also enabled leaders to rest safely, a tactic described by one impatient second as 'infernal dangling'. It also increased the chance of a fall breaking the rope, ironically one of few eventualities that ensured the second's survival. Another danger was that the rope might jam and pull off the leader.

The crux of Black Chimney was the final pitch, a vertical crack containing two wedged stones. Harland untied from the rope and Ashley passed the end behind the first chockstone so that the leader was safeguarded when he retied and started to climb. To reach the second stone Harland climbed onto Ashley's shoulders, who then pushed his right foot high enough to enable him to grasp the crucial hold. Black Chimney was originally graded Exceptionally Severe by Ashley, one of only five Skye climbs in this category.

On his previous visit to Sron na Ciche, Ashley Abraham had spotted the unclimbed line of the Cioch Direct. Back at Sligachan this 500ft (150m) of steep gabbro below the Cioch would not leave his thoughts. Though the rest of his party were preparing to leave for home, he managed to persuade Harland to extend his stay. The weather remained fine and settled as they returned to Glen Brittle to stay overnight with Colin Phillip. The next morning saw Harland confidently building a cairn at the start of the route. The initial chimneys were an obvious weakness to start with, but at half-height these blended into a vertical band of rock where the way was not so clear. The last of the chimneys, for many years known as the Bell-mouth Chimney, is regarded as the climb's crux. Here their confidence in the reliability of gabbro was tested as a massive block they had just climbed over fell to the screes. Badly shaken, they followed a slab gangway leftwards beneath overhangs, past a jumble of boulders and then across a slab to a good belay below two parallel cracks of impeccable gabbro. It appeared that you had to start up the right crack and then, at half-height, somehow transfer to the left. A shoulder assisted Harland to start the initial crack but he had difficulty making the crucial transition:

> Harland had got his left foot and hand across, but seemed to find a difficulty in making up his mind to swing over. I had him splendidly belayed, however, so there was little danger, but his position was one of great strain, and I shouted to him to get across before he tired. 'I'm not quite sure that my left hand will hold me,' he gasped. Just then his left foot slipped away, thus settling his indecision. All his weight suddenly came on his left hand for a moment, a moment of great excitement. A second later and he got his right hand above his left, and was then able to pull up on his arms reaching a higher hold, and thence a small ledge on the outside of the crack. After a 'breather' he went straight upward to a sloping ledge, above which rose a great expanse of slab.[16]

Easy climbing now led to the terrace: 'We congratulated each other, and swore it was the best climb we had either of us done, the stiffest, the most interesting.' From here 'a fresh route was devised on the Cioch Gully side of the pinnacle', probably the prominent slanting crack (South-West Face, Moderate). These rocks above the terrace, between Cioch Nose and Cioch Gully, are poorly documented: in 1908 Abraham stated that 'three or four ways up it have been discovered and climbed'.

Significantly, no photographs exist for Cioch Direct, the most celebrated of all their Skye climbs. The seriousness of the undertaking, and a small party of two, left photography too risky and impracticable. Not content with the first ascent of one of Britain's classic climbs, they were determined to cram as much as they could into the day, their last of the trip. They considered tackling one of the other 'last great problems' in the area: the Crack of Doom, originally known as Hanging Chimney, or the great unclimbed Western Buttress of Sron na Ciche where Abraham had spotted the line eventually taken by Median.

However Cioch Direct had taken its toll on nerve and muscle and they settled for an ascent of Cioch Gully with its unusual Letterbox Pitch. After regaining the terrace they tackled the airy mantelshelf of Cioch Nose, one of the routes first climbed earlier in the week by the Rucksack Club party of Steeple, Woodhead and Bowron. (This explains why Ashley, in his book, devotes twelve pages to Cioch Direct and one sentence to Cioch Nose.) From the top of the Cioch Abraham and Harland continued into Eastern Gully and eventually gained the summit ridge.

They then descended Sron na Ciche's shoulder until they were able to cut back along the western continuation of the Cioch Terrace. Here, to conclude a memorable day, they explored some now neglected features such as the Finger, a wobbly pinnacle. Ashley's comment was, 'I must personally confess to a feeling of relief when I ultimately found myself on the top and not the top on me.' The Finger was first climbed in 1904 by J C (James) Thomson, a chartered accountant from Glasgow. This was the first rock climb to be recorded on Sron na Ciche and Thomson would have been more than aware of the still 'undiscovered' Cioch jutting out from the cliff below.

Abraham and Harland then ascended The Flake, a large boulder which had fallen from above to block the terrace. On its top they found the cairn left by Collie and Mackenzie the previous June: 'After a delightful half-hour's siesta on the top, we crossed the foot of a minor gully and regained the crest of the mountain by way of the ridge forming its left wall.'[17] On the photo-diagram of Sron na Ciche in the 1923 SMC guide there is a climb marked as Flake Traverse which starts up the right side of the Flake and ends near the top of Central Gully, though the route is not described in the text.

The rock-fall on Cioch Direct was not an isolated occurrence. Although holds on gabbro are generally very sound, the rock is as susceptible as any to large rock-falls and slips. When W H Murray climbed Cioch Direct in 1937 he and Kenneth Dunn were severely shaken by a massive rock avalanche nearby. On the same holiday Murray had another near escape when traversing the Main Ridge with James Banford. On Sgurr Dearg, in thick mist, they mistakenly set off down the false ridge from the summit. After a hand-traverse across an overhang the mist cleared to reveal both their mistake and a massive drop below. They hastily returned the way they had come. They were no sooner clear of the overhang when it 'silently keeled over into the void in blocks like cottages'.

Peter Bicknell visited Skye in the 1930s, experiences he related in a radio programme: 'I remember sitting eating lunch at the foot of the great precipice on Sgurr Sgumain, when a boulder about the size of a grand piano landed a few feet in front of us and burst like shrapnel, pitting the face of rock behind us.' In 1965 an enormous rock-fall from the Cioch Upper Buttress was seen and heard as far away as Glen Brittle. In 1997 the terrace approach to the Cioch Slab was affected by falling blocks from Eastern Buttress. Six years later the large projecting block below Cioch Direct's parallel cracks, known as the Yardarm, fell to the screes. In 2011 there was a fatality on the same climb due to rocks dislodged by the leader below the crux chimney and for a while climbers were advised to avoid the route until a safety assessment was made.

It's not just Coire Lagan. Back in 1897 at the SMC camp at Coruisk, John Rennie witnessed two enormous rock-falls with a 'noise like thunder': one on Sgurr Dubh Mor, the other on the cliffs of Druim nan Ramh above the loch. In 1996 a massive rockslide on the latter cliffs left an enormous white scar, visible from several miles, and removed much of the 1962 route Coruisk Slabs (Severe). Lightning strikes have also created physical changes to exposed sections of ridge. In recent years the Bad Step on Am Basteir, the Imposter on Clach Glas, and the

Inaccessible Pinnacle have all been altered to some degree (the answer to Munro-baggers' prayers is for a direct hit on the latter, reducing its height to below that of Sgurr Dearg!)

For the remainder of 1907, Ashley Abraham was engrossed in the final preparation of his manuscript. The publication of William Douglas's Skye guide in the September 1907 issue of the *SMC Journal* induced him to make one last trip, that October, to finalise his research and fill the remaining photographic gaps. As well as Henry Harland and brother George, he was accompanied by A W (Arthur) Wakefield, a Kendal doctor who established the Lake District Fell Record (the precursor of the Bob Graham Round) in 1905. Wakefield was also a member of the 1922 Everest Expedition where he failed to shine, not solely due to his inability to acclimatise well, but also because he was suffering undiagnosed post-traumatic stress disorder, then known as shellshock, from his experiences in the First World War. After the traditional warm-up of Pinnacle Ridge they made a new climb on Knight's Peak (North Face, Difficult) which started up some enjoyable chimneys before finishing by a narrow arête.

They then hired two ponies to help transport their gear down Glen Sligachan where they set up camp near Loch an Athain. Inspired by an account in their SMC guide of a climb on Bla Bheinn's north face, the four set off the next morning to get to grips with this mountain's less frequented Pinnacle Ridge (Moderate). However the higher they got on the climb the more the angle seemed to lie back and, after checking their description, they realised too late it related to an ascent under winter conditions (by William Inglis Clark, T E Goodeve and Harry Walker in April 1905). On the descent into Coire Dubh, Ashley and another of the party, most likely Harland, were determined to make up for this anticlimax. Although it was now twilight they started up a gully on Clach Glas's West Face, finishing in almost total darkness. It was given the apt name of Consolation Gully (Moderate).

The cold, wet weather of that autumn's visit dampened even Ashley's enthusiasm for camping out in the Cuillin. George was never as keen on tents as his brother: 'Space forbids a description of the discomforts of camp under such conditions.' On the other hand he was a pioneer motorist (he used clutch fluid to oil his boots) who favoured the use of a vehicle to avoid further nights in 'a sodden mass of flattened canvas'. George probably owned the first resident motor car in the Lake District, a Sunbeam Mabberley that he bought in 1900. Two years later, after the brakes failed giving him a broken collar bone, he switched to an Alldays. He wrote several books on motoring which he treated just like climbing: Honister Pass in the Lake District has 'several steep little pitches and one awkward corner rather less than half-way up the ascent'.

He even did first ascents, driving the first car to make it over Wrynose and Hardknott Passes. He repeated this feat with his friend and fellow motoring enthusiast Andrew 'Sandy' Irvine. George gave Irvine crucial support for selection to the ill-fated 1924 Everest Expedition. George's daughter Enid recalled the circumstances: 'When we went over Hardknott and Wrynose he said to my father quite out of the blue, "You know I'd love to go on this coming Everest expedition" and father said "Why not?" which completely floored Sandy. However, father got in touch with various people he knew who were interested in the expedition or planning, and they took him right away.'[18] To many on the 1924 expedition, however, it remained a moot point that someone who had never even set foot on the Cuillin could be considered as George Mallory's partner for a crack at mountaineering's greatest prize.

The advent of the car revolutionised access to the hills. In Skye, prior to the First World War, there was little public transport; many hotels, including Sligachan and Broadford, now acquired their own transport to take guests to and from the steamer, and the hills. When John Campbell opened his own hotel in Broadford in 1908, guests had access to two cars which could be utilised to reach the likes of Bla Bheinn and Clach Glas. Around 1910, for transport between the Sligachan Inn and Portree, you had the choice of a waggonette holding six passengers, or a more expensive motor car taking five. By the 1930s guests at Sligachan were picked up at Portree harbour in a yellow Rolls-Royce. Early mountaineers who drove to Skye include G B Gibbs (from Sunderland in a Renault) and William Inglis Clark (from Edinburgh in an Arrol-Johnston). The surgeon Edred Corner drove from London to Skye in 24 hours but took another three hours for the notoriously rough going on the final leg from Sligachan to Glenbrittle.

As well as open drains, jaywalking sheep and startled crofters, early motorists had to contend with two main cruxes on the road to the Cuillin: the Kyle of Lochalsh ferry where vehicles were transported on two precarious planks balanced across the gunwales (this continued until 1928 when a purpose-built, one-car turntable ferry was introduced) and the infamous sand and gravel hill, Druim nan Cleochd, between Luib and Sconser. The 'wretched surface' of the latter was eventually bypassed in 1927 with the construction of the coastal Moll road until the existing road was built to the west of the original climb. It was now a commoner sight to see motorists attempt to negotiate the potholes, ruts and fords of the stone-strewn Glen Brittle 'road'. George Abraham used his 10-horsepower Alldays to convey his party gingerly through and over the obstacles to the newly available accommodation at Mary Campbell's cottage with its en suite sheepdogs, hens and pet Westies: 'Limited accommodation can certainly be had at Mr Campbell's (the shepherd), but the room there, which is dining-, smoking-, and bed-room in one, leaves much to be desired.'[19]

After an ascent of Window Buttress and climbs either side of Banachdich Gully, Ashley Abraham's mind drifted back to the warm days of June 1906 when he was sunbathing at the lochan in Coire Lagan; when he was continuously drawn to the conspicuous challenge of Sgurr Mhic Choinnich's West Buttress

(Difficult) but had not enough time to tackle it. Ashley decided to put this to rights but now conditions were very different. They set off up the climb during a wild autumnal hailstorm; the rocks were wet and cold with hailstones settling in the crevices. The upper chimneys proved formidable in the ferocious wind. Chilled to the bone they were thankful for the sudden finish, just a few feet from the summit where there was shelter from the gale on the lee side of the ridge.

George Abraham's last recorded visit to Skye was in 1920 as part of a large contingent of the Fell and Rock which divided themselves between the Chisholm and Campbell households. Abraham, along with Henry Harland and Geoffrey Summers, created a direct line to the summit of Knight's Peak, now recorded as a variation to North Face (Difficult). Over on Clach Glas they took up the obvious challenge of B Gully (Severe). After eight pitches in the confines of the gully they moved right to climb fine slabs before re-crossing the gully towards the summit, almost 2,000ft (610m) of varied and interesting climbing. Five years earlier W N Ling and E (Edward) Backhouse, a bank manager from Stockton, put up Central Buttress (Difficult) to the left of B Gully where, at half-height, they avoided a vertical wall by a chimney on the left. In 1920 Abraham's party took on this difficulty directly with George commenting, 'This needed rubber footgear.'

Rock-Climbing in Skye was published in 1908, price one guinea. It rapidly sold out, establishing the Abraham brothers as leading exponents in one of the most challenging of photographic genres. The book's witty and informative style, combined with spectacular action photographs, ensured fine reviews, 'The mystery of Skye is now fully unveiled.' The *Glasgow Herald* stated: 'A volume which cannot be too strongly recommended to the attention of all who propose to choose Skye for the scene of their mountaineering feats.' The book's innovative format included a graded list, stars for recommended routes, and a map in an endpaper wallet. It was soon referred to as the 'Bible according to Abraham'. Enthused readers rummaged pockets for tram tickets to mark must-do routes. Dramatic accounts of the likes of Slanting Gully and Cioch Direct precipitated a rash of repeats and caused reviewers like Naismith to comment that it 'will be apt to cause the reader to wedge himself across his arm-chair while he gropes about for a good hitch'.[20]

Rock-Climbing in Skye strongly influenced climbers' choice of route well into the 1950s. Between 1907 and 1911 George Abraham was also busy, producing four more climbing books and a host of magazine articles. He was helped by his wife Winifred, a cousin of O G Jones and a fine climber herself, who often ghosted for George from his rough notes. (She is commemorated in Winifred's Pinnacle on Aonach Dubh in Glen Coe, one of several climbs the couple did on their honeymoon in 1901.) *British Mountain Climbs,* published in 1910, became a huge commercial success. Still in print in the 1940s, young enthusiasts could learn about Clogwyn du'r Arddu in Snowdonia: 'It cannot be said that this imposing mass possesses much interest to the rock climber.' The Abrahams even experimented with cine films, creating a five-minute travelogue for Pathé Review, an ascent of Napes Needle. In 1936, when Ashley was 60 and George 64, the brothers did their last climb together, their favourite, New West on Pillar.

The period surrounding the publication of *Rock-Climbing in Skye* brought the twilight of Skye's golden age. Abraham's book, hot on the heels of the Cioch's discovery, saw 'the cragsman's Mecca' of Sron na Ciche becoming the main focus of attention, as the trajectory of pioneering on Skye shifted from Sligachan to Glen Brittle, and from the Scottish Mountaineering Club to the newly established clubs from south of the border, most notably the Rucksack Club and the Climbers' Club.

Chapter Seven

The British Alps

After the Easter Meets of 1903 and 1905, the SMC were no longer the driving force they once were on Skye. Younger, more active groups from south of the border, like the Climbers' Club (formed 1898) and the Rucksack Club (formed 1902), now began to dominate the new climb lists. (Early members of the Climbers' Club were often subject to ridicule since the term 'climber' was seen as derogatory by 'proper mountaineers'.)

Flicking through any Cuillin guidebook the names Steeple and Barlow invariably come to the fore. E W (Everard) Steeple and George ('Guy') Barlow are synonymous with the mountains during the early part of the twentieth century. Steeple was a bank manager from King's Norton in Birmingham. Contemporaries often commented on his shy and unassuming nature, 'a reserved and lonely soul but with a quiet and entertaining sense of humour'. J H B. Bell of the Scottish Mountaineering Club concurred: 'Steeple was a modest, retiring man, but pure gold when you got to know him.' He developed into one of the Cuillin's most prolific pioneers, the 'High Priest of Skye', with around forty new routes between his first and last visits in 1907 and 1924 respectively.

Barlow, who was often addressed as 'GB', was originally from Gravesend in Kent but was educated in London where his science teacher, O G Jones, introduced him to climbing. Barlow went on to become a physics lecturer at Birmingham University, and it was in this city that he first became friends with Steeple. After visiting the Cuillin several times independently, the pair joined forces in 1910 to create the distinctive Skye brand of Steeple and Barlow. Steeple was the leader on most, if not all, of their Skye climbs. The partnership was further cemented through their editorship, along with Harry MacRobert, of the seminal 1923 SMC guide *The Island of Skye*.

Previously climbers based themselves at Sligachan, with its good links to the steamer, for the start and end of their holiday, transferring to Glen Brittle for the middle part of their stay. A ghillie and pony were hired to transport heavier baggage to the glen while, lightly laden, it was possible to walk over Bealach a' Mhaim, take in a climb in Coire na Creiche, and then traverse part of the Main Ridge before descending for dinner at your new accommodation in the village.

As Sligachan was now increasingly perceived as a poor choice of base, remote from the centre of things, Steeple and Barlow established operational HQ at the cosy den of Cuillin Cottage in Glen Brittle, a thatched cottage located between the present-day campsite and Glen Brittle House. Here, from around 1906 until her death in 1947, Mary Campbell provided homely shelter for many well-known climbers, initially in cramped box beds though later an annexe was constructed as lounge and sleeping quarters. Another regular guest, Inverness-based lawyer H C (Herbert) Boyd, looked forward to her Highland hospitality: 'True it is no hotel, and it is somewhat difficult to reach; but once you are there, and if you are content with the simple accommodation and homely fare of the shepherd's cottage, with its stores of scones, fresh eggs and unlimited supplies of rich milk, your lot is one to be envied.'[1] With four beds Mary Campbell doubled the accommodation available in the village; there was also Mr McRae the gardener (2 beds) and Mr Nicolson the gamekeeper (2 beds).

Glen Brittle was now the first choice of base for climbing activists. A new younger generation were keen to avoid the expense of Sligachan – where there was no alternative budget accommodation – and were impatient to get to grips with the recent cutting edge climbs in Coire Lagan. But what was the best way of getting there? Some tried the train to Mallaig, excursion steamer to Loch Scavaig, and then the steep hike over Bealach Coire na Banachdich. Some came by motorbike. Others got the *Dunara Castle*, one of the steamers servicing the west coast of Skye, disembarking at Carbost or Struan. Leslie Shadbolt and Alistair McLaren based themselves at Sligachan but kept a rucksack of kit at Glen Brittle to give them the option of finishing at either location.

Although both Steeple and Barlow joined the Climbers' Club in 1907, Steeple's earliest visits to Skye are with Rucksack Club parties (he did not officially join until 1911). The club was formed in October 1902 as a Lancastrian alternative to the Yorkshire Ramblers. Their first outing to Skye, in June 1905, comprised H E Bowron from Liverpool, W Heap, Walton Tattersall and Robertson Lamb. Blessed with very dry weather they managed the second ascent of Waterpipe Gully Direct as well as the first ascent of Third-Fourth Gully (Very Difficult) on Sgurr nan Gillean, a route that had persistently turned back strong parties. Although probably climbed by Collie prior to 1890, a rock-fall had subsequently altered the gully leaving a very loose and tricky pitch. When W Naismith and W W King attempted this 'last great problem' in 1898 they were eventually forced to take to the rocks on the right, a route now known as North Face (Difficult).

Slimy chimneys, mossy chockstones and dank through routes are avoided if at all possible by today's climbers, but the Edwardians appeared to approach them with a degree of chary relish. In early ascents throughout the British Isles a similar scenario was played out: a small group of men gathered below an enormous capstone and, between drips from the roof, discussed tactics. For the Rucksack party the overarching problem of Third-Fourth Gully was no different. Heap revealed how a plan was formulated to support Lamb's attack: 'Bowron took up his position in the cave and fastened both Lamb's rope and mine around him. Tattersall then wedged himself securely at the cave end of the ledge and held both ropes. Meanwhile Lamb had donned scarpetti. I stood up near Tattersall and made myself as firm as possible. Lamb stepped from Tattersall's shoulders on to mine and then slowly on to my up-stretched hands, but only found one handhold.'[2] After over an hour of these shenanigans, using different permutations of personnel, an alternative solution was spotted by Tattersall and eventually led by Robertson Lamb, '12 feet of difficult and dangerous climbing'.

Guy Barlow's first visit to the Cuillin was in August 1906 with H B (Harry) Buckle, a rope well known for their 1902 discovery of the classic Gashed Crag (Hard Difficult) on Tryfan in North Wales. When they climbed the Cioch by way of the first complete ascent of Cioch Gully (Very Difficult) Barlow and Buckle were unaware of Norman Collie's explorations. After the climb they were keen to quiz Collie about the cairn on the pinnacle's summit, but found him 'aloof and unapproachable'.

The next June (1907) Steeple was part of a visiting Rucksack Club party that included H E Bowron, and A G (Arthur) Woodhead from Bolton. With no published guidebook, visiting climbers found it difficult to obtain any information on Skye climbs. Although there was the occasional article on the Cuillin in magazines and journals, the most reliable source remained conversation or correspondence with those in the know. (It is a real testament to the early pioneers that participation in this potentially lethal sport, with so little accurate information available, resulted in so few accidents.) Charles Pilkington, an early supporter of the Rucksack Club, informed Bowron, Steeple and Woodhead what he knew of Collie's original route to the Cioch. Arthur Woodhead later recorded how they attempted to reach the Cioch by way of Cioch Gully but, like Collie, were stopped by the gully's last pitch:

> Dr Collie had been unable to reach the neck behind the pinnacle, and we found an apparently impossible pitch cutting us off from it; so, profiting by his experience, we set off along a convenient little terrace leading round the pinnacle. Dr Collie's plan, we understand, was to traverse round to the other side, ascend to a point above the pinnacle, and then descend again to the neck by a slanting traverse.
>
> As we went round the terrace, however, we found a place at which we thought the pinnacle itself might be directly climbed. The ridge proved to be uninviting, but at the top of the chimney, on the left, a V-shaped groove ran upwards across the face of the pinnacle, and the rib forming its outer lip, though obviously difficult, seemed to be worth trying. Fortunately there was a splendid belay near the lower end of the groove, so the leader started up the slab, using the rib at first as a handhold. At the end of the rib a badly shelving platform was reached, and a final arm-pull landed the leader in safety close to the top.[3]

This final section sounds very much like Cioch Nose (Very Difficult) and, if so, would be the first ascent, predating Abraham and Harland's ascent by several days. (The Rucksackers' last climb on Skye was Central Gully; Abraham and Harland repeated this three days later, and on their final day did Cioch Direct and the Cioch Nose.) The ascent of Cioch Gully and Cioch Nose was a fine achievement as Woodhead recalled: 'Steeple led us throughout the day's vicissitudes with nerve and good temper, even under the most watery conditions.' When Francis Greig's party repeated Cioch Nose the next year (1908), in dry conditions, they thought it merited the hardest grade then available 'Exceptionally Severe'.

Steeple, Bowron and Woodhead managed a substantial amount of climbing on Skye considering their limited knowledge of the mountains and that 1907 was one of the wettest summers on record, as Woodhead confirms: 'To avoid repetition, it may be taken for granted throughout the following account that it was raining either continuously or at intervals, unless otherwise stated.' On their only dry day they were delighted with the South Crack of the Inaccessible Pinnacle. Steeple and Woodhead also attempted Little Gully (Difficult) which they mistook for the start of Cioch Direct, but abandoned the climb as it was getting dark. This route was eventually climbed by Guy Barlow the next year (1908) and was known as 'Dr Barlow's Gully' up until the Second World War.

From a climber's perspective, the years 1907 and 1908 saw pivotal changes in the Cuillin: the popular John Campbell left Sligachan, and on the hills mountaineers were not as welcome as they once were. On a more positive note the first climbing guidebooks became available. William Douglas's guide, *The Island of Skye,* appeared in the September 1907 *SMC Journal.* It dealt comprehensively with the peaks and climbs near to the traditional base of Sligachan though coverage of the Glenbrittle end of the range remained sketchy: Sgurr Sgumain and Sron na Ciche were dispatched in a dozen lines while the newly discovered Cioch only got a mention.

On a diagram in his guide, Douglas marked two 'Easy routes to Sgurr Sgumain': one was the North-West Ramp while the other followed the line of Frankland's Gully, a Hard Severe not climbed until 1925. After the first ascent of the former climb in 1896, J H Bell and the Napier brothers drew a sketch in the Sligachan Climbers' Book, labelling the climb, wrongly, as the North Ridge of Sgurr Sgumain. The latter route was also often confused with the mountain's West Buttress Route and consequently there was a degree of muddle over the relative locations of these climbs.

After his visit in June 1907 Arthur Woodhead wrote an article in the *Rucksack Club Journal,* 'In the South Cuillin,' in which he attempted to sort out the aforementioned confusion, as well as outline the latest developments in Glen

Brittle. He provided the first detailed description of Sgumain's North Ridge (Moderate), evidence of a possible first ascent. This climb, like most of their excursions, was done in wet weather with the hardest section proving to be the rock-band about halfway up: 'The climbing of this wall proved really difficult. We started a few paces to the right of the ridge and ascended obliquely, bearing to the right. The difficulties were of the usual character: ledges sloping outwards, scarcity of belays and damp rocks.'

Woodhead also recorded an ascent of West Buttress Route (Difficult) on Sgurr Sgumain which started directly up the slabs in the lower corrie to join Pilkington's original 1890 line higher up. On this climb Woodhead, Bowron and Steeple were accompanied by Robertson Lamb, a Cheshire timber merchant who remained a bold and technically proficient rock climber until late in life; on a visit in 1919 he contributed Flutings Climb (Difficult) on Sgurr nan Gillean (possibly mistaken for Forked Chimney).

The publication of Abraham's classic, *Rock-Climbing in Skye,* in 1908 eclipsed all previous information sources. This inspirational book contained a bumper 330 pages of historical research, first-hand accounts and dramatic photographs. Waterpipe Gully, Slanting Gully and Cioch Direct became must-have ticks. If there was now a reliable record of what had been done, conversely, areas ripe for new routes also became more apparent.

Although the main impetus for pioneering was now coming from south of the border, the warm summer of 1908 saw a brief resurgence of activity by the SMC. One club member, Edinburgh stationer Francis Greig, was fired up by Abraham's account to make the second ascent of Slanting Gully. In common with the Abraham brothers, Greig has a narrow ledge on the Crowberry Ridge in Glen Coe named after him. With the help of a recalcitrant local donkey his party established a camp near the Fairy Pools from where they set out in hot weather for Slanting Gully which didn't disappoint, 'One of the best climbs to be had anywhere.' After five hours in the gully they descended for the perfect end to a perfect day, 'A right royal feast of cold tongue, pears, and cocoa was soon spread out on the grass.' Greig's party also managed the first ascent of Hidden Gully (Difficult) on the west face of Sgurr a' Ghreadaidh where the slim Greig had the physical attributes required to lead the regulatory through-routes, caves and chimneys. On the descent one of the party received a nasty gash on the head from a falling rock which was stitched at Cuillin Cottage using a sewing needle and fishing line.

Others in the SMC, though, did not care for wild camping with donkeys and continued to enjoy the carnal comforts of Sligachan. The summer of 1908 saw a steady stream of club members at the Inn including the Reverend A E Robertson who finally managed an ascent of the Inaccessible Pinnacle, the main stumbling-block in his attempt to climb all the Munros. That August W W King was back on the island, keen as ever to get to grips with the confines of a Cuillin chimney. On Bruach na Frithe he led William Inglis Clark and his daughter Mabel on the first ascent of North Chimney (Very Difficult). At one difficult chockstone King was forced to swing into space and climb the rope until, almost exhausted, he eventually regained contact with the rock. The next month Arthur Russell and Frank Goggs claimed the first ascent of An Stac Chimney (Moderate). For a while this was a popular approach to the Inaccessible Pinnacle but the chimney proved to be exactly the right width to jam rucksacks, providing an added dimension to the term 'gripped'.

In September 1908 Buckle and Barlow were also back in Glen Brittle. They investigated the gullies on the Stone Shoot Face of Sgurr Thearlaich which provided them with a selection of interesting chimney pitches. Although the best of their finds, Gully D (Very Difficult), was done in descent, it was still deemed acceptable to claim the route as a valid first ascent. However, according to the *SMC Journal* (1911) some of these gullies had already been climbed but not recorded. As no further details were forthcoming Buckle and Barlow remain in print as the first ascentionists. They later created West Central Gully and Arete (Very Difficult) on Sron na Ciche but the spoilsports of the SMC again pointed out that the gully section had been climbed previously.

Chimney and gully climbs like these were bread and butter to the early mountaineers. Specific techniques were devised to surmount their characteristic challenges in much the same way as, for example, climbers of the 1970s analysed how best to ascend cracks. W W King developed special twisting techniques to overcome chimneys of an awkward width, described as 'muffin struggles'. Consequently, many of these 'old-fashioned' routes can often create problems for the modern climber as they may have originally been ascended using arcane methods not described in modern instruction manuals. Their grades, especially in areas like Skye where they have had few ascents, should often be taken with a pinch of salt.

In June 1909, Steeple and Bowron discovered a Cuillin classic. They were aware that, back in 1906, Ashley Abraham had spotted potential on Sron na Ciche's extensive Western Buttress. Although conditions remained unrelentingly wet, and it was their eighth consecutive day climbing, they were still up for the challenge. Starting up a crack-line near Central Gully they ascended the full 1,200ft (350m) of the face to give Western Buttress Direct (also called West Route on early diagrams). Now known as Median (Very Difficult) this mountaineering route has an alpine character that contains a little of everything: walls, chimneys, slabs, gullies and cracks. The next day they did the second ascent of Cioch Direct which Steeple reckoned concentrated more quality climbing into its length than any other Cuillin climb he knew of.

The next month Guy Barlow was back in Glen Brittle when he claimed three new lines: Black Chimney (Very Difficult) in Coire na Banachdich, (originally called Black Cleft), Eastern Wall of Central Gully (Very Difficult) on Sron na

Ciche (originally named Hexagon Block and Central Gully Arete), and 'Central Buttress by traverse from Cioch'.

Most mountaineers were too caught up with the rock climbing to bother recording the local scene, but one Rucksack Club member who did was A E Barker from Colchester:

> Glen Brittle is one of these spots which seem to have preserved their primitive simplicity and loneliness, and to have been left behind in the rapid march of civilisation. The hamlet consists of one house of modern appearance and a score of primitive crofters' cottages, each of one storey, built of large rude stones, roughly thatched, and with a curious wooden chimney [probably a herring barrel]…We were met soon after we started by some of the women from the crofters' cottages carrying on their backs large wicker baskets or 'creels', fastened with cords across their shoulders, and heavily laden with the peat they use for fuel.[4]

During Easter 1910, Steeple and Bowron joined forces in North Wales with Guy Barlow and A H (Harry) Doughty, a friend from Derbyshire who was an early access campaigner for his local crags, to produce the classic Grooved Arete (Hard Very Difficult) on Tryfan. That autumn the same party set off for Skye where they set up camp in Coire a' Ghreadaidh after getting permission from Colin Phillip, who was renting the shooting rights as part of his lease of Glen Brittle House. They were very fortunate with the glorious, midge-free September weather. Between climbs they restocked supplies at Mary Campbell's where the newlywed Mr and Mrs Buckle were currently in residence.

It turned out to be a week of sustained gully climbing characterised by a succession of attic windows, projecting capstones and converging walls. The undoubted highlight was the discovery of a bristling ten-pitcher on the Coruisk side of Sgurr a' Mhadaidh, South-East Gully (Severe). Climbed during a spectacular temperature inversion, complete with Brocken spectres, Steeple considered this one of the most memorably beautiful days he ever had in the mountains; the cloud level remained at 2,500ft all day, stretching from horizon to horizon with the tops of all the major peaks peeking through. Due to a late start Doughty and Bowron decided to withdrew at the crux pitch, a wise decision as Steeple and Barlow were forced to complete the final pitches by moonlight.

They were all back together for Eagles Gully (Grade 3) on Sgurr Eadar da Choire, named after a 'colony of eagles' they disturbed. Early accounts of rock climbing in the Cuillin often recount eagles being startled by climbers or vice versa. Ashley Abraham recalled one such incident on the first ascent of Black Chimney on Sgurr nan Gillean. While on a solo traverse of Bidein Druim nan Ramh Steeple took the wrong route; to regain the correct line he was forced to crawl along a narrow ledge, and just at this moment an eagle glided through the gap about a metre above him, 'Which of us was most startled I do not know.' Steeple recalled how he plastered himself against the rock thinking something was falling towards him.

John Mackenzie was once descending the craggy north side of Bla Bheinn when he found the remains of hare and ptarmigan strewn about. Nearby he noticed an eyrie with several eaglets. The adult female soon arrived at the nest, followed by the male which promptly began to attack him; he only managed to escape through his ability to descend rapidly down very steep ground. The growth of sheep farming meant these close encounters became a rare occurrence as a bounty was offered in an attempt to eradicate the birds. In 1858 a sea eagle with a wingspan of 7ft 9in (2.36m) was shot in the Cuillin and sent to a taxidermist in Inverness. Donald Cameron, the tenant farmer at Glenbrittle farm (1863-84), claimed to have shot over thirty eagles in the Cuillin area. The last breeding pair of sea eagles, before reintroduction, was recorded in Skye in 1916.

In 1908 John Campbell left the manager's post at Sligachan to run Campbell's Hotel (sometimes referred to as the Temperance Hotel) near Broadford Pier. Donald Macdonald took over day-to-day business at Sligachan assisted by Bella Stewart, later manageress of the Royal Hotel in Portree. Macdonald, a large man with a red beard, was known as 'Tormore' after a farm he owned near Armadale. He was a close friend of Alexander Smith who mentions him in one of his poems, 'Edinbain'.

Donald Macdonald was Lord MacDonald's factor from 1872 until 1880 when he was responsible for the clearance of much of Sleat. Later on he was factor at Glendale where he reputedly carried a revolver for his own protection; he was lambasted by Lord Napier for his heavy-handed treatment of the crofters there. After Macdonald's sequestration and death in 1912, John Campbell was assigned the lease of Sligachan in May of the following year. In 1928 he bought the business from the MacLeods of Dunvegan and it remains in Campbell family hands today.

During Macdonald's tenure at Sligachan there was a more proprietorial attitude from landowners regarding access to the hills; the open-armed welcome and cosy arrangements of the 1903 and 1905 SMC Easter Meets were now a thing of the past. The SMC held a further Easter Meet at the Inn in 1911 but no accommodation was forthcoming at Camasunary, although 'permission obtained to explore Clach Glas and Bla Bheinn'. Fortunately the SMC had Colin Phillip among their ranks and through his largesse Glen Brittle House was placed at the club's disposal. The week of the meet turned out to be a very stormy one with many parties' plans thwarted by conditions on the tops.

Alexander Cameron was a close friend of the new innkeeper and in his *Handbook to the Isle of Skye* (c.1912) gives a picture of the hotel around this time:

One of the morning sights at the Sligachan Hotel is the organisation of parties for the mountains. John Mackenzie, the famous guide, is early astir, and can be seen wending his way round the bend which hides Sconser from the hotel, as early as eight o'clock. Before setting out he has done a good day's work on his croft, but this in no way incapacitates him for the remainder of the day on the mountains. John has been forty years the Coolin guide. When he reaches the hotel in the morning he is eagerly consulted by guests as to the probable chances of the weather. His advice is usually taken and Mackenzie has never advised any serious climbing if in his judgement the meteorological conditions are unfavourable.

The family guiding tradition was maintained by one of John Mackenzie's nephews, Rory. In June 1909 Rory made the first ascent of Am Basteir Chimney (Very Difficult) with J Martin from Glasgow, one of many to spot his potential: 'Rory is a worthy successor to John, and should in time be the best climber of all the Mackenzies.'[5] They didn't start the climb until 6pm after waiting over an hour for heavy rain to ease. Chilled by the quantity of water coming down the rocks and then their sleeves, they avoided the central section of the chimney by ledges on the left. The next year (1910) Paul Scoones, a maths master at Eton, straightened the line out and, the following summer, provided a variation finish to the right, North Face (Difficult). That March Rory also guided J M (James) Wordie, the geologist on Shackleton's ill-fated *Endurance* expedition, when they completed a wintry ascent of Sgurr nan Gillean.

The summer of 1911 proved a momentous season on Skye with some exceptional achievements on the hills. Ironically Steeple and Barlow missed out, taking a break from their customary visit to the island. Although the spring and autumn of 1911 were poor, the core summer months provided some brilliantly sunny weather. A fine June enabled Leslie Shadbolt and Alastair McLaren to achieve what many thought was impossible. Both of them were inspired by the books and articles of the Abraham brothers to visit Wasdale Head where they first met in 1903; McLaren was on his way by bicycle from North Wales back home to Scotland.

Leslie Shadbolt was initially employed in the family Portland cement business near Uxbridge, but after the firm was taken over in 1912 he worked for a brush company. He was asked by his friend George Mallory to join the 1924 Everest Expedition, an invitation he was forced to decline. McLaren's background was very different, an archetypal Highlander who wore the kilt and played the bagpipes. A sheep farmer at Inverardran near the foot of Crianlarich's Ben More, he often used his rock climbing skills to rescue cragfast sheep. Leslie Shadbolt would affectionately recall his friend: 'He moved through the Highlands, a splendid and romantic figure which in a curious fashion seemed to shrink a little and lose something vital whenever he came down to the cities and plains.'[6]

From 1906 onwards Shadbolt and McLaren started to explore the Cuillin, sometimes accompanied by Shadbolt's brother and sister. With his brother they attempted a route on the Bhasteir Tooth which they had mistaken for King's Cave Chimney. The chimney eventually led to an enormous roof where they noticed a hole above them, the start of a narrow tunnel. This was led by Shadbolt's brother, the smallest of the party, but took the others three hours of effort, removing debris, before they were able, 'to reach the outer air lying flat on our backs and wriggling like snakes'. Originally called North Chimney, this unusual route has been known as Shadbolt's Chimney (Very Difficult) since the 1996 SMC guide.

Ashley Abraham repeated the climb in 1907 finding it harder and the subterranean passages even more complicated than its famous neighbour. The route's popularity was not helped by Paul Scoones' comments in the Sligachan Climbers' Book in 1909: 'In my opinion the climb is most risky, I found two at least of the jammed stones in the cave that moved slightly and any considerable movement of one block might result in the imprisonment of the climber. It would be a matter of immense difficulty to release anyone held captive in such cramped quarters and the result might be a horrible and lingering death.' The climb developed its own mystique, with some old hands at Sligachan briefing Cuillin newcomers: 'Shadbolt's, you know, makes an entertaining descent. I'll not say any more.'

From around 1896 onwards a lot of speculation circulated as to the possibility of traversing the Main Ridge in a single expedition. This would involve eight miles (13km) and 10,000ft (3000m) of ascent and descent between the first and last peaks of Gars-bheinn and Sgurr nan Gillean. There were also four miles (6km) and 3,000 ft (900m) from Glen Brittle to the summit of the first peak, and a similar distance in descent to Sligachan. Most of the route was exposed and serious scrambling interspersed with harder sections of rock climbing like the Thearlaich-Dubh Gap, the Inaccessible Pinnacle and the Bhasteir Tooth.

In October 1896 Colin Phillip wrote to William Douglas that if he required assistance with the compilation of his list of Cuillin peaks he should consult Collie, 'who has traversed the ridge from end to end several times'. There were persistent rumours that within recent years the bulk of the Main Ridge had been traversed. William Brown thought it highly unlikely this had been completed in a single expedition: 'It is said that the whole ridge has been traversed end to end in one day; but ordinary climbers will agree that this is a feat for the gods, who can step from mountain top to mountain top. Three long summer days would ordinarily be required to complete the circuit.'[7]

This became more of a possibility in 1898 when two crucial parts of the jigsaw were slotted in place: King's Chimney on Sgurr Mhic Choinnich and Naismith's Route on the Bhasteir Tooth. One man harbouring the ambition of being first to traverse the Main Ridge was the writer John Buchan (it was initially assumed any attempt would start at Sligachan):

> The whole of the ridge has been traversed repeatedly, but the conquest of it in one day still remains the unfulfilled ambition of many mountaineers. A young and very active man in hard training might possibly achieve it by starting before dawn from Sligachan Inn on some long June day, and finishing on the screes of Coir' a' Ghrunnda well after sunset; but it would be a feat of more than common endurance. For many parts are serious climbing, and I do not envy the lot of a man who, with ten hours' work, had to face the awkward direct descent of Sgurr Mhic Choinnich or cross the Alasdair-Dubh Gap in a fading light.[8]

Ashley Abraham elaborated on the qualities required for success:

> Amongst other things he would need to have exceptional physique and staying power: to be a quick, skilful and neat rock climber (particularly he would need to be neat, for otherwise his hands would be torn to pieces before he got halfway); to possess an intimate knowledge of the entire length of the ridge and a familiarity with its various *mauvais pas*. Perfect weather, a light rope to double for descents and a carefully arranged commissariat would be essential.[9]

Leslie Shadbolt and Alastair McLaren fulfilled most of Abraham's criteria for this much sought-after objective though they were unfamiliar with the long central section between Sgurr Thearlaich and Sgurr a' Mhadaidh. When they left Glen Brittle at 3.30am on 10th June 1911 they were both in extremely good shape after an energetic week climbing throughout the range. They reached Garsbheinn in two-and-a-half hours and didn't even stop for a break, continuing to Bealach Coir' an Lochain before halting for breakfast. McLaren set the pace and punctiliously kept timings to monitor progress, for example 'roping up in gap, one minute'. Despite including summits like Caisteal a' Garbh-choire which today's climber usually avoids, they were two and a half hours ahead of schedule at Sgurr Dearg. Initially they had some mist but with the weather now set fair they realised there was plenty of time to complete the expedition before nightfall, so they consequently eased their pace.

With only one bottle of water between them they endured a rasping thirst until the descent off the ridge to the 'long dreamt of' gurgling springs in Fionn Choire. According to his partner McLaren then led Naismith's Route on the Basteir Tooth, 'seemingly as fresh as when he started'. They reached Sgurr nan Gillean at 6.25pm, a very impressive time (top to top) of 12 hours 18 minutes, one most present-day parties would be more than happy with. Two hours twenty minutes of this was spent in halts.

At the age of 88, on the sixtieth anniversary of the first traverse of the Main Ridge, Shadbolt looked back fondly to that momentous day: 'We were very lucky to succeed as there were large sections of the ridge we had never seen. Fortunately it was a perfect day and quite clear. My stalwart and well-tried companion Alastair McLaren was as always a tower of strength. It was a great day for both of us.'[10] The successful traverse, in such an extraordinary time, created something of a sensation. It was inevitable it would be done but few imagined so soon or in such fine style. Ashley Abraham was suitably impressed, stating that '10th June 1911 witnessed one of the most remarkable feats of endurance, and mountaineering and climbing skill, ever accomplished in our home mountains.'[11]

In September 1911, three months after Shadbolt and McLaren's Main Ridge Traverse, J M A (James Merriman Archer) Thomson produced one of the finest weeks of pioneering ever seen in the Cuillin. Thomson was one of the leading climbers at Geoffrey Winthrop Young's get-togethers at Pen-y-Pass near the top of the Llanberis Pass in Snowdonia. These Christmas and Easter gatherings began in earnest around 1907 and were attended by up to sixty guests until the First World War brought them temporarily to an end. They featured much communal singing with songs composed to celebrate, or gently mock, participants and any events of note.

These were seminal occasions in developing British rock climbing. Most leading English, Welsh and Irish climbers participated in the exchange of ideas and information in this transitional period when climbers were moving out of gullies and chimneys on to slabs and faces. The emphasis was changing from arm strength towards the ability to balance; outcrop training was encouraged. An attractive but little known mountain range on the Isle of Skye was one of the topics under discussion. Winthrop Young had made several visits to the summer gatherings at Glen Brittle House and was highly influential in guiding some of his Pen-y-Pass protégés north to the Cuillin, most notably Archer Thomson, Siegfried Herford, Conor O'Brien and George Leigh Mallory.

When Archer Thomson arrived on Skye in September 1911 the fine weather of early summer was well and truly over. His climbing achievements here are especially noteworthy as there were few occasions when, if it was not actually raining, the rocks had time to completely dry. The son of a clergyman, Thomson was headmaster at Llandudno County School in North Wales. His capacity for introspection was legendary but was symptomatic of a depressive illness from which he suffered a breakdown in 1908. In rock climbing circles, Thomson was regarded as one of the most adroit of the new balance school with its slow controlled movement; he was compared by Winthrop Young to a chess player planning ten or twelve moves in advance. In 1894 there were only twelve rock climbs in all of Snowdonia. Within two years Archer Thomson doubled this number and by 1908 created a dozen new routes on Lliwedd alone, a cliff previously regarded as impossible. His systematic exploration and perfection of the balance technique heralded a breakthrough in the standard of climbing possible. Areas of rock without apparent features, at a high angle and with poor or no belays were now tackled regularly. He would introduce these developments to the Cuillin.

Thomson was accompanied to Skye by two regular partners from his current exploration of Lliwedd: H O (Humphrey) Jones 'the Welsh Mallory', and E S Reynolds. Jones was an outstanding chemist, a collaborator with Sir James Dewar, and one of the youngest Fellows of the Royal Society. The previous month (August 1911), along with Winthrop Young, Jones had his most successful Alpine season with several major first ascents. At the close of the season he teamed up with Thomson to traverse the Matterhorn twice in three days, taking in the Zmutt Ridge. Winthrop Young went on to say: 'He [Thomson] was so much impressed by the possibility of combining speed with climbing grace and security that, when he subsequently led a notable series of first ascents in Skye, he climbed at a pace, and with a finish and safety, that his companions maintain they have never seen approached on difficult rock.'[12] Thomson's Skye party was brought up to six with the addition of Leslie Shadbolt, Alistair McLaren and Jones's sister, Bronwen.

At the Sligachan Inn they did not hit it off with the proprietor, Donald Macdonald, due to climbing on the Sabbath and their very early starts. The first two days, both wet and windy, were spent exploring Sgurr nan Gillean's pinnacles where, in various permutations, they put up three new routes. The next day found them in Harta Corrie creating new lines either side of Raeburn's Route on An Caisteal. Shadbolt and McLaren chose South Buttress (Difficult) which the former described as, 'A delightful expedition, without any great difficulty but requiring care throughout. The start, immediately above what appeared to be a great overhang, at once emphasised the airy nature of the whole climb.' To the right, across South Gully, Thomson and Jones found themselves frequently climbing on smooth, slippery basalt (Archer Thomson's Route, Difficult). Both parties reported finding practically no belays in 1,200ft (370m). For many years the grade 'Skye Diff' had the same catch-all cachet as 'Scottish VS' where you had to be prepared for anything. Both of the above routes are in the former category.

After three wet but productive days at Sligachan, Archer Thomson's party moved base to Glen Brittle. As was the custom, weather permitting, they hoped to take in a climb in Coir' a' Mhadaidh on the way there. Thomson, Jones and Shadbolt decided to tackle the rocks between Slanting Gully and Deep Gash Gully. This was Thomson's favourite type of climbing, a steep open face like Lliwedd with possible options to the left or right at any vertical or overhanging sections. They scrambled up to the foot of a Severe chimney which Thomson led with confidence. Easier climbing then brought them to what they all considered the hardest part of the climb, a series of exposed moves where you could look straight down to the cairn they had built at the start of the route.

Thomson left a description of the crux in the Sligachan Hotel Climbers' Book: 'Twenty feet higher is an excellent belaying bollard; above and to the right of this a smooth, slippery slab of ten feet was met with and at the top of this tilted table is a basalt cube with a similarly sloping surface. Three steps are taken up the slab and the block grasped at two of the corners, a knee is placed upon it and an erect position is assumed gradually. The operation requires the utmost care and circumspection.' After Thomson's lead they were soon all together at what Shadbolt described as a 'pale green cave'. Before starting out on the climb they had studied the face in order to trace out the best line. From below the most problematical part seemed a band of overhangs, the point they had now reached. The tension was relieved when Thomson found a way through up a steep rib on the left which was fortuitously furnished with good holds.

Both Thomson and Shadbolt went on to state that the climb, now known as Archer Thomson's Route (Severe), was the finest and the hardest they knew of in Skye. Leslie Shadbolt was highly impressed by Thomson's calculated performance on such a complex cliff (the climb was dispatched in 2 hours 20 minutes), and his ability to continue coolly not knowing what was coming next. Shadbolt admitted he could never have led the route himself, nor had he the ability to work out such an intricate line. The climb is still a challenge to the route-finder today: the 1996 SMC guide gave the following succinct description: 'Using route-finding skills, try to find the easiest way up the cliff.'

After a night in Glenbrittle they walked up to Coire Lagan where Thomson was not so impressed by Sron na Ciche: 'The face, despite its terrific aspect from a distance, was now seen to be much broken, and no climb so continuously resistant as that on the face of Sgurr a' Mhadaidh will ever be found.' They chose to tackle the Western Buttress where they appeared to be unaware of the two existing climbs: Median, and West Central Gully and Arete. They started out as a party of six but, after some lunch, split into two ropes of three. Spoilt for choice on such an extensive face they went on to create two parallel lines: Zigzag (Difficult), and Chimney and Crack Climb (VS). Thomson, at the time one of Britain's finest rock climbers, was very taken by the quality and difficulty of Chimney and Crack Climb. Now largely neglected, he considered the 110ft (33m) crux crack harder than anything in North Wales at the time, even comparing it to the Mummery Crack on the Grepon. The 1923 SMC guide elaborated on the difficulties: 'It was climbed with the right foot in the fissure, and both hands grasping the edge. At a height of about 90 feet a foothold for the left foot gave a minute's rest, but the crack still continued, and the strain was not relaxed till a projecting bulge was surmounted after a struggle.'

The next day it was back to Coire Lagan for an attempt on the Cioch's imposing Upper Buttress. The line in question had for long been an ambition of Shadbolt's but was again eventually named after the lead climber as Archer

Thomson's Route (Very Difficult), the third climb of the week given the same name. This was not Thomson's fault as he was opposed to personal names for climbs and had suggested 'Cioch Buttress Climb'. The climb's first difficulty was a protruding corner which Thomson tackled on the right using a finger-hold to get established on the slab above. The next pitch involved removing two loose blocks before the party of six could regroup on a sloping stance below the final exposed rib. The total time for the ascent was one and a half hours.

On their way back to Sligachan they made a direct ascent of Slanting Gully, Thomson's seventh consecutive new climb in as many days; a real tour de force for the taciturn 48-year-old considering the poor weather and that he had no prior knowledge of the mountains: 'By choice or by chance we had climbed for a week on virgin rocks; their scale impressed us as magnificent, and their quality as excellent beyond previous experience in Britain.'[13]

The next summer, on his way to the Alps, Thomson visited his younger brother, Herbert, in Surrey. Thomson was due to attend a dinner function but his brother arrived home to find him sitting in the dark, an empty tumbler at his side. He had drunk a bottle of carbolic acid: 'Suicide while of unsound mind'. Around the same time Humphrey Jones and his wife Muriel, on honeymoon in the Alps, were both killed when their guide slipped on Mont Rouge de Peuteret.

Another of Winthrop Young's inner circle was the blond, blue-eyed Siegfried Herford. The enigmatic Herford (he may have been autistic) visited Skye in 1912 when he was 21, two years before his mould-breaking lead of Central Buttress on Scafell, the high-water mark of pre-war British climbing (originally Hard Very Severe, now E1 after the loss of the crucial chockstone). Since 1909 Herford was an engineering student at Manchester University, specialising in aeronautics, and rubbing shoulders with the likes of Wittgenstein. Herford was accompanied in Skye by his regular partner John Laycock, a Runcorn lawyer who compiled the first major guide to gritstone. Due to poor weather the pair failed to fulfil their potential in the Cuillin, but their journey north must be one of the most convoluted ever made.

Leaving Manchester at 11pm they had to change trains twice in the middle of the night. The West Highland Line from Glasgow to Mallaig provided a couple of missed connections (at one point their train was travelling back towards Glasgow), leaving them stranded at Bridge of Orchy station on Saturday evening with no trains till Monday. To pass the time they walked to Glen Coe for an ascent of Crowberry Ridge Direct. When they eventually reached Mallaig (no regular Skye ferry yet) they hired a boat to Armadale, and then walked to the Point of Sleat where they hoped to get a fishing boat to Rum and finally connect with a vessel for the island of Soay. They eventually managed to reach Rum but there were complications with catching the steamer. A fishing boat took pity on them and landed them on Skye at An Leac, opposite Soay. This probably explains their unusual choice of campsite, a few miles south of Glen Brittle 'in the middle of a bog'. When their flysheet was blown away one night, they were forced to sort things out stripped naked in order to preserve their only dry clothes, sets of pyjamas.

The location of their base also explains why they were attracted to explore the rarely visited Coire nan Laogh, between Sgurr na Eag and Gars-bheinn, where they had spotted potential from the fishing boat. Here they climbed three new gullies which they named A, B and C, though modern guidebooks refer to them as West, Central and East. Laycock recorded how a 100ft (30m) pitch below the start of East Gully (Difficult) gave him as much pleasure as anything else they did on Skye. This included effortless ascents of a wet Cioch Direct, a wet Slingsby's Route on Sgurr nan Gillean as well as Slanting Gully, their only dry day. There is a photograph of Herford on Slingsby's Route with his jacket elbows torn to absolute shreds. All of these routes were approached on foot from their campsite and this high level of fitness contributed to these cutting-edge climbs failing to live up to their reputation; even Cioch Direct seemed an anti-climax compared to Crowberry Direct which Laycock described as 'emphatically superfine'.

At the Pen-y-Pass gatherings there was also a small Irish contingent, led by Winthrop Young's cousin, Page Dickinson, which occasionally sailed over to North Wales on Conor O'Brien's yacht. Another of the group, W B Yeats, was not invited to Wales as Young felt his poetic sensibility would be a liability on the rocks. O'Brien's godson, the writer and diplomat Conor Cruise O'Brien, who was named after him, went on to describe the sailor, 'I have never seen a human being who looked more like a gorilla.' In 1923, O'Brien set off in his ketch *Saoirse* bound for New Zealand to join a mountaineering party. As he arrived too late, he continued around Cape Horn to reach Dun Laoghaire harbour almost two years to the day from when he left; the first person to sail around the world in his own yacht by way of the clipper route round Cape Horn (Joshua Slocum used the Magellan Strait). *Saoirse* remained his only home until he sold her in 1940.

In the summer of 1912, O'Brien anchored at Loch Scavaig with fellow Dubliner, E L (Ernest) Julian. Julian was a high flyer. Aged 27 he became Reid Professor of Law at Trinity College, Dublin, a position held by two future Irish Presidents, Mary Robinson and Mary McAleese. The previous Christmas Julian created panic at Pen-y-Pass when he and N E Young got completely lost and spent the night under a small boulder near the summit of Crib Goch. In times of crisis the Edwardians turned to their classical education for answers. This pair, in a stoical attempt to keep warm, took turns to stand outside and recite Homer. The event was characteristically celebrated by O'Brien with the composition of a song 'The Search Party'.

On Skye O'Brien and Julian walked along Loch Coruisk and then up into Coireachan Ruadha where they intended to explore the uncharted acres of Sgurr Dearg's north-east face. In the wet and slippery conditions they took a rightwards-trending line from the lowest slabs towards a prominent rock tower near the top of Sgurr Dearg. They recorded this serious mountaineering route (O'Brien and Julian's Climb, Severe) in the Sligachan Climbers' Book: 'The climb is exceedingly steep and as the rock is largely basalt the holds are small and often slippery. The whole face is swept by water and a party caught anywhere on the climb in heavy rain would be in a very dangerous position.'

Three days later, again in wet conditions, O'Brien and Julian tackled Mhic Choinnich's North-East Gully (VS) probably the hardest climb yet tackled in the Cuillin. A hundred years after its first ascent the 2013 SMC guide commented: 'The climb is unchecked and the grade likely to be considerably higher.' The Irishmen found that the main difficulties were concentrated in a vertical 150ft (45m) section, approached by an easy but sensational hand traverse across the top of an overhanging flake. A crack then led into a slabby corner which proved the crux, a pull-up on tiny holds into a small, steeply sloping shelf. They only succeeded in grappling their way up this greasy problem because of a good hitch, 10ft up, with which the leader could be protected. They concluded their notes with: 'From a spectacular point of view this is perhaps the finest gully in the Cuillin. The damp state of the rock increased the difficulty, but even under the best conditions it must rank as one of the severest climbs in the mountains.' Many would agree. In August 1951 Bill Brooker and Mike Dixon, at the end of a fortnight's holiday in which they had completed many of Skye's hardest climbs, including the first ascent of Crack of Dawn, failed on North-East Gully. The next month Dixon and Dan Stewart completed the climb, what they thought was probably the second ascent, and felt a great deal of respect for the pioneers.

In the years prior to the First World War, Steeple, Barlow and Doughty continued to systematically explore Sron na Ciche and the remaining Skye gullies. The recording of their routes is increasingly sophisticated including the innovative use of photo-diagrams. In the summer of 1912 Steeple and Doughty reached Mary Campbell's cottage by way of Loch Coruisk, then the steep tramp over Bealach Coire Lagan to Glen Brittle where they met up with Barlow at their favourite base. Their first new route was the steep West Gully (Very Difficult) on the unclimbed Ghrunnda face of Alasdair, a good climb with eight short but strenuous pitches in quick succession. They found the rock here sound, contrary to the contemporary reputation for looseness on south-facing cliffs in the Cuillin.

Their next new route was Direct Route (Severe) on the 'magnificent' Eastern Buttress of Sron na Ciche, the finest climb any of them had yet done on Skye, snatched during a lull in a stormy August: 'The route is one of absorbing interest, as few of the pitches can be seen from those which precede them, and there is a constant feeling of glorious uncertainty as to the nature of the difficulties ahead. The superlative quality of the rock and the many fine situations lend a charm to the climb, which is only tempered by regret that the buttress is not as high as its more westerly neighbour.'[14]

After Doughty's departure, Steeple and Barlow went on to ascend the neighbouring Chimney Route (Difficult): 'This climb, though less difficult than the Direct Route, is full of interest, the situation, on the outer edge of the great left wall of the gully, being very striking.' They also had a long held ambition to girdle the whole of the Sron na Ciche cliffs, and they delayed their intended departure to see if the wind would let up and allow them to make an attempt. Steeple later admitted, 'there is something very thorough about a Skye gale which compels one's admiration'. After five stormy days the winds eventually abated and, though it was still raining steadily, Steeple and Barlow decided to set out on this marathon jaunt of over 3,000ft (910m).

Starting in the Sgumain Stone Shoot they traversed right across Eastern Buttress, climbing down the 'serpentine chimney' in the process; then across the Cioch Slab to the neck behind the Cioch where they descended a narrow, slanting chimney they had discovered in 1909. They eventually topped out near the finish of Median, creating a Very Difficult that linked up several interesting sections of the face. The expedition was described in the 1996 SMC climbing guide as 'a real expedition for jaded palates'. When Hirst, Fraser and Bishop repeated the Girdle Traverse in 1915 they recommended it be tackled in the opposite direction (right to left) as the climbing on the Western Buttress felt an anti-climax in comparison with some of the earlier sections.

The next summer (1913) Steeple and Barlow returned to Glen Brittle to be blessed with a long spell of hot weather. It was so warm they started up one lengthy climb on Sron na Ciche at 8pm They devoted most of their break to exploring the rarely visited crags on the Coruisk side of the range. As these cliffs were generally east-facing, a conventional post-breakfast start from Glen Brittle meant you were already in the shade by the time you reached the foot of the climbs. To maximise any time in the sun, Steeple and Barlow made alpine starts from Glen Brittle, frequently as early as midnight, often taking an hour's nap in the heather before commencing to climb. On this occasion exceptionally dry conditions enabled them to double the number of climbs in Coir' an Uaigneis, with Second-Third Gully (Very Difficult) selected for particular praise.

The following month (September) saw the Rucksack Club party of J B (Ben) Meldrum and two brothers, William and Jesse Wallwork, arrive on the island. William Wallwork developed a great affection for the solitude offered by the Cuillin, but soon realised they were a very different proposition from English hills with few well-trammelled paths or even cairns to mark the way. Meldrum, a mechanical engineer who took part in the second ascent of Scafell's Central Buttress, was renowned as a late developer. A resolute bachelor he gamely held his nerve until succumbing to matrimony at 90. He was elected an honorary life member of the Alpine Club on his hundredth birthday, and later became something of a celebrity when he had to resit his driving test after an accident. Meldrum lived to be 107.

In the Cuillin the three Rucksackers soon found themselves under the wing of Harold Raeburn who had recently returned from an expedition to the Caucasus. When Raeburn supported Meldrum's application to join the SMC he stated: 'I consider him one of the very best rock climbers I know.' Raeburn had the use of Colin Phillip's shooting cabin at An Leac opposite Soay, a base which provided a fine view into Coir a' Ghrunnda. An Leac was also where a heather fire was lit to notify islanders on Soay when a boat was required; a different heather knoll was reserved for each family so they knew whose responsibility it was to ferry folk across.

Raeburn inveigled the Rucksackers to join him in tackling a new climb on the north face of the isolated Sgurr Coir' an Lochain. When they attempted to ascend this imposing buttress directly from the lowest point they were consistently forced left onto steep slabs, probably joining the upper part of Norman Collie's Original Route. They took nearly four hours for the ascent, leisurely by Raeburn's frenetic standards. He summed the route up, 'Hitches are not abundant and great care is always necessary.' Although Raeburn's Route is graded Very Difficult, repeat parties should expect some harder sections, though few crowds. Harold Raeburn reckoned they were the first to visit the summit since the mountain was first climbed in 1896. Raeburn also went on to record an ascent of the broken buttress on the Coir' an Lochain face of Sgurr Thearlaich (North-East Ridge, Moderate). When he recommends this route as an alternative to the 'somewhat difficult passage' of the Thearlaich-Dubh Gap, he is doubtless thinking back to his own dramatic crossings in the blizzard conditions of 1903 and 1905.

With the outbreak of the First World War, in August 1914, the Alps became out of bounds. Many mountaineers were caught out and had to hurriedly pack for home. Harold Raeburn had an epic five-week journey back from the Caucasus. With the Alps now unavailable the Cuillin were mooted as a fine alternative; there were few visitors about so accommodation at Sligachan was much easier to secure. But even here it was hard to escape the hostilities as convoys with destroyer escorts steamed up and down the Minch. William Galbraith of the SMC arrived on the island as many young Skyemen were sailing off to the war aboard the *Gael*. Few would return. The Skye Company of the Cameron Highlanders was decimated overnight at Festubert in May 1915. One who fell, shot through the neck, was Ronald Macdonald, a Portree solicitor and SMC member who, barring John Mackenzie and the other guides, was regarded as the greatest local expert on the range.

In 1915 Steeple and Barlow arrived in Skye earlier than usual, in April, to find the holy grail of modern British mountaineers, the Cuillin Ridge, in pristine alpine condition. After a day climbing the Alasdair Stone Shoot on perfect snow they ascended the west face of Sgurr a' Ghreadaidh, ground they had explored under summer conditions in 1910. (The Eton party of Tatham, Porter and Benson made two unsuccessful attempts on this face in similar conditions at Easter 1892). Steeple went on to relate how they then traversed the narrow crest of Ghreadaidh which, in good conditions, provides one of the finest winter ridge climbs in Britain:

> Mounting into the south branch of Coire a' Ghreadaidh, we kicked and cut up a steep snow-slope to the foot of the Diagonal Gully, continuing up its snow-filled bed. When this became too icy for a rapid advance we broke out on the left, ascending by mixed snow and rock on the face of the mountain, and, re-crossing the gully near its top, gained the main ridge a little to the right of the south summit. The shattered ridge northward was traversed in a snowstorm, which added to the excitement, but put the camera out of action. There is no actual climbing on the ridge, but it is so narrow and broken that it is always interesting, and clad in ice and snow it is super-excellent.[15]

Two days later Steeple and Barlow made an unrecorded winter ascent in Coire na Creiche, 'a zigzag route up the easterly slabs of Mhadaidh', possibly South Buttress. They also made an ascent of the classic gash of Sgurr nan Eag's Chasm: 'Its architecture is of a most imposing character, and the astounding upward curve of its great left wall is perhaps unique in the Cuillin.' The 1923 SMC guide described the first ascent conditions as 'partially filled with snow', though Barlow and Steeple's earlier account suggests the climb was banked up: 'The gully when reached was also found to contain a vast quantity of snow which completely masked the pitches we had previously seen.'[16] They were so taken by this atmospheric climb they resolved to repeat it in summer conditions, a chance to find out what delights were hidden underneath the snow and ice.

An opportunity came in 1919 when, accompanied by Doughty, they found four complex chockstone pitches. Steeple recalled the second pitch as providing the most difficulty: 'The cave possesses a through route which, however, is not easy to reach except by means of a human ladder.' A chimney in a vertical wall then led to the last pitch where there was a 'tier of immense blocks wedged overhead'. This complicated pitch, now regarded as the crux, ends at the distinctive rock archway that is often scrambled over on the traverse of Sgurr na Eag. By exiting the Chasm under this you can make the unusual claim of starting a climb in one corrie and finishing in another.

In September 1915, William Wallwork returned to Skye with H M (Harry, but only to close friends) Kelly and John Wilding, a hardworking organiser for the Rucksack Club. Kelly was a powerfully built figure who was one of the leading Lake District lights in the 1920s, especially associated with Pillar Rock. Kelly's private life seems shrouded in mystery though rumour had it he worked as a civil engineer. When they reached Skye, Wallwork, Wilding and Kelly set off for

Glen Brittle on foot from Kyleakin, spending their first night in Broadford. They then opted to walk to Glen Brittle by way of Camasunary and then around the coast. Like many before and after, they underestimated the time required for this, spending an unplanned night in the heather. Once at Glen Brittle they were some of the first climbers to stay at what became a Cuillin institution, Mrs Chisholm's post office at Bualintur, the western part of the village reached across a wobbly suspension bridge over the river. (This was occasionally swept away by winter storms.) Looking from the Coire Lagan path above the Glen Brittle campsite, the post office was the leftmost of the cottages on the far side of the River Brittle.

Agnes Chisholm was originally from Gartocharn on Loch Lomond and moved to Glen Brittle after her marriage to Malcolm Chisholm in 1912. That summer she started to take in guests. Although there were only sixteen visitors in her first season, she soon became a much-loved fixture of the Skye climbing scene. The 'very sprightly' Mr Chisholm tended to stay in the background (there were rumours of being henpecked), making an appearance when visitors required postcards, stamps, or parcels of excess gear to be sent home.

Although Mrs Chisholm's developed into an important focal point for climbers in Glen Brittle, it was a long way from the once handy peaks above Sligachan. Undeterred, the Rucksack Club party set off on foot from the cottage for ascents of Pinnacle Ridge and Naismith's Route on the Bhasteir Tooth. Kelly noted the latter as, 'A long round for a 100-foot climb'. With regard to footwear, this was a transitional period when nailed boots were generally worn for climbing, but plimsolls carried for any particularly hard sections. On Cioch Direct's crux chimney Kelly succeeded in rubbers after Wallwork failed wearing boots.

The Rucksackers had hoped to try Archer Thomson's Route on the Cioch's Upper Buttress. Failing to locate this, they decided to attempt what they thought might be a new route. The result was the exposed Slab and Crack, now known as Wallwork's Route (Very Difficult), for years under-graded as an infamous 'Skye Diff'. They surprised themselves in reaching the top as the climb appeared so desperate from below. It was Kelly's first new route, and up until publication of the 1958 SMC climbing guide was often referred to as 'Kelly's Route'. However the crux was led by William Wallwork, wearing rubbers, with the heavier boots carried in a rucksack by the last man. Wallwork later related how he followed an initial trap dyke to a mantelshelf:

> The mantelshelf was quitted by its left corner, and a short chimney with three jammed stones ascended to a small cave. Thence the wall on the left is climbed to a chimney of easy angle with a sheer wall on its left and a staircase of rock on its right. After this chimney comes the most difficult pitch of the climb. One bears slightly to the left to go between a huge sloping slab and the left wall; the slab is mounted, and from a precarious stance on its sloping summit the crack which rises above is attained with difficulty by means of

small holds on the left wall; the ascent of the crack is the end of the climb.[17]

After 25th July 1916 the area north of a line between Inverness, Invermoriston and Kyle of Lochalsh became a 'Special Military Area' and those visiting were required to apply for a permit. (However the whole area could be circumvented by the train to Mallaig and steamer to Skye.)

One group who visited Skye at this time were exempt as they were members of the armed forces. This party was organised by David Pye who was inspired to visit the Cuillin after attending one of Norman Collie's lectures at the Alpine Club. Currently serving as an engineer with the Royal Air Force, Pye got together a small group of friends, all regulars at Pen-y-Pass, for a visit in July 1918. During much of the Second World War Pye was Director of Scientific Research with the Air Ministry for which he was later knighted. He features in the movie *The Dam Busters* where he is played by Stanley Van Beers. David Pye was an old friend of George Mallory's at Cambridge, and became his first biographer with the 1927 book *George Leigh Mallory*.

For the Cuillin trip Pye invited Mallory, currently home from the war on extended sick leave (the aggravation of an old climbing injury to his ankle) and his wife Ruth. The couple had married in 1914, a relationship described by their best man, Geoffrey Winthrop Young, as 'too good to be true'. George Mallory was part of the pre-war Cambridge set that included Rupert Brooke, James and Lytton Strachey, Geoffrey and Maynard Keynes; proto-hippies challenging the social and sexual conventions of the day. After university Mallory joined the staff of Charterhouse School where one of his pupils recalled an unlikely Himalayan hero: 'He was pale and to our unskilled eyes, weedy, far from athletic. He taught English and really seemed to enjoy poetry. Discipline, he had no idea of keeping. On one occasion he was put on the floor and we sat on his head.'

At Inverness the Mallorys met up with Pye and the final member of the team, Cuillin veteran Leslie Shadbolt. Early in the First World War Shadbolt was an officer in the Hood Battalion, a close-knit cadre that coincidentally also included Rupert Brooke as well as fellow poet Patrick Shaw-Stewart. They are commemorated in a piece of navy doggerel, 'The Hood Alphabet': 'Shaw-Stewart and Shadbolt both start with an S: one excels at finance, and the other at chess.'[18] They all attended Brooke's funeral on the Greek island of Skyros after he died of blood poisoning on the way to Gallipoli.

An isolated shower at Kyle of Lochalsh was the last rain Pye and his friends would see for eight days. Shadbolt, the only one who had been to Skye before, recommended they try Archer Thomson's Route in Coir' a' Mhadaidh. However, once roped up at the foot of the cliff, the impetuous Mallory struck out on a steep line to the right, the easier but no less intricate Pye and Mallory's Route (Very Difficult), 'Of good belays there are few.'

The Mallorys were inveterate skinny dippers and as the pressure rose, each day dawning hotter than the last, no opportunity was lost for bathing in sea, burn or loch (with mixed nude bathing the etiquette was that men were expected not to look). When they moved their base from Sligachan to Glen Brittle, it was a long and exhausting day; over Druim nan Ramh to Loch Coruisk and then a climb up the north face of Sgurr Coir' an Lochain which Pye later described: 'There are several really difficult pitches, and towards the top some of the most delightful slab climbing I know, varied by sensational ledge walking and some elegant chimneys.' They then climbed over Bealach Mhic Choinnich and down Coire Lagan to, first a swim in the sea, and then some welcome supper at Mrs Chisholm's.

The next day Ruth Mallory chose to rest in the glen while Pye sunbathed on the Cioch's summit, watching Mallory and Shadbolt's progress on a new route the pair were attempting on the Upper Buttress: 'Mallory led Shadbolt up what we thought at the time was a new climb running straight up the face from the start of Mr Archer Thomson's route, which traverses up to the right.'[19] This route description and the fact they found a cairn at the top suggests a repeat ascent of Wallwork's Route. However David Pye's account in the *SMC Journal* is illustrated by photographs on which he has marked their explorations. His dotted line avoids the obvious weakness of Wallwork's to instead follow some impressive ground to its left.

The final day of Mallory's stay was directed at climbing Sron na Ciche's Western Buttress direct from the screes, as most of the existing routes crept in from the right. The assiduous Mallory spent six hours trying to solve the problem of his Slab and Groove (Very Difficult); the most time-consuming section was trying to find a way through the water-worn slabs above Central Gully. A year later the route was repeated by Bower, Meldrum and Solly who commended it as 'probably the finest buttress climb in Skye'. After the well-defined start, many repeat parties created numerous variations, both deliberate and accidental.

Mallory's week in Skye was rounded off with 'a glorious bathe' on the way to Sligachan before his return to England and, soon after, the Western Front for the final months of the war. His place in Skye was taken by Geoffrey Bartrum, a member of Ashley Abraham's party in June 1907. Bartrum would join Pye and Shadbolt as they checked the reputations of the Exceptionally Severe courses in Abraham's graded list. Only Waterpipe Gully Direct passed the test.

The exceptionally warm weather enabled David Pye and Leslie Shadbolt to have eight consecutive days climbing on gabbro. They now had a well-deserved rest. The next day was their last in Glen Brittle and they had big plans. Climbs which have names prior to their first ascent generally display a certain strength of character. The unclimbed Crack of Doom, the sweeping, curved crack above and to the right of the Cioch, had been an ambition of most leading climbers who had visited the island. Barlow and Buckle, George Mallory and the Abraham brothers had all inspected the climb's infamous crux. Pye and Shadbolt had one last chance to take up the challenge. Rested and on top form they completed their warm-up climb, Cioch Direct, in an hour and a quarter. At the foot of Crack of Doom, Pye assessed the view upwards:

> I felt certain these lower pitches would go; they looked as if one could in time have wriggled up them, even without holds, but then there was that forbidding looking stretch at the top, black and greasy and apparently holdless; it was necessary to keep a big reserve of energy for that. There is a chock-stone about halfway, and one felt that at least one could reach that and have a rest …There are no holds at all on the right wall, which here becomes black and slimy. The left wall is dry, and it is possible to find just sufficient hold on it to raise oneself steadily and positively by the feet, with no wriggling. It will be interesting to learn how the pitch strikes other parties.[20]

He did not have long to wait. The next July (1919) George Bower made a repeat ascent: 'This is without doubt, the most difficult climb we did during the holiday, the sort of climb one vows never to revisit, except in nightmares.' With opinions like this, Crack of Doom developed a formidable reputation. When the traditional British grading system was introduced to Skye in 1948 it was the only climb given Very Severe, the highest grade then available. The ominous name only added to its aura, and it remained *the* route to aspire to well into the 1950s. Later down-graded to Severe, it now appears to have stabilised at Hard Severe.

During the First World War, at Gallipoli in June 1915, Leslie Shadbolt was wounded by a bullet in the left arm, but patently made a good recovery after being shipped to hospital in Alexandria. Many others who feature in the story of the Cuillin weren't so lucky. Professor Julian enlisted with the Dublin Pals, arriving in the searing heat of Suvla Bay with no maps and no orders, no water and little ammunition. The Irishmen threw stones and the Turks threw back grenades. One of Julian's men, Private Wilkins, caught five and threw them back. The sixth blew him to pieces. Julian was shot in the back and died the next day, the third anniversary of North-East Gully on Sgurr Mhic Choinnich. The Gurkhas also fought at Gallipoli: Harkabir Thapa was killed, Charlie Bruce was severely injured.

During trying times the editor of the *Rucksack Club Journal* tried to maintain morale: 'It has occurred to me that if we suspend publication it will be placarded all over Germany as proof that England is unable to carry on.' On the Western Front Harry Walker, one of the Dundee cousins, died at the Battle of Loos. Siegfried Herford, whose mother was German, was killed by a grenade near Bethune in 1916. Nigel Madan died on the Somme; Alastair McLaren was seriously injured at Arras and would never climb again.

Back in London, John Buchan was head of propaganda, Director of Information, choreographing a campaign to quash pacifist sentiment and maintain the impression of a just war against a heinous enemy. Harrison Barrow of the 1897 Coruisk camp, a Quaker, wrote an anti-war pamphlet, *A Challenge to Militarism,* and was jailed for six months in Pentonville Prison for refusing to submit the leaflet to government censors. Mallory's mentor, Geoffrey Winthrop Young, had a leg amputated above the knee after being hit by a shell in Italy. T E Goodeve died in Palestine. G P Baker lost three sons. Charlie Inglis Clark, father to a new-born son, was killed in Mesopotamia in the last year of the conflict. The telegram read: 'He died from gunshot wounds to the head received in action.' Geoffrey Howard, an SMC member, reflected every climber's thoughts:

> I wonder if the war will ever end and give us leave to walk among the hills again. I want to feel the good Scottish rain running down my neck; I want to feel great screaming winds roaring down the glen; I want to hear Willie Ling say for the ten thousandth time, 'It's a fine day but saft.' In a word, I want a big Easter Meet in peacetime, and I want – but there, the rain has stopped, and the evening paper has come, and the war and its work are still our masters.[21]

Chapter Eight

Goodbye to all That

After the First World War, there were two Britains: composed of those who had fought in the conflict and those who hadn't. With newspapers and letters heavily censored, non-combatants had still little inkling regarding the realities of modern warfare and often showed little compassion or understanding for its participants, who faced further ignominy for having survived while others' loved ones hadn't. The writer Robert Graves, a close friend of George Mallory's, related in his autobiographical *Good-bye to All That* (1929) that many soldiers on leave found it a relief to return to Flanders, so skewed was the perception of the war back home. At the end of hostilities, British life was dominated by over one and a half million injured veterans: amputees, facially disfigured, homeless, unemployed, blind, shell-shocked and insane; hollow-eyed men who couldn't or wouldn't talk about the past.

The 1920s was a listless, melancholic decade as people, many numbed by grief, came to terms with the slaughter in their own different ways. In Skye, few families were left untouched; often whole communities were decimated. The MacLeod estate sold off large parts of Minginish to the government; much of the village of Portnalong originates from this time when landless veterans from Lewis and Harris were offered plots for houses there. The estate retained Glen Brittle, the Cuillin and Soay, while the greatly reduced Glen Brittle Farm was let to the Wisharts from Elgin until 1929 when the MacRae family, who are still in residence, became tenants.

Some of the first climbers to return to Skye after the war were C F ('Charlie') Holland, H R C (Herbert) Carr and Dorothy Pilley. In August 1919 they met up at Mrs Chisholm's post office ('one large bed, take four if their knees are slightly bent'). Herbert Carr, who was introduced to climbing by Holland, described his fellow schoolmaster as, 'A short, stocky sharp-featured man, with a grin that reminded one of the famous gargoyle on Notre Dame and a laugh that became more and more Rabelaisian after the second or third pint.'[1] Prior to the war Holland was a workman-like climber despite contributing to major events like the first ascent of Scafell's Central Buttress. During the conflict, in which he was awarded a Military Cross, his right elbow was smashed by a piece of shrapnel, an event that paradoxically seemed to galvanise his climbing career.

For any lulls in the Flanders bombardments Carr had taken with him George Abraham's *British Mountain Climbs* and *The Complete Mountaineer*. Dorothy Pilley had several first ascents to her credit including the North Ridge of the Dent Blanche in 1928, and the Victoria Memorial on Armistice Day 'with the help of a soldier and a sailor'. She was a journalist with political aspirations who became a noted authority on Chinese culture, religion and art. She preferred to be called plain 'Pilley', as was the current post-suffragist fashion. Adventurous to the last she spent her final New Year at the Glen Brittle Hut, aged 92, drinking gin till the early hours.

Holland had a reputation for recklessness and, at a time when the dictum decreed the leader never fell, was quite happy to take a tumble. He had a warning cum catch-phrase: 'I'll be off in a minute.' In Holland's opinion the longer the fall the safer it was. The only time he hurt himself was when he fell two inches on Dow Crag in the Lake District. In fact he became quite proud of his ability to accomplish them with a degree of panache, recounting them with the same relish most people saved for the crux moves.

While in Skye, Holland would add two serious peels to his tally. The first was on the final committing moves of Cioch Gully when, hands numbed by wet holds, his strength failed him for the final strenuous heave, as Pilley recalled: 'Holland, skin unbroken and composure unruffled, rose to his feet and began to look for his pipe.' This pitch developed a reputation, with even Menlove Edwards, one of the most powerful climbers of his day, falling off in 1931. Charlie Holland's second fall was on Shadbolt's Chimney on the Bhasteir Tooth when he suddenly found himself hanging upside-down in space. Ironically, this last spill removed the remaining adhesion in his wounded arm which he claimed was considerably improved by the experience. In later years Holland lied about his age to serve in the Second World War. Caught in the bombing of the London Blitz, he reflected on happier times in Skye:

> An air raid of considerable magnitude is now going on, and in the variety of strange noises that is assailing my ear drums my mind has become a jumble of conflicting memories; at one moment I am hurtling through the air into the welcoming arms of Richards, only to find myself up in Skye and hanging at the end of a rope on the Bhasteir Tooth, held up by the strong arms of Pilley; in the same moment I am reclining among the boulders below the top pitch of the Cioch with the rest of the party a good deal higher; their laughter still rings in my ears; they say now that it was due to relief at my escape, but I am sure there was a good deal of genuine amusement in it, and I hope there was.[2]

The highlight of Carr, Holland and Pilley's stay of 1919 was a new route to the right of Cioch Direct, West Face Climb, now known as the classic Cioch West (Severe). In the corrie below, Steeple and Barlow followed their progress through a telescope, and later complimented them on their achievement and invited them back to their den at Mary Campbell's. Holland was an advocate of the thinner alpine line which was lighter than alpine rope but had half the breaking strain. Its main advantage was minimising the 'pull' on long run-outs, though on Cioch West's breezy traverse Herbert Carr was not convinced:

> Nor did my misgivings prove groundless. Holland climbed easily up a twenty-foot chimney, which sprang from the left-hand end of the ledge, hitched the rope (or, I should say string) over a pinnacle and with a long stride to the left started off along an exposed traverse. One or two places gave him some trouble, and I began to experience all those sensations usually associated with a dentist's waiting room. Finally he reached a broader ledge, drew up the slack after him, and disappeared from view round the corner to re-appear later, thirty feet higher, with a curt order for me to come on. Over my feelings and flounderings on that traverse I would draw a veil.[3]

The next year (June 1920) the Fell and Rock were back in Glen Brittle. Among them was Howard Somervell, a stocky Kendal surgeon who had a traumatic introduction to his profession among the casualty clearing stations of the Battle of the Somme. He joined Mallory on the 1922 Everest Expedition and again two years later when resident in India as part of forty years' service as a medical missionary. In 1924 he attained 28,000 feet without oxygen. Somervell was renowned for his stamina. The publisher Peter Hodgkiss teamed up with him in the Lake District in the 1950s 'when he was 60-odd and climbing at VS with speed and confidence'.

On 20th June, a hot and sultry day, the 30-year-old Somervell set out to attempt the Main Ridge with club-mate Graham Wilson from Tynemouth. They reached the summit of Gars-bheinn in just over two hours but by Sgurr na Banachdich Wilson was finding the pace too hot. After suffering violent cramps he was forced to drop out, leaving Somervell to continue alone. Despite the heat he had no water bottle, sustaining himself with fluid from the occasional snow patch, supplemented by his hometown mint-cake. He soloed Naismith's Route to complete the second successful traverse in 10 hours 29 minutes: 'Another time, with a water bottle and a pound of raisins, I think I could knock another hour off the time, but the chief disability was thirst and unappetising bannock.'[4] When Graham Wilson eventually reached Sligachan the seat of his breeches was completely worn through by the abrasive gabbro, an embarrassment soon forgotten after the magnum of champagne Somervell had waiting.

The respect in which Somervell's feat was held is reflected in one climber's comment: 'Took us that time side to side!' After such an exhausting experience most people would be glad to rest on their laurels and put their feet up. Not Howard Somervell. He was on top form and the next day joined a party for an ascent of Slanting Gully. With Wilson he then completed the much-feared Crack of Doom with few problems, 'formidable but most enjoyable', before creating what he thought was a new route on Knight Peak's north-east face.

Although Howard Somervell considered the Main Ridge Traverse the finest expedition outside the Alps he had noticed (in common with George Abraham) something even more challenging, the possible continuation to include Bla Bheinn and Clach Glas. On his traverse Somervell had actually continued to Sgurr na-Uamha which he regarded as the true termination of the Main Ridge. This extra exertion, a cruel dogleg 180 degrees from the long-salivated refreshments at Sligachan, did not catch on. Although Somervell's traverse has been recorded as the first solo completion, it can scarcely be regarded as such since he was partnered by Wilson for the first, more technical half.

Two months after Somervell's impressive achievements, Skye had a Swiss visitor, Ery Lüscher, a biochemist currently based at Cambridge University. Lüscher had wide experience of the Alps where he began climbing in 1911 as a 17-year-old. He first heard about the Cuillin's charms from Norman Collie. Largely alone, he became increasingly enamoured with their changing moods, making some impressive solo ascents (complete with yodelling). These, often in wet conditions, included Slanting Gully, Cioch Gully and South Crack, his third ascent of the Inaccessible Pinnacle. On his initial visit to the pinnacle when he climbed its West Ridge wearing socks as it was streaming with water, he gave a top-rope to two young members of the Cairngorm Club who thought his performance on the rock 'little short of miraculous'.

The next day Lüscher went from Mrs Chisholm's to Sligachan by way of a solo ascent of Waterpipe Gully followed by a direct descent from Bidein's Central Peak towards Druim nan Ramh. To gain this prominent ridge from the top of the Central Peak you traditionally retraced your steps towards the West-Central gap to gain a ledge system on the Coruisk side. However, from the summit cairn Dr Lüscher, kept going east along a sharp ridge and then descended the impressive prow through a combination of down-climbing and double-roping. This steep section of cliff was first climbed in ascent, in July 1945, by a party led by G H Townend and G C Curtis, better known for their Arran climbs such as Sou'wester Slabs.

Towards the end of his three-week stay Lüscher teamed up with J H Bell, the croquet-playing SMC president (1922-24), to traverse the only part of the ridge he had not managed to cover, from Sgurr Dubh an Da Bheinn to Alasdair. They accomplished this by way of the Dubh Ridge, starting and finishing at Sligachan as all accommodation at Glen Brittle was fully booked, an increasingly common problem. Lüscher's other achievements include a repeat of Slingsby's Route on Sgurr nan Gillean's Third Pinnacle, as well as adding two eponymous routes to its right: Luscher's No. 1 (Very Difficult) and Luscher's No. 2 (Difficult). His first route follows a prominent chimney: 'To pass the chockstone of the top pitch I had to climb with the right arm and leg in a narrow crack on the left of the stone and left leg and arm on the left wall. There was a difficult move getting the right arm from below the chockstone and reaching a hold on the top of the stone.'[5]

The 1920s was a golden age for the Rucksack Club. With their liberated and anarchic attitudes they challenged the more conservative values of the older-established clubs. Winthrop Young remembered 'the admirable blend it presented, elements of university and of industry intermixed with the right proportion of originals and oddities'. Olympian Chris Brasher, a club member for over twenty years, depicted them as 'specialists in extreme journeys'. One of their leading activists was the wiry A S (Fred) Pigott. Like Charlie Holland, Pigott was seriously wounded in the First World War. Considering the resultant disability to his hand (amputation was considered) his subsequent climbing achievements are remarkable. These include participation in the first ascents of three Very Severes on Clogwyn du'r Arddu in North Wales: Longland's Climb, Pigott's Route and Narrow Slab. He was one of the first to experiment with inserting pebbles (usually selected from a nearby stream) in cracks, and slinging them for protection. A Stockport sugar merchant, he was a courteous and modest man though very determined and focused on the rocks. The long-time secretary of the Mountain Rescue Committee, he helped establish a network of Mountain Rescue Posts throughout the country for which he was awarded the OBE in 1964. These included two in Skye: Glen Brittle House and Sligachan Hotel, where stretchers and rucksacks of medical equipment were stored and maintained.

Fred Pigott and John Wilding arrived on Skye in June 1921, the middle of three successive climbing holidays in Scotland that produced Crypt Route (Very Difficult) in Glen Coe and Pigott's Route (Mild Severe) in Coire Mhic Fhearchair in Torridon. In Skye they completed the steep Direct Finish to Crack of Doom (Hard Severe) which George Bower had previously failed on. For a while this was known as Pigott's Continuum. The next day they put up two adjacent Very Severes on the Inaccessible Pinnacle, Route I and Route II.

In the 1920s, little or no thought was wasted on route names. The names of rock climbs are a fascinating reflection of contemporary climbing culture, but the 1920s are an anachronism with the most boring route names ever despite log books, like those at Glen Brittle House and Mrs Chisholm, putting modern equivalents in the shade with their imaginative wit and creative flair in the form of poems, limericks, sketches and cartoons. However, one of Pigott's later routes, Caravan Route (Hard Severe), does have a story behind it. In 1949 he was back on Skye, part of a touring holiday on which he introduced his son Geof to some of his old haunts. Together they put up a new route on Sron na Ciche's Eastern Buttress which started up the first pitch of the Girdle Traverse. Geof Pigott recalled this family holiday, explaining the climb's unusual name:

> My father, mother and I had borrowed Wilson Hey's (of mountain rescue fame) folding Rice caravan which formed a trailer for towing. We camped in Glen Brittle and enjoyed some of the classic Cuillin routes. We spotted the line of Caravan Route and it made an interesting little climb. On the way home, beyond Sligachan, the towing bracket broke and Hey's caravan very luckily came off the road above the long drop to the sea at the only spot for miles where it could be rescued unscathed.[6]

Enquiries were made to purchase the Cuillin in honour of those who died in the First World War. They were not for sale, although an assurance was given that access would always be available for mountaineers. (Many in the 1920s were advocating the Cuillin as a National Park.) As an alternative the SMC decided that a set of guidebooks to the Scottish mountains, what became known as the District Guide series, would make a fine memorial to fallen members. (There was also a General Guide, published in 1921, which made Munro's list available to the general public.) Editors were appointed for each region. Steeple and Barlow were the ideal candidates to help with the Skye volume, but first they had to become members of the SMC. Their applications, proposed by Henry Alexander and seconded by Robert Jeffrey, were submitted to the relevant committee on 28th October 1921. The first page of Steeple's application was a foolscap list of first ascents in the Cuillin, 'all above led'. The SMC committee made the following notes (the discrepancies in ages were possibly due to the applications being initially considered prior to the war).

> **Steeple.** Age about 28, [actually about 40] started climbing 1907. A great many ascents in Skye. A leader of numerous first ascents. Several snow climbs in the Coolin, Ben Nevis, Aonach Mhor, Bidean etc and several guideless climbs in Switzerland.

> **Barlow**. Age about 30, [actually about 38] started climbing in 1906, numerous first ascents in Coolin including a few under snow conditions. Several guideless climbs in Tyrol, no great snow experience

Most of their guidebook research was done between 1920 and 1922 when they also managed to climb 18 new routes. They were occasionally joined by Harry Doughty who had been taken prisoner-of-war in 1918. Their headquarters continued to be Mary Campbell's where the regime was described by Pigott and Wilding in 1921: 'We were quickly made aware of the fact that the ménage was run on the lines laid down by Steeple and we were expected to live up to its high tradition.'[7] In B H Humble's evocative classic *The Cuillin of Skye*, there is a photograph of Doughty and Barlow relaxing in their box beds, replete after one their host's belt-loosening evening meals. Dorothy Pilley elaborated further on their domestic arrangements:

> Here when a large meal ended, tea and eggs in dozens would appear. But Steeple and Barlow beat this. Not content with the tea and eggs in surplus, their hospitality produced a plum pudding boiled in their own billy. It had been gurgling therein succulently all through the meal. Whether it had come to Glen Brittle in one of their locally notorious parcels or had been somehow created by them there I never knew. These parcels were nicely calculated not to exceed either in weight or dimensions the maximum allowed by the Post Office regulations and yet not to fall short of it. They were elegantly encased in a distinctive buff-coloured material and soundly stitched. You could recognise them a long way off. In a stream of such parcels their entire luggage, gear and provisionment would arrive, harbingers appearing some considerable time before Steeple and Barlow themselves.[8]

Barlow had a tent, specially made to withstand Skye gales, which was used for high camps to maximise climbing time in the remoter corries. They also used Doughty's tent: 'The owner informs us that it is possible to stand upright in it, if one stoops low enough.' Steeple recalled one occasion when a whole tent was blown away leaving the occupants shivering on the groundsheet in a downpour. Flooding is another common camping hazard in the Cuillin as the thinness of the soil is unable to soak up much moisture. When the water table rises large areas rapidly become waterlogged. Those wanting to camp in the hills, or around Loch Coruisk or Loch Scavaig, were expected to obtain prior permission. In 1910 Steeple and Barlow were allowed to camp in Coir' a' Ghrunnda; in 1912 Coire Lagan, and in 1919 were some of the first to camp in the remote and atmospheric Coir' an Lochain ('without permission').

Steeple and Barlow often as not imbued their day on the hill with a brew-up in the Cuillin corries using a spirit stove. The popularity of stopping for a cuppa, along with mountain interests like photography, botany and ornithology, reflected a more leisurely approach to a day on the hill. This also created a new topographical feature, the tea boulder, hand-picked for specific qualities like shelter from wind, ergonomic backrest, handy water supply and expansive view. The pair were not alone in regarding the newly available Thermos flask as a convenience too far, a vacuous gimmick with unpleasant smell-retentive qualities, an unwelcome threat to the tea-making ritual with its hard-won mastery of alfresco infusion rates.

Hill snacks included tins of sardines (remember the key!), savoury meat lozenges, dried fruit, potted meat pastes and the age-old favourite, cheese or jam sandwiches. To Mrs Chisholm's eternal relief, the innovation of the weatherproof sandwich tin spelt an end to murmurs about sodden and unpalatable bannocks. Harold Raeburn rarely left the road without a full ration of his favourite acid drops.

Boulders were also used for climbing practice: limbering up before a route or while waiting for the kettle to boil. On the approach to Coire Lagan there was a requisite warm-up on the Matterhorn Boulder near where the path splits off to the Sron na Ciche cliffs. There is film footage, shown on BBC Alba's Cuillin documentary *An Culithian* (2005), of John Mackenzie working out the correct sequence to its Hornli Ridge.

In lower Coire Lagan, Steeple, Barlow and Doughty discovered Parallel Cracks Route (Very Difficult) on Sron na Ciche in 1920, 'a capital climb' with a fine chimney pitch and unusual for the Western Buttress in having an independent line. The same summer they claimed Terrace Gully (Severe) on Sgurr a' Ghreadaidh's Coruisk face, first spotted the year before from the summit of Sgurr Coir' an Lochain. Although some pitches remained wet despite a week of dry weather, they rated it one of the best Skye gullies. Two years later, Steeple and Barlow returned to climb the rocks on the right which provided Terrace East Buttress (Difficult), a drier alternative to the gully.

That summer's main focus, however, was the exploration of a major new cliff, the Ghrunnda face of Sron na Ciche, first noticed by Steeple when he descended the corrie in 1909. Although less imposing than its northern equivalent the new crag received much more sunshine. With its great sweep of glaciated slabs and absorbing view towards the islands of Rum and Canna, Coir' a' Ghrunnda had always been a favourite choice for a visit or as an approach to the peaks on the adjacent ridge. With a dozen new climbs, Steeple and Barlow made it a fine climbing venue in its own right. On their first explorations in 1920 they were initially attracted to the more broken North Crag with Stack Buttress Direct (Difficult) the best of four routes recorded, an excellent excursion with a fine crack pitch of rough rock on the final tower. Slab Buttress (Moderate) also provided a pleasant scramble on coarse gabbro slabs to the summit of Sron na Ciche.

The more compact South Crag has since become much more popular. Of the eight routes pioneered there, White Slab (Very Difficult) became a well-trodden classic. Steeple described it: 'This route, the last to be discovered, makes the finest climb on the crags. It is continuously difficult, and occasionally sensational, but the rock is good throughout, and the climbing varied and attractive. In fact, of the face climbs with which I am acquainted, I know of none on which the standard of difficulty and interest is so well maintained.'[9] Also of merit were Central Buttress (Difficult) giving 'very captivating climbing of some difficulty', the pleasant Green Recess Chimneys (Very Difficult) and Owl Chimney (Difficult) named after a pinnacle in the rake above that resembled a watchful owl.

On the south face of Alasdair, to the left of the Thearlaich-Dubh Gap, Steeple had previously attempted a route to the right of West Gully but was defeated by an overhanging nose. In July 1921, Steeple successfully bypassed this difficulty on the left to create Central Route (Severe): 'The climb is exceptionally severe and demands a sustained effort on the part of the leader.' Over on the Coruisk side of the ridge, on Sgurr a' Choire Bhig, Steeple, Barlow and Doughty explored two unexceptional gullies, but recommended the area as 'well worth a visit, as good and interesting climbing on splendid gabbro may be combined with a walk through three of the finest corries in the Cuillin'.

The same summer (1921) they finally managed Final Tower Direct (Hard Severe) on Sgurr Sgumain, a fine finish to routes on the West Buttress. Although they had visited the foot of this climb several times conditions were always either too cold or too wet. Originally named Terminal Tower, this climb developed something of a reputation as many subsequent parties found it either hard to locate, or difficult to follow the original line. This was due not only to the climb's reserved location, tucked away at the left end of the terrace, but also because of the frugal description, just two sentences: 'The route works upwards across the north face of the tower, trending back to the right near the top. The climb is somewhat severe, on the very rough but clean-cut rock, with few holds.'[10]

With the help of Harry MacRobert, Steeple and Barlow fleshed out Naismith's pre-war climbing notes to complete the SMC guidebook, *Island of Skye*, which was published in July 1923. The *Geographical Journal* reviewed it as 'one of the most perfect types of Guide-book of its class hitherto published'. The most immediate improvement was a series of excellent crag diagrams by Steeple, often juxtaposed with the relevant photographs. There was a larger format gatefold version for Sron na Ciche, copies of which could be purchased separately. However, close inspection revealed some irregularities. For example, on the Cioch Upper Buttress information from David Pye's photo-diagram in the 1919 *SMC Journal* had been uncritically transposed to the new guide's version. Wallwork's Route was still missing although a line approximating to Integrity was shown. Given the prominence of this diagram it is highly likely, in the 26 years until its credited ascent in 1949, that other climbers stumbled onto, if not up, the classic line of Integrity.

Steeple and Barlow's text was supplemented with photographs by Howard Priestman, A E Robertson, and J R Young, as well as sketches by Godfrey Wilson and Fred Jackson. Although the new guidebook did not immediately galvanise activity like its 1907 predecessor, it formed an illustrated package that was pored over by the next generation of climbers who would follow the dotted lines or examine the blank spaces in-between. The new guide retained the Skye numerical grading system.

Howard Priestman, a Bradford textile consultant and great lover of the Cuillin, produced a map at three inches to the mile based on his own photographic triangulation. Housed in an endpaper pocket, his map simplified the alignment of the ridge and the position of the main summits, but appeared somewhat anodyne and rudimentary compared to Alfred Harker's earlier version. During the 1920s, the OS Popular Edition also became available, the first OS maps to use colour and to have 50-foot contours. Although visually attractive these provided little additional help for navigating the complexities of the Main Ridge. They did, though, add some new mountain names to the OS Cuillin lexicon, such as Sgurr Beag, An Stac, Sgurr Coir' an Lochain, Sgurr Dubh Mor and Sgurr Dubh Beag.

Steeple and Barlow's research for the new guide meant spending a lot of time on Skye and inevitably sitting out a lot of bad weather in the cramped, cabin-fevered confines of Mary Campbell's. J H B (Jim) Bell recalled them spending inclement days in Coire Lagan having a competition to find Ordnance Surveyors' bench marks (an arrow-like mark often cut on a rock), each scoring a point when they found one. When this entertainment palled they proposed competing rain gauges in different corries with the loser having to forfeit his late-evening supper of scones and boiled eggs.

Colin Phillip once pointed out that the height of Sgurr Thearlaich had not been properly surveyed, leaving the possibility it might be higher than Sgurr Dearg and even the Inaccessible Pinnacle, the two highest after Sgurr Alasdair. Barlow became increasingly obsessed with solving this problem, developing his own esoteric, one-man levelling technique to calculate the correct heights of the peaks. He finally reckoned Thearlaich to be marginally lower than Sgurr Dearg. However, his most significant finding was that Sgurr Dearg was actually 28ft (9m) lower than the OS calculation, and that many other OS heights were inaccurate. Indeed, those originally given by Collie and Harker often seemed nearer the mark.

For Barlow the whole experience had a profound and lasting effect. When the 1956 *SMC Journal* was reviewed in the *American Alpine Club Journal,* the reviewer was mystified to find, 'nine pages of mathematical formulas and logic seriously attempting to prove that it might be possible to view one Scottish range (the Cuillin) from another (the Cairngorms) 100 miles distant (both are under 4,000 feet elevation).'[11] Yes, it was Barlow.

Guy Barlow's rucksack was for many years preserved in a reliquary at the Glen Brittle Memorial Hut. When the hut was refurbished in 2016 it was donated, along with his rope, to the Scottish Mountain Heritage Collection. For carrying items on the hills the earliest recorded visitors to the Cuillin often favoured a wicker fishing basket, a useful receptacle for geological and botanical specimens. For his two-month Highland walking tour in 1836 James David Forbes used a leather knapsack with a piece of waterproof oilskin to protect the contents: spare clothing, toiletries, books and two geological hammers, a total weight of 15lb (7kg). In the late nineteenth century a party heading off to repeat Forbes's ascent of Sgurr nan Gillean, or the more challenging Pinnacle Ridge, would have lunch in one pocket, tobacco pouch and pipe in another, taking turns to carry the rope coils over a shoulder.

By the 1920s rucksacks were more popular. Women often preferred a satchel. Working-class climbers could only afford the square 'government surplus' ex-army packs, often complete with bloodstains from the trenches. Compared to the Victorian knapsack the more triangular-shaped rucksack had adjustable leather straps as opposed to webbing (Ellis Carr and J H Wicks had a long-running debate over this key issue), allowing the centre of gravity to be lowered which Harold Raeburn advocated as important on steep ground. Specialist mountaineering versions soon became available such as Dexter's alpine model which had leather loops for ice axes and a mackintosh lining. The latter might not be sufficient for persistent Skye deluges, and jaconet or oiled silk bags were often used to further protect contents. These included the tea-making paraffinalia: stove, nested canteen and infuser; as well as items for dealing with any emergency that might arise during a long summer day: spare braces, whisky or brandy flask, sticking plasters, Kola chocolate and candle lantern. The best type of the latter was the Italian Excelsior variety which folded to the size of a guidebook. Lessons were learned from parties who became separated in the dark: one with the lamp, one the candles, the other the matches.

At Sligachan, John Campbell had overseen a programme of improvements and refurbishment. There was now electric lighting throughout the hotel; private sitting rooms were available for guests, and motor cars could be hired for excursions. Reception was stocked with tobacco, chocolate, fishing tackle, walking sticks and postcards. The hotel's season was consolidated from May till September with the last three months constituting peak season. In the less frequented months of May and June there were cheaper weekly rates. Meals now had set times with breakfast at 8.30am and dinner at 7.45pm.

In June 1923 the SMC held a week-long meet at Sligachan but, despite the stimulus of a new guidebook, there was still little stomach for hard climbing. For the time of year there was a lot of snow about, though later in the week the sun began to clear it from the rocks. One of the attendees was the Reverend Aubray Ronald Graham Burn who was hoping for assistance with the trickier Cuillin summits to enable him to become the first person to ascend all the Tops in Scotland over 3,000ft. A reserved and lonely soul, Ronnie Burn was a classical scholar, shabbily dressed with a pronounced hunchback, who spent some of his life in a hostel for the homeless. Burn's sole rock climbing experience was four years earlier, a few days on Scafell with C F Holland. To obtain the help he required for the Skye peaks he was willing to sacrifice his dignity and put himself at the mercy of the younger, more mischievous contingent of the SMC that included J H B Bell and E C (Edward) Thomson.

Jim Bell was a chemist specialising in papermaking, an unconventional character who could and would expound at length on a wide variety of topics. Someone once said of Bell, 'The advantage of Jimmy is that any story you invent about him is almost sure to be true.' The arrival of the garrulous Bell to the SMC in 1922 was just the fillip Scottish mountaineering needed to finally come out of mourning. But just occasionally they may have regretted it. Bell, from a coal-mining area of Fife, had strong left-wing views and when speaking at a Marxist rally was introduced as 'Dr Bell of the Scottish Mountaineering Club'. The June SMC Meet of 1923 was his first visit to Skye.

Burn, whom Bell described as 'a rabid collector', was disappointed with their first day, the still snowy peaks of the Main Ridge from Bruach na Frithe to Bidein, as it only included one Munro. After the peaks at the north of the range were ticked, including an ascent of Knight's Peak by way of a wintry Pinnacle Ridge, Burn, Bell, Philip and Thomson moved south to tackle, amongst other peaks, the oft-dreaded Inaccessible Pinnacle. Here Bell adopted his natural role as ringleader: 'By common conspiracy we persuaded Burn that he must stand upright on the small block on the summit, or he could not be credited with having climbed this important peak.'[12]

They spent the night at Mary Campbell's. Bell, who knew which side his bannocks were buttered on, was particularly taken by this home from home; she would often insist on darning his socks. He later wrote: 'Glen Brittle has never lost that charm for me. The Alps have shown me scenes grander, or on a larger scale but Skye has (alone), between her ugly moods which have a grandeur all their own, been able to show me scenes perfect in colours of crag, moor, sea and sky.'[13] Next morning it was over the tops of Banachdich, Ghreadaidh and Mhadaidh for a large dinner at Sligachan around midnight. On 8th June the plucky Burn even joined Edinburgh lawyer George Sang to claim a new climb, North Face Direct (Difficult) on Bla Bheinn. Six weeks later, on the summit of Beinn a' Chroin near Crianlarich, he achieved his ambition of becoming the first person to climb every Munro and Top: 'I believe I am the first and only one to have done everything.'

The next year (June 1924) the younger SMC members met up again in Skye. Joining them was new member J Rooke Corbett, prophetic advocate of the mountain bike, first to repeat Burn's feat of doing Munros and Tops, and creator of the next eponymous ticking level, the Corbetts. Skye has two Corbetts: Glamaig and Garbh-bheinn. A Bristol tax inspector with a long black beard 'of almost Assyrian magnificence', he did not publish his list of Scottish mountains between 2,500ft and 3,000ft himself, but after his death his sister passed it on to the SMC. In the *Rucksack Club Journal* he was lampooned in a spoof article, 'In the High Grampians with Beard and Bicycle'.

In the Cuillin, Corbett and Bell teamed up to explore King's Cave Chimney only to find the passages blocked, 'an old bleached rope hung down from the lower cave'. That autumn H M Kelly found likewise, the beginning of the end in the popularity of this iconic Cuillin climb. Bell and Corbett climbed Naismith's Route instead but on the way back the competitive Bell was disgruntled to find himself outpaced by Corbett on the moors. In his diary he noted: 'I could get even with him on the rocks.' The chance came the next day on the complex contours of Bidein, but from here on they parted ways: Corbett to Sligachan, and Bell to Mary Campbell's to join other SMC members including Burn with whom he climbed Window Buttress: 'I photographed Burn coming up a pitch but he has not seen the photo and may not want to.'

Another SMC character was W A (William) Morrison, a scientific analyst from Edinburgh where he was once called out to a rescue on Salisbury Crags, and reputedly arrived on his bicycle wearing pyjamas. On wet Glen Brittle days Morrison entertained the household with his penny whistle, or set about repairing Mary Campbell's collection of clocks. Ironically he had little sense of time himself being frequently benighted, including one occasion on the summit of Sgurr a' Ghreadaidh. This was in 1920 after a new, direct version of Collie's South-East Ridge (Difficult) with close friend, Edinburgh solicitor D H (Douglas) Menzies. Cunningly deploying string for tiny hitches, too small for their rope, they followed a narrowing ledge that curved upwards to join the original route above a rickety arete: 'Sitting in the cave, the second could hear a grunt of satisfaction, from which could be gathered gabbro had been struck.' At the summit they celebrated the first ascent with their last scone, 'just enough light was diffused to enable us to distinguish each other'.

As secretary of the Alpine Club in 1953, Basil Goodfellow was involved in much of the behind the scenes work for the successful Everest Expedition. He was part of a group who were influential in the controversial replacement of the original leader, Eric Shipton, with John Hunt, another regular guest at Mrs Chisholm's. In 1924 Goodfellow arrived in Skye with Frank Yates, a fellow member of the Rucksack Club. Both were fresh from graduation at Cambridge and were keen to traverse the Main Ridge. Born in Manchester, Yates went on to become one of the greatest statistical scientists of his generation, specialising in the field of experimental biology. Deplorable weather forced the pair to spend a frustrating week in Glen Brittle waiting for favourable conditions.

Getting an accurate weather forecast was not easy. In fact up to the Second World War one of the most reliable forecasts was provided by Mrs MacRae at Glenbrittle House: if no packed lunches appeared by 10am you could be assured rain was not far away. Although the MET Office started back in 1854, it was geared primarily towards mariners, and from the 1920s aviation. In the Scottish press weather forecasts, prior to the Second World War, originated in London and were out of date by the time they were seen by the reader. By 1923 there were daily BBC radio forecasts of a general nature. For more detailed information the

SMC *General Guide-Book* (1933) advised:

> A special forecast can be obtained by a reply-paid telegram addressed 'Weather London,' or by phone, London, Holborn 3434, Extension 62, or by writing in advance to the Director, Meteorological Office, Air Ministry, Kingsway, London, WC2, enclosing payment for the telegram. It is not usually worthwhile to ask for a forecast beyond the following day, though on special occasions, for example in settled fine weather or cold wintry spells, it may be possible to issue an outlook for two or three days.

On 17th July Goodfellow and Yates eventually achieved their goal of the Main Ridge in a time of 12 hours 50 minutes, the first traverse to be completed in a north to south direction. However this was neither for novelty nor a new record. At Glen Brittle they had given up waiting for settled weather and decided to head for home. From Sligachan a 5.30am start was required to catch the steamer at Portree. Waking up to unexpectedly dry conditions they spontaneously changed plans and set off for the ridge. In mist the whole way, they used the detailed description in the new SMC guide as a navigational aid until the last peak, Garsbheinn, where they were rewarded with their only view of the day. A few years earlier Allan Arthur, after traversing much of the ridge in thick mist, suggested that the names of the peaks should be left in bottles at the summit cairns, so you knew where you were.

For Goodfellow and Yates much time was wasted searching for the top of descents like Naismith's Route and King's Chimney. Descending into the Thearlaich-Dubh Gap they were some of the first to use the classic abseil, a technique recently introduced from the Dolomites. The term abseiling did not become popular (it was German) and 'roping down' continued to be used. The technical standard of the gap was raised by having to climb up the short side where the rock is often greasy in the wet. The mist did have its advantages – it kept them cool and preserved pools of drinking water. Despite a 35-minute delay on Sgurr nan Eag when they lost their way, they completed the expedition in only half-an-hour more than Shadbolt and McLaren: 'Mrs Chisholm's kindness to us in preparing a meal and beds, arriving as we did unexpectedly at midnight, was beyond all praise.'

On the same day as Goodfellow and Yate's completed their traverse, J H B Bell and F S (Frank) Smythe were making the first ascent of West Ridge of the Cioch (Severe). This followed the rib bounding the left side of Cioch Gully, providing a couple of mantelshelf problems before finishing up the previously climbed rocks to the right of Cioch Nose. West Ridge of the Cioch, originally graded Difficult, appears to vanish into the ether, not surfacing in rock climbing guides until 1996, as a Severe. It was the first of seventy new routes Bell put up in Scotland; the last was Pillar Buttress on A'Mhaighdean with his wife Pat in

1950. She once described her husband: 'Jim was five foot seven, slightly built and very tough.'

Look up J H B Bell in an index and somewhere he'll be stripping off and jumping into loch, sea or river. Iain Ogilvie related how he and Bell were in a party intent on the first summer ascent of the North Post of Coire Ardair. It was a scorcher of a day and they first had a bathe in the corrie lochan. The other two got dressed, but not Bell—he just put on his boots and started up the route.

Bell and Smythe (Bell was four years older) first bumped into each other at Wasdale Head in 1921 when Smythe introduced Bell, still a relative novice, to some of the harder Lake District climbs. A difficult childhood (his father died when he was an infant), and some negative educational experiences, gave Smythe an insecurity that left him with a reputation for petulance and irritability. He often claimed he was a 'sickly child' who later suffered heart problems. But this was not true. Smythe went on to study engineering, including hydro-electricity in Austria, before joining the RAF. After being discharged as medically unfit in 1927 he took refuge in the mountain environment.

In September 1923 Howard Somervell was asked to sound Smythe out for possible inclusion on the 1924 Everest expedition. He reported back: 'A bad mountaineer, always slipping and knocking stones down, and an intolerable companion.' Raymond Greene, a fellow member of the successful 1931 Kamet expedition, where he extracted one of Smythe's teeth under a rum anaesthetic, found: 'In temperament he was more highly strung than his rather shy and reserved manner might suggest.' One of his biographers, Harry Calvert, succinctly summed him up, 'Smythe was a misfit.'

In July 1924 Bell and Smythe arranged to meet up at Sligachan. Smythe went to Skye by train while Bell travelled north on his motorbike. At Spean Bridge station Bell decided to ambush Smythe by standing on the arriving platform and shouting 'Good Morning!' as he passed by. They were reunited at Mary Campbell's where regular tenants, Steeple and Barlow, were already ensconced.

Steeple and Barlow occupied the cottage while Bell and Smythe were relegated to the annexe, a corrugated shed by the burn. They were all together for meals when the more experienced pair furnished them with information and advice for attempting the Main Ridge. Steeple and Barlow, imaginations overwrought after too many wet Skye days, initially encouraged them to try something more novel like visiting all the Cuillin corries in a day, or swimming in all the lochans. For the Skye veterans this was one of their last active visits to Skye before they transferred their mountaineering affections to the Lofoten Islands and other areas of northern Norway. Barlow, aged 44, married a Norwegian and eventually retired to Wales. Their final recorded routes in Skye, climbed that July, were Terrace West Buttress (Difficult) on Sgurr a' Ghreadaidh and Owl Buttress Left (Very Difficult) in Coir' a' Ghrunnda.

After several more wet days Bell and Smythe completed the first ascent of

West Ridge of the Cioch. The next day there were rumours that two Cambridge students had done the Main Ridge for the first time in a north to south direction. They popped over to Mrs Chisholm's to meet Goodfellow and Yates and hear their story. Enthused by what they heard they resolved to set out themselves for an attempt early next morning:

> Mary Campbell very kindly offered us breakfast at 2am. The great morning arrived. Mary Campbell was better than her word and eggs, tea, etc. appeared at 1.30am. A more dismal prospect could not be imagined. A fine thick rain was falling. The heavens were black and the clouds came down to within 200 feet of sea level. We retired to bed to read novels and I went to sleep. At 4.30am Smythe wakened me with the news that Alasdair and Sgumain were showing. We set off about 5.15am.[14]

For the first half of the ridge, Bell and Smythe enjoyed perfect conditions of sunshine tempered by a cool breeze. All went smoothly until a delay at King's Chimney when Smythe insisted on trying to climb the wet rock wearing rubbers. Bell took over and led it successfully in nails. It eventually developed into a warm day when their only source of water was what they could suck from small pools or drips with a length of rubber hose they carried. On the enervating grind up Bruach na Frithe the breeze failed them and they began to suffer from the heat. By the final peak Smythe, who unlike Bell had not descended to the spring in Fionn Choire for a drink, was unable to eat due to dehydration. His relief was enormous when he eventually managed to gulp down some water in Coire a' Bhasteir.

For the Alps aluminium or leather water bottles were an essential piece of kit but were regarded as unnecessary on wet British hills. Here the only locally available receptacles were made of glass, usually beer or soda bottles; Shadbolt and McLaren, ever the class act, used a wine bottle for their 1911 Traverse. There were more ingenious solutions to the problem. Some of Norman Collie's slides show wooden barrels being hauled up the Sron na Ciche cliffs on ropes, to be placed strategically to catch and store rainwater for use during dry spells.

Smythe and Bell's was the fourth successful Traverse to be recorded. Their time was 10 hours 40 minutes, only eleven minutes more than Somervell: 'We reached Sgurr nan Gillean at seven pm, but took a long time for the leisurely descent to Sligachan where they gave us a grand dinner, after Smythe had borrowed a pair of trousers for use whilst his own were being mended. It was a great ambition fulfilled, which we did not neglect to celebrate before retiring somewhat unsteadily to bed up a narrow and steep staircase at the back of the hotel, the most difficult pitch of the day.'[15]

On the evening prior to their last day in Glen Brittle they noticed the long shadows on Sgurr Sgumain highlighting a vertical crack. Curiosity piqued, they investigated this the next day to create West Trap Route (Severe). One of the most distinctive landmarks on the cliffs of Sgurr Sgumain is a large white section of rock (actually lichen) known as the White Blaze. Bell and Smythe took a line to its right where a 'formidable, vertical chimney' provided one of few breeches in the defences of a steep wall. This led to the recurring feature of the climb, a trap dyke, the most continuous Bell had ever seen. At one point it went straight up for nearly 70ft (21m) like a staircase that was entirely unsupported on one side.

When Bell reached the shattered pinnacles at the top of the route there could only be one finish, a second ascent of Final Tower Direct (Hard Severe). Bell later admitted that he was too preoccupied by the route's difficulty and exposure 'to take adequate heed of the details'. But he reckoned it was without doubt harder than Crack of Doom, the current benchmark of Cuillin severity. In 1948 he repeated Final Tower Direct along with his wife Pat, and Colin Allan when his respect for Steeple and Barlow's ability was further cemented. This time Bell was able to thoroughly recall the climb:

> After fifty feet of scrambling we were up against the sheer wall. Above us was a terrifying chimney, so much undercut that there seemed to be no way of even reaching its base. Again the gabbro was rough and excellent. Climbing straight over steep slabs to the left, there was just enough holds for pulling up into the niche below the chimney, and there was even a spike for a belay. I cannot say how I managed to lead the chimney itself. I remember pulling up with all my weight on a spike of gabbro which projected somewhat *downwards* towards me. This sounds ridiculous, of course, and was only possible by reason of the rough, sharp crystals which projected everywhere from the surface of the rock. Another spike protruded against my body, and I had to swing round past it to the right in order to raise myself sufficiently to secure a foothold on the right wall of the chimney. The next move had to follow at once, but when the left foot was planted on the other side, I could rest for a moment. The remainder was orthodox but very strenuous.[16]

Since the 1890s, an increasing number of women, like Pat Bell, were enjoying the delights of the Cuillin. The 1890 Alpine Club 'expedition' included Mrs Slingsby, Mrs C Pilkington and Mrs E Hopkinson. Naismith's sister was yet another woman paving the way, one of the first to traverse lengthy sections of the ridge. In 1893 she was just beaten to first female ascents of Am Basteir, Bhasteir Tooth and Clach Glas by Mrs Sidney Williams who also accompanied her husband on the second (direct) ascent of the Dubh Ridge. Other female activists included Mrs T K Rose, the first female to record Pinnacle Ridge (in August 1895), and Evelyn

Heathcote who did several climbs with her brother, J Norman Heathcote. There were also the accomplishments of mother and daughter, Jane and Mabel Inglis Clark. In 1911, Bronwen Jones raised the bar as far as standards were concerned. Her ascent of Chimney and Crack on Sron na Ciche is one of the first, if not *the* first record of women pioneering VS in Britain's mountains.

Up to the First World War, female climbers on the Cuillin were almost without exception accompanied by male siblings or spouses. The war changed womens' lives dramatically proving they could pass muster working in the likes of munitions factories. It was now socially acceptable to drive cars, drink and smoke in public, wear lipstick and participate in energetic sports. Swooning or fainting were no longer the done thing when confronted by the priapic precipices of the Inaccessible Pinnacle. The new independent woman was now starting to record 'manless' ascents despite the often powerful social constraints—it was still considered bold to wear trousers; Dorothy Pilley created a hullabaloo when she refused to change into a skirt for dinner at Sligachan. The Fell and Rock Climbing Club was the only mainstream English club to encourage women to join, the Cairngorm Club had been doing so since its inception in 1887. The SMC would reluctantly bow to pressure in the 1990s.

Mabel Barker was a gypsy-like figure from the Lake District who seemed to exist solely on tea and cigarettes, 'slim and sunburned and her hair… coiled in Catherine wheels over her ears'. She was introduced to climbing by Millican Dalton, Borrowdale's 'Professor of Adventure'. In August 1925 Barker drove to Skye on her Excelsior motorbike to join her climbing companions, H V Hughes and C D (Claud) Frankland, a Leeds headmaster. Frankland was a late starter who only began climbing when he was 31, but soon developed into one of the best rock climbers in the country, especially renowned for his hard solo ascents at Almscliff in Yorkshire. He was so disillusioned with the standard of safety offered by roped climbing that he regarded soloing as a more responsible approach.

In Coire Lagan, Barker, Frankland and Hughes had intended to climb Collie's Route on Sgurr Alasdair but in the misty conditions found themselves starting up a steep gully. This would turn out to be the first route to tackle Sgumain's impressive North Buttress. As the direct start looked wet and uninviting, Frankland climbed a pinnacle on the right before traversing back into the gully by a tricky mantelshelf. Higher up there was another traverse which reminded Frankland of the Collie Step on Scafell. Barker found these moves especially hard as it was her first time on rock for seven months. By the top of the climb the mist cleared and they were able to orientate themselves and figure out where they were: Sgurr Sgumain not Sgurr Alasdair. They named their new climb 'Big Wall Gully' after its imposing right flank.

After several sorties to the Coruisk area where they stayed in a dilapidated corrugated iron hut, Hughes suggested they should try the Main Ridge from

THE BLACK CUILLIN

here as it would be the first time the Main Ridge was done as part of a logical circuit, starting and finishing at the same place. It would also be the first female Traverse. Barker and Frankland made a determined attempt to complete this but conditions proved far from ideal. They had no proper rope, 'Just a clothes-line for lowering rucksacks.' In the mist, despite searching for over three hours, they failed to find a way onto Sgurr na Banachdich from Sgurr Dearg. But they made a pact to try again.

The next summer (August 1926) Barker and Frankland returned to Skye for another attempt. Leaving Coruisk at 5am they were at the top of Gars-bheinn two hours later where conditions seemed no better than the previous year: mist, rain and strong wind. It turned out to be a day of volatile weather trending towards a gradual improvement. By the Inaccessible Pinnacle the rain had stopped; by Sgurr a' Mhadaidh the weather appeared to be settling down. Ascending Bruach na Frithe there was a last hailstorm, while on Sgurr nan Gillean they were rewarded with a temperature inversion. After descending into Lota Corrie there remained only a race against darkness to reach their camp at Coruisk. Barker had fulfilled her ambition of being the first woman to do the Main Ridge returning to the starting point the same day.

Two weeks later Frankland wrote to Barker: 'We must be the first at the complete ridge walk including Blaven and Clach Glas. You and I can do it in dry weather. Rubbers will solve it.'[17] The next year (1927), while Frankland and Barker were climbing Chantry Buttress (Very Difficult) on Great Gable, a hold broke and Frankland was killed when his head struck the rock. His body was found with the piece of rock still clutched in his hand. He is buried in the small graveyard at Wasdale Head. In his honour the Skye climb was renamed Frankland's Gully (Hard Severe).

In 1928 there was the first testosterone-free Main Ridge Traverse. Lilian Bray, along with Dorothy Pilley, was one of the first women to climb guideless in the Alps, and was also a founder member of the all-female Pinnacle Club in 1921. At the age of 89 she took the chairlift to the top of Cairngorm and then walked back to Aviemore, some twelve miles. A forthright and somewhat formidable woman, she was accompanied in the Cuillin by the Wells sisters, Biddy and Trilby, 'always said in that order'. On their first Main Ridge attempt at Whitsun 1927 they were joined by Dr Catherine Corbett, sister of J Rooke Corbett, but were forced to descend after an icy bivouac on Sgurr a' Ghreadaidh when their flask of tea froze solid.

The Pinnacle Club party tried again the next Whitsun but without Dr Corbett. After leaving two caches of food, water and spare cardies, they set out from Mrs MacRae's in Glen Brittle at 2.30am. In stark contrast to their previous attempt this was the warmest day of the year, indeed the hottest weather Bray had ever experienced on British hills: 'The day turned out hot, cloudless and absolutely airless. We left the Pinnacle at 12.30, the heat was really terrific, and the rocks almost too hot to touch, our mouths so dry we could hardly speak.'[18] On the long grind up Bruach na Frithe the heat finally took its toll as one of the party announced they could not manage another step: 'We lay down in our tracks.' By 3.30am they were back on their feet in the cool early morning air to complete the ridge at 9am, a total of thirty-and-a-half hours, much of it in roasting conditions with little fluid. They all agreed that tea at Sligachan never tasted so good.

One woman was crucial to mountaineering in Skye throughout this period. Many climbs and ridge traverses were made possible by Mrs Chisholm's hospitality and invariably fuelled by her ham and eggs, and take-away bannocks. Her kindness, as well as her baking, was remembered with fondness by generations of visitors to the wonderful mountains on her doorstep. Isabel Dickson of the Ladies Scottish Climbing Club tells us more of her triumphs in the face of adversity:

> Without appearing aggressively efficient, Mrs Chisholm conducted a lifelong struggle against circumstances which would have daunted many a stout heart. On an open peat fire she could cook a more than welcome three-course dinner, which seemed to be miraculously ready however late we came. I happen to know that, after a certain hour, members of her family were strategically posted to watch for movement on the green slopes. But that was only one step in a comprehensive campaign; there were bannock and crowdie for sandwiches when the bread failed to arrive and the butter was short; there were the 'annexes' to accommodate extra guests; there was the judicious manipulation of bookings to avoid incompatibility in the sitting-room.[19]

Climbing-wise the 1920s settled into a more relaxed decade in comparison to the highly competitive Edwardian period. In the event of biting Atlantic gales it was now acceptable, though not yet entirely guilt-free, to spend the day sipping well-sugared tea, nibbling scones around the peat fire, listening to the rain rattle off the corrugated-iron roof of Mrs Chisholm's porch and, between trips to tap the barometer, discuss the thorny issues of the day. Were the new, hard steel tricounis causing excessive scratching on the rock of the Cuillin? Was using plimsolls on easier climbs tantamount to cheating? Did the current nails versus rubbers debate approach the ferocity of the belt and braces rumpus of the 1870s? Did scree-running and the standing glissade merit full Olympic status? Mabel Barker and Frankland had left a cache of food and water at the Inaccessible Pinnacle on their first ridge attempt. This was seen by some as unsporting. It was an option rejected by Goodfellow and Yates.

The 1920s saw a great improvement in gear. Successive Everest expeditions made available close-woven windproof fabrics, better designed tents and eiderdown sleeping bags. Gear was lighter too. In 1927 a Rucksack Club party used a two-and-a-half pound (1.1kg) tent at Coruisk compared to the 40 lb

(18kg) tent and 175 lb (53kg) of equipment taken there by Martin and Arthur Gimson of the Climbers' Club in 1906. By the 1920s clothing was lighter and more loose-fitting, moving away from tweeds towards more functional flannels. Harold Raeburn's sister, Ruth, advised female climbers: 'The modern athletic girl does not need to be told that the ordinary corset is undesirable.' Women either bought men's trousers specifically for climbing or borrowed a pair of Oxford bags from a male friend.

In 1888 Thomas Burberry patented gabardine in which the yarn was waterproofed prior to weaving. Though only really shower proof, this produced a light windproof garment that repelled snow and was able to breath. Its innovative design included underarm gussets that enabled climbers to reach for holds without the jacket riding up. It was even made into tents for the expeditions of Scott and Amundsen. Use on the 1924 Everest Expedition, meant Burberry and Jaeger were the designer labels to be seen in at Sligachan and other fashionable mountaineering centres.

The more impecunious made do with battered sports jackets and mangled blazers, regulating the temperature by the number of jerseys, or fastening the collar with a safety pin. In his 1923 book, *First Steps to Climbing,* George Abraham bemoaned this slipping of standards: 'Discarded army outfits and tunics have been much in evidence and the appearance of many cragsmen has become deplorable.'

Mackintosh capes and oilskins were often the only defence available against Skye downpours. A E Robertson, however, felt he had found the answer, encasing himself in a German-made Wettermantel. Hill-goers at this time were prepared to put up with bad conditions and more philosophical about getting wet, relying on a change of clothes at the end of the day. Sartorial self-expression was often reserved for headgear: glengarries, Balmoral bonnets, Nansen hats, cycling caps, knitted Tam o' Shanters, Dexter Climbing Caps, deerstalkers, balaclava helmets and alpine-style felt hats. Trousers and jackets came and went but favourite hats formed a lifelong bond with their owners. In Hebridean gales wide-brimmed versions could be anchored down using a large handkerchief.

George Bower wrote an article (*FRCC Journal* 1917-18) where he laid down the foundation for modern belaying methods. He advocated the use of a shoulder belay to replace the rope being passed over a hitch by the second. However many climbers still did not feel the need to anchor themselves. Bower thought otherwise, and used his vivid 'cork from a bottle' metaphor to emphasise the importance of also tying oneself to the rock.

Light, close-fitting footwear and outcrop training were pushing climbing standards steadily upwards but with little corresponding improvement in leader protection. The leader's utter insecurity, especially on face climbs, was seen as itself a source of safety as it coldly emphasised the consequences of a fall. Slings were occasionally carried as 'independent loops' for the indirect belay, but as yet they had not been adapted for running belays. In this little progress had been made since the Victorians. With rising standards and longer run-outs serious accidents inevitably occurred; there was a fatality on Cioch Direct in 1922. Death in the mountains was still a rare occurrence though inevitably followed by a long period of salutary reassessment. The death of a party of four on Scafell in 1903, all personal friends of the Abraham brothers, was one such tragedy that had resonances nationwide among the close-knit mountaineering community.

In the later half of the 1920s, pioneering of new routes in the Cuillin dried to a trickle. Some of the most regular visitors at this time were students from Cambridge and Oxford Universities who often met up in Glen Brittle when their exams were over. One of the few first ascents to be made was on 24th June 1927 when F W (Francis) Giveen, a former Oxford student, took a direct line up the sound rock of Sgurr nan Gillean's Fourth Pinnacle to create West Face Direct (Hard Severe). The climb was originally done in five pitches with the crux near the end of the original fourth pitch, about 100ft (30m) up: 'Eventually the leader reaches a stance immediately under a large overhang, on a two-inch ledge. Here he can rest but there is no belay, and he must with extreme difficulty traverse about fifteen feet to the right, and go up about five feet over a nose on small sloping holds to a platform with a good belay.'[20] The last pitch involved climbing 'a steep slab of magnificent rock'.

Giveen was ostracised by the participants of not one, but two major sports. All motor sport on public roads was banned on the British mainland in 1925 after a time trial in the Chilterns when Giveen's Bugatti ran off the road and broke a spectator's leg. A few months after the first ascent of Giveen's Route he became a further *persona non grata* after an incident on Craig yr Ysfa in Snowdonia when he abandoned two companions in a blizzard who later died of exposure. He went to bed, then ate a leisurely breakfast before going to raise the alarm. Raymond Greene, elder brother of the novelist Graham, subsequently blackballed him from the Climbers' Club. Outraged, Giveen resolved to shoot Greene. In Oxford, in May 1930, he did shoot someone, a Thames diver's assistant, who some thought he had mistaken for Greene. Giveen then fatally turned the gun on himself.

In the interest of balance it should be noted that behaviour in Cambridge circles was equally delinquent. The month after Giveen's suicide, Sandy Wollaston, who had met Norman Collie's party at Sligachan in 1899, was murdered. After being doctor on the 1921 Everest expedition, Wollaston gave up medicine to become a tutor at King's College, Cambridge. One of his students, Douglas Newton Potts, was absent from college for over a week, then a serious offence. According to the press Potts spent the time in London with Miss Madge Miller, 'a golden-haired night club dancer'. A policeman questioned the student in Wollaston's rooms as to the reasons for his non-attendance. Infuriated by the interrogation Potts drew a revolver and killed the detective, then Wollaston, then himself.

In the five years after Giveen's West Face Direct, until 1932, there was only one new route recorded in the Cuillin, North-East Gully (Severe) on An Diallaid, climbed in 1929 by two unarmed Cambridge students, P M Barclay and J A (Arthur) Ramsay. Ramsay was originally from Ayrshire and went on to become professor of comparative physiology at Cambridge.

Through the 1920s there was a decline in the number of new routes on Skye, as was the case almost throughout Scotland. This was not unrelated to the economic crises of the time which were not just an urban phenomenon. The exceptionally wet weather of 1924 resulted in an almost total failure of the hay, corn and potato harvests in the Hebrides. In addition the peats had not been able to dry so people were without food, fuel or the ability to feed their animals. The SMC petitioned its members for contributions to a Skye Relief Fund: 'Very great distress prevails in the Isle of Skye among many of the crofters owing chiefly to the exceptional wetness of the last season. It has been a source of very great happiness to many SMC members and others to express their gratitude for such halcyon memories by combining in a "Climbers' Contribution" to the fund for relieving distress in the island.'[21]

The miners' strikes of the 1920s led to great disruption in the steamer services with many visitors, like the SMC's A G (Archie) Hutchison, hiring fishing boats from Mallaig to Loch Brittle. Hutchison was one of the instigators in the establishment of the Junior Mountaineering Club of Scotland (JMCS). This was formed to create a focal point for Scottish climbers not in a club, as well as providing training up to SMC entry qualification. The idea was first discussed by Hutchison, R N (Dick) Rutherford and Arthur Rusk on a trip to the Alps. The club was formally brought into existence in August 1925 at the Narnain Boulder on the Cobbler with chairman Rusk proposing the constitution while still in his sleeping bag. The first Skye Meet was in June 1926, camping at the Banachdich Burn, when C E (Eddy) Andreae cycled all the way from Glasgow to Skye and back. This reflected a change of style that the JMCS and other younger clubs brought to Scottish mountaineering in the 1930s as a sense of fun and vitality temporarily returned to the hills.

Chapter Nine
Always a Little Further

By the early 1930s, the hiking craze was in full swing as thousands of young people made their escape from the grime and asperity of Scotland's industrial lowlands. To the urban working class the nomadic tramp was a romantic symbol of freedom from long hours of mundane and poorly paid work. In the newly accessible outdoors many tried to emulate this uncluttered, if malodorous, lifestyle. Sleeping bags were a luxury affordable to few; blankets were often discarded in favour of lighter and more versatile newspapers which could be stuffed up jerseys and crumpled down trousers. The four-season *Glasgow Herald* was reckoned to have the best thermal qualities.

This era was encapsulated by Alasdair Borthwick's evocative classic *Always a Little Further*, first published in 1939. Sandy, one of Borthwick's hapless companions who led the hard side of the Inaccessible Pinnacle 'on his first day on a mountain', survived a potentially fatal fall on Sgurr Mhic Choinnich to become Alexander Mackendrick, director of the Hollywood masterpiece *Sweet Smell of Success* and the Ealing comedies *Whisky Galore* and *The Ladykillers*.

The outdoor movement was encouraged by an upsurge in the growth of walking, climbing and cycling clubs, and was underpinned by public-spirited organisations like the Scottish Youth Hostel Association (SYHA), Holiday Fellowship, Scottish Rights of Way Society and Scottish Ramblers' Federation. A spate of guidebooks, tramping books and the affordable Popular Edition Ordnance Survey maps provided accessible information for planning weekends and holidays. Instructional books for the outdoors often included patterns for making your own tent, anorak etc. The offices, shops and factories of the industrial towns and cities were full of workers daydreaming of lunch-time on Saturday, packing frying pans, blankets and spare socks into rucksacks, and heading for the hills.

Improved public transport and cheap excursion tickets helped foster the explosion of exploration in the new-found countryside. It was only during the longer summer holidays, however, that it was feasible to get as far as Skye, and to many young unemployed the Cuillin remained an almost unattainable Shangri-la. (In 1933 the unemployment rate in Glasgow was 30 per cent.) In contrast, the 1930s were something of a golden age for the middle-classes with cheap second-hand cars, reasonably priced hotels, and affordable high quality equipment like eiderdown sleeping bags, mountain tents and windproof anoraks.

Any talk of the outdoors in Scotland in the 1930s is guaranteed to bring up one name – Jock Nimlin. A shipyard crane driver (in good visibility he could see the Cobbler from his cab), Nimlin led one of the hardest pre-war Scottish climbs, Raven's Gully (HVS) in Glen Coe, and became the leading light of a new breed whose accommodation of choice included caves and barns. His spartan outdoor lifestyle epitomised the interwar years and his ethos of hard-living nonconformity provided a rugged role model for future generations. With Bill Dougan, a Glasgow butcher who announced his presence on the hills with his ever present bugle, Nimlin formed the Ptarmigan Club. In July 1931 the pair headed for Skye.

The Ptarmigans and similar small clubs like the Creagh Dhu (formed 1930) Tricouni (1931) and the Lomond (1933) took great pride in their ability to construct a howff with whatever material was at hand. It was Nimlin who adopted the word 'howff', the old Scots for a cosy inn, as the name for a natural shelter in the hills. Look under any large boulder in the Arrochar hills, and Nimlin and his friend Ben Humble will have been there before. They also built many of these dosses in the Cuillin corries and around Loch Coruisk, enabling them to temporarily live in the mountains rather than descend each evening to the valleys. To Nimlin this was part of an ongoing tradition going back to Robert the Bruce, Rob Roy and Bonnie Prince Charlie.

Once at Sligachan, Nimlin and Dougan showed their usual initiative in improvising a suitable base for the hills, as Nimlin later related: 'Well, we found a pile of builder's rubble lying quite close to the hotel and we found two wooden trestles and we carried them across the moor to a little peat shed, and we put the trestles against the side of the peat shed and then we collected some planks and we laid them across the entrance; we slept on the ground but we had a pile of heather underneath us and we stayed there I think for about eight days, sleeping under what appeared to be a pile of rubble.'[1]

From their newly-constructed base, Nimlin and Dougan spent a week exploring the Cuillin, including a night out on Sgurr Dearg to watch the sunrise. Characteristically they claimed to have spent 24 hours in the hills with only a slice of bread and two sardines between them. In the evenings they cooked a meal on their Primus, brewed-up in blackened billy-cans and enjoyed a smoke around their peat fire. Down the road at the Sligachan Hotel there was a growing realisation that little profit was to be made from this new breed of impecunious hill-goer and that the future lay with a more affluent, tweedier clientele. In 1930 the corrugated annexe incorporating the famous smoking-room was demolished to make way for a more luxurious new wing incorporating the second lounge with its distinctive curved windows, giving panoramic views of the Black and Red Cuillin. It was the end of an era. The writer H V Morton described the new accommodation: 'Here are salmon-fishers, deer-slayers, artists in oil and watercolour, mountaineers, and the clipped voice of that which was once the

English ruling class.'[2] Glen Brittle would now be the destination of choice for most of the new hiking fraternity.

During the 1930s there were few radical improvements in equipment for rock climbing yet standards continued to rise, primarily due to the increasingly widespread use of gym shoes. Manila hemp remained the standard rope until after the Second World War. Longer ropes became more popular, as did the use of lightweight line, especially in winter. The indirect belay, where the inactive end of the rope was passed around a spike or natural chockstone and tied back into the waistline with an overhand knot, superseded the direct belay where the active rope was fed out over hitches. Protection that originated in the 1920s, like the jammed knot and inserted pebble, continued to evolve but were often deemed best left to the experts.

There was also the start of a more trenchant analysis of climbing methods rather than a blind reliance on balance or strength. Techniques that once seemed esoteric, like hand jamming and the photogenic layback, became more mainstream. The use of slings gradually gained acceptance though there was an initial resistance to karabiners, possibly due to their association with pitons on the continent. On the likes of the Inaccessible Pinnacle, slings were readily adopted as an abseil anchor, though many continued to drape the rope over the prominent flake above the short side's crux, as this saved having to leave a sling behind (it was the Great Depression after all!).

By the end of the Second World War, nylon ropes became available. Instead of tying directly to this with a bowline knot, Ken Tarbuck, from the Wirral, suggested a hemp waistline as a rudimentary harness to which the main rope was attached by way of a karabiner and an adjustable, shock-absorbent knot he had specifically invented. Tarbuck visited Skye in June 1932 when he created a variation to Shadbolt's Chimney on the Bhasteir Tooth that avoided the tortuous through-route of the original excursion. (Outside Variation, Very Difficult).

A few weeks after Tarbuck's visit, Ernest Wood-Johnson arrived on his motorbike in Glen Brittle with pillion passenger and regular climbing partner, C Astley Cooper. These friends were described by Sid Cross as 'tremendous company radiating an atmosphere of good humour, wit and friendliness'. Wood-Johnson was a regular visitor to Skye, often accompanied by his brother George who, along with Frank Smythe, was a member of the 1933 Everest expedition. 'Uncle Ernie' as he was known to friends, also climbed on gabbro with the visiting American mountaineer Elizabeth Knowlton, a participant on Willy Merkyl's 1932 Nanga Parbat expedition. Like many American visitors to Britain she was flummoxed to hear discussion, often in mixed company, on the merits of wearing rubbers when climbing.

Together, they made a new variation to Mallory's Slab and Groove, one of many the climb propagated during the 1930s. At the start of the climb Wood-Johnson asked her whether she minded if he called her 'George', as 'Miss

Knowlton' was very formal and 'George' was what he was used to. In the wet conditions they had difficulty following the original route, not for lack of consulting the guidebook as Knowlton confirmed, 'I have frequent memory-pictures of Wood-Johnson braced on narrow ledges with his head bent over its fast-soaking pages, as the rain pelted down on him.'

In June 1932, Wood-Johnson and Cooper returned to Skye with D Lewers when they camped at a favourite spot by the river above Glen Brittle Lodge. They had ten days in which to bring their climbing ambitions to fruition. Their initial day produced the first of four new routes climbed, a line on the Western Buttress of Sron na Ciche. The final, crux pitch, a steep wall that constantly pushed the climber out of balance, provided the route's name, Cooper's Gangway (VS). When Cooper wrote about the new climb he apologised for wearing rubbers; this was still a controversial issue that would not go away.

On his previous visits to the Western Buttress of Sron na Ciche, Wood-Johnson noticed that the huge diamond-shaped slab above the start of Central Gully had never been tackled directly. It was circumvented on the left by Trap Face Route (VS) but he reckoned the unclimbed slab could provide a direct start to this route. Trap Face Route was first ascended in 1914 by James Burrell and C N Cross when, in seven hours, they claimed not to have touched gabbro the length of the climb. The climb was graded 4, the highest available in the Skye numerical system, with the crux a smooth, vertical chimney. If Mallory's Slab and Groove was easy to get lost on, Trap Face Route was even more spoilt for choice. For a while guidebook writers all but gave up trying to demarcate the correct border controls, blending together a direct version in 1976, also graded Very Severe.

Wood-Johnson reckoned that a direct ascent of the diamond slab might be devoid of belays for the full 300ft (90m). For this eventuality he purchased 400ft (120m) of stout fishing line, 'as sold on a frame in seaside shops', to haul the main climbing rope. He hoped this might enable him to ascend the slab direct to its apex, as otherwise the rope drag on such a long run-out could render the climb impossible. On 22nd June his unorthodox technique worked to create Central Slabs (Severe), a line he considered similar in character to Mallory's Slab and Groove, but steeper and harder.

This part of the Western Buttress has a confused history. In earlier guidebooks Wood-Johnson's climb has possibly been documented too far to the right. His description has it ascending the slabs directly to where Trap Face Route crosses West Central Gully. Fifty years later he looked back on it as the most enjoyable and perhaps the best new climb he had ever done: 'Our new route was the perfect rock climb; that is, one in which the detail is lost in the joy of being there, and the only clear climbing memory is of the poetry of movement'. Wood-Johnson was 'in the zone':

I tied on the line and started the climb. After a few feet the others were out of sight below a small overhang. I was on my own and it was wonderful to be there, already with that clear insight which sometimes comes at the end of a climb but rarely at the beginning. I was climbing above my normal standard and it continued free and carefree. I do not remember any of these sharp or flat holds which are so welcome, only abrasive rounded footholds, nor any of those small cracks one expects in a large slab. There was a good standing place at about a 100 feet but no belay, so I climbed on. I was now really high up and the climb became more enjoyable the higher I went. I felt light and capable and free from anything that might disturb the quiet pleasure of being on that delightful route.[3]

There followed a couple of days' rain, after which Wood-Johnson's party managed the first ascent of Owl Buttress Right (VS) on the South Crag in Coir' a' Ghrunnda. Two days later they returned to Sgumain's North Buttress where there was an impressive area of unclimbed rock to the right of Frankland's Gully. They had attempted a route up the centre of this buttress the previous week but had only made ten feet of progress in two hours. The steep face is crossed by two terraces sloping from left to right. The initial problem was how to gain the lower of the terraces where a dark, overhanging corner looked as though it might provide access to the upper terrace. Starting near the bottom of Frankland's Gully they managed to weave a way through the overhangs, steep and exposed but with large holds where it mattered, to the first of the terraces. From here a steep crack, to the left of the dark corner, brought them to the second terrace where they continued directly up some loose rock to complete Wood-Johnson's Route (VS).

The next month, July 1932, saw the ascent of another large unclimbed buttress when Alan Horne and H V Hughes explored the triangular face at the back of Sron na Ciche's Amphitheatre. Horne, an actuary student, was one of the early driving forces in the establishment of mountain rescue posts in Scotland. Hughes, from the Midlands, was a leading member of the Rucksack Club. Looking up at the Amphitheatre face, the pair saw that the cliff comprised three sections: the lower slabs led to an overhanging wall which was cut off from the upper tier by a terrace. Splitting the overhanging wall was a prominent crack jammed with three large boulders. Intrigued, they climbed Mallory's Slab and Groove to the terrace where, to the right of the Flake, they started on the upper part of what became Amphitheatre Wall (VS), a route described in the 1958 SMC guide as 'a formidable climb of continuous severity'. One of the advantages of nailed boots was that they left distinct scratches on the rock, making the way easier to follow. Wearing plimsolls, Horne and Hughes were concerned for those repeating the route, so they marked each belay point by scratching a cross and Roman numeral on the rock.

At the top, after enjoyed some absorbing climbing, they resolved to return at the earliest opportunity to investigate the lower sections and complete the route. In true Skye fashion it rained continuously until the day earmarked for setting off for home. That morning the weather looked promising so they changed plans and headed back to Sron na Ciche. Unfortunately a sudden downpour saw the rocks streaming with water and they opted for Cioch West instead. By the top of this climb it was warm enough for sunbathing. They decided there might still be time to try their original objective, and by 5pm were roped up at the lowest rocks, this time wearing boots for the expected wet rock. The initial slabs proved harder than they looked, leading to two 'embryonic chimneys' which were climbed to a good stance below a slanting crack on the left. Horne and Hughes found this pitch hard and, with only a hundred feet of rope, became concerned that they may have cut off any chance of retreat. Relieved at finding a good thread belay, they now focused on what lay above, the meat of the route, the crack with the jammed boulders:

> To pass the blocks jammed in the chimney and crack, one has to climb out and over them in unusual and exposed positions rather like climbing over a gargoyle at the top of a building. The third block turns out to be resting on the floor of a corner, and we made a good stance, twenty-five feet above the foot of the crack. The through route is narrow and twists. The weightier member of our party had partly to undress before succeeding in his struggles. There was hardly room for two on the ledge and the leader had to move immediately the second emerged, a safe movement, however.[4]

That same summer (1932) SMC member Campbell Steven was struggling to figure out the crux moves of North Chimney on the Bhasteir Tooth. He eventually noticed two figures watching him from the screes below. One of them shouted up instructions on how to locate the key handhold high on the left wall. Steven later discovered that this timely assistance had come from one of the first ascentionists, Leslie Shadbolt.

Shadbolt and McLaren were on a return visit to Skye, this time accompanied by a young architect, Peter Bicknell, who felt very privileged to be joined on some Cuillin classics by the pioneers. He was also one of a select few to be taken into the confidence of Professor Collie. On 28th August Peter Bicknell completed the Main Ridge in a new record time of 8 hours 1 minute, even having enough energy to finish down Pinnacle Ridge.

On his Main Ridge Traverse Bicknell, like Howard Somervell, initially had a supporting partner. This was Alan Hodgkin, older brother of Robin who was also on Skye at the time laid up with a broken leg. Alan Hodgkin was a member of the Cambridge secret society, the Apostles, and later a Nobel Prize-winning biologist. Unfortunately he had to drop out at the Inaccessible Pinnacle. After waiting fifty years for a Nobel laureate to tackle the In Pin, three came along together! The previous summer (June 1931) Jim Bell was part of what must be the brainiest party to set foot on the Cuillin. Bell, who had a DSc in chemistry, was accompanied on the Inaccessible Pinnacle and other classics by both Paul Dirac, the 1933 Nobel Physics Prize winner, known as 'the British Einstein', and Igor Tamm, the 1958 physics laureate, and father of the well-known Soviet mountaineer Evgeny Tamm. Bell had met Professor Tamm on a visit to the Caucasus in July 1930.

In 1934 Peter Bicknell repeated the Main Ridge Traverse in the opposite direction with his brother Claud, taking 14 hours from Sligachan to Glen Brittle. This made him the first person to do the ridge twice, and first to do it in both directions. The brothers left the inn after breakfast and were back in time for dinner: 'We treated it as an ordinary climbing day, except for a rather early start and a little more food than a packet of sandwiches in our rucksacks. It was a poor day with mist and wet rocks most of the way.'

In the early 1930s there was a series of annual meets to Skye by the Cambridge University Mountaineering Club who based themselves at Mrs Chisholm's post office. Trips to the 'Misty Isle' were often planned at home in a buoyant mood of optimism: a traverse of the Main Ridge on sun-kissed gabbro finishing effortlessly at Sgurr nan Gillean before descending in a smouldering sunset to a coterie of beaming admirers. However, once on the island, the realities of Skye weather and island lifestyle didn't take long to kick in. The first day of the 1933 Cambridge Meet saw them take part in a gruelling rescue. Later, there was a trip to Rum for a change of rain.

The Cambridge parties produced several new variations to existing classics, but the main achievement was by K W Simmonds who, on 11th July, completed the first entirely solo traverse of the Main Ridge in 10 hours 40 minutes. After bivvying on the summit of Gars-bheinn he set off at 4.50am, reaching the cairn of Sgurr nan Gillean at 3.30pm. For the bulk of the ridge the weather was showery and misty with Simmonds attempting to navigate by compass. Following Howard Somervell's example, he continued to Sgurr na h-Uamha and, impressively, managed to return to his tent in Glen Brittle the same evening.

By the mid-1930s, the predominance of English accents in the glen was replaced by the less comprehensible brogue of the Glasgow area as a wide range of budget accommodation sprung up to cater for the influx of walkers and climbers. The Scottish Youth Hostel Association was formed in 1931. Two years later the little Glen Brittle school and school-house, along from Mrs Chisholm's, was converted to a rough and ready summer hostel. This became the Skye base for many Tricouni and Creagh Dhu members including Alastair Borthwick, Alex Small and Andy Saunders, whose high-spirited antics created a laughter-filled common room. In bad weather they helped out the warden, Bill Neil, by humping bags of coal across the river, bringing in water, washing dish towels and other odd jobs. Neil, unlike many of his colleagues, was described as 'absolutely free from all traces of officialdom'. Alex Small later compiled 'The Walkers' and Scramblers' Cuillin' a short guide that was incorporated into the SYHA *Guide to Isle of Skye*.

After two seasons the hostel was forced to close as it was required once again as a school. To fill the accommodation gap the Sutherlands, down the track opposite Glen Brittle House, opened an unofficial hostel with a kitchen in a corrugated-iron outhouse where they provided a couple of large Primus stoves for cooking. Likewise, Mary Campbell started her own 'Campbell's Seaside Hostel' – described by B H Humble as 'a wooden hut equipped something on the hostel style and boasts two armchairs, the spoils of a derelict motorcar'. Mrs Chisholm's was still going strong: mornings found residents making a post-porridge assessment of the mist level on the tops, or a leisurely shave at the water tub outside the bedroom window. In the evenings, after dinner, many of those staying elsewhere in the Glen congregated at the cottage to share tales of their day on the hill or to find climbing partners for the following day.

The blossoming outdoor scene ensured companies like Thomas Black of Greenock, the tent manufacturers, were thriving. In Glen Brittle camping was no longer discouraged, and Blacks' tents like the Palomine, the Guinea (named after its original price) and the Tinker (designed for wild camping), became a regular feature of the summer landscape: near the beach, beside the Banachdich Burn above Glen Brittle House, among the gorse by the River Brittle, as well as overflow accommodation at houses taking in guests. Over at the Sligachan end of the range, a well-used camping spot was around Alltdearg cottage (known as Cuillin Lodge until around 1900), currently unoccupied and boarded up.

Going to the farm for a jug of milk became a fondly remembered holiday ritual and fresh eggs and vegetables were also available there. For more exotic provisions the shop at Carbost delivered twice a week to the glen. Campers washed out by rain storms, eaten by midges or whose tents were trampled and chewed by the cows, gravitated to the sanctuary of the MacRaes' barn. Hugh MacRae came to Glen Brittle from Glenelg in 1924 as a shepherd to Frederick Wishart. He was farm manager until he became tenant in 1931 when he took over the lease of Glen Brittle House. The next year Hugh and Nancy MacRae opened the lodge, as it was often called, as a boarding house, and from this time it became an important focus for mountaineers in the glen. The couple became famed for their warm-hearted hospitality to hill-folk and their unstinting support and genuine concern when accidents occurred. Hugh MacRae was often left to organise rescue parties with what volunteers he could muster. Alex Small wrote of him: 'Despite the vigorous demands of farming in such a rough area he was always ready to give precedence to rescue and recovery no matter how inconvenient to his own affairs. Even when complaining about campers stealing his potatoes, he did so with wry forbearance.'[5] Glen Brittle House continued to take in guests until 1974.

For several summers in the early 1930s J E B (Jerry) Wright used Glen Brittle House as a base for his guiding business. Wright was a controversial figure, the founder of Lakeland Mountain Guides, who claimed to be England's first professional guide. He raised the hackles of at least three major climbing clubs: the Fell and Rock for his high-profile commercialism in the Lake District, 'his propaganda methods smack of American advertising and the cheap press'; the Scottish Mountaineering Club for criticising the stretcher they maintained at Glen Brittle House, and the Alpine Club for daring to suggest that some of Norman Collie's classic climbs might be a tad loose. Wright was jailed as a conscientious objector during the First World War and consequently felt comfortable in the role of outsider.

In his book *Mountain Days in the Isle of Skye,* Wright included a sketch map of the Cuillin, the first to demarcate sections of the Main Ridge into 'Easy Walking', 'Rough Scrambling', and 'Rock Climbing'. When his book was published in 1934, an anonymous *Alpine Journal* reviewer used any excuse to put in the critical boot: 'The narrative is full of expletives, slang and breezy conversations between the author and his various companions. He appears to be on intimate terms with especially the lady members of his parties; at all events, he refers to them in conversation and text by their Christian names. This is his affair.'[6] The poet Hugh MacDiarmid was more objective in *The Spectator*: 'Except for the SMC's guidebook, there has been a lag of a quarter of a century in the documentation of Skye climbing, and this book does much to rectify it.'[7]

In his poem 'Direadh III', Hugh MacDiarmid uses the summit of Sgurr Alasdair as a vantage point to survey the Cuillin range which he sees as a metaphor for contemporary Scotland; the Inaccessible Pinnacle represents the difficulties to be overcome if the people of Scotland are to fulfil their potential. The Raasay-born Gaelic poet Sorley MacLean also flew the red flag over the Cuillin, making them an embodiment of the international revolutionary movement. MacLean was inspired by his friend MacDiarmid's poem, 'A Drunk Man Looks at the Thistle', to write 'An Cuilithionn' (The Cuillin), described as 'a defiant affirmation of Gaelic cultural pride'. In MacLean's poem the heroic outlines of the mountains form a potent symbol of stoicism, hope and aspiration, rising 'on the other side of sorrow', above the 1930s threat of Facism, and the people of Skye's recurrent struggle with subjugation, famine and clearance. When Sorley MacLean taught at Portree High School, from 1934 until 1937, he often coped with the pressures of the job by escaping to the peace and quiet of the Cuillin.

In the outdoors of 1930s Scotland you were rarely far from talk about politics, especially socialism and its potential for positive change. Yet, despite card-carrying hordes wandering seemingly willy-nilly over privately-owned land, it was surprising how little conflict occurred. What the toffs were not prepared to tolerate, however, was disruption of the autumn stalking season. On a visit to Skye the radical Labour MP Tom Johnston, the man responsible for driving ahead the post-war Highland hydro-electric schemes, witnessed an example of this, an experience he related in a speech at the House of Commons, in December 1936:

> The last time I was in the Isle of Skye, going down the hill towards Sligachan, I saw, copied and photographed a notice stuck in a tree in the following words: 'Warning to trespassers and visitors. The soft-nosed bullet carries far and inflicts a nasty wound.' Visitors are warned to keep away. It is common knowledge that lands have been closed, that roads have been closed and that everything possible has been done to turn vast tracts of the Highlands of Scotland into a wilderness, a sportsman's paradise.[8]

The guide Jerry Wright was a life-long socialist, another reason he was unpopular with the climbing establishment. He did several significant climbs in Skye including a winter ascent of North Chimney (III) on Bruach na Frithe. On Knight's Peak, with W Bruton, he also repeated Giveen's West Face Direct, creating a hard direct start (VS) up a prominent red slab. Two days later he completed a Severe traverse of Am Basteir's north face, one hundred feet below the ridge, 'rotten rock, loose holds, dangerous under any conditions'. Wright probably also made the first ascent of the exhilarating Arrow Route (Difficult) up the centre of the Cioch Slab. He mentions two ascents of this route, which he named Cioch Slab Central Face and graded Severe, prior to 1934: one solo wearing plimsolls, and a roped ascent when he was able to reach a belay by using 200ft (60m) of line.

Arrow Route was not named until Ian Allan's credited ascent in 1944. Allan later re-climbed the route and, with a sharp stone in one hand, scratched large arrows onto the rock (visible for many years from the top of the Cioch) to show the way up the featureless slab. Although open to variation and nowhere technically difficult, Arrow Route remained a serious undertaking until the advent of camming devices in the 1980s. The original route took a bold line directly up the slab yet in the 1958 SMC rock climbing guide was only graded Moderate. Along with the neighbouring routes, Slab Corner and Cioch Nose, it was regarded as a variation of Collie's Route, not meriting a separate route description, just a brief mention in the introduction. This lack of accurate information ensured the regular sight of a rope of two, no runners between them, climbing simultaneously up the slab in a desperate attempt to reach a belay.

One of J E B Wright's regular clients in Skye was Elizabeth Coxhead, a journalist and writer best known for her 1951 novel *One Green Bottle*. An earlier book *June in Skye* (1938) was based on visits to Glen Brittle, set in and around the Cuillin where Glen Brittle Lodge becomes Glen Dhunan Lodge and Mrs

MacRae is transformed into Mrs MacCulloch. The story revolves around the attraction between Beatrice Smith, a novice climber from London, and Robert, an experienced mountaineer from the black tenement slums of Glasgow. The plot employs all the essential ingredients of a climbing holiday in Glen Brittle in the 1930s: wet days passed in books, jigsaws and board games; boat trips to Loch Scavaig or the Small Isles with Ian MacCulloch, a thinly disguised Ewen MacRae, and a trip to the bar at Sligachan (Alt-na-Strachan Hotel) 'the inevitable lodestar of every Skye expedition'.

Elizabeth Coxhead divides the motley house-party by their climbing ability into 'Stone Shooters' and 'Bad Steppers', after the two most popular routes up Sgurr Alasdair. One evening the lodge residents become concerned over Beatrice and Robert's late arrival from a climb on the Cioch. A rescue party is organised, an opportunity for the SMC stretcher to make its literary debut, 'a collapsible affair of canvas and bamboo which looked compact and light, but was in fact most disconcertingly heavy'. The young couple are eventually found safe and well. They had decided on an all-night dalliance at the summit of Sgurr Alasdair. It's a will-they-won't-they romance story with a series of twists and turns, eventually resolved at the very last page on the platform of Glasgow's Queen Street Station. (They will). Elizabeth Coxhead took her own life at the age of 70.

In *Mountain Days in the Isle of Skye* Jerry Wright provides a flavour of mountain rescue in the Cuillin in the early 1930s. Greater numbers on the hills led to a corresponding increase in accidents which were reported in the press with graphic headlines like 'Holiday Death Fall', 'Fatality on Ben Cioch', and 'Companions See Body Hurtle Past Them'. On a wet day in September 1933, after completing an ascent of Archer Thomson's Route on the Upper Cioch Buttress, Jim Bell and Con O'Grady were tackling the Bad Step on Alasdair's South-West Ridge when O'Grady fell. Bell made a quick assessment: 'He was badly hurt, unable to put his right foot to the ground and unable to take much weight on his left. At first he thought I could help him back over Sgumain but this was soon seen to be impossible. I left what spare clothing I had with him and proceeded downwards as quickly as possible for help. The time was about 6pm and the weather was calm and improving.'[9] O'Grady had broken both ankles. On the way to get help Bell bumped into Alfred Wood and Tom Barlow who had just finished a climb. Bell and Barlow returned to help keep the casualty comfortable while Wood ran down to Glen Brittle House to raise the alarm. Here there was a large contingent relaxing after dinner in the drawing room. Wright, by far the most experienced in mountain rescue, started to get things organised:

> In a very short time the whole household of Glen Brittle Lodge had tasks assigned to them, and preparations for the rescue party were soon on foot. Ropes were taken down. Electric torches were gathered together. Food and drink came from the kitchen. Whisky, brandy, rum, first-aid appliances, sweaters, waterproofs, oranges, sandwiches and Thermos flasks found

their temporary resting places in a dozen rucksacks. A long pole rolled with canvas and blankets were brought from the barn. (This we were told was the stretcher.) It weighed about fifty pounds. Murray Lawson and Alexander Harrison, who had just returned from a climb, prepared this cumbersome object for its long journey. In less than twenty minutes fourteen of us, including two Highlanders, were ready to start.[10]

The rescue party reached O'Grady in under two hours. Bell had earlier descended the stone shoot and directed everyone he could find in the corrie to come and help. Apart from bandages there was an almost complete lack of medical equipment, most notably morphine. Alcohol was used to anaesthetise the Irishman for the bone-rattling descent, first over Sgurr Sgumain then down the shoulder of Sron na Ciche. Climbing ropes were cut up to lace the casualty into the stretcher as well as create four hauling ropes, which were invaluable in negotiating the short rock step to gain the summit plateau of Sron na Ciche. The stretcher party eventually reached Glen Brittle at 7am. Wright reckoned it was the hardest rescue he had ever been involved in.

A day on the hill with Jim Bell was always memorable, and often unorthodox. In June 1934, camping on the shore of Loch Slapin, Bell and his friend Colin Allan went off for an after-dinner stroll, in ordinary town shoes, up the nearest hillside to admire the view down the loch. This inexorably developed into an overnight traverse of Sgurr nan Each, Garbh Bheinn, Clach Glas and Bla Bheinn: 'There was just enough difficulty to keep us from becoming drowsy.'

The next June (1935) Bell and Allan decided to try a new line on Sgurr Coir' an Lochain. They caught a boat leaving from Loch Brittle at 10am for Loch Scavaig. Arrival here demanded a long swimming session at Bell's favourite pool in the sandy bay near the Bad Step. This was followed by a leisurely lunch and an afternoon snooze until 5pm when they decided to start out for their climb up the steepest buttress on Sgurr Coir' an Lochain. Here they ran into 'serious difficulties' at a steep groove where they could make no headway. It was almost dark when they decided to rope down to reach the ground. With enveloping mist and darkness they set out for Bealach Coire Lagan, but when they gained the Main Ridge they realised they were not at the right location. They started to descend, hoping for the best, but were constantly forced right onto slabby rocks; once below the mist they realised they were not in Coire Lagan, but Coire na Banachdich where they should have kept well to the left under the cliffs of Sgurr Dearg. Colin Allan had a shock of white hair and was frequently asked if this was due to climbing with Bell.

The 1930s saw the establishment of the Main Ridge Traverse as one of the country's most prestigious challenges, an attainable ambition for any British climber worth their salt. For every successful ridge completion there were (and still are) many failures. One particular script is often adhered to: a small error is made early in the day, exponentially precipitating a crisis near the end, usually around Naismith's Route on the Bhasteir Tooth, and generally involving one or more of wetness, dryness, or darkness.

The photographer C D Milner and G F (Gilbert) Speaker, whose equipment consisted of a rope and two pounds of chocolate creams, were forced to omit the Tooth due to a terrific storm. It was torrential rain that forced the Aberdeen climbers, W A (Bill) Ewen and G R (Roy) Symmers, to abandon their attempt and escape to a wet tent in Glen Sligachan, an experience described by Symmers as 'sodden oblivion'. Even in the 1950s ridge completions were rare enough for those in the Sligachan lounge to troop out and applaud the successful party as they coyly hobbled across the tarmac of the A863.

Many climbers were now keen to gain the kudos of being first to extend the expedition to include Clach Glas and Bla Bheinn, creating what became known as the Greater Traverse. Among them were J H B Bell and Colin Allan. Their first attempt was in June 1934 when all went well until Bidein where there was a perceptible change in the weather; the mist set in and they decided to give up the attempt. The next year, two days after their adventures on Sgurr Coir' an Lochain, they were determined to have another go. They were awake for 1am, left Glen Brittle at 1.50am, and were stripped to the waist with the heat by 3am. As they climbed Gars-bheinn there was an ominously scarlet sunrise with spectacular light effects. By Sgurr Dubh an Da Bheinn it was extremely hot, 'I noticed that Allan started snoring during this halt.' True to form there was a sudden deterioration approaching the Bhasteir Tooth, with a rising wind and scudding rain. At Sgurr nan Gillean they decided to call it a day and set off over the Bealach a' Mhaim for Mary Campbell's where they arrived at 9.15pm, 19 hours 35 minutes after setting off. Bell and Allan had included the ridge outliers Sgurr Dubh Mor and Sgurr Sgumain and up to the Second World War this became an alternative format. Bell was now the second person to have done the traverse twice, but the prize of the Greater Traverse remained.

Jimmy 'Hamish' Hamilton was another who harboured ambitions of the Greater Traverse. In 1936 he led a Tricouni Club party on the first ascent of Agag's Groove on Buachaille Etive Mor, one of Scotland's most celebrated climbs. The Tricounis, unlike many clubs, welcomed female members. They met to make their weekend plans at Cranston's tea rooms in Glasgow as many pubs barred women. Hamilton would fail on his attempt on the Greater Traverse but he did complete a solo of the Main Ridge, Glen Brittle to Glen Brittle, in 22 hours 30 minutes. This round trip was accomplished several times during the inter-war period; not for aesthetics or a new record but due to the practicalities of returning to base at a time of few cars and limited public transport.

After the closure of the Glenbrittle youth hostel in 1934, the Tricounis transferred their allegiance to Glen Brittle House. Here, any lah-di-dah affectation was soon broken down by this influx of colourful characters from *Always a Little*

Further, including the charismatic Hamilton, Margaret 'Midge' Stewart and Alex Small, as well as the author himself, Alastair Borthwick and his brother Jim. To the traditional parlour games were now added discussion of philosophy and politics, and high jinks like abseiling from trees and sewing up pyjama arms and legs. The club song 'Minnie the Moocher' was added to the repertoire of musical turns which Alex Small described in his diary: 'Mr Cole ransacked Gilbert and Sullivan, the Wells sisters of Pinnacle Club and Main Ridge fame warbled quietly, the Broadbents embarked on interminable ballads, the Humbles crooned in diapason. Alastair renewed all his favourites. The whole house quivered with sound.'

The Tricounis were inspired by the early pioneers to climb the Bhasteir Tooth by Naismith's Route and descend by King's Cave Chimney. On closer acquaintance, Alex Small thought the Tooth resembled the prow of a giant ship and imagined how satisfying it would be to smash a bottle of champagne across the massive bow and watch it slip away into the mist. A while later this prospect was not so appealing as he found himself trapped inside the bowels of the cliff, an incident humorously recorded by Borthwick in *Always a Little Further*, 'The Corking of King's Cave'. The next day Hamish Hamilton lead Borthwick and an extricated Small up Cioch Direct where he characteristically belayed with one hand while playing his mouth organ with the other.

On a later visit to Skye a Tricouni team tackled Cioch West. At the start of the second pitch Alex Small was making a move left when a large flake, the size and shape of a coffin, slid down on top of him. The rock broke his leg, swept him off the rock, and cut through the rope in two places. He had a compound fracture of the fibula and tibia; there was a gaping wound on his shin and his boot was at right-angles to its normal position. The rest of the party helped keep him warm while others went to raise the alarm. A stretcher team, including Ewen and Gideon MacRae, soon arrived from the lodge. In four hours they brought the casualty to Glen Brittle House which he entered through the front window. Here the doctor, 'after a brief dissertation on the folly of climbing', administered chloroform on a towel before setting and splinting the bones. That very morning, a new pair of climbing boots arrived in Glenbrittle for Small—it would be almost two years before he was able to wear them.

Through the 1930s the options for travelling to Skye improved dramatically. The train and steamer continued to operate a connecting service: Glasgow 5.50am, Mallaig 12.30pm, Kyle 2.45pm, Portree 4.45pm. For many years the Mallaig-Portree steamer was the much-loved *Glencoe*, the grandmother of the MacBrayne fleet with an ancient single-cylinder steeple paddle engine. However, some mountaineering clubs chose to hire a fishing boat which had the advantage of transporting you directly to Glen Brittle or Loch Scavaig. When a Rucksack Club party arrived off the train at Mallaig, they were directed towards the Soay-based *Minerva*. 'She was about 30 feet long and so broad in the beam that not her most ardent admirer could have called her racy. Perhaps the fact that it had not rained for ten minutes stimulated our enthusiasm, for we greeted her as though she were the Cunard White Star's latest effort.'[11]

The Rucksackers eventually reached Loch Brittle after an unscheduled night on Soay and mid-sea engine repairs that involved a greasy hair comb and a length of sticking plaster. From its island base the *Minerva* continued to make trips from Loch Brittle to Loch Scavaig, providing a convenient approach for those wishing to undertake the traverse of the Dubhs or to visit the hitherto forbidden island of Rum. Others who arrived by sea included E W Hodge, a wealthy lawyer from the Lake District who led sea-mountaineering parties to the Hebrides, often mooring at Loch Brittle or Loch Scavaig. In much the same vein, M B Nettleton was a teacher who led outdoor education groups on sailing cum climbing trips to the likes of Knoydart, Rum and Torridon. In April 1934 one of his parties anchored their yacht in Loch Scavaig, 'a grand base, although it becomes a grim prison for a boat in bad weather'. After roping up in their dinghy near the Bad Step, they set off for the summit viewpoint by way off a series of slabs of rough, sound rock, the first route to be recorded on the miniature mountain of Sgurr na Stri.

Through the 1930s there was a steady increase in the numbers of motorists in the Highlands with a consequent improvement in the roads. The route to Skye was complicated by the need to use ferries like Ballachullish, the Aird Ferry at Dornie (until a bridge was built in 1940) and finally a one-car turntable ferry at Kyle of Lochalsh. During the 1930s increased demand on the latter led to first a two-car ferry, then a second ferry to run simultaneously. In 1935 the first vehicular ferry started at Kyle Rhea. All of these were expensive for cars. None of the ferries operated on Sunday making a weekend visit impossible. For non-motorists the cheapest method was an excursion train ticket from Glasgow to Mallaig, the new four-car Mallaig-Armadale ferry (started 1935), then bus to Sligachan where you could either wait for Neil Beaton's bus, or tramp over the Bealach a' Mhaim, to Glen Brittle. But for a couple of years buses, steamers and trains had more exotic competition.

Between 1935 and 1938, the MacRaes' hayfield in Glen Brittle, next to the present-day campsite, was re-designated as an airstrip with initially two, then three return flights from Glasgow's Renfrew Airport. One of few locations in Skye where an aircraft could land, it had the advantage of an uninterrupted approach over the sea from the south-west, the most likely direction for bad weather. Sleepy Glen Brittle was for a few hectic years the focus of the Northern and Scottish Airways route development in the Western Isles.

After a leisurely breakfast in Glasgow it was now possible to enjoy a freshly buttered batch of Mrs MacRae's scones for elevenses at Glen Brittle House. The MacRaes' son Ewen was Aerodrome Manager, clearing the runway of potential hazards, organising passenger transport and refuelling the aircraft from a tank at the back of his Humber car. The flights brought all sorts of advantages such as air ambulances being able to evacuate casualties of climbing accidents.

R M Lawrie and D A Rait of the St Andrew's University Mountaineering Club were some of the lucky few to experience this, the ultimate approach to the Cuillin, as well as a useful aerial reconnaissance for their club meet in Glen Brittle. For the flight, aboard a Spartan Cruiser II, they were supplied with all the requirements deemed necessary for early passenger air travel: tartan travel rugs, headache pills, American chewing gum. The flight lasted one hour ten minutes and afforded glorious views of all that was best in Scottish scenery: Loch Long, Loch Awe, Ben Cruachan, Glen Coe, Ardnamurchan and the white-capped peak of Rum:

> In the distance in a shimmering haze were the Outer Hebrides, low on the horizon, and before us the Black Cuillin, strangely puny and unimpressive from this height. We began to descend and in a series of spirals came down over Loch Brittle; a final vertical bank, a few feet it seemed above the loch, then a bump which sent us fifty feet into the air, and then we were racing up to the hut which is dignified by the name of airport. It was a quarter of a mile to the Sutherland's bungalow, but the others still had ten miles of moorland over the Mam. We emerged into a sunny day, but up in the corries the waterfalls were silent and icebound.

The recently formed St Andrews University Mountaineering Club held Easter Meets to Skye in both 1935 and 1937. One highlight of the earlier meet was an ascent of a verglassed Cioch Gully, described by the club's first secretary J D B (John) Wilson: 'The two top pitches gave us good sport, especially the ultimate. I have a vivid recollection of someone's nails taking a fair grip on my scalp, the sound of an ice-axe grating in a crack, and, after what seemed an age of suspense, a half-gasp, half-shout of triumph.'[12] Lawrie and Rait's return flight to Renfrew Airport was just as exhilarating:

> On 23 March we returned after renewing our acquaintance with the Cuillin at close quarters. The day was clear and completely windless, and before leaving the pilot asked us if we would like a trip round the Cuillin, a thing rarely possible owing to air currents. We set off up Glen Brittle, with the peaks and corries just beside us, in and out of the corries, over ridges and peaks we went, lifting and falling alarmingly as we met pockets and eddies. It was more than exhilarating, especially as we would occasionally skid and sideslip violently near the rocks. Into the great Tairneilear Corrie, a wonderful sight with the

gash of Waterpipe Gully splitting Sgurr an Fheadain from top to bottom. Then round the west shoulder, the splendour of the Pinnacle Ridge met our eye. Over Sligachan we turned, the conditions were too bad for Coruisk. Back over the Main Ridge, now above the peaks, an unforgettable experience.[13]

Two years later (1937) the Cuillin were plastered in snow when those attending the St Andrews meet realised that these conditions increased the standard dramatically. The likes of Sgurr Dubh Mor and Sgurr Thearlaich now became serious undertakings under snow and ice, while even the normally docile Sgurr na Banachdich started to show some teeth. One group managed a third of the way up the long side of the Inaccessible Pinnacle before they were stopped by an exposed knife edge of snow and ice. George Collie, the club secretary, went so far as to say that this virtual winter backwater provided better training for the Alps than even the famous winter precipices of Ben Nevis. The glorious weather saw ascents of Banachdich Gully (III), and the Thuilm Ridge of Sgurr a' Mhadaidh (III), which in places provided an exposed arete of snow overlooking an enormous drop into Deep Gash Gully.

But it was the Junior Mountaineering Club of Scotland (JMCS), particularly the Glasgow Section, that would be most strongly associated with the pre-war years on Skye. This was primarily through the writing of two of its members, W H (Bill) Murray, who worked in a Glasgow bank, and his friend B H (Ben) Humble, a Dunbartonshire dentist who was one of eight brothers. The JMCS held both official and informal meets in Glen Brittle through the 1930s when they helped re-establish the Scots as prime activists in the Cuillin.

Ben Humble first visited Skye in July 1929 with George MacKay, when they spent a fortnight touring the island on foot. At the end of the holiday they approached Glen Brittle over the hill-track from Loch Eynort, which was then open moorland with no trees. The spectacular, and unexpected, view of the Cuillin became engraved on Humble's mind, an epiphany that changed the direction of his life. The next day the pair climbed Sgurr Alasdair by the Stone Shoot, a route recommended by John Mackenzie with whom they had serendipitously found accommodation at 19 Sconser earlier in their trip. From here the 25-year-old Humble had written home:

Well, Father, here we are, sixteen miles today and still going strong, enthusiasm unabated, blisters commencing! We were very lucky to get in here, for the owner John Mackenzie is the only resident professional guide for mountaineering in Skye. The cottage is just a but and ben, and we are sleeping in the loft. Mackenzie is a wonderful old veteran. No living man knows the Skye mountains better, for he has spent a lifetime among them. He is well over seventy, but still acts as a guide and goes daily with climbing parties to the top of some peak or other, and it is real climbing! It is absolutely necessary to be roped together. He gave us many good tips, and showed us many of his climbing treasures, including a map of the Cuillin which had been presented to him.[14]

On a later visit to Sligachan, Humble was thrilled to meet the other half of the famous climbing partnership. A car drew up at the hotel and an old man stepped out, 'Tall he was and upright, a notable figure in any company and that nose was unmistakable. It was Professor Collie!'[15] Humble's visits to Skye sowed the seeds of a lifelong interest in the island that generated a trilogy of books: *Tramping in Skye*, a hiking guide published in 1933, *Songs of Skye* (1934), and the classic *Cuillin of Skye* (1952). *Tramping in Skye* proved a great success making Humble something of a Skye guru among outdoor folk, the focus of much enquiry regarding climbs, shops, accommodation etc. The year after publication a 'Humble's Tearoom' opened in Portree but the author was deflated to find himself still presented with a bill.

W H Murray joined the JMCS late in 1935, a purple patch for the club that saw seasoned members, who were expected to move on to the SMC, choosing to remain with the 'junior' club. In May 1936 Murray and his brother-in-law Archie MacAlpine began climbing with the more experienced Bill MacKenzie who worked in the same bank as Bill Murray (but a different branch). MacAlpine was a fine rower while MacKenzie was a also a keen sportsman who in his younger days played for his home-town football team, Elgin City. The addition of solicitor Kenneth Dunn created the iconic quartet that still resonates as the epitome of Scottish mountaineering past. In 1936 Murray was 23 years old, Dunn 25, MacKenzie 28 and MacAlpine 30.

Murray's first visit to Skye was in June 1936 when he was still a relative novice. The trip was a catalyst for his first book, *Mountaineering in Scotland* (1947), a classic that would inspire generations of British climbers. Several chapters of the book, and its sequel *Undiscovered Scotland* (1951), recount Murray's visits to Skye between 1936 and 1939. However the one that crops up most is the warm summer of 1936 when Murray travelled to Skye with Ross Higgins. On the steamer from Mallaig they bumped into other JMCS members, Douglas Scott and Rob Anderson, who both worked at the Templetons carpet factory in Glasgow, and who were also heading for the Sutherlands' bunkhouse in Glen Brittle. Scott and Anderson left the vessel at Armadale to catch the bus for Sligachan where they walked, in the rain, over Bealach a' Mhaim to Glen Brittle. Murray and Higgins remained aboard the steamer until Portree. Douglas Scott, later a professional photographer, wrote up events in his diary:

Monday 15th June. We went to Sutherlands as arranged. Not a bad place really, they try to run it like a hostel, with dozens of little rules stuck up all over the place. 1/6 per night, one cooks meals in a draughty little shed.

Tuesday 16th June. Still grey and hopeless looking outside so we got up late. When we did eventually get up we met Higgins and friend [Murray] just climbing down from the loft where they had been sleeping with a crowd of cyclists. We decided to join forces. We were last for breakfast in the shed and spent a long time over it. Mrs Sutherland put another fire in our room and the four of us lay around while our clothes dried and Rob and Ross provided discussion and argument.

After getting on the wrong side of Mr Sutherland for neglecting the washing-up, they set up their tents by the River Brittle. As the weather got hotter, more and more time was spent swimming and sunbathing. Murray, characteristically, could not cope with the inactivity and made a solo ascent of Banachdich. On the Friday they were joined by Archie MacAlpine and his wife Margaret (Murray's sister) who had managed to drive from Glasgow in a day after booking the Mallaig ferry by telegram. With only a weekend to spare, MacAlpine was keen to cram in as much as possible. The next day he and his brother-in-law did Abraham's Climb, and then the round of Coire Lagan, exploits Murray described in the 'Coire Lagain' chapter of *Mountaineering in Scotland*.

Ben Humble and Ian Maitland also motored to Skye but used the recently opened vehicle ferry at Kyle Rhea, celebrating their arrival on the island with a warm-up climb on Sgurr nan Gillean and high tea at Sligachan. Humble wrote about the latter in his diary: 'We were just finishing when the dinner gong went and all the old colonels and their ladies trooped in!' They then drove to Glen Brittle and soon had their tents up beside Murray's party. Their warm welcome was partially due to their ample supply of citronella, the most effective midge repellent at the time.

After MacAlpine's departure, Murray teamed up with Humble who was ten years his senior. Through this unlikely pairing Humble discovered a patient, and long-suffering model for his photographs while Murray acquired a colourful character to enliven his climbing tales. With the weather warm and settled Humble was keen to emulate the feats of his hero, Sheriff Nicolson and his midsummer wanderings over moonlit peaks. He decided to recruit Murray to the cause.

During the Second World War, after he was taken captive in North Africa, Murray was determined to survive life in the Prisoner-of-War camps by reliving, through writing, his precious memories of the Scottish hills. After spending days staring at a blank piece of paper, his mind locked onto these carefree, pre-war days in Skye, the June heat wave of 1936, the very first lines of *Mountaineering in Scotland*:

It was ten o'clock at night, in Glen Brittle. The June sun had left our little cluster of tents, which nestled behind a screen of golden bloom between the Atlantic and the Cuillin. Eastward, the peaks were written along the sky in a high, stiff hand. High above us, the brown precipice of Sron na Ciche, which reacts chameleon-like, to every subtle change of atmosphere, was dyed a bright blood-red in the setting sun.

I watched the lights fade from the rocks and white evening mist begin to creep around the hills, then I thought of having supper and retiring with a pipe to my sleeping bag. But in this hope I had reckoned without my friend, B H Humble; his head, adorned by a dilapidated panama, emerged of a sudden from the door of a nearby tent. The lighted eye, the mouth upturned at the corners, the warm colour—they all bore witness to a recent brain-storm. Humble had given birth to an idea. I regarded him with profound suspicion.[16]

By 10.30pm they had left their tents. Two hours later they were bivouacking on a ledge in Coire na Banachdich. At 2am they were awake and soon moving off north along the ridge to discover what they had assumed to be mist was actually cloud. By Sgurr a' Mhadaidh their unorthodox timetable rewarded them with a superb sunrise above a temperature inversion. Murray described it as the most magnificent sight he had ever seen: the cloud forming a vast sea at 2,500ft, flowing between the now isolated tops of the Cuillin horseshoe. Humble had forgotten spare film but six years later, in a POW camp, Murray could recall every detail: 'Down in the basin of Coruisk, the cloud-surface at once flashed into flame, as though a stupendous crucible were filled with burning silver. The twenty turrets of the Cuillin, like islands lapped by fire-foam, flushed faintly pink. The shade crimsoned. Within a space of minutes, the rocks had run the gamut of autumn leafage, "yellow, and black, and pale, and hectic red".'[17]

In his diary Murray stated: 'thereafter our route to Coruisk would be as roundabout and inconvenient as Humble's evil ingenuity could devise'. At Loch Scavaig they were offered hospitality aboard the MacBrayne steamer *SS Loch Nevis* which was disembarking sight-seers to view Loch Coruisk. Unshaven, and dressed in ragged climbing breeches and braces, they created something of a sensation among the female passengers who queued up to have their photographs taken with these wild men of the mountains. Replenished and refreshed after a large meal and two pints of cold beer in the first-class dining saloon, Murray and Humble set off up the boiler-plate slabs of the Dubh Ridge to reach Glen Brittle almost exactly 24 hours after their departure. Humble summed up the day in his diary, 'This will rank as the finest mountain excursion I have ever had.'

A few days later Humble, Maitland and Murray decided to visit the famed Cioch. The mist they encountered early in the day dissipated at the Cioch Terrace to provide another spectacular temperature inversion. Referring to Humble, Murray noted: 'An orgy of photography now took place.' The holiday on Skye cemented Humble's ambition to write a new history of Cuillin mountaineering. It also provided a dramatic cover photograph for his book, *The Cuillin of Skye*, 'the picture of a lifetime', of Bill Murray on the summit of the Cioch with the sun setting on the clouds behind.

Humble had no tripod, lens hood or exposure meter, and Murray's patience was sorely tested as he posed for over an hour until the photographer was satisfied. Humble eventually ran out of film. As mentioned above, the airfield brought all sorts of benefits. Humble asked the pilot if he would do him a favour. He could, and a couple of new spools duly arrived the next morning. The airstrip eventually closed in 1938 primarily due to the state of the Glen Brittle road which still had no bridges over the rivers. Hamish Hamilton, who travelled to the glen by motorbike, described it as the 'wildest conjunction of ruts and boulders in all Skye'.

Ben Humble suffered increasingly from deafness. While rock climbing he developed a system of rope tugs to communicate. His disability affected his speech and on one occasion he was mistakenly arrested for drunk driving and incarcerated in Glasgow's infamous Partick Marine police cells. His release was only secured after the forthright Bill MacKenzie, who lived locally, vouched for his sobriety. Humble was eventually forced to give up dentistry entirely and rely on writing to earn a living. He became a prolific author who rehashed all his favourite topics: the Arrochar Alps, mountain indicators (a craze of the day), youth hostels and howffing, under various pseudonyms in a wide-ranging number of periodicals. He even introduced youngsters to howffing with an article in *Boys Own*. When *Cuillin of Skye* was finally published it was reviewed in the *Geographical Journal* (July 1953): 'Herein is the history of their exploration, not dry and dusty as some histories are, but lively as the air of the mountains and warm-blooded as the personality of the author.'

Murray returned to Skye in June 1937 when he climbed regularly with the powerful Kenneth Dunn (the one in his climbing tales always forgetting his boots). Despite disappointing weather they managed to successfully tackle some of the harder climbs like Crack of Doom as well as classics like Shadbolt's Chimney, described by Murray as, 'a corkscrew tunnel twisting and turning this way and that through total darkness'.

He only recorded one new route in Skye, the eponymous Murray's Climb (Difficult). Browsing through the SMC guidebook six months earlier, he noticed a description of Sgurr na h-Uamha: 'There is no record of an ascent of the steep, south-westerly buttress facing Sgurr Dubh'. This became the main objective of their 1937 Skye holiday and all other routes were regarded as preparation for this unclimbed challenge. Sensing a change in the weather Murray brought forward their attempt in case there was a sudden and prolonged deterioration. There was. The buttress comprised a series of bristling overhangs which they turned by traversing ledges to the left or right until they could find a crack or corner that would take them to the next tier. By the final rocks the wind had increased to gale force, making it difficult at times to breathe or maintain contact with the rock.

This was the precursor of a fierce storm that lasted three days.

By the mid-1930s the race was on in earnest to be first to do the Greater Traverse, linking the Main Ridge Traverse with Clach Glas and Blaven in a single expedition of 12 miles (19km) and over 13,000ft (4000m). First to achieve this were Ian Charleson, a bank manager from Oban, and W E (Ted) Forde, from Edinburgh, on 12th June 1939. They had realised that to succeed on such a long and complex objective you needed extensive and thorough planning. They intended to establish two camps where they could have some rest and shelter: one at the foot of Gars-bheinn, to facilitate the start, and the second at the mouth of Harta Corrie, to provide rest and replenishment before the final energy-sapping ascent of Clach Glas and Bla Bheinn. The next part of the strategy was to use their first week on Skye to recce the ridge, increase their fitness and leave caches of food and drink at Sgurr Dearg and Bidein.

On the allotted day they left their first camp at 1.30am. On the ascent of Gars-bheinn, although it was almost mid-summer, there was frost on the grass and patches of ice on the rocks. They even had snow underfoot for part of the day; a bottle of water left at Bidein was cracked by the frost. They used Shadbolt and McLaren's times as a template, and carried a full size alarm clock in case they fell asleep when they stopped for rests. At 8.30am they reached Sgurr Dearg and their first cache of food: cheese, dates, chocolate and oranges, but it was too cold to linger long. Charleson led the last major difficulty, Naismith's Route, in his socks. When they reached the tent in Harta Corrie they had reservations about continuing. After a rest and meal they felt revitalised enough to tackle the last leg, and eventually shook hands on the summit of Bla Bheinn at 11.12pm. Their time, top to top, was 20 hours 7 minutes, a fine achievement in poor conditions where careful planning and good judgement had paid dividends.

That summer (1939) three other versions of the Greater Traverse were completed. On 23rd July a Wayfarers' Club team started with Bla Bheinn and Clach Glas before tackling the Main Ridge south to north, finishing in a time of about 23 hours. They included Sgurr Dubh Mor and Sgurr Sgumain which Charleson and Forde had omitted. In September a party from Nottingham climbed all the Cuillin Munros in one trip. After sleeping out on the summit of Bla Bheinn, they set off at 5.30am to traverse the Main Ridge north to south, including Sgurr Sgumain but omitting both Clach Glas and Gars-bheinn.

Bill Murray had had his eye on the Greater Traverse since his first visit to Skye in 1936. In 1937 he completed the Main Ridge Traverse in 12 hours with James Banford, but could not find anyone interested in taking on the extended challenge. In 1939 he discovered a willing partner in R G (Gordon) Donaldson from Bearsden, who would have been no more than 18 years old at the time.

Donaldson later studied medicine at Cambridge. In 1941 he was responsible for two fine climbs on Buachaille Etive Mor: Bottleneck Chimney and Hangman's Crack, but later fades from climbing records. Plans for an Alpine trip were scrapped as August 1939 was earmarked for the Greater Traverse. They spent ten days getting themselves into shape: starting the day with a hard climb like Slanting Gully or Slingsby's Route, then a long section of the ridge, and finally 'a gargantuan feast at base camp'.

On the designated day they left Glen Brittle at 9.30pm and proceeded by torchlight until the Thearlaich-Dubh Gap where favourable conditions prevailed for the rest of the Main Ridge. Like Charleson and Forde they had established a provisioned tent in Glen Sligachan where copious measures of the performance enhancing Mummery's Blood, a potent cocktail of Bovril and navy rum (the navy bit is important) were prescribed for the final leg up Clach Glas and Bla Bheinn. They finished the Greater Traverse in a new best time of 19 hours top to top (27 hours tent to tent), an achievement they celebrated at Sligachan with a meal and bottle of champagne.

With the start of the Second World War, in September 1939, Kyle of Lochalsh was renamed 'Port ZA', a major centre for mine-laying operations in the North Atlantic. The view from the Cuillin tops once again featured what one local described as 'big, ugly, grey ships': mine-layers with battleship escorts heading for the Denmark Strait. Skye residents had to carry identity cards and a 'certificate of residence in a protected area'. Cairns were built in the MacRaes' field in Glen Brittle to prevent enemy planes landing. The windows of civilian aircraft were blacked out so you couldn't observe troop or ship movements. The prevailing obsession with spies meant it was an offence for anyone in the West Highlands to be in possession of binoculars or a telescope without special permission; even weather forecasts were classified as secret information.

To leave or enter the island you also required a travel permit which were generally not issued for mountaineering purposes. Staying locally Bill Wood did not require one. Originally from Aberfeldy, Wood was exciseman at Talisker Distillery, a dream job for a climber who enjoyed a dram. Elizabeth Coxhead wrote another novel set on Skye, *A Wind in the West* (1949), which contains a pen-portrait of Wood. In 1939 he did a first ascent on Sgurr a' Mhadaidh which he named after his occupation, Gauger's Gully (Difficult).

If not resident on Skye, getting a travel permit was not easy. One successful applicant was the distinguished geologist N E (Noel) Odell who taught at a number of universities, including Cambridge and Harvard. In October 1917, on a combination of honeymoon and sick leave after being injured by the detonation of an unexploded bomb, he climbed a snow-covered Inaccessible Pinnacle using his geological hammer to chip away the ice. In June 1935 he was a member of a party, led by George Mallory's daughter, Clare, which put up a new variation to Waterpipe Gully. The next year, with Bill Tilman, Odell made the first ascent of

Nanda Devi, the highest summit yet climbed.

In 1943 Odell was geologising on Marsco searching for the rare marscoite, a peculiar blend of rock produced by the reaction of basic gabbro and acidic granite. In the course of his exploration he created the first new route in the Red Cuillin, Odell's Route (Difficult). Odell's name would be better known if, on Everest's North Col in June 1924, he had not been passed over as George Mallory's partner in favour of the much less experienced Andrew 'Sandy' Irvine. Odell was interested in spiritualism and, when he wrote Howard Somervell's obituary in the 1976 *Alpine Journal,* mentions that he (Odell) received a 'message' purporting to come from Sandy Irvine and saying they reached the summit and the accident occurred on the way down.

There were supernatural forces at work on Skye too. Loch Coruisk, due to its inaccessibility, had always been a prime source for eerie tales of the paranormal. In 1813 John MacCulloch recalled how his oarsmen were too frightened to venture from the shore into the bowl of Coruisk, considering it the 'haunt of the Water Demons'. There was a Faustian tale of a local man who, near the loch, sold his soul to the Devil for gold and precious stones; there was also the legend of the 'Cave of the Ghost'. In the 1920s, J A Macculloch, a Portree minister, wrote that the area was home to 'a fearful shape, half-human, half-goat, with long hair, long teeth and claws'. Many dismissed this as mistaken identity, a brief glimpse of a wild camper or howff-dweller. On a sea-mountaineering trip to Coruisk in 1937, M B Nettleton had a strange experience. Eating lunch halfway up the Dubh Ridge, his party were surprised to hear the distinctive scratching of nailed boots approaching from below:

> At the same time a feeling of great uneasiness overcame us, although nothing had been (or normally is) further from our minds than the occult, and to break the spell we confidently advanced to the edge of our broad ledge to meet the unexpected stranger from below. The sounds had just ceased, and not only was no stranger visible, but it was fairly clear that the ground in the direction of the sounds was steep to an almost incredible degree. There was nothing to block our line of vision, and in the utter stillness the sense of a hostile influence now grew so overpowering that, despite the fine weather, we abandoned our climb, and descended in most indecent haste by the easiest ledges we could find down to Garbh Choire.[18]

During the Second World War, Sandy Wedderburn, one of the Cambridge University students who visited Skye, and his younger brother, Tommy, led groups of soldiers in mountain warfare training in the Cuillin. (Coincidentally, Tommy Wedderburn, Bill Murray, and another Cuillin activist, Alastair Cram, all ended up in the same POW camp where they established one of the more esoteric mountaineering clubs. The British Mountaineering Council was formed around this time and Murray recalled how they would have joined, 'had communications been better'.) The schoolhouse at Torrin was requisitioned as a base. Armed troops scaled many of the classic routes, and in 1942 there was a mock invasion at Camasunary, where the lodge was used as an officers' billet for Catalina flying boat crews hunting U-boats in the Atlantic. The goal of the invasion was to attack and capture the enemy headquarters at the Sligachan Hotel, no doubt to the wry amusement of one elderly professor. In the mid-nineteenth century a shepherd from the Torrin area reported seeing a troop of soldiers on the hills dressed in unusual uniform, including red hats, of no known British regiment. The tale became part of local oral tradition. During the Second World War the same soldiers were seen again, the Parachute Regiment training in the Cuillin.

Prior to the war, Camasunary was let as a fishing lodge where anyone catching a sea trout over 8lb had to draw or paint its likeness on the wall (these can still be seen). In 1914, R L Thomson sold the Strathaird estate to the Johnson family who were the current owners. Stephen Johnson spent his formative summers at the remote lodge. During the Second World War he was captured when his plane crashed into the Zuiderzee in the Netherlands. In an interesting parallel to W H Murray, he too was drawn to writing a book in his POW camp, *Fishing from Afar*, recalling his angling escapades among the Cuillin. He later designed a popular fishing fly called the Camasunary Killer.

In 1944, the restrictions on movement through the Highlands were lifted in time for some of the finest weather in living memory. One visitor was a conscientious objector, J M (Menlove) Edwards, a Liverpool psychiatrist himself suffering from mental illness. That summer Edwards had an extended holiday at Glenbrittle Lodge, 'Mixed rain and sunshine this month. Climbs, coast walking and boat. Also days reading and slacking. A grand time.' On 30th-31st May he greatly reduced the record for the Greater Traverse, with a ridge time of approximately twelve-and-a-half hours (Gars-bheinn to Bla Bheinn). The homosexual son of a vicar, his inner conflicts, together with some professional failures, began to rack up the psychological strain. Edwards was already in the throes of schizophrenic breakdown when he set out from Glen Brittle on a spontaneous solo attempt on the Greater Traverse. Feats of endurance on the mountains and at sea appeared to alleviate his symptoms.

Edwards had no watch, so we only accurately know his starting and finishing times. He carried no water bottle and his only food was one of Mrs MacRae's packed lunches. He left Glen Brittle at 8am, traversed the Main Ridge south to north reaching the summit of Bla Bheinn at sunset; he returned around the coast in the dark, arriving back at Glen Brittle House at 8.30am, 24 hours after he left. His brief note in the Glenbrittle Lodge logbook reads: 'Main Ridge walk plus Garbh-bheinn to Blaven.' Menlove Edwards took his own life in 1958. Like homosexuality, suicide was illegal in Britain until the 1960s.

Two months after Edward's record-breaking feat Sydney Thompson, an RAF

Flight-Lieutenant, reduced the time to 11 hours 40 minutes. Thompson did not have a rope, nor did he have caches of food or water, carrying all his own provisions. He left Glen Brittle at 4.50am and followed the Main Ridge to Sgurr na h-Uamha. After Bla Bheinn he went over Druim Hain to Coruisk and then around the base of Gars-bheinn back to his starting point. He regarded this last section as the worst part of the trip. On an earlier visit to the Cuillin, in July 1938 with Lake District activist Jim Haggas, Thompson also made the first complete ascent of Eastern Gully (VS) on Sron na Ciche, oftened abseiled as a descent from the Cioch area.

Throughout the war Ben Humble continued to entertain and inform his readers with tales of Sheriff Nicolson, howffing in the Cuillin and climbing on the Cobbler. One of his articles was entitled, 'To a Prisoner of War':

Dear Bill,
Skye wouldn't see us this year, but perhaps next summer we'll again camp in Glen Brittle that delectable glen and cragsman's paradise. Mrs C, postmistress and hostess to generations of climbers, wrote to me recently and said: 'The Coolin are in grand condition, and there is no one to climb them.' She too looks forward to that first summer after the war. What a rush to Skye then! And whatever may happen in Europe the Coolins are changeless and will welcome us all back after the war.[19]

The north face of Am Basteir and the Bhasteir Tooth

The first pitch of Naismith's Route (Severe) on the Bhasteir Tooth

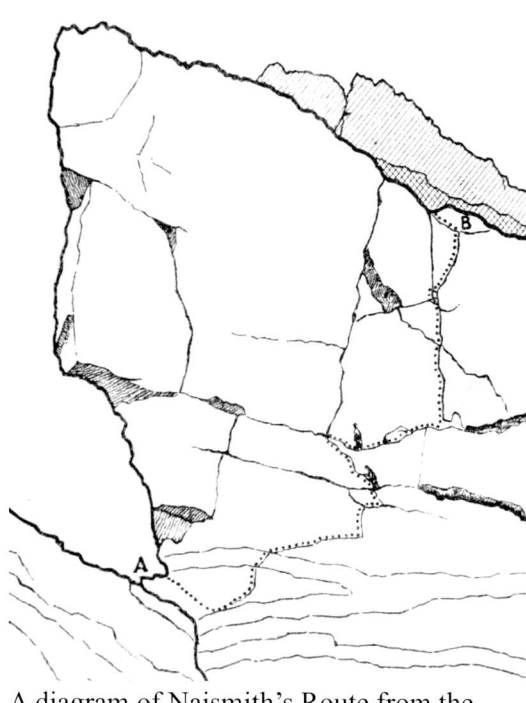

A diagram of Naismith's Route from the first SMC guide to Skye (1907)

VIRGIN PEAKS FOR THE MOUNTAINEER WITHIN OUR OWN SHORES.

Scaling the Peaks of the Isle of Skye

Written and Illustrated by George D. Abraham, Author of "The Complete Mountaineer," Member of the English Climbers' Club and the Swiss Alpine Club.

One of the most interesting peaks in Skye is Sgurr nan Gillean, and as half of our party were new to Skye our first few days proved it to be of using for those remarkable gendarmes, and before long to be vanquished. On the top we were fortunate to see the spectre of the Brocken, a somewhat common sight on the damp and misty isle. When we began the descent the clouds blotted out everything, and on consulting our compass we had a striking example of the magnetic nature of the rocks. A few yards below the top on the western ridge the needle pointed due south-west instead of north. This erratic behaviour nearly led us into difficulties, but fortunately one of the party recognised some rocks of unusual shape on the ridge; this saved us possibly from a night out on the precipitous face of the peak. As it was darkness fell ere we got off the mountain. We learnt once more that the Coolin rocks are hard, the ridges are long, and that winter days in Skye are short.

Next day we made a new route up the face of Knight's Peak, which is the name given in honour of a well-known professor to the adjacent summit of Sgurr nan Gillean on its northern side. The lower part proved the most interesting, and the struggle up some splendid chimneys hindered us from forgetting the bruises we had received the previous evening. Near the top a narrow knife-edge arête of rock made a splendid finish; the views downwards into the huge chasms on either hand were wonderful. They made us move circumspectly and take special care to avoid using loose holds for hands or feet.

The following morning we were out of bed in the small hours, and as the rosy gleam of sunrise was tipping the tops of the White Coolin with a golden glow we were trudging away down the wild recesses of Glen Sligachan, where night still lingered. The party was augmented by two ponies carrying our camping outfit, and a gillie who had charge of us all (judging by the Gaelic expletives to let loose when we persisted in making short cuts across some boggy sections). We were bound for a few days exploration and climbing on Clach Glas and Blaven, a detached and lesser-known portion of the Black Coolin. Our "guide" left our goods and chattels at the foot of the ridge between the two peaks, and we struck upwards into the wild recesses of Lonely Corrie en route for Clach Glas, which boasted several routes.

The real sunrise had not belied its warning of storm. A strong gale was already blowing up aloft and was driving clouds eastward across the sea from the north-west. At first we were sheltered, but on a on the main ridge we had a foretaste of what old Boreas held in store for us higher up. Nevertheless, the conditions were dry, and by skirting the various gendarmes on the west side we secured fair shelter. The Great Tower soon loomed straight ahead, looking almost inaccessible with its vertical cliffs of dark and remarkable outline. On this account it has been appropriately called "the Matterhorn of Skye." The resemblance was accentuated that winter morning by the snow and ice festooning the giant cliffs. Forsaking the ordinary route we made the direct ascent of the impossible-looking pinnacles below the Great Tower, and then forced a way straight up the face of this from the well-marked col at its foot.

Our reception on the summit was a "cooling" one, and the descent on the exposed further side of the peak seemed scarcely feasible. However, we finally consigned ourselves to the care of a fragile-looking ridge which dipped over into a cloud-filled abyss, whence the storm arose, now with a shriek and anon with a roar as it caught us in full force. At such times movement was impossible. Like Brer Rabbit we lay low and clung to the sharp ridge of rock until the lull came between the blasts. Through breaks in the spindrift on the left we caught glimpses of the sea some thousands of feet

A TYPICAL COOLIN SUMMIT IN THE ISLE OF SKYE
The "Inaccessible Pinnacle" on the top of Sgurr Dearg

Ashley Abraham

Previous page: An article by George Abraham in *The Sphere* (1908)

Top Right: The diagonal line of Cioch Direct

Bottom Right: Approaching the Parallel Cracks pitch on Cioch Direct

George Abraham

E W Steeple and A H Doughty relaxing at Mary Campbell's cottage

Direct Route (Severe) on Sron na Ciche's Eastern Buttress

E W Steeple and party on the Bealach a'Mhaim in September 1910

William Wallwork

Right: Wallwork's Route (Very Difficult) on the Cioch Upper Buttress, first climbed in 1915

Ben Humble and Bill Murray with a group of admirers at Loch Coruisk

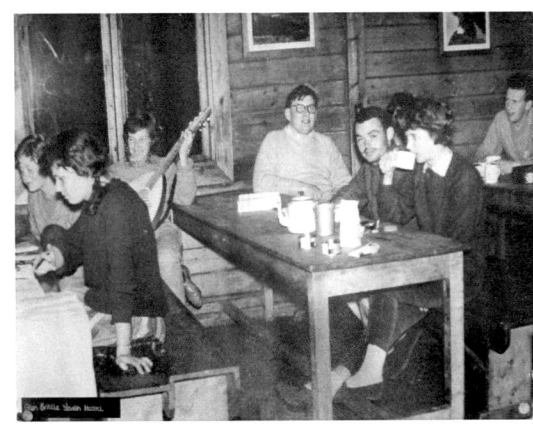

Clockwise from above: The common room at Glenbrittle Hostel around 1970, Bastinado (E1) on Cioch Buttress, Trophy Crack (E1) on Cioch Upper Buttress, An SYHA guide to Skye from the 1960s
Opposite page: Vulcan Wall (HVS) on Sron na Ciche's Eastern Buttress

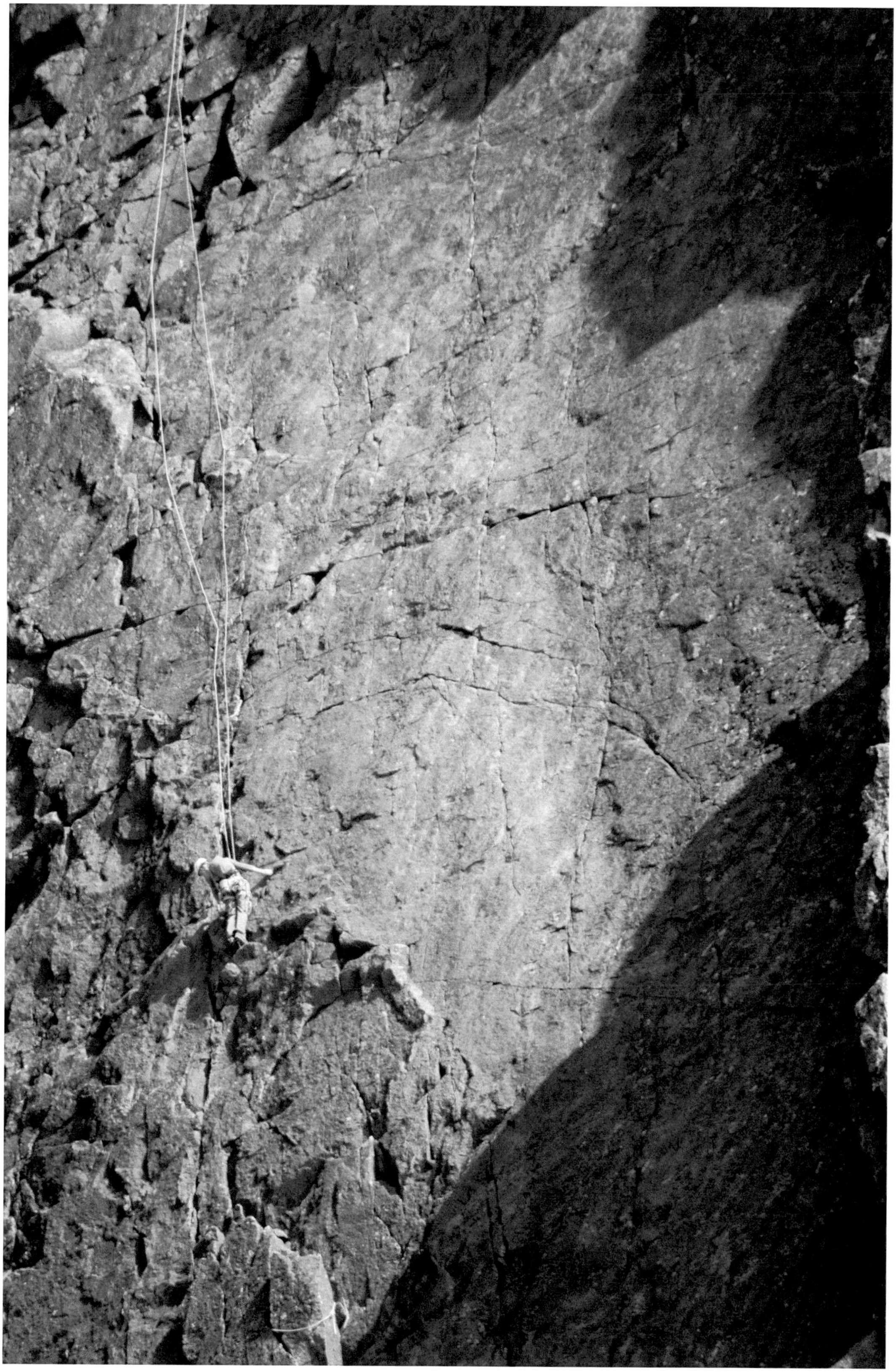

The view north from Bruach na Frithe

Tom Patey on a winter traverse attempt in 1962. (Photo: Richard Brooke)

Phill Townsend on an early ascent of King Cobra (E1) on the north face of Sgurr Mhic Choinnich (Photo: John Harwood)

Chapter Ten

The Magic of Skye

On 11th May 1945, four German U-boats, one flying the swastika, the other three the black flag, sailed down the Inner Sound to surrender at Kyle of Lochalsh. The war was finally over.

Post-war Britain was a place of great austerity with strict rationing and widespread financial hardship. One of few things readily available were ex-War Department supplies which were improvised, 'Make Do and Mend', to fulfil many of life's requirements including gear for the outdoors: silk parachute material for tents (and wedding dresses), sewn-up army blankets for sleeping bags, groundsheets with a hole for the head as waterproofs. It's no coincidence that the post-war Scottish weekender had an distinctly military mien: khaki shirts and drill trousers, kilts, black berets and ex-military rucksacks. The latter were eventually replaced by the lighter Bergen or Buckta packs. By the 1950s the serious hiker and climber had a more pacifist look: the ubiquitous fawn anorak with kangaroo map pocket, climbing breeches, hand-knitted bobble hat, known in Scotland as a 'toorie'. Better-off hill-goers could afford the more expensive Grenfell jacket, 'as used on the 1936 Everest Expedition', a Burnley-made cloth that was windproof and breathable, a worthy successor to Burberry.

After John Campbell's death in 1941, his brother Charles acted as manager at the Sligachan Hotel until the end of the war when his son Ian took over. Along with his wife Fiona, Ian Campbell continued the tradition of hospitality that the hotel was famed for. In May 1955 they hosted the second Everest reunion when Sir John and Lady Hunt also traversed the Main Ridge.

As Ben Humble predicted, visitors started to pour onto the island with the first chance of a holiday for years. Sligachan became something of a transport hub as folk changed buses for destinations around the island, including Glen Brittle. The vehicles were barely able to cope with the sudden influx of tourists as Donald Gillies, a chronicler of Skye events, confirmed:

> The summer tourist to Skye has become numerous this month. Every boarding house and hotel in the island is reported full. The rationing system, which is still in force, has been a great hardship on those that board visitors. A

great number of hikers and cyclists are on the roads from morning till night. Mountain climbers have also exceeded former years. About ten buses meet the steamer at Armadale and four or five buses from Kyleakin.[1]

Glen Brittle House, now ablaze with the newly available electric lighting, was soon back to its pre-war occupancy rate. In 1946 visitors from Dundee's Grampian Club provided a flavour of life at the lodge: 'There was MacRae the farmer, Nancy and Minnie, his daughters, who ran the establishment; John, Minnie's husband who helped; Ewen, Gideon and Ronnie, the sons; Joan, commonly called Seonaid, and Ann, the maids, old Miss MacCrimmon, Chisholm the roadman, John-Willie, a helper, Rory the Post, and residents who dropped in for a cup of tea.'[2]

Half a mile up the glen there was now a commodious new youth hostel which would soon take over from Glen Brittle House and Mrs Chisholm's as the main focus for hill lovers on Skye. Glenbrittle hostel was built in 1939, just in time to be closed for the duration of the Second World War. It was part of a chain along Scotland's west coast that was designed to be within walking distance of each other. Costing a shilling a night they provided affordable accommodation for young people from the cities, 'hotels for hikers'.

Sleeping over eighty, in bunks three-high, the Glen Brittle building was pre-fabricated in Oslo and slotted together on brick foundations without the use of nails. Apart, as the local joke went, the one the joiner used to hang his coat on. The kitchen was a shelf under the stairs for primus stoves; washing facilities comprised a lead-lined area with cold taps and enamel buckets. There was no drying room until the 1960s. A much anticipated treat was a food parcel from home or a trip to Portree for a high tea. A ceilidh dance in a village hall was the perfect antidote for extended periods of bad weather. Many visitors, however, had no inkling that Scottish country dancing was far more dangerous than rock climbing.

Hostel wardens often ruled with a rod of iron, martinets who manipulated the communal chores, usually of the mopping, sweeping, chopping variety, to provide suitable punishment for miscreants. Contemporary Scottish Youth Hostel Association handbooks were refreshingly customer-hostile: 'During the day you should be on the road to the next hostel or else out walking or climbing. It is the only time the warden can get any peace.'

The hostels were mostly self-catering which, until the end of food rationing in 1954, often meant corned beef and 'Pom' (a war-time dried potato), powdered egg, sardines and cod roe. This enriched the existing miasma of tobacco smoke, blistered feet, sweaty socks, and left-over kipper skins in blackened frying pans: 'No frying pans on the table!'; 'Thinks he's 'itler he does.' There was a rush to finish the evening meal and get the singing started when hostellers, many high on cocoa and biscuits, crowded around the stove for renditions of *The Hiking*

Song, Mhairi's Wedding, Uist Tramping Song or *The Road to the Isles*. Altogether now!

Sure by Tummel and Loch Rannoch and Lochaber I will go
By heather tracks wi' heaven in their wiles.
If it's thinking in your inner heart, the braggart's in my step,
You've never smelled the tangle o' the Isles.
Oh the far Cuillins are puttin' love on me,
As step I wi' my crummack to the Isles.

Down in the peace and quiet of the village, the indefatigable Mrs Chisholm and her family continued their traditional Highland hospitality. Many entries in her visitors' book are generous in their praise of her and her family: 'Mrs C is as charming and gracious as ever, Malcolm just as friendly and Mary just as cheerful. We are unfortunate not to see Morag this time.' Mrs Chisholm's daughter Mary started to court one of the Soay boatmen, Ronald MacDonald, and duly became Mary MacDonald. After the death of Mrs Chisholm, in 1953, the couple took over the running of the post office, taking in guests until the late 1970s. Ronald, one of the great characters of the Glen Brittle scene, ran boat trips in *The Hetty* from Loch Brittle, an ad hoc, fingers-crossed service for Rum or the Coruisk area, perhaps with an hour or two stop on Soay to explore the island. Ronald had no licence to carry passengers and the police were constantly trying to catch him with an uninsured, and often overloaded, cargo of tourists. However he and Mary devised a signalling system using the washing line to warn of any police presence in the glen.

For several decades the Soay boatmen provided important transport links for those visiting the Cuillin. MacBraynes were responsible for services to Soay when small boats put out from the island to meet the Loch Scavaig excursion steamer while passengers were ashore visiting Loch Coruisk. These would bring you to Glen Brittle for 4pm, three to four hours faster and a lot cheaper than the Mallaig-Kyle-Portree steamer and then Ewen MacRae's bus service to the glen (the Glen Brittle road was finally surfaced in 1952). At the head of Loch Scavaig new steps were constructed to help people disembark. From Elgol several boats provided trips to see Coruisk, including the *Silver Spray*, *Paragon*, *Morag* and *Otter*. However, as the peak visitor season coincided with the busiest time for fishing and crofting, few committed themselves fully to the tourist trade. Another who provided boat trips was Ted Comber, husband of locally-based author Lillian Beckwith.

With petrol rationing in force until Whitsun 1950, one solution to travel difficulties remained the train to Mallaig and then finding a vessel to take you to Loch Brittle or Loch Scavaig. The first summer after the war, a group of the Glasgow-based Lomond Club, including Ben Humble and Jock Nimlin, hired a boat from Sandy Maclean. On the stormy five and a half hour crossing Nimlin had time to observe the skipper: 'The only guide to his emotions was the speed at which he puffed his pipe. When we reached the lee of Soay his pipe was fairly reeking as he debated whether to shelter overnight on the island or try for a landing in Loch Brittle which has no pier or jetty. He decided to try the latter course.' They eventually went aground on a gravel bank in Loch Brittle: 'Sandy's pipe was fuming.'

Despite most of the Lomonds being seasick, everyone was delighted at a return to peacetime normality and a chance once again to climb on gabbro. The first day fulfilled all of Humble's expectations as the club climbed Window Buttress and then the Inaccessible Pinnacle. The next day Humble was babysitting the two-year-old Dorothy Nimlin in Coire Lagan (she had been camping and howffing since she was three months old) as her parents climbed on the Cioch. The Nimlins were not long back when there was news of an accident on Sgurr Thearlaich. A Polish soldier traversing the mountain had been knocked off balance by a dislodged stone and fell out of sight over the cliffs on the Coruisk side. A party of Lomonds set off immediately only to find that the casualty was dead, killed instantaneously by a fall of over 600ft (180m). The Lomonds' speed and competence in locating the casualty saved many from a night out on the hill.

Humble cadged a lift into Portree with the police officers investigating the accident. It was the responsibility of the police to monitor mountain rescue incidents but they were not supplied with the specialist equipment required, and were often expected to scale the Cuillin in their police uniforms and regulation boots. (In the early 1950s they were reduced to asking RAF Kinloss Mountain Rescue Team to help them out with ice-axes, ropes and protective clothing.). After being offered a cell for the night Humble returned next day to Glen Brittle in the hearse recovering the body, 'holding on to the coffin with one hand and holding a dozen kippers in the other'.

The next year (1946) the Lomonds organised an islands meet. After catching the steamer from Mallaig for a few days exploring Rum, they arranged for the Soay fishermen to transfer them to Glen Brittle. Their luggage comprised four tents, seven hefty rucksacks and a pram. On this visit Humble was determined to tick off Bla Bheinn, a mountain he had many tantalising sights of but never managed to climb. Unfortunately the promised boat for Loch Scavaig failed to arrive in Loch Brittle, but someone then suggested: 'Just draw a line on the map from Glen Brittle to Bla Bheinn and we'll try and follow it.' At 4am Nimlin, Humble and Davie Easson left camp in a cold, misty dawn without sleeping bags, blankets or stoves, characteristically intending to improvise whatever they could find for warmth and shelter.

After crossing Bealach na Banachdich they breakfasted at a fine howff they discovered on the Coruisk side of the col. Lunchtime saw them at another potential howff under a large boulder on the east side of Loch Coruisk. Of all Scottish mountain areas Nimlin regarded the Cuillin as having the finest potential for howffs, a passion he expanded on in the *SMC Journal*: 'There is a deep satisfaction to be found in howff-building, a sense of conformity with the primal nature of the mountain scene.'[3] (Directions to one famous howff, the Arrochar Caves, concluded with, 'then keep walking till you smell kippers').

At Loch Coruisk Nimlin's building regulations were followed to the letter: remove large stones from floor (best tool was a flattened soup tin to scrape loose the soil), draught-proof by plugging holes with moss and peat, level floor and cover with bracken and heather, make door of groundsheet hung over wedged tree branch. The hills were often forgotten in the excitement of creating the ultimate penthowff.

They finally managed to reach the summit of Bla Bheinn at 8pm. It was dark by the time they were off the hill and ensconced for the night in a draughty cave at Loch Scavaig. They tried to keep warm lying around a fire made from the plentiful wood washed ashore from torpedoed and mined shipping. The trip was another treasured memory for Humble, marred only by the loss of his favourite beret on the return leg to Glen Brittle. When *The Cuillin of Skye* was published in 1952, it was dedicated 'To Jock and Davie and howffing days'.

The same holiday, the Lomonds' plans were again waylaid when a walker was reported missing from Sligachan, leaving no note of his intended route. Search parties continued without success for several weeks. Two years later, in May 1948, a skeleton in corduroy shorts, tropical shirt and brown leather jerkin was found on the slopes of Sgurr Hain by Ian Campbell and Willie MacPherson. The remains were identified as the missing man, 26-year-old Captain Maryon, an accountant from Kent. A well-constructed pyramidical cairn, built by a close friend, now marks the spot. It was a mystery how the body remained undiscovered for so long as it lay just a hundred yards from the main Sligachan-Loch Coruisk path.

Between 1925 and 1945 there were 46 fatalities on the Scottish mountains. Seven of these were in the Cuillin with three occurring in the two years before the war. Between 1945 and 1961 there were over 30 fatalities in Skye alone. In 1945 the Gritstone Club donated a new Thomas stretcher for Glen Brittle House; much lighter than the original, it had extended handles, straps to distribute weight, and wooden runners. The new stretcher was comfortable and easy to handle. There was also a Thomas splint which helped prevent amputation, but the bandages in the first aid kit were poor quality and often broke during splinting.

By the 1950s, there was some semblance of an official rescue team on Skye with John 'Jonags' MacKenzie, a Portree postal worker, leading a group of local police as well as volunteers like Sandy Innes, Calum McInnes, Willie MacPherson, Ian Campbell at Sligachan and local GP, Dr MacDonald. MacPherson was the farmer at Crossal, one of the unsung heroes of mountain rescue in the Cuillin. His obituary in *The Clarion of Skye* stated: 'No search party was considered safe without his presence.'

Often as not rescues were carried out by an enthusiastic but inexperienced band of hostellers and campers. In September 1951, two students discovered a climber lying near Collie's Ledge with severe injuries. The casualty was able to tell them he had fallen from the ridge late in the afternoon the previous day. It was the third call-out of the week. Sergeant Glendinning contacted a 20-year-old medical student, staying at Glen Brittle Hostel, who had helped on the earlier rescues. The student organised what medical supplies he could, and a team of six from the hostel were first to reach the casualty about 9pm. In appalling weather and fading light it was felt inadvisable to move him. One of the group was Cambridge geology student Mike O'Hara, pioneer of climbs on the Etive Slabs and Carnmore Crag, who later wrote an account of the incident:

> A few feet down the screes we found our man, almost invisible in his khaki anorak. Darkness was upon us. A flashing torch announced the arrival of the others. It fell and went out. It was the only torch. For Ray this was a bad moment. As a medical student it was his responsibility to decide what we could best do for the now unconscious man. Eventually we stripped him as far as practicable, and slid him with infinite care into his sleeping bag on the stretcher. There was no means of ascertaining whether he had suffered head injuries or not. Should we give him morphine? We tried to feed him coffee, without success. He was groaning occasionally, deathly white, and puffy in the face from shock. We gave him the morphine and drank the coffee ourselves, huddled around the stretcher waiting for the others to arrive. Alone we could not risk moving him. It was over thirty hours since he had fallen. An hour later, Ray leant over and felt his pulse. 'He's dead,' he said. I felt no sensation beyond that of cold and misery.[4]

In winter there were few visitors about and any accident victims were almost entirely dependant on local people for assistance. Roger Gray, the Portree optician, had long dreamt of a snowy ascent of Sgurr Alasdair's Stone Shoot. In March 1955 perfect conditions arrived with crisp winter skies and snow down to 1,000ft (305m). After a memorable ascent of Skye's highest peak, Gray and his companion, bank clerk Dougie Meldrum, turned to retrace their steps. Attempting a roped glissade they lost control on the icy surface and both tumbled down the gully.

Glissading is an exhilarating method of descending snow using the boot soles as a form of ski. For connoisseurs the glissade was a much anticipated and elegant finale to a winter's day on the hill, but for those unfamiliar with pace control, the blindside turn, and somersault arrest, it became a byword in accident reports. One instructional book noted: 'There are three types of glissade: standing, sitting and involuntary, and they often follow each other in quick succession.' In the Alasdair Stone Shoot they only came to a halt when Meldrum's ice-axe, still attached by his wrist-loop, fortuitously caught between two rocks.

Gray suffered a broken femur but Meldrum, despite fractured ribs, managed to descend to Glen Brittle for assistance. The advance rescue party of John Mackenzie, Jimmy Dewar, George Bennett and Alastair MacLennan, a local constable, arrived about midnight. After Bennett attached a splint, the casualty was lowered gingerly down the gully on ropes wrapped around ice-axes planted in the snow. They reached the lochan around dawn when they were reinforced by a contingent from RAF Kinloss led by Dan Stewart. Fourteen hours after his accident, Roger Gray reached Glen Brittle House where he was greeted by Mrs MacRae, who had been up all night looking after the rescue parties, with a very welcome cup of tea. Gray later became a prominent peace activist and was arrested in 1986, three months before his death at the age of 70, during a CND demo at Coulport.

The late 1940s and early 1950s saw a flourishing of university climbing clubs. One of the most active on Skye was the Edinburgh University Mountaineering Club, formed in 1938. One of its early activists was Derek Haworth, a medical student who was reckoned by Hamish MacInnes to be one of the finest rock climbers of his generation. After his graduation Haworth disappears from climbing records: he first worked as a surgeon on cruise ships before emigrating to Canada in 1953.

The Cioch Upper Buttress had been largely ignored as regards new routes since Crack of Doom back in 1918. In May 1947, Haworth teamed up with I ap G Hughes (nicknamed 'Yappy' after his Welsh initials) to put this to rights. Haworth and Hughes created two fine climbs in a single day: Doom Flake (Severe) and Crack of Double Doom (VS). The latter is one of the best climbs of its grade on the island.

Two years later (1949), Haworth and Hughes were back to claim one of Skye's most enduring classics, Integrity, a direct line through some unlikely looking territory on the Cioch Upper Buttress. Initially regarded as one of the best Very Difficults in the range, Integrity now weighs in as a four-star Very Severe. The climb was named two years later by Dan Stewart who was unaware it had been climbed previously.

Another climber active at this time was Cym Smith, the great-nephew of O G Jones. Smith was a prominent figure in post-war British climbing until his death in a motorcycle accident in Edinburgh in the early 1950s. In 1949 he put up two new climbs: an eponymous Severe on Sgurr na h-Uamha, and Rib of Doom (VS) the rounded arete to the left of Crack of Doom. (The original description of Rib of Doom was hard to follow and several variations were made by mistake; the best of these is the HVS Sternum climbed by Davie Gardner and Dog Holden in 1979). For a while it was popular to try and tick off all four 'Doom' climbs in a day, known as 'Doing the Dooms'.

Later in the summer of 1949 Hamish Nicol and Alan Parker tried to solve the seemingly intractable problem of Deep Gash Gully on Sgurr a' Mhadaidh. Nicol was a medical student at Oxford where his regular climbing partner was Tom Bourdillon. Nicol was a reserve for the 1953 Everest Expedition while Bourdillon was selected and reached the South Summit. Deep Gash Gully was first attempted by William Naismith and G B Gibbs in 1898 when they were bamboozled by the formidable second pitch. Ashley Abraham, who twice came to Skye with this as his prime objective, stipulated his criteria for a successful ascent: 'The rocks should be dry; they themselves should be in good climbing trim; and, above all, they should be sufficiently experienced men to know when to turn back. The turning back will probably be the chief feature of their expedition.'[5] Many leading climbers had come away empty-handed, including Leslie Shadbolt, E W Steeple and W H Murray.

When Nicol and Parker arrived at the foot of the first pitch their first impressions didn't bode well: 'It looked awful: a 40-foot overhang, left wall overhanging, right wall a sheer glass-smooth slab, the back parts well irrigated by unseen sources above.' After deciding to take on the obstacle directly, Parker managed to get a sling on the chockstone at the lip of the overhang. Using this for aid he lunged for an obvious handhold at the edge and then mantelshelved strenuously onto the chockstone: 'The second pitch inspired no greater enthusiasm than did the first. It was seventy-foot high, a narrow cave-chimney, whose lip generously overhung its base, perhaps by as much as twenty feet.'[6] Again there was no way of evading the direct challenge. You were forced to back and foot up and out to the lip of the overhang where 'a massive bollard can be grasped'.

More jammed stones, undercut chimneys, overhangs and jets of cold water led to the Thuilm Ridge where, bedraggled, soaked and filthy, they celebrated the conclusion of one of Skye's most protracted campaigns, now graded Hard Very Severe.

Around the same time as the first ascent of Deep Gash Gully, Richard Brooke and Dave Davidson were staying at Jock Nimlin's howff at Loch Coruisk. Brooke was a member of Ed Hillary's party on the 1956-58 Trans-Antarctic Expedition when he had Mount Brooke named after him. From their base the steep outline of Sgurr Coir' an Lochain inspired them to attempt a new line on this remote peak, what became Shelf Route (Severe), as Brooke relates:

> Our original idea was to attempt the north ridge direct by a steep chimney we could see leading round onto the extremely steep west face. After a half-hearted attempt to reach the foot of this chimney we traversed back to the left and found a line of weakness running up to the left which we followed for 150 feet (200 feet above foot of rocks) from where a long shelf ran out to the right. The shelf, outward sloping but rising only slightly, was about six

feet wide to start with but higher up, where the vertical upper wall receded, it was thirty to forty inches from outside to inside edge. The first pitch was easy but the second I didn't like at all. Dave put on his rubbers (mine had been left at the howff) and led it brilliantly. His boots in my sack made an awkward burden.

The pitch got steadily harder, culminating in a very hard bit in rounding a corner in layback fashion. The slabs were hard and smooth and almost totally lacking in positive footholds. The belay was a miserable affair and the stance negligible. Dave went on, first upwards, then a long traverse to the right along the top of the slabs to some broken rocks at almost the extreme right of the shelf. These two pitches were both about 100 feet with no runners. With much care I removed my nailed boots and tied them to my waist loop. In stockinged feet the slabs lost much of their sting. Dave went up very steep rocks for forty feet before reaching a stance and hauled up rucksack and boots. I led a twenty foot wall of slabs to the right with a hard move at the top after which easier rocks and scrambles led to the top. We traversed across the head of Coir' an Lochain to Bealach Coir' an Lochain and then followed the main ridge to Gars-bheinn.[7]

In the mid-1940s a series of hard winters meant classic routes like Sgurr nan Gillean's Pinnacle Ridge were in pristine condition. Since the late 1930s there had been an upsurge of interest in Scottish winter climbing boosted especially by the writings of W H Murray. Standards rose rapidly, helped by the use of tricouni-nailed boots, long lengths of the lighter alpine line and the innovative use of home-made head-torches. (One of the first British climbers to use a head-torch was Archie MacAlpine who got the idea through his work as a dentist). Winter belays were still very basic, often simply sticking the ice axe in the snow and wrapping the rope around it. Despite the transport difficulties there was the occasional winter sortie to the Cuillin.

Like its summer ascent, the date of the first winter ascent of Pinnacle Ridge is difficult to pin down. The Alpine Club team of Gibson, Morse, Wicks and Carr have a sound claim at Easter 1892 when 'the surroundings were wintry in the extreme'. At the 1911 Easter Meet three SMC parties climbed the route when they were troubled by snow and ice from the Third Pinnacle onwards. In *Mountain Days in the Isle of Skye*, Jerry Wright provides information on climbs he has done, including details of Pinnacle Ridge, 'Ice conditions, 6 hours'.

Bill Wood stated that both Pinnacle Ridge and the West Ridge of Sgurr nan Gillean were done twice in 'the great winter of 1947'. This was the coldest winter of the century (the coldest February for 300 years) when there were ice floes in the North Sea and Highland sheep farmers lost a quarter of their flocks. In the Cuillin conditions were superb. The first 1947 ascent was by Lord Malcolm Douglas-Hamilton and Donald MacIntyre when they climbed much of Pinnacle

Ridge over two days. Basing themselves at Alltdearg, Lord Malcolm's cottage below Sgurr nan Gillean, they also traversed several sections of the Main Ridge where MacIntyre was yet another to fail on the Inaccessible Pinnacle's ice-sheathed West Ridge.

After MacIntyre left for home Douglas-Hamilton teamed up with Bill Wood of Portree to make a complete ascent of Pinnacle Ridge as the fine weather continued. Douglas-Hamilton was impressed how the climb was transformed by winter conditions; the easy ledges of summer disappearing under high-angle snow-ice which required almost continuous step cutting and accentuated the sense of exposure. The next year (March 1948) Tom Weir and Arthur MacPherson also made a winter ascent of Pinnacle Ridge when they found the crux to be the final section to the summit of Sgurr nan Gillean which, plastered in snow and ice, required long run-outs of delicate climbing and careful route selection. In conditions like these Pinnacle Ridge (IV) provides one of the finest winter routes in the country.

In his ten years on Skye Bill Wood amassed an unrivalled knowledge of the mountains, especially in winter when he made ascents of all the main summits and ridges but, as he pointed out, 'not all at once!' After their ascent of Pinnacle Ridge, Douglas-Hamilton and Wood descended the West Ridge where they used a 30-foot line to lasso and pass the Gendarme. This was a technique Wood also brought into play on what was probably the first winter ascent of the Inaccessible Pinnacle's West Ridge when the target was the block above the sloping ledge, 'a most exasperating experience'. Wood also made a conventional winter ascent of the pinnacle's long side in three pitches, now graded III/IV.

Before leaving the 1940s, mention must be made of one of its enduring characters, William Arthur Poucher. A bench outside the Sligachan Inn is dedicated to him: 'A renowned mountain photographer who loved the wild places.' Walter, as he preferred to be called, trained as a chemist and became chief perfumier with Yardley where he negotiated six months leave per year. Every May he headed north from Surrey to photograph the Cuillin with his cherished Leica. His definitive textbook, *Perfumes, Cosmetics and Soap*, was scrupulously avoided by most mountaineers of the time, certainly those staying in howffs, but *The Magic of Skye*, first published in 1949, became a highly collectable classic. The book was double the thickness of others in the series and his own personal favourite, reviewed in *The Scotsman* as 'a deluxe portfolio of pictures'. Other reviewers, however, were less enamoured by his flowery verbiage. An amiable eccentric, Poucher was renowned for wearing long red socks, eye-shadow, blusher and gold lamé elbow gloves (the socks drew the most derision), yet happily socialise with Skye's less outré walkers and climbers.

When photographing the Cuillin he was prepared to wait hours for the right light, time he used to test out Yardley's products against Skye's robust cyclonic weather and voracious midges. In 1980 Poucher was the innocent cause of what

TV viewers voted their most shocking chat-show moment. Wearing full slap of blue eyeliner, lipstick, rouge and a perfume 'created especially for tonight', Poucher recounted how, during the Battle of the Somme, he was responsible for the burning of amputated arms and legs. The chat-show host, Russell Harty, responded: 'Is that why you got into the perfume industry when you got back?' Sadly, we will never know the answer because Harty had unadvisedly turned his back on PVC-clad singer Grace Jones who, smarting at the lack of attention, began to assault him.

During the 1950s, there was an increasing polarisation between walkers and climbers. Many of the clubs that now dominated climbing would not have welcomed Poucher as a member. However, equipment as well as techniques, even sock colour, continued to develop. There was now the gradual introduction of new products specifically designed for the fast-evolving sport of rock climbing, like hawser-laid nylon ropes which were shock-absorbent, stronger and more pliable when wet than manila hemp. Two or three slings were carried for runners and belays with the thinnest nylon (5mm) used for threading small natural chockstones.

Ex-military steel karabiners, often called snap-links, became widely available and, combined with improvised techniques like the drilled-out machine nut, knotted sling and inserted pebble, helped improve protection for leaders. When Don Whillans climbed Crack of Double Doom in 1956 his second, W P L Thomson, recalled how 'Don led out right, diagonally into the mist, attaching runners and artificial chockstones at 50-foot intervals.'[8]

One post-war Cuillin route celebrates the availability of all this new kit. The more you have the more there is to lose, especially on polished cruxes like the Thearlaich-Dubh Gap. The party who made the first ascent of the gully on the Coruisk side of the gap came across a treasure trove of gear dropped by gripped leaders above. Each pitch provided more booty than the last, hence the name for the new climb, Aladdin's Route (Difficult).

One of the first of the new student generation to make their mark on Skye was A C (Anthony) Cain from Liverpool, known as Ginger due to his shock of red hair. In 1950, when he was a student at Leeds University, Cain hitched to Glen Brittle where, at the Sutherlands' bunkhouse, he met up with Brian 'Doddy' Dodson, a medical student at Guy's Hospital who was later a GP in Somerset. On the south face of Sgurr Alasdair, they unsuccessfully attempted the corner now taken by Con's Cleft, then started up another route to the left. This line was first noticed by Harold Raeburn in 1914 when he described it as a 'double-barrelled crack'. Cain and Dodson succeeded in climbing the route, calling it Commando Crack (Hard Severe), described in the 2011 SMC guide as, 'One of the best climbs in the Cuillin'. Cain went on to recount its discovery:

Further left there was a steep section of cliff where we noticed a chimney and crack line taking a very direct way between overhanging caves. I started up what turned out to be a good, strenuous climb on excellent rock involving very varied chimneying and crack climbing with the outcome never obvious or the difficulties too great. When a problem arose there was always a solution to it by moving left or back right. This makes for intriguing and enjoyable climbing.[9]

Another student who regularly stayed at the Sutherlands' bunkhouse was G H (Godfrey) Francis from Inverness, known as 'Goff', a leading activist with the Oxford University Mountaineering Club. After graduating in geology Francis worked as a scientist at the British Museum, and was a regular contributor of new climbs in Skye until his death on Pillar Rock in 1960, aged 33, from lightning-induced rock-fall. His first new climb in the Cuillin was White Slab Direct (Severe) on Sron na Ciche's South Crag, in April 1950, when he added a new start as well as a serious direct finish up the edge of the slab itself.

Francis also noticed that there was an unclimbed line to the left of Cioch Direct, separated from it in the upper part by a large plinth. In September 1957 he persuaded the affable Ian MacNaught-Davis to join him for an attempt on what became Cioch Grooves (HVS). 'Mac', from Wakefield in Yorkshire, was well known as Joe Brown's frequent climbing partner in the 1960s. At this time pitons were occasionally carried but ostensibly only for emergencies or for a new route. If pegs were used there was a protocol that they were always mentioned in the route description (this was not always done). There was still a stigma attached to their use as MacNaught-Davis was about to discover:

The attraction was the long corner above the real difficulties. I led up to what turned out to be the crux section below the corner. It had been difficult (or impossible) to place much reliable protection in the lead up to the crux with the gear we had available. So I decided to bang in a peg just below the hard bit. This was very difficult to do and the peg didn't go in very far and I wasn't at all sure that it would sustain a fall. I descended back to where Goff was belaying and we swung on the rope to see how safe it was. I eventually succeeded in leading it and found it hard. The longish corner above turned out to be much easier than we had expected and this was a bit disappointing. Of course we were criticized by the Scots for using a peg for protection but I believe that people who did it subsequently were grateful that the peg was there (and tested!).[10]

Godfrey Francis was joined for several other new Cuillin lines by E A (Ted) Wrangham, an old Etonian and Northumbrian landowner who was regarded as one of the world's foremost experts on Japanese art. On an expedition to the Pamirs in 1962 he was asked by Soviet climbers what he did for a living. He replied that he was a collective farmer: 'My peasants farm, I collect.' He is credited as the visionary behind Kielder Water, northern Europe's largest man-made lake, work for which he was awarded the OBE.

In June 1952, Francis and Wrangham put up the atmospheric Shining Cleft (Hard Severe) on Sgurr a' Mhadaidh as well as Petronella (VS) on Sron na Ciche. The latter route is named after a Scottish country dance and similar footwork may be required. The next year Ted Wrangham made solo first ascents of Central Buttress (Very Difficult) Marsco's second recorded route, and North Buttress (Difficult) on An Caisteal. He observed: 'Happily the supply of great unclimbed buttresses in the Cuillin is far from exhausted.'

Three days after Ted Wrangham's ascent of North Buttress the rescue teams were once again busy. On the western slopes of Bla Bheinn the body of an 18-year-old woman was found with unusual injuries. A fortnight later two rock climbers, Marion Bradford and Roberta Symes, fell on the same mountain after their rope was deliberately sliced through by a third party. One of the women was dead, the other in a coma at Camasunary where police hoped she would soon regain consciousness and reveal the name of the killer. This is the plot of Mary Stewart's 'romantic suspense' novel *Wildfire at Midnight* in which Alexander Nicolson's dream of a comfortable hotel at Camasunary comes true. It's a real-life murder mystery weekend set at the time of the Coronation when residents huddled around the wireless listening for news of progress on Everest. But among them is a homicidal maniac slowly working his way through the guests.

Through the late 1940s and early 1950s the colourful world of Cuillin geology continued to flourish. Among those keen on studying the Tertiary igneous rocks of Skye were the geology staff of Durham University. These included Mary Stewart's husband, Frederick (Fred) Stewart, later professor of geology at Edinburgh University. He was a cousin of the actor Stewart Grainger (real name James Stewart, hence the change). At Durham, Fred Stewart's professor was Lawrence Wager, a keen Morris dancer who had been a student of Alfred Harker at Cambridge in the 1920s. When Noel Odell dropped out of the 1933 Everest expedition he was replaced by 'Waggers' who went on to equal Norton's altitude record of 28,200ft without using supplementary oxygen. He and Wyn Harris found the ice-axe belonging to Sandy Irvine. After the war Wager's geological interests shifted from Greenland to Skye where, along with Fred Stewart and star student G M (Malcolm) Brown, he began to reinvestigate Harker's work on the Skye granitic complexes.

Another geologist studying the Cuillin around this time was Peter Zinovieff. In 1956 he and his half-brother, Patrick Skipwith, were camping in Harta Corrie while undertaking geological mapping of the area. Zinovieff later invented the VCS3 synthesizer and was described by Jon Lord of the band Deep Purple as 'a mad professor type. I was ushered into his workshop and he was in there talking to a computer, trying to get it to answer back.'

In Skye, in days of yore, the MacLeods and the MacDonalds liked nothing better than a bloodthirsty clan fight in a Cuillin corrie. The Bloody Stone in Harta Corrie commemorates one such occasion around 1395 when the MacDonalds were victorious and the bodies of the slain were reputedly heaped around the boulder. At two in the morning something made Skipwith throw back the tent-flap. On the other side of the burn were dozens of kilted Highlanders moving across the hillside. A similar thing happened a few nights later.

All outdoor-minded young people were eager to make the most of the post-war freedom after years of stringency and restrictions (even trouser turn-ups were banned to save material). Lack of money did not deter their ambitions. Every major climbing area had a focal point catering for young, hard-up climbers, many of whom could not afford sleeping bags or tents: the Wall End Barn in Langdale, Cameron's Barn in Glen Coe, and the Cromlech boulders in Snowdonia. In Glen Brittle Hugh McRae provided basic accommodation in his barn, the building with distinctive stairs at the gable end. The climbers' den was in the attic space which doubled as a hayloft, so the amount of floor-space for sleeping diminished rapidly during the hay-making season. Many of the climbers would help out around the farm.

MacRae's barn attracted young activists from all over Britain, itching to experience the magic of Skye. There was a regular contingent of gritstone-trained, flat-capped English climbers like Dennis Gray, Neville Drasdo and Mike Dixon, many of whom were still at school. Hitchhiking was the pragmatic solution to post-war travel difficulties, until you could afford a motor-bike, and often provided as many adventures as the rock climbing. However it made regular climbing partnerships difficult as in far-flung Glen Brittle several days might separate the arrival of a team of two. On his first visit in 1949 Dixon took four days to reach Skye from his home near Leeds. Still top of the wish list were Crack of Doom and Mallory's. Before he left home Dixon purchased a 130ft quarter weight (5mm) rope, both for its lightness and because he reckoned this length was required to tackle the now iconic Slab and Groove.

Another regular visitor to Glen Brittle was Bill Brooker, a tall rugby-playing Aberdonian with enormous hands. The Brookers, like many families from North-East Scotland, were involved in tea planting in India where Bill was born. Aged 17, Brooker hitched to Glen Brittle where he teamed up with Pat Walsh who had a tent made from parachute material. But he had forgotten the poles and was using tree branches instead.

On a trip up to the Main Ridge, Brooker and Walsh noticed the impressive profile of the North Face of Sgurr Mhic Choinnich, 'a great discovery'. They later investigated this more closely when they attempted what became the classic Fluted Buttress (this was originally the name given to the whole cliff). When they reached the first band of overhangs it started to rain and, with water flowing down the rocks, they were forced to abandon the climb. Mike Dixon and Neville Drasdo also made some tentative explorations hereabouts, but they too were thwarted by wet weather.

The next summer (1950) Brooker and Dixon, who was again on his school holidays, joined forces for another attempt on Fluted Buttress. They approached the cliff down what they aptly named Rotten Gully. Due to a late start they didn't have enough time for their original plan but instead made the first ascent of the less serious North-East Buttress (Very Difficult). The next day they returned to their main objective. At their previous highpoint Mike Dixon traversed further to the right where he was able to find a way through the overhangs. Above, the buttress reared up into vertical flutes of rock separated by three steep cracks. Wearing nailed boots Dixon chose the central crack but was eventually forced to admit defeat, exhausted, and with fingers numbed by the wet and cold rock. Any further attempts on the climb were thwarted by more foul weather and a protracted rescue in Harta Corrie.

Over at Sligachan, Charlie Gorrie and Iain Ogilvie, who had first met as students at Edinburgh University, were hoping to traverse the Main Ridge. As part of their preparations they tackled Sgurr a' Ghreadaidh's South-East Ridge, attracted by its then reputation as a splendid climb, reputedly one of the longest in Britain. After an arduous day they were only back at Sligachan for five minutes when a young man arrived with news of an accident. He and his sister, Mary Duncan, had set out from Glen Brittle to cross the Main Ridge to Sligachan by way of Harta Corrie. Mary had fallen on the descent, receiving head injuries, and was unconscious.

The ensuing search and rescue would display many of the shortcomings of well-intentioned but uncoordinated rescue attempts that were all too common before local rescue teams became more organised and better funded through the next two decades.

Ogilvie and Gorrie realised it was imperative to reach the casualty before dark. Some of those at Sligachan had already left to go over Bealach a' Bhasteir. Others wanted to have dinner first. Ogilvie took charge, organising an advance party that included Duncan and a doctor. A large team of helpers were on their way from Glen Brittle by bus, including Mike Dixon and Bill Brooker. The latter would later recall the incident as the worst night he had ever spent on a Scottish mountain.

There was still a little daylight left when the advance party arrived at where Duncan thought his sister lay, but ominously he conceded that he did not recognise any features and concluded that it must be the wrong location. It was soon dark and heavy rain started to fall, blown up the corrie by a strong wind. The advance party had little food and few torches. The doctor was soaked through as he had no waterproof, just a sweater. Huddled behind a rock, they saw the lights of the Glen Brittle party below but they were heading in the wrong direction, sidetracked by flashing lights and shouts from yet another group on the slopes of Sgurr na h-Uamha. Iain Ogilvie descended to redirect this party who were led by shepherd Willie Macintosh [MacPherson?]. Ogilvie later recorded the events of the night:

> It was very dark and cold now, and further search was useless until dawn. Willie MacIntosh knew of a large pile of boulders near the Lota Corrie waterfall and we made our way there with difficulty over half a mile of rough country. At 11.30pm I crawled with ten others under a huge supported block. The rest of the party, now about thirty strong, found other blocks and we settled down for a very uncomfortable night. Outside our inefficient shelter we had both a gale and a thunderstorm. Inside was a burn below and wet dripping slab above. We were cramped, cold and wet. Once we all went out to stretch our legs but soon retreated again. At least we were out of the wind.
>
> Willie started to organise things at 4.15am, some in Harta, some in Lota. Unfortunately just as we were up to the top of the fall, two stray members of the search party started to shout between the two groups and each group mistook this for a messenger from the other to report a find and we came down again and they stopped looking. Once in Lota Corrie the real messenger arrived to say they had found her, unconscious but alive, in Harta Corrie within 200 yards of the night's shelter.[11]

The casualty was carried down on the stretcher using three shifts of ten people, and once on easier ground, five shifts of six. About two miles from Sligachan they were met by the long-awaited relief party with food and hot tea. Sadly it was all in vain as Mary Duncan died two days later without regaining consciousness. Ogilvie thought it was the hardest 24 hours he'd ever had on the hill, reckoning they had expended more energy than the traverse of the Main Ridge.

Once recovered from the ordeal, Brooker and Dixon were impatient to have another crack at Fluted Buttress, but yet more wet weather meant it was a week after their initial attempt before they were able to have another shot at solving the problem. On this occasion Dixon discovered a gangway on the right which now constitutes the route's exposed crux:

> I brought Bill up to a small stance and tried to break out on the wall on the right. Below, the rock fell sheer to the tumbled bed of the North-East Gully, but thirty feet of vertical rock above would lead us past the overhangs. This way past the flutes was the hinge upon which the route depended. Slowly I

eased myself from the shelf on to the wall and began to move delicately up and to the right on a line of small shaky holds. At last I pulled out on to the easement above the flutes. Above us lay a broken section and we climbed quickly till we reached a depression in the face below the steep rocks of the final tower. (12)

On this last section, the Direct Finish, Brooker had a miraculous escape. He was leading a holdless groove, made greasy in the rain that had just started to fall, when he was forced to swing left on the only good hold, a large spike:

As I swung across on the spike it snapped and I skidded down the slab. Near its base my feet caught on something and I managed to regain my balance. The big rock spike went whistling down the cliff, touching the rope on the way. Fifty feet below me, Mike Dixon had no idea how close we were to oblivion as his belay would have held nothing. I still don't know how I stopped. I must have hit some sort of wrinkle on the slab. I saw the scratches made by my nails but there were no obvious holds.[13]

Fluted Buttress was originally graded Hard Severe but is now HVS, as is the Direct Finish. After Brooker left for home Dixon teamed up with Tom Shaw, on yet another cold and wet day, to explore the possibilities of Bealach Buttress across Rotten Gully from Fluted Buttress. They were initially rebutted on an attempt on Black Cleft but succeeded on Hourglass Crack (VS) named after the distinctive crux, 'the narrows', where the climber is forced out of the crack. Mike Dixon became increasingly enamoured with this wild Coruisk side of the range, what he called 'the Forgotten Corrie', and introduced various partners to climbs like Fluted Buttress and North-East Buttress. As he pointed out, these were the first explorations in the corrie since 1912.

The next summer (1951) Bill Brooker and Mike Dixon again joined forces for a line they had noticed to the left of Fluted Buttress: 'A terrific crack curved up the wall and soared into the mist, an awe-inspiring sight.' This became Crack of Dawn (HVS), a fine climb on clean, sound rock. Dixon led the crux because, as a gritstone-trained climber, he was more at home on steep cracks than Brooker. From the platform at the end of the second pitch they continued by a steep chimney directly above, but Brooker took note of the corners on the left for future reference. Seven years later he climbed these with Dick Barclay to produce Dawn Grooves (HVS). Mike Dixon later reflected on his time in Glen Brittle when he regarded their climbing equipment as 'worse than basic':

It seemed to rain every morning and Bill and I would cut logs for Hugh MacRae with a two-handed saw. For this we got lunch as we had little money for food. About 1.00pm we would set out to climb on the wet rock. Sometimes it was so windy we were forced to choose sheltered routes like Waterpipe Gully despite the guidebook recommending a week's dry weather. Belays were restricted to natural features like spikes or chockstones. However on Fluted Buttress we had a couple of bent, home-made pegs which we hammered into cracks with rocks. On one stance I remember clearing a ledge of stones before realizing I had disposed of all my 'hammers'. Not only was equipment poor but I had inadequate clothing, sometimes just a rugby jersey. We often reached the tops at twilight but this was OK as it was Skye. In deference to the MacRaes there was no climbing on a Sunday which I used to write up the routes in the logbook.[14]

Here are some of Dixon's comments from the Glen Brittle House logbook:

Waterpipe Gully: 'Plenty of water, plenty of loose rock.'
Amphitheatre Wall: 'One of the finest routes on the Sron, on perfect rock with excellent steep climbing. Climbed just after heavy rain, but the rock dried out very quickly. The standard is consistent throughout, each pitch a delight in itself.'
Crack of Dawn: 'Rock clean, grease-free and sound throughout. Lower section steep with fine moves and situations. VS in rubbers. Time 3 hours.'

In the summer of 1953 Bill Brooker continued his exploration of the Coruisk faces with Tom Patey, a 21-year-old medical student from Ellon near Aberdeen. As a reward for helping out around the farm on their off days, Brooker and Patey were promoted to a 'private room' in the MacRaes' barn. On the left flank of Bealach Buttress they produced Thunderbolt Shelf (Severe) named after a lightning flash that occurred during the climb. Two days later found them exploring the unclimbed Coruisk face of Sgurr na Banachdich. Despite some shattered rock the Aberdonians put up four new routes in one day: South Twin (Difficult), North Twin (Severe), Midget Ridge (Moderate) and Clouded Buttress (Severe). This last route was 'a very good climb that comes out almost on the summit', but the pick of the bunch was the easiest, Midget Ridge, a fine scramble that in places narrows to a knife-edge.

Although all the newly available climbing equipment was successfully refined for use on British rock, one problem area remained. Few accounts about the Cuillin during the 1950s were complete without a furrowed-brow reference to footwear. Despite plimsolls being widely used since the First World War, many rock climbers adhered to nails even for high standard climbs where it was essential that you placed the boot deliberately onto the foothold, holding it stock-still as you moved up. Mike Dixon wore tricounis when he led Fluted Buttress as this had smoother basalt sections where gym shoes didn't grip in the wet. The next year on Crack of Dawn he wore gym shoes but took his tricounis with him for any damp sections. This became a popular compromise with the surplus footwear carried by the second and sent up on the rope as required.

During the 1950s nailed boots had competition from rubber soles, called Vibrams after their Italian inventor Vitale Bramani. Lighter and better insulated they gradually replaced nailed boots though some diehards swore by tricounis in winter into the 1970s. One of the first climbers to try out these new rubber soles in Skye was J H B Bell. In May 1948 he used the British-made Itshide 'Commando' version and was more than happy with their performance. Bell wore them to lead the South Crack of the Inaccessible Pinnacle while his partner, Colin Allan, opted for socks. A few days later they were joined by Bell's wife Pat, along with Robert and Mabel Jeffrey, for the classic Jeffrey's Dyke (Difficult) on Sgurr Mhic Choinnich. Mrs Jeffrey had another first ascent in the Cuillin, North Chimney on Bruach na Frithe, climbed forty years earlier when she was Miss Mabel Clark.

The first ascent of Jeffrey's Dyke is surprisingly late considering such an obvious line in a popular corrie; it was commented on by Woodhead and Steeple in 1907. The party of five found the general standard to be about Difficult with a couple of harder sections higher up. Here they had to contend with hail and snow showers as well as 'mild electrical discharges' when Bell had to resort to using Allan's shoulder at one steep pitch, 'the storm being at its height'. Jim Bell concluded that his rubber soles gave a satisfactory grip in the dry and the wet, on both gabbro and trap. However not everyone would agree, and some went so far as to nail a few tricounis around the edge of their Vibram soles.

After graduating from Aberdeen University, Brooker taught geography before working at the extramural department of his old university. His native Cairngorms were one of the last bastions of nailed boots. The isolated Aberdonians were regarded as footwear fundamentalists, reluctant to embrace any technical innovation. (John Cunningham joked that they were slow to adopt crampons as it would mean having to cut a larger step). By the time Brooker started to use Vibrams, leading climbers elsewhere were wearing lightweight, rubber-soled rock boots called PAs after their French designer Pierre Allain. Of all the innovations in equipment these probably did most to foster the rapid rise in standards. But Brooker continued to mourn the passing of the tricouni, 'Something was lost, you know, when climbers stopped using nails.'

In June 1954 Mike Dixon, now a professional photographer who gained international recognition as a specialist in photographing antiquities, was back in Skye when fine weather allowed him to create five new climbs in three days on Bealach Buttress. He was drawn again to the prominent chimney that separated the buttress from the sheer wall to its left. His initial assessment was of a Very Difficult climb with some short harder sections. Three hours later he and John Monks reached the top of what they called Black Cleft (VS) after 'pitch after pitch of hard, exacting, strenuous and impressive climbing'. The next day they returned for the first ascents of two obvious lines to which they had already given names: The Bow (VS), to Hourglass Crack's bowstring, and Lost Arrow (VS) due to a huge chockstone shaped like an arrowhead:

> The Bow proved a really enjoyable climb, on pleasant rock with some fine positions. The steep overhanging crack gave some fine technical climbing, delicate and strenuous at the same time. It was not easily won. Once more I borrowed John's Vibrams for this pitch, and he followed in gym shoes. Above the overhang the crack continued up the corner of the large clean slab which had attracted our interest from below, and soon led us to the Upper Terrace, with the deep recesses of Hourglass Crack on our left.[15]

The Glasgow Fair holiday weekend in July 1956 saw the arrival in Skye of a boisterous Creagh Dhu team, bringing with them their high Glen Coe climbing standards. While the island had waited a long time for its first Extreme, it now got two in the space of a day. John Cunningham, a Clydebank shipyard welder, was near the height of his climbing powers which peaked with ascents like Bluebell Grooves (E4) and Carnivore (E3) both on Buachaille Etive Mor in Glen Coe. Cunningham's hard exterior was to mellow with the years, unlike his route on Sron na Ciche, Bastinado (E1), which still requires the same forceful approach it did then. Here he was accompanied by club-mates John Allen and Bill Smith.

Pat Walsh started climbing at 14 when introduced to the Creagh Dhu by Chris Lyon who got him a job at John Brown's shipyard in Clydebank. His thick spectacles and chubby appearance belied a powerful physique capable of the hardest lines, exemplified by Club Crack (E2) on the Cobbler, a route many stellar Creagh Dhu names failed to follow. His Cuillin legacy is a vertical gritstone-like crack to the right of Integrity: 'Hamish MacInnes tried Trophy Crack before me but couldn't make it. He left a piton in, as I did the climb I took it out and that was my trophy. Harry Mackay was my second. The same day Johnny Cunningham did Bastinado so the next day we repeated each other's climbs.'[16]

That the working class, Clyde-built Creagh Dhu could invite an Edinburgh architect to join their ranks, speaks volumes for Jimmy Marshall. A seminal figure in Scottish mountaineering, Marshall became an honorary member of the club in 1987. One of his earliest first ascents, his only one on Skye, was Toolie Grooves (VS) in Coire na Banachdich in June 1953. Marshall, George Hood and Charlie Donaldson arrived on Skye via Soay. (It was the week the island was evacuated with many Glen Brittle folk helping the islanders pack their belongings onto the SS *Hebrides* for a new life on Mull). Charlie Donaldson recorded their new route in his diary:

George Hood and I left by 4.30am train for Skye. Jimmy Marshall had left on Friday morning to hitchhike there. At Mallaig, George and I met Geddes the owner of Soay who was talking a small party by sea to Glen Brittle. He offered to take us for 10 shillings each which we accepted; about three hours to Glen Brittle via Soay. Camped about 5pm on flattish spot above crossing on Allt Banachdich. Jimmy arrived about one hour later. We went up Coire na Banachdich and George led Window Buttress.

We then descended to the foot of a very steep buttress which we spotted higher up the corrie. The lower rocks overhung and higher up bulged in even greater overhangs. We roped up and after three unsuccessful attempts Jimmy finally forced a way up a groove at the right-hand side of the lowest rocks. This led into the very hard-looking gully which we had mistaken for Black Chimney. From the top of this pitch a high-angled, awkward traverse led out onto the face of the buttress. A further not too difficult pitch followed. Severe climbing then led up under the great overhang before moving right onto a steep sloping slab. The top of this slab led to a groove, overhanging at the bottom and with a projecting nose on its left – terrific exposure. Fifth and final pitch led up crack and then wall to the top of the buttress. Probably about 350 feet on excellent gabbro, at least Hard Severe in vibrams.[17]

Later in the 1950s, Jimmy Marshall was mentor to a group of talented young climbers emerging in the Edinburgh area. One of these, Robin Smith, developed into one of the finest British climbers of the twentieth century, certainly one of the most precociously talented Scotland has ever produced. In *Hard Rock* half of the entries from mainland Scotland are Smith routes.

Robin Smith first came to Skye, the island he described as 'wedding of thrusting rock and sucking sea', in September 1957 at the start of his second year as a philosophy student at Edinburgh University. The meet was also attended by 75-year-old Professor Graham Brown who had discovered a kindred spirit in Smith. Brown is best known for his exploration of the Brenva Face of Mont Blanc with Frank Smythe; for many years the pair had a rancorous feud over their respective contribution to these classic routes. Brown allowed the EUMC to have the run of his large Old Town home where he lived surrounded by piles of fish and chip wrappers, and used matches, spending nights in his sleeping bag on a camp bed. In the Cuillin he climbed Cioch West with Graham Dewar while one of the other students, most likely Robin Smith, ascended Cioch Direct and Arrow Route wearing Wellington boots.

To the left of the Chasm on Sgurr nan Eag, Robin Smith discovered an unclimbed line of cliffs, 'over 300 feet high and very vertical'. Here, with Hugh Kindness, he did the first ascent of Left Edge (E1) which he compared to Rib of Doom on Sron na Ciche. Like most Smith routes Left Edge is an architecturally alluring natural line. He is also credited with soloing the nearby Ladders (VS), 'very good pitches doubtfully connected', but his route description also contains phrases such as 'shoulder useful' and 'piton belay', terms not normally associated with a solo ascent.

The 1957-58 *EUMC Journal* concluded: 'There is probably no place left in Britain with such scope for new routes as the Cuillin of Skye. Although the popular cliffs like Sron na Ciche are really worked out, there are still faces all over the place, three times the size of Rannoch Wall and without a route.' In 1960 Smith returned to Skye with Geoff Milne to make the first ascent of Thunder Rib in Coir' a' Mhadaidh. His route description was for many years wryly quoted as a model of brevity: 'Thunder Rib. 1,000 feet. Very Severe [now E1]. The fine rib on the left of Deep Gash Gully. Follow line of least resistance.'

In 1960, Robin Smith was also part of an SMC group who introduced visiting Soviet climbers to the Cuillin from a base at the Coruisk Hut, an occasion he recorded in his inimitable style: 'Scavaig stravaiged around the beetling Cuillin. They hove to. Still with this crew, we lent a hearty hand to heave-ho chests and firkins to the Hut. Skye! Mecca to these chaps, all in a froth for Gabbro. Of an evening we four put an end to the Crack of Dawn to lend that route some matter and form. The Russians tight-roped the razor ridge, they cut their feet to ribbons. "At home we haff not such feats" they said, dismayed.'[18] It was on a reciprocal visit to the Pamirs two years later in 1962 that Smith was killed in a fall, aged 23. An anonymous obituary in the 1961-62 *EUMC Journal* stated: 'The mood of happy disorganisation in which he climbed is reflected in his articles. Written in an original and humorous style, they reveal his character far better than any eulogy. Even writing theses lines, one can hear his sardonic laughter.'

Aid climbing in the British Isles is as old as rock climbing itself. One early example was Norman Collie's ascent of Moss Ghyll on Scafell in 1892 when he hacked a hold at the crux. When foreign climbers later hammered pitons into British rock it sparked the mountaineering equivalent of a diplomatic crisis. Aid has always been controversial, but in the 1950s it had its day in the sun primarily due to methods promoted during the war for cliff assaults as well as exposure to glossy American magazines where it was very much in vogue: 1958 saw the first ascent of The Nose at Yosemite in California.

J E B Wright was one of many outspoken critics of this new fad for 'steeple-jacking'. In his instructional book *The Craft of Climbing* he wrote: 'The pegging of any new route which is less then Very Severe is a disgraceful act; it is even more disgraceful in Scotland where thousands of new routes are waiting to be done, routes which will make superb free climbs.' Although highly contentious, some argued that the occasional peg was justified if it created a worthwhile route; a laudable attempt to break new ground.

In 1953 the fashion for aid climbing was introduced to Skye from the USA by Maynard Miller of the American Alpine Club. Miller has two claims to fame: he was technical adviser on John Carpenter's 1982 cult movie *The Thing* – about an extraterrestrial that infiltrates an Antarctic research station. He was also one of the first scientists to identify hard evidence of global climate change as a result of human industrial activity: 'We told the world about it but nobody believed us except the US Navy.' Miller, a member of the successful 1963 Everest West Ridge Expedition, conducted research on Alaska's vast Juneau Icefield since the 1940s in the longest continuous research program on climate change. His conclusion?: 'We're going to be in one heck of a mess, I can guarantee that.'

In the early 1950s Maynard Miller was a Fulbright Fellow at Cambridge University where he befriended fellow geologist G H Francis. On a visit to Skye the pair created the Cuillin's first artificial climb, Magic Casement on Sron na Ciche's Eastern Buttress. The crux, a fierce-looking vertical crack, was overcome using channel pegs and stirrups. It is now climbed free at HVS.

The scene was now set for Hamish MacInnes to introduce the continental grading system for aid climbs: A1, A2, A3 and A4. MacInnes, whose mother came from Skye, maintained a high profile for many years as writer, equipment designer, international mountain rescue expert, and safety adviser on films like *The Eiger Sanction*. His National Service in the Austrian Tyrol gave him a taste for artificial climbing. In Scotland pegs were not unknown. The odd one had been used by J H B Bell and W H Murray but MacInnes, never shy of courting controversy, was the first to wholeheartedly embrace the new artificial ethos.

Through the summers of 1957 and 1958, MacInnes flouted the established ethics with a series of controversial aid climbs on Skye. For many of these he teamed up with Ian Clough who was also instructing on Jerry Wright's Mountaineering Association courses based in Glen Brittle. Clough was nicknamed 'Dangle' after his penchant for practicing aid climbing. Clough's National Service in the RAF led to a three-year stint with the Kinloss Mountain Rescue Team, commemorated in the name of Kinloss Gully (VS) on Sron na Ciche. Every Whitsun, from around 1953, the Kinloss team stationed themselves at the MacRaes' barn.

MacInnes and Clough, augmented at times by John Temple, Don Pipes, John Alexander and others, produced a host of artificial climbs as well as some fine free routes. MacInnes often specifically identified hard crack lines conducive to artificial climbing, but also used aid on largely free routes where short hard sections intervened. On Sron na Ciche's Eastern Buttress, Creag Dhu Grooves (E3 free) was provocatively recorded as HVS, a grade that did not officially exist in Scotland until 1977. Its name was originally spelt Creagh Dhu Grooves (as in the club) but the first 'h' was lost prior to inclusion in the 1969 SMC guide. The climb's second and third pitches were tackled using pegs, expansion bolts and industrial nuts (thread drilled and slung on nylon line) for aid, 'two bulges are interesting'.

Strappado (HVS) took the steep wall to the right of Creag Dhu Grooves starting up the right side of a huge flake. (Strappado, noun: torture by hoisting to a height and letting fall to the length of the rope.) The original description for the third pitch states: 'Artificial climbing for 40 feet up fault. Where dyke joins small fissure on slight overhang traverse right (sling and etrier on bollard). Attain ledge and do tension traverse from piton (removed).'

On the North Buttress of Sgumain MacInnes, Clough and Alexander used three pitons to overcome the rotten overhang of Prometheus, giving access to areas of better rock for routes like Prokroustes (HVS) and Theseus (HVS). The classical name theme continued with Styx (HVS) on Sgurr Dearg's South Buttress, so called after the underground stream running behind the rock. Many of these climbs offer a rich vein for mountaineering archaeologists as jammed bolts, shipyard pitons and other homemade engineering ephemera can still be discovered where they were hammered home.

In the summer of 1958, MacInnes continued to attack overhanging sections of gabbro with his peg hammer, known affectionately as 'The Message'. To the left of Integrity he deployed bolts, pegs and tension traverses to create Atropos, given an original grade of A3. These antics were recorded by the pioneering female alpinist Nea Morin:

> That evening coming down Eastern Gully we heard sounds of ironmongery high above us. This was Hamish MacInnes, 'Piton Hamish or MacPiton', which we thought a most appropriate nickname. During the day he was instructing for the Mountaineering Association, so he was only free in the evenings. Now he was trying out a new artificial route on the Cioch Upper Buttress and he and his friends were making an unconscionable row, hurling blocks of rock about, dropping pitons and karabiners. They bellowed us to get across beneath them quickly; we needed no urging. From far down the Coire Lagan we could still hear great cries of 'beee-low!' followed by the alarming crump and clatter of falling rocks shattering the still evening air.[19]

The next day, 30th May, MacInnes was back on Sron na Ciche with Ian Clough and John Temple for the first ascent of the classic Vulcan Wall (A2, HVS free), the first route to tackle the great slab between Kinloss Gully and Creag Dhu Grooves. It was succinctly recorded by MacInnes as 'sustained difficulty, eight hours'. The previous year (1957) John Temple, who with Clough also added two direct finishes to Sunset Slab on Sgumain, made two attempts on the line of Vulcan Wall. Near his limit, he managed to get up the initial strenuous corner but, climbing with a near novice, decided to call it a day and abseil off. Failure often grates and the next day Temple was keen to return for another shot. On this attempt he got no higher but had the compensation of recovering the krab he had left by abseiling directly from the sling.

The next summer Temple was invited to join Clough and MacInnes, whom he had met that Easter during a rescue on Ben Nevis, for a further attempt on

Vulcan Wall. He was dismayed to watch Clough aid the first pitch that he had already led free, and then witness MacInnes's modus operandi on the second pitch, 'I was bemused rather than aghast that he then murdered the pitch.'[20]

Although Clough and MacInnes produced many other artificial climbs and variations, some quality free climbs were also created. Two days after Vulcan Wall they were joined by Don Pipes for free ascents of the pleasant Depravity (VS) on the Cioch Upper Buttress and the classic Grand Diedre (VS) a prominent corner on the Thearlaich-Dubh Buttress of Sgurr Alasdair. Another MacInnes discovery was Aesculapius (Hard Severe), high in Coire na Banachdich, which catches the evening sun and can be combined with a visit to the Inaccessible Pinnacle.

By July 1958 MacInnes had left Skye and a sense of serenity once again returned to the rocks of Coire Lagan. The same month, on the steep buttress between Cioch Direct and Cioch West, D Gregory and R Hutchison of the Lomond Club put up Crembo Cracks (HVS), a climb as good as, and as hard as, many of MacInnes and Clough's creations. Crembo Cracks symbolised the end of an era with the Lomond pair wearing Vibrams as they followed a trail of nail marks which stopped at the poorly protected crux (chalk marks often end here too).

In the last two years of the 1950s two long-awaited events came to fruition. In 1948 there was a revised second edition of the 1923 SMC guide, with a 24-page appendix of new climbs which at last introduced the standard British grading of Easy, Moderate, Difficult, etc to replace the anachronistic Skye numerical system. As the new guide was fairly bulky, the foreword promised a separate pocket-sized rock climbing guide to be published soon. There was a convention that descriptions of new climbs were always checked prior to inclusion in a guidebook. With rising standards and a spate of hard new routes in the Cuillin, it was increasingly difficult to find the personnel to do this. In 1951 the guidebook editor stated in the *SMC Bulletin*: 'It is essential that a rock climbing guide to Skye be ultimately published, and the Club Committee have approved this. I therefore appeal for volunteers to join a team that I am trying to form, to cover the Coolin peaks and corries.'

Dan Stewart was one of those who helped out, in the process making early repeats of North-East Gully, Cioch Grooves, Fluted Buttress, Crack of Dawn and Forgotten Groove, the last three in a single day with Pat Vaughan. Contained within distinctive maroon boards, the *Climbers' Guide to the Cuillin of Skye*, compiled by Bill MacKenzie with diagrams by Donald Mill, eventually surfaced in 1958 after what the Fell and Rock Climbing Club described as 'an elephantine period of gestation'. It was still very welcome despite the traditional grouses over inaccuracies, lack of index and graded list. Curiously, a new grade of Moderately Difficult was introduced between Moderate and Difficult.

Grading has always been a source of controversy. In England and Wales there was a uniform acceptance of detailed pitch by pitch descriptions. In Scotland the rights of the route-finding enthusiast and climber-explorer were rigorously upheld. For example, South Gully on Sgurr a' Mhadaidh is 700ft (210m) long but the description in the 1948 SMC guide consisted of only nine words: 'There are about twelve pitches. Rock sound, scenery excellent.' In Bill MacKenzie's 1958 guide the description of the nearby Archer Thomson's Route is even shorter, with its 900ft (270m) summed up (inaccurately) as: 'Straightforward climb directly up the cliff to the summit.'

In his 1949 guide, *Glencoe and Ardgour*, W H Murray explained: 'The ideal rock-guide is one that gives at most an indication of a climb's existence, a clue to its whereabouts, and a vague description of what the mountaineer may expect to encounter.' This was not so that English climbers got lost, but to foster judgement through a calculated compromise between detail and vagueness. Scottish climbers have always been keen to express their separate identity, but Scottish mountains *were* different: more remote, less frequented and more serious – none more so than the Cuillin. The 1958 Cuillin guide was one of the last to grade climbs for nailed boots, though if Vibrams or rubbers were the recommended footwear this was mentioned in the text. For example, Crack of Dawn was 'a rubber climb for dry conditions' and Doom Flake, 'Severe in rubbers'.

In May 1959 the much-discussed possibility of a hut at Coruisk (in actuality Scavaig) became a reality. Since the 1890s an Alpine-style hut here had long been mooted by the likes of Ashley Abraham and William Brown as the perfect solution to the long approach walks. Local builder Lachlan MacKinnon, using existing foundations and chimney, battled through illness, storms, rain and midges to have it completed by September 1958. The hut is a memorial to David Monro and Peter Drummond Smith, both killed on Ben Nevis at Easter 1953. Although maintained by the Glasgow Section of the Junior Mountaineering Club of Scotland, it was owned by the trustees until bequeathed to the club in the 1970s. It was to provide a critical impetus to exploration on the Coruisk side of the range.

Chapter Eleven

The Sixties and Seventies

The opening of the Coruisk Hut prompted a flurry of activity to investigate the lower-lying crags now easily accessible from this new base. The most obvious objective was Mad Burn Buttress, well seen through the hut window, offering quick-drying routes on perfect gabbro. Members of the Glasgow Section of the Junior Mountaineering Club of Scotland were first to exploit the possibilities here.

In December 1962, there was a New Year meet of the Glasgow JMCS at Kintail Lodge Hotel where one of their number, ex-submariner Norman Tennant, was proprietor and chef. On 30th December Nigel Robb and Ken Bryan took the ferry to Skye for the first ascent of Subsidiary Gully and West Face (IV) on Knight's Peak, a fine sustained climb that was a significant pointer to the potential for quality winter climbs in the range. Bryan, an industrial radiographer and one of Scotland's up and coming climbers, emigrated to Canada but was tragically killed in a car crash. Once the pair returned to Kintail Lodge there was little time to celebrate the ascent of Skye's first grade IV. Just as they were about to sit down to dinner, there was a phone call to say that there had been a serious accident in the Cuillin involving a Glasgow University Mountaineering Club (GUMC) party staying at the Coruisk Hut. Robb, Bryan and Jim Simpson grabbed some chicken legs and squeezed into Norman Tennant's Mini Cooper to catch a specially laid-on ferry for Skye.

A party of three of the GUMC had left the Coruisk Hut to traverse the Dubh Ridge prior to the traditional Hogmanay celebrations. There was brick hard snow above 2,000ft (610m) and one of the party lacked crampons; on the descent off Sgurr Dubh Mor into An Garbh-choire they all fell, roped together, down an icy gully. The next day a search party from the club found two bodies but one of the climbers, medical student John Methven, was still alive. George Wallace ran to Glen Brittle to raise the alarm. Fortuitously Hamish MacInnes, now leader of the Glen Coe Mountain Rescue Team, was staying with John Campbell at Cuillin Cottage. MacInnes, vastly experienced in mountain rescue, would later regard this as his most memorable call-out, 'the longest and most protracted rescue ever enacted in Scotland'. He immediately instigated rescue proceedings by contacting the JMCS party in Kintail, an RAF Kinloss team he knew was based at Glen Nevis for the New Year, as well as the local Skye team, largely police personnel with a sprinkling of civilians. Most of the RAF team had to be rounded up from Fort William pubs, many the worse for wear.

There was a great deal of confusion among the various search parties as to the location of the accident (this was prior to the introduction of radios). At night, with lighting limited to hand-held torches and Tilley lamps, and in extremely icy conditions, they investigated several possible sites but found no sign of the casualties. Eventually, Hamish MacInnes's party descended to the Coruisk Hut where they learnt the sad news that Methven had passed away not long after Wallace left to get help. The rescue teams, over 35 personnel, succeeded admirably in evacuating the bodies from 2,500ft, down some of the most challenging terrain in the country, a task compounded by snow, ice and mid-winter darkness. Finally Bruce Watt's Mallaig-based *Western Isles* was chartered to evacuate the bodies by sea from the Coruisk Hut.

This tragic accident had a strong bearing on one of the most contentious environmental conflicts of the 1960s which became known as the 'Coruisk Affair'. The proposals first came to light when Sandy Cousins, a marine engineer who was secretary of the Association of Scottish Climbing Clubs, learnt that a Manchester-based Territorial Army unit had requested permission to use the Coruisk Hut. With little or no public consultation they intended to implement a scheme to speed up rescue in this remote area. Mountain rescue records for Skye occasionally mention dinghies having to be manhandled from Loch Scavaig to Loch Coruisk to aid the evacuation of casualties from this side of the range.

The new plan involved the construction of an unsurfaced road from Kilmarie to Camasunary, wire suspension bridges over the Rivers Camasunary and Scavaig, and 'improvement' of the path from Camasunary to Coruisk by blasting the Bad Step to create a three-foot wide path with rock steps. The Mountain Rescue Committee of Scotland was against the scheme and thought the money could be better spent. However, in June 1968 all of these proposals were carried out with one exception – there was no alteration to the Bad Step.

Despite extensive enquiries there was great difficulty in establishing where the proposals originated. In a letter to the press Christopher Brasher pointed a finger of blame at the landowners for giving the project their blessing. In a reply to Brasher's letter Walter Johnson stated robustly that in the 54 years his family had owned the estate they had agreed to only three 'development' suggestions, out of many, and these were done in good faith as being of benefit to all: the building of a landing place to help tourists disembark to see Loch Coruisk, the construction of the JMCS climbing hut, and the building of the bridges and track.

Sandy Cousins eventually came to the conclusion that wilderness areas in Scotland were not safe in sympathetic hands, as had naïvely been assumed, and that existing conservation bodies were not as effective as they could be in defending them from inappropriate development. In the 1960s there was little awareness of the quality or fragility of wild land, and the threats it faced. Those who care about the Cuillin owe a great deal to Cousins who stoically battled bureaucracy to obtain greater consultation with which opponents of the scheme could put across their case. It was probably only Cousin's observation that blasting the Bad Step might result in the whole cliff collapsing that saved this famous feature from destruction.

There is a further connection between explosives and the Glasgow JMCS. The term Tartan Army is nowadays used for the inebriated but good-natured fans of Scotland's football team, but in the 1970s it had more sinister connotations. When the Prime Minister, Ted Heath, reneged on a promise to implement a Scottish Assembly, there ensued a bombing campaign targeting oil pipelines and electricity pylon lines by what the press dubbed the 'Tartan Army'. (Some have speculated that the whole affair was designed to blacken the name of a resurgent Scottish National Party.) The JMCS's Hamish Henderson was one of five charged with conspiracy and offences involving explosives. He was tried at the High Court in Edinburgh in September 1976 and cleared of all charges. The next year Henderson and another of the club's activists, Curly Ross, made the first ascent of the appositely named Gael Force (HVS) in the secluded south branch of Coir a' Ghreadaidh.

In the 1960s, affordable cars and cheaper petrol made getting out to the hills an easier proposition. Long weekends and summer holidays saw fully loaded Triumph Heralds, Hillman Imps, Ford Anglias, and all manner of beat-up vans, heading for more distant venues like Skye. To the west of the Great Glen most roads were still single track until the mid-1960s. Once at Kyle of Lochalsh the ferry could only accommodate four to six cars, and at the height of the tourist season there could be red-misted delays of several hours (at peak periods 12 hours was not unusual – often the only sunny spell of the holiday). The service struggled to cope until larger 28-car ferries were introduced in 1970. In 1964 MacBraynes started a large car ferry, the *Clansman*, on the Mallaig–Armadale route (initially summer only), providing another option for getting to Skye.

During the 1960s, flower power began to exert itself in the mountains as the dull khaki anoraks and black berets of the 1950s were replaced by counter-cultural cagoules and hallucinogenic orange balaclavas. Hemp was now something to be smoked rather than tied onto. A crude layering system evolved: string vest, woollen plaid shirt and Fair Isle pullover, topped by an outer shell of the aforementioned cagoule which trapped a condensation engine-room of sauna-like humidity. This remained a problem until more breathable fabrics like Gore-Tex became available in the 1980s.

The 1960s saw ex-War Department equipment being replaced by more specialised items of gear: purpose-designed nuts like the Peck Cracker, the Acorn and Moac; rock climbing boots like EBs, an improved version of the PA; and shock-absorbent Kernmantel ropes. Safety was increased with better belaying techniques, climbing helmets, screw-gate karabiners and the use of double ropes.

A feature of the 1960s was the emergence of a number of close-knit, hard-climbing clubs like the Edinburgh Squirrels, a counterpoint to similarly anti-establishment groups in Glasgow. Aberdeen's anarchic spirits found a ready home in the Etchachan Club. In the latter Tom Patey developed into one of the great characters of post-war British mountaineering.

Through the 1950s, Patey dominated Cairngorm mixed climbing along with Bill Brooker, producing routes like Mitre Ridge (V,6) and Eagle Ridge (VI,6). He was recommended by Bill Murray for the successful Everest Expedition in 1953 but rejected as too young. In 1960 Patey joined up with Chris Bonington for a Highland route-bagging holiday. Bonington remembers this as 'one of the best holidays I've ever had':

> My first climbing trip with Tom Patey was in the summer of 1960, just after I got back from my first Himalayan expedition to Annapurna II. We travelled up to Scotland together on the train and had a wonderful mountain Odyssey in the Highlands. We climbed eleven routes in a fortnight, of which ten were new. Perhaps our greatest classic was the Nose of the Cioch on Applecross, which we graded Difficult. This was followed by a visit to Skye where we climbed King Cobra on the Coireachan Ruadha Face and gave it a VS grade. Once again I've climbed it since and found it a very beautiful route and quite challenging.
>
> This was followed by Whispering Wall on Sgurr a' Mhadaidh, given a V Diff. [this route developed something of a reputation and was re-graded Severe], and then King's Cave Wall and Outside Edge Continuation on the Bhasteir Tooth. The grand finale was a route on Am Basteir [West Wall] which we gave a Severe grade, and we soloed. I very nearly died on this when a hold gave way and I nearly swung off. Our final climb was the first ascent of the Cathedral on the rocks around the Old Man of Storr in north Skye. I also of course took up winter climbing with Tom, usually he was climbing solo, me doing my best to catch him up, carrying the rope, trying to persuade him to put it on.[1]

Tom Patey was aware that Bill Brooker had avoided the steepest part of Dawn Grooves on the right which, if straightened out, looked as though it would provide superlative climbing. When they reached the foot of the crag, however, Bonington spotted something even better, a sweep of rock to the left of Crack of Dawn where a line of unclimbed corners ran the height of the cliff. They decided this was the route to go for. It turned out to be probably the hardest rock climb Patey had attempted; his scrabbling style was more suited to vegetative Cairngorm granite than technical gabbro niceties. Bonington, wearing the newly available PAs, successfully tackled the 5b crux, a smooth and exposed groove, while Patey led through the next easier pitch up to a wide ledge below the bulges that marked the start of pitch five. When Bonington tackled these Patey described him as like a young eagle about to take flight for the first time. They eventually reached a peg belay before the final difficulties where there are two prominent spikes that look like fangs, which is why they named it King Cobra (E1).

Until the 1960s, the winter potential of the Cuillin was a relatively unknown quantity. The 1958 Scottish Mountaineering Club publication, *Climbers' Guide to the Cuillin of Skye,* admitted, 'knowledge of winter climbing is very sketchy'. The achievements of the Victorians and Edwardians were either never fully acknowledged or forgotten. William Naismith's opinion that it was doubtful whether much snow was ever likely to be found, still held sway. Even Norman Collie had been dismissive. After visiting Skye at Easter 1897 he wrote to William Douglas that snow 'utterly spoilt the Coolin, brought them down to second rate Alps'.

However there was the occasional dissenting voice. In the 1940s, Tom Weir spent his winter army leaves at Glen Brittle, on one occasion traversing the ridge from Sgurr Dearg to Sgurr a' Mhadaidh, 'one of the most perfect things I have ever done in my life, a day of absolute bliss. You couldn't have had better conditions if you'd prayed for them'. Save for opinions like this, a reputation for being too mild for consistent winter conditions persisted. Throughout much of the post-war period there was an air of neglect with winter activity in the Cuillin at best patchy. With no Sunday ferries until 1965, and few winter holidays, the range continued to be quiet and relatively untrodden out with the busy summer season.

However, the traverse of the Main Ridge under winter conditions (the Winter Traverse) slowly but surely evolved into a major objective, the Holy Grail of British mountaineering , if only it could be caught in suitable condition. This required a complex and rarely attained set of circumstances to come into alignment.

Mike Dixon made two unsuccessful attempts, first in December 1956 with Barry Cliff, and again in February 1963 with Eric Herbert. In early February 1962 Tom Patey, now a GP in Ullapool, had a try with naval officer Richard Brooke, a fellow member of the 1958 Rakaposhi expedition. All of these attempts followed the traditional south to north direction which entailed tackling the often iced-up chimney on the Thearlaich-Dubh Gap's long side.

When Brooke and Patey arrived on Skye in the doctor's battered red Skoda, heavy snow blocked the road at Carbost, resulting in the inevitable late-night ceilidh: 'Tom made good use of his accordion and we eventually settled down in a hay barn at 2am' Next day they walked through the snow to the Campbells' cottage in Glen Brittle. Brooke remembers how they set off on their ridge attempt early the next morning:

> Away about 5.40am by torchlight. The walk across the moor to Garsbheinn was hard. Deep soft snow all the way, but superb down views. Took five-and-a-half hours. Another fine day with little if any wind. Although some of the Main Ridge was blown clear of snow, there was a lot of powder snow on all sheltered ledges. No compacted snow and only one or two patches of ice. We never had to kick or cut steps; I don't think we ever put crampons on. The Thearlaich-Dubh Gap was difficult with new snow and the descent from Thearlaich to the Mhic Choinnich gap was the most difficult section of the day. We climbed King's Chimney as though for summer and then on up the Inaccessible Pinnacle. By then the sun was near the horizon. A bivouac was mentioned. Tom may have been serious – I was not. We had no bivouac equipment whatever and only a couple of jerseys, soaking wet feet, no spare socks and no stove. Tom, typically, was not even carrying a rucksack. We went down in the last of the gloaming.[2]

Tom Patey left Skye slightly disillusioned as the hard-won ridge crest was stripped bare of snow by the wind: 'I doubt whether satisfactory winter conditions for the Main Ridge ever obtain.' Based locally, Bill Wood knew better. In the ten winters he'd lived on Skye, Wood had done all the summits and ridges under snow and ice, including the West and East Ridges of the Inaccessible Pinnacle. Despite wanting to achieve the first Winter Traverse himself, he magnanimously shared his extensive knowledge of the winter Cuillin in the 1962 *SMC Journal*. Here he succinctly compressed his experience into a few paragraphs, giving those interested an accurate template for completing the traverse under snow and ice.

Significantly, he advocated a north to south approach as many of the technical problems could be avoided by abseil. He advised a 4am start from Sligachan, ascending Sgurr nan Gillean by the Tourist Route before daybreak; climbing by torchlight was necessary at the end of each day if the traverse was to be completed in two days. Wood also pointed out what to abseil, how snow and ice affected various parts of the route, what side of the ridge to avoid difficulties on, what equipment to take; as well as suggesting specific solutions for particular problems such as combined tactics (Central Peak of Bidein) and lassoing (West Ridge of Inaccessible Pinnacle).

In February 1965, Tom Patey was inspired to have another try at the Winter Traverse, this time with Eric Langmuir, Brian Robertson and Graham Tiso whose name is now familiar in the chain of outdoor stores he founded. Their attempt mirrored much of Wood's advice but, despite perfect conditions, ended prematurely with Tiso hanging upside down on the Bhasteir Tooth after his crampon got entangled in the abseil rope. A week later Patey and Robertson were back for another attempt along with Hamish MacInnes and Davie Crabb, currently a winter climbing instructor in Glen Coe. Since 1950 MacInnes had already made six winter attempts on the Main Ridge, on one occasion donning crampons as early as Kintail in order to push his car over ice on the old road above Dornie.

The four left Sligachan at 6am and with iron-hard ground underfoot made rapid progress up through Coire a' Bhasteir. They planned to avoid the longer Tourist Route on Sgurr nan Gillean by ascending the West Ridge, leaving their rucksacks at the col. Characteristically Patey set off on his own to climb the final section of Pinnacle Ridge. In perfect conditions of hard snow and little wind they made good progress, following their old footprints over Bruach na Frithe and An Caisteal to Bidean Druim nam Ramh. Here the technically difficult north ridge of the Central Peak was turned on the Glen Brittle side. Although there are no other major difficulties on the central section between Bidein and Sgurr Dearg, a series of problems are encountered that could severely delay a roped party. The four decided that soloing was the most effective way to deal with this, but it was a solution that required absolute concentration since a simple slip could easily be fatal. The Winter Traverse has been described as superb ridge climbing interspersed with a series of terrifying abseils.

By early afternoon it began to cloud over with a few snow flurries. On Sgurr a' Mhadaidh one of Crabb's crampons broke in two and he and MacInnes seriously considered abandoning their attempt. However, after roping up they decided to push on over Ghreadaidh's knife-edges, one of the winter highlights. With darkness falling they managed to catch up with the others at their prearranged bivvy site on Sgurr na Banachdich. The next morning, after caching surplus gear, MacInnes tackled the time-consuming West Ridge of the Inaccessible Pinnacle despite the rocks being plated in ice. As usual Tom Patey couldn't wait and wandered round to investigate the long side. Soon he was committed regretting he'd no rope or belayer:

> There was no sense in hanging on indefinitely for a last-minute reprieve, so I chose to continue while I still had some strength. As so often, no sooner had I made this resolution when everything suddenly clicked. Crampon points bit tenaciously into thin wafers of water-ice, woollen gloves clamped down firmly on rounded verglassed holds and before I even had time to consider the penalties of failure, I was already over the difficulty and scrambling up the last few feet to the top.[3]

Although often bypassed, the East Ridge of the Inaccessible Pinnacle, at grade III/IV, constitutes one of the technical cruxes of the Winter Traverse. From the summit of the pinnacle Patey dropped a rope down the short side to speed up the progress of the other three. At Sgurr Mhic Choinnich the awkward abseil down King's Chimney, taken by the original party, can be avoided by traversing Collie's Ledge. If banked up with snow this provides spectacular situations similar to the Eastern Traverse of Tower Ridge on Ben Nevis. When they reached the top of the Thearlaich-Dubh Gap, MacInnes used Bill Wood's lasso technique to safeguard the ascent of the other side: 'I took a gamble and hurled a loop of rope across the narrow gap to a frozen boulder on the lip, luckily it caught first time and using this as a handrail we managed to climb the other side with the minimum of delay.'[4]

This hard problem (technical Grade 6) is now often avoided by descending the Thearlaich-Dubh Gully to Coir' a' Ghrunnda, and then rejoining the Main Ridge beyond the difficulty. For Patey, Robertson, MacInnes and Crabb, however, a last abseil from the top of the short side brought easier ground and eventually, at Gars-bheinn, success on what Patey described as the greatest single adventure in British mountaineering.

A few months later MacInnes and Crabb were asked by the BBC to participate in a televised ascent of the Matterhorn to commemorate the centenary of the first ascent. There was a large international press conference beforehand where participating mountaineers were asked in turn to recall their most memorable climbs. To the consternation of continental correspondents, Crabb's choice was the Cuillin Winter Traverse for which, he cheekily added, the Alps provide valuable training.

Just two days after the first Winter Traverse the feat was repeated, again in perfect conditions, by Graham Tiso and James 'Elly' Moriarty. Tom Patey's humorous and evocative account in his classic book, *One Man's Mountains*, inspired many others to attempt this expedition of a lifetime. One of these, Des Rubens, confirmed Patey's opinion of the route's quality: 'Imagine winter climbing conditions so good that the pleasure of every movement over step, slab, bulge, and rib is enhanced by rock-solid névé. Add an intensely blue, cold sky and choose for your climbing, not the confined, slow progress up a corrie wall but the unadulterated luxury of continual movement, with views from Barra to Ben Nevis.'[5]

The first winter Greater Traverse was achieved by John McKeever and Nigel 'Yorky' Robinson during a spell of fine settled weather in April 1988. Despite the lateness of the season there was still a heavy snow covering with some ice on north-facing slopes. Starting at 4am from a bivvy in Coire a' Ghrunnda, they took the Main Ridge from south to north. After two more bivvies, on Sgurr a' Mhadaidh and in Am Fraoch-choire, they finished on the summit of Bla Bheinn at 11am on 4 April. Their traverse included ascents of the TD Gap, East Ridge of the In Pinn and Naismith's Route on the Bhasteir Tooth.

While the Winter Traverse was now established as one of the highlights of

British mountaineering, the summer Main Ridge Traverse began to evolve into a hill-running challenge. On 27th June 1960, Les Kendall from Carlisle smashed Dan Stewart's record for the Main Ridge by almost two-and-a-quarter hours with a time of 4 hours 33 minutes. Kendall wore kletterschuhe and had a two-pint water cache at Sgurr Dearg. This was a phenomenal time considering he had no prior knowledge of the mountains and the slower, though easier, Lota Corrie Route was taken. Despite conditions deteriorating towards the end of his run, Kendall finished with considerable panache by descending Pinnacle Ridge in thick mist. One person who hoped to beat Kendall's time was Eric Beard from Leeds. A talented endurance athlete, by 1963 Beard held the Lakeland 24-hour Fell Record with 88 miles (142km), 56 summits, and 33,000ft (10,000m) of ascent in just under 24 hours. He now turned his competitive instincts to the Cuillin Main Ridge.

In the spring of 1963, Beardie, as he was universally known, beat Kendall's time with a new record of 4 hours 9 minutes. Details of Beard's run were initially hard to find as he recorded them, while working as an instructor at Plas y Brenin in North Wales, in the Locked Book at the Pen-y-Gwryd Hotel which had restricted access (and little obvious connection with Skye). It was popularly thought he avoided the Inaccessible Pinnacle but this was not the case. Some confusion even existed over the year as it was often quoted as 1967. Eric Beard was killed in a car crash in 1969 at the height of his athletic powers, only a few days before an attempt on the world 24-hour track record. For some time racing against the clock in such a dangerous environment as the Cuillin was seen as controversial; Beardie's run helped make the Main Ridge Traverse a legitimate competitive target.

In 1963 John Harwood climbed with Eric Beard at Glen Brittle while he trained for his ridge attempt: 'A few days before his record attempt I climbed with him on Sgurr Dearg with the rain pouring down. After informing me that he was 'off form', he proceeded to race up the crag giving a cheerful commentary on different things as he did so.'[6] Harwood was a regular visitor from the West Midlands, putting up nearly twenty new climbs in the Cuillin through the 1960s and 1970s before he became disillusioned by the continually wet weather that often as not coincided with his visits. He helped to bring some maturity to the neglected Sgurr a' Ghreadaidh corries where, to a handful of older classics like Hidden Gully Buttress (Very Difficult), he added eight harder climbs. His first visit to Skye was as a teenager in 1963 when he booked a week-long Scottish Youth Hostel Association (SYHA) rock climbing course based at Glen Brittle Youth Hostel. Harwood stayed on at the end of the course and, in the space of two weeks, went from being a novice to leading the revered grade of Very Severe. He even put up a new, direct start to Parallel Cracks Route (Severe) on Sron na Ciche (wearing walking boots) with friends Dave Robbins and Hamish Small (son of A C D Small).

The SYHA climbing courses were very popular, contributing to the youth hostel becoming the social hub of the outdoor scene in Glen Brittle through much of the 1960s. One of few areas of employment for professional mountaineers at the time, the courses attracted some of the best climbers around. These included 'Elly' Moriarty, school-friend and early partner of Dougal Haston, who moved to Glen Brittle in the early 1960s to be warden at the hostel (the nickname comes from his elegant climbing style). Described as 'a curly-haired giant', he did the second ascent of King Cobra in 1963.

In 1964, John Harwood, now a student at Birmingham University, returned to Glen Brittle Hostel along with Dave Robbins to work as climbing instructors. In their spare time, despite terrible weather, they managed a couple of new routes: Varicose (VS) on the South Face of the Inaccessible Pinnacle and, two weeks later, Goliath Buttress (HVS) on Sgurr a' Mhadaidh:

> I had spotted a big, unclimbed buttress up in Coir' a' Mhadaidh and Dave and I went to try it on our day off. Unfortunately, 1964 was a really bad summer (three dry days in two months in the Cuillin) and it was showering as we walked up. Nevertheless, we started up and reached the first terrace of Goliath Buttress before having to traverse off because of the wet rock. Even as far as we got was quite impressive and I made Dave more nervous (not intentionally) by dropping stones from the first terrace and timing them to see how far we were up the route! A week later, on our next day off, we were blessed by a good day and made short work of the climb to the first terrace. The crux was still wet but I put a peg in and managed to get over the overhang after which there was only one more hard pitch to the top. We were jubilant. After all, a 1,200-foot new route can be pretty impressive to young lads.[7]

In June 1965 there were two events, coincidentally on the same weekend, which would have a significant and long-lasting effect on the development of mountaineering in the Cuillin. On Sunday 6th June fourteen people were arrested after a stern Presbyterian barricade, presided over by the Reverend Angus Smith, tried to prevent cars boarding the first Sunday ferry at Kyle of Lochalsh. Watched by several hundred onlookers they held out for half an hour: 'Cheers came from the crowd as police began to remove demonstrators one by one. Six police were needed to carry away a huge man… A bystander advised the Chief Constable, when he had extricated himself from the fray, to summon up a bulldozer. Gaelic expletives were torrential.'[8] As an air of calm returned to Kyle of Lochalsh, many folk in Glen Brittle were waking up after a night of celebration.

The long-awaited Glen Brittle Memorial Hut finally opened its doors. After the Second World War the British Mountaineering Council chose to establish a memorial for those 'who found strength in the hills to sustain them even to death'. Post-war restrictions delayed any firm decision as to its format until 1955 when it was decided to build a national mountaineering hut for the use of all clubs. The SMC suggestion for a location at Glen Brittle was accepted. There had been previous attempts to establish a hut there. In 1947, after the death of Mary Campbell, the owner agreed in principle to a lease of her cottage as a climbing hut, but there were problems as to who would manage it, and the proposals eventually fell through.

For the new BMC Hut, the MacLeod Estates agreed to donate land with a nominal annual feu of one shilling when requested. It never was. The hut was completed with much voluntary labour and donated material; a prime mover was Harry Spilsbury who did much of the interior finishing himself. The hut was formally opened by Dame Flora MacLeod on 5th June 1965. In attendance were the MacRae family who had done so much for climbers in the glen and who, since the opening, have held the keys of the hut and taken a kindly interest. Others raising their glasses (a crate of Talisker was donated by the distillery) included Cuillin veterans Fred Pigott, who was treasurer of the hut appeal fund, and Howard Somervell. The first booking secretary was Bill Wallace who held the position until 1969 when Dan Stewart filled in for a few months. Jim Simpson then took on the post which he held for the next 28 years.

Simpson was approached to produce a new climbing guide to the Cuillin comprising two volumes: the first was to include the Glen Brittle corries while the second covered the Sgurr nan Gillean area, Bla Bheinn and the Coruisk corries. He personally checked about three-quarters of the routes, and for the others used reliable sources like Ian Clough. Simpson attempted to simplify over-subscribed areas like the Western Buttress of Sron na Ciche, and to also use the recommended list of routes to encourage climbers to expand their horizons and explore areas other than the well-trodden Coire Lagan classics. He admitted, though, that many new climbs had not been recorded, and that many of those that had were in reality variations of existing routes.

The first series of SMC rock climbing guides were in plain maroon boards. The 1960/70s New Series were colour-coded with pictorial covers. Simpson's Skye guides had distinctive orange spines with the second volume featuring an iconic cover shot of Bill Brooker leading a repeat ascent of Crack of Dawn (black beret, white tennis shoes, no runners). Prior to 1958, Scottish rock climbs were graded for nailed boots. The new Skye guides demonstrated how, in the 1960s, grades were now for climbers wearing Vibrams in dry conditions, or rock boots for the hardest climbs. (The Cairngorms were naturally an exception where Malcolm Smith's guidebooks reflecting the area's home-grown ethos and tradition: 'A pitch proving too difficult in nails should be climbed in socks.') In Simpson's guides the six standard climbing grades were used but with no sub-division into, for example, Mild Severe and Hard Severe, despite these grades being used in MacKenzie's 1958 Skye guide. The Scottish grading system still had a ceiling at VS which was offset by the inclusion of a graded list, but only for recommended routes.

The SMC still encouraged succinct route descriptions compared to the more detailed versions south of the border. The upshot was that many visitors to the Cuillin stuck to recommended routes as the graded list provided the reassurance of more accurate information on what difficulties to expect, especially at VS which was, with ever-rising standards, an increasingly broad church. 'Scottish VS' became notorious as an all-embracing Caledonian climbing experience where almost anything could be encountered; the first ascentionists were sometimes regarded as a better guide to difficulty than the grade and description. Graded lists encourage ticking. Conversely any climbs not on the recommended list were increasingly neglected, and the favoured few like Cioch Direct and Eastern Buttress's Direct Route developed more and more of a sheen. It was not until 1977 that the HVS grade was introduced in Scotland; the next year Extremely Severe was adopted, and by 1979 Scotland was in line with England and Wales with the open-ended E1, E2, E3, etc.

With the new Sunday ferry and the BMC Hut, the summer of 1965 was a busy one on the Cuillin cliffs. That July John Harwood was back in Glen Brittle with Hamish Small when they discovered four new climbs in three days in Coire a' Ghreadaidh. After the first ascent of Virgin Arete (VS) on the Summit Buttress of Sgurr a' Ghreadaidh, they arrived back at the hut to find John Cunningham in residence. Harwood eagerly peered over to see what the legendary Creagh Dubh climber looked like:

> I wasn't that impressed for he just seemed a slim guy who didn't cut the heroic image. Then I saw what he was doing. He had two piles of blade pegs and was taking them one at a time from the first pile, straightening them in his fingers and putting them on the second pile. One day we went out to Mhic Choinnich and did the superb Dawn Grooves while Bill Sproul and Johnny Cunningham were leading the third and fourth ascents of King Cobra. Anyway Bill was in awe of Cunningham and when he knocked some rocks down was very worried he might hit Cunningham. But all was well for they missed, but the fact that a small lump hit me (a Sassenach) was not worth a comment![9]

Others in the Creagh Dhu were also active on Skye. In Coir' a' Ghrunnda John McLean, Bill Smith and Willie Gordon climbed two new lines: the chimney-crack of The Asp, Skye's first E2, and the adjacent Con's Cleft (E1). If rock climbs resemble their first ascentionists then a degree of caution should be exercised before embarking on one of the McLean brand. Respectfully and accurately known as Big McLean, he was described by fellow Creagh Dhu'er Davie Todd as 'this super-arrogant and confident and thirsty and nasty character McLean, a big snarly bastard in an oilskin jacket'.[10] The name of Con's Cleft is ironic in that McLean's club-mate Con Higgins (who reckons the year of the first ascent was 1962, the same Glasgow Fair holiday they put up Torro on Ben Nevis) first noticed the potential here and was none too happy when McLean claimed the route in a pre-emptive strike.

The Edinburgh Squirrels were also active in Skye during the summer of 1965. One member, Alasdair 'Bugs' McKeith, best known for his role in the development of Canadian ice-climbing, created a new climb on Caisteal a' Garbh-choire. This pinnacle contains one of the largest exposures in Britain of peridotite, an iron-rich mineral that literally rusts into large holds, making it one of the easiest rocks to climb. It also explains MacKeith's route name, Lumps (Very Difficult) an example of the 1960s' trend towards more idiosyncratic route names. Another Squirrel, Jim Renny, was part of the team who discovered The Snake (HVS) on Sron na Ciche's Eastern Buttress. This sinuous seam of basalt was described in the 1969 SMC guide as 'well protected by runners'. A widespread comment was that someone had missed out a 'not'. Jim Renny recalls the day of the first ascent:

The Snake was climbed on 9 August 1965 after first climbing Cioch Gully with Jim Hall and then Integrity with Jim and Bill Sproul; Integrity being a magnificent route. Bill then suggested we try the unclimbed line which is now The Snake. The line was very obvious and climbed up the middle of a steep buttress. I led the first pitch and Bill the next two. We all found it a really enjoyable route and a pleasant VS. We called it The Snake both because it was basically a trap dyke fault which from a short distance away looked like a snake and also in keeping with the nomenclature of other Skye classics such as The Asp and King Cobra.[11]

In 1967, John Harwood hitch-hiked back to Skye. When his climbing partner failed to show up he spent much of the time exploring the Cuillin on his own, looking for areas with potential for new routes. The next summer he returned with Roger High when fine weather allowed them to put this information to good use; in a highly productive week they created six new climbs. Harwood's explorations in the Cuillin reflect his extensive knowledge of the mountains and are characterised by climbs in remote and sequestered corners of the range. Their first new route was Scimitar (VS), a corner line named after its shape, on Sgurr a' Ghreadaidh's Summit Buttress. Harwood led the crux traverse using a peg runner. High seconded with their boots in a rucksack, enabling them to descend to the other side of the Main Ridge for Peridot (HVS). This is still Sgurr Thormaid's only rock climb, named after its dyke of distinctive rock.

The next day saw Harwood and High on the Coruisk side of Sgurr Mhic Choinnich for the first ascent of Magpie Cracks (VS) on the Lower Cliff. After an off-day due to wet weather, by long tradition spent going round the shops in Portree, they discovered Leviathan (E1) on Sgurr nan Eag, a committing route that finds a way through the overhangs between the two existing Robin Smith creations: Left Edge and Ladders. A diagonal line between overhangs meant retreat from the upper pitches could be problematical. Roger High was a bit overawed by the situation and Harwood had to take over the lead on two occasions, precipitating a near argument, 'the only strained incident in 35 years of climbing together'. Their final two new routes were on Marsco: The Boojum (HVS) and The Snark (VS), the latter containing some memorable pitches on rock reminiscent of Chamonix granite.

Pete Thomas was another who had done their stint as a SYHA climbing instructor. Originally from Liverpool, he moved to Skye where he eventually became a full-time mountain guide, and also set up one of Scotland's first independent hostels, the Croft Bunkhouse at Portnalong. Thomas was leader of the Skye Mountain Rescue Team until 1971. John MacLeod then held the fort for a year until the responsibility passed to Gerry Akroyd. Originally from Lancashire, Akroyd moved to Glen Brittle in 1972 where he established a guiding business. In 2010 he was awarded an MBE for his services to the Skye Mountain Rescue Team.

During the 1960s the annual number of rescues was usually in single figures. However, in June 1968, there were two serious climbing accidents on the same day, both in Coire Lagan. The first of these was on the Direct Route on Eastern Buttress when a climber fell 80ft and suffered fatal injuries. Pete Thomas was soon on the scene. The RAF Kinloss Team were fortuitously in attendance at the MacRaes' barn. After a tiring day on Bla Bheinn, they were about to pack up and leave when they got the call-out for the incident. The recovery of the body and evacuation of the survivors proved particularly challenging due to the difficulty in accessing the scene of the accident. After strapping the casualty into the stretcher, Pete Thomas and the RAF personnel were about to start the carry-off to Glen Brittle when they heard the sound of the second accident across on Western Buttress. Six of them then hurried to this incident.

On Amphitheatre Wall a climber from Leeds had gone off-route and became cragfast, unable to move up or down. His second tried to reach him but was eventually forced to belay on a small ledge some distance below. The leader soon tired and fell. Although held by the rope he was killed instantly. The second was soon shouting for help as he was being slowly 'strangled' by the 16-stone of his companion dangling on the end of the rope. One of the RAF team, along with a civilian climber, managed to reach the casualty and ease the strain on the second. The rescue team then lowered the casualty 600ft to the base of cliff.

Despite improvements to the rescue teams, climbers were often still reliant on each other when accidents occurred. Protection for routes was frequently barely adequate and a leader fall could often spell an injury of some sort. Consequently, leading Severe at this time still commanded a great deal of respect. Living and working in the glen, John Harwood was able to give a flavour of the Skye climbing scene at the time, when the all-important pub was fifteen twisty, sheep-filled miles away (24km) at Sligachan:

> One aspect of climbing in these days which has changed a lot is mountain rescue. In these times there was little organisation and, when an accident occurred, every climber in the area would leave their climbs and come to help. It was a chastening experience for a teenager to deal with bloodied victims and, later, corpses.
>
> Two walkers had fallen off near the top of Sgurr Alasdair and bounced over 1000 feet down. You can imagine how beat up they were. But the worst was when we tried to put one on the stretcher to carry them down. They had only been dead an hour or so and their lungs were full of air which gurgled up through the blood as we lifted them. It was terrifying!
>
> The most impressive rescue, however, was when we were called out at dawn to rescue someone who had fallen on Sgurr nan Gillean. His mate had a broken ankle and collarbone and various other injuries, but had crawled down through the night to raise the alarm at Sligachan. What was really impressive about his effort was that the weather was so bad that we had to use ropes to cross the streams as we went up with the stretcher next morning. Unfortunately his heroism was in vain as his companion had been killed in the fall.
>
> One of the local characters around in the 1960s was Ronald McDonald who ran the post-office. Ronald was fond of a 'wee dram' and was always keen to accompany the climbers on their weekly outing to the Sligachan Hotel. We would hire Sutherland's mini-bus and career off on a Saturday night, returning well into the small hours of Sunday. Since Sutherland himself had also been entering into the party spirit, it was a wonder we always seemed to successfully drive back at all! Ronald would be 'three sheets to the wind' and often we had to insist that he stayed at the Youth Hostel rather than venture back over the footbridge to his home. But he and his fellow locals were great fishermen and, if you could persuade them to go out on an 'off' day, there would always be plenty of herring for tea.[12]

During the 1960s, pubs were an increasingly important element in the rapidly expanding outdoor scene. Every major mountaineering centre in Britain, with the notable exception of Glen Brittle, had its own traditional climbers' bar. In Skye the Sligachan public bar, located in what is now the micro-brewery, provided an often crammed focal point for those in need of a restorative pint or two of Tartan Special or Harp Lager. The menu was limited to toasted sandwiches. A loud bell for last orders, just before 10pm, saw a stampede to the bar for double rounds and a large carry-out. The lounge bar ensured a more refined experience: the wearing of boots was not allowed and, more deviously, beer was only sold in half-pint measures. This was intended to keep out the riff-raff but could be counter-productive as any resident who enjoyed a pint was forced to join the melee in the bar. There was no official campsite at Sligachan until the 1980s, and prior to this most folk camped informally around the bridges.

Unlike the Great War, the Second World War appeared to do little to advance the cause of British women in mountaineering terms. In fact the 1950s (and the 1960s and 1970s) were a very male-dominated era, especially in Scotland where female activists were particularly thin on the ground. Bucking the trend was Gwen Moffat, the UK's first accredited female mountain guide who lived on Skye for a while in the 1950s when she worked as an instructor on the Mountaineering Association courses based in Glen Brittle. In 1947, with David Thomas, she had put up Lagan Route (VS) on Sgurr Dearg's South Buttress.

In 1968 John Harwood noticed that Moffat, now an established writer and something of a celebrity, was a fellow-guest at the hostel: 'She seemed a bit stand-offish at first but, once she realised we were doing new routes each day, suddenly became very interested in us, and awaiting eagerly for us to get back (which was later and later each evening!)' Eight years later, in 1976, Moffat used her knowledge of the Skye climbing scene to write *Over the Sea to Death*, a combination of detective story and climbing adventure set in an 'imaginary valley near the Cuillin mountains'.

The tale focuses on Glenbrittle House which becomes Glen Shirra House. The reactionary hotel owner, known as 'the Colonel', is resentful of the permissive Swinging Sixties infiltrating the peace and quiet of the glen as layabouts on national assistance lounge about the campsite with loud transistor radios (a cutting-edge piece of technology that didn't need to be plugged in).

In the evening the Glen Shirra House bar became a popular rendezvous for local guides and other mountaineers. These included Melinda Pink, Gwen Moffat's amateur sleuth, who soon has several suspicious deaths to investigate. Nowadays mountain guiding can seem a somewhat routine affair: helping Munro baggers tick off the In Pin, or scramblers to achieve their ambition of a Main Ridge Traverse. In *Over the Sea to Death*, Moffat creates a more dramatic scenario. When a dead body is found in a plastic bivvy bag near Mrs Chisholm's cottage (known in the book as 'Rahane'), Miss Pink reckons that the local guides, one of whom is having an affair with their client, may be implicated. Then one of the guides is found murdered near Eas Mhor, the waterfall above Glen Brittle House…

Over in the crime-free Coruisk corries, Fluted Buttress, Dawn Grooves and King Cobra were by now established classics, but there was still plenty potential for further quality routes. One of the best was initiated in 1974 by the powerful Lakeland team of Jeff Lamb, a Carlisle joiner, and pharmacist Pete Botterill, who climbed the cracks and corners to the left of Dawn Grooves to produce Mongoose. Three years later Mick Fowler incorporated a clean-cut groove to create Mongoose Direct (E1): 'I didn't know about the earlier route Mongoose and thought the whole climb was new. In fact though, all we had done was straightened out the earlier route. I seem to recall Pete Botterill telling me that they tried the direct line but it was too wet when he was there.'

During the late 1950s, the St Andrews University Mountaineering Club explored the tier of cliffs below the Fluted Buttress area. For some years this crag, now known as the Lower Cliff, was referred to as 'J Buttress' after its annotation in the 1958 climbers' guidebook. The St Andrews students produced Chemist's Constitutional (Very Difficult) and St Andrews Crack (HVS), the latter using some aid. An attempt on the still unclimbed Great Gully was abandoned when a rock fall almost obliterated one of them and shortened their rope by ten feet.

Since the late 1950s the St Andrews University Mountaineering Club had congregated at Glen Brittle Youth Hostel as soon as their exams were over. Like many visiting clubs they used Ronald MacDonald's services to ferry parties round to the Coruisk side of the range. On one trip to Rum a misunderstanding left two students stranded on the island and they had to find their own way back to Skye via Mallaig 'at great expense'.

By the mid-1960s there was a decline in the popularity of youth hostels among climbers who increasingly preferred the less-regulated regimes of climbing huts or campsites. This was reflected in the annual gathering of St Andrews students who transferred their allegiance from Glen Brittle Hostel to the new campsite near the beach. The 1960s saw a great improvement in tent design. Blacks' tents, such as the Arctic Guinea and Good Companion, now had competition from newer companies like Andre Jamet and Vango (an anagram of Govan, the part of Glasgow where the company originated).

One of the main St Andrews activists in the 1960s was Phil Gribbon, later professor of physics at the same university. Although brought up in Belfast, Gribbon was born in France. One summer, on his way to the Alps, he was arrested by French police as a deserter attempting to evade national service, and was incarcerated near Marseilles for several months, the focus of a minor diplomatic incident.

In 1966 Gribbon discovered a spectacular, unclimbed 300ft (90m) prow of weathered gabbro close to the Bla Bheinn-Clach Glas col. A 200ft (60m) crack, undercut at the base, split the pinnacle before finally petering out in a smooth headwall. In rainy conditions Gribbon made a tentative, but ultimately frustrated, attempt on the crack with Helen McSpoadlum. For the next two years he anxiously scanned the new routes section of the *SMC Journal* to see if his secret had been uncovered.

The chances were that it hadn't. Most climbers in the 1960s sped past the

Elgol turn off at Broadford in a rush to get to where it was all happening, Glen Brittle. There was an air of neglect around Bla Bheinn where there had been little new activity since the First World War. In the 1958 SMC guide there were no routes harder than Moderate. On Clach Glas the first new climb since the 1920s was Penelope (Very Difficult) done by Hamish MacInnes as a break from his 1958 pegging frenzy. Gribbon himself described the area as, 'a lost land, full of doubtful Diffs and impossible Mods'. However, in the 1960s there were stirrings of activity as two strong teams claimed new routes on the East Face of Bla Bheinn near Gribbon's coveted line. In August 1961, Tom Patey and R Harper produced Chock-a-Block Chimney (Hard Severe), 'a fine old-fashioned climb with much thrutch and a murky through route'. To the right of this Dan Stewart and Donald Bennet put up The Horn (Severe), on the east face of Naismith's Half-Crown Pinnacle, in 1967.

By June 1968, Gribbon reckoned the time was right for another crack at his line. He got together three other St Andrews students: Bill Band, Neil Ross and Wilf Tauber, to put Bla Bheinn well and truly back on the map with The Great Prow (VS), the only Cuillin inclusion in Ken Wilson's *Hard Rock*, the definitive compendium of contemporary test-pieces. The obvious choice to lead the first, crux pitch was Wilf Tauber, a tall somewhat reserved English literature student who only began climbing two years earlier after starting university. As well as an exceptionally long reach (in *Hard Rock* Gribbon calls him Superspan) he had tremendous drive and determination. As they geared up at the foot of the crack, Tauber put on his rainbow-coloured helmet and selected some pegs 'in case'. He was belayed by Neil Ross, sheltered to one side in case of falling rocks. Phil Gribbon stepped back to monitor progress:

> Thirty feet up the problems were noticeable even to the bystanders as Tauber placed his 'chockstone' in the crack, runnered it and groaned; basically there was a left wall with a ragged groove edge on the right: with wide-bridging he got to another chockstone, a swinging-out move up on it with one foot, to get lodged awkwardly under a bulge. There he extended like a rubber snake reaching up high into the crack, the bulge pushing him out, his toes on sloping ledges under the bulge, then the fast move sequence to his third runner where with a side hold on the left edge and a reach to the first good hold on the stone above he swiftly crept up a steep left slab wall. 'Mild VS!' he murmured, but Band and I were raising our eyebrows in disbelief, which is one of the troubles of sitting at the bottom and getting gripped in anticipation.
>
> At 100 feet he started hurling boulders off to disclose a fine belay, and it was Neil's turn to embark on the first pitch which he did in fine style but with vital variations imposed by the normal person's inability to reach to infinity. When everything was set, Tauber embarked again but now with gross understatements about the technical difficulties of the crack; first there was

a corner with a right swing outwards, then after his one and only runner a layback action on the crack leading to the last hard stretch where the crack narrowed and steepened and was climbed by the standard bridging technique with toes on poor holds on the left wall and with back on the right. 120 feet out, he stopped near the top of the splinter and with much derisory comment on the quality of the rock he deigned to put on a belay-of-sorts at the finish of another fine section of the route in the severish grade.

It was now Bill Band's turn to reach the first belay which he did without too much effort, but I at the screes was not convinced and still ran around chewing pastilles, smoking mini-fags and photographing frantically. Neil then went up to the splinter top, mouthing disgust at Tauber's belay and finding a neat chockstone in the back of the crack, where he sat down and prepared to watch the next crucial pitch. We were now stuck unless it was possible to follow the twin grooves across the left wall in a spectacular traverse, so Tauber polished his PAs and started sidling across, now watched by the gallery of Clach Glas traversers with their ill-chosen comments. Wherever there was a piece of loose rock on a minute hold it would drop downwards with a flick of the Tauber toe, but could not disturb the inert Band who had gone to sleep at his belay. It was beautiful to watch our route going up, and now as the traverse was done it became quite certain that we would make it to the top. Perched high on the pinnacle he moved up the easiest pitch of the route, over a ledge and round left under the final nose. Ignoring the shattered rock which was reported to be too bad for pegs, Wilf went up to find a seat and to wait for me to start on the first pitch, and then when I had started he moved right to the edge of the nose, pulled up on a jammed block, and the climb was made. [13]

As Tauber reached the top, the whole party were strung out along the length of the route with Gribbon still on the screes, 300ft (90m) below. Easier than it looked, the climb was originally graded Hard Severe, though later upgraded to Very Severe. Tauber went on to create two other fine routes on Sgurr Sgumain. On 12th June 1970, with A Robertson, he put up Reluctance (Hard Severe) to the left of Prometheus. A year to the day later he was back at the foot of the crag with J S Shade. Tauber felt that Dan Stewart's Direct Route did not live up to its name and resolved to tackle the impressive, unclimbed wall it avoided. The result was Grannie Clark's Wynd (E1), known to golf enthusiasts as a road that crosses The Old Course in St Andrews. The Great Prow should have been called 'Splinter' but another claim by Ian Clough, who repeated the climb three months later, was received first and it was too late to change the name in the new SMC guide.

Clough worked as a climbing instructor in Skye around this time and, after the controversies of the 1950s, had cleaned up his act to produce some quality free lines. To be fair, Clough's climbing career reflected what was happening in

Britain as a whole, with the 1960s a transitional period between the occasional over-pegging of the 1950s and the free climbing ethic of the 1970s. In 1964 he put up two adjacent routes on Sron na Ciche's Eastern Buttress with A Nicholls: Searcher (Very Difficult) and Shangri-La (VS). The latter, described in the 1996 SMC guide as 'a superb classic climb', contains a Cuillin curio, a Damoclean block lashed in place with a hawser.

Ian Clough joined forces with Hamish MacInnes to establish a guiding business, the Glencoe School of Mountaineering. Through the summers of 1968 and 1969 they returned to Skye to exploit the potential still evident on Clach Glas and Bla Bheinn. But one prime target remained, the prominent chimney-corner on the wall to the left of The Great Prow. Dave Alcock, an engineer who switched to being an outdoor instructor, recalls the first ascent of this feature:

> It was a week's climbing holiday with brilliant weather when Martin Boysen and I went north, meeting up with Hamish MacInnes and Ian Clough accidentally. Hamish was quite secretive as to the 'plums' available, as he called them. New routing was very secretive in those days, and there were many crag Xs. However, we drove up to Skye with them and it became obvious that Hamish was after the line of Jib, so Martin and I started up what has since become Stairway to Heaven. It transpired that Hamish and Ian failed to do their route, so Martin and I traversed into Jib and completed the climb. I guess Stairway to Heaven was hard going and Jib seemed available and in the bag to us, so to speak, especially after Hamish had failed.[14]

Clough and MacInnes eventually followed Boysen and Alcock up the route using a variation start. Many regard Jib (E1) as a finer climb than its coffee-table neighbour The Great Prow. Boysen and Alcock also claimed Bargain Offer (E1) which takes the wall to the left of Clough's Cleft. Without telling the others, MacInnes and Clough furtively set off for the Mainreachan Buttress on Fuar Tholl in Torridon where they knew there was a lot of unexplored rock. The route names there: Investigator, Sherlock, Snoopy, etc celebrate Boysen and Alcock's detective work in managing to surreptitiously follow them from Skye and beat them to some of the choice lines on their secret crag.

By the late 1960s, many activists from south of the border chose to spend their holidays in Scotland, often influenced by Tom Patey's explorations in the north-west Highlands where the swathes of unclimbed rock came as a breath of fresh air compared to the increasingly minuscule gaps between gritstone climbs. One of those was Ginger Cain who, since his ascent of Commando Crack in 1950, had lived in Canada where he was employed as a fire lookout in Banff National Park. Cain developed an interest in painting, and on his return to Britain in 1965 worked as a mountain guide in North Wales while trying to establish himself as an artist. He later moved to Scotland, opening a studio in

Plockton where many of his attractive prints featured the Cuillin. He eventually returned to Wales as his wife threatened to leave him on account of the amount of rain in Wester Ross.

On visits to Coir' a' Mhadaidh, Ginger Cain noticed an impressively steep and hitherto unclimbed section of the face to the right of Slanting Gully. On the upper part of this 800ft (360m) crag was an obvious corner but direct access was barred by a band of overhangs at 200ft (60m). Word of the possibilities here had got around with both Joe Brown and Robin Smith making unsuccessful attempts. Cain twice managed to reach the overhangs, on one occasion with Elly Moriarty, but failed to crack the problem.

By 1967, Cain was keen for another attempt on the line, especially as good quality chrome-molybdenum steel pegs were now widely available. After easily persuading Chris Boulton to accompany him, the pair set off in a Renault 4 van on the long drive north from Wales. On Skye conditions seemed ideal as it had not rained for over a month. Once started on the climb they made quick progress to the stance below the overhangs. Here Cain watched as Boulton attempted to crack the crux pitch:

> The serious stuff now lay ahead. It was Chris's turn to lead and he gathered up all the gear: slings, nuts, pegs and hammer and stepped up onto the wall on the left and proceeded to go up. A tricky mantelshelf was passed and he reached the area below the large overhang where the angle relaxed. He was able to put in a peg in the crack at the back of this break as a runner and also to protect me on the wall below, as he now started to move left along the slabby break until he reached its end, where it petered out at the top of a corner with an overhanging lip forming its far wall which he now had to climb over to reach a slab above. There was an old ring peg here that he could use as a runner (Joe Brown told me later that he had left this peg to abseil back from after an attempt via the corner directly below).
>
> The move onto the far wall was the hardest on the climb. None of the holds were quite satisfying and after one had launched onto the wall it was necessary to move up onto still unsatisfying holds while still out of balance until a foot could be reached out left onto a sloping ledge and a pull out until a standing position on it could be gained. After this it got easier as a steep corner led straight up but gave an opportunity to bridge and ease the strain a little. A move out of the corner brought a stance and a peg was placed to belay. I followed up, finding the climbing very hard; the crux move was as hard as or harder than anything that I had ever done.[15]

Cain led the next pitch to the finish by way of the large corner of Shining Cleft. The new route, probably the hardest climb on Skye at the time, was named Thor (E2) from Coir' a' Tairneilear (the thunder) as well as matching Robin

Smith's Thunder Rib. Chris Boulton was highly impressed by both the route and the amount of potential that remained on such a prominent cliff. He returned to Skye five years later, in 1972, accompanied by Paul Nunn and Bob Toogood, a Sheffield tool-maker. Paul Nunn had a big presence, six foot two with thinning sandy hair and a loud, rumbustious laugh. He was an early star of the Alpha Mountaineering Club where his nickname was 'Angus McFungus' after early attempts at a beard.

Fred Zinneman, the Hollywood director (*High Noon, From Here to Eternity*) made his final film on location in the Alps, *Five Days in Summer*, in which Sean Connery plays an aging Alpinist. Hamish MacInnes, in charge of safety, was at a rare loss when asked who might make a suitable climbing double as he had never seen a James Bond film and had no idea what the actor looked like. The role was eventually given to Paul Nunn, also part of the safety team.

On the way north to Skye, Boulton, Nunn and Toogood stopped off at Hamish MacInnes's cottage in Glen Coe (later notorious as one of Jimmy Savile's homes). Here Hamish, after spreading out an array of Cuillin photographs, recommended a visit to Bla Bheinnan and an ascent of Jib. The next day, with this intention in mind, they piled into Nunn's Renault 16 and sped off up the A87 for the ferry at Kyle of Lochalsh.

Once they reached the foot of Bla Bheinn's East Face, however, they were attracted by a slanting ramp that reminded them of Moss Ghyll Grooves on Scafell. After starting up Clough's Cleft, they moved left to gain the ramp by a wide bridging move, then a high step followed by a delightfully delicate slab. Now out of the shade and in the heat of the sun, and with no-one else about, it reminded Nunn of Cloggy in the late 1950s. They continued up poorly protected slabs to below a soaring jamming crack which Nunn led to a final sting in the tale.

After this climb, which they named Ecstasis (E1), Boulton introduced the others to Coir' a' Mhadaidh and the bulging cliff to the right of Thor. Here the crucial consideration was the angle of the rock between the overhangs; if these sections were slabby Nunn reckoned it might be possible to link them together and complete a route through the steeper areas of rock. The first pitch provided 150ft (45m) of pleasant slabs to a basalt dyke that took them through an overhang. A hanging slab now led to a small stance where, above, they could see a banana-shaped ramp that offered the only option through the steepest of the overhangs, as Nunn related:

> There was a little wall first of about 20 feet which was really good climbing, and then a long slab which we had to climb downwards, which was eventually cut off completely as it tapered to nothing at all. This barrier just hung out in space, and the ramp started above it. I went out there and couldn't make head or tail of it at all. I spent a long time trying to use aid to climb this barrier; trying to use rurps and all sorts of things. Just one point of aid was really

what you wanted, but in this basalt you couldn't get anything that would stay in. We didn't get up and went away, and that seemed like the end of it.[16]

It wasn't. Nunn returned to the problem at Easter 1974 with Paul 'Tut' Braithwaite and Martin Boysen. The tall and gangly Boysen, a Manchester biology teacher, was one of the most respected rock climbers of his day. Like Nunn he had showbiz credentials, as climbing double for Clint Eastwood in *The Eiger Sanction*. Tut Braithwaite, lank hair and droopy moustache, was an art school dropout from Oldham who made his living as a painter and decorator. Like Boysen he was a regular on Chris Bonington's Himalayan expeditions. They were all on good form and with luck this would be their fifth new route in five days. Paul Nunn pointed out how they could traverse in from the right to the high point of three years ago. He described what happened next:

> Tut belayed me from about eighty feet away through the runners. Then Martin came along and stood on my shoulders. He threw some loose stuff off the end of the overhanging wall, grabbed a big jug and was able to swing out and into the bottom of the ramp. It was amazing because it went out like a banana with all the bottom cut away; the whole thing had gone and it was straight into this overhang, climbing almost straight out, but in fact you were climbing on a slab. Martin climbed up and had a couple of good runners to start, so it wasn't too serious, though there was quite a lot of rope drag from the runners. We had a peg runner towards the end, and did some delicate climbing round a corner. We ended up bridged across a groove and belayed, in that uncertain situation where you're on the end of nowhere on a very overhanging mass of crag, with a possibility of climbing out but not quite sure how hard it's going to be, depending on what the rock's like. To get us over the combined tactics bit, Martin had a sling hung round a jug. It was a very good pitch, climbing up the open groove at about VS, getting to the top and traversing a great open wall right across nowhere, over Tut's head really, and again over another overhang to come out on some slabs. In a way it was over. Martin brought Tut up and the rest was great.[17]

The climb was named Megaton (E1) and, despite the 'Abraham shoulder', partnered Thor in a chapter of *Extreme Rock*. Unfortunately the crux ramp, freed at 6a, fell to the screes some years later leaving a section of blank and unstable rock. In the hot summer of 1976 Boulton and Nunn completed the Coir' a' Mhadaidh triptych with the fierce central line of Quark. (Its one point of aid was freed by Tom Prentice and Calum Fraser in 1984 to give a grade of E3 5c.) Paul Nunn could not believe his luck in discovering yet another major line on the same cliff. On the crux, an exposed traverse across a steep wall, he found himself hardly able to move due to rope drag. After struggling to reach a narrow slot, he half-sat, half-hung from the belay. Above, there was a flat, smooth roof that still left the outcome in doubt:

> At last, with trepidation, I touched the underside of the roof, standing up on small holds. Three fingers of my right hand locked into a damp undercling, too high above my face to feel secure. The other hand excavated some small loose rock chips next to the attached hand, gradually working towards the entry of a fourth finger. Then a small sliver of rock flirted out under the leverage, and I saw light through a thread leading to the fingerlock. There was a breathless, timeless little struggle as a sling slid through and emerged near my attached hand five inches to the right. Clip, it was in the bag![18]

Chapter Twelve

The Competitive Edge

During the late 1970s and early 1980s there was a rapid rise in the standard of rock climbing, coinciding with a strong ethical backlash against the use of aid. In Skye, climbers started to eliminate aid points from MacInnes routes like Penitentiary Grooves (E1), Styx (HVS), Vulcan Wall (HVS) and Creag Dhu Grooves (E3). This process continued as a number of factors conspired to generate a sharp increase in the standard of free climbing: a series of fine summers, the introduction of chalk, (a highly contentious topic at the time), and the development of systematic training. There were also technical improvements to equipment such as dynamic ropes, belay devices, 'sticky rubber' soles for rock boots, better designed nuts, camming devices and, to a sigh of relief from male climbers, testicular-friendly harnesses.

In Scotland, in the 1980s, these developments coincided with the emergence of a group of young climbers dedicated to advancing standards and relieving existing routes of aid points. Those active in the Cuillin included Murray Hamilton, Pete Hunter, Dave Cuthbertson, Gary Latter and Rab Anderson. Much of their energy initially focused on Sron na Ciche, especially its Eastern Buttress, where there was a concentration of old aid routes as well as subtler weaknesses.

In May 1980, there was an outburst of activity by Edinburgh University students, especially Pete Hunter and Cameron Lees. Their first new climb was Slow Riser (HVS) a fine, direct line on Marsco's South-West Buttress. On Sron na Ciche's Eastern Buttress they completed another two new lines: Strappado Direct (E2), a harder, more assertive version than the original, and, two days later, the bold and atmospheric Spock (E3) which took on the arete to the left of Vulcan Wall. The day between these two climbs, 17th May, was a busy one, as Cameron Lees relates:

> We were on a ten-day visit in the middle of a superb spell of weather. Pete knew the island like the back of his hand and the line of Krugerrand (E3) was well overdue for an ascent and it was top of his list of things to do. I seem to remember an old peg halfway out of the crack under the roof indicating that someone had tried it before, on aid I think. By getting the outside edge of your right foot on the one foothold on the wall beneath the roof you could finger-jam out and reach the crack above. The crack above was definitely the

hardest bit though and it was Pete that managed to lead it.

It was all good fun because it was hot and sunny and quite a crowd were watching from the Cioch, so we had to succeed! Also, Rob Milne and Duncan McCallum were nearby doing a new route on the Amphitheatre face and Adam Kassyck and Mathew Priestman from Edinburgh University were also doing a new route over to the left [Vanity E2], so it was a good atmosphere with everyone being pushed a bit. Spock was a bit more foreboding, much quieter and shadier. Again, I seem to remember a rusty old wire on the first pitch so somebody must have tried it before.[1]

Brought up in Colorado, Rob Milne was a key figure in advanced technology research when he was for a time Chief Artificial Intelligence Scientist at the Pentagon. In 2005 Milne tragically died near the summit of Everest, the final peak in his quest to climb the Seven Summits, the highest point on each of the continents. Duncan McCallum was later a TV presenter of adventure sports programmes. Milne and McCallum's route was based on a little-known MacInnes aid climb called Prolepsis, as Milne recalls:

We walked into Sron na Ciche and I had no idea what we might do. It was Duncan who led the way. I am not sure if he knew the wall had potential and scoped out the line when we arrived or if he had already spotted it. I remember that a hold broke off on the first pitch, causing Duncan to slip but not fall, hence the name Hang Free (E2). The route has some fine double cracks up high and this is what attracted us. I led them and found the climbing great. That same weekend we did a new route, Val (Very Difficult) in Coire na Banachdich. After soloing about on Window Buttress we didn't find much of interest until we spotted some nice clean rock and did this route. We went out of our way a bit to make the route hard and interesting. The rock was great.[2]

The modern free-climbing ethos was epitomised with visits to Coire Lagan by Dave Cuthbertson during the summer of 1982. 'Cubby', as he is popularly known was one of Scotland's finest all-round mountaineers, producing routes of a difficulty never seen in the country before. Requiem (E8) on Dumbarton Rock, climbed over a week in 1983, was a contender for hardest rock climb in the world at the time. In June 1982, Cuthbertson made two visits to Skye, first with Duncan McCallum, and then with Glaswegian Gary Latter, as Latter relates:

My first visit to Skye was in 1982 with Cubby when we climbed four new routes over the weekend of 19-20 June. The first day we climbed Confession (E4), The Chambre Finish to Vulcan Wall (E2) and Magic (E4). Cubby had tried Magic before (I think the previous weekend) and had left a nut on the initial crux crack. I remember I couldn't get it out seconding, and he abseiled down to remove it. He was keen to get it out, as it obviously made the route easier to repeat! We climbed The Team Machine (E4) the following day. Cubby had cleaned both Confession and I think Magic. Unknown to me at the time, Duncan McCallum had also cleaned The Chambre Finish the previous weekend. I only found this out years later in conversation with McCallum.[3]

Through this period the remoter Coruisk corries again remained largely unaffected by the scrutiny for new routes elsewhere. On the Coireachan Ruadha faces there was an average of one new summer climb per decade. The contribution for the 1980s was Lightfoot (E3) created by Murray Hamilton, Rab Anderson and Pete Whillance, a leading Lake District activist. During 1982 and 1983 this trio were at the forefront of a controversial style of new routing where steep, unclimbed sections of cliff were first identified and then pre-cleaned by abseil. Rab Anderson explains how, in June 1983, they transferred these tactics from their main focus, Creag an Dubh Loch in the Cairngorms, to the mountains of Skye. On Sron na Ciche, and other cliffs, they had difficulty in locating similar large areas of steep, unclimbed rock:

> However, from down below, Bealach Gully Buttress looked big and continuous and appeared to offer what we were looking for. At 250 feet plus, two pitches of 140 feet, it must be one of the biggest single, uniform pieces of rock in the Cuillin. In those days we were cleaning routes with long static ropes. Pete had one and Murray had one. The next day we returned and Murray dropped a rope down and started cleaning. It was usual for me to clean the upper pitch on a climbing rope and for one of the others to go lower on the static. Murray finished and we abseiled in on the single 300-foot static. It seemed the easiest way to approach because it is a hell of an awkward place to get to.
>
> I remember the abseil being quite airy and quite scary. Vertical for the first half and then, when it went out over the roof, completely in space. Every now and again you would spin round and get a full panorama of the Cuillin with a huge amount of exposure between your legs. There is a wall below the shelf and steep scree below so the sense of exposure is keenly felt. I had abseiled big routes on Creag an Dubh Loch but nothing matched the exposure on the abseil down to Thunderbolt Shelf (hence the route name after the Clint Eastwood film *Thunderbolt and Lightfoot*). Murray led both pitches. The climbing was superb. The small belay ledge above the roof was situated in a tremendous position. I certainly rate Lightfoot (E3).[4]

Although Anderson, Hamilton and Murray had problems finding areas suitable for the extremely hard climbs they were trying to create, Colin Moody, a fish farmer on Mull, had a knack for finding quality climbs at a more amenable standard in the most obvious of places. These included Piety (VS) and Mistral Buttress (VS) on Sron na Ciche, as well as a HVS on Sgurr Sgumain called Raynauds (his poor circulation led him to giving up winter climbing). In July 1994 Moody found himself in Skye with no climbing partner, so a friend put him in touch with Steve Hill. They went on to make the first ascent of Helen, a three-star E3 taking the fierce arete between Trojan Groove (HVS) and Spartan Groove (E1). Another fine Moody discovery was Pocks (E3) on Sron na Ciche's Eastern Buttress, a protracted saga that started in June 1988:

> George Szuca was living in Onich. We had a great day on Aonach Dubh, then another in Glen Nevis with Ian Taylor. We loaded my bike up that evening and set off for Skye. Got a puncture at Fort William, unloaded the bike and hitched back to Onich. Got the puncture fixed the next day and didn't want to waste the day going to Skye. Did The Bat, drove to Skye and camped in Coire Lagan. Did some great routes including the first pitch of Pocks. (George didn't believe it was new.) There were plenty of pock holds beside the crack. I tried the second pitch with a hammer (!) for scraping the moss. Dropped the hammer which nearly hit George, then gave up. The mist came in the next day so we went to Kilt Rock. Neil Smith, Roger Lupton and I did Uhuru a few years later and I got keen on the route again so Neil and I came back a couple of weeks later to add a second pitch and complete the route.[5]

Sron na Ciche's Eastern Buttress continued to be a main focus of interest, providing an especially fine crop of E3s. In 1979 Dougie Mullin and Murray Hamilton added Enigma (E3) to the left of The Snake. In 1990 Kev Howett, the Mountaineering Council of Scotland's first National Officer, and journalist Tom Prentice, found Uhuru (E3) the central crack between Vulcan Wall and Dilemma. Howett returned in 2001 with Scott Muir for Clinging On (E4) which starts up Dilemma but finishes directly where that route turns diagonally right:

> After doing Uhuru in 1990 with Tom Prentice, I noticed the obvious hairline crack that runs direct up the wall above the initial crack of Mick Fowler's Dilemma and vowed to return. It took me eleven years! It was the first new route of the year and the finest rock route I'd done for months. The weather was awful, heavy rain, and the Cuillins had only just started to open up after Foot and Mouth. I abseiled it to check the line (but did not check the gear or practice moves). We waited for the rock to dry and the sun to come around onto the wall. As a result the bit I thought would be hard was easy and vice versa. It took me two hours to lead the 55m pitch of sustained 5b/5c with a 6a crux near the top. My feet were in agony but it was a good way of getting back into the swing of things.[6]

Even the Cioch was having a modern makeover. In 1978 Murray Hamilton and statistician Geoff Cohen made the earliest of several claims for the first free ascent of Overhanging Crack (E2), on the imposing wall overlooking Slab Corner. Five years later the Aberdeen-based rope of Douglas Dinwoodie and Graeme Livingstone, a leading Scottish team of the 1980s, climbed the crack in the Cioch's small frontal face to give Erotica (E3), a good route with a well-protected crux. To its left Grant Farquhar, a psychiatrist, and Gary Latter added the spectacular arete of The Highlander in 1989, the first E6 in the range. Gary Latter:

> Grant Farquhar and myself had tried the compelling line of The Highlander in June 1988, initially on-sight. I recall Grant falling from the difficult finishing moves pulling over onto the easy slab at the top of the arete, and shredding my new rope. I also remember climbing other routes later that weekend, including Enigma, then racing down the hill and driving furiously to catch the last (9.00pm) ferry back at Kyleakin. I think we managed to get from the base of the cliff to the ferry in an hour and a quarter. We went back up the following year (1989) and completed the route.[7]

The Highlander was named after the cult, Oscar-free Sean Connery film, described by one critic, 'As rubbish goes it is excellent.' Connery plays a sixteenth-century aristocrat who is mentor to Connor Macleod, teaching him swordsmanship in various spectacular Highland locations including the Cuillin. The movie *Highlander* also provided the name for The Gathering (E8), a very serious route by Dave MacLeod (no relation) up the frontal arete of the Cioch. MacLeod, a Bearsden-born sport scientist, produced Rhapsody at Dumbarton Rock in 2006, the world's first recognised E11 trad route. He even moved house so he could be near the project. On The Gathering there is no protection till the 'thank God' spike near the top, and a fall would undoubtedly prove fatal – unless you're one of the immortals featured in the film.

The *Highlander* theme continues with The Prize (E2), named after the ultimate power of the immortals, first climbed by Ben Wear and James Sutton in 2003. Three years later Sutton produced a guide to bouldering in the Cuillin, *Gabbrofest*, containing over 150 problems. (Wilfred Coats of the SMC was one of the first to realise the quality of bouldering in Coire Lagan, writing enthusiastically about it in the late 1920s.)

As well as *Highlander*, the Cuillin have starred in several other films including David MacDonald's 'forgotten classic', *The Brothers* (1947), an eerie tale of lust and murder involving a rancorous feud on a Hebridean island. *The Brothers* starred Patricia Roc who was fresh from Hollywood and a romance with Ronald Reagan. Reviews of the film often begin with an intriguing hook: 'Why is a man floating in the middle of a Highland loch with a herring tied to his head?' A trailer of highlights might include Miss Roc skinny-dipping in Loch Scavaig and, in Loch Coruisk, one of the most bizarre methods of execution you will ever see.

In Alexander Mackendrick's *Laxdale Hall* (1953), filmed across the Inner Sound on Applecross, the villagers petition for an improved road to their remote community. When a Parliamentary delegation suggests they all move to a newly built town, one villager retorts: 'No view of the Cuillins and no river? Man, I would rather live in Hell than in a place like that.'

In the 1970s Michael York starred in the movie *Zeppelin* about a prototype airship on a secret mission to attack the Scottish coast, played with great aplomb by Loch Coruisk and the surrounding mountains. In 2007 the Cuillin also provided the premise for the very first Gaelic feature film, *Seachd: the Inaccessible Pinnacle,* directed by Simon Miller. This was the story of a young boy's relationship with his grandfather after his parents are killed in a climbing accident on the Inaccessible Pinnacle. It was a low budget affair as Angus Peter Campbell, who plays the grandfather, admitted, 'I even had to grow my own beard.' Much of the 2015 movie *Macbeth*, starring Michael Fassbender, used locations around Sligachan.

But it was *Highlander* that first brought the Cuillin to a worldwide cinema audience. Hamish MacInnes filmed the spectacular swordfight scene on the top of the Cioch. Paul Nunn was part of the safety crew responsible for the camera equipment that was flown up to the pinnacle in nets below a helicopter. One of the loads was not linked together properly, and when the net opened Nunn was horrified to see the contents, including a state of the art movie camera, cascade past several startled climbers onto the screes below.

Clive Rowland was an early climbing partner of Paul Nunn when they were students together at Sheffield University in the 1960s. After moving to Inverness, where he opened a climbing shop, Rowland developed two cliffs in the Cuillin. The first was Sgurr Fheadain, left of Waterpipe Gully, the other was Creag Druim Eadar da Choire on Garbh-bheinn where, along with Paul Nunn and others, he developed some fine new routes. In 1990 John MacKenzie and Graham Cullen added further quality lines here including Cuckoo Waltz (E1) and Rites of Passage (E1).

MacKenzie, who also answers to the 'Earl of Cromartie' and 'Baron Castlehaven', was the first clan chief to edit a climbing guide, *Rock and Ice Climbs in Skye,* published in 1982. Although a selective guide, this was the first Skye version to use E grades. In 1996 the Scottish Mountaineering Club published a comprehensive guide in two volumes, *Skye and the Hebrides*. The first volume, by John MacKenzie and Noel Williams, covered the whole of Skye and introduced technical grades. Back in the 1970s there was an experimental moratorium on the recording of climbs in selected areas of Scotland, an attempt to try and preserve the exploratory mountain experience. On Skye, Sgurr na Stri was 'closed' in 1977, as was Sgurr Coir' an Lochain the following year. By the publication of the

1996 SMC guide this initiative had been quietly forgotten, as was a bias against the recording of short climbs (under 45m, then the standard rope length) in mountain areas.

The 1996 guide also confirmed the trend towards development in areas outwith the Cuillin, like Neist Point and Kilt Rock. However quality mountain routes were still being discovered in long-established venues on or near the Main Ridge, like the Bhasteir Tooth and the Inaccessible Pinnacle. On the former, the striking face to the left of Naismith's Route had long attracted speculative glances. In May 1953, the 23-year-old Jimmy Marshall investigated the possibilities as one of his partners, Charlie Donaldson, recalled: 'We all climbed to the boulder ledge on Naismith's Route. Jimmy then made a very delicate traverse left to a tiny stance in an open corner, which we had hoped might be a chimney. Once a piton was inserted as a belay, I followed along to the stance but further progress was impossible.'[8]

The face was eventually climbed by Steve Hill and Tom Dickson in July 1989 to give Rainbow Warrior (E3). A friend of theirs had previously failed on the route and offered them the line which they did 'on-sight and chalk-free'. A few years later, round on Am Basteir's North Face, Martin Moran discovered two hard chimneys. He felt that, 'for atmospheric and challenging mountain rock the place takes some beating'. Moran describes the first climb:

> Hung, Drawn and Quartered (E3): this big chimney line on Am Basteir was climbed with Ian Dring a long-time climbing friend from Cheshire in September 1996. The line had drawn my attention many times during ridge traverses, a stunning trap dyke. After a long dry spell we could hope it would be dry. Pitch one was the crux, 6a moves up an overhanging slot just right of the main chimney; Ian led and fell trying to clear fine rubble off the finishing holds, having already snapped most of the basalt fresco off the wall below. I went up, rested on a nut and cleared the ledge so that he could lead it clean on a second attempt. Pitch 2 was a delightful little ladder dyke; pitch 3 the magnificent trap dyke, gently overhanging for 18m and sustained at 5b/c. Big danger of knocking stones off on to unsuspecting walkers on the screes below. Pitch 4 an easier continuation dyke to a final capstone. A prime contender for Skye's finest chimney route. We gave it E4, having dealt with all the problems of on-sight leading but perhaps E3 is enough. Two hours late in getting back home for a planned meal out with our wives, so the route name reflects our fate on arriving home that night as much as a derivative from Am Basteir, the Executioner.

The other big chimney line, 40m to the left, The Squeeze Box (E2), was climbed with Andy Nisbet in June 1997; not as good a route but still a most entertaining day out; pitch one is quite serious wall climbing at 5b. Then the slim torture tube itself, led by Andy and just wide enough to admit an unsuspecting body – a tour de force of bodily contortion, definitely 5b. Then a remarkable through route in a cave which had looked all but impossible to surmount. We gave it E3 but again on reflection E2 is probably fair. Amazing that no one had climbed on the north cliff before us.[9]

Even the seemingly worked-out Inaccessible Pinnacle was yielding quality new routes. In 1999 Mike Lates, a local guide since 1993, stumbled on a three-star crack line round on the unfrequented north side of the pinnacle. He called it The Naked Saltire (E2), claiming it 'the straightest line in Skye'. The name celebrates an incident the previous day when two of his female clients, apparently serial exhibitionists, posed in the nude behind a Scottish flag for a souvenir photograph on the summit. Lates reveals how he discovered the route:

> I'd been stashing water for a Cuillin ridge traverse earlier in the year and couldn't believe that I'd never even noticed the line. It was dripping and full of black slime, but an undeniably stunning, protectable route. I suppose nobody normally has any reason to wander under the dark dank wall apart from for a quick nervous pee. The only clue to its existence is that South Crack follows the same fault on the opposite side of the Inaccessible Pinnacle. The corner line is undercut by a 10-foot band of basalt. It took two attempts to work out a sequence of three lunges, which brought me into the niche in the bottom of the main corner. I'd carried a wire brush to try to remove some of the dried black slime from the walls, but there was no need as the sharp crystals of the gabbro poked right through to give perfect friction. Invisible from below, a series of positive, square-cut, horizontal ledges kept appearing on the left wall. Small pebbles dropped well behind Icky's head as the crack soared up and out.
>
> Laying away brought positive edges into reach, a chance to get back in balance and a plethora of protection possibilities. Run-outs grew with my confidence and the holds just kept appearing from the blank looking wall to my left. A two-foot section of basalt on the right wall proved solid enough for the single foothold needed on it, and forewarned me that some caution may be needed 'over the top'. A deserted Coire Lagan was bathed in evening light as I popped my head over the crest.[10]

Mike Lates also assisted Gordon Stainforth with his portfolio of mountain photographs, *The Cuillin*, published in 1994. Stainforth previously worked in the film industry where, for example, he was music editor on Stanley Kubrick's *The Shining*. From his home in Derby he made eight photographic trips to Skye in one year that involved 15,200 miles (24,500km) of driving, 191,700 feet (58,500m) of climbing and 115 rolls of film. Out of 150 days, the Main Ridge was only clear on 71. On one occasion, Stainforth was trapped by storms and high rivers at the Coruisk Hut for four days. The production of one particular image required complicated computer projections as well as the use of walkie-talkies.

Despite the exposure generated by Stairway to Heaven's inclusion in *Extreme Rock* in 1987, Bla Bheinn and Clach Glas had another of their periodic quiet spells through the 1980s and 1990s. Gary Latter, however, had noticed possibilities. In June 1997 he joined Grant Farquhar and Paul Thorburn to produce Finger in the Dyke (E5), a series of cracks in the 'obvious dyke-infested arete' left of The Great Prow. At the time it was the hardest multi-pitch route in the Cuillin. All three climbers led a pitch apiece with Thorburn tackling the initial crux section. A rope access worker, Thorburn was nicknamed 'Stork' by fellow climbers due to his profile while he characteristically balanced on one leg to put his rock boot on the other.

The standing on one leg theme continues. In 1978 the Strathaird estate, which includes Bla Bheinn and Clach Glas, was bought by Ian Anderson, lead singer and flautist with prog rock band Jethro Tull. (A track on their *Stormwatch* album 'Dun Ringall' is named after a local Iron Age hill fort.) Anderson set up home at Kilmarie House where he established a successful salmon farm business. In 1994 he magnanimously agreed to sell the 15,000-acre estate to the John Muir Trust who currently manage the area.

On the estate near the foot of Bla Bheinn's south ridge stood Camasunary, one of Scotland's most spectacularly situated bothies. In 2016 the original building was reclaimed by the owner, Alan Johnson, as a private dwelling. He provided funds for a replacement, a custom-built structure which was located a kilometre to the south. The new bothy provided a grand view of the Cuillin but had no fire or stove, a stipulation made by the owner after several break-ins to the nearby farm house by people looking for fuel.

The essence of bothying is to get ensconced around a roaring fire, drink whisky and tell tall tales about bothy ghosts, gymnastic mice and unlikely hill exploits. In December 1982, after a typically wet day on Bla Bheinn, brothers John and Paul Rasher with friend Paul Robson were doing just that, when the meditative glow of the bothy fire was abruptly shattered, as Paul Rasher explains:

> Moments later I looked out the window to see the entire bay was illuminated with a deep red light, we could see right across to the other side, even the rabbits running for their burrows. Simultaneously, a thundering started to grow in intensity from a loud low rumble to a screaming that made our ears pop and the bases of our spines hurt. I threw myself to the floor honestly thinking that a nuke had gone down on the mainland and this part of its flash effect; at this point part of the ceiling by the door fell down with a crash and

the outer and inner windows were shaking violently. John grabbed his knife and jumped into the corner seriously believing that someone was booting the door down.[11]

At 8pm a USAF F-111 had crashed into the south face of Sgurr na Stri, above the bothy, creating a huge orange fireball that slowly rose to illuminate the whole of the Main Ridge for over five minutes. A team from RAF Kinloss led by David 'Heavy' Whalley had an epic journey to reach Camasunary by helicopter. With the wild winter weather they were forced to fly low near roads to get updates on their navigation and had a near miss with some electricity lines. Around the bothy there was a strong smell of fire and aviation fuel in the air. In the dark, with heavy snow falling, Paul Rasher led the RAF team to the crash site. Both of the crew were killed; they are commemorated in a memorial at Elgol.

About a mile north of Camasunary bothy lies Sgurr Hain Crag where, in the warm summer of 1990, Tom Walkington and Alistair Cunningham developed five new routes, commenting that there was 'scope for dozens more'. Walkington also saw the potential of the Coir'-uisg Buttress of Sgurr a' Mhadaidh, an unclimbed cliff he described as 'the most awesome wall of rock in the UK'. First to take on this obvious challenge, in May 2007, was leading Lake District climber Dave Birkett. Film-maker Alastair Lee described Birkett's ascent of Skye Wall (E7/8), the hardest route yet climbed in the Cuillin: 'Protection is difficult to arrange on the mostly blank wall as many of the thin cracks flair. The crux section involves a thin undercling and some imaginary foot holds well above any protection. The scariest section of the climb is above the crux which involves a thin flake which must be handled with extreme care.'

After Birkett took a potentially serious fall, in increasingly hot conditions, it was decided to take a break. Two days later, as the heat wave continued, Birkett again fell from the crux moves but his time it seemed to galvanise him as without thought of a rest he overcame the problem in fine style.

The next month (June 2007), the continuation of the warm settled spell saw further outstanding achievements with two of Scotland's best climbers adding another two routes in the Coruisk basin. Guy Robertson and Pete Benson first had a look at the Skye Wall area, putting up Paradise Found (E2) before, the next day, completing the much sought-after Rainman (E5) on Bealach Buttress, 'a tremendous route up the smooth right side of the big vertical wall'. Rainman is regarded by many as the best E5 in the Cuillin.

Two days after Dave Birkett's ascent of Skye Wall, 4 May 2007, Es Tressider broke the record for running the Main Ridge. By the 1980s Eric Beard's 1963 time of 4 hours 9 minutes had lost its aura of invincibility and was now seen by an elite group of hill runners as an attainable target, there for the beating. First to take on the challenge was 25-year-old Andy Hyslop on 7 May 1984. Conditions were ideal with dry rock, good visibility and a light breeze. Hyslop

THE BLACK CUILLIN

had two support points en route and navigated using small route cards pinned to his sleeves. At the Inaccessible Pinnacle his time was almost exactly that of Eric Beard's, but by the final col below Sgurr nan Gillean he had 14 minutes left in which to beat it. He managed to reach the summit cairn in 9 minutes to create a new record of 4 hours 4 minutes.

Hyslop then set out to dispel any confusion that may have existed after Beard's run by laying down a set route and style, clarifying the challenge for other runners. This required the cairns of all the Munro summits, and the tops of Bidein, to be touched; previously most record traverses had not included Sgurr Dubh Mor. All the rock climbing sections, like the Inaccessible Pinnacle, King's Chimney and the Thearlaich-Dubh Gap were to be soloed without support or the use of ropes. Feeders and pacers could, however, be used.

Two years later, Del Davies and Paul Stott of Eryi Harriers in North Wales knocked 15 minutes of Hyslop's time. This was an impressive achievement considering their limited experience of the ridge. It inspired Martin Moran to have a try at the record, but he had to wait till a suitable weather window coincided with a day off from work. This left him no time to organise a support team. In June 1990 he was helped by his knowledge of the ridge as a mountain guide to substantially reduce the record to 3 hours 33 minutes:

> I left Glen Brittle at 08.10am, jogged and walked to Gars-bheinn eating sandwiches and drinking Cremola strawberry foam mix, then set off at 10.30am (I'd wanted a witness to sign me off at the start but no-one was around). A cool light NW airflow with high cloud gave ideal running conditions. I carried nothing except a spare thermal top; no water or food.
>
> Main event was a serious tumble on a narrow section descending Mhic Choinnich, slipped facing out and rapped my shin badly drawing blood and a bruise. Slowing towards end largely out of a fear of getting 'bonked' through lack of liquid. The idea of doing a sub 3.30 did occur but the main thought was to finish safely and I was delighted to be so far inside the existing record. Surprised an old Yorkshire guy when springing up on to the top of Am Basteir. He grasped 'Bloody hell' as I scuttled past him. Later when walking back to the Fionn Choire on the way to get my car from Glen Brittle I passed him talking about me to another walker: 'Bugger just came up out of nowhere,' he was saying, 'with nowt bloody on!'[12]

Moran's run ignited Andy Hyslop's interest in regaining the Main Ridge record. Closely examining the terrain to fine-tune his route, he discovered that much of his previous line was too contrived; it was often faster to stick to the ridge crest. On 25 May 1994, ten years after his initial record-breaking run, he set off from the starting line, the cairn on Gars-bheinn. Wearing a heart monitor, all went well until he reached the Bhasteir Tooth: 'Suddenly I was a minute down on schedule, and the unacceptable face of failure stared me in the face. Adrenaline jolted me to climb Naismith's Route faster than was safe. With anxiety building, I tripped, stumbled and grasped past the final obstacles leading to the summit of Sgurr nan Gillean.' [13] He had beaten Moran's time by just 10 seconds (coincidentally Moran, out guiding that day, was one of the people he rushed by). Not satisfied with such a close margin, Hyslop returned three months later to chip another 35 seconds off his previous best.

When Es Tresidder first visited Loch Coruisk, aged 14, and saw the Cuillin skyline silhouetted by the evening sun, it instilled an ambition to one day run the ridge. An environmental building consultant, he waited several years for the requisite conditions to run the Main Ridge on-sight. By the time he succeeded, in May 2007, aged 27, he had become very familiar with the complexities of the route. His first try was in the autumn of 2006 when he was rained off at the Thearlaich-Dubh Gap. This attempt had its compensations as Blair Fyffe recalled after helping Tressider recce parts of the ridge:

> The next day we headed up to the Bhasteir Tooth so Es could check out Naismith's Route which he planned to solo in his running shoes on his ridge record attempt. We trudged up on a grey and cloudy morning, and arrived on the ridge in the mist. We started on Naismith's route, going up it, down it, and back up it again. By this time, there was a hint of blue through the cloud and we decided to have a look at a new line, essentially a super direct version of an existing E3, the Rainbow Warrior. As I had lead most of the lines at Elgol the previous day, Es got the lead. He headed up as the mist, which had been swirling about, began to clear and the sun poked through. Es continued up steadily, launching confidently up onto the blank looking wall above the ledge, where Rainbow Warrior traverses left. Fortunately gear and holds did appear, and he was soon on the top. It had cleared up by that point, and I seconded in the bright sunshine. There was still some dampness in the groove of Rainbow Warrior, which made it feel hard, but the warm and dry headwall above was a joy to climb.[14]

A photograph of Tressider and Fyffe's route, Captain Planet (E4), was selected for the cover of the Mike Lates' 2011 SMC climbing guide. Tressider's next attempt on the Main Ridge record was on 30 April 2007 when he managed a very credible time of 3 hours 59 minutes despite problems with the heat when he ran out of water at Bidein. Throughout the next week the failure gnawed at him. He decided he had to return for another go. He had two days off work, probably his last chance of the year. A plan evolved: 'Early train to Glasgow, sprint across town, long bus journey to Skye, meet Ben, drive to Glen Brittle, walk up on to the ridge, a few last-minute checks of a section of the route where I lost time on previous attempt, sleep on ridge, wake, run ridge, hitch-hike home'.

Tressider used the internet to ask for support, especially with water drops at the Inaccessible Pinnacle and Bruach na Frithe. He chose to bivvy on Garsbheinn which left him fresher, and the earlier start time of 6.21am meant fewer people would be about. He wore custom-made fell-running shoes with sticky rubber. Once started he regularly compared his split times with those of Andy Hyslop. At the cairn on Sgurr Dearg he realised he had opened a sizeable gap. By Sgurr na Banachdich he was eight minutes up and knew the record was there for the taking, as long as he didn't make a mistake or hit the wall. However, by Bidein he had lost all but one minute of his advantage:

> I gritted my teeth and put in a major effort going over An Caisteal and up Bruach na Frithe, only to find myself fifteen minutes ahead again! I was met there by Wendy Donnelly with some more water and half a banana. For the only time in the whole day I went into the mist coming off Am Basteir. I panicked a bit in the confusion, but soon found familiar rock for the climb up Sgurr nan Gillean. I reached the summit a very happy man in 3 hours 17 minutes 28 seconds, taking nearly 15 minutes off the record…The day turned out to be one of the most spectacular I've ever seen. The valley was slowly enveloped in a sea of mist, leaving the ridge the only thing floating above in the sunshine. It was like running in heaven.[15]

For a long time Es Tressider thought his record safe, as the combination of an exceptional hill runner with the required rock climbing skills was relatively rare. None of the current runners who were faster than him had the necessary climbing ability. One of the features of this particular challenge is that you can't just turn up and have a go; a lot of time and hard work have to be invested in preparation due to the complex nature of the route with its almost endless potential for shaving off a second or two here and there. It is significant that runners have now broken down the Main Ridge into 13 distinct legs, so that split times can be analysed and compared.

With the emergence of Fort William runner Finlay Wild, through his win of the 2010 Ben Nevis Race and breaking of the long-standing Glamaig Hill Race record in 2012, Tressider realised that he now had serious competition. Wild, a GP practicing in Inverness, was one of Britain's best hill runners, particularly fast over rough ground, and also a rock climber. When he made his intentions known about tackling the Main Ridge record, Tressider generously helped with information. A refreshing feature of hill running is the friendliness, lack of ego, and degree of co-operation among potential rivals.

In 2013 Finlay Wild ran the Cuillin Main Ridge on four occasions, breaking Tressider's record two, arguably three times. On 9th June, in perfect weather, he completed the Traverse in 3:10:30. However, on the final descent it dawned on him that he had failed to touch the cairn of Sgurr Mhic Choinnich despite passing within 10m of it. Later the same day he reascended the mountain to check out what had happened, eventually discounting his time on very strict ethical grounds.

The next weekend (16th June) Wild was highly motivated to make up for this mistake. He left the summit of Gars-bheinn at 5am. Despite the promised forecast for fine weather failing to materialise, he decided to persevere in misty and slightly damp conditions. At the Thearlaich-Dubh Gap Wild considered giving up, but eventually decided to take his time and safely negotiate the often greasy descent into the gap. Due to his recent knowledge of the ridge, route-finding continued to go well. At Bidein he checked his split times from the week before to find he was four minutes behind. At Bruach na Frithe he was very near Tressider's 2007 split. Wild managed to reach Sgurr nan Gillean in a new record time of 3:14:58., beating the previous best time by 2 minutes 30 seconds.

Once rested and recovered from this major achievement, he reckoned that breaking 3 hours 14 minutes was possible if the rocks remained dry; he even thought 3 hours 5 minutes feasible if he could get back while his memory of the route was fresh. Three months later a short window of fine weather coincided with his weekend off, a perfect opportunity, probably the last of the year. On Saturday 12 October he touched the cairn on Gars-bheinn at 12 noon and set off in near perfect conditions: few people about, dry rock and not too hot.

By Sgurr Mhic Chionnich he was 9 minutes ahead of his own record splits. The last hour of the run evolved into a sustained push to try and break the sub-3-hour barrier. At Sgurr a' Ghreadaidh there was near disaster when the zip to his supply of jelly babies jammed. He managed to rip it open and regain access to this vital energy source. By the top of Am Basteir he had 10 minutes left to break 3 hours; by the Window, just below the summit of Sgurr nan Gillean, one minute: 'This time I knew I had done it. No doubts about summits touched, or route taken, I surveyed the ridge, counting off each top in the sunshine. I did some shouting.' Wild had taken 15 minutes off his own record, breaking the 3 hour barrier with a time of 2:59:22.

Not content with this achievement, Finlay Wild created a new record for the Winter Traverse of 6:14:17 with Tim Gomersall in February 2016. Their time was helped by parties before them who had broken trail and excavated abseil points. Wild led the short side of the TD Gap (VI) which is often avoided. Two years later, on 26 February 2018 Uisdean Hawthorn knocked over an hour off this when he set off from Sgurr nan Gillean just after 8am and arrived at Gars-bheinn in a time of 4:57:7. This was an unsupported attempt with minimum planning where Hawthorn seized an opportunity due to good weather and conditions.

With the start of front-pointing in the 1970s, there was little pattern to winter developments in the Cuillin as activists found their feet in what was, apart from the Winter Traverse, still largely unknown territory. Attention eventually focused on what was popular at the time, major gully lines like Waterpipe Gully and Deep Gash Gully, as well as any prominent icefalls in condition. The opening of the Skye Bridge in 1995 saw a noticeable upturn in pioneering with a consequent consensus over what areas provided the most consistent conditions. A return of severe winters in the late 2000s saw Skye play its part as Scottish winter climbing reached unprecedented new levels of difficulty. With this rise in standards it was felt the Scottish winter grading system needed a revamp. In 1993 a two-tiered system similar to the summer E grades was introduced, with an overall grade (Roman numerals) and a technical grade (Arabic numbers) for example, Deep Gash Gully (VI,7).

Through the 1970s, there was sporadic winter activity in the more accessible Glen Brittle corries with the pick of the bunch being Roger Robb and M. Donn's North-West Ridge of Sgurr a' Ghreadaidh (II). In 1974 there was a futuristic winter ascent of Cioch Direct (V) not recorded until the 2011 SMC guidebook. In the early 1980s Clive Rowland demonstrated further winter potential with routes like Frankland's Gully (V) on Sgurr Sgumain and White Wizard (III/IV) in the atmospheric Harta Corrie. But it was Waterpipe Gully that was seen by many as one of the outstanding winter prizes. As is often the case several parties converged on the route around the same time. First on the scene, in February 1986, were the Aberdonian pairing of Brian Findlay and Greg Strange whose main objective had been the Winter Traverse. Greg Strange relates what happened:

> The next morning was beautiful, clear blue skies and a hard frost. It remained like that for at least the next four days. Our plan was to climb Sgurr nan Gillean by the Tourist Route, descend the West Ridge then continue the traverse as normal. As we got higher so the snow got deeper until we reluctantly accepted that it would take forever to do the ridge in these conditions. (There were drifts up to five feet deep above 2,500 feet.) At this point we noticed a fine icefall near the centre of the two-tiered cliff which curved up below the south-east ridge and, despite our lack of climbing gear, decided to try this as a consolation. On the steeper ground we found good neve and near perfect ice. Lament (III/IV) seemed a suitable name in the circumstances
>
> We spent the second night in the car in Glen Brittle and decided to take a look at Waterpipe Gully on the Sunday. We knew the climb only by reputation and had no pre-conceived ideas as to what it would look like or how hard it would be, although we assumed that since it was VS and still unclimbed in winter it might be a bit stiff. The first section from the bottom was a deep narrow chimney, icy, but still running with water. We could have climbed it but would have got very wet in the process so decided to take the right-

hand rib. After about 300 feet of very snowy but easy mixed climbing we re-entered the main gully only to be confronted by even deeper powder. Gullies full of powder have never been our thing so we descended and returned to Glen Brittle.

That night as we strolled on the snow-covered beach we re-considered the situation and concluded that a first winter ascent of this famous Skye gully was worth another look. Besides, there had been no fresh snow and no appreciable wind for two days. We went back the next day and climbed the whole thing, encountering only one major pitch, where a series of iced chockstones had to be negotiated. As we descended in the late afternoon we spotted two tiny figures progressing slowly along the main ridge and felt pangs of envy. We had been two days too early and now had to return to Aberdeen.[16]

Four days later, Doug Scott and Colin Downer, a former miner, arrived at the foot of Waterpipe Gully. Doug Scott, an ex-teacher from Nottingham, is best known for his 1975 ascent of Everest's South-West Face with Dougal Haston. In 1979, along with Jim Duff, Scott put up Skye's first recorded grade V (now VI), The Smear in Coir' a' Mhadaidh. This prominent icefall connects Foxes' Rake with the Upper Rake and was probably not repeated for over thirty years. Due to a big freeze following the Aberdonians' ascent, Scott and Downer were able to climb Waterpipe Gully in its entirety, confirming a feeling of anti-climax as it succumbed at an unexpectedly mild grade IV. The hardest and longest pitch was the initial crux section, bypassed by Strange and Findlay as it was unfrozen. The remainder of the gully consisted of a series of short pitches separated by easy snow. The very next day a Londoner called Mick Fowler arrived ominously on the scene.

To Fowler commitment, adventure and the lure of the unknown were as integral a part of the game as they were anathema to the newer ethos of sports climbing. His idiosyncratic approach was summed up in the first ascent of a frozen ice-fall on St Pancras Station (the result of a leaking toilet) with second, Mike Morrison, belayed to a parking meter. Mick Fowler first visited Skye in June 1977 when he and Phil Thomas created several fine climbs in the space of a few days. Their first new route was Stairway to Heaven (E5) on Bla Bheinn which took on the huge unclimbed wall between Jib and The Great Prow. Classic status was ensured with inclusion in *Extreme Rock*. Fowler relates in the book how, to negotiate the crux, he had to trust a precarious ledge that might or might not hold his weight:

> Desperate climbing on tiny holds placed me in a position where I could clear the debris from the ledge with my right foot; the ledge itself seemed quite stable and, as I couldn't hang on the wall any longer anyway, I gently eased my

weight on to it. My heart was in my mouth, but, no detectable movements of the ledge occurred, and standing in balance by now, I was more than a little pleased to find a solid spike a little higher which acted as a most welcome runner. The wall above looked far from easy but led without incident to a slanting gangway providing an excellent stance.[17]

On Sron na Ciche, Fowler and Thomas also created a new line based on MacInnes and Clough's Atropos (E1) which, since its first ascent, had suffered a massive rock-fall. On the same cliffs they produced Grooves Eliminate (E2) and Dilemma (E3), the latter foreseeing the potential of Sron na Ciche's Eastern Buttress. Fowler's comments on these last two routes are brief and to the point, 'Just went there, saw obvious gaps and climbed them.' Grooves Eliminate, originally named The Nipple by Fowler and Thomas, was one of several 1950/60s aid routes that were not properly recorded.

In winter, Fowler, a tax assessor, became renowned for his 1,300-mile (2,400km) round trips from London in search of undeclared Scottish ice. His record is eleven consecutive weekend trips. There were four drivers, all fully dressed for ice climbing, taking three-hour shifts for both driving and keeping the driver awake with climbing quizzes, leaving six hours to try and sleep. En route they only allowed themselves one break, Ma Shepherd's transport cafe near Penrith, where they obtained an up-to-date weather forecast and purchased food for the weekend: cheese rolls for breakfast on Saturday, ham rolls for Sunday, the theory being that cheese dries out faster than ham.

In March 1986, Mick Fowler asked his father, on holiday in Skye, if he would monitor and report on ice conditions. George Fowler's call to London was made at 7pm. Early the next morning Mick Fowler and Vic Saunders were at the foot of the climbs. Their main objective was Waterpipe Gully but Fowler senior had failed to notice the line of footsteps up the gully. They had unluckily arrived the day after Scott and Downers' ascent. After making the second complete winter ascent, Fowler and Saunders then descended into Coire na Creiche for an unroped ascent of South Gully (III/IV), first climbed by Ginger Cain and G Wallace in 1979.

They then moved right to the Amphitheatre where, up and left of The Smear, they came face to face with Icicle Factory (V), a continuous ice runnel capped by overhanging icicles. As they had left one rope and most of their gear at the foot of South Gully, they soloed the initial pitches before tying onto their single 9mm rope for the upper section. This culminated in the crux overhang, two huge icicles. By transferring, on improving ice, from one icicle to the other, Fowler was able to gain the frontal face and, eventually, easier ground.

Vic Saunders, a Gordonstoun-educated architect, was referred to as 'Slippery Vic' by Fowler and his circle of friends, since he could be hard to pin down. In the *Alpine Journal* (1980) Saunders gave his own take on the route, 'a wonderful ephemeral line of blue ice with three free-standing icicle pitches and a final blue umbrella which felt like climbing up the inside of a giant frozen jellyfish'. With descriptions like this the Icicle Factory became a much sought-after objective.

The next day, along with Chris Watts, Fowler and Saunders made the first ascent of White Wedding (IV), an icefall on the west face of Sgurr a' Ghreadaidh. They now faced a 600-mile overnight commute back to work in London for Monday morning which Saunders recalls: 'We left Skye at 4pm and were in bed in London by 2am, covering the drive from Kyle to Fort William in one hour. The next day Chris Watts was so tired that when he got into his (new) car he did not notice the wheels had been stolen, and it was up on bricks, until he had been revving up the engine for at least ten minutes.'[18]

As Chris Watts was trying to get his car started, back on Skye two young climbers were heading into trouble. This incident would demonstrate one of the hazards of winter climbing in the Cuillin where proximity to the sea meant conditions could change extremely rapidly. That day the freezing level shot up from sea-level to 9,000ft (2,750m) in a matter of hours, stripping the thick layer of snow and ice that had coated the likes of Icicle Factory and White Wedding.

The two climbers intended to ascend Sgurr nan Gillean by the Tourist Route, but in poor visibility started up Pinnacle Ridge by mistake. Not realising their error, they abseiled off the Third Pinnacle thinking they were going down into Lota Corrie. Descending from the gap between the Third Pinnacle and Knight's Peak one of them slipped and broke a leg. His companion dug a snow-hole, left the casualty in a sleeping bag with plenty of food and clothing, and rushed to Sligachan to raise the alarm.

When the callout came in the late afternoon, the Skye Mountain Rescue Team assembled at the inn. The weather was deteriorating with lashing wind and rain. Normally a helicopter is scrambled, and the time prior to its arrival used to gather information about the incident. On this occasion a yellow Sea King was already in the vicinity and immediately began to ferry team members into Lota Corrie, the location given for the casualty. No sign of the missing climber was found and, as conditions were deteriorating rapidly, the search was called off at 9pm.

The helicopter was only able to pick up half-a-dozen or so of the rescue team from the corrie. It then developed a fault and was forced to fly below 50ft (15m), navigating by its lights; so fierce was the wind the chopper was at times forced to fly backwards. The rest of the team had an even bigger epic returning to base. They had to wade the freezing, chest-deep waters of the River Sligachan in full spate, having to link arms as large blocks of ice hurtled downstream in the darkness, threatening to knock them off balance and sweep them away.

Around midnight the messenger was re-interviewed and the truth dawned – the team had been looking in the wrong corrie. At first light operations were resumed in the correct location with the assistance of search and rescue dogs.

They eventually came across a scene of jumbled blocks of snow and ice, more avalanche debris than anyone present had ever seen in the Cuillin. But there was still no sign of the casualty. Around noon the dogs found a Mars Bar, then a helmet, suggesting he may have been avalanched from his bivouac during the night. After probing the debris it was not long until a body was discovered.

Martin Moran, originally from Tyneside, had moved to Strathcarron in Wester Ross to start a guiding business. Living near to many prize winter lines, it was particularly galling that the London-based Mick Fowler could beat him to them: Pipped at the Post (V) on Fuar Tholl celebrates one such occasion. After this fait accompli Moran began to exhibit signs of paranoia at the sight of north London registration plates on remote Highland verges. One of Moran's main ambitions was the first winter ascent of Skye's spectacular Deep Gash Gully (VI,7) on Sgurr a' Mhadaidh, considered by many to have the makings of Skye's finest gully climb. In February 1991 Moran succeeded in climbing the route with Martin Welch; it proved a formidable undertaking that stretched both men to their limit:

> Skye's answer to Raven's Gully of Glen Coe, but steeper and considerably harder. End of a fine spell; a big front arrived mid-morning and we climbed the route in a constant stream of spindrift with verglas everywhere. The lower cave gave a technical chimneying section, but the upper pitches were far more impressive, a big iced groove leading to a tiny belay under a hanging chimney and capstone. Establishing myself in the hanging chimney involved falling across the gap and planting both hands on the far side with the prospect of a fall direct on to the belay if the move failed. At the time it seemed the hardest thing I'd ever done in winter but the appalling conditions probably enhanced my impression. A scary mantelshelf gained sufficient height to reach axes into ice and the final capstone overhang was relatively straightforward. Now dark so we topped out about 8pm in a fierce southerly gale; crawled over the summit and into Coire a' Ghreadaidh past fresh avalanche debris. Torrential rain down in the glen.
>
> A few weeks later Andy Nisbet called me to say that Mick Fowler had done the route a few days before us, denying us this major coup. Worse still he only gave it grade V; but everyone knows that Mick's winter grades are somewhat traditional and unreasonably harsh so our suggested VI,7 has stuck.[19]

Andy Nisbet occasionally worked for Martin Moran, often guiding clients along the Cuillin Ridge. Originally from Aberdeen, he was undoubtedly the most prolific pioneer of Scottish winter climbs. After his death in an accident on Ben Hope in the winter of 2019, Moran described Nisbet as 'undoubtedly the greatest and nicest character with whom I have ever climbed or worked'. (Moran himself was killed a few months later in an avalanche on Nanda Devi.) Guiding the Cuillin Main Ridge in 1995 Nisbet noticed, when descending Sgurr na Banachdich, how much winter potential there was on Sgurr Dearg's large north-east face below the Inaccessible Pinnacle.

The next winter (1996) Nisbet's interest in this cliff was rekindled when he noticed ropes left over from a rescue, blowing in the wind across the face. The previous May two climbers had got lost and ended up abseiling down the face. However their ropes jammed and, unable to free them, they became cragfast above overhangs near O'Brien and Julian's Climb. Due to atrocious weather (even some snow) the pair were not located by rescue teams until after spending two nights out on the cliff. Suffering hypothermia, they were eventually lowered to the foot of the crag where one of the climbers tragically died.

In March 1996, Nisbet teamed up with Brian Davison to try and create the first winter route on the face. Davison, a Durham-born research scientist, was regarded by Nisbet as the finest mixed climber in the country through the 1990s. Nisbet went on to describe their winter ascent of O'Brien and Julian's Climb (VI,5) as 'a fantastic route':

> Conditions were great with lots of ice and I like wandering about on a big face trying to get up, which might not be everyone's cup of tea, but I thought it was a three-star route. I had to work that evening so the pressure of time added to the excitement as well. We slept in the car and set off before dawn but in the end I was half-an-hour late. As a V. Diff. in the guide we thought we would do it quickly, but it turned out to be much harder and longer than we thought. We just couldn't believe how we got a 1000-foot grade VI out of a 270-foot V. Diff. The rescue team had obviously been surprised too when they had had to aid up most of the way to the lads. Left loads of gear too, the second pitch was like a sports climb! After the hard lower section there was pitch after pitch of grade III mostly on ice in spectacular positions.[20]

The development of climbing in the Cuillin has always been influenced by improved communications with the mainland. With the Skye Bridge opening in October 1995 access to Skye changed dramatically for the better with winter weekends no longer proving a problem. However the new bridge was highly controversial, a toll bridge which protesters claimed was the most expensive in Europe; there were over 500 arrests for refusing to pay. In December 2004 the Scottish Executive purchased the bridge for 27 million pounds, just in time for a massive Hogmanay celebration on the now toll-free crossing. Although this brought ease of access it didn't necessarily bring good winter conditions.

Main activists now included the Argyllshire team of Dave Ritchie, an engineer from Oban, and regular partner Mark Shaw, as well as locally-based guides Mike Lates and Martin Moran. Lates' first new winter climb was the popular Escape from Colditz (III) on Bla Bheinn. Through the 1990s Sgurr nan Gillean, Clach Glas and Bla Bheinn were the main focus for new winter routes with Ritchie and Shaw at the forefront of this long-overdue development. Until the ascent of B Gully (IV) by Ritchie and Steve Kennedy, in January 1991, no winter climbs had been recorded on either Bla Bheinn or Clach Glas since before the First World War. Soon after the opening of the Skye Bridge, Ritchie created two fine lines on Bla Bheinn: Virgo (IV) in December 1995 with I Stevenson, and Birthday Groove (IV) in March 1996 with Mark Shaw.

The degree to which the Cuillin had been neglected in winter can be seen by the fact that Sgurr nan Gillean, 150 years after its first ascent, had only three recorded winter climbs: West Ridge, Pinnacle Ridge, and Bryan and Robb's West Face on Knight's Peak. It was soon realised that snow and ice added distinct character to many of the long-neglected rock climbs which now provided excellent short winter lines. Martin Moran was particularly active here; some of his best efforts include Flutings Climb (IV) and West Ridge of Knight's Peak (III), both done on the same day, as well as Forked Chimney (IV) and Luscher's No. 1 (IV). This revival of interest in these early climbs brings one era of the mountains full circle, back to where much of it began when Norman Collie watched Stocker and Parker on Sgurr nan Gillean in 1886.

Dave Ritchie and Mark Shaw went on to discover that another neglected area, the North Face of Am Basteir, came regularly into winter condition. In March 1999, on consecutive days, they put up Deadline (III) and North Face (IV), both of which utilise the exposed ledge systems that characterise the cliff. Dave Ritchie summarised their explorations here: 'On Am Basteir the most memorable route was a winter ascent based on North Face Route, one which we called White Spirit. Although the technical difficulties were short, the positions steadily improved with a memorable protectionless traverse along a narrowing ledge leading into The Squeeze Box. The climb would almost certainly be harder without good snow-ice on the ledges.'

After a series of mild and disappointing winters, December 1999 brought the best conditions for years. Inevitably Mick Fowler was back on the road to Skye to take advantage, this time with Paul Ramsden. In the Cuillin they claimed two more prime winter targets, both coincidentally first climbed in summer by Tom Patey. On the first winter ascent of Deep Gash Gully, Fowler could not have failed to notice the imposing line of Whispering Wall (VI) on the gully's right wall. Originally graded Very Difficult (now Severe) this was a climb that saw frequent failures in summer. Fowler recalls that on the first winter ascent they followed the lower two-thirds of the summer line before trending right: 'The crux, second pitch was led by Paul Ramsden; a really good lead as it seemed desperate to me. He protected it (poorly) with one of those ice sky-hook things.'[21]

This steep and exposed winter line was in contrast to the next day's offering, Chock-a-Block Chimney (V) on Bla Bheinn, an often wet and greasy rock climb that reeked of winter potential. On the second pitch Fowler realised that the rocks on the right offered the only viable alternative, but once above the problem it proved difficult to regain the original chimney line which higher up became almost subterranean: 'A good route. It was on my list for over ten years before we managed to get it in condition. I had been up to it at least once before but not actually tried it.' On the same day that Fowler and Ramsden were grappling with Chock-a-Block Chimney, Dave Ritchie and N Nelson made the first winter ascent of Am Basteir Chimney (IV). The thought of Fowler prowling about Bla Bheinn galvanised Ritchie into action there to claim one of his long-held ambitions:

> For years I had often looked up at Clough's Cleft, up and right of the Great Prow of Bla Bheinn, and wondered if it would make a good winter route. The guidebook certainly talked about a route which rarely dried in summer, this fact being supported by the presence of ice noticed several times when exploring other routes nearby on Bla Bheinn and Clach Glas. Spurred on by news of a winter ascent of the adjacent route, Chock-a-Block Chimney, in December 1999, and with exceptional conditions prevailing across Scotland during the first week of March 2000, three of us succeeded in climbing Clough's Cleft. We found three pitches of excellent icy mixed climbing, superb rock scenery and a fine outlook. The day was made all the more memorable by fine weather, beautiful summit views and the onset the following day of a major thaw which stripped all but the highest crags for the rest of the winter![22]

Dave Ritchie went on to describe Clough's Cleft (V,6) as probably the best route he had climbed in the Cuillin. Another fine winter discovery was the Stone Shoot Face of Sgurr Thearlaich, initially developed by Ritchie, Mark Shaw and Neil McGougan. Due to its relatively high altitude this venue appeared to offer fairly consistent conditions as Ritchie explains:

> The winter of 2001-2, I climbed a trio of good chimney/gullies on the Stone Shoot Face of Sgurr Thearlaich. These were Gullies B (VI,6), C (III) and D (V,6). Gully B provided a memorable ascent not only by being the second route of the day with a nocturnal finish, but also because of the fine technical climbing towards the top of the first pitch. Perhaps Buckle, Barlow and Doughty climbed chimneys with great ease as their description talks of three easy pitches to start. In winter, at least, the main chimney low down was by no means easy, in fact it proved to be one of the hardest and technically interesting pitches I have encountered on Skye! I had also been keen to try Gully D for some time, intrigued by their description of the first

pitch as being the 'piece de resistance'. Although the summer description talks of a route only gradually improving, in winter we found the route to have sustained interest and a fine crux pitch to finish at the top.[23]

In February (2000) Dave Ritchie and Neil Marshall put up White Dreams (IV,5) the first winter climb on the south-facing Lota Corrie face of Sgurr nan Gillean, a good choice for cold, cloudy conditions. That same weekend the Cuillin had its own *Touching the Void* episode. Jay Stewart and Kathy Lipson were tackling the Inaccessible Pinnacle's East Ridge in the prevailing icy conditions. As Lipson was leading the second pitch it started to snow heavily. She slipped and fell. Sitting at the belay Stewart felt a violent jerk from the rope. Looking down she could see a motionless red fleece dangling below. Stewart held on as long as she could but ultimately had no option but cut the rope.

In Val McDermid's 2010 crime novel, *Trick of the Dark*, Charlie Flint, a clinical psychiatrist and forensic profiler, has Jay Stewart earmarked as a serial killer. Ten years after Lipson's fatal fall, Flint visits Skye with a friend to finally investigate the incident. After booking into a local hotel, an opportunity for some lesbian libido and Stornoway black pudding (but not at the same time), they interview members of the 'Glen Brittle Mountain Rescue Team'. They uncover crucial clues that may have far-reaching significance...

In the non-fiction world the first decade of the twenty-first century was characterised by extremely mild winters when many Scottish ski centres were almost forced out of business. However the decade ended with some of the coldest winters for many years, and as climbers were forced to venture out of the gym something had changed. Increasingly milder and inconsistent weather had reduced the reliability of good conditions for front-pointing, leading to an upsurge of interest in modern mixed climbing where the required conditions could be produced by a single cold snap rather than the more complex freeze-thaw cycle needed for ice climbing. This, combined with dry tool training, led to a greater number of people tackling the top end routes.

With the most snow for over a decade, the winter of 2007-8 would be one to remember. On 11th January 2008 Pete MacPherson, Graham Briffet and Mike Lates took advantage of excellent conditions to make the first winter ascent of Grand Diedre (VI,6) on the Thearlaich-Dubh Buttress. MacPherson, who runs a climbing shop in Inverness, reported: 'I headed up the first pitch expecting it to be the crux, but found great hooks in the crack at the back of the corner all the way. On the right wall of the corner there was very helpful icy rime, which took a mono [point] just nicely. If there wasn't any icy rime on that wall the pitch would have been a lot harder!'[24]

The next day Guy Robertson joined Glasgow doctor Mark Garthwaite for an investigation of Sgurr Mhic Choinnich's North Face. After leaving Glen Brittle they were on the crest of the ridge by 7.30am where the dawn broke to reveal conditions similar to those encountered on Grand Diedre, a good covering of icy hoar (unusual in the Cuillin). After considering various options they plumped for Dawn Grooves (VII, 8). Guy Robertson: 'We thought a summer VS would maybe give us a VI or VII, so we were slapped in the face a bit! It was a very sustained route, with superb climbing all the way. I was pretty chuffed with our ascent – we didn't hang about. There was a pitch of 6, three of 7, and two of 8, all of them very sustained, so eight hours was rapid enough. That's the great thing about climbing in January – it puts a spring in your step!'[25]

The next winter (2008-09) started early with blizzards in October. The next month Martin Moran and Nick Carter managed a winter ascent of the highly technical Hung, Drawn and Quartered (VIII,8) on Am Basteir. They found the chimney plastered in verglas, one of the best sealants for keeping the basalt intact, but which also compromised the generally good protection. Not long after the route had a second winter ascent by Pete MacPherson and Ian Parnell. The former found the climb, especially the third pitch, a serious proposition with some marginal hooks on sloping holds. However, with MacPherson's robust training regime, the route stood little chance:

> I'd put on a big harness and pull a van behind me, and then Roddy would have a huge diameter rope off of a ship tied to the van and I'd have to pull it towards me, hand over hand for fifty metres. Then straight after that I'd knock shit into a tractor tyre with a massive sledge hammer, a minute on the left hand, a minute on the right, back and forth, back and forth.[26]

The next two winters offered some exceptionally cold, stable weather when there was a massive leap in the standard of modern mixed climbing throughout Scotland. The 2009-10 season was described as 'the mother of all winters', the coldest on record in northern Scotland, a sustained freeze from December through to the middle of March when daytime temperatures at road level struggled to get above zero. Urban pavements were so icy some hospitals ran out of plaster for broken limbs.

One of the best discoveries of 2009 was North Face Direct (IV) on Bla Bheinn by Dave Ritchie and Mark Shaw. In January 1910 exceptionally snowy conditions allowed Simon Richardson and Iain Small, a conservation stonemason, to do The Great Prow (VII,8) on Bla Bheinn. Richardson recorded this first winter ascent in his authoritative blog *Scottishwinter.com*:

> We ploughed up through thigh-deep snow on Blaven looking for something icy to climb, but were drawn to The Great Prow that was draped in powder. It gave an absorbing winter climb that became increasingly icy as we reached

the top. The crux was as per the summer route and overall we felt the route to be VII,8. We finished in the dark and gingerly down climbed Scuppers Gully, fearful that it would avalanche, before starting the long slippery drive home.[27]

In December 2010, Guy Robertson and Greg Boswell, who started climbing aged 13 in 2004, did a winter ascent of Black Cleft (VI,7). After sorting out gear for a 3am start from Glenbrittle, they slept in the car as temperatures dropped to minus 20. With dawn breaking as they reached the crest of the Main Ridge, they were able to assess what was in condition on the Coruisk side. Their prime objective wasn't in nick but Black Cleft was. This long sought-after objective proved quite a technical climb despite its traditional appearance, as Boswell confirmed: 'Even though it was a last hope option the route was totally awesome and gave a good variety of wall climbing and winter chimneying. The route was sustained but never super difficult so we decided to give it VI,7 and we both agreed that it was one of the most enjoyable routes we had done in a while.'[28] Robertson added: 'We felt very privileged to climb such a fine route in such an outstanding corrie, and so early in the season as well. Descending from Coire Lagan in the last moments of daylight, the sun setting over a snow-clad Isle of Rum, with a storm brewing over the Outer Hebrides, forming an angry backdrop to the cobalt sea, was amazing.'[29]

The same day, over on the Bhasteir Tooth, Pete MacPherson, Martin Moran and Francis Blunt joined forces for the Outside Variation of Shadbolt's Route (VI,7), as MacPherson recorded: 'I have to say it's the weirdest route I have ever climbed. The chimney disappears right into the back of the Tooth where a through route leads out to the other side. I chose to head out the other way towards the light. This involved extreme chimney/caving out under a 8-10 metre roof before heading up into the upper squeeze chimney. It involved the strangest of contortions and a massive rack of 16-foot slings and cams up to size 6! Getting gear in was desperate as I could hardly move without getting jammed or tangled in the rope! It's almost impossible to grade, however VI/VII,7 with a pinch of salt is about right.'[30]

Postscript

Mention has previously been made of the Bad Step controversy in 1968, but threats to the Cuillin's unique qualities will always be with us. In 1995, MacLeod Estates made an application for planning permission to construct a visitor centre in Glen Brittle, incorporating an 80-seater restaurant. The proposal was eventually shelved after an outburst of protest over such an inappropriate development. It is only through objections from the MacRae family and other villagers that Glen Brittle has avoided the imposition of a public house.

In 1997, a planning application was made by Man Friday Helicopters to construct a heliport at the Sligachan Hotel as a base for a tourist helicopter service. This involved a single flight path: down Glen Sligachan, over to Coruisk, and back across Harta Corrie; taking ten minutes and proposed six hours a day, six days a week. Over 1,500 letters of objection were received on grounds of visual intrusion, noise pollution and the disturbance of protected bird species. The protests were successful in that the Campbell family at Sligachan severed their connection with the helicopter company.

Anyone scanning the newspaper adverts in April 2000 might have been surprised to note the following: 'For Sale, Scotland's most famous mountain range. An area of international scenic, recreational and national importance.' On 22nd March, John MacLeod, the 29th chief of Clan MacLeod, placed the Cuillin on the market for a price of £10 million pounds in order to finance repairs to the roof of his ancestral home, Dunvegan Castle. Tenant farmers such as Hugh MacRae in Glen Brittle only heard about the sale when it was announced in the media. Conservationists and land valuation experts alike regarded the valuation as ludicrously overpriced, over four times the going rate for similar land elsewhere. MacLeod was seen by many to be offering a speculative sale, hoping to capitalise on a perceived demand for land by government. Snowdon had recently been purchased by the National Trust for the highly inflated price of £3.65 million.

Doubts soon emerged that the clan chief might not actually own the Cuillin. When the Crown Estate Commission came under increasing pressure to investigate the legitimacy of MacLeod's ownership, the estate agents suspended sale proceedings. In July 2000 the Crown Estate Commissioners decided not to mount a legal challenge, despite the fact that John MacLeod appeared to possess no formal title to the disputed territory. They argued there was not enough evidence to dispute the ownership in court and as no one had contested it since 1611 there was little chance of it being successfully contested now.

Doubts remained and the Ramblers Association commissioned Alan Blackshaw to undertake some historical research into the ownership claim. He unearthed some discrepancies: the original grant of land in 1611 did not specifically mention the Cuillin, nor did subsequent title deeds including the present one (1966). Some title deeds suggested that the eastern boundary of the MacLeod estate was actually within Glen Brittle and consequently MacLeod did not hold any valid title deed to the Coruisk side of the range, or indeed much of the Glen Brittle side. (In 1883 Alexander Nicolson and the Napier Commissioners were told that these Cuillin hill pastures were common grazing).

In July 2001, with no concrete offers, MacLeod proposed a deal where he would 'gift' the mountains to the nation if a proposed charitable trust pay for repairs to the castle. However, any agreement seemed ill-advised while confusion over ownership remained.

Since Bonnie Prince Charlie squelched his way down a dark Glen Sligachan many paths in the Cuillin have been substantially improved. The other side of the coin is that, as in many areas worldwide, the growing footfall that this encourages has diminished the sense of remoteness, a quality in increasingly short supply.

More recently, Skye's popularity as a tourist destination has put pressure on the island's infrastructure: roads, parking, toilet facilities etc. Unless more creative solutions are found, attempts to solve these problems can have widespread negative ramifications. One area particularly affected has been the Fairy Pools in Glen Brittle, below the Cuillin. Expanding parking facilities here or widening the road could simply bring the same problems to Glenbrittle village, creating pressure there for more parking, which in turn could generate a demand for developments like cafes, pubs, interpretation centres etc, and, in this scenario, the unique charm of Glenbrittle could be lost forever.

Whereas previous generations had problems finding information on the Cuillin, the level of detail now available is probably due some scrutiny as to its effects on the mountain experience. We all have a duty to promote mountains appropriately and responsibly, and help protect fragile areas like the Cuillin. In the words of the late Tom Weir: 'We all have to do our bit, no matter how small.'

References

The following abbreviations have been used:

AJ, Alpine Journal
EUMCJ, Edinburgh University Mountaineering Club Journal
FRCCJ, Fell and Rock Climbing Club Journal
LSCCJ, Ladies' Scottish Climbing Club Journal
NLS, National Library of Scotland
SMCJ, Scottish Mountaineering Club Journal
TGSI, Transactions of the Gaelic Society of Inverness

Chapter 1

1. Quoted in Ronald Macdonald, 'The Island of Skye in 1764, as Described by John Walker', *TGSI* 27 (1912), p.109.
2. Robert Jameson, *Mineralogy of the Scottish Isles* (Edinburgh, 1800), p. 2:72.
3. Thomas Pennant, *A Tour in Scotland, and Voyage to the Hebrides, 1772* (London, 1772), p. 1:287.
4. James Boswell, *Boswell's London Diary 1762-1763*, (London, 1974), p. 32.
5. *Lumsden and Son's Steam-boat Companion to the Western Isles* (Glasgow, 1831), p. 156.
6. Alexander Smith, *A Summer in Skye* (Hawick: Byways Books, 1983), p. 24.
7. J.E. Portlock, *Memoir of the Life of Major General Colby*, 1809. Quoted in *Scottish Studies* 7 (1963), p. 12.
8. John MacCulloch, *The Highlands and Western Isles of Scotland*, (London, 1824), p. 3:471.
9. MacCulloch, John, 'Corrections and Additions to the Sketch of the Mineralogy of Skye', *Trans. Geological Society of London* 3 (1817), p. 183.
10. John MacCulloch, *The Highlands and Western Isles of Scotland*, (London, 1824), p. 3:471.
11. Ibid. p. 3:474.
12. J.G. Lockhart, *Memoirs of the Life of Sir Walter Scott* (Edinburgh, 1837), p. 4:310.
13. J.L. Robertson, *Scott's Poetical Works* (London, 1904), p. 475.
14. William Daniell, *Voyage round Great Britain* (London, 1825), 2:37.
15. Ibid. 2:35.
16. Joseph Mitchell, *Reminiscences of My Life in the Highlands* (Newton Abbot, 1971), p. 1:219.
17. *Life and Letters of the Reverend Adam Sedgwick* (Cambridge, 1890), 1:305.
18. Charles Lesingham Smith, *Journal of a Tour in Scotland* (Edinburgh, 1838), p. 52.
19. Papers of James David Forbes, St Andrews University Manuscript Collection, msdep 7, Incoming letters, 1836, No. 26, 1 July 1836.
20. J.D. Forbes, 'Notes on the Topography and Geology of the Cuchullin Hills', *Edinburgh New Philosophy Journal* 45 (1846), p. 80.
21. Quoted in F. Cunningham, *James David Forbes, Pioneer Scottish Glaciologist* (Edinburgh, 1990), p. 216.
22. A. Geikie, 'Memoir of the late James David Forbes', *Edinburgh Geological Society*

(Edinburgh, 1869).
23. *Black's Tourist Guide to Scotland* (Edinburgh, 1856), p. 399.
24. Henry Cockburn, *Circuit Journeys* (Edinburgh, 1842). p. 121.
25. 'Mr Fixby's Visit to Skye', *Bentley's Miscellany* 36 (1854), p. 251.
26. *North Wales Chronicle,* 24 September 1859.
27. George Anderson and Peter Anderson, *Guide to the Highlands and Western Islands of Scotland* (Inverness, 1863), p. 251.
28. Alexander Smith, *A Summer in Skye* (Hawick: Byways Books: 1983), p. 106.
29. William Knight, *Memoir of John Nichol* (Glasgow, 1896), p. 155.
30. *Black's Tourist Guide to Scotland* (Edinburgh, 1856), p. 395.
31. James Leitch, *St James Magazine* 15:3 (1866), p. 497.
32. *Inverness Advertiser*, 12 February 1856.
33. Charles Simpson Inglis, 'A Pedestrian Tour in the Highlands, 1856', *SMCJ* 18 (1927), p. 63.
34. C.R. Weld, *Two Months in the Highlands, Orcadia and Skye* (London, 1860), p. 356.
35. Ibid. p. 375.

Chapter 2

1. J. Veitch, 'In Memoriam: The Late Sheriff Nicolson', *SMCJ* 2 (1893), p. 257.
2. Ibid. p. 254.
3. Mary R.L. Bryce, *Memoir of John Veitch*, (Edinburgh, 1896), p. 95.
4. Alexander Nicolson, 'Skye and Sgurr nan Gillean in 1865', *SMCJ* 2 (1892), p. 104.
5. Sligachan Hotel Climbers' Book, Acc. 11538 (16), NLS.
6. *The Scotsman,* June 1872.
7. *Good Words,* July 1875.
8. Quoted in *TGSI* 52 (1980-82), p. 444.
9. Alexander Nicolson, *Verses*, (Edinburgh, 1893).
10. W. Naismith, letter to W. Douglas, 3 September 1892, Acc. 11538 (40), NLS.
11. J. Veitch, 'In Memoriam: The Late Sheriff Nicolson', *SMCJ* 2 (1893), p. 254.
12. James Leitch, 'Three Weeks in Skye') *St James's Magazine*, 15 (1866), p. 495
13. Charles Pilkington, 'The Black Coolins', *AJ* 13 (1888), p. 442.
14. Lawrence Pilkington, 'The Inaccessible Pinnacle', *SMCJ* 22 (1939), p. 63.
15. Charles Pilkington, 'The Black Coolins', *AJ* 13 (1888), p. 435.
16. Ibid. p. 435.
17. Ibid. p. 439.
18. A.H. Stocker, 'Alpine Notes', *AJ* 13 (1887), p. 265.
19. Reginald Broomfield, Sligachan Hotel Visitors' Book, 4 September 1886, Acc. 11538 (15), NLS
20. Sligachan Hotel Visitors' Book, Acc. 11538 (15), NLS.
21. Clinton Dent, *Mountaineering* (Badminton Library), (London, 1892), p. 344.
22. Charles Pilkington, 'The Black Coolins', *AJ* 13 (1888), p. 445.
23. Charles Pilkington, 'Sgurr Alasdair', *SMCJ* 1 (1891), p. 141.
24. W.P. Haskett Smith, *Climbing in the British Isles; Wales and Ireland*, (London, 1895), p. viii.
25. Sligachan Hotel Visitors' Book, Acc. 11538 (15), NLS.
26. Charles Pilkington, 'Sgurr Alasdair', *SMCJ* 1 (1891), p. 142.
27. J.N. Collie, 'On the Height of Some of the Black Cuchullins in Skye', *SMCJ* 2 (1893), p. 172.

Chapter 3

1. J.N. Collie, 'Ascent of the Dent du Requin', *AJ* 17 (1893), p. 18.
2. Ibid. p. 13.
3. G.W. Young, 'Obituary of N. Collie', *Himalayan Journal* 13 (1943), p. 116.
4. J.N. Collie, 'The Island of Skye', *AJ* 23 (1918), p. 163.
5. *The Times*, 3 September 1851.
6. Charles Weld, *Two Months in the Highlands, Orcadia and Skye,* (London,1860), p. 380.
7. H.T. Munro, 'Note to Prof. Heddle's Paper', *SMCJ* 5 (1898), p. 114.
8. Ashley Abraham, *Rock-Climbing in Skye,* (London, 1908), p. 195.
9. Sligachan Hotel Climbers' Book, Acc. 11538 (16), NLS.
10. J.N. Collie, 'On the Height of Some of the Black Cuchullins in Skye', *SMCJ* 2 (1893), p. 168.
11. Alexander Nicolson, 'Skye and Sgurr-nan-Gillean in 1865', *SMCJ* 2 (1892), p. 105.
12. G.W. Young, 'Norman Collie (In Memoriam)', *AJ* 54 (1943), p. 63.
13. J.N. Collie, 'The Island of Skye', *AJ* 32 (1918), p. 165.
14. Ibid. p. 166.
15. A.E. Maylard, 'A Day in the Cuchullins', *SMCJ* 2 (1892), p. 5.
16. A.E. Robertson, (A. Ernest Maylard: 1855-1947), *AJ* 56 (1948), p. 275.
17. W. Douglas, 'Island of Skye', *SMCJ* 9 (1907), p. 332.
18. A.E. Maylard, 'A Day in the Cuchullins', *SMCJ* 2 (1892), p. 3.
19. Thomas Fraser Campbell, 'In Memoriam: George Gilbert Ramsay', *SMCJ* 16 (1921), p. 23.
20. W. Brown, 'Coolins in 96', *SMCJ* 4 (1897), p. 204.
21. W. Naismith, letter to W. Douglas, 21 Sept 1896, Acc. 11538 (41), NLS
22. J.N. Collie, 'A Reverie', *SMCJ* 5 (1898), p. 99.
23. Norman Collie, 'On the Canadian Rocky Mountains North of the Yellowhead Pass', *AJ* 26 (1912), p. 16.
24. Martin Conway. Quoted in C. Bruce, *Himalayan Wanderer,* (London, 1934), p. 89.
25. Quoted in Derek Cooper, *Skye,* (London, 1970), p. 64.
26. G.W. Young, *AJ* 54 (1943), p. 62.
27. Gilbert Thomson, 'The Club in Retrospect', *SMCJ* 22 (1939), p. 21.
28. J.N. Collie, 'The Island of Skye', *AJ* 32 (1918), p.168.
29. Ibid. p.169.
30. Ibid. p. 169.
31. G.W. Young, *AJ* 54 (1943), p. 62.
32. Quoted in W.C. Taylor, *The Snows of Yesteryear,* (Toronto, 1973), p. 165.
33. Dorothy Una Ratcliffe, 'The Isle of Mist', *Irish Monthly* 50: 592, (October, 1922), p. 423.
34. Quoted in Victorian Studies, Vol. 37: 2 (Winter, 1989), p. 261.
35. J.N. Collie, 'John Mackenzie', *SMCJ* 20 (1933), p. 125.
36. Quoted in Affleck Grey, *The Grey Man of Ben MacDhui,* (Aberdeen, 1970), p. 3.
37. Hugh D. Welsh, 'John Norman Collie', *Cairngorm CJ* 15 (1939), p. 201.

Chapter 4

1. Malcolm Ferguson, *Rambles in Skye,* (Irvine, 1885), p. 83.
2. *Cornhill Magazine,* April 1895, p. 376.
3. Charles Pilkington, 'The Black Coolins', *AJ* 13 (1888), p. 445.
4. A.E. Maylard, 'A Day in the Cuchullins', *SMCJ* 1 (1892), p. 3.

5. C.F. Gordon Cumming, *In the Hebrides*, (London, 1886), p. 402.
6. W. Naismith, 'The Pinnacle Route', *SMCJ* 2 (1893), p. 287.
7. Charles Pilkington, 'Sgurr Alasdair', *SMCJ* 1 (1891), p. 142
8. Ashley Abraham, *Rock-Climbing in Skye*, (London, 1908), p. 37.
9. Clinton Dent, 'The Rocky Mountains of Skye', *AJ* 15 (1890), p. 436.
10. Ibid. p. 436.
11. J.H. Gibson, 'Easter in the Cuillins', *SMCJ* 2 (1893), p. 223.
12. Ibid. p. 217.
13. Ibid. p. 220
14. Ibid. p. 220.
15. Letter from W. Naismith to W. Douglas, 18 October 1892, Acc. 11538 (40), NLS.
16. Alexander Nicolson, 'Skye and Sgurr nan Gillean in 1865', *SMCJ* 2 (1892), p. 102.
17. *Murray's Handbook for Scotland*, (1894), p. 392.
18. A. H. H., 'A Day's Hill Climbing in Skye', *The Field*, 5 Oct 1895.
19. Sligachan Hotel Climbers' Book, Acc. 11538 (16), NLS.
20. F.W. Jackson, 'Clach Glas, Skye', *SMCJ* 4 (1896), p. 21.
21. Quoted in Finlay MacLeod (ed.), Togail Tir (Marking Time), (Stornoway, 1989), p. 98.
22. W. Douglas, 'Sgurr Dubh', *SMCJ* 4 (1896), p. 163.
23. Quoted in C. Ralling, *The Voyage of Charles Darwin*, (London, 1978), p. 23.
24. A.E. Robertson, 'Dr Alfred Harker', *SMCJ* 22 (1939), p. 143.
25. Quoted in Alfred Harker, *The West Highlands and the Hebrides*, (Memoir by Albert C. Seward), (Cambridge, 1941), p. xx.

Chapter 5
1. J. Rennie, 'Gars-bheinn, Skye', *SMCJ* 4 (1897), p. 177.
2. W. Douglas, 'Sgurr Dubh, Skye', *SMCJ* 4 (1896), p. 162.
3. W. Douglas, 'The Climbers' Camp at Coruisk', *SMCJ* 5 (1898), p. 13.
4. A.E. Robertson, Diaries, Volume 1, p. 64 (23 June 1896), Acc. 11538 (137), NLS.
5. A.H. MacKay, 'Vignettes of Earlier Climbers', *SMCJ* 24 (1950), p. 170.
6. A.H. MacKay, 'Vignettes of Earlier Climbers', *SMCJ* 24 (1950), p. 171.
7. Diary of Arthur Russell, 'Summer Holiday 1898'. Personal communication with George R. Russell.
8. Ashley Abraham, *'Rock-Climbing in Skye'*, (London, 1908), p. viii.
9. G.D. Valentine, 'At Sligachan, the Classic Age', *SMCJ* 23 (1945), p. 236.
10. John Buchan, 'The Knees of the Gods', *SMCJ* 23 (1943), p. 83.
11. John Buchan, *Memory Hold the Door*, (London, 1940), p. 133.
12. John Buchan, *Mr. Standfast*, (New York, 1919).
13. John Buchan, 'In the Heart of the Coolins', *Blackwood's Magazine*, 1906, p. 760.
14. John Buchan, *The Three Hostages*, (Boston, 1924).
15. A.E. Robertson, 'Alpine Mountaineering in Scotland', *Chambers Journal*, (1906).
16. W.N. Ling, 'Harold Raeburn', *SMCJ* 22 (1939), p. 47.
17. W.N. Ling, 'Easter (1903) in Skye, (1) Sligachan to Glen Brittle by the Dubh Ridges', *SMCJ* 7 (1903), p. 302.
18. Harold Raeburn, 'Ridge-walking on the Coolins at Easter, 1905', *SMCJ* 9 (1906), p. 64.
19. 'Harry Walker: In Memoriam', *SMCJ* 14 (1917), p. 30.

Chapter 6
1. Ashley Abraham, *Rock-Climbing in Skye*, (London, 1908), p. viii.

2. G.W. Young, 'Ashley Abraham', *AJ* 58 (1952), p. 404.
3. Ashley Abraham, *Rock-Climbing in Skye,* (London, 1908), p. 102.
4. Ibid. p. 214.
5. Ibid. p. 275.
6. George Abraham, *The Complete Mountaineer,* (London, 1907), p. 252.
7. Harold Raeburn, *Mountaineering Art,* (London, 1920), p. 19.
8. Francis Greig, 'Sgurr Alasdair', *SMCJ* 11 (1911), p. 348.
9. Ashley Abraham, *Rock-Climbing in Skye,* (London, 1908), p. 231.
10. Ibid. p. 188.
11. Ibid. p. 129.
12. Ibid. p. 131.
13. Ibid. p. 136.
14. J.M.A. Thomson, 'A Week's Exploration on the Coolin', *AJ* 26 (1912), p. 30.
15. Ashley Abraham, *Rock-Climbing in Skye,* (London, 1908), p. 236.
16. Ibid. p. 250.
17. Ibid. p. 259.
18. Enid Abraham, Transcript of interview, Ambleside Oral History Group, 1999. www.aohg.org.
19. Ashley Abraham, *Rock-Climbing in Skye,* (London, 1908), p. 237.
20. W. Naismith, 'Review: Rock-Climbing in Skye', *SMCJ* 10 (1908), p.175.

Chapter 7
1. H.C. Boyd, 'Midsummer in Glen Brittle', *Cairngorm CJ* 6 (1909), p. 60.
2. W. Heap, 'A New Climb in Skye', *Rucksack CJ* 1 (1904-05), p. 13-17.
3. A.G. Woodhead, 'In the Southern Cuillins', *Rucksack CJ* 1 (1907), p. 81.
4. A.E. Barker, 'A Day's Walk in Skye', *Rucksack CJ* 1(1910), p. 263.
5. Sligachan Hotel Climbers' Book, Acc. 11538 (16), NLS.
6. L.G. Shadbolt, 'Alasdair McLaren (1880-1950)', *SMCJ* 24 (1951), pp. 339-341.
7. W. Brown, 'The Coolins in 96', *SMCJ* 4 (1897), p. 195.
8. John Buchan, 'In the Heart of the Coolins', *Blackwoods Magazine,* 1906, p. 755.
9. Ashley Abraham, *Rock-Climbing in Skye,* (London, 1908), p. 158.
10. L.G. Shadbolt, 'The First Traverse', *SMCJ* 30 (1972), p. 87.
11. A.P. Abraham, 'Coolin from End to End', *FRCCJ* 2 (1911), p.184.
12. G.W. Young 'J.M. Archer Thomson', *AJ* 27 (1913), p.70.
13. J.M.A. Thomson, 'New Climbs in the Island of Skye'*, SMCJ* 12 (1911), p.31.
14. E.W. Steeple, 'New Expeditions in the Coolin', *Climbers' CJ* 1 (New Series) 1912, p. 26.
15. E.W. Steeple, 'Wanderings in Skye', *FRCCJ* 4 (1917-18), p. 134.
16. G. Barlow and E.W. Steeple, 'The Chasm of Sgurr nan Eag', *SMCJ* 15 (1920), p. 257.
17. W. Wallwork, 'Extracts from a Skye Diary', *Rucksack CJ* 3 (1916), p. 111.
18. Quoted in Leonard Sellar, *The Hood Battalion, (*London, 1995).
19. D.R. Pye, 'A Fortnight in Skye', *SMCJ* 15 (1919), p.137.
20. Ibid., p.144.
21. G.E. Howard, 'The Rain of Peace', *SMCJ* 15 (1918), p.23.

Chapter 8
1. Quoted in R. Clark, E. C. Pyatt, *Mountaineering in Britain,* (London, 1957), p. 153.
2. C.F. Holland, 'Air Raid Symphony', *FRCC Journal* 35 (1941), p. 23.
3. H. Carr, 'A New Climb on the Cioch', *Rucksack CJ* 4 (1920), p. 104.

4. T.H. Somervell, 'Main Ridge Traverse', *SMCJ* 15 (1919), p. 342.
5. Sligachan Hotel Climbers' Book, Acc. 11538 (16), NLS.
6. Geoff Pigott, letter to the author, July 2001.
7. A.S. Pigott and J. Wilding, *Rucksack CJ* 9 (1941), p. 313.
8. Dorothy Pilley, *Climbing Days,* (London, 1935), p. 101.
9. E.W. Steeple, G. Barlow and H. MacRobert, *Island of Skye,* (Edinburgh, 1923), p. 95.
10. E.W. Steeple, 'Some New Climbs from Glen Brittle', *SMCJ* 16 (1922), p. 160.
11. *American Alpine Club Journal*, 1957, p. 217.
12. J.H.B. Bell, *Progress in Mountaineering,* (Edinburgh, 1950), p. 176.
13. J.H.B. Bell, Diaries, Acc. 9960, NLS.
14. J.H.B. Bell, Diaries, Acc 9960, NLS.
15. J.H.B. Bell, *Progress in Mountaineering,* (Edinburgh, 1950), p. 123.
16. J.H.B. Bell, *Progress in Mountaineering,* (Edinburgh, 1950), p. 184.
17. Quoted in Jan Levi, *And No-One Woke up Dead*, (Ernest Press, Glasgow, 2006), p. 164.
18. Quoted in Shirley Angell, *Pinnacle Club,* 1988, p. 31.
19. Isabel Dickson, 'In Memoriam: Mrs Chisholm', *LSCCJ,* 1952, 50.
20. E.W. Steeple, G. Barlow and H. MacRobert, *The Island of Skye,* (Edinburgh, 1948), 131.
21. G.M. Fraser, 'The Skye Relief Fund', *SMCJ* 17 (1924), p. 41.

Chapter 9
1. Billy Kay, *Odyssey*, (Edinburgh, 1980), p. 82.
2. H.V. Morton, *In Search of Scotland,* (London, 1929), 206. Copyright © Marion Wasdell & Brian de Villiers.
3. E. Wood-Johnson, 'The Fishing Line', *FRCC Journal,* 1981, p. 195.
4. A. Horne, H.V. Hughes, 'The Amphitheatre Wall', *SMCJ* 20 (1933), p. 21.
5. Alex Small, 'Hugh MacCrae', *SMCJ* 31 (1978), p. 436.
6. 'Review: Mountain Days in the Isle of Skye', *AJ* 46 (1934), p. 436.
7. The Spectator. Reprinted with permission from The Spectator (1828) Ltd.
8. *Hansard*. Commons, 16 December 1936.
9. J.H.B. Bell, Diaries, Acc 9960, NLS.
10. J.E.B. Wright, *Mountain Days in the Isle of Skye,* (Edinburgh,1934), p. 187.
11. J.G. Dent, 'A Short Cut to Glen Brittle', *Rucksack CJ* 8 (1936), p. 158.
12. J.D. Wilson, 'The Spring Cuillin', *SMCJ* 23 (1943), p. 63.
13. R.M. Lawrie, St Andrews' University Mountaineering Club Logbook, U7911/Mountaineering, Volume 4, p. 8. .
14. Quoted in Roy Humble, *The Voice of the Hills,* (Edinburgh, 1995), p. 42.
15. B.H. Humble, *The Cuillin of Skye,* (London, 1952), p. 113.
16. W.H. Murray, *Mountaineering in Scotland,* (London, 1947), p. 1.
17. Ibid. p. 4. 4 lines.
18. Quoted in Affleck Grey, *The Big Grey Man of Ben Macdhui,* (Aberdeen, 1970), p. 55.
19. B.H. Humble, 'To a Prisoner of War', *The Field,* 2 October 1943.

Chapter 10
1. Donald Gillies, *Annals of Skye,* July 1945, p. 44.
2. Grampian Club records, Dundee University archives, MS 138/13/1
3. J. Nimlin, 'Mountain Howffs', *SMCJ* 24 (1948), p. 2.
4. M. O'Hara, 'Night and Day', *Cambridge Mountaineering,* 1956, p. 21.
5. Ashley Abraham, *Rock-Climbing in Skye,* (London, 1908), p. 127.

6. Hamish Nicol, Deep Gash Gully, *Alpine Annual,* (London, 1951), p. 139.
7. Richard Brooke, letter to author, June 2002.
8. W.P.L. Thomson, St Andrews University MC Logbook, Volume 11, p. 16. U7911/Mountaineering
9. A.C. Cain, unpublished manuscript.
10. Ian McNaught-Davis, letter to author, June 2001.
11. Iain Ogilvie, Acc. 11851 (3), NLS.
12. C.M. Dixon, 'The Forgotten Corrie', *SMCJ* 25 (1952), p. 6.
13. W.D. Brooker, personal communication with author, 2002.
14. C.M. Dixon, personal communication with author, 2002.
15. C.M. Dixon, 'The Forgotten Corrie Again', *SMCJ* 25 (1955), p. 308.
16. P. Walsh, letter to author, July, 2001.
17. Charles L. Donaldson, extract from diary, through correspondence with C.J.M. Loftus.
18. Robin Smith, 'A Week in the Hills', *SMCJ* 27 (1961), p. 174.
19. Nea Morin, *A Woman's Reach,* (London, 1968), p. 178.
20. John Temple, 'Failing on Vulcan Wall', *SMCJ* 41 (2010), p12.

Chapter 11
1. Chris Bonington, letter to author, October 2001.
2. Richard Brooke, letter to author, March 2002.
3. Tom Patey, 'The First Winter Traverse of the Cuillin Ridge', *SMCJ* 28 (1965), p. 69.
4. H. MacInnes, 'The Last Great Problem', *Scotland's Magazine,* July 1965, p. 22.
5. Des Rubens, 'Space-time Excerpts from the Hills', *SMCJ* 32 (1987), p. 420.
6. John Harwood, personal communication with author, August 2001.
7. John Harwood, personal communication with author, August 2001.
8. (The Times, 7 June 1965.)
9. John Harwood, personal communication with author, August 2001.
10. Jeff Connor, *Creagh Dhu Climber,* (Glasgow, 1999), p. 112.
11. Jim Renny, letter to author, July 2001.
12. John Harwood, personal communication with author, August 2001.
13. Phil Gribbon, St Andrews University Mountaineering Club Logbook, 14, p. 110. U7911/Mountaineering.
14. Dave Alcock, letter to author, March 2002.
15. A.C. Cain, unpublished manuscript.
16. Nunn, Paul, 'Desert Island Climbs, Megaton', *Crags* 17 (1972), p. 28.
17. Ibid., p. 28.
18. Nunn, Paul, 'Skye Wars', in Chris Bonington (ed.), *Great Climbs,* (London, 1994), p. 65.

Chapter 12
1. Cameron Lees, letter to author, July 2001.
2. Rob Milne, letter to author, June 2002.
3. Gary Latter, letter to author, August 2001.
4. Rab Anderson, letter to author, July 2001.
5. Colin Moody, letter to author, July 2001.
6. Kevin Howett, *On the Edge* 115, p. 78.
7. Gary Latter, letter to author, August 2001.
8. Charles L. Donaldson, extract from diary, through correspondence with C.J.M. Loftus.
9. Martin Moran, letter to author, April, 2002.

REFERENCES

10. Mike Lates, letter to the author, 2002.
11. Paul Rasher, 'Plane Crash at Camasunary', *Mountain Bothy Association Journal*, No. 67, December 1983.
12. Martin Moran, letter to author, April 2002.
13. A. Hyslop, *Climber and Rambler,* August, 1995.
14. Blair Fyffe, personal communication with author, June 2012.
15. Es Tressider, 'Cuillin Ridge Record', www.es-on-ice.co.uk, 5 May 2007.
16. Greg Strange, letter to author, March 2002.
17. Ken Wilson & B. Newman, (eds), *Extreme Rock,* (London, 1987), p. 13.
18. Vic Saunders, letter to author, May, 2002.
19. Martin Moran, letter to author, April, 2002.
20. Andy Nisbet, letter to author, July 2001.
21. Mick Fowler, letter to author, May 2002.
22. Dave Ritchie, letter to author, June 2002.
23. Dave Ritchie, letter to author, June 2002.
24. Quoted in Simon Richardson, 'Scottish Winter Notes 2007/8', *SMCJ* 40 (2008), p. 189.
25. Quoted in Simon Richardson, 'Scottish Winter Notes 2007/8', *SMCJ* 40 (2008), p. 189.
26. Ian Parnell, 'Northern Lights', *Climb*, December 2010, p. 25.
27. Simon Richardson, www.scottishwinter.com, 12 January 2010.
28. Greg Boswell's Blog, 3 December 2010.
29. Guy Robertson, www.scottishwinter.com, 9 December 2010.
30. Pete MacPherson, www.scottishwinter.com, 3 December 2010.

SOURCES

Chapter 1
(Louis Albert Necker), Obituary, *Inverness Courier,* 5 Dec 1861.
'Thomas Grierson', *Cairngorm CJ,* XI (1920), p. 19.
Clarke, R.W., *The Victorian Mountaineers* (London, 1953), p. 45.
Cooper, Derek, *Road to the Isles* (London, 1979).
Douglas, W. (ed.), 'Early Descriptions of Skye', *SMCJ,* V (1899), pp. 205-230.
Drummond, Hugh, 'Scientist of the Mountains', *Scotland's Magazine,* December 1964.
Eyles, V.A., 'Louis Albert Necker, of Geneva, and his Geological Map of Scotland', *Trans. Edinburgh Geological Society,* XIV, pp. 93-127.
Finley, Gerald, *Landscapes of Memory; Turner as Illustrator to Scott* (London, 1980).
Forbes, J.D., 'Louis Albert Necker', *Proceedings of Edinburgh Royal Society,* V (1863).
Forbes, J.D., *Travels Through the Alps of Savoy,* (Edinburgh, 1843).
Geikie, A., *Scottish Reminiscences* (Glasgow, 1904)
Grenier, Katherine Haldane, *Tourism and Identity in Scotland, 1770-1914* (Aldershot: Ashgate, 2005)
Harker, Alfred, 'On Some Old Maps', *SMCJ,* XIV (1916), pp. 65-71.
Henderson, Philip, *Swinburne, Portrait of a Poet,* (London, 1974).
Hobsbaum, Philip, 'Gift in Prison', *Scottish Book Collector,* VI (1999), pp. 14-16.
Hunter, James, *On the Other Side of Sorrow,* (Edinburgh, 1995).
Samuel Johnson, *A Journey to the Western Islands of Scotland* (London: Penguin, 1984)
MacCulloch, John, *A Description of the Western Islands of Scotland,* (Glasgow, 1819).
MacCulloch, John, 'Sketch of the Mineralogy of Sky', *Trans. Geological Society of London,* I (1816), pp. 1-111.
MacCulloch, John, 'Corrections and Additions to the Sketch of the Mineralogy of Sky', *Trans. Geological Society of London,* III (1817), pp. 156-192.
MacTaggart, K., 'Challenging Summits', *Discover Scotland,* III (1990).
Martin, Martin, *A Description of the Western Islands of Scotland, circa 1695,* (London, 1716).
Mitchell, Ian, 'Putting the Cuillin on the Map', *Climber Magazine,* May 1995.
Mitchell, Ian, *Scotland's Mountains before the Mountaineers,* (Edinburgh, 1983).
Monro, Donald, *Description of the Western Isles of Scotland,* (Edinburgh, 1805).
Nicolson, Alexander, 'Alexander Smith', *Good Words,* 5 Jan 1867.
Reed, Laurance, *The Soay of our Forefathers,* (Edinburgh, 2002).
Shairp, J C., Tait, P.G., & Reilly, A.A., *Life and Letters Of James David Forbes,* 1873.
Smart, Robert N., *An Index to the Correspondence and Papers of James David Forbes (1808-1868),* St Andrews University Library, St Andrews, 1968.
Smith, Alexander, 'How we went to Skye', *Blackwoods Magazine,* February 1859, pp. 155-164.
Smith, Alexander, 'Rambling about the Hebrides', *Temple Bar,* March 1862, pp. 481-491.
Smith, G.A., 'The Work of Prof. James D. Forbes', *SMCJ,* III (1895), pp. 309-315.
Stevens, E.H., 'James David Forbes', *AJ,* LIV (1944), pp. 372-378.
Valentine, G.D., 'Sligachan and Some Early Visitors', *SMCJ,* XXIII (1944), pp. 117-133.

Chapter 2

(Alexander Nicolson), Obituary in *Glasgow Herald*, 13 Jan. 1893.
(Charles Pilkington), Obituary in *SMCJ*, XV (1920), pp. 259-61.
(Lawrence Pilkington), Obituary in *SMCJ*, XXIII (1942), pp. 41-42.
'Henry Chichester Hart', *Irish Naturalist*, XVIII (1908), pp. 249-254.
'Knight's Peak, Sgurr nan Gillean', *SMCJ*, XIV (1916), p. 94.
Brown, H.M., 'Remembering a Cuillin Pioneer', *SMCJ*, XXXV (1995), pp. 620-624.
Cameron, A.D., *Listen to the Crofters, the Napier Commission and Crofting a Century Ago*, (Stornoway, 1986).
Evidence taken by Her Majesty's Commissioners of Inquiry into the Condition of the Crofters and Cottars in the Highlands and Islands of Scotland, Volume I, (London, 1884).
Fionn (Henry Whyte), 'Gaelic Men of Letters', *Celtic Monthly*, XVL (1908), pp. 91-93.
Gordon-Cumming, Constance F., 'Notes of a Wanderer in Skye', *Temple Bar*, 1883, pp. 75-92.
Hart, Henry Chichester, 'Arabis Alpina in Skye', *Journal of Botany*, 1887.
Heddle, M. F., *The Mineralogy of Scotland*, (Edinburgh, 1901).
Humble, B.H., 'In the Beginning', *Climber and Rambler*, July 1974.
Knight, W., *Some Nineteenth Century Scotsmen*, (Edinburgh, 1903), pp. 363-367.
Mackenzie, Alexander, *Isle of Skye in 1882-83*, (Inverness, 1883).
Mitchell, Ian., *Mountain Footfalls*, (Edinburgh, 1996).
Naismith, W., 'Three Days Among the Cuchullins', *SMCJ*, I (1891), pp. 56-62.
Naismith, W., 'Bidein Druim na Ramh', *SMCJ*, XII (1912), pp.173-176.
Nicolson Alexander, *The Scotsman* 1872: June 14, June 25, July 16.
Nicolson, Alexander, *Good Words*, 1875, pp. 344-350, 384-392, 457-462, 561-568.
Nicolson, Alexander, *Gaelic Proverbs*, Ian MacDonald (ed.), (Edinburgh, 1996).
Nicolson, Alexander, *History of Skye*, (Portree, 1994).
Willink, Henry, 'An Early Climb on Blaven', *SMCJ*, XVI (1922), 171-173.

Chapter 3

'In Memoriam: W.W. King, (1862-1959)', *SMCJ*, XXVII (1960), pp. 81-86.
Bell, J.H.B., 'Prof. J. Norman Collie', *SMCJ*, XXII (1939), pp. 80-81.
Bicknell, P., *AJ*, LIV (1944), pp. 339-347.
Brunskill, W., 'Sgurr Dearg Pinnacle, Skye', *SMCJ*, II (1892), pp. 134-135.
Clark, R.W. & Pyatt, E.C., *Mountaineering in Britain*, (London, 1957).
Clark, R.W., *Six Great Mountaineers*, (London, 1956).
Collie, J.N. & Stutfield, H.E.M., *Climbs and Exploration in the Canadian Rockies*, (London, 1903).
Collie, J.N., 'A Chuilionn', *SMCJ*, IV (1897), pp. 259-266.
Collie, J.N., 'Colin Bent Philip (1856-1937): In Memoriam', *SMCJ*, XIX (1932), pp. 408-409.
Collie, J.N., 'Dreams', *Cairngorm CJ*, XV (1942), pp. 205-215.
Collie, J.N., 'Independence', *Cairngorm CJ*, XV (1939), pp. 15-17.
Collie, J.N., 'John Mackenzie', *AJ*, IVL (1934), p. 198.
Collie, J.N., 'Reminiscences', *FRCCJ*, VII (1926), pp.214-218.
Collie, J.N., *Climbing on the Himalaya and other Mountain Ranges*, (Edinburgh, 1902).
Garden, Wm., 'Norman Collie: In Memoriam', *SMCJ*, XXIII (1943), p. 95.
King, W. W., 'Some Early Climbs in the Cuillin', *SMCJ*, XXVI (1956), pp. 37-39.
MacTaggart, Ken, 'Scotland's Last Mountain', *SMCJ*, XXXVI (1997), pp. 234-239.

McOwan, Rennie, 'Cuillin Climbing Companions', *Scots Magazine,* March 2000, pp. 240-245.
Mill, Christine, *Norman Collie, A Life in Two Worlds*, (Aberdeen, 1987).
Mummery A. F., *My Climbs in the Alps and Caucasus,* (Oxford, 1936).
Pilkington-White, T. Col., 'Camped Out under the Cuillins', *Blackwoods Magazine,* 1889, pp. 211-222.
Robertson, A.E., 'A.E. Maylard 1855-1947', *SMCJ,* XXIV (1948), pp. 61-63.
Slater, S.D., 'Alfred Ernest Maylard (1855-1917) Glasgow Surgeon Extraordinaire', *Scottish Medical Journal,* 1994, pp. 86-90.
Smith, Edwin W., 'The Past President: H. D. Welsh', *Cairngorm CJ,* XVI (1946), pp. 57-59.
Welsh, Hugh D., 'Symphony', *Cairngorm CJ,* XV (1939), pp. 149-160.

Chapter 4
'Dr Alfred Harker, F. R. S.', *Geological Magazine,* 4 July 1917, pp. 289-293.
'W.C. Slingsby: In Memoriam', *Yorkshire Ramblers' CJ,* VI (1930), pp. 66-69.
Adamson, Prof., 'Hill-Climbing in Skye', *Cairngorm CJ,* I (1895), pp. 181-191.
Booth, Martin, *A Magick Life,* (London, 2000).
Douglas, W., 'Names, Heights, and Positions of the Coolin Peaks', *SMCJ,* IV (1897), pp. 209-213.
Geikie, A., *The Ancient Volcanoes of Britain,* (London, 1897).
Harker, Alfred, 'Glaciated Valleys in the Cuillins, Skye', *Geological Magazine,* VI (1899), pp. 196-201.
Harker, Alfred, 'Ice-erosion in the Cuillin Hills, Skye', *Trans. Royal Soc. Edin,* XL (1901-02), p. 239.
Harker, Alfred, 'Notes on the Cuillin Hills', *SMCJ,* VI (1900), pp. 6-13.
Harker, Alfred, 'On Some Old Maps', *SMCJ,* XIV (1916), pp. 65-71.
Harker, Alfred, *Tertiary Igneous Rocks of Skye,* (HMSO, 1904).
Oldroyd, David R., *The Highland Controversy,* (London, 1990).
Phillip, C.B., 'Nomenclature of the Cuillin', *SMCJ,* XIV (1916), pp. 11-18.
Phillip, C.B., Letter to William Douglas, *SMCJ,* VIII (1904), p. 137.
Tough, W., 'Sgurr nan Gillean', *Cairngorm CJ,* I (1894), pp. 57-64.

Chapter 5
'Fatality on Sgurr nan Gillean', *Cairngorm CJ,* IV (1903), p. 237.
'Sligachan Easter Meet, 1905', *SMCJ,* VIII (1905), p. 251.
Baker, E.A., 'A Walk Over Blaven', *Climbers' CJ,* II (1900), pp. 108-110.
Barclay, W., 'On the Ridges of the Coolins', *Cairngorm CJ,* V (1906), pp. 187-195.
Barrow, Walter, 'The 1897 Meet on S.S. *Erne*' *SMCJ,* XXII (1939), pp. 29-31.
Bell, J.H.B, 'A. E. Robertson, 1870-1958', *SMCJ,* XXVI (1959), pp. 362-366.
Brown, W., 'The Coolins in 96', *SMCJ,* IV (1897), pp. 193-208.
Clark, J., *Pictures and Memories,* (Edinburgh, 1938).
Clark, W. Inglis, 'Stormy June Days in Skye and on Ben Nevis', *SMCJ,* VI (1901), pp. 218-225.
Clark, W. Inglis, 'The Coolins (Notes)', *SMCJ,* V (1898), pp. 144-145.
Crocket, K.V. & Fowler, J.R.R., 'Of Beer and Boats', *SMCJ,* XXXVI (1997), pp. 380-383.
Dalton, Ida F., 'First Recollections of Skye, 1893', *LSCCJ,* 1929, p. 61.
Dangar, D.F.O. & Blakeney T. S., 'John Thom: Mountaineer', *AJ,* LXV (1960-62), pp. 199-

207.
Douglas, W., 'Sir Hugh T. Munro: In Memoriam', *SMCJ*, XV (1919), pp. 214-219.
Garden, W., 'Mr. Whincup's Fatal Accident in the Coolins', *SMCJ*, VII (1902), pp. 41-42.
Gibbs, G. Bennett, 'August at Sligachan', *SMCJ*, V (1899), pp. 164-175.
Gillion, Stair, 'Lord Tweedsmuir: In Memoriam', *SMCJ*, XXII (1940), pp. 200-205.
Glover, G.T., 'William Inglis Clark', *AJ*, VL (1933), p. 148.
Hankinson, Alan, *Mountain Men,* (London, 1977).
Jacob, Mike, 'Harold Raeburn, the Final Journey', *SMCJ*, XL (2008), pp. 41-51.
Leicester, Mark, 'Correspondence to Fred Jackson', *SMCJ*, VIII (1905), pp. 84-85.
Ling, W.N., 'Harold Raeburn', *AJ*, XXXIX (1927), pp. 126-129.
Ling, W.N., 'Harold Raeburn', *SMCJ*, XVIII (1927), pp. 26-31.
Maylard, A.E., 'Only a Beautiful Day on the Hills', *SMCJ*, VIII (1905), pp. 299-303.
Orr, Donald M., 'An Expert Cragsman', *SMCJ*, XXXVI (1997), pp. 240-243.
Parker, J.A., 'Sir Hugh T. Munro', *SMCJ*, XXII (1939), p. 45.
Dualchas, Portree.
Penny, Scott Moncrieff, 'Cloudless March Days in Skye', *SMCJ*, VI (1901), pp. 167-171.
Raeburn, Harold, 'Skye - The Castles from Harta Corrie', *SMCJ*, IX (1906), pp. 101-102.
Robertson, A.E., 'Mountain Memories', *SMCJ*, XXIV (1949), pp. 81-84.
Smith, Janet Adam, *John Buchan,* (London, 1979).
Smith, W.C., 'Sligachan Meet, Easter, 1903', *SMCJ*, VII (1903), pp. 280-284.
Thompson, R.E., 'A Fortnight in Skye', *Climbers' CJ*, II (1899), pp. 25-31.
Tough, Wm., 'Bidein-nan-Ramh', *SMCJ*, III (1895), pp. 284-287.
Williams, Sidney, 'Blaven', *SMCJ*, VI (1901), pp. 129-130.

Chapter 6
'Review; Rock Climbing in Skye', *Rucksack CJ*, I (March 1909), p. 198.
'Review; Rock Climbing in Skye', *AJ*, XXIV (1948).
Abraham, A.P., 'Henry Harland', *FRCCJ*, XV (1908), pp. 280-281.
Abraham, A.P., 'Rock Climbing in Britain', *Wide World Magazine,* March 1899.
Abraham, G.A., 'Our Adventures in the Black Coolin', *World Wide Magazine,* IXXX, 1912.
Abraham, G.A., 'Photographing Britain's Mountains', *Cassell's Magazine,* September 1904.
Abraham, G.A., 'Virgin Peaks for the Mountaineer within our own Shores - Scaling the Peaks of the Isle of Skye', *The Sphere,* 21 March 1908, pp. 249-252.
Abraham, G.A., *British Mountain Climbs,* (London, 1909).
Abraham, G.A., *Modern Mountaineering,* (London, 1933).
Abraham, G.A., *On Alpine Heights and British Crags,* (London, 1919).
Abraham, G.A., 'My Most Thrilling British Climbs', *Fry's Magazine,* April 1912.
Abraham, G.A., *Mountain Adventures at Home and Abroad,* (New York, 1910).
Griffin, A.H., 'The Keswick Brothers', *Climber and Rambler,* September 1975.

Chapter 7
Abraham, G.A., *Modern Mountaineering,* (London, 1933).
Arthur, Allan, 'Some Memories and Long Days among the Scottish Mountains during the Last Fifty Years', *SMCJ*, XXIII (1944), pp. 153-161.
Bagley, A.L., 'The Western Buttress of Sgurr Sgumain', *FRCCJ*, III (1914), pp. 74-77.
Barclay, W., 'On the Ridges of the Coolins', *Cairngorm CJ*, V (1907), p. 195.
Brockbank, Philip, 'A Short History of the Rucksack Club, 1902-1918', *Rucksack CJ*, 1977, pp. 78-99.

Buchanan, J.H., 'Some Memories of Skye', *SMCJ*, XIV (1917), pp. 170-177.
Burrell, J. & Cross, C.N., 'Sron na Ciche, Trap Face Route', *SMCJ*, XIII (1915), p. 176.
Carr H.R.C. & Lister, G.A., *The Mountains of Snowdonia,* (London, 1925), p. 76.
Clark, R. & Pyatt, E.C., *Mountaineering in Britain,* (London, 1957).
Doughty, A.H., 'Guy Barlow', *FRCCJ*, 1969, pp. 177-178.
Gibbs, G. Bennett, 'A Trip to Sligachan and Glen Brittle', *SMCJ*, X (1908), pp. 47-50.
Gimson, A.M., 'Camping in Skye', *Climbers CJ*, IX (1906), pp. 98-104.
Greig, Francis, 'Sgurr Alasdair', *SMCJ*, XI (1911), pp. 344-350.
Greig, Francis, Midsummer Days in Skye, *SMCJ*, X (1909), pp. 199-214.
Hirst, J., 'Sassenachs in Skye', *SMCJ*, XIV (1916), pp. 1-6.
King, W.W., 'SMC. in Skye in 1908', *SMCJ*, X (1909), p. 226.
Lamb, Robertson, 'Notes', *SMCJ*, IX (1907), p. 288.
Laycock, J., 'Impressions of Skye', *FRCCJ*, III (1914), pp. 61-64.
Levack, John R., 'A Week's Climbing in Skye', *Cairngorm CJ*, VI (1908), pp. 87-94.
Levack, John R., 'A Week at Sligachan', *Cairngorm CJ*, VII (1909), pp. 19-26.
MacRobert, H. & E. W. Steeple, *SMCJ*, XXII (1941), pp. 384-385.
MacRobert, H. & Steeple, E. W., 'Skye (Notes)', *SMCJ*, XIII (1914), pp. 58-59.
MacRobert, H., 'Glen Brittle in June', *SMCJ*, IX (1907), pp. 159-166.
MacRobert, H., 'Night up There', *SMCJ*, XXII (1941), pp. 280-282.
Parker, J.A., 'The Cuillins in a Week', *SMCJ*, X (1908), pp. 131-138.
Pye, David, *George Leigh Mallory,* (Oxford, 1927).
Robertson, David, *George Mallory,* (London, 1969).
Shadbolt, L.G., 'Early Days in Skye', *Climbers CJ*, 1956, pp. 190-196.
Shadbolt, L.G., 'The Cuillin Main Ridge', *SMCJ*, XI (1911), pp. 326-329.
Steeple, E.W., 'A Week in Coire Ghreadaidh', *Rucksack CJ*, II (1911), pp. 5-15.
Steeple, E.W., 'June Days in the Coolins', *Climbers CJ*, XII (1909), pp. 15-23.
Steeple, E.W., 'The Gullies of Coire an Uaigneis', *SMCJ*, XIII (1914), pp. 13-16.
Steeple, E.W., 'The South-East Gully of Sgurr a' Mhadaidh, Skye', *Climbers' CJ*, XIII (1910), pp. 34-36.
Steeple, E.W., 'Wanderings in Skye', *FRCCJ*, IV (1917-18), pp. 129-136.
Thomson, J.C., 'Wanderings on the Cuillin', *SMCJ*, XII (1912), pp. 129-136.
Thomson, J., 'The Eastern Faces of Blaven and Clach Glas, Skye', *SMCJ*, XIII (1915), pp. 282-286.
Treacher, Keith, *Siegfried Herford, An Edwardian Rock-climber,* (Glasgow, 2000).
Wallwork, W., 'A First Visit to Glen Brittle', *Rucksack CJ*, II (1914), pp. 290-295.
Yeld, G., 'The Cuillin Hills', *AJ*, XXIII (1907), pp. 611-616.
Young, G.W., *Mountain Craft,* (London, 1920).
Young, G.W., *Mountains with a Difference,* (London, 1951).
Young, G.W., Noyce, W. F. & Sutton, G (eds.), *Snowdon Biography,* (London, 1957), p. 37.

Chapter 8
'C.D. Frankland', *Yorkshire Ramblers' CJ*, V (1929), pp. 311-313.
'Extracts from Sligachan Climbers' Book', *SMCJ*, XVII (1925), p. 220.
'Summer Meet 1924, Skye', *SMCJ*, XVII (1924), pp. 91-93.
Abraham, G.A., *Modern Mountaineering,* (London, 1933).
Allan, Elizabeth, *Burn on the Hill,* (Beauly, 1995).
Baker, E.A., *British Highlands with Rope and Rucksack,* (London, 1933).
Barker, M., 'Camp at Loch Coruisk', *Yorkshire Ramblers' CJ*, V (1922-24), pp. 198-203.

Barker, M., 'The Third Round, or Ridge-Walking in Skye', *FRCCJ*, VII (1926), pp. 219-227.
Barlow, G., 'The Relative Heights of the Cuillin Peaks', *SMCJ*, XVI (1923), pp. 244-249.
Bell, J.H., 'Skye Notes', *SMCJ*, XVI (1921), pp. 88-90.
Bell, J.H., 'The Dubhs and Sgurr Alasdair from Coruisk', *SMCJ*, XVI (1921), pp. 4-11.
Bower, G., 'Sgurr Alasdair and Sron na Ciche', *SMCJ*, XV (1920), pp. 284-286.
Calvert, Harry, *Smythe's Mountains*, (London, 1988).
Carr, H.R.C., '1919, C. F. Holland's Year', *Climbers' CJ*, 1981, pp. 75-80.
Giveen, F.W., 'The Fourth Pinnacle, Sgurr nan Gillean', *SMCJ*, XVIII (1927), p. 122.
Goodfellow, B.R., 'The Cuillin Ridge', *Rucksack CJ*, V (1925), pp. 261-264.
Goodfellow, B.R., 'Wanderings in Scotland', *Oxford and Cambridge Mountaineering*, 1924, pp. 26-34.
Greene, Raymond, *Moments of Being*, (London, 1974).
Harrison, Alex., 'A Pilgrimage to Skye', *SMCJ*, XVIII (1927), pp. 19-22.
Hartley, H., 'Alfred Sefton Pigott', *AJ*, 1980, p. 262.
Howard, G.E., 'Summer Meet at Sligachan', *SMCJ*, XV (1919), pp. 227-230.
Hughes, H.V., 'A New Gully Climb on Sgurr Sgumain' *SMCJ*, XX (1934), pp. 190-191.
Hutchison, A.G., 'Summer Days in Skye', *SMCJ*, XVII (1926), pp. 329-336.
Kirkman, N.F., 'Alfred Sefton Pigott', *Rucksack CJ*, 1979, pp. 69-73.
Lüscher, E., 'A Summer Holiday in Scotland', *SMCJ*, XVI (1922), pp. 99-106.
Odell, N., 'Theodore Howard Somervell', *AJ*, 1976, pp. 272-273.
Parry, C.W., 'Four Novices in Skye', *SMCJ*, XVII (1925), p. 224.
Pigott, A.S., 'On Skye', *Rucksack CJ*, IV (1922), pp. 262-266.
Sang, G., 'Climb on North Face, Blaven', *SMCJ*, XVI (1923), pp. 326-329.
Smith, Ken, 'A Profile of George Bower', *Climber and Rambler*, October 1980.
Somervell, T.H., 'Climbing in the North-West Highlands', *FRCCJ*, V (1920), pp. 113-118.
Steeple, E.W., 'Notes', *SMCJ*, XVI (1921), pp. 48-49.
Wilding, John, 'A Cuillin Day', *Rucksack CJ*, VI (1927), pp. 58-64.
Wilding, John, 'The Cuillins (with Meldrum)', *Rucksack CJ*, V (1924), pp. 228-230.
Williamson, A.M.M., 'Climbing in Skye in Wet Weather', *Cairngorm CJ*, X (1922), pp. 150-159.

Chapter 9
'CUMC Meet, Glen Brittle', *SMCJ*, XX (1933), p. 151.
'Skye Meet, 1933', *SMCJ*, XX (1933), pp. 223-226.
'Traverse of the Coolin Ridge', *SMCJ*, IXX (1932), pp. 428-429.
Angell, Shirley, *The Pinnacle Club*, (The Pinnacle Club, 1993).
Bicknell, P., 'Skye', *AJ*, LIV (1944), pp. 337-347.
Borthwick, A., *Always a Little Further*, (London, 1939).
Charleson, Ian G., 'Traverse of the Cuillin Ridge and the Ascent of Blaven and Clach Glas', *SMCJ*, XXII (1939), pp. 127-133.
Cooper, C. Astley, 'Some New Climbs in Skye', *FRCCJ*, IX (1932), pp. 135-141.
Cox, David, 'Early Years', *AJ*, 1980, p. 91.
Cram, A.L., 'April Climbing in Skye', *SMCJ*, XIX (1932), pp. 392-398.
Cumming, S.M., 'Sligachan, Easter 1936', *SMCJ*, XXI (1936), pp. 122-123.
Dunn, J.K.W., 'Bhasteir Tooth', *SMCJ*, XX (1935), pp. 369-371.
Ewen, W.A., 'The Road to Glen Brittle', *Cairngorm CJ*, XIV (1937), pp. 201-207.
Forsyth, Nancy, 'In Skye', *LSCCJ*, 1938, pp. 32-35.
Gordon, Seton, *Highways and Byways in the Western Highlands*, (London, 1935).

Greenwood, A.M., 'Summer Meet, 1934, in Skye', *Cambridge Mountaineering,* 1936, pp. 52-53.
Hirst, John, 'Sassenachs in Skye', *SMCJ,* XIV (1916), pp. 1-6.
Humble, B.H., 'High Coolin Dawn', *SMCJ,* XXI (1937), pp. 197-199.
Humble, B.H., *The Cuillin of Skye,* (London, 1952).
Humble, B.H., *Tramping in Skye,* (Glasgow, 1933).
Kemball-Cook, R.B., 'Summer Meet, 1935, in Skye', *Cambridge Mountaineering,* 1936, pp. 63-64.
Littlejohn, Anne, 'The Greater Traverse', *LSCCJ,* 1959, p. 24.
MacAskill, Ewen, 'Portrait of Jock Nimlin', *Climber and Rambler,* September 1983.
Murray, W.H., *Undiscovered Scotland,* (London, 1951).
Odell, N.E., 'Marsco', *SMCJ,* XXIII (1944), pp. 192-193.
Perrin, Jim, *Menlove,* (London, 1985).
Reid, D.L., 'Sron na Ciche, Engineers' Slant', *SMCJ,* IXX (1932), pp. 382-388.
Tarbuck, K., 'North Chimney, Bhasteir Tooth', *SMCJ,* IXX (1932), p. 426.
Tebbutt, Joan, 'The Ridge', *LSCCJ,* 1938, pp. 19-23.
Thomson, I.D.S., *May the Fire be Always Lit, a Biography of Jock Nimlin,* (Glasgow, 1995).
Wedderburn, E. A. M., 'Summer Meet, 1933, in Skye', *Cambridge Mountaineering,* 1934, pp. 72-76.
Wood-Johnson, E., 'On Sron na Ciche', *FRCCJ,* VIII (1928), pp. 7-11.
Wood-Johnson, E., 'The North Buttress of Sgumain, West Face', *Wayfarers' CJ,* I (1928-33), pp. 83-86.

Chapter 10
Bell, P., 'Jeffrey's Dyke, Sgurr Mhic Coinnich', *LSCCJ,* 1952, pp. 48-49.
Brooker, W.D., 'A Visit to Skye Fifty Years Ago', *SMCJ,* XXXVI (1997), p. 244.
Brown, G.M., ed. J.G. Capewell, 'The Tertiary Igneous Geology of the Isle of Skye', 1969.
Cairns, H.J.F., 'Skye in August', *Climbers' CJ,* 1945-46, pp. 23-26.
Cook, F.L., 'Skye 1947', *FRCCJ,* XV (1948), pp. 211-214.
Davidson, B., ''Tis the Far Coolin', *Oxford Mountaineering,* 1959, pp. 53-56.
Desmond, V.J., 'The Skye Ridge', *Rucksack CJ,* 1954, pp. 235-242.
Douglas-Hamilton, M., 'The Cuillins Under Snow', *AJ,* LVI (1945), pp. 382-385.
Donald Gillies, Annals of Skye 1938-48, Eilean A Cheo; A Factual Record of an Island and its People, 5 vols.
Gray, Dennis, *Rope Boy,* (London, 1970).
Humble, B.H., 'Glen Brittle', *Scotland's Magazine,* July 1954, pp. 31-33.
Humble, B.H., 'We go in Search of Blaven', *Scotland's Magazine,* May 1956, pp. 18-21.
MacKenzie, W.M., *Climbers' Guide to the Cuillin of Skye,* SMC, (Edinburgh, 1958).
Nicol, Hamish, 'Deep Gash Gully', *AJ,* LVII (1950), pp. 542-544.
Poucher, W.A., *The Magic of Skye,* (London, 1949).
Waghorn, Tom, 'Walter Poucher', *Climbers' CJ,* 1988, p. 127.
Weir, Tom, 'Snow on the Cuillin', *SMCJ,* XXIV, pp. 181-185.
Whitehouse, H.D., 'A First Visit to Skye', *Cairngorm CJ,* XV (1945), pp. 289-292.

Chapter 11
'The Coruisk Affair', *SMCJ,* XXIX (1969), pp. 111-120.
Beatty, John, 'The Winter Traverse of the Cuillin of Skye', *Rucksack CJ,* 1977, pp. 34-43.

Bennett, K., 'A Week in Skye', *FRCCJ,* 1973/74, pp. 153-157.
Broadhead, Dave, 'Another Winter Traverse of the Cuillin Ridge', *EUMCJ,* 1973, pp. 12-14.
Brooker, W. D. & McInnes, H., 'Thomas Walton Patey: In Memoriam', *SMCJ,* XXIX (1971), p. 433.
Forster, John, 'Glen Brittle Memorial Hut', *Achille Ratti CCJ,* 1996.
Harben, R., 'Skye: the Ridge', *Yorkshire Ramblers' CJ,* 1964, pp. 296-300.
Harwood, John, 'An Aim Fulfilled', *Birmingham University Mountaineering Club Journal,* 1966, pp. 62-64.
Keir, Sally, 'The Best Route in Skye', *Pinnacle CJ,* 1985-87, pp. 43-46.
MacInnes, Hamish, *Call Out,* (London, 1973).
McInnes, H, 'The Last Problem', *Scotland's Magazine,* July 1966.
Moffat, Gwen, 'The Cuillin Ridge', *Scotland's Magazine,* June 1966.
Porter, Mollie, 'The 25-Hour Day of Beardie', *Climber and Rambler,* April 1969.
Smith, David, 'Skye', *Yorkshire Ramblers' CJ,* 1973, pp. 40-43.
Waller, Ivan, 'Cuillin Double', *Climber and Rambler,* March 1978.
Waller, Ivan, 'Skye with George', *Rucksack CJ,* 1975, pp. 35-40.
Walton, Ian, 'The Maids Have All Gone From Glen Brittle', *SMCJ,* XXXVI (1997), pp. 249-251.
Wilson, Ken & Newman Bernard (eds), *Extreme Rock,* (London, 1987).

Chapter 12
Hamilton, Dave, 'A Skye Sensation', *Climber and Hill Walker,* February 1991.
Hyslop, Andy, 'Rocking and Running on the Black Cuillin', *Climber,* July 1984.
Hyslop, Andy, 'Running the Ridge', *Climber,* May 1995.
Moran, Martin, *Scotland's Winter Mountains,* (Newton Abbot, 1991).
Moran, Martin, 'Winter Epics', *Climber and Hill Walker,* November 1992.
Stainforth, Gordon, *The Cuillin of Skye,* (London, 1994).
Williams, Noel, *Skye Scrambles,* SMC, 2000.

INDEX

Abraham Werner 17
Abraham, Ashley 11, 61, 66-67, 74, 87-88, 99, 101, 119, 124, 134, 137, 139, 143, 147-168, 172-175, 177-180, 191, 196, 198, 215-216
Abraham, George, 137, 143, 147-151, 153-159, 161-163, 165-168, 196-198, 215
Abraham's Climb 157
Accidents 229-30, 232, 248-51, 259-60, 271-2, 312-3
Admiralty Survey 40-41, 48-49
Advocates' Library 43
Aesculapius 269
Agassiz, Louis 13
Aladdin's Route 255
Alasdair Stone Shoot 122, 187
Alcock, Dave 290
Alexander, John, 267
Allain, Pierre 263
Allan, Ian, 228
Alpine Club 10-11, 40, 75, 78, 80, 90, 97-102, 108-110, 122, 140, 148, 151, 156, 204, 207, 211, 227, 253, 266
Alpine Journal 58, 60-61, 66, 80, 85, 97, 99, 101, 227, 242, 311
Alps 57, 59, 68, 198, 206, 210, 213, 217
Always a Little Further 219, 231, 232
Am Basteir 127, 129, 132, 211, 228, 274, 301, 305, 307-08, 315-316, 318
Am Basteir Chimney 316
Amphitheatre Arete 89
Amphitheatre Wall 223, 284
An Caisteal 277
An Garbh-choire 271
An Stac 174
An Stac Chimney 174
Anderson, Ian 303
Anderson, Rab 295, 297
Anderson's Guide 37, 40
Andreae, C E (Eddy) 217
Arch Gully 150
Archer Thomson, J M 160

Archer Thomson's Route 181-182, 189-190, 270
Arrow Route 228, 265
Arrowsmith, Aaron 10, 20-21
Atropos 311

B Gully, Clach Glas 127, 167, 315
Backhouse, Edward 167
Bad Step 94-96, 229, 230, 233, 272-273, 321
Baddeley's Guide 95, 108
Baker, G P 128
Ball, Richard, 77
Balmoral 74
Baly, E C C (Cyril) 70, 72, 87, 90
Banachdich Gully 132, 144, 235
Band, Bill 288-289
Barclay, Dick 261
Barker, A F. 175
Barker, Mabel 212
Barlow, George (Guy) 169, 170-172, 174-175, 177, 185-188, 191, 197, 200-204, 209, 211
Barrow, Harrison 102, 125-126, 193
Barrow, Walter 102
Barton, Claude and Guy, 5/15
Bartrum, Geoffrey 159-160, 191
Bastinado 264
Battle of the Braes 12, 51
Bealach a' Mhaim 49, 59, 130, 133
Bealach Mhic Choinnich 104
Bealach na Banachdich 248
Beard, Eric 279, 304, 305
Beckwith, Lillian 247
Beinn na Caillich 17, 20
Bell, J H B 169, 172, 198, 204, 206-211, 225, 229- 231, 263, 267
Bell-mouth Chimney 162
Ben Nevis 130, 140, 145, 152, 268, 270, 278, 283
Bennet, Donald 288
Benson, A C 106

INDEX

Benson, Pete 304
Berry, Natalie 12,
Bhasteir Gorge, 101
Bhasteir Tooth 76-77, 95, 97, 101, 105-106, 113 127, 131, 133, 139, 149, 153-154, 164, 175, 178, 189, 191, 196, 211, 221, 224, 231-232, 274, 276-278, 301, 305-306, 319
Bicknell, Peter 224
Bidein Druim nan Ramh 44, 47, 56, 58, 60, 63, 149-150, 164, 166, 198
Big Wall Gully 212
Binns, A H 153, 156-157, 159-160
Birkett, Dave 304
Birthday Groove 315
Bla Bheinn 17, 21, 32-33, 35, 37-39, 56, 78, 82, 90, 94, 100, 111-112, 114, 119, 127, 140, 144, 150, 165-166, 213, 230-231, 240-241, 243-244, 248-249, 257, 278, 281, 284, 287-288, 290, 292
Black Chimney, Coire na Banachdich, 174-175
Black Chimney, Sgurr nan Gillean, 162
Black Cleft 261, 263, 319
Black's Tourist Guide 36, 38
Blackadder, John 20
Blackshaw, Alan 322
Blaeu, Joan 15, 49
Bonington, Chris 11, 274, 293, 345, 348
Bonnie Prince Charlie 15, 33, 220, 332
Boots 158-9, 262-3, 281
Borthwick, Alasdair 219, 225, 232
Boswell, Samuel 9, 17-18, 33
Botterill, Pete 286-287
Boulton, Chris 291-293
Bower, George 191-192, 199
Bowron, H E 170-175
Boyd, H C 170
Boysen, Martin 290, 293
Braithwaite, Paul 293
Brasher, Chris 199, 272
Bray, Lillian 213
British Mountaineering Council 280-282
Broadford 19, 27, 29, 33, 35-36, 38, 64-47, 127, 134, 166, 176, 189, 288
Broke, Reverend G 170
Brooke, H Sinclair 74
Brooke, Richard 252
Brooke, Rupert 135, 190, 275

Brooker, Bill 185, 274, 281
Broomfield, Reginald 61
Brown, Joe 256, 291
Brown, Professor Graham 265
Brown, William 122, 125-126
Brown's Climb 126
Bruach na Frithe 56, 94, 106, 113-114, 174, 206, 210, 213-214, 228, 277, 306-308
Bruce, Charles 79, 85-86
Brunskill, Walter 110
Bruton, W 228
Bryan, Ken 271
Buchan, John 11, 135-138, 179, 192
Buchanan, Robert 18
Buckle, H B 88, 171, 174-175
Burke, Edmund 10
Burn, Reverend A R G B 205
Butters, John Alexander 48
Byron, Lord 9

Cadell, Francis 25
Cain, A C (Ginger) 255, 290-291
Cairngorm Club 69, 91, 128, 198, 212
Cairngorms 204, 274
Caisteal a' Garbh-choire 75, 179
Calder, Trish 87
Camasunary 12, 21, 23, 25, 30, 36, 94-95, 102, 113, 138-139, 142-144, 176, 243, 257. 272, 303-304
Cambridge University Mountaineering Club 225
Cameron, Alexander 176
Cameron, Donald 49, 176, 187
Campbell, Ian 249
Campbell, John 134, 138, 166-167, 172, 176, 205
Campbell, Mary 170, 175, 185, 197, 200, 204, 206-207, 209-210, 226, 231, 281
Campbell, Robin 115
Camping 102-3, 105, 138, 201, 226
Captain Planet 306
Caravan Route 199-200
Carbost 107, 112, 117, 275
Carlyle, Thomas 46
Carmichael, Alexander 112
Carpenter, John 266
Carr, Ellis 205
Carr, H R C 195-197

Cartography 20, 56-57
Central Buttress, Coir' a' Ghrunnda 195
Central Buttress, Marsco 202
Central Gully 161-162, 164, 172, 174-175, 182, 191
Central Route, Alasdair-Thearlaich Cliffs 203
Central Slabs, Sron na Ciche 202
Charleson, Ian 240-241
Chemist's Constitutional 287
Chimney and Crack Climb 182
Chimney Route 186
Chock-a-Block Chimney 288, 316
CIC Hut 78
Cioch Direct 162-164, 167, 172-174, 184, 189, 192, 197, 216, 256, 265, 269, 282, 309
Cioch Grooves 256, 269
Cioch Gully 88, 161, 163, 171-172, 196, 198, 208
Cioch Nose 161, 163, 172, 228
Cioch Slab 162, 228
Cioch West 12, 197, 224, 232, 265, 269
Cioch, The 12, 85-89, 161-164, 167-168, 171-175, 182-184, 186, 189, 191-192, 224, 228-229, 232, 234, 238-239, 244
Clach Glas 64, 102, 111-112, 114, 198, 211, 213, 224, 228-229, 232, 234, 238-239, 244
Claude glass 25
Clearances, The Highland 34, 48-9, 51-4
Cliff, Barry 275
Climbers' Club 98, 102, 112, 118, 123, 168-170, 215-216
Climbing techniques 132,155,199, 215, 220-2, 266-8
Clinging On 298
Clinton Dent 98, 101, 102
Clothing 106-7, 215, 245, 273
Clouded Buttress 262
Clough, Ian 267-269, 281, 28-290, 292
Clough's Cleft 316
Cockburn, Lord Henry 33-35
Cohen, Geoff 299
Coir a' Ghreadaidh 132, 273
Coir' a' Ghrunnda, 31, 32, 79, 179, 185, 187, 201, 202, 209, 278, 282, 201-202, 209
Coir' a' Mhadaidh 31, 48, 56
Coire a' Bhasteir 71-72, 149, 153
Coire Banachdich 132
Coire Dubh 144
Coire Lagan 21, 32, 49-50, 60, 63, 67, 100, 111, 130, 141-142, 156-158, 164, 166, 170, 182, 185, 189, 191, 201-202, 204, 212, 248, 268-269, 281, 284
Coire na Banachdich 230, 238, 264-265, 269, 296
Coire na Creiche 56, 96, 100, 104, 150, 159, 169, 188
Coire nan Laogh 184
Coire Riabhach 21, 32
Coireachan Ruadha 297
Colby, Thomas 19, 22, 350
Coleridge, Samuel Taylor 9
Collie Step 212
Collie, Norman 11, 58, 60, 63-72, 74-92, 98, 104, 107, 109, 110, 113- 115, 118, 98, 104, 107, 109-110, 113-115, 118, 121, 123, 125, 128-129, 134, 144-145, 148, 149, 156, 159, 161, 162, 164, 170, 171, 178, 187, 190, 224, 227-228, 235-236, 250, 266
Collie's Climb 81
Collie's Corner 92
Collie's Ledge 65-67, 104
Collie's Route 89, 156, 161-162, 228
Collier, Joe 80, 83
Combined tactics 154, 162
Commando Crack 255
Con's Cleft 12, 282, 347
Confession 296, 297
Connery, Sean 292
Consolation Gully 165
Cooper, C Astley 221-222
Cooper's Gangway 222
Corbett, Catherine 213
Corbett, J Rooke 206, 213
Corlett, W E 66, 82, 111, 118, 130
Corrie, Hamish 91
Coruisk 93-95, 97, 102-105, 107, 113-114, 122-125, 138-142, 144, 149-151, 164, 198, 201-203, 212- 214, 271-272, 281, 283, 286-287, 321-322
'Coruisk Affair' 272
Coruisk Hut 271-272
Coruisk Slabs 164
Cousin's Buttress 140
Cousins, Sandy 272-273
Coxhead 228, 229, 241

INDEX

Crabb, David, 11, 276-278
Crack of Dawn 185, 261-262, 266, 269-270, 274, 281
Crack of Doom 191-192, 198-199, 211, 251, 258
Crack of Double Doom 12, 251, 255
Craig, David 9, 13
Crampons 142-3, 263
Cram, Alastair 224
Creag Dhu Grooves 267-268, 295
Creagh Dhu Mountaineering Club 220, 225, 264, 267
Crembo Cracks 269
Crosskey, Reverend Henry 38
Crowley, Aleister 11, 109, 141
Cuchulain 18
Cuckoo Waltz 300
Cullen, Graham 300
Culloden 15-18, 26
Cumming, C F Gordon 98
Cunningham, John 263-264, 282
Cuthbertson, Dave (Cubby) 295-296

Daniell, William 10, 21, 23, 24, 25
Darwin, Charles 115
Davidson, Dave 252
Davies, Del 305
Davison, Brian 314
Dawn Grooves 274, 282, 286, 287, 318
Dawson, R K 19
Deadline 315
Deep Chimney 138
Deep Gash Gully 131, 181, 252, 266, 309, 313, 315
Deep Purple 257
Dent, Clinton 98, 100-102
Depravity 269
Diagonal Gully 188
Dickson, Isobel 214
Dilemma 298, 311
Dinwoodie, Dougie 299
Dirac, Paul 225
Direct Route, Sgurr Sgumain 282, 284, 289
Direct Route, Sron na Ciche 185-186,
Disarming Act 16
Dixon, Mike 185, 258-259, 261-263, 275
Dobson, J F 131-132
Dodson, Brian 255

Donaldson, Charlie 264, 301
Donaldson, Gordon 240-241
Doom Flake 251, 270
Dougan, Bill 220
Doughty, A H (Harry) 175, 185, 186, 188
Douglas, William 111, 113-114, 117-119, 122, 125-126, 130-131, 172
Douglas-Hamilton, Lord Malcolm 253-254
Downer, Colin 310-311
Drasdo, Neville 258-259
Dring, Ian 301
Druim Hain 22, 28, 35, 37, 47, 95, 113, 116
Druim nan Ramh Ridge 60, 63, 102, 105, 149
Dubh Ridge 124-125, 140, 271
Dunn, Kenneth 236, 239
Dunvegan 43, 48, 62, 130, 139, 321

Eagles Gully 175
Easson, Davie 248
East Gully 175, 184-185, 192
Eastern Gully 161, 163, 244
Eastern Wall 174
Eckenstein, Oscar 148
Ecstasis 292
Edinburgh 16-17, 25-26, 29-30, 33, 37, 43-45, 55, 68
Edinburgh Squirrels Climbing Club 274, 283
Edinburgh University Mountaineering Club 251
Edwards, J M (Menlove) 243
Elgol 12, 16, 25, 33, 35, 48, 54
Enigma 298-299
Equipment 214, 255, 273, 295
Erotica 299
Errington, Lindsay 13
Escape from Colditz 315
Everest 145, 154, 158, 161, 165, 166, 197, 207, 209, 214-216, 221, 242, 245, 252, 257, 267, 274
Evers, F P 77

Fairy Pools 173, 322
Falcon, T A 121, 123
Farquhar, Grant 299, 303
Fell and Rock Climbing Club 89, 98, 161,

167, 197, 212, 269
Ferguson, Malcolm 94
Final Tower Direct 203, 211
Findlay, Brian 309
Finger in the Dyke 303
First World War 187, 192-3, 195-6
Flake Traverse 164
Fleming, Fergus 13
Fluted Buttress 259, 260, 261, 262, 269, 286, 287
Flutings Climb 173, 315
Forbes, James David 20, 29-32, 73, 74
Forde, W E 240-241
Forgotten Groove 269
Forked Chimney 131, 136-137, 315
Fowler, Mick 298, 310-313, 315-316
Foxes' Rake 133, 159
Francis, Godfrey H 256-257, 267
Frankland, C D 214
Frankland's Gully 213, 223, 309
Free Solo 12
Fyffe, Blair 306

Gael Force 273
Gardner, Davic 251
Gars-bheinn 21, 25, 32, 41, 56, 124, 136, 143, 225, 231, 240, 243-244, 253, 276, 305-306, 308
Gauger's Gully 241
Geikie, Archibald 32, 34, 43, 55, 115-117
Geological Society 21
Geology 16-17, 19-20, 31-2, 115-7, 257-8
George IV 26
Gibson, John Henry 103-106, 109
Gillon, Stair 136
Gilpin, William 9, 13, 24
Girdle Traverse of Sron na Ciche 186
Giveen, F W 216-217
Gladstone, William 46-47, 53
Glamaig 15, 17, 20, 52, 86, 92
Glamaig Hill Race 86, 307
Glasgow University Mountaineering Club 271
Glen Brittle 9, 11, 48-50, 58-59, 62- 65, 122-123, 128, 130, 132, 139, 141-142, 144, 150, 152, 154, 156, 159, 161-162, 164, 166, 168-169, 170, 172, 174-176, 178, 179-181, 183, 185-186, 189, 191, 195-201, 204, 206-208, 210, 213, 216, 221-222, 225-231, 233-241, 243-251, 255, 258-261, 264-265, 267, 271, 275, 277, 279, 280-282, 284-288, 305-306, 309-310, 317, 321-322, 353-354, 357
Glen Brittle House 50, 62, 65, 87, 89-90, 96-97, 100, 102, 104, 110, 116-117, 122, 139, 141-142, 170, 175-176, 180, 199, 226-227, 229, 234, 243, 246, 262
Glen Brittle Memorial Hut 280
Glen Brittle Youth Hostel 10, 246, 280, 285, 287
Glen Coe 26, 34
Glen Nevis 9, 271
Glen Sheil 18
Glen Sligachan 16, 20, 22, 30, 34-37, 40, 150, 165, 231, 241
Glenelg 93, 226
Goethe 33
Goggs, F S 174
Goliath Buttress 280
Goodeve, T E 144, 193
Goodfellow, Basil, 207-208, 210, 214
Gorrie, Charlie 259
Grading 82, 269-70, 281-2, 300, 309
Grainger, Stewart 257
Grampian Club 246
Grand Diedre 13, 317
Grand Tour 10, 17, 26, 34, 340
Grannie Clark's Wynd 289
Grant, Duncan 127
Graves, Robert 195
Gray, Dennis 258
Gray, Roger 250
Gray, Thomas 9
Greater Traverse 231, 240, 241, 243
Green Recess Chimneys 202
Greene, Raymond 209, 216
Greg, Walter 96, 102-103, 121
Greig, Francis 157, 159-160
Gribbon, Phil 287-289
Gritstone Club 249
Grooves Eliminate 311
Gully B, Sgurr Thearlaich 316
Gully D, Sgurr Thealaich 174
Gully E, Sgurr Thealaich 63
Gunn, Neil 112

INDEX

Half-Crown Pinnacle 82, 111-112, 288
Hallitt, Arthur W 121, 123
Hamilton, 'Hamish' 231
Hamilton, Murray 295, 297-299
Hamish's Chimney 132
Hang Free 296
Harkabir Thapa 85
Harker, Alfred 116-119
Harland, Henry 153, 154, 156-157, 159, 160, 162, 163-165, 167
Hart, H C 64-68, 77
Harta Corrie 57, 58, 60, 64, 130, 138, 181, 257, 258, 259, 260
Harty, Russell 255
Harvie-Brown, J A 73
Harwood, John 279-280, 282-284, 286
Haskett Smith, Walter 61-62, 65, 68, 103, 112, 125, 148
Hastings, Geoffrey 69, 80, 98, 100-101
Haston, Dougal 310
Haworth, Derek 251
Hawthorn, Uisdean 308
Heap, W 170
Heathcote, Evelyn 130, 212
Heathcote, J Norman 81-82, 130
Heathcote's Gully 130
Heddle, M F 73
Heelis, James 62-63
Helen 298
Henderson, Hamish 273
Henry, Alexander 344, 347
Hepburn, David 44-45, 51
Herbert, Eric 275
Herford, Siegfried 180, 183-184, 192
Hidden Gully 173
Hidden Gully Buttress 279
Higgins, Con 282
High, Roger 283
Highland Land League 51
Hill, Steve 298, 301
Hillary, Sir Edmund 252
Hodge, E W 233
Hodgkin, Alan 224
Hodgkiss, Peter 197
Holden, Dog 251
Holland, C F (Charlie) 195-197, 199, 205
Hood, George 264-265
Hopkinson, Edward 98, 101, 103

Horne, Alan 223, 224
Hourglass Crack 261, 264
Howard, G E 193
Howell, E B 81-82
Howett, Kevin 198
Howffs 220, 248-9
Hughes, H V 212, 123-224
Hughes, I ap G 251
Hulton, Eustace 57, 59-61, 63
Humble, Ben 64, 201, 220, 226, 235-239, 244-249
Hung, Drawn and Quartered 301, 318
Hunt, Alfred William 123
Hunt, Sir John 245
Hunter, Pete 295
Husabost 43, 51
Hutchison, A G 217
Hutton, James 17
Hyslop, Andy 304-307

Icicle Factory 311-312
Inaccessible Pinnacle 12, 41, 46, 49, 57-63, 65, 68, 71, 75, 78, 83, 89-90, 99-100, 104, 110-111, 114-115 128, 130, 132, 142, 144, 149-150, 156-157, 165, 172-174, 178, 198-199, 204, 206, 212-214, 219, 221, 224-225, 227, 235, 241, 248, 254, 263, 269, 276-277, 279-280, 300-302, 305-306, 314, 317, 341, 355, 359, 361
Inglis Clark, Charles 40, 74, 127-128, 132, 134, 138-139, 142, 144, 152, 165, 166, 174, 193, 350, 355
Inglis Clark, Jane 127-128
Inglis Clark, Mabel 174, 263
Inglis Clark, William 128, 132, 134, 138-139, 142
Integrity 12, 251, 264, 268
Irvine, 'Sandy' 166

Jackson, F W (Fred) 110-112
Jameson, Robert 16-17
Jeffrey's Dyke 263
Jethro Tull 303
Jib 290, 292
Johnson, Samuel 9, 17-18, 24, 355
Johnson, Stephen 243
Johnston, Tom 228
Jones, Bronwen 181, 212

Jones, Grace 255
Jones, H O 160, 181
Jones, O G 118, 147-148, 153-154, 160, 167, 169, 181, 183, 251, 255
Julian, Professor L 184-185, 192
Junior Mountaineering Club of Scotland 217 235-236, 270-273

Kassyck, Adam 296
Keats, John 39
Kellas, A M 70, 145
Kelly, H M (Harry) 188-189
Kelsall, J 121, 123
Kempson, Reverend E 79
Kendall, Les 279
Keynes, Maynard 190
Kidson, E R 112, 118
Kindness, Hugh 265
King Cobra 274-275, 280, 282-283, 286
King, William Wickham 76-79, 121, 129-133, 169, 170, 173-174, 178
King's Cave Chimney 206, 232
King's Chimney 67, 104, 129-132, 133, 178, 206, 276, 277
Kinloss Gully 267-268
Knight, William Angus 45-46, 68, 99
Knight's Peak 46, 90, 165, 167, 271, 312, 315
Knowlton, Elizabeth 221-222
Krugerrand 295
Kyle of Lochalsh 166, 233, 241, 245, 273, 280, 292

Ladies' Pinnacle 89
Lady of the Lake 10, 24, 89
Lagan Route 286
Laidlaw, Henry 62
Lake District 57, 60-61, 68
Lamb, Robertson 170-171, 173
Lates, Mike 302
Latter, Gary 295-296, 299, 303
Lawrie, R M 234
Laycock, John 183-184
Lees, Cameron 295
Left Edge, Sgurr nan Eag 265
Lesingham Smith, Charles 28-29, 37, 158
Leviathan 283
Lightfoot 297

Little Gully 172
Livingstone, David 35
Livingstone, Graeme 299
Loch Coruisk 10, 15, 20-26, 29-35, 46, 47, 50, 51, 58, 60, 63, 93, 95, 97, 102, 104, 107, 113, 114, 220, 238, 242, 247-249, 252, 272, 300, 306
Loch Eynort 48
Loch Katrine 10, 23, 340
Loch Scavaig 22, 24-25, 32-33, 35-36, 39, 47, 64, 93-95, 102, 113, 124-125, 142, 170, 184, 247-249, 272, 300
Loch Slapin 94, 111
Lomond Mountaineering Club 220, 247-249, 269
Lost Arrow 264
Lota Corrie 31, 51, 57, 77, 78, 80, 82, 127, 131, 143, 149, 312, 317
Lota Corrie Route 79-80, 109, 127
Lumps 283
Lüscher, Ery 197-198
Luscher's No. 1 101, 199, 315
Luscher's No. 2 199
Lyon in Mourning 16
Lytton Strachey, Giles 11, 135, 190

MacAlpine, Archie 236-237
MacCulloch, John 19, 20-22, 33-34, 63, 115, 229, 242
Macculloch, Reverend John 242
MacDiarmid, Hugh 227
MacDonald family 21, 48, 52-54, 59, 258
MacDonald, Alexander 52-54
MacDonald, Flora 15, 37
MacDonald, Ronald (Glen Brittle) 247, 284
MacDonald, Ronald (Portree) 187
MacInnes, Hamish 11, 251, 264, 267-269, 271, 272, 276-278, 288, 290, 292, 295-296, 300, 311
MacIntyre, Donald 253-254
MacIntyre, Duncan 30-31, 44
Mackay, A M 131
Mackay, Harry 264
MacKendrick, Sandy 11, 219
Mackenzie, Archie 74, 117
MacKenzie, Bill 236, 239, 269-270
Mackenzie, Donald 74, 112, 121, 124

INDEX

Mackenzie, John 11, 50, 52, 58, 61- 69, 72-74, 76- 79, 82, 85, 88- 92, 121, 124-125, 130, 132-133, 136, 138, 144, 158, 164, 176-177, 187, 202
MacKenzie, John 'Jonags' 249
Mackenzie, Murdo 74, 89, 111
Mackenzie, Rory 74, 177
MacKinnon, Sir William 54
Maclay, James 128
Maclay's Gully 129
MacLean, Sorley 50, 53, 227
MacLennan, John 39-40
MacLeod, Dave 12, 299
MacLeod, John 284
MacLeod, the Clan 12-13, 21 176, 258, 281, 284, 322
MacNaught-Davis, Ian 256
MacNiven, John 124
MacPherson Angus 45, 58, 73
Macpherson, Captain, OS 56
Macpherson, James 18-19, 27, 357
MacPherson, Pete 317-319
MacPherson, Willie 249
MacRae, Alexander 49-50
MacRae, Ewen 229
MacRae, Hugh 226, 261
MacRae, John 125-126
MacRae, Nancy 226
MacRobert, Harry 169, 203
MacWhirter, John 26
Mad Burn Buttress 271
Madan, Nigel 161, 192
Magic 296
Magic Casement 267
Magpie Cracks 283
Main Ridge Traverse 102, 130, 152, 160, 164, 169, 178- 80, 197-199, 204, 206-210, 212-213, 224-225, 227, 230-231, 232, 235, 240-241, 243- 245, 254, 258-260, 275-279, 283, 286, 301-302, 304-307, 314, 319
Mallory, Clare 241
Mallory, George 70, 86, 91, 135, 145, 161, 166, 177, 180-181, 190-191, 193, 195, 197, 221-223, 241, 242, 258
Mam a' Phobuill 16
Marsco 16, 349
Marshall, Jimmy 264-265, 301
Marshall, Percy 111
Marshall, William 111
Martin Martin 15
Martin, J 177
Maryon, Captain 249
Matterhorn 10, 44-45, 59, 62, 150, 157, 202, 278
Maylard, A E 77-78, 97, 114
McCallum, Duncan 297
McCulloch, Horatio 37
McKeever, John 278
McKeith, Alasdair 'Bugs' 283
McLaren, A C 135, 160, 177-182, 224, 240
McLean, John 282-283
Median 174, 182, 186
Megaton 293
Meldrum, Dougie 250
Meldrum, J B 250-251
Menzies, D H 207
Methven, John 271-272
Midget Ridge 262
Mill, Donald 269
Miller, Maynard 11, 266-267
Milne, Rob 296
Mistral Buttress 298
Mitchell, Ian 13
Mitchell, Joseph 27
Moffat, Gwen 286
Mongoose Direct 287
Monks, John 263
Monro, Donald 15
Moody, Colin 297-298
Moran, Martin 301, 305-306, 313-315, 318-319
Morewood, E. Palmer 139, 141
Moriarty, James (Elly) 278, 280, 291
Morin Nea 268
Morrison, W A (William) 207
Morse, G H 103, 105
Morton, H V 220
Mountaineering Council of Scotland 298
Mrs Chisholm 195, 198-199, 202, 207-208, 210, 214, 225-226, 246-247
Muir, Scott 298
Müller, Johann 9
Mullin, Dougie 298
Mumm, Arnold 85
Mummery, A F 11, 69, 71, 81, 84, 105
Munro, Hugh 49, 73, 75, 90, 128, 135, 142,

144
Murchison, Roderick 28
Murray, W H 164, 230, 235-237, 238, 239, 240, 242-243, 252-253, 267, 270, 274
Murray's Climb 239

Naismith, William 55-56, 62-63, 81, 83, 99, 103-104, 107, 110-114, 118, 123, 127-133, 148, 153, 167, 170, 178-179, 189, 197, 203, 207-208, 211, 252, 275, 278, 288, 301, 305-306
Naismith's Route 131, 133, 178-179, 189, 197, 207-208, 231-232, 240
Naked Saltire 302
Napier Commission 122-123, 125, 132
Napier, J S 79, 122-123
Napier, R 79, 122-123
Napoleonic Wars 19, 26
National Trust for Scotland 321
Necker, Louis Albert Necker (de Saussure) 30-3, 359
Nettleton, M B 233, 242
Nicol, Hamish 252
Nicolson, Alexander 26, 37, 41, 43-51, 53-55, 57, 63, 68, 105, 107, 110, 112, 119, 124, 129, 138, 237, 244, 257, 322
Nicolson's Chimney 44
Nimlin, Jock, 220, 247-249, 252
Nisbet, Andy 301, 313-314
North Buttress, An Caisteal 257, 268
North Chimney, Bruach na Frithe 174, 178, 224, 228, 263
North Face Direct, Bla Bheinn 206, 318
North Face, Am Basteir 176-177, 301, 315
North Face, Bla Bheinn 170, 177
North Face, Knight's Peak 165, 167
North Ridge, Sgurr Sgumain 172-173
North Twin 262
North-East Buttress 259, 261
North-East Face, Sgurr na h-Uamha 64
North-East Gully, An Diallaid 185, 192, 217
North-West Buttress, Sgurr a' Mhadaidh 82
North-West Corner, Inaccessible Pinnacle 78
North-West Ramp, Sgurr Sgumain 111, 122, 172

North-West Ridge of Sgurr a' Ghreadaidh 132
Nunn, Paul 292-293

O'Brien and Julian's Climb 314
O'Brien, Conor 180, 184-185
O'Grady, Conn 229-230
O'Hara, Mike 250
Oban 4, 47
Odell, N E (Noel) 241-242
Odell's Route 242
Ogilvie, Iain, H 209, 259-260
Old Man of Storr 274
Ordnance Survey 50, 56-57, 75, 77, 97, 105, 112-115, 119, 204, 219
Original Route 82-83, 187
Ossian 18-19, 22, 24, 30, 33, 34, 360
Over the Sea to Death 286
Overhanging Crack, The Cioch 299
Owl Buttress Left 209
Owl Buttress Right 223
Owl Chimney 202
Oxford University Mountaineering Club 256

Paddy and Mick's Route 60
Paradise Found 304
Parallel Cracks Route 202, 279
Parker, A G 61, 71, 81-83, 252
Parker, Alan 252
Parker, J A 81-83, 127
Patey, Tom 11, 262, 274-278, 288, 290
Penelope 288
Penitentiary Grooves 295
Pennant, Thomas 17, 20, 360
Peridot 283
Petronella 257
Phillip, Colin 113-115, 118, 161-162
Piety 298
Pigott, Fred 199-200, 281
Pilkington White, Colonel T 56, 102
Pilkington, Charles 49, 57-60, 62-64, 66, 68, 97-102, 110-112, 124, 127, 144, 171, 173
Pilkington, Lawrence 58-60
Pilkington, Mabel 100
Pilkington's Gully 62, 144
Pilley, Dorothy 11, 195

INDEX

Pinnacle Club 213
Pinnacle Ridge 72, 77, 79, 82- 84, 99, 100, 104, 108-109, 111, 128, 136-137, 141, 144, 149, 152, 165, 205-206, 211, 224, 235, 253-254, 312, 315
Pipes, Don 267, 269
Photography 147-52, 203, 233-9, 254-5
Pocks 298
Pont, Timothy 10, 15
Porter, H E L 161
Porter, T C 106
Portree 15, 27, 30-31, 33-34, 39, 46, 48, 52-53, 93-95, 97, 126, 139, 149, 152, 161, 166
Poucher, W A 254-255
Prentice, Tom 293, 298
Priestman, Howard 102, 203
Prokroustes 268
Prolepsis 296
Prometheus 268, 289
Ptarmigan Club 220
Pye and Mallory's Route 190
Pye, David 190-192

Quark. 293
Queen Victoria 33, 38
Quiraing 47

Raeburn, Harold 101, 126, 130, 133, 140-145, 152, 154, 156, 181, 187, 255
Raeburn's Route 152, 181, 187
RAF Kinloss Mountain Rescue Team 248, 284
Rainbow Warrior 301, 306
Rainman 304
Ramblers Association 322
Ramp Route 127
Ramsay, Professor G C 43, 70
Ramsay, Professor W 70, 84, 87
Ramsden, Paul 315-316
Rasher, Paul 303-304
Raynauds 298
Red Cuillin 17, 19, 20-21, 52, 112-113, 116, 119-220, 242
Reid, W A 83
Reluctance 289
Rennie Hut 125
Rennie, John 124-127, 164
Renny, Jim 283

Reynolds, E S 181
Rib of Doom 251, 265
Ritchie, Dave 314-318
Rites of Passage 300
Robb, Nigel 271
Robbins, Dave 279-280
Robert the Bruce 23, 36
Robertson, A E 11, 78, 90, 116, 118, 127-128, 138, 141-142, 170-171, 173, 203, 215
Robertson, Brian 276
Robertson, David 91
Robertson, Guy 304, 317-19
Robinson, Nigel 278
Robson, George Fennel 25
Rock Climbing in Skye 11, 99, 119, 124, 147-148, 150, 152, 154, 160, 167-168, 173
Romantics 17-18, 24-26
Ropes 68, 80, 156, 221
Rose, T K 103, 112
Ross, Neil 288
Rowland, Clive 300, 309
Rubens, Des 278
Rubha an Dunain 49
Rucksack Club 88, 98, 161, 163, 168-172, 175, 186, 188-189, 192, 199, 206-207, 214, 223, 233
Rucksack Club Journal 172, 192
Rucksacks 107, 204-5, 245
Ruskin, John 9, 13, 123
Russell, A W 133, 174

Sang, George 206
Saunders, Vic 311
Schama, Simon 10, 13
Scimitar 283
Sconser 11, 50, 52, 54, 72, 106, 139, 158, 166
Scoones, Paul 177
Scott, Doug 310
Scott, Sir Walter 10, 13, 21-26, 33, 35-36
Scottish Mountaineering Club (SMC) 38, 43-44, 55-56, 60-61, 63, 67, 75-82, 87, 90, 98-99, 103-106, 108-114, 116-119 122, 124-126, 128-129, 132-143, 150-152, 156, 160, 161, 164-165, 168-169, 172-174, 176, 178, 182, 185-189, 191, 193, 198, 200, 203-208, 212, 217, 223-224, 227-229, 236, 239, 249, 253, 255, 266-267, 269-270, 275-276,

281-283, 287-290, 299, 301, 306, 309
Scottish Youth Hostel Association 219, 225-226, 246, 279-280, 284
Seachd: the Inaccessible Pinnacle 300
Searcher 290
Second-Third Gully, Sgurr a' Mhadaidh 154
Second-Third Gully, Sgurr nan Gillean 83
Second World War 237, 242-45
Sedgwick, Adam 28
Sgumain Stone Shoot 186
Sgurr a' Choire Bhig 124
Sgurr a' Fionn Choire, 82
Sgurr a' Ghreadaidh 57, 64-65, 105, 109, 118, 173, 187, 202, 207, 209, 213, 259, 308-309, 312
Sgurr a' Mhadaidh 56-57, 60, 64-65, 76, 78, 82-83, 90, 95, 97, 100, 105, 109, 113, 150, 159, 175, 179, 182, 235, 238, 241, 252, 257, 270, 274-275, 277-278, 280, 304, 313
Sgurr Alasdair 41, 49-50, 60, 63, 66, 75, 77, 79-81, 86, 97, 100, 103, 106, 150, 156-157, 159, 204, 212, 227, 229, 235, 285
Sgurr an Fheadain 121
Sgurr Beag 30, 362
Sgurr Coir' an Lochain 82-83, 187, 191, 202, 204, 230-231
Sgurr Dearg 49, 56, 58-59, 61-62, 204, 213, 275, 277, 279, 286
Sgurr Dubh 50, 60, 64, 122, 124-125, 139-141, 143, 231, 235, 239-240
Sgurr Dubh Beag 64, 124-125, 140-141
Sgurr Dubh Mor 50, 60, 271, 305
Sgurr Dubh na Da Bheinn 101, 114
Sgurr Eadar da Choire 175
Sgurr Mhic Chionnich 49, 63, 65-67, 69, 77, 128, 142, 167, 178-179, 192, 258, 263
Sgurr na Banachdich 49, 56, 67, 77, 105, 113-114, 117-118, 166, 197, 213, 314
Sgurr na h-Uamha, 74, 82, 152
Sgurr na Stri 10, 300, 304
Sgurr nan Eag 124, 143, 283
Sgurr nan Gillean 10, 19, 21, 29-31, 37, 40, 70-72, 75, 77-78, 82-83, 96, 101, 106-108, 115, 118, 149, 152, 170, 173, 175, 177-179, 181, 184, 225, 231, 237, 253-254, 276-277, 281, 285,
Sgurr Sgumain 50, 56, 97, 100-101, 104, 111, 119, 122, 130, 141, 172-173, 203, 210-212, 230-231, 240
Sgurr Thearlaich 97, 104, 114, 150, 174, 179, 187, 235, 316
Sgurr Thormaid 69, 283
Sgurr Thuilm 48, 64
Shadbolt, Leslie 170, 177-182, 190-192, 221, 224, 239-240, 252
Shadbolt's Chimney 178, 196, 221, 239
Shadbolt's Route 319
Shangri-La 290
Shaw, Mark 314-315
Shaw, Tom 261
Shaw-Stewart, Patrick 190
Shelf Route 252
Shining Cleft 257, 291
Sibbald, Sir Robert 15
Sid's Rake 127
Simmonds, K W 225
Simpson, Jim 271, 281
Skipwith, Sir Patrick 257
Skye Bridge 13, 309, 314-315
Skye Mountain Rescue Team 249, 284, 312
Skye Wall 304
Slab and Groove 191, 221 223, 258
Slab Buttress 202
Slab Corner 162, 228, 299
Slanting Gully 154, 156, 159-161, 167, 173, 181, 183-184, 198, 241, 291
Sligachan 9, 11-12, 15-16, 18- 22, 27-31, 34-40, 44-52, 54, 55- 68, 71-74, 76-83, 86, 89, 90-105, 107-112, 116-117, 121-123, 126-128, 130, 133-135, 137, 138-145, 149, 150, 152-154, 156, 159, 162, 165-166, 168-170, 172-173, 176, 178-179, 181-183, 185, 187, 189, 191, 197-200, 205-210, 212, 214-216, 220, 225-226, 228-229, 231, 233, 235-237, 241, 243, 245, 249, 254, 259-260, 276-277, 285-286
Sligachan Hotel 134, 199, 220, 243, 245, 321
Sligachan Inn 27-28, 35, 39, 48, 56, 68, 73, 78, 86, 89, 94-95, 97-99, 110, 123, 128-130, 133-135, 137-138, 140, 149, 161, 166, 173, 176, 179, 181
Slingsby, William Cecil 70, 98, 153
Slingsby's Route 101, 198, 241
Slow Riser 295

Small, Hamish 281-282
SMC Journal 99, 105, 110-112, 114, 117-118, 132, 139, 152, 165, 172, 174, 191, 203-204, 249, 276, 287
Smith Alexander 9, 13, 18, 22, 37-38, 176
Smith, Bill 264, 282
Smith, Cym 251
Smith, Malcolm 281
Smith, Robin 265, 266, 284, 291
Smythe, F S (Frank) 208-211, 221
Solly, Godfrey 80, 128-129, 142, 145
Somervell, Howard 197-198, 209-210, 224-225, 242, 281
South Buttress 181, 188
South Crack 156, 157
South Gully, Coir' a' Mhadaidh 311
South Ridge, Sgurr na h-Uamha 82
South Twin 262
South-East Gully, Sgurr a' Mhadaidh 175
South-East Ridge 259
South-East Ridge, Sgurr a' Ghreadaidh 259
South-East Ridge, Sgurr na h-Uamha 81
Spar Cave 26, 29, 34-36, 39
Spartan Groove 298
Spock 295-296
Sproul, Bill 282-283
Sron na Ciche 161-164, 168, 172, 174, 182, 185-186, 191, 199, 202-203, 210, 212, 222-224, 230, 238, 244, 279, 281, 283, 290, 295-298, 311
St Andrews Crack 287
St Andrews University Mountaineering Club 234, 287
Stack Buttress Direct 202
Stairway to Heaven 303, 310
Steamers 34, 46, 93-4, 126, 152, 232-3, 247
Steeple, E W 160-161, 163, 169-177, 185-188, 197, 200-204, 209, 211, 252, 263
Stephens, Fred 85
Sternum 251
Stevenson, Robert 23
Stewart, Dan, 251, 269, 279, 288-289
Stewart, Fred 257
Stocker, A H 61, 71, 78
Stone Shoot 229, 235, 250
Storr Pinnacles 47
Stott, Paul 305

Strange, Greg 309-311
Strappado 267
Strappado Direct 295
Strathaird House 33
Strome Ferry 46, 47
Styx 268, 295
Sublime, the 10, 24, 26
Subsidiary Gully 271
Sunset Slab 100, 268
Sutherland family, Glenbrittle 226, 234, 236-237
Sutton, James 299
Swinburne, Algernon Charles 11, 38, 364
Szuca, George 298

Tamm, Evgeny 255
Tarbuck, Ken 221
Tatham, H E W 106
Tattersall, W 170
Tauber, Wilf 288-289
Telford, Thomas 26-27, 34
Temple, John 267, 268
Tennant, Norman 271
Terrace East Buttress 202
Terrace Gully 202
Terrace West Buttress 209
The Asp 282-283
The Bow 264
The British Mountaineering Council 242
The Brothers 299
The Chambre Finish 296
The Chasm 188
The Finger, , 6/15
The Flake 164
The Gathering 12, 299
The Great Prow 288-290
The Highlander 299
The Horn 288
The Lord of the Isles 10, 23-26
The Naked Saltire 302
The Nipple 311
The Prize 299
The Smear 310, 311
The Snake 12, 283
The Snark 284
The Spur 82
The Squeeze Box 301, 315
The Team Machine 297

The Thirty-Nine Steps 137
The Three Hostages 136-138
Thearlaich-Dubh Gap 12, 76, 78-80, 101, 114, 122, 130, 140-141, 143-144, 155, 157, 178, 187, 203, 208, 245, 255, 269, 275-276, 278, 305-306, 308, 317
Theseus 268
Third-Fourth Gully 170
Thom, John 137
Thomas, Pete 284
Thomas, Phil 310-311
Thompson, Roger 123
Thompson, Sydney 243-244
Thomson, E C 206
Thomson, Gilbert 108, 129
Thomson, J C 160
Thomson, J M A 162, 164
Thomson, John 10, 21, 26, 180-183, 189, 190-191
Thomson, R L 138-139
Thomson, W P L 235
Thor 291-293
Thorburn, Paul 303
Thuilm Ridge of Sgurr a' Mhadaidh 160
Thunder Rib 266
Thunderbolt Shelf 262
Tiso, Graham 276, 278
Todd, Davie 282
Tolmie, Frances 49
Toogood, Bob 292
Toolie Grooves 264
Torrin 19, 25, 33, 35-36, 47, 93-94, 243
Tough, Wm 110, 122
Tourist Route 108
Trap Face Route 222
Travers, Morris 70, 87
Tressider, Es 306
Tribe, W N 73
Tricouni 220, 225, 231-232
Trodhu 32
Trojan Groove 298
Trophy Crack 264
Turner, J M W 10, 25, 33, 340
Two Pitch Gully 161

Uhuru 298
Upper Rake, Sgurr a' Mhadaidh 90

Val 296, 317
Valentine, G 134
Vanity 296
Varicose 280
Vaughan, Pat 269
Veitch, John 43, 45-49, 51, 55
Virgin Arete 282
Virgo 315
Vulcan Wall 268-269, 295-296, 298

Wager, Lawrence 257
Wakefield, A W (Arthur) 165
Walker, Charles 140, 142
Walker, Harry 140, 142, 144
Walker, Horace 59-63
Walker, Reverend John 16
Walkington, Tom 304
Wallwork, Jesse 186
Wallwork, William 11, 186, 188, 189, 191
Walsh, Pat 258, 264
Waterpipe Gully 82, 114, 118, 121-123, 135, 153, 155, 173, 198, 262, 300, 309-311
Waterpipe Gully Direct 170, 191
Watts, Chris 312
Wayfarers' Club 240
Wear, Ben 299
Weather forecasts 207-8
Wedderburn, E A M 242
Weir, Tom 254, 275, 322
Welch, Martin 313
Weld, C R 40
Wells, Biddy 213
Wells, Trilby 213
Welsh, Hugh 91
West Buttress 159, 167
West Buttress Route, Sgurr Sgumain 100, 111
West Buttress, Sgurr Mhic Choinnich 167
West Central Gully 174, 182
West Face Direct, Knight's Peak 216-217
West Face, Knight's Peak 271
West Gully, Alasdair-Thearlaich Crags 185
West Trap Route 211
Western Buttress Direct 174
Whillance, Pete 297
Whillans, Don 255
Whincup, Alexander 138
Whispering Wall 315

White Dreams 317
White Slab 202
White Slab Direct 12, 256
White Spirit 315
White Wedding 312
White Wizard 309
Whymper, Edward 10, 105
Wicks, J H 103
Wild, Finlay 11, 307-308
Wilding, John 199-200
Williams, Alfred 124-125, 127, 149
Williams, Noel 300
Williams, Sydney 79, 127
Wilson, Godfrey 203
Wilson, Graham 197-198
Wilson, J D B 234
Wilson, John 39
Window Buttress 89, 166, 207, 248, 265
Winkworth, Stephen 69
Winthrop Young, Geoffrey 71, 76, 89, 98, 131, 147, 159, 180-181, 183-184, 190, 193, 199
Wollaston, A F R (Sandy) 86
Wood, William 241, 254, 276, 278
Woodhead, A G 171-173
Wood-Johnson, Ernest 221-223
Wood-Johnson's Route 222-223
Woolley, Hermann 98, 100-101
Wordsworth, William 9
Wrangham, E A 256-257
Wright, J E B 227-230

Yates, F 207
Yorkshire Ramblers 98
Young, G W 71, 76, 89-90, 180-181, 183
Younghusband, Francis 70

Zigzag 89, 182
Zinneman, Fred 292
Zinovieff, Peter 257

ALSO FROM CALUM SMITH
IN RYMOUR BOOKS

In 1889, the bloody and battered body of Edwin Rose, an English tourist, was found concealed under a boulder on Goatfell on the Isle of Arran. This is a fascinating account of the murder that scandalised Victorian Scotland and its aftermath.